THE
INDONESIAN ECONOMY
IN TRANSITION

The **ISEAS – Yusof Ishak Institute** (formerly Institute of Southeast Asian Studies) was established as an autonomous organization in 1968. It is a regional centre dedicated to the study of socio-political, security and economic trends and developments in Southeast Asia and its wider geostrategic and economic environment. The Institute's research programmes are the Regional Economic Studies (RES, including ASEAN and APEC), Regional Strategic and Political Studies (RSPS), and Regional Social and Cultural Studies (RSCS).

ISEAS Publishing, an established academic press, has issued more than 2,000 books and journals. It is the largest scholarly publisher of research about Southeast Asia from within the region. ISEAS Publishing works with many other academic and trade publishers and distributors to disseminate important research and analyses from and about Southeast Asia to the rest of the world.

THE
INDONESIAN ECONOMY IN TRANSITION

Policy Challenges in the Jokowi Era and Beyond

EDITED BY

HAL HILL • SIWAGE DHARMA NEGARA

ISEAS YUSOF ISHAK INSTITUTE

First published in Singapore in 2019 by
ISEAS Publishing
30 Heng Mui Keng Terrace
Singapore 119614
E-mail: publish@iseas.edu.sg
Website: <http://bookshop.iseas.edu.sg>

The responsibility for facts and opinions in this publication rests exclusively with the authors and their interpretations do not necessarily reflect the views or the policy of the publisher or its supporters.

ISEAS Library Cataloguing-in-Publication Data

Hill, Hal, 1948–
    The Indonesian Economy in Transition : Policy Challenges in the Jokowi Era and Beyond / Hal Hill and Siwage Dharma Negara.
    1. Indonesia—Economic policy.
    2. Indonesia—Economic conditions—1997–
    3. Joko Widodo, 1961–
    4. Indonesia—Politics and government—1998–
    I. Negara, Siwage Dharma.
    II. Title.
HC447 H642   2019

ISBN 978-981-4843-06-5 (soft cover)
ISBN 978-981-4843-10-2 (e-book, PDF)

Typeset by Superskill Graphics Pte Ltd
Printed in Singapore by Mainland Press Pte Ltd

CONTENTS

FOREWORD
Lessons for Indonesia from East Asia

I am pleased to be able to write the Foreword for this important and timely book on the Indonesian economy. As we know the country is currently entering the five-yearly elections cycle that will set the political stage for the subsequent five years.

The book aims to shed light on whether Indonesia has presently embarked on a new development model. In this piece I would like to share with you my reflection, inevitably quite subjective, on a related but somewhat narrower issue. The question I am going to raise is what Indonesia could learn from the experience of the East Asian countries. I will relate it to the changing environment of policymaking in Indonesia in the past six decades or so, half of which time I had had the privilege to observe the process from the ring side, so to speak, and subsequently found myself increasingly drawn into the ring. I will conclude with a tentative suggestion on how Indonesia could improve its policy performance in the coming years.

Let me begin by clarifying what I mean by the East Asian countries. In this group I include Japan, Taiwan, South Korea, Singapore, Hong Kong and, more recently, China and now perhaps also Vietnam. This group in my view is unique because in their quest for development they carried out similar strategies with similar outcomes.

I am aware that within that group individual countries differ in their experiences and in their specific policies with regard to their important sectors such as industries, trade and finance. Nonetheless, we can readily identify some basic commonalities in their approaches to development. For the purpose of this talk I will pick two of them.

The first is this. From the early stages of their development these countries consistently placed high in their agenda the upgrading of three strategic areas, namely, education, bureaucracy and infrastructure. The first two — education and bureaucracy — have roots in the Confucian precept about the basic role of the state, while the third is an enabling element. The pursuit of these three objectives constitutes a crucial part of their development stories.

Their strategy emphasizes the "supply side" development with the goal of progressively raising the country's "productive capacity". In the literature three factors, namely, human resources, institutions and infrastructure, have consistently stood out as prime determinants of a country's development in the long run. The success of the East Asian countries with their strategy corroborates this view.

I am raising the issue of long-term productivity and supply to highlight what I see as an apparent lop-sidedness of policy discussions and policy practice in Indonesia, especially in the past twenty years or so (my time in government not excepted). By default or by design they tend to be dominated by short-term issues and are too demand-oriented. For example, when policymakers talk about growth, more likely than not the focus is on how to raise it this year or the next and the way to do that is primarily by juggling the components of aggregate demand or spending, almost taking for granted the supply side. Such a mode of thinking — appropriate for market analysts but grossly inadequate for development policymakers — when it translates into policy practice would inevitably have far-reaching consequences. The fault, though, seems to lie not so much in the policymakers as in the politics of the country. We will come back to this issue, but presently let me say a bit more about those three factors.

To raise the quality of a country's human resources over the long run, the law of population dynamics requires us to focus on taking care of our children and youth — the next generation. The principal instrument for it is a fully integrated, well-targetted education-cum-health intervention scheme applied to all children right from their earliest ages through their teens. The key words here are fully integrated and well-targetted.

The East Asian focus on creating an effective bureaucracy is an important lesson. Too often we hear how bureaucracy has often become a drag on, rather than a prop of, development. Yet too few countries have seriously and systematically carried out the all-important task of reforming their bureaucracies. In reality the task is much greater than reforming government bureaucracy. To sustain the impacts, other important public institutions, among which the legal institutions are the most critical, must be concurrently reformed.

Being more tangible, building the third element of the "trilogy" — physical infrastructures — should be a more straightforward task. But even here a clearer statement of priorities is imperative. What we want to build is not just a collection of unrelated pieces of infrastructure but effective networks of infrastructure that jointly serve: (a) to raise the general productivity of, and lower the transaction costs across, the economy; (b) to support the other two objectives (human resources and institutional development); and (c) very importantly for young nations, to integrate various parts of the economy into a more unified national entity. A good plan of infrastructures development must therefore contain a strategic vision of the needed infrastructure networks in, say, the next twenty to thirty years.

Pursuing with resolve and efficiency that trilogy of development is a clear lesson that Indonesia could learn from the East Asian experience.

The second feature of the East Asian experience does not provide a ready guide for action but it is an important lesson nonetheless. It relates to the choice of policy frameworks and the supporting institutional set-up. The East Asian countries decided right from the outset to adopt some sort of "corporatist" model in which business enterprises continued to be relied on as the main actors in the economy, while the state assumed a strong and active coordinating and guiding role.

In their case such an approach required a bureaucracy and political system that enabled the state to discharge its activist role. That is why, at the early stages of their development, necessarily their bureaucracies tended to operate in the top-down mode and their political regimes were not democratic. It was only at later stages of their development that some of those countries began to embrace full democracy and a less rigid bureaucracy.

The important thing to note is that during the critical stages of their development they were freed from the problem of "shortermism" that often afflicts democracies, especially the young ones. Their strategic plans were somehow spared from the vagaries of discontinuities and abrupt swings that often follow election cycles. Political gridlocks that cause delays and indecision in policymaking did not appear to be their main problem. They therefore could better channel their administrative and social energies into solving long-term issues that really matter for development. True, the journeys of the East Asian countries were far from smooth sailing. Mistakes were made and social and economic costs, often quite substantial, were incurred. But the bottom line is that somehow the essential foundations for their sustained development got built.

We may note that Indonesia in fact had its own experience with a similar regime, with a slightly different twist. More than three decades under the New Order, Indonesia had witnessed significant progress on its economic and social fronts, thanks to the implementation of systematic development policies overseen by a group of capable and dedicated technocrats working under the umbrella of a not quite democratic but stable political regime. Progress begets new aspirations. As living conditions improved the calls among the populace for greater say and participation in politics became increasingly vocal. There was also a growing perception that rent-seeking activities and corruption among the elite had been growing unchecked.

Alas, the needed political reforms never came. The 1997/98 financial crisis provided a trigger for the subsequent social and political upheavals that eventually led to a regime change. The *Reformasi* reinstated a full electoral democracy, the separation of state powers, the system of checks and balances in government and free press. But on the more operational levels something important is lost. A group of dedicated technocrats overseeing policies is no more, and the established mode ensuring continuity of policies over time has vanished.

That is the general picture. Let us now delve a little deeper.

In terms of human resources development, the New Order had recorded a quantum leap in education and health areas, at least compared with the situation at the beginning of the era. However, the 1997/98 crisis had caused a serious setback in these sectors, only to recover very slowly thereafter. The population and technological dynamics have made the task we are facing now weightier by the day. In the midst of the current technological revolution the Indonesian labour force is still dominated by unskilled labour. On the quality of school education, international surveys have consistently placed Indonesia well behind any of the East Asian countries. And despite all the efforts the percentage of stunted children remains the highest in the region. These are just a few facts that should serve as a compelling reminder that more resources, better planning and execution and above all stronger political commitment are desperately needed to do the big catching up.

The second element of the trilogy has not fared any better. I have to say that the New Order institutional development has never been given the weight it deserves. Efforts to reform the bureaucracy have been patchy. It is not so much a lack of ideas as a lack of sustained commitment to systematically implement them. Evidence keeps emerging that important parts of the central and regional government bureaucracies act more as a drag on development. In the progress in legal reform there is also still much to be desired.

The records of infrastructure development are somewhat better. During the New Order, wide-ranging infrastructures were built and the standards of infrastructure services in Indonesia were *on par* with its neighbours in the region. But again the crisis of 1997/98 had brought about a collapse in infrastructure spending which as percentage of GDP has not recovered to its New Order level to this day. We should duly recognize, though, the serious efforts by the present administration to accelerate infrastructure development.

It has been two decades now since Indonesia first launched its *Reformasi*. The pertinent question to be asked is whether a democratic polity as we currently have could and would evolve to be one that supports higher gear development. For many of us, the preferred answer is likely to be yes. As hopeful as we might be, though, it is important to keep our feet on the ground. We should constantly remind ourselves of the following basic truths: that democracy *per se* does not guarantee development, that development can only come from rising long-term productivity, that long-term productivity is determined by the quality of the nation's human resources, its public institutions and its networks of infrastructure, and also we must never forget that without development democracy itself is unlikely to survive.

What we need is a "development-oriented" democracy. One that is not merely understood as a competitive game of acquiring power but also one that is animated by collective consciousness and higher desire to achieve common progress. A democracy that is not hostage to "shortermism". One that can produce and execute a rational blueprint for the nation's long-term development. A democracy that is not saddled with gridlocks, delays and indecision. A democracy that delivers results. Such a democracy, or a close approximation of it, is indeed possible. But, just to remind ourselves, the onus falls on those who have faith in democracy to make such a regime a living reality. If history is any guide, the journey would likely be long and challenging, requiring constancy of purpose and a reservoir of collective wisdom to maintain the delicate balance between freedom and order along the way.

As we travel along that road, we will be faced with the practical question: what should we do while our democracy is still in the process of consolidation? Given the state where we are now, let me try out some very preliminary thoughts on the issue in the hope that they will spark discussions and, who knows, perhaps also actions.

First, adopt the trilogy as the overarching theme of the national development efforts. Prepare a strategic blueprint for the three components, taking a planning horizon of, say, twenty years to come. Prepare a more specific plan of actions for its first ten years and fully worked-out programmes for its first five years. This last-mentioned part of the plan should in principle be ready for execution by the new Cabinet on its first day in office.

That constitutes the base plan. On top of that we may add whatever other themes (such as policies on industry, trade, finance, social welfare and national security) deemed necessary to make the blueprint a more complete development plan. Needless to say, the plan must be of first-rate quality, not just another bureaucratic product, as it serves as the main conduit for reintroducing the essential elements of effective policies that have been lost, namely, order, focus, coherence, rationality and continuity.

You may also need a radical restructuring of the Cabinet. There may be seven coordinating ministers corresponding to seven areas of responsibilities: human development, bureaucratic reform, legal reform, infrastructure development, social welfare, economic-cum-finance, and national security. Each coordinating minister is "field commander" with the sole mission of making the goals in his or her area of responsibility a reality. Sufficient coordinating power and perhaps also some line authorities should be vested with the coordinating ministers to enable them to optimally mobilize the relevant operational ministers to help achieve those goals. Unlike the current set-up, the main job of operational ministers is to implement policies as directed by the coordinating ministers, not to contrive their own goals and policies.

There is one more thing. Our own experience and that of other countries confirm that some sort of institutionalized mechanism of control, that independently and objectively evaluates the execution of policies on the ground and directly reports to the President, is indispensable. Alas, this matter is too often not given its due weight at the cost of performance.

Finally, here is an almost redundant reminder: the proposed scheme will come to naught if the strategic slots are not filled with persons who know their jobs and know how to get the jobs done through teamwork.

By now some of you may be wondering why such a top-down scheme. The scheme may be thought to be appropriate for an authoritarian regime with central planning but not for a democracy which cherishes initiatives and participation of its citizens. My whole narrative is meant to underscore the importance of what have been missing in policymaking in this country, namely: order, focus, coherence, rationality and continuity. They are absolutely crucial for effective conduct of policies in any political system, be it a democracy or not. When missing, they must somehow be rewired into the system lest the country diminish into Socrates' proverbial ship that is forever condemned to go adrift in the open sea.

Boediono
Former Vice-President of Indonesia

ACKNOWLEDGEMENTS

It is a pleasure to acknowledge the many people who contributed generously to this volume, and without whom it could not have been completed.

First and foremost, we would like to express our gratitude to the twenty-five contributors, for their fine papers and their willingness to respond quickly and helpfully to our numerous editorial requests. Special thanks go to former Vice-President Boediono, for kindly agreeing to open the conference and to writing the Foreword.

We are indebted to the many staff of ISEAS – Yusof Ishak Institute, who as usual combined generous hospitality with smooth and efficient organization. What a wonderful institution it is! We wish it well for its next fifty years and beyond. Director Choi Shing Kwok opened our 21–22 March workshop. Karthi Nair and her team ran the administration, as always with great charm and attention to detail. Ng Kok Kiong, Rahilah Yusuf and Pritish Bhattacharya oversaw the editorial production quickly and efficiently. Francis Hutchison and Cassey Lee played a helpful facilitating role.

We are grateful to our friends Chatib Basri and Mari Pangestu for kindly providing endorsements.

We also want to thank the additional chairs and discussants at the conference who supported our workshop, including Soedradjad Djiwandono, Tham Siew Yean, and Khatarina Naumann.

This publication comes at a crucial time in Indonesian history. It is on the cusp of its fifth national and regional elections in the democratic era. We hope that in some small way the papers in this volume might contribute to informing the scholarly and policy communities in the country, and to the many people outside Indonesia with an interest in this fascinating and important country.

Hal Hill and Siwage Dharma Negara
Canberra and Singapore
October 2018

ABOUT THE CONTRIBUTORS

Ridho Al Izzati is Junior Researcher at SMERU Research Institute, Jakarta.

Titik Anas is Founder of Presisi Indonesia; and Lecturer at Padjadjaran University, Bandung.

Luhur Bima is Senior Researcher at SMERU Research Institute, Jakarta.

Gerrit J. Gonschorek is PhD candidate at the Institute of Economics, Department of International Economic Policy, University of Freiburg, Germany.

Natasha Hamilton-Hart is Professor in the Department of Management and International Business at the University of Auckland, New Zealand.

Hal Hill is the H.W. Arndt Professor Emeritus of Southeast Asian Economies, Arndt-Corden Department of Economics, Crawford School of Public Policy, ANU College of Asia and the Pacific, Australian National University, Canberra.

Ellisa Kosadi is Research Assistant at the Indonesia Project, Arndt-Corden Department of Economics, Crawford School of Public Policy, ANU College of Asia and the Pacific, Australian National University, Canberra.

Ari Kuncoro is Professor of Economics and Dean, Faculty of Economics and Business, University of Indonesia, Jakarta.

Sandra Kurniawati is Research Specialist in the National Team for the Acceleration of Poverty Reduction, Office of the Vice President of Republic of Indonesia.

Chris Manning is Honorary Associate Professor, Arndt-Corden Department of Economics, Crawford School of Public Policy, ANU College of Asia and the Pacific, Australian National University, Canberra.

John McCarthy is Associate Professor at the Crawford School of Public Policy, ANU College of Asia and the Pacific, Australian National University, Canberra.

Siwage Dharma Negara is Senior Fellow in the Regional Economic Studies Programme and Co-coordinator of the Indonesia Studies Programme at the ISEAS – Yusof Ishak Institute, Singapore.

Arianto A. Patunru is a Fellow in the Indonesia Project, Arndt-Corden Department of Economics, Crawford School of Public Policy, ANU College of Asia and the Pacific, Australian National University, Canberra.

Devanto Pratomo is Senior Lecturer at the Faculty of Economics and Business, Brawijaya University, Malang.

Arief Ramayandi is Lead Economist in the Economics Department, Asian Development Bank, Manila.

Budy P. Resosudarmo is Professor at the Indonesia Project, Arndt-Corden Department of Economics, Crawford School of Public Policy, ANU College of Asia and the Pacific, Australian National University, Canberra.

Wilmar Salim is Chair of Graduate Study Program at the Department of Regional and City Planning, School of Architecture, Planning and Policy Development, Bandung Institute of Technology, Bandung.

Günther G. Schulze is Professor of Economics at the Institute of Economics, University of Freiburg, Germany; and Adjunct Professor at the Arndt-Corden Department of Economics, Crawford School of Public Policy, ANU College of Asia and the Pacific, Australian National University, Canberra.

Mulyadi Sumarto is Assistant Professor in the Department of Social Development and Welfare and Center for Population and Policy Studies, Universitas Gadjah Mada, Yogyakarta.

Daniel Suryadarma is Deputy Team Leader at RISE Programme in Indonesia, Jakarta.

Asep Suryahadi is Director of SMERU Research Institute, Jakarta.

Eve Warburton is Visiting Fellow in the Indonesia Studies Programme at the ISEAS – Yusof Ishak Institute, Singapore.

Maria Monica Wihardja is an Indonesian economist.

Thaliya Wikapuspita is a researcher at Presisi Indonesia.

Asri Yusrina is Researcher at SMERU Research Institute, Jakarta.

1

SETTING THE SCENE
The Indonesian Economy in Transition — the Jokowi Era and Beyond

Hal Hill and Siwage Dharma Negara

1.1 INTRODUCTION

It is now more than twenty years since one of the most decisive and important turning points in Indonesian economic and political history. The year 1998 was one of exceptional turbulence, hardship and uncertainty. The seemingly impregnable thirty-two-year Soeharto presidency came to a sudden end on 21 May. The economy and the currency were in free-fall. An acrimonious relationship had suddenly emerged with international financial institutions. There were nasty conflict episodes, mostly with serious ethnic dimensions. Almost one million of its citizens were internally displaced. There were various "Yugoslav" scenarios of territorial disintegration. Most important of all, there was no institutional roadmap to guide the country through the vacuum that Soeharto's hasty exit had created.

Viewing the country through the gloomy lens of that era, it is perhaps no exaggeration to state that the economic and political developments over the intervening two decades have been little short of miraculous. Crises of this depth and severity have often set countries back for extended periods, but Indonesian per capita income had recovered to pre-crisis levels by 2004. The country is now regarded as one of the most vibrant democracies in Southeast Asia and in the Muslim world. It has maintained its territorial integrity. There have been four rounds of credible national elections, while democracy has also taken root in the more than 500 subnational jurisdictions. A far-reaching programme of decentralization has been implemented. The economy has returned to at least a moderate growth rate of around 5 per cent per annum. Inflation is well under control, and the macroeconomic framework looks secure. The authorities navigated the 2008–09 global financial crisis with little difficulty. The economy is in much better shape than the resource-exporting members of the much-hyped BRICS (Brazil, Russia, India, China and South Africa) group. Indonesia is recognized as a significant regional power through its membership of the G20 and other international fora.

Yet in important respects Indonesia is still a country in transition, and one that faces major development challenges. It is still a relatively young democracy, in the process of establishing durable institutions that will be needed to underpin an upper middle-income economy. Its ambitious decentralization programme is still being bedded down into an effectively operating system of government. Tens of millions of its citizens live below or precariously above a meagre poverty line. The economy is not growing fast enough to quickly eradicate poverty and destitution. Perhaps paradoxically, inequality has risen appreciably during the democratic era. There are daunting environmental challenges. Corruption remains an ever-present and serious problem.

President Joko Widodo — widely known as Jokowi — was narrowly elected to office in 2014 with high expectations. The seventh president of the republic lacked family name, military background and wealth, itself an impressive reminder of the country's democratic progress and resilience. Jokowi campaigned successfully as an effective local government leader, with a reputation for clean and pragmatic administration. His agenda was to accelerate economic growth, overcome the country's massive infrastructure deficit, and eradicate poverty. He promised a professional Cabinet. His first major economic policy decision was a very significant one, to dramatically reduce the crippling fuel subsidies.

Almost five years later, what can be said about his record? Inevitably, as the papers in this volume document, the outcomes have been mixed. Most of Indonesia's major development issues are not amenable to quick solutions in a single-term presidency. Moreover, Jokowi had the misfortune to be elected just as the decade-long super commodity boom was fading. For growth to be maintained and the social policy agenda implemented substantial reform was required. In the event, Jokowi has been a decisive president in some respects, but he has not been the major reformer that some of his supporters had hoped for. He has lived up to his commitment to prioritize infrastructure, and continue with the popular social policies, including health (*"kartu sehat"*), education (*"kartu pintar"*) and village grants. His personal integrity has been beyond reproach. He has maintained the stable macroeconomic policy settings of his predecessors.

Yet in other respects his policy narratives and achievements have struggled to make the transition from local to national government, in part reflecting the "rainbow coalition" of competing interests and diverse views that constitute his Cabinet. He has wavered on international economic policy, between pragmatic openness and economic nationalism. One obvious manifestation has been his three very different trade ministers, resulting in little progress in rolling back the increasingly protectionist policies that had been introduced during the commodity boom. The continuing very weak tax effort means that the government is not able to effectively fund the public services and social transfers that the community expects. A one-off tax amnesty hardly constitutes major fiscal reform. Microeconomic reform has also proceeded erratically: simplified business licensing procedures have been introduced, yet the sixteen "reform packages" in totality have not amounted to much. The continuing flow of cases before the Corruption Eradication Commission, the KPK, is testimony to the struggle to improve governance standards. Many observers fear a rising tide of political and social intolerance, especially towards "minority" groups. The result has been an economy that has continued to progress, but the "new normal" for economic growth appears to be 5 per cent, considerably slower than Jokowi's campaign pledge of 7 per cent.

Moreover, the international economic environment that Indonesia faces continues to be uncertain and at times volatile. The normalization of monetary policy in the rich economies, especially the United States, and the threat of an increasingly disorderly trading environment increase the vulnerability of commodity exporting emerging market economies. The rising global energy prices of 2018 should be a positive development for Indonesia. But unless the government is willing to allow domestic prices to follow international trends, paradoxically these higher prices will place even greater stress on the budget as the energy subsidies again blow out.

The papers in this volume address these and other issues at this crucial juncture of Indonesian history, as the country approaches its fifth national elections of the democratic era. Section 1.2 provides an overview of recent economic developments. In section 1.3 we examine "Jokowinomics", that is, economic policies and performance during the administration of President Joko Widodo, asking in particular whether they could be characterized more by continuity or by change. Section 1.4 provides a sketch of the contents of the volume, while the concluding section sums up.

1.2 THE INDONESIAN ECONOMY: AN OVERVIEW

1.2.1 Historical Context

Indonesia has achieved sustained economic growth only since the late 1960s. From 1966 to 1996, that is the Soeharto era, growth averaged 7.3 per cent per annum. The economy then contracted severely during the Asian Financial Crisis (AFC), 1997–99, including by 13.4 per cent in 1998. The economic momentum was then restored from 2000 onwards, with an average annual growth this century of 5.1 per cent. As a result, per capita GDP has risen rapidly over the past half-century, by more than sixfold.

Although there is no obvious comparator for Indonesia,[1] the country belongs to a very small group of mainly East Asian economies that have achieved exceptionally rapid growth for a sustained period. Two major World Bank studies (1993, 2008) illustrate this proposition. The Bank's "miracle" study (1993) singled out seven East Asian economies, including Indonesia, for their very high growth. The Growth Commission (2008) report asked the question, which economies over the preceding century had grown exceptionally fast, defined as GDP growth averaging at least 7 per cent for at least a decade. The authors concluded that there were just 13 economies among the 150 for which they could obtain reliable estimates. Indonesia was one of these 13, for the period 1966–96.

Nevertheless, Indonesia has not grown as fast as China, and the four newly industrializing economies (NIEs) (and earlier Japan), which achieved such rapid growth that per capita income since around 1960, has risen 12–16 fold. By contrast, the increase for Indonesia and other high-growth Southeast Asian economies has been a still very respectable 6–8 fold.[2] Table 1.1 compares Indonesia and three of its middle-income neighbours, Malaysia, the Philippines and Thailand. Since 1960 Thailand has been the most dynamic economy, with per capita income rising almost tenfold, whereas the Philippines has been the laggard with an increase of just 2.5 times. Indonesia and Malaysia adopt intermediate positions. Over the course of this century, however, their growth rates have been almost identical. For some periods Malaysia and Thailand have grown more quickly, but as open economies they were more seriously affected by the Global Financial Crisis (GFC).

1.2.2 The Economy under Jokowi

The "new normal" for the economy under Jokowi has been around 5 per cent annual growth. Growth has been stable, but well below the president's 7 per cent target. This rate is somewhat slower than that of the commodity-driven Susilo Bambang Yudhoyono (SBY) era, but comparable to its ASEAN neighbours (Figure 1.1): in recent years, somewhat slower than the Philippines and Vietnam, but faster than Thailand.

Indonesia struggles to create enough decent jobs. Some 3–4 million persons enter the labour market each year, in addition to the backlog of widespread underemployment. It is true that official unemployment has been declining gradually, to around 6 per cent. But this is relatively high compared to ASEAN neighbours (Figure 1.2), and the official definition does not take account of the many employed persons who are seeking additional

TABLE 1.1
The ASEAN Four: Comparative Economic Growth, 1960–2015

Country	2015 GDP per capita (Constant 2010 US$)	GDP per capita ratio between		
		2015 and 2000	2015 and 1980	2015 and 1960
Indonesia	3,834	1.8	3.5	6.6
Malaysia	10,878	1.6	3.3	7.7
The Philippines	2,640	1.6	1.6	2.5
Thailand	5,775	1.7	4.1	10.1

Source: WDI.

FIGURE 1.1
Economic Growth in Selected ASEAN Countries, 1990–2017 (%, year on year)

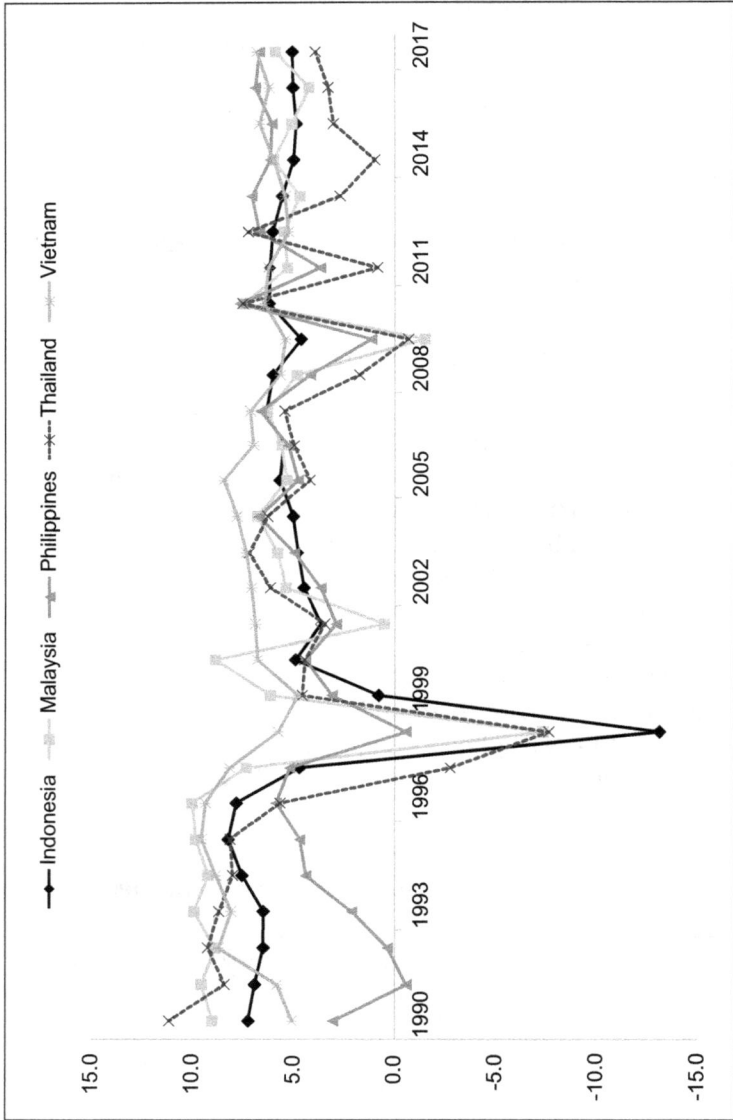

Source: CEIC, ASEAN section.

FIGURE 1.2
Unemployment Rate in Selected ASEAN Countries, 1990–2017 (%, year on year)

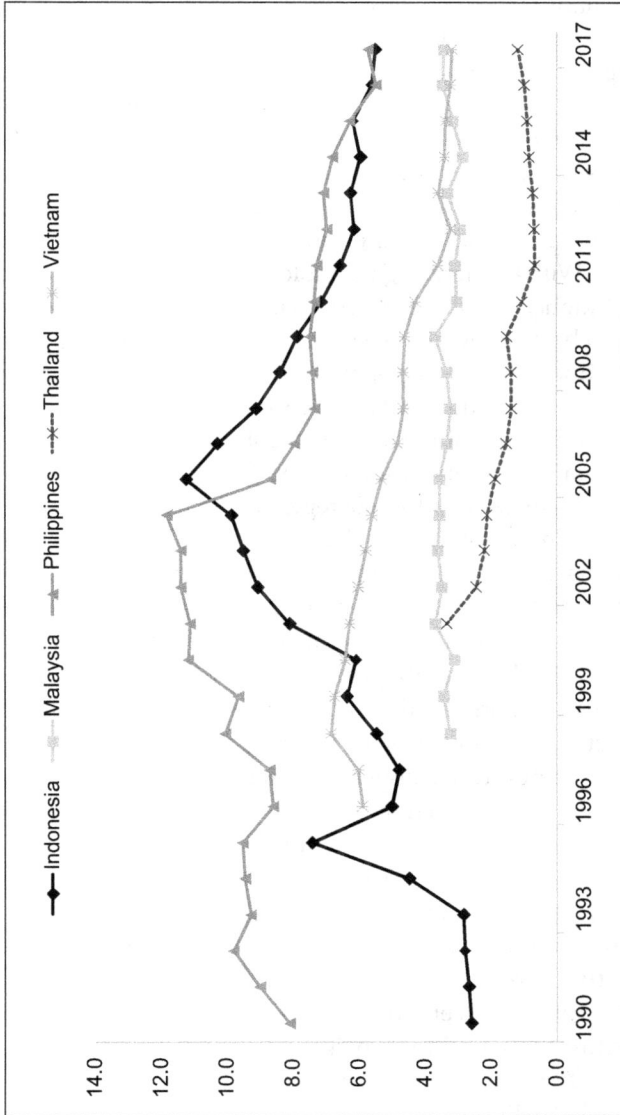

Source: CEIC, ASEAN section.

employment. The sluggish employment record partly reflects the growth slowdown after the commodity boom and the decade or more of jobless growth in manufacturing. However, as Manning and Pratomo (Chapter 11) argue, there are hopeful recent signs that manufacturing employment is picking up. Consistent with general patterns of structural change, the share of agricultural employment continues to decline, by almost 10 percentage points in the past decade. The main driver of employment growth has been services, including trade and tourism (Figure 1.3). Notably, the two countries in Figure 1.2 with the most regulated labour markets, Indonesia and the Philippines, have higher unemployment than their less regulated neighbours. With accelerating technological change, especially in IT-related activities, Indonesia will need to equip its labour force for the challenges that lie ahead, in basic educational skills, in vocational education and training, and in lifetime training opportunities. As Kurniawati et al. (Chapter 10) show, in spite of significantly increased funding over the past decade, Indonesia's educational performance continues to lag.[3]

Indonesia's inflation outlook is comfortable (Ramayandi and Negara, Chapter 3). Historically Indonesia registered relatively high rates of inflation compared to most of its neighbours, necessitating frequent nominal depreciations of the rupiah to maintain international competitiveness. However in recent years it has managed to narrow the gap (Figure 1.4). Inflation is of course first and foremost a monetary phenomenon, and thus arguably Bank Indonesia (BI) is insufficiently "monetarist" in its approach. But it could also be argued that the country's relatively closed trade regime and the high costs of logistics in this archipelagic nation have complicated BI's mission. Import restrictions on key food commodities (rice, beef, wheat, sugar, salt, soybeans, etc.) have pushed up domestic prices.[4] Moreover, the gradual (and commendable) reduction in energy subsidies, at least during the first three years of the Jokowi administration, increased administered inflation for periods of time, as shown in Figure 1.5.

Indonesia faces a huge infrastructure deficit, and improved infrastructure was a key campaign commitment of Jokowi (Salim and Negara, Chapter 9). Ever since the AFC, Indonesia has underinvested in infrastructure compared to its neighbours, even including the Philippines (Figure 1.6). According to Bappenas estimates, Indonesia needs to spend about Rp4,800 trillion (approximately US$356 billion) over the period 2015–19 to achieve its targets. It further calculates that the central and regional governments can finance only about 41 per cent of this amount.

FIGURE 1.3
Indonesia: Employment by Sector, 1990–2017 (% of total employment)

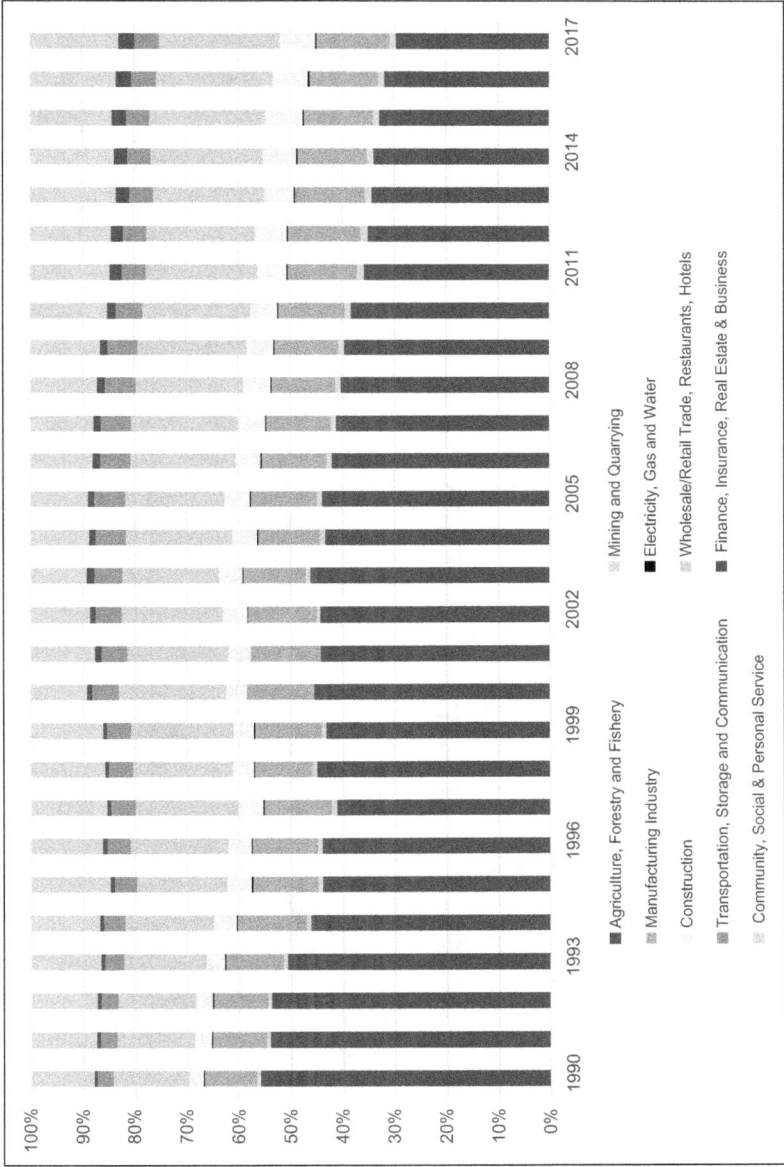

Source: BPS via CEIC.

FIGURE 1.4
Inflation Rate in Selected ASEAN Countries, 1990–2017 (%, year on year)

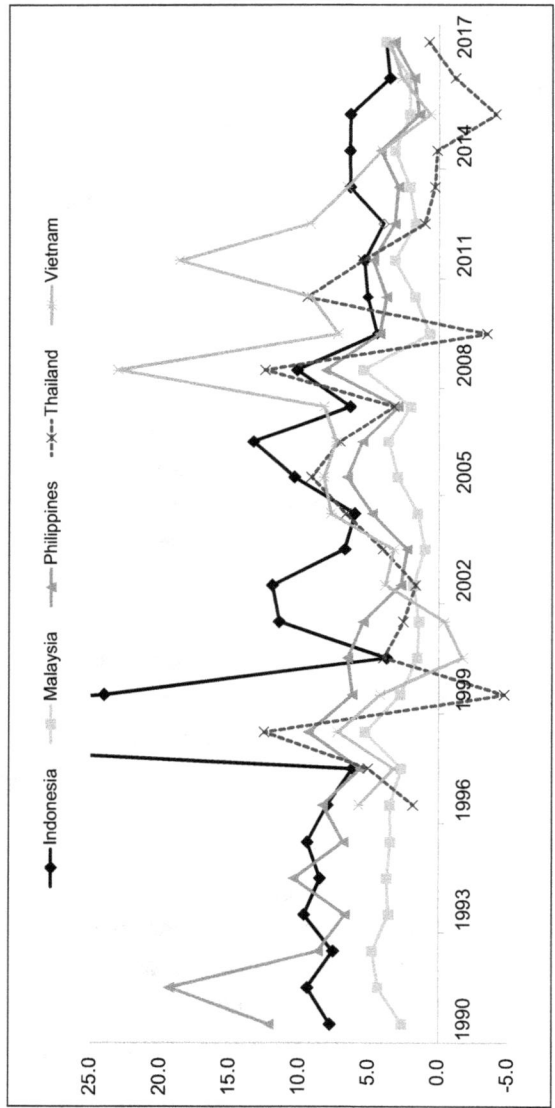

Source: CEIC, ASEAN section.

FIGURE 1.5
Indonesia: Monthly Inflation Rate, 2014–18 (%, year on year)

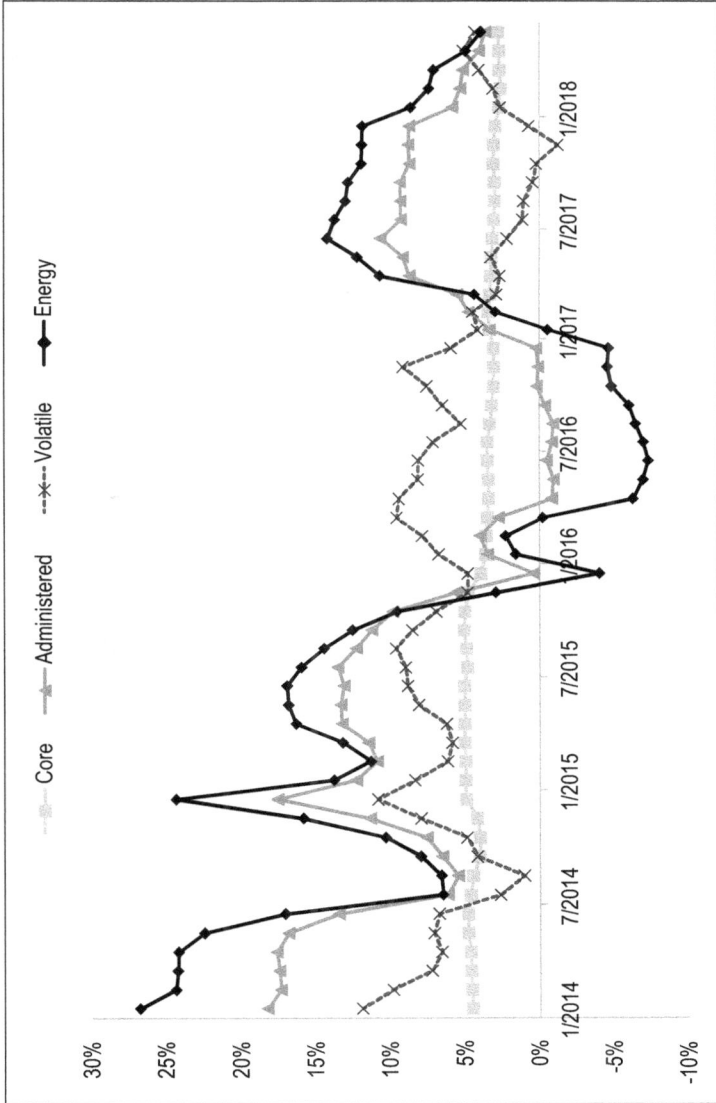

Source: CEIC, ASEAN section.

FIGURE 1.6
Infrastructure Spending in Selected ASEAN Countries, 2010–18 (% of GDP)

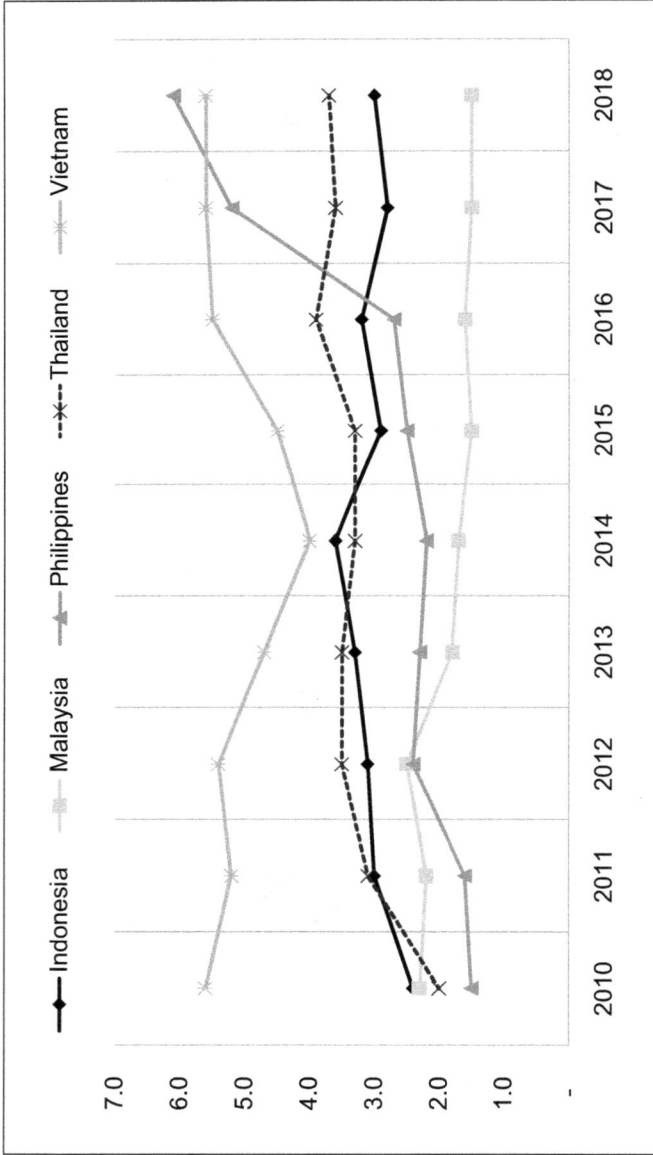

Note: 2017 and 2018 figures are forecasted figures. Indonesia's figures are budgeted data (not realized). They include 25% of total regional government budget for infrastructure.
Source: CEIC, HSBC.

The rest will have to come from state-owned enterprises (SOEs, 22 per cent) and the private sector (37 per cent). At least through to the mid-point of the Jokowi presidency, infrastructure spending remained low, at about 18.5 per cent of the total state budget, equivalent to 2.8 per cent of GDP. Not surprisingly, given the financial constraints and the policy uncertainty, the private sector has not been able to match its target. Foreign investors also await a more reassuring and predictable policy environment. Nevertheless, Jokowi has gradually matched his campaign rhetoric. As Figure 1.7 shows, his government's infrastructure spending has been rising since 2015, and is projected to reach Rp388 trillion in 2018, equivalent to 2.8 per cent of GDP. The increase has been financed by reduced subsidies, although these are likely to increase in the current year unless the government is willing to allow fuel prices to adjust to the higher international levels. Meanwhile, the government has continued to implement the 20 per cent and 5 per cent targets for education and health respectively, as mandated by Laws 20/2003 and 36/2009.

However, official infrastructure expenditures remain hobbled by Indonesia's anaemic tax effort. The country has one of the lowest tax/GDP ratios in the region, at about 10.3 per cent (Hamilton-Hart and Schulze (2016) and Ramayandi and Negara, Chapter 3). This is in spite of a succession of tax initiatives over the years, including the 2016–17 tax amnesty programme, which at best resulted in a one-off boost to revenues. The inescapable reality is that Indonesia's fiscal space is severely limited: a weak tax effort; about one-third of the national budget being passed on automatically to local governments (whose own revenue-raising efforts are also weak); the 3 per cent fiscal deficit limit; the education and health spending mandates as noted; some of the "low-hanging fruit" of subsidy reform already completed; and the large (and inflexible) allocations to civil servants' salaries.

With little progress on the tax effort, the restoration of investment grade from several key ratings agencies, and continuing low global interest rates, not surprisingly there have been mounting calls for the government to relax the fiscal deficit limit and embark on more aggressive international borrowing for infrastructure. In principle, borrowing for investment projects with rates of return higher than the cost of borrowing makes sense. Undoubtedly Indonesia has many infrastructure projects that would easily meet this benchmark. Moreover, Indonesia's public debt is low by regional and international standards (Figure 1.8), thanks to the remarkably

FIGURE 1.7
Indonesia: Budget Allocations across Key Sectors, 2005–17 (% of total budget)

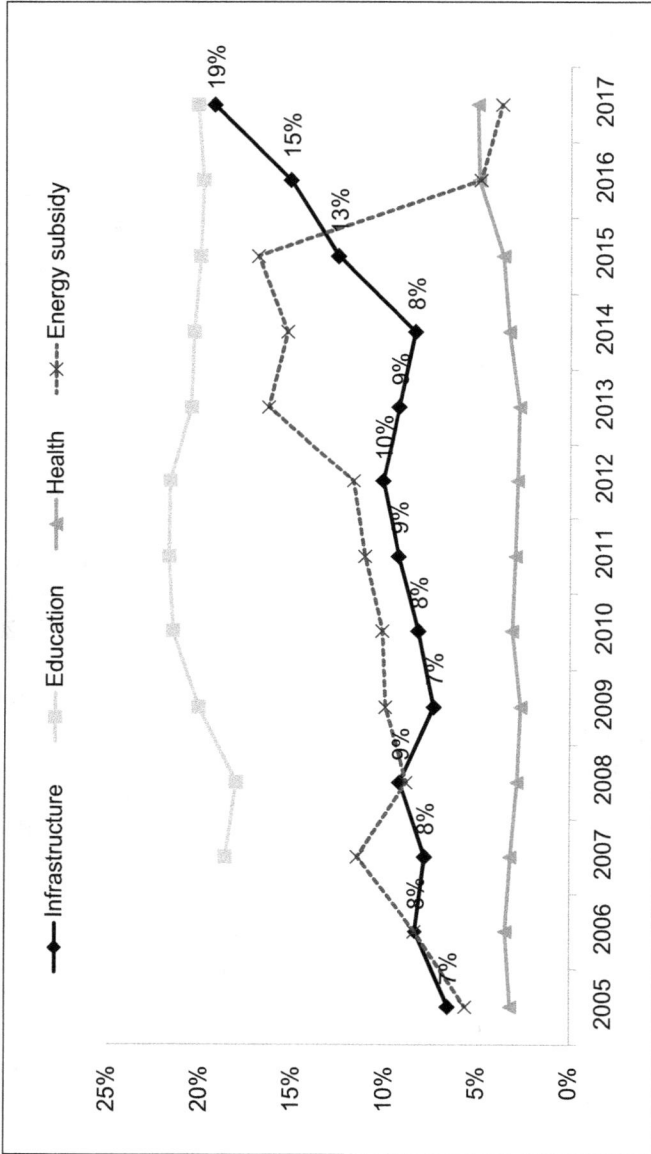

Source: DG Budget via CEIC.

FIGURE 1.8
Public Debt of Selected ASEAN Countries, 1990–2017 (% of GDP)

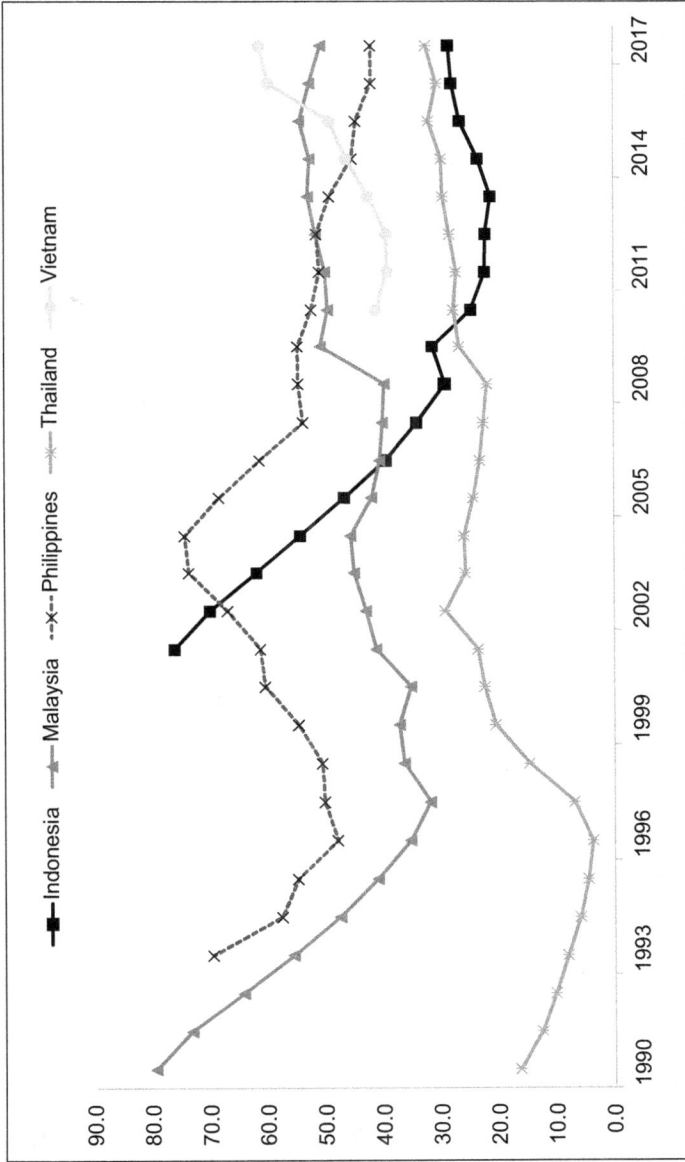

Source: CEIC, ASEAN section.

successful fiscal consolidation that has occurred since the AFC (Figure 1.9). In spite of recent calls to relax the deficit and debt ceiling, there are powerful contrary arguments. Indonesia's macroeconomic policy framework has served the country well since the AFC, including its management of the GFC. There is also the question of whether it has the institutions to absorb and spend a large increase in its infrastructure budget. In addition, with reform, a lot more private funding could be mobilized. Moreover, debt has become a controversial political issue, with public commentators focusing (wrongly) on the country's total public debt (the left axis in Figure 1.9) rather than its size relative to GDP (the right axis).

Slower economic growth and rising inequality have renewed public apprehension about the slow pace of poverty reduction. There is concern that the increasing inequality over the past two decades may weaken social cohesion and heighten social instability. In response, governments in the democratic era have introduced various social programmes aimed at achieving more inclusive growth. These include land redistribution to landless farmers, housing for the urban poor, credit for micro and small business, health care and education assistance for low-income households. These and related issues are discussed extensively in the chapters that follow, by Suryahadi and Al Izzati (Chapter 12), McCarthy and Sumarto (Chapter 13), Kurniawati et al. (Chapter 10), and Manning and Pratomo (Chapter 11).

As these chapters show, the impact of the various social programmes has been mixed. The percentage of the population below the poverty line has been declining very slowly in recent years, while the Gini ratio, which rose sharply through to around 2012, has declined slightly in recent years (Figure 1.10). According to the official BPS estimates, based on the national poverty line, there were 27.7 million poor people in March 2017, equivalent to 10.6 per cent of the population. The expenditure Gini ratio was 0.39. There is therefore still some progress required to achieve the Jokowi campaign promises of a poverty rate of 7–8 per cent and a Gini ratio of 0.36 by the end of 2019.

1.3 "JOKOWINOMICS": CONTINUITY AND CHANGE

Some world leaders come to be defined by their policies. In the case of Japan, for example, there is Prime Minister Abe's "Abenomics" and the "three arrows", of monetary stimulus, fiscal flexibility, and structural

FIGURE 1.9
Indonesia: Public Debt by Sources, 2001–07 (US$ million)

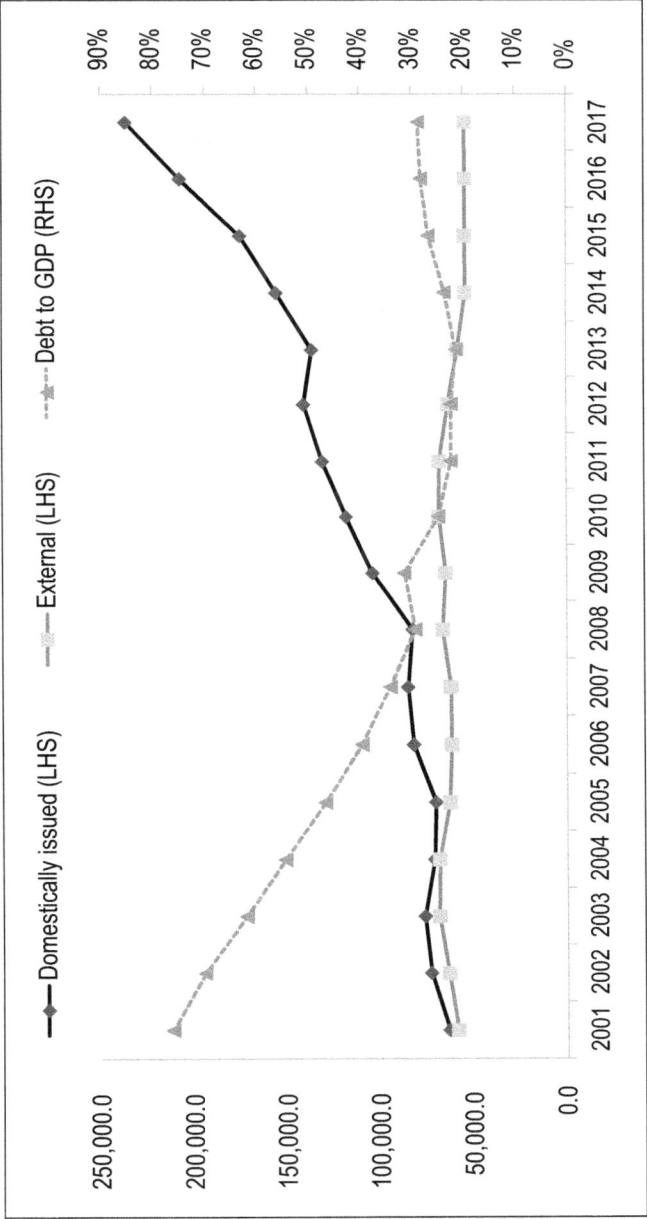

Source: CEIC.

FIGURE 1.10
Indonesia: Poverty and Inequality, 2000–18

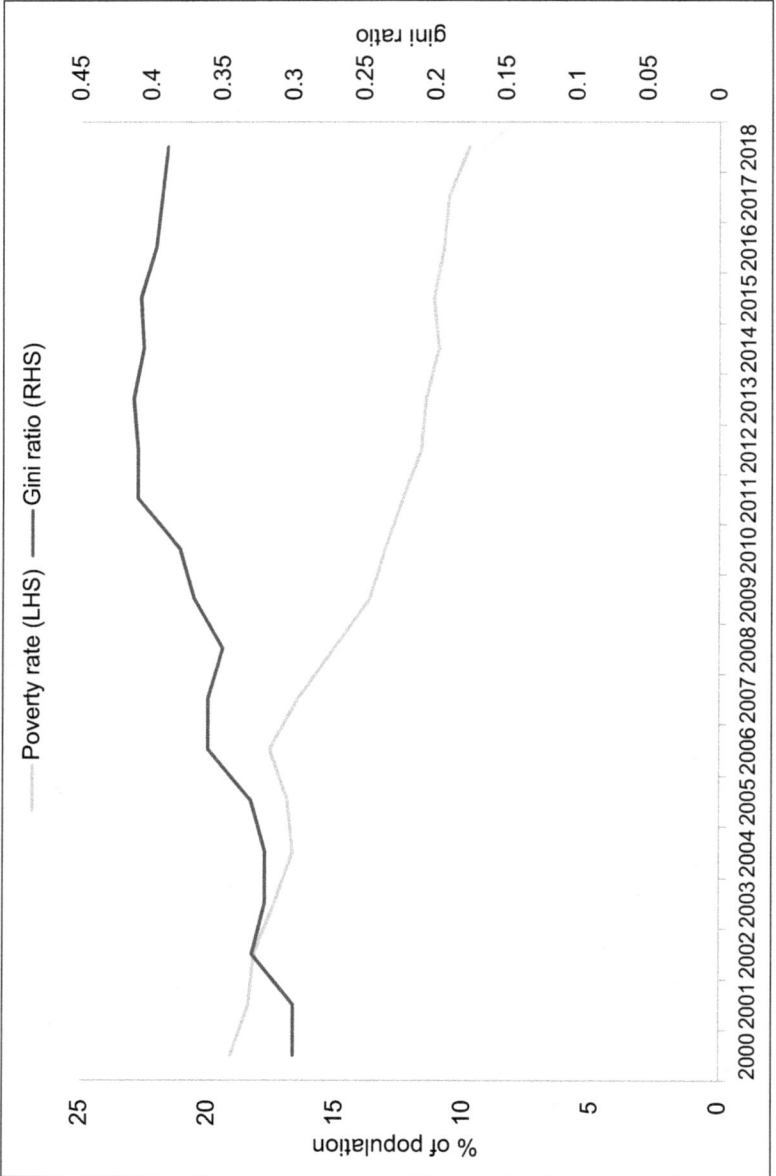

— Poverty rate (LHS)   —— Gini ratio (RHS)

Source: BPS, CEIC.

reform (Ito et al. 2018). President Trump's economic policies have focused on increasing the fiscal deficit (at a time of full employment) through large tax cuts, and mercantilist trade policy focused on bilateral trade deals with countries that have trade surpluses with the United States (Corden and Garnaut 2018).[5]

What about President Jokowi? The term "Jokowinomics" is in common parlance in Indonesia. Does it have any substance? Obviously the president has left his mark on the country, through particular policy initiatives, through his selection of Cabinet members and other senior government officials, and through his style of government. But are there distinctive and significant departures from his predecessors that go beyond the rhetoric of campaign speeches and Independence Day addresses? Has he set Indonesia on a new development trajectory with different policy priorities and modalities? We briefly address these questions and draw out examples from the chapters that follow. Our main conclusion is that the continuities in economic and social policy are greater than the changes. In making this judgement, the main comparison is obviously with the two-term SBY era (on which see Aspinall, Mietzner and Tomsa (eds, 2015)), by which time Indonesia had overcome the devastating economic crisis of 1997–99 and the country's democratic institutions and processes were more or less established. It is also important to take account of changing external circumstances, a factor of particular relevance to Jokowi's presidency since he took office just as the massive commodity boom was coming to an end.

President Jokowi has not articulated a detailed vision, philosophical or programmatic, of where he wishes to take Indonesia. His goals, as for example articulated in his *Nawacita* (nine priorities) and major speeches, include poverty alleviation, rural development, economic nationalism, infrastructure, maritime development, and clean government. He is seen as a pragmatic president who gets things done, as he did as mayor of Surakarta and (briefly) as governor of Jakarta. He set an ambitious growth target which, as we observed above, the country has fallen well short of. To further evaluate his record it is useful to survey policies, approaches and outcomes across the major areas of government.

Perhaps the clearest illustration of continuity is with respect to *macroeconomic policies* (Ramayandi and Negara, Chapter 3). There is very little that distinguishes him from the SBY era: he has appointed respected technocrats to the key positions of Minister of Finance and Governor of Bank Indonesia, the fiscal rule that deficits not exceed 3 per cent of GDP has been adhered to, and the monetary policy settings of a floating exchange rate, inflation targeting and an open capital account have been maintained. The weak tax effort has persisted. There was a bold effort to control fuel subsidies in his first budget but, apart from increased infrastructure expenditure, made possible by the reduced subsidies, thereafter there has hardly been a significant change in expenditure or revenue priorities. The Jokowi administration has also broadly followed similar policies with respect to the regulation and supervision of the financial sector (Hamilton-Hart, Chapter 5).

The continuities are also evident in the case of *trade and commercial policy*. The president and his administration have continued the ambivalence on trade policy that was evident especially in the second SBY administration, as Patunru (Chapter 6) demonstrates. Jokowi actually had three trade ministers in his first three years, and their stances ranged from highly protectionist to liberal-reforming and then back to a more inward-looking approach. The goals of "food sovereignty" and "self-sufficiency" (the terms are sometimes used interchangeably) remain paramount (Wihardja, Chapter 14). Indonesia has tended to take a back seat on regional and international trade initiatives. It did not join the Trans-Pacific Partnership (TPP), it has not played a leadership role commensurate with its size either in ASEAN or the Regional Comprehensive Economic Partnership (RCEP). It has not signed on to the Information Technology Agreement II (ITA II) (which governs global trade in electronics). Perhaps fortunately, it has not signed a bilateral trade deal of any significance. A similar ambivalence is evident in foreign investment policy.

The one major break from the past is a determined effort to simplify the complex regulatory regime. Jokowi's impatience with bureaucracy is well known, and the investment board's (BKPM) procedures have been simplified. This has resulted in the country's much-publicized ascent up the ranks of the 190 countries in the World Bank's annual Ease of Doing Business (EODB) calculations, from 106 in 2016 to 91 in 2017 and to 72 in 2018.[6] Nevertheless, at the sector level, much-needed reform is still needed (Kuncoro, Chapter 7; and Anas and Wikapuspita, Chapter 8).

Infrastructure was a major Jokowi campaign commitment and, as Salim and Negara (Chapter 9) show, expenditure has been rising through his term, once the subsidy reforms provided the fiscal space for increased spending. The differences should not be overstated, however. Local government infrastructure spending is often not rising commensurately. It is not evident that the much-vaunted *Poros Maritim Dunia* (Global Maritime Fulcrum) will transform inter-island shipping and connectivity. Land acquisition issues remain complex. Efforts to engage the private sector, including foreign investors, have resulted in mixed outcomes. Major projects continue to encounter serious problems, such as the China-backed Jakarta–Bandung high-speed rail project.

On relations between the *central and regional governments*, Jokowi has had to juggle conflicting forces. With his background in local government, he is instinctively supportive of local initiative and autonomy. Yet as Schulze and Gonschorek (Chapter 4) show, here too the reform agenda is a sizeable one, and little major reform has been enacted in his term. One-third of the national budget flows through to subnational governments, mostly on a formula-driven basis, yet many of these governments have little to show by way of improved service quality. Local revenue efforts also remain weak, with the large vertical imbalances in the system providing a strong inducement for these governments to pass the responsibility of unpopular taxation measures back to the central government. Significant reforms are said to be under consideration, but they have yet to materialize.

With regard to *social policy*, as noted, poverty has declined very slowly and the Gini ratio has remained high. There is of course no evidence to suggest that these outcomes can be attributable to President Jokowi, either in the positive or negative sense. The slow poverty reduction is primarily the result of slower growth in the context of the now elevated inequality. His administration's social policies have essentially been more of the same, basically adopting the same set of social policy initiatives of the SBY era, with some rebadging. As Chapters 10 to 13 on poverty, education and the labour market show, the relatively small conditional cash transfer programmes, formerly known as *Bantuan Langsung Tunai* (Unconditional Cash Transfers) and now referred to as *Program Keluarga Harapan* (literally Hopeful Families Programme), have achieved some success in targeting the poor, but this is a complex technical and social issue, and mis-targeting is therefore inevitable. The funding guarantees for education and health have been maintained. There is slow progress towards a rudimentary national health scheme, albeit with major gaps in coverage and a chronic under-supply of the requisite professional skills. Inter-jurisdictional coordination is required for effective service delivery. The labour regulatory regime has become more predictable. The important work of the government's principal social policy think-tank, known as TNP2K, located within the office of the vice-president, appears to have been somewhat marginalized.

Jokowi reportedly takes *environmental* issues quite seriously, but there have been few significant policy developments. He combined the portfolios of environment and forestry, which dismayed environmental activists. Illegal deforestation and over-fishing evidently remain rampant. The occasional high-profile destruction of illegal foreign fishing ships is no substitute for a coherent marine management strategy (Resosudarmo and Kosadi, Chapter 15). There has been no concerted action, or regional leadership, on climate change. Nevertheless, the major investments now underway in urban mass transit should at least lead to some gradual improvement in air quality in the major cities.

While Indonesia's democracy remains vibrant, and election processes and results are largely credible, the country's *formal institutions* are still relatively weak (Warburton, Chapter 2). Perhaps not surprising given the complexities involved, legal institutions are developing very slowly, as illustrated by the various comparative international metrics. Bureaucratic reform has been minimal. The highly popular anti-corruption commission (KPK) is frequently under assault by the legislature, and is more tolerated than supported by the administration. Nevertheless, supporters of the Jokowi presidency, and for that matter SBY also, can at least point to the fact that the president has not lurched significantly in the direction of authoritarian leaders like Presidents Trump, Putin, Erdogan and Duterte.

In sum, there is much to admire about President Jokowi. Unlike many among the Indonesian political class, he has great personal integrity. Unlike many of the country's elite, he sets an example in modest living. He achieved office without the usual credentials of dynasty, military or wealth. He rarely if ever displays the arrogance and hubris found among many world leaders. He retains the common touch. His adroit management of the 2014 election campaign illustrated his extraordinary political dexterity. He not only led a party accustomed to opposition and sentimentally attached to the Sukarno legacy and family, but he also faced off an aggressive and richer opponent, while also nullifying the dark politics and innuendo directed at him.

It is no exaggeration to state that Jokowi is arguably the most attractive head of state in contemporary ASEAN. It is true that he has little interest in international affairs, other than in the realm of commercial deals, and that he does not appear comfortable on the international stage. But this can hardly be counted as a criticism. What matters is the quality of his domestic governance, and his ability to at least manage the country's ASEAN and bilateral relationships, especially with the great powers. In this regard he has proven to be quite effective.

Jokowi's strategy is one of small steps — getting things built, removing bureaucratic obstacles for business, backing initiatives for the poor, and good housekeeping. He is not a reforming leader, nor has he appointed reformist ministers, with a few notable exceptions such as his finance minister. There is no coherent strategy of how to translate the 7 per cent growth target into action. He does not have a vision of an internationally oriented Indonesian economy. His social vision is commendable, but it too translates into action in a sporadic and half-hearted manner. His support for protectionist food policies, for example, inflates the domestic price of rice and pushes more Indonesians into poverty than would otherwise be the case (Patunru, Chapter 6; Wihardja, Chapter 14).

Perhaps this judgement is too harsh. Indonesia is an extraordinarily difficult country to govern. At the national level, presidents need to form coalitions of parties and vested interests that are united by little more than opportunism. They have to manage the more than 500 local governments, all democratically elected and many with independent fiscal resources. The sectarian politics behind the removal in 2017 of his one-time Jakarta running mate, Basuki Tjahaja Purnama or Ahok, threatened to polarize the nation. And, as noted, Jokowi had the misfortune to assume office just as one of the largest commodity booms in Indonesian history was coming to an end, which necessitated managing the expectations of an electorate and political class that had grown accustomed to the largesse created by the boom.

1.4 THIS VOLUME

Collectively, the papers in this volume address a number of dimensions that are key to understanding the economic changes in, and challenges for, the Indonesian economy as it seeks to attain high-income status.

This volume opens with an "insider" view. Boediono, who served as vice-president during SBY's second term (2009–14), and before that held all major Cabinet-level economics posts during the Soeharto and democratic eras, provides his reflections on what Indonesia could learn from the experience of the East Asian economies. He includes Japan,

Taiwan, South Korea, Singapore, Hong Kong and, more recently, China and also Vietnam in the group that is unique because, in their quest for development, they carried out broadly similar strategies with similarly successful outcomes.

Relating the East Asian approach and outcomes to his own experiences, Boediono concludes that for Indonesia to improve its policy performance in the coming years, it needs to make progress in three strategic areas, namely, education, bureaucracy and infrastructure. Well-targeted education-cum-health interventions are necessary to raise the quality of Indonesia's human resources over the long run. Moreover, he argues, institutional reform is needed to create an effective bureaucracy that can promote development. And finally, an effective network of infrastructure with a good long-term plan of infrastructures development is key to support the first two goals.

Following this introductory, scene-setting chapter by the editors, Chapter 2 by Eve Warburton discusses whether Indonesia had entered a new era of "developmentalism" under Jokowi. She argues that over the course of the past decade, Indonesia's economic planning has become increasingly "developmentalist" in orientation. Aspects of this model have deep roots in Indonesian history. But a more self-conscious developmentalist agenda re-emerged during President Susilo Bambang Yudhoyono's second term in office (2009–14). This chapter suggests that, under President Jokowi, a new developmentalism has crystallized further and, arguably, become a defining feature of Indonesia's political economy. To advance this argument, Warburton draws upon studies of the "new developmentalism" in middle-income and emerging economies. The strategy is characterized by a normative commitment to an activist state that can engineer fast economic growth, direct industrial upgrading, and ensure economic redistribution. However, she argues that developmental agendas should be distinguished from developmental outcomes. For Indonesia, she argues, state-led programmes for industrialization and inclusive economic growth have often fallen short. Warburton also highlights some structural constraints upon the new developmentalism in Indonesia, with a particular focus upon politics. Specifically, she identifies patronage and clientelism as fundamental challenges to an effective state-led developmental model. Successive Indonesian governments, Jokowi's included, have taken a cautious approach to the political problems that undermine their developmental goals.

In Chapter 3, Arief Ramayandi and Siwage Dharma Negara examine Indonesia's macroeconomic trends and challenges. The chapter discusses the evolution of Indonesian economic management post AFC by concentrating mainly on fiscal and monetary policy in dealing with both internal and external economic challenges. Then it looks at the evolution of macroeconomic management during the two most recent administrations. They highlight fiscal and monetary policy management post the GFC to provide a discussion of whether or not the manner and the style of macroeconomic policy management has changed under the Jokowi presidency. Overall, they argue that there is continuity: that is, the Jokowi administration has also sought to maintain a prudent fiscal rule, a flexible exchange rate regime, an accommodative monetary policy, and an open capital account. In particular, monetary policy is directed towards maintaining exchange rate stability and achieving inflation targets. The two administrations have also faced similar challenges of weak tax revenue and pressure to achieve a balance between fuel subsidies and other social expenditure priorities. What is different, arguably, is that the Jokowi administration faces more complicated external challenges stemming from a combination of lower commodity prices of Indonesia's main exports, increased protectionism around the world, and rising interest rates in advanced economies, particularly the United States. These factors have put Indonesia's macroeconomic stability under pressure in recent years. The chapter also discuss the prospects and challenges that the economy is facing to reform its fiscal structure in this uncertain international economic environment.

Gerrit J. Gonschorek and Günther G. Schulze's Chapter 4 examines Indonesia's intergovernmental fiscal transfer system. They look at the size, allocation mechanisms, and the economic rationale for the various transfer schemes. Their chapter describes some substantial changes in institutional arrangements and in relative magnitudes of the transfers effected by the Jokowi administration. It assesses to what extent the government has shifted the policy stance on fiscal decentralization. It also analyses the effectiveness and efficiency of the existing system including the recently implemented reforms. They observe a significant increase in overall funds transferred to the regions, which demonstrates a commitment to fiscal devolution to the subnational level. The implementation of village funds, they argue, extends Indonesia's fiscal decentralization even further. The new scheme may be the biggest change so far in the intergovernmental transfer system under President Widodo. However, instead of solving more urgent problems, such as increasing the local own source revenue or the overall quality of spending, it devolves more funds and fiscal responsibilities to another level of local government. Therefore, they argue that the policy has shied away from the more far-reaching (but necessary) reforms of the intergovernmental fiscal transfer system. In the implementation of village funds, in particular, the design has been found to be suboptimal.

Chapter 5 by Natasha Hamilton-Hart looks at how well Indonesia's banking and financial systems serve the needs of savers and business. She argues that financial sector performance in recent years has shown a marked improvement in many areas. Financial stability indicators are mostly robust, suggesting a relatively resilient banking sector. The interventionist policies aimed at promoting financial inclusion and growth introduced by the Jokowi administration have so far not been excessively costly. Moreover, a degree of inefficiency may be the price to pay for financial stability. This chapter explores some of the policy and structural sources of inefficiency in the banking sector as they have developed over recent years. Hamilton-Hart shows that Indonesia's banking sector is structurally segmented, with limited competition among the largest banks and a competitive but constrained mid-size bank segment.

Arianto Patunru discusses Indonesia's rising economic nationalism in Chapter 6. He shows that protectionism started to come back in the early 2000s and that, despite some reform initiatives, economic nationalism is in general amplified under the Jokowi administration, and that in all likelihood it will continue to do so in the near future. He examines the political-economic factors that might explain the re-emergence of protectionist measures under Jokowi's presidency. Using the case of fuel and rice as illustrations, Patunru shows that, while economic nationalism might pay politically, it is however detrimental to the poor. It is therefore in Indonesia's interest to resist the continuing push for protectionist policies.

In Chapter 7, Ari Kuncoro discusses trends and challenges in the manufacturing sector. He argues that Indonesian manufacturing has gone from being an export-driven sector to become dependent on the growth of domestic demand. The commodity boom, which was present from 2005 until 2012, has created the familiar "Dutch-disease" problem, in which the booming commodity sector has reduced the incentive for manufacturing exports as domestic demand is readily available. This chapter shows that Indonesia's manufacturing exports are based on fewer and fewer products, which are dominated in particular by palm oil. It also discusses how Indonesia's manufacturing has lagged behind its neighbours in exploiting the international value chain. This is because the country's industrial policies are becoming more inward-looking. Kuncoro argues that traditional sectors like textiles and automotive products are still promising. However, to effectively promote manufacturing exports, Indonesia needs to improve its logistics, lower non-tariff barriers and improve the quality of its human resources.

Some of these challenges are also evident in Indonesia's services sector, which is examined in Chapter 8 by Titik Anas and Thaliya Wikapuspita. They argue that Indonesia has not paid enough attention to this sector. Although services is the largest employer of labour, its contribution to GDP is below the world average. Its productivity is also lower than that of the manufacturing sector. The policies towards services have been relatively more restrictive than those of manufacturing, particularly on foreign investment and workers. The restriction on foreign investment and workers limits its domestic capacity, which in turn translates into a persistent services account deficit and weakened competitiveness in general. During President Jokowi's term, the policies towards the services sector have remained restrictive, notwithstanding new polices on foreign investment in 2016 and foreign workers in 2018. Further foreign investment liberalization, relaxing the list of occupations open to foreign workers, and reforming the tertiary education sector are among the main agenda items for the next government. Reforms in these areas will have the potential to improve the performance of the services sector in particular and modern business in general.

Chapter 9 by Wilmar Salim and Siwage Dharma Negara examines the progress, challenges and policies regarding infrastructure development in Indonesia. The Jokowi administration is ambitious in its plans to develop the country's infrastructure. The authors argue that, compared to the previous administration, the Jokowi government has taken a more pragmatic approach to execute infrastructure development. One of its major policies has been to shift budget allocations away from fuel subsidies and towards infrastructure. Moreover, there have been continued efforts to reform the needed regulatory and institutional aspects to expedite infrastructure development. Notwithstanding this strong political commitment, overall, the progress is not as smooth as hoped for. Limited resources and capacity require the administration to re-evaluate the number of national strategic projects and to be more selective in prioritizing any infrastructure projects. Moreover, this chapter argues that the national strategic projects must be linked more closely to national development plans that have longer time-frames, such as the National Spatial Plan and sectoral master plans. This is necessary to achieve integrated regional development, and to build Indonesia from the periphery, as outlined in the *Nawacita*.

In Chapter 10, Sandra Kurniawati, Daniel Suryadarma, Luhur Bima and Asri Yusrina look at the education system in Indonesia. After successfully improving access to education in the early 1990s, with virtually universal primary school completion and similarly positive trends at the secondary level, Indonesia began investing to improve learning outcomes since 2005. For almost a decade, the country has been spending about one-fifth of its public funds on education. Teachers have received significant salary increases through the certification programme. However, using international test results, this chapter shows that improvements in learning levels are too small to justify the significant investments to date. It argues that without adding accountability measures that focus on learning outcomes, there is little chance that the investments will provide significant returns in the form of substantially improved learning outcomes.

Related to education, in Chapter 11 Chris Manning and Devanto Pratomo review developments in the labour market during the Jokowi presidency. It is set in the context of changing employment, wages and productivity since the Asian Financial Crisis and the policies pursued during the previous Yudhoyono government. They argue that Jokowi's approach has been positive for employment and wages, although less so for labour productivity. Formal sector jobs have been growing quite rapidly and have recovered somewhat in manufacturing, while the downward trend in unemployment has continued. Reform of the minimum wage setting processes has not endeared the president to vocal union groups. But it appears to have moderated the minimum wage increases in the country's main industrial centres. At the same time, a wider wage gap has emerged between permanent and casual workers and this could have contributed to rising inequality.

Chapter 12 by Asep Suryahadi and Ridho Al Izzati examines Jokowi's social assistance programmes. These have given the poor access to education and health services as well as food and cash transfers, and grants for villages as mandated by the Village Law. They assess the implications of these initiatives for poverty and inequality by correlating economic growth with real per capita household consumption growth by quintile at the district level. This chapter shows that economic growth became less pro-poor during the first three years of the Jokowi government, as indicated by the lower growth elasticity of consumption of the poorest 20 per cent of the population. By contrast, those of the middle quintiles have increased significantly and that of the richest 20 per cent the most of all. This indicates that the poor have been less connected to economic growth compared to the middle class and the rich. In turn, this implies that Jokowi's poverty and inequality reduction strategy, through the expansion of social assistance programmes and grants for villages, does not appear to be sufficient to help the poor. Hence, the authors argue that a complementary strategy to connect the poor to economic growth through job creation and income generation is needed.

Addressing a similar set of issues, John McCarthy and Mulyadi Sumarto in Chapter 13 look at distributional politics in Indonesia, where social protection policies are rapidly expanding. They discuss the dilemma of "layering", "nesting" and social fit in Jokowi's poverty policies. Their chapter discusses two programmes most relevant to the poor, the rice-for-welfare and the conditional cash transfer programmes. They draw attention to the tension between a layered approach to social protection, where new institutional arrangements are placed on top of or alongside existing ones, and a "nested" approach where the principles of a community's own distributional arrangements are located within wider state arrangements. The chapter concludes that Indonesia is still in search of a welfare regime that fits with the country's political-economic situation and cultural practices. It suggests that improving the "social" and "institutional fit" of social protection policies will involve working towards a more polycentric approach where the state-supported targeting logic accommodates the social ethics and moral concerns of rural people.

Chapter 14 by Maria Monica Wihardja discusses Indonesia's food policy with special focus on rice. She argues that Indonesia's food policy has a macroeconomic dimension, as it has implications for inflation, for fiscal policy, and it also affects the trade balance. It is central to the government political base, as a failure to manage food policy has the potential to disrupt politico-socio-economic stability. The author examines Indonesia's food value chain, and key policies and programmes under the

Jokowi administration. Posing the question, "has Indonesian food policy failed?", the chapter also examines the shortcomings and challenges facing policymakers to improve the efficiency of the sector.

The final chapter by Budy P. Resosudarmo and Ellisa Kosadi discusses Indonesia's environmental policies during the Jokowi era, with special reference to the country's controversial illegal fishing war. In view of Indonesia's immense environmental challenges, the authors argue that it is time the country started seriously dealing with this issue. SBY clearly showed the world that he was willing to meet this challenge by making climate change policy a top national priority. It remains questionable whether Jokowi has also been willing to do so, despite the controversial war on illegal fishing, led by his minister of marine affairs and fisheries, which has attracted considerable domestic and international media attention. This chapter argues that, in general, Jokowi so far has not significantly improved the management of Indonesia's environment. It is also difficult to determine how much the campaign has been able to reduce the size of illegal fishing. The impact of this illegal fishing war on the national formal fishery sector has been relatively small. The impact might be significant at a local level but only in a few areas in Eastern Indonesia. Moreover, while this local impact could have benefited small-scale fishing operations, it has negatively affected larger operations.

1.5 SUMMING UP

Indonesia is both on the move and at the crossroads. Its citizenry is immeasurably better off than just two generations ago. Its last serious crisis was two decades ago. Since then, living standards have progressed. The country is comfortably within the middle-income group. It has achieved what in retrospect was a remarkably smooth transition from authoritarian rule to democracy, together with a major devolution of power and resources to the regions. Its national borders are secure, and it is recognized throughout the world as a major emerging power.

But it is also at the crossroads, facing the choice between a dynamic and internationally oriented economy and society, and a slower growing, more inward-looking economy, and possibly a less tolerant society. The choices it makes in the coming years will therefore be decisive. The chapters in this volume lay out an agenda for policy reform, to achieve faster economic growth, economic stability, stronger institutions, more liveable cities, better connectivity across a vast archipelago, more inclusive development, and environment sustainability.

Indonesia clearly needs to accelerate its economic growth in order to reach high-income status. With a GDP per capita of US$3,878 in 2017, it will take the country at least two decades of sustained growth acceleration to reach this level, and longer still if the recent growth trajectory persists. Current global economic uncertainties and disruptive technological changes also require policy responses that not only enhance growth but also promote inclusive outcomes. The fourteen chapters that follow provide wide-ranging insights into some of the deep economic and institutional reforms that are required to meet these challenges.

Notes

1. In the 1970s the usual comparator was Nigeria, given its size, tropical location and endowment of energy resources. Around 1970 Nigeria's per capita income and its human capital were somewhat higher than Indonesia's. However, the two countries parted company thereafter. By 1990, Indonesia's per capita income was three times that of Nigeria.
2. See Perkins (2013) who draws out this distinction.
3. For recent analyses of the Indonesian labour market, see also Allen (2016) and Dong and Manning (2017).
4. See Patunru and Rahardja (2015), Patunru (Chapter 6) and Wihardja (Chapter 14).
5. How far these characterizations can be taken is a moot point. Commenting on Prime Minister Mahathir's election victory in May 2018, the cover of the June edition of the *Malaysian Business* magazine described it as "The Rise of Rakyatnomics", a term that remains ill defined, as is the similar Indonesian term *"Ekonomi Rakyat"* (People's Economy).
6. While an increase of this magnitude must be regarded as significant, the analytical rigour of the EODB estimations has come into question following the high-profile resignation of the Bank's chief economist in 2017 over alleged politicization of the numbers.

References

ADB. *Meeting Asia's Infrastructure Needs*. Manila: Asian Development Bank, 2017.
Allen, Emma R. "Analysis of Trends and Challenges in the Indonesian Labour Market". ADB Papers on Indonesia No. 16, March 2016.
Aspinall, Edward, Marcus Mietzner and Dirk Tomsa, eds. *The Yudhoyono Presidency:*

Indonesia's Decade of Stability and Stagnation. Singapore: Institute of Southeast Asian Studies, 2015.

Bappenas. *Rencana Pembangunan Jangka Menengah Nasional (RPJMN) 2015–2019* [National Medium-Term Development Plan 2015–2019]. 3 vols. Jakarta: Bappenas, 2015.

Corden, M. and R. Garnaut. "The Economic Consequences of Mr Trump". *Australian Economic Papers* 51, no. 3 (2018): 1–7.

Dong, S. and C. Manning. "Labour Market Developments at a Time of Heightened Uncertainty". *Bulletin of Indonesian Economic Studies* 53, no. 1 (2017): 1–25.

Fossati, Diego, Hui Yew-Foong, and Siwage Dharma Negara. *The Indonesian National Survey Project: Economy, Society, and Politics*. Trends in Southeast Asia, no. 10/2017. Singapore: ISEAS – Yusof Ishak Institute, 2017.

Hamilton-Hart, Natasha and Günther G. Schulze. "Taxing Times in Indonesia: The Challenge of Restoring Competitiveness and the Search for Fiscal Space". *Bulletin of Indonesian Economic Studies* 52, no. 3 (2016): 265–95.

Hill, Hal and Deasy Pane. "Indonesia and the Global Economy: Missed Opportunities?". In *Indonesia in the New World: Globalisation, Nationalism and Sovereignty*, edited by A.A. Patunru, M. Pangestu and M.C. Basri, pp. 267–93. Singapore: ISEAS – Yusof Ishak Institute, 2018.

HSBC. "ASEAN Economics: When Reforms Meet Politics". *HSBC Analysis* (2017).

Ito, Takatoshi, Kazumasa Iwata, Colin McKenzie and Shujiro Urata. "Did Abenomics Succeed?". *Asian Economic Policy Review* 13, no. 1 (2018): 1–22.

Kementerian Keuangan. "Buku II: Nota Keuangan & RAPBN 2018". 2018 <https://www.kemenkeu.go.id/media/6665/nota-keuangan-apbn-2018-rev.pdf>.

Manning, Chris. "Jokowi Takes His First Shot at Economic Reform". *East Asia Forum*, 13 September 2015 <http://www.eastasiaforum.org/2015/09/13/jokowi-takes-hisfirst-shot-at-economic-reform/>.

McCawley, Peter. "Infrastructure Policy In Indonesia, 1965–2015: A Survey". *Bulletin of Indonesian Economic Studies* 51, no. 2 (2015): 263–85.

Patunru, Arianto. "Jokowi Needs a More Realistic Tax Target". *East Asia Forum*, 23 August 2016 <http://www.eastasiaforum.org/2016/08/23/jokowi-needs-a-more-realistictax-target/>.

———— and Sjamsu Rahardja. "Trade Protectionism in Indonesia: Bad Times and Bad Policy". *Lowy Institute Analysis*, 30 July 2015 <http://www.lowyinstitute.org/files/patunru_and_rahardja_trade_protectionism_in_indonesia_0.pdf>.

Perkins, D.W. *East Asian Development: Foundations and Strategies*. Cambridge, MA: Harvard University Press, 2013.

Ray, David and Lili Yan Ing. "Addressing Indonesia's Infrastructure Deficit". *Bulletin of Indonesian Economic Studies* 52, no. 1 (2016): 1–25.

Tempo. "Terkejut Pencabutan Subsidi Setrum". 23 July 2017, pp. 82–83.

Warburton, Eve. "Indonesia: Why Economic Nationalism Is So Popular". *Lowy Interpreter*, 25 August 2015 <http://www.lowyinterpreter.org/post/2015/08/25/Indonesia-Why-economic-nationalism-is-so-popular.aspx>.

————. "Jokowi and the New Developmentalism". *Bulletin of Indonesian Economic Studies* 52, no. 3 (2016): 297–320.

World Bank. *The East Asian Miracle: Economic Growth and Public Policy*, Washington, D.C.: World Bank, 1993.

————. "The Growth Report: Strategies for Sustained Growth and Inclusive Development". Commission on Growth and Development, World Bank, Washington, D.C., 2008.

————. *Indonesia: Avoiding the Trap — Development Policy Review 2014*. Washington, D.C.: World Bank, 2014.

————. "Indonesia Economic Quarterly: Closing the Gap". October 2017.

————. *Doing Business 2017: Equal Opportunity for All*. Washington, DC: World Bank, 2017.

2

A NEW DEVELOPMENTALISM
IN INDONESIA?

Eve Warburton

2.1 INTRODUCTION

Scholars have had difficulty characterizing the economic orientation of the contemporary Indonesian state. Following the devastating Asian Financial Crisis (AFC) of 1997–98, the Indonesian government opened up many parts of its economy, and pursued a neoliberal economic model recommended by its lenders, the International Monetary Fund and the World Bank. At the same time, many sectors remained characterized by high levels of state intervention and market distortion. Despite the democratic transition and the new government's pursuit of liberal economic policies to ensure competition, transparency and accountability, old oligarchs and predatory state actors maintained much political and economic power. State capacity has also continued to vary enormously across ministries and regional governments, and problems of coordination and communication

This article was first published in *Journal of Southeast Asian Economies* 35, no. 3 (December 2018).

mean that different state bodies often pursue contradictory economic policy paths. As a result, since the end of the New Order, analysts have variously identified the new democracy as being "neoliberal" (Aspinall 2012), "quasi-developmental" (Sato 2017), "oligarchic" (Hadiz and Robison 2013), "nationalist" (Patunru and Rahardja 2015), or some combination thereof.

Yet, this chapter argues that over the course of the past decade, a discernible developmental model has (re)emerged. To advance this argument, the study draws upon a body of literature on the "new developmentalism" in middle-income and emerging economies. The new developmentalism is characterized by a normative commitment to an activist state, and a rejection of neoliberalism's blind faith in small government (Khan and Christiansen 2010; Trubek et al. 2013; Schneider 2015; Döring, Santos and Pocher 2017). Economic policy is underpinned by the idea that states should intervene in markets in order to stimulate economic growth, direct industrial upgrading, and ensure economic redistribution. The new developmentalism is heterodox and flexible, and state activism is supplemented by selective support for aspects of an orthodox and liberal economic strategy. It is a paradigm associated with emerging economies such as China, and often Brazil (at least during the first decade of the 2000s), where activist states seek to transform their country's comparative advantage, and graduate to a higher-income status.

Aspects of this model have deep roots in Indonesian history.[1] But, a more self-conscious developmentalist agenda re-emerged during President Susilo Bambang Yudhoyono's second term in office (2009–14). The chapter suggests that under President Joko "Jokowi" Widodo, the new developmentalism has crystallized further and, arguably, become a defining feature of Indonesia's political economy. It specifically points to the Jokowi administration's emphasis on an activist industrial policy, its obsession with moving up international rankings, the renewed focus upon state-owned enterprises (SOEs) as engines of economic growth, and the institutionalization of state-funded welfare and social protection programmes.

At the same time, one must distinguish between developmental *agendas* and developmental *outcomes*. Successive post-New Order governments have overseen steady growth, a stable democratic regime, and incremental improvements on a range of international indices measuring governance quality and socio-economic outcomes. Ultimately, however, progress has been slow, stilted and uneven, and many ambitious state-led programmes for industrialization and inclusive economic growth have fallen short. Like many other middle-income emerging economies, Indonesia faces a set of structural and institutional challenges that make state-led developmentalism difficult. In the economic sphere, the country still relies heavily on primary commodity exports, and post-boom conditions have placed pressure on the state budget and, therefore, upon President Jokowi's developmental agenda. High levels of labour informality and a stagnant manufacturing sector continue to hold back transformative economic growth.

The second key challenge is political. Policymaking in post-New Order Indonesia remains subject to the distortionary effects of patronage politics, and the country's political elite has shown little enthusiasm for extending or improving mechanisms for transparency and accountability. Despite high expectations, during his first term in office, President Jokowi has taken a conservative approach to such problems. The current government's emphasis upon growth, infrastructure, and investment, has eclipsed any substantive agenda for bureaucratic, legal and anti-corruption reform. The new developmentalism in Indonesia is thus narrow, and in some ways shallow. While seeking to reach new heights on global economic rankings, successive administrations have proven unable to overcome the political problems that undermine developmentalist agendas.

A brief caveat should be taken into account. Some scholars use the concept of a new developmentalism with a normative objective, in order to recommend a particular policy path for emerging economies.[2] In this chapter, the term is used in a positivist sense. The goal is to characterize existing patterns and trends in Indonesian economic policymaking during the post-Soeharto period, and to identify the political and economic constraints upon developmental agendas.

The rest of this chapter is structured as follows. The second section explores an emerging literature on the new developmentalism. The subsequent section makes the case for its application to contemporary Indonesia, with particular reference to industrial policy, SOEs and state-subsidized welfare schemes. This section also reflects upon the quality of these economic programmes and the fiscal constraints upon developmental agendas. The fourth section turns to look at political constraints, and identifies the fragmenting effect of patronage and clientelism as a fundamental challenge to an effective state-led developmental model. The final section concludes.

2.2 THE NEW DEVELOPMENTALISM: AMBITIONS AND AGENDAS

The idea of a new developmental paradigm has gained increasing academic currency over the past decade. Scholars deploy the term as a means to define and explain the economic strategies of middle-income and emerging economies in the twenty-first century (Schneider 2015; Döring, Santos and Pocher 2017). As Schneider (2015) puts it, "what differentiates developmental states from other states — nearly all of which seek to promote growth — is that developmental states are designed to shift a country's global ranking rapidly and permanently". To achieve such rapid growth, developmental states actively intervene in the economy to engineer new comparative advantage, invest in industrial upgrading, and move their economy's sectoral bias away from low value-added production (Khan and Christiansen 2010).

The new developmentalism is marked by a more "heterodox" set of goals and prescriptions that blend aspects of liberal orthodoxy with a commitment to state interventionism (Bresser-Pereira 2009).[3] Where the old developmentalists were "inward looking", contemporary developmentalism responds to and embraces globalization (Khan and Christiansen 2010). In an assessment of a new developmentalism in Brazil, Carrillo (2014) explains how such an approach involves "increased government intervention in market activities, particularly in the drafting and executing of industrial policies, as well as providing capital to private firms in order to support their expansion and enhance their market position". Under a new developmentalism, the state embraces free and open trade policy and seeks access to international markets for state and private national companies to promote their products and enable their direct investments abroad (Döring, Santos and Pocher 2017). Studies on China, for example, emphasize how, through a policy of state activism, the country has successfully moved up global value chains in commodity production (Gallagher and Shafaeddin 2011). At the same time, China has opened up its economy significantly, selectively liberalizing key sectors, investment policy and trade policy, too (Hsueh 2016).

The new developmentalism also responds to the socio-economic problems common to middle-income and emerging economies. Within this paradigm, the state is viewed as a crucial tool for redistribution, and state-run welfare programmes and social subsidies are key ingredients in the new model. To return to the Brazilian example, scholars point how the government's pro-poor cash transfer programmes and other welfare interventions meant that Brazil's growth, primarily during the first decade of the twenty-first century, was broadly inclusive (Carrillo 2014; Trubek et al. 2013). In short, the new developmentalism is characterized by government intervention in domestic markets, state support for domestic companies and SOEs, and state-run programmes for economic redistribution — supplemented with a selective embrace of more orthodox liberal policies.

Developmentalist "ambition" and intervention, however, must be analytically separated out from developmental "effectiveness" (Schneider 2015). For middle-income and emerging countries, the challenges of executing a developmentalist model are many. Doner and Schneider (2016), for instance, identify high levels of inequality, poverty, and labour informality as structural problems that many middle-income economies face, and which make public investments in economic upgrading, research and development, and even in tertiary education, more difficult for governments to justify. The ubiquity of patronage politics and clientelism in many middle-income countries similarly fragments the coalitions of societal, business and state actors that are necessary for successful execution of a developmental agenda (Doner and Schneider 2016; Carrillo 2014). As a concept, therefore, the new developmentalism is defined not only in terms of its ideational orientation and policy agenda, but also in terms of a common set of institutional problems and structural constraints.

2.3 A NEW DEVELOPMENTALISM IN INDONESIA?

The concept of a new developmentalism can help to make sense of economic policymaking in contemporary Indonesia and account for its contradictions and, ultimately, its limited success. Over the past two decades, Indonesia has maintained a commitment to macroeconomic stability, savings and a (relatively) open trade policy. The country has continued to climb on indexes measuring ease of doing business, investment and trade policies, and has also improved slowly on global measures of government effectiveness. The Index of Economic Freedom 2018, for example, ranked Indonesia the sixty-ninth freest economy in the world out of 180 countries, classifying it as "moderately free" (Index of Economic Freedom 2018). Indonesia was placed fifteenth out of the forty-three Asia-Pacific countries, which, according to the report, means "its overall score is above the regional and world averages".[4] Such outcomes indicate not just prudent economic management, but even a disposition for a liberal and relatively open approach to economic planning.

Yet, analysts regularly point to an increasing volume of statist and nationalist economic interventions over the past five to ten years (Patunru and Rahardja 2015; Warburton 2017). This fusion of a selective liberal orthodoxy with economic nationalism is best understood within the framework of the new developmentalism. This section outlines the Indonesian government's activist approach to industrial policy, the expansion of SOEs in the economy, and the institutionalization of state-run social welfare schemes. It also looks briefly at the structural and fiscal constraints that have frustrated many of these developmental policy agendas.

2.3.1 Industrial Activism

An interventionist industrial policy was revived during the second term of President Yudhoyono (2009–14). As was the case at previous points in Indonesian history, a commodities boom gave the government fiscal freedom to pursue an activist approach towards its industrial goals. This approach was expressed most clearly in the Master Plan for Acceleration and Expansion of Economic Development 2011–2025 (MP3EI), and in a new Industry Law (3/2014), which laid out a vision for a value-added economy that could move the country beyond its reliance on raw commodity exports. It was claimed that Indonesia would "transform into a developed nation in the twenty-first century and [enter] the top ten advanced economies in the world by 2025 and the top six by 2050" (Sato 2017). This was a self-conscious effort to move Indonesia up global economic rankings via industrial intervention.

The MP3EI and the new Industry Law promoted non-tariff measures and tax incentives to direct investment downstream across a range of sectors, from raw commodities industries, petroleum refining, car manufacturing to telecommunications technology (Sato 2017). The most controversial policy associated with this industrial push was the ban on raw mineral exports, executed by the Yudhoyono government in early 2014. The ban was framed as a crucial innovation to promote a downstream mineral smelting industry in Indonesia's mining sector, which until this point had been driven almost entirely by the export of unprocessed minerals (Warburton 2018). Similar restrictions and taxes were placed on other raw commodities like rattan and cacao as well, in order to engineer a new place for Indonesia further up the global commodity chain (Patunru and Rahardja 2015).

The plans and policies laid out in the MP3EI were, for the most part, sustained by the Jokowi administration, though rebranded and tweaked in various ways. From petroleum refining to mobile phone production, the Jokowi government has continued to play an activist role in the economy in order to compel investment towards higher value industries.[5] Arguably, however, the most important feature of Jokowi's plan for industrialization and economic growth has been his emphasis upon building and modernizing Indonesia's physical infrastructure, in order to reduce the logistical costs of doing business around the archipelago. During the Yudhoyono period, infrastructure investment was weak and construction progress was painfully slow. Projects stalled due to land acquisition problems, regulatory bottlenecks, low-quality contractors and generally poor planning (see Salim and Negara, Chapter 9). When Jokowi took office, he promised more action and better results. The new government reallocated a large tranche of state money from fuel subsidies such that spending on public infrastructure doubled between 2014 and 2018 from 8.4 to 18 per cent of the state budget (Salim and Negara, Chapter 9). Jokowi set out to add another 35,000 MW of electricity to the grid, and build 5,000 km of railways, 1,000 km of toll roads, and twenty-four seaports.

There is little doubt that Jokowi has gone much further than Yudhoyono in terms of prioritizing and funding infrastructure development. However, Jokowi's industrial vision for an infrastructure boom and value-added economy has also suffered various financial and political problems. First, attracting private and foreign investors into new industrial sectors and infrastructure projects has been difficult. As part of a series of economic reform packages, the government tried to remove many bureaucratic obstacles for private investors (Amin 2015). Deregulation and debureaucratization of the economy have been central to the president's political message during his first three years in office, and he has achieved notable results. According to the World Bank's 2018 Ease of Doing Business survey, Indonesia improved nineteen positions compared to the previous year and now sits at seventy-two on the list (World Bank 2018).

But on closer inspection, levels of investment in key sectors have remained below the targeted levels, and below what the government needs to realize is industrial boom. For example, the government allocated approximately US$25 billion of the state budget for new infrastructure projects, state-owned companies have been tasked with US$48 billion worth of new contracts, and US$83.5 billion was slated to come from private investors (*Straits Times* 2018). But as was the case during the Yudhoyono period, private businesses have shown limited interest in the capital-intensive, long-term projects that the government is offering. The author could not obtain precise figures on the realization of private investment into infrastructure over the past three years, but in general domestic and foreign investment realization sits at between just 30 to 40 per cent, according to the government (*Straits Times* 2017). Darmin Nasution, Coordinating Minister for Economic Affairs, publicly acknowledged that, "only 31 per cent of pledged domestic investment and 27 per cent of foreign investment has been realized over the past decade" (McBeth 2018). According to one report, "the government counted a total of 190 cases ... between 2010 and 2017 ... where investors decided not to continue with their investment plans even though they had already obtained a principle license (*Izin Prinsip*) from the Investment Coordinating Board (BKPM)" (*Indonesia Investments* 2018).

Part of the problem is that Jokowi's economic reforms have focused primarily upon cutting red tape to speed up processes for establishing a business, registering property and improving access to credit. These are the changes that have largely been responsible for the increase in Indonesia's competitiveness on the World Bank index. However, for businesses to want to make large, long-term investments in capital-intensive projects — like building toll roads, ports and railways — they need regulatory and legal certainty. Regulations relating to taxation, local content, foreign staffing requirements, and legal protections for long-term investments, are all highly discretionary in Indonesia and prone to regular revision. For this reason, investment realization remains low.

In some sectors, investment has, in fact, decreased. The energy sector is one such case. Investment in oil and gas exploration has declined since Jokowi came to office, from US$1.3 billion in 2013 to under US$100 million in 2016 (*Katadata* 2017). This decline has persisted despite the government's rhetorical commitment to increase exploration and production in order to reduce the country's reliance on expensive crude and petroleum imports.

The tepid response from investors can in part be attributed to low oil prices, but companies are also turned off by land acquisition problems, contract extension concerns, and ongoing changes to the contract system itself (*Katadata* 2017).

Industrial interventions, such as export restrictions, domestic market obligations, and local content requirements are also subject to regular revision (Zain 2017; Munthe and Asmarini 2018). An illustrative example comes from the mining sector. In January 2017, President Jokowi relaxed the 2014 mineral export ban, despite initially expressing his enthusiasm for the downstream strategy. The state-owned miner, Antam, had suffered a blow to its profits when the raw nickel ore ban was introduced. The Jokowi government decided to allow ore exports in order to help boost the company's bottom line. Businesses in the smelting sector were incensed; their investments had been contingent upon the ban, which ensured a captive domestic market for raw mineral ores (Warburton 2018). In general, such a discretionary and ad hoc approach to industrial intervention has meant that investment has been lower than expected, and much lower than what is needed for the industrial boom that Jokowi seeks.

2.3.2 Renewed Emphasis on the State-Owned Sector

A second core feature of Indonesia's new developmentalism is the renewed emphasis on expanding the economic role of SOEs. During the early Yudhoyono years, the government made regular commitments to reduce the number of state companies. In reality, however, the sector remained largely unreformed. In key sectors such as electricity provision and petroleum distribution, the state electricity provider, *Perusahaan Listrik Negara* (PLN), and the national oil company, Pertamina, have maintained a monopoly. Studies show that SOEs own more and have a greater market share in the contemporary Indonesian economy that they did prior to the liberal reforms introduced at the end of the New Order (Carney and Hamilton-Hart 2015; Sato 2017).

State-owned companies have been central to President Jokowi's economic agenda. First, in pursuit of fast-paced infrastructure development, President Jokowi tasked state-owned construction companies with most of the large, strategic projects (Setiaji and Suroyo 2017). Funds borrowed from the World Bank, as well as China and Japan, have been used to finance projects that are being built by SOEs, including new airports, roads, railroads. The much-vaunted Bandung–Jakarta high-speed rail link, for example, is being built by a consortium of Chinese and local SOEs using a US$4.5 billion loan from the China Development Bank (Setiaji and Suroyo 2017).

Beyond infrastructure, the government also laid out a plan to establish state-owned holding companies in strategic sectors, including the mining, oil and gas, infrastructure, and financial services sectors.[6] The goal is to pool state companies' assets, such that new holding companies can leverage more capital, expand their domestic and overseas investments, and eventually become global corporate champions (*Insiders Stories* 2017). In the extractive sectors, the Jokowi government has pushed state companies to take shares or take over strategic, foreign-owned mineral and hydrocarbon projects as the contracts of foreign companies begin to expire (Warburton 2017). Pertamina, for example, was handed the contract for the Mahakam Block, the country's most strategic gas block, which had previously been operated by France's Total and Japan's Inpex. To maintain and expand gas production at Mahakam, Pertamina has allocated US$1.7 billion for 2018 (Singgih 2018). Inalum, a state-owned mining company, meanwhile, is poised to acquire a controlling share in Freeport Indonesia's Grasberg gold and copper mine in Papua, an acquisition that will cost upwards of US$4 billion.

Again, however, developmental ambition appears stronger than developmental capacity. Indonesia's state enterprises have had to borrow large sums of money in order to execute strategic projects and acquisitions. In 2015, the government injected US$3 billion into its state companies. But Jokowi must manage a yawning budget deficit and the government cannot afford to capitalize its state companies for the projects and roles they have been assigned. Instead, the government has sought new ways to increase state companies' assets and, therefore, their access to credit. The establishment of holding companies is one such mechanism. Both Pertamina and Inalum were in the process of being transformed into sectoral holding companies at the time of writing, in order to help them access the credit needed to take over foreign resource projects. The government has also encouraged state enterprises to engage in creative accounting strategies. For example, PLN used a new accounting method in 2016 that allowed it to "value its fixed assets at their current market price, rather than their purchase price as had previously been the case", which had the effect of adding an extra US$50 billion of equity to the company's ledger (Guild

2018). In 2017 and 2018, PLN went on to borrow an extra US$3 billion (Guild 2018). The company is in desperate need of extra funds, not only to invest in President Jokowi's planned electrification projects, but also to manage the costs of rising electricity prices, which the government ordered PLN to absorb so that Indonesian consumers were not hit by the price hike.

The renewed emphasis on state-owned companies, and the tasks these enterprises have been dealt, have left both the companies and the government financially exposed. Outside analysts, and even members of the executive, have expressed concern over state companies' mounting debt (Guild 2018). The Finance Minister, Sri Mulyani, even formally warned PLN that its debts were becoming unsustainable (Jefriando 2017). More broadly, the government's stated goal of transforming its state companies into global and professional corporate giants will be harder to achieve if those companies are forced to make inefficient business decisions and take on heavy debts, in order to meet the government's economic agenda and political objectives.

2.3.3 State-Run Welfare Schemes

A third feature of Indonesia's post-New Order economic model is the institutionalization of a state-sponsored welfare system. As was the case in the developmental states of Korea and Taiwan, democratization in Indonesia provided openings for societal groups and reformist politicians to demand more state investment in social protection and safety nets. From 2004, in the area of health cover, the Yudhoyono government introduced the *Jamkesmas* scheme (formally *Askeskin*), which "dramatically increased health care coverage ... covering about 86 million persons out of a total population of 245 million in 2013, at a total cost of Rp8.29 trillion, about US$861 million" (Aspinall 2014). An even more encompassing social security system began in 2011, under the BPJS (Social Security Administering Agency), which provided individual health cover and workplace insurance. The system requires employer and employee donations, but the state subsidizes coverage for low-income citizens. Jokowi, once in office, poured more funding into, expanded, and in some cases rebranded, the central government's welfare schemes.[7] These distributive programmes have contributed to a real expansion in citizens' access to healthcare and social security, and by 2018 BPJS was serving over 190 million members — 60 per cent of whom are recipients of the government subsidy — making it among the largest social insurance schemes in the world (Heriyanto 2018).

The institutionalization of universal coverage was, according to Aspinall (2014), a product of democratization, and the opening up of the policymaking process to social forces, non-government organizations (NGOs), unions, healthcare activists and scholars, together with a parliament which "was generally welfarist and statist on economic matters". Programmes to expand access to basic education and welfare provision attracted a broad coalition of support and, as a result, state-run welfare schemes are now a central and permanent feature of the post-New Order state.

Despite this, economic growth over the past two decades has not been broadly inclusive. The poverty headcount has steadily declined from 23.4 per cent in 1999 to 11.2 per cent in 2014 (Yusuf and Sumner 2017). But on other measures of poverty, the figures are less impressive. When it comes to improving labour informality, underemployment, and unemployment, consecutive Indonesian governments have struggled to make progress. According to a study by Yusuf and Sumner (2017), for indicators on living standards and assets, "there was unequivocal and impressive progress ... [but there was] little improvement in employment growth since the late 1990s". Levels of labour informality as a proportion of the labour force have remained more or less the same, even since the 1970s (Kim, Sumner and Yusuf 2017). The growth that accompanied the resources boom from approximately 2003 to 2013 also produced a sharp rise in inequality, upon which the state's distributive programmes had little discernible impact.

State welfare programmes also face serious financial challenges. For example, in the years since its inception, the BPJS budget deficit has grown at an alarming pace. By 2016, the institution was in deep financial stress due to "out-of-control financing and unpaid contributions" (Rakhmat and Tarahita 2017). The deficit hit Rp9.7 trillion (or just over S$880.9 million) in 2016 (Rakhmat and Tarahita 2017). As a result, BPJS has failed to reimburse hospitals for their patients' procedures, which places enormous pressure upon Indonesia's already resource-poor hospital system.

State welfare schemes are a core feature of Indonesia's developmental paradigm, which has provided Indonesian citizens — and particularly the poorest citizens — with a remarkable increase in access to basic workplace and health insurance, as well as subsidized education. However, these programmes have not been accompanied by significant improvements in social equity. In other developmental economies such as Brazil, inclusive growth and a decline in inequality was achieved through "a combination of rising wages, increasing formal-sector jobs growth, and expanding social protection" (Carrillo 2014). Indonesia's developmental model is yet to motivate such a shift away from the informal sector, which is a fundamental means via which a country advances to a higher income status.

2.4 POLITICAL CONSTRAINTS ON DEVELOPMENTAL AGENDAS

The discussion so far has highlighted how a state-led developmental model faces a complex set of fiscal constraints and structural economic challenges in Indonesia. Recently, however, scholarship on the middle-income trap has turned attention to the political conditions that stunt transformative growth in countries like Indonesia. In their influential work on the political causes of the middle-income trap, Doner and Schneider (2016) argue that countries such as Indonesia lack the supportive and coherent political coalitions necessary for difficult institutional reform, like reforms for developing an efficient and merit-based bureaucracy, or for establishing effective mechanisms for transparency and accountability. Institution-building is so elusive for many lower and middle-income countries, because of the fragmentation that characterizes political and social groups within the state and within the economic sphere (Doner and Schneider 2016).

What is the nature and cause of this fragmentation? Comparative studies indicate that in countries with political systems characterized by high levels of clientelism, personalism and patronage, bureaucratic reform and economic upgrading are inherently difficult (Doner and Schneider 2016; World Bank 2015). Indonesia's experience confirms these propositions. Aspinall (2012), for example, has described the Indonesian state as "a nation in fragments". Aspinall found the source of this fragmentation in the ubiquity of patronage and clientelism, which he suggests are the "organizing principles" of Indonesia's political life:

> [P]atronage is defined as a material resource disbursed for particularistic purposes and for political benefit, typically distributed via clientelist networks, where clientelism is defined as a personalistic relationship of

power. Clientelistic networks devoted to the distribution of patronage have long been central features of Indonesian politics … [T]he weakening of alternate modes of organizing and imagining political identity have helped to heighten this feature of the political economy and made patronage the most important glue of political relations in Indonesia.

The patronage that defines political relations splinters institutions that are crucial for the state's developmental ambitions, and undermines coalitions for reform. Take, for example, the bureaucracy. The democratic era produced new patterns of patronage distribution and politicization at the various levels of government, and interventions to improve the quality of state services often clash with the clientelistic systems that underpin Indonesia's sprawling bureaucracy. For example, when it comes healthcare, according to Aspinall (2014):

> … the health care system is a site of major corruption in Indonesia. The media is full of reports about corruption scandals in public hospitals, involving everything from skimming off funds in construction projects, equipment purchases, and pharmaceutical orders, to manipulation of patient or staffing data and outright theft of equipment. As elsewhere in the public sector, such corruption is integral to the system, and is critical to the manner by which staff are recruited, promoted, and assigned tasks within it.

Rosser (2018) paints a similarly bleak picture of Indonesia's education system. He demonstrates the distortionary effect that patronage and clientelism have had on the quality of Indonesia's education provision, and argues that perverse incentives have undermined teacher quality and entrenched resistance to new merit-based systems that would restructure the sector.

Politicization of Indonesia's bureaucracy also undermines attempts to improve the quality of state services. In the regions, incumbent district and provincial heads often view the civil service as a source of partisan support (Rosser 2018). Since direct local elections began in 2005, local leaders have used their authority over the bureaucracy to compel government employees to mobilize their networks and collect votes during election season. Individuals whose loyalty is in doubt are regularly demoted to less senior positions. To quote Aspinall (2014) again, in the healthcare system, "the links to the political system are also clear, with local health bureaucrats being political appointees who are expected to furnish their superiors with kickbacks and support them in election campaigns". Pisani (2013) makes similar observations about local education services based on her ethnographic work in regions throughout the country: "For the district head or mayor, creating teaching posts is a way of thanking people who helped with the election or who otherwise deserved a small-to-medium-sized favour."

The picture looks similar at the national level. The distribution of ministerial posts for patronage purposes was a definitive feature of Yudhoyono's approach to government. During the Yudhoyono decade, ministries were effectively "leased out" to political parties in the process of negotiating a governing coalition (Mietzner 2013). Ministries with authority to issue business licenses or procurement contracts, like the Ministry of State-Owned Enterprises, Ministry of Transport, and ministries that oversee natural resource industries, are highly sought after by political party elites. Party leaders view these "wet" ministries as a crucial instrument to raise funds for party activities (Mietzner 2013). The institutional effect of this system is that ministries become fiefdoms, and senior bureaucratic positions are negotiated between competing networks of vested interests and politico-business elites. Against this backdrop, interventions to improve quality and performance through merit-based promotions system have faced opposition from senior figures within bureaucracies (both national and regional) who benefit from the status quo.

President Jokowi's brand of developmentalism is characterized by a conservative approach to such political institutional problems. Despite high expectations at the start of his presidency, the Jokowi administration has not made transparency, accountability or law reform a political priority. For much of his first term in office, the president has favoured political stability over a disruptive reformist agenda. For example, bureaucratic reform has been reduced to a vaguely defined programme of *revolusi mental* or "mental revolution", which encourages positive thinking, nationalism and hygiene among civil servants. The government's plans to rationalize and downsize the bureaucracy by 300,000 positions also appear to have stalled (*Straits Times* 2016). Perhaps the clearest example comes from the Ministry of State-Owned Enterprises. Despite Jokowi's ostensible goal of transforming the SOEs into engines for economic growth, the government has made decisions and appointments that expose the ministry to politicization. For example, Rini Soemarno's political position within the administration casts a shadow over the government's claim to be rationalizing and modernizing its state companies. Rini is one of the president's strategic political allies, and her support was critical to his success back in 2014. She helped to organize and finance Jokowi's presidential campaign in 2014 (Power 2016), and distributed senior positions on SOE boards to prominent actors from the Jokowi campaign, in what appeared to be an obvious act of patronage distribution (Aziza 2017). Since taking up her ministerial post, she has also regularly reshuffled and restructured state companies' leadership boards in search of pliable and loyal individuals.

Institutions designed to ensure transparency and accountability have struggled to manage the enormous task which they have been dealt. The country's political elite have done little to extend or improve the relevant mechanisms that were established in the early years of *Reformasi*. Indonesia has a solid cast of regulatory bodies, most of which were established as part of the broader democratic transition after 1998: The Corruption Eradication Commission (Komisi Pemberantasan Korupsi, KPK); the Business Competition Supervisory Commission (Komisi Pengawas Persaingan Usaha, KPPU); the Ombudsman; and the Financial Auditing Agency (Badan Pemeriksaan Keuangan). These agencies perform their tasks in politically difficult circumstances, and invariably face resistance and threats from vested interests within the business and political elite. And they must do so with limited resources. Under such conditions, their capacity, understandably, various widely.

Let us look briefly at the KPK. Since it began operations in 2003, the KPK has remained one of the country's most visible and popular institutional products of the *Reformasi* era (Butt 2015). Its sting operations have put many high-profile politicians, judges, bureaucrats and business people behind bars. The KPK is, therefore, regularly targeted by Indonesia's political elite and law enforcement. Throughout the Yudhoyono period, and in the early years of the Jokowi administration, KPK commissioners were intimidated and arrested by police, and the DPR made several attempts to curb the body's powers of investigation. President Yudhoyono himself never spearheaded attacks on the KPK, nor did he explicitly support campaigns to check the Commission's authority. However, as Butt (2015) concludes, "there is little evidence that [Yudhoyono] contributed much to the success of [the] KPK. He rarely stepped in to defend them when they came into conflict with powerful and resentful political players."

President Jokowi has offered a similarly weak defence of the KPK in the face of fresh attacks (Muhtadi 2015). For example, in February 2018, the DPR passed revisions to the 2014 Law on Legislative Bodies (the MD3 Law). The revisions make prosecuting and investigating legislators more complicated, and provide legislators with powers to take legal action against people or institutions it feels have defamed or insulted them (Robet 2018). President Jokowi allowed the revisions to pass, despite widespread opposition from the country's academics and activists. Jokowi's approach to the KPK has been passive, choosing neither to defend nor explicitly undermine it. The KPK's mandate and its powers of investigation are perpetually at the risk of being eroded by a political class that seeks to maintain and protect opportunities for rent seeking and patronage distribution.

The KPPU provides another example of the plight of Indonesia's watchdogs. The KPPU receives far less media attention than the KPK, and its record has been more mixed. Like KPK, the KPPU was a product of the post-Soeharto reforms, and was established under the 1999 Anti-Monopoly Law. While it deals primarily with bid-rigging in tenders, mostly in the construction and infrastructure sectors, it has also increased its investigations into uncompetitive mergers and acquisitions, cartel behaviour and price-fixing. Some assessments cast the KPPU's investigations as mostly independent, and free from interference from either political or corporate interests. However, there have also been cases where large companies have leaned on, or offered incentives to, KPPU commissioners in return for a favourable ruling on their case (Reuters 2009). Davidson (2016) also speculates that several high-profile cases against the foreign acquisition of domestic companies were politically motivated, and designed to benefit specific domestic state-owned and private domestic companies. Beyond the vulnerabilities of the KPPU itself, the commission's decisions can also be turned over in the courts, which are themselves notoriously corrupt. The KPPU's most serious challenge, however, is the sheer enormity of its task. The vast majority of cases it handles — upwards of 70 per cent — are for suspect tenders (KPPU 2016). Between 2000 and 2016, the KPPU managed to file 189 cases against companies involved in bid-rigging, or an average of eleven cases per year (KPPU 2016). Such figures indicate that the regulator is barely scratching the surface of a problem that sits at the heart of Indonesia's political economy.[8]

2.5 CONCLUSION

Contemporary Indonesian economic planning displays the core features of a "new developmentalism" that scholars have identified in other parts of the world, both in terms of policy agenda and rhetorical framing. Jokowi, in particular, has articulated a vision for fast-paced, inclusive economic growth. Three areas of economic planning stand out as reflecting the new developmental paradigm — industrial activism, expansion of SOEs, and the institutionalization of state-run welfare schemes. The objective of an activist state is to move Indonesia quickly into a higher stratum within global economic rankings. And although institutional reform in Indonesia has been slow, it has been persistent. Indonesia's trajectory on most international indices that measure government capacity, ease of doing business, and perceptions of corruption, all tell a relatively positive story about the nation over the past two decades.

On closer inspection, however, the new developmentalism is, in many ways, dysfunctional. Political factors constitute a major source of this dysfunction. Comparative research tells us that patronage-based and personalistic political systems make structural reform immensely difficult (Doner and Schneider 2016; Carrillo 2014). Jokowi's developmental focus has eclipsed an agenda for political or legal reform. Observers expected his presidency to breathe new life into the institutions responsible for transparency and accountability. But, in fact, the president has proved to be immensely conservative. This approach, ironically, undermines the institutions that are necessary for the fast-paced developmental success that President Jokowi so desires.

Notes

1. During the New Order period (1967–98), the state was sometimes characterized as a "repressive developmental" regime (Feith 1981). The transition to democracy after 1998 was followed by a period of economic liberalization and privatization.
2. See, for example, Bresser-Pereira (2009).
3. This literature demarcates the old developmentalism of the twentieth century from the contemporary developmentalist approach that took root in countries such as Brazil, Argentina and Mexico. The old developmentalism of the 1980s emphasized import substitution as the core strategy to catch up with industrialized nations. In contemporary middle-income countries, developmentalism is concerned with the industrialization of export-oriented sectors, and the pursuit of foreign markets.
4. The full report can be accessed at <https://www.heritage.org/index/country/indonesia>.
5. In some cases, industrial interventions have produced results. For example,

tough local content requirements compelling phone companies to manufacture their handsets locally appear to have engineered something of a boom. According to one report, "prior to the imposition of the requirement in 2013, there was no real phone manufacturing industry in Indonesia. The following year, fifteen companies — including Samsung and China's Oppo Electronics — applied to the Industry Ministry for production license" (*Thailand Business News* 2018). The government now claims that over 60 million handsets were produced in Indonesia in 2017 — a remarkable increase from the 5 million produced back in 2014 before the local content rules had made their mark (Novalius 2018).

6. Such plans, in fact, began in the late Yudhoyono years to consolidate ineffective SOEs, divest some shares in the better ones — while retaining the state's majority stake — and boost the healthier ones through mergers and acquisitions. Momentum, however, increased markedly under President Jokowi as part of his greater emphasis on SOEs as engines for fast-paced development.

7. Indonesians in the low socio-economic brackets now have three separate cards entitling them to state subsidized services: Kartu Indonesia Sehat (Healthy Indonesia Card, which is a rebranding of BPJS); Kartu Indonesia Pintar (Education Indonesia Card, which covers set costs for the poorest Indonesian school children); and Kartu Indonesia Keluarga (the Family Indonesia Card, which provides a cash transfer to the poorest families).

8. Rigged tenders are the bread and butter of patronage politics in Indonesia. According to van Klinken and Aspinall (2010) "construction projects are a major focus of collusive and predatory behaviour ... Provincial and district parliaments are full of contractors ... and contractors are prominent in the campaign teams for directly elected district heads and governors". From the national level and down into the regions, the discretionary distribution of business contracts acts as a political currency, and a binding agent for political alliances.

References

Amin, Khoirul. "A Year of Mixed Seasons for External Trade". *Jakarta Post*, 31 December 2015 <http://www.thejakartapost.com/news/2015/12/31/a-year-mixed-seasons-external-trade.html>.

Aspinall, Edward. "A Nation in Fragments: Patronage and Neoliberalism in Contemporary Indonesia". *Critical Asian Studies* 45 (2012): 27–54.

———. "Health Care and Democratization in Indonesia". *Democratization* 21, no. 5 (2014): 803–23 <https://doi.org/10.1080/13510347.2013.873791>.

Aziza, Sari Kurnia. "Banyak Relawan Jokowi Jadi Komisaris BUMN, Menteri Rini Bilang Karena 'Kebetulan'". *Kompas*. 24 October 2017 <https://ekonomi.

kompas.com/read/2017/10/24/105550626/banyak-relawan-jokowi-jadi-komisaris-bumn-menteri-rini-bilang-karena>.

Bresser-Pereira, Luiz Carlos. "From Old to New Developmentalism in Latin America". In *Handbook of Latin America Economics*, edited by Jose Antonio Ocampo. Oxford University Press, 2009.

Butt, Simon. "The Rule of Law and Anti-Corruption Reforms under Yudhoyono: The Rise of the KPK and the Constitutional Court". In *The Yudhoyono Presidency: Indonesia's Decade of Stability and Stagnation*, edited by Edward Aspinall, Marcus Mietzner and Dirk Tomsa, pp. 175–95. Singapore: Institute of Southeast Asian Studies, 2015.

Carney, Richard W. and Natasha Hamilton-Hart. "What Do Changes in Corporate Ownership in Indonesia Tell Us?". *Bulletin of Indonesian Economic Studies* 51, no. 1 (2015): 123–45 <https://doi.org/10.1080/00074918.2015.1016570>.

Carrillo, Ian R. "The New Developmentalism and the Challenges to Long-Term Stability in Brazil". *Latin American Perspectives* 41, no. 5 (2014): 59–71.

Davidson, Jamie S. "Indonesia's New Governance Institutions: Accounting for Their Varied Performance". *Asian Survey* 56, no. 4 (2016): 651–75 <https://doi.org/10.1525/as.2016.56.4.651>.

Doner, Richard F. and Ben Ross Schneider. "The Middle-Income Trap: More Politics than Economics". *World Politics* (2016): 1–37.

Döring, Heike, Rodrigo Salles Pereira dos Santos and Eva Pocher. "New Developmentalism in Brazil? The Need for Sectoral Analysis". *Review of International Political Economy* 24, no. 2 (2017): 332–62 <https://doi.org/10.10 80/09692290.2016.1273841>.

Feith, Herb. "Repressive-Developmentalist Regimes in Asia". *Alternatives: Global, Local, Political* 7, no. 4 (1981): 491–506 <https://doi.org/10.1177/0304375482 00700406>.

Gallagher, Kevin and M. Shafaeddin. "Government Reform and Industrial Development in China and Mexico". In *Towards New Developmentalism: Market as Means Rather than Master*. Routledge, 2011.

Guild, James. "Jokowinomics vs reality: A look at PLN". *New Mandala*, 4 April 2018 <http://www.newmandala.org/jokowinomics-vs-reality-look-pln/>.

Hadiz, Vedi R. and Richard Robison. "The Political Economy of Oligarchy and the Reorganization of Power in Indonesia". *Indonesia* 96, no. 1 (2013): 35–57 <https://doi.org/10.1353/ind.2013.0023>.

Heriyanto, Devina. "BPJS Kesehatan, Health for All Indonesians". *Jakarta Post*, 7 April 2018 <http://www.thejakartapost.com/academia/2018/04/06/qa-bpjs-kesehatan-health-for-all-indonesians.html>.

Hsueh, Roselyn. "State Capitalism, Chinese-Style: Strategic Value of Sectors, Sectoral Characteristics, and Globalization". *Governance* 29, no. 1 (2016): 85–102 <https://doi.org/10.1111/gove.12139>.

Indonesia Investments. "Indonesia Misses Out on Billions Because of Troubled Investment Climate". 12 January 2018 <https://www.indonesia-investments. com/news/todays-headlines/indonesia-misses-out-on-billions-because-of-troubled-investment-climate/item8488?> (accessed 18 April 2018).

Insiders Stories. "Rini Soemarno: SOEs Holding Strong and Efficient". 22 September 2017 <https://theinsiderstories.com/rini-soemarno-soes-holding-strong-and-efficient/>.

Jefriando, Maikel. "Kenapa Sri Mulyani Sangat Was-Was Dengan Utang PLN?". *Detikfinance*, 27 September 2017 <https://finance.detik.com/energi/d-3660358/kenapa-sri-mulyani-sangat-was-was-dengan-utang-pln>.

Katadata. 2017. "Investasi Menurun, Cadangan Migas Susut". 12 April 2017 <https://katadata.co.id/infografik/2017/04/12/investasi-menurun-cadangan-migas-susut>.

Khan, Shahrukh Rafi and Jens Christiansen. *Towards New Developmentalism: Market as Means Rather than Master*. Routledge, 2010.

Kim, Kyunghoon, Andy Sumner and Arief Anshory Yusuf. "How Inclusive Is Structural Change? The Case of Indonesia". ESTC GPID Research Network Working Paper, no. 3. Economic and Social Research Council and Global Challenges Research Fund, 2017.

McBeth, John. "Public trumps private in Widodo's Indonesia". *Straits Times*, 12 October 2017 <http://www.atimes.com/article/public-trumps-private-widodos-indonesia/>.

Mietzner, Marcus. *Money, Power, and Ideology: Political Parties in Post-Authoritarian Indonesia*. Honolulu: University of Hawai'i Press, 2013.

Muhtadi, Burhanuddin. "Jokowi's First Year: A Weak President Caught between Reform and Oligarchic Politics". *Bulletin of Indonesian Economic Studies* 51, no. 3 (2015): 349–68 <https://doi.org/10.1080/00074918.2015.1110684>.

Munthe, Bernadette and Wilda Asmarini. "Indonesia Puts New Shipping Rules on Hold as Coal Buyers Wait". *Jakarta Globe*, 28 February 2018 <http://jakartaglobe.id/news/indonesia-puts-new-shipping-rules-hold-coal-buyers-wait/>.

Novalius, Feby. "Impor Turun, Produksi Ponsel Nasional Capai 60 Juta: Okezone Economy". Okezone, 17 February 2018 <https://economy.okezone.com/read/2018/02/17/320/1860745/impor-turun-produksi-ponsel-nasional-capai-60-juta>.

Patunru, Arianto and Sjamsu Rahardja. "Trade Protectionism in Indonesia: Bad Times and Bad Policy". Lowy Institute, 2015 <http://www.lowyinstitute.org/publications/trade-protectionism-indonesia-bad-times-and-bad-policy>.

Pisani, Elizabeth. "Medicine for a Sick System". Inside Indonesia (blog), 25 January 2013 <http://www.insideindonesia.org/medicine-for-a-sick-system-2>.

Power, Thomas. "Cashing In". New Mandala (blog), 8 August 2016 <http://www.newmandala.org/cashing-in/>.

Rakhmat, Muhammad Zulfikar and Dikanaya Tarahita. "Indonesia's Prize Health Insurance System Mired in Debt". *Asia Sentinel*, 20 November 2017 <https://www.asiasentinel.com/society/indonesia-health-insurance-system-debt/>.

Reuters. "Indonesia Anti-Trust Official Charged with Graft". 10 February 2009 <https://in.reuters.com/article/indonesia-corruption/indonesia-anti-trust-official-charged-with-graft-idINJAK3415520090210>.

Robet, Robertus. "Beyond the Bounds of Democracy: DPR Consolidates Its Power". Indonesia at Melbourne (blog), 22 February 2018 <http://indonesiaatmelbourne.unimelb.edu.au/beyond-the-bounds-of-democracy-dpr-seeks-to-consolidate-its-power/>.

Rosser, Andrew. "Beyond Access: Making Indonesia's Education System Work". Lowy Institute for International Policy, 21 February 2018 <https://www.lowyinstitute.org/publications/beyond-access-making-indonesia-s-education-system-work>.

Sato, Yuri. "State, Industry, and Business in Indonesia's Transformation". In *Southeast Asia beyond Crises and Traps: Economic Growth and Upgrading*, edited by Boo Teik Khoo, Keiichi Tsunekawa and Motoko Kawano. Springer, 2017.

Schneider, Ben Ross. *Designing Industrial Policy in Latin America: Business-State Relations and the New Developmentalism*. Palgrave Macmillan, 2015.

Setiaji, Hidayat, and Gayatri Suroyo. "Private Sector Left in Dust in Indonesia's Infrastructure Push". Reuters, 20 October 2017 <https://www.reuters.com/article/us-indonesia-economy-infrastructure/private-sector-left-in-dust-in-indonesias-infrastructure-push-idUSKBN1CP12B>.

Singgih, Vincent. "Pertamina Takes over Mahakam from Total, Inpex". *Jakarta Post*, 1 January 2018 <http://www.thejakartapost.com/news/2018/01/01/pertamina-takes-over-mahakam-from-total-inpex-.html>.

Straits Times. "Indonesia's Bureaucratic Dead Wood: The Jakarta Post". 7 June 2016 <https://www.straitstimes.com/asia/se-asia/indonesias-bureaucratic-dead-wood-the-jakarta-post>.

———. "Indonesian President Jokowi Roots for Private Investment to Develop Infrastructure and Natural Resources". 17 October 2017 <https://www.straitstimes.com/asia/se-asia/indonesian-president-jokowi-roots-for-private-investment>.

———. "Jokowi Chasing $196b to Fund 5-Year Infrastructure Plan". 27 January 2018 <https://www.straitstimes.com/asia/se-asia/jokowi-chasing-196b-to-fund-5-year-infrastructure-plan>.

Thailand Business News. "Rapid Growth of Indonesia's Manufacturing Sector". 4 January 2018 <https://www.thailand-business-news.com/asean/indonesia/66974-rapid-growth-indonesias-manufacturing-sector.html>.

Trubek, David M., Helena Alviar Garcia, Diogo R. Coutinho and Alvaro Santos.

Law and the New Developmental State: The Brazilian Experience in Latin American Context. Cambridge University Press, 2013.

van Klinken, Gerry and Edward Aspinall. "Building Relations: Corruption, Competition and Cooperation in the Construction Industry". In *The State and Illegality in Indonesia*. Brill, 2010 <https://doi.org/10.1163/9789004253681_009>.

Warburton, Eve. "Resource Nationalism in Post-Boom Indonesia: The New Normal?". Lowy Institute for International Policy, 2017 <https://www.lowyinstitute.org/publications/resource-nationalism-post-boom-indonesia-new-normal>.

————. "Nationalism, Developmentalism and Politics in Indonesia's Mining Sector". In *Indonesia in the New World: Globalisation, Nationalism and Sovereignty*, edited by Mari E. Pangestu, Chatib Basri and Arianto Patunru, pp. 90–108. Singapore: ISEAS – Yusof Ishak Institute, 2018.

World Bank. "Doing Business 2018: Reforming to Create Jobs, Economy Profile Indonesia". 2018 <http://www.doingbusiness.org/~/media/WBG/DoingBusiness/Documents/Profiles/Country/IDN.pdf>.

Yusuf, Arief Anshory and Andy Sumner. "Multidimensional Poverty in Indonesia: How Inclusive Has Economic Growth Been?". *Arndt-Corden Department of Economics Crawford School of Public Policy, ANU College of Asia and the Pacific* (No. 2017/09). June 2017.

Zain, Winarno. "More Reforms Needed, but Will Jokowi Take the Risk?". *Straits Times*, 2 August 2017 <http://www.straitstimes.com/asia/se-asia/more-reforms-needed-but-will-jokowi-take-the-risk-the-jakarta-post-columnist>.

3

MACROECONOMIC MANAGEMENT
Success and Challenges

Arief Ramayandi and Siwage Dharma Negara

3.1 INTRODUCTION

At the start of his presidency, Joko "Jokowi" Widodo promised that Indonesia would achieve a 7 per cent economic growth within three years of his administration. His plan was to achieve this through a combination of infrastructure development, improved budget allocation and efficiency of spending, increased private sector participation in the development and financial sector deepening. Four years later, the economy seems to be stuck at a 5 per cent growth rate, leaving the impression that the 7 per cent target is too hard to come by, if not impossible.

Jokowi's government, however, inherits the legacy of macroeconomic conditions from its predecessors, particularly those resulting from the substantial change post the devastating Asian Financial Crisis (AFC) 1997–98. Analysing the current government achievement without considering the conditions that preceded it will not be an objective approach. The AFC was a significant game changer to the management of the Indonesian economy. The economy underwent a series of economic reforms that provided it with better resilience when facing the Global Financial Crisis (GFC).

The Indonesian economy took a big hit during the AFC. GDP fell by over 10 per cent at the peak of the Crisis in 1998, inflation soared to above 50 per cent, and it took a while before the economy eventually recovered to the level of economic activity it had before the Crisis. In about a decade prior to the AFC, Indonesia massively liberalized its banking sector through its second banking liberalization package in October 1988 (Pakto 88) that brought substantial liquidity deepening impact to the economy. The financial deepening impact, however, came at a cost of the country's heightened vulnerability to financial shocks especially when coupled with inadequate financial supervision. Combined with a practically pegged exchange rate regime,[1] the economy had quietly built up a substantial risk of financial vulnerability that culminated in late 1997 when authorities had to acknowledge defeat in holding its overvalued currency and had to go through a considerable overhaul in the banking sector.

Post-crisis, Indonesia went through a series of reforms. It underwent a rapid political democratization process which was both beneficial for the country's future but taxing to the economic recovery processes at the same time. A rapid move towards fiscal decentralization changed the ball game for fiscal interventions by passing more authority to the local government in decision-making. While these reforms are certainly positive in general, the transformation due to the political and fiscal reforms require systemic adjustments that would take time before the whole economy can adapt to both transformations appropriately. The mismatch time between the transformations and the appropriate adaptation to the new system has somewhat contributed to holding back the pace of recovery from the Crisis.

On the economic management side, a number of important decisions were made. Most notable reforms in monetary policy include the move towards a freely flexible exchange rate regime and a more independent central bank. Not too long after, a fiscal rule that limits budget deficits to a maximum of 3 per cent of GDP was introduced in 2003. All these paved the way for more prudent macroeconomic management practices in the country, which eventually ensured its readiness to weather external shocks as large as the GFC relatively well.

To provide a fair discussion on the performance of Jokowi's administration in managing the economy, the chapter steps back a little to look at some recent historical conditions and past policy decisions that led to the foundation for the set of economic challenges that Jokowi has to face in his era of presidency. To begin, we start off with questions that are related to how the economy has performed and been managed post the AFC, the kind of global environment that underlies this performance, and factors that helped the economy weather the GFC effects. Then we move on to focus more on the issues on whether Jokowi's administration has introduced any substantial changes to the way the economy is managed and whether or not they have been effective to propel the country's growth momentum.

In light of these questions, the next section will begin with a discussion on the evolution of the Indonesian economy around the AFC by concentrating mainly on the aspects of fiscal and monetary management in dealing with both internal and external challenges. Section 3.3 will delve deeper into the evolution of macroeconomic management during the last two administrations. In particular, highlighting fiscal and monetary policy management post the GFC to provide a discussion about whether or not the style of the macroeconomic policy management has changed under Jokowi's presidency. Having discussed this, section 3.4 will move on to discuss the prospects and challenges that the economy is facing going forward. The chapter concludes by providing some general assessments based on the issues covered and provides relevant policy implications.

3.2 THE 1997–98 ASIAN FINANCIAL CRISIS

After being devastated by the AFC, Indonesia continues to struggle to find its way back to its initial path of high economic growth and observes low growth in its industrial sector (Kuncoro, Chapter 7). It took at least five years for the economy to come back to the level of GDP it attained before the Crisis. At the same time, authorities strived to stabilize its macroeconomic fundamentals through a combination of prudent fiscal management and monetary policy.

In the years leading up to the AFC, GDP significantly outpaced its potential trend and opened up growing output gap, defined as a difference between the actual GDP and its trend, before it plunged deeply during the peak of the Crisis (Figure 3.1). This vast build-up of output gap created severe macroeconomic imbalances and high inflationary pressures on the economy. Price pressures were evident when inflation averaged at nearly 10 per cent prior to the AFC.

FIGURE 3.1
Output Deviations from Trend: 1993–2017

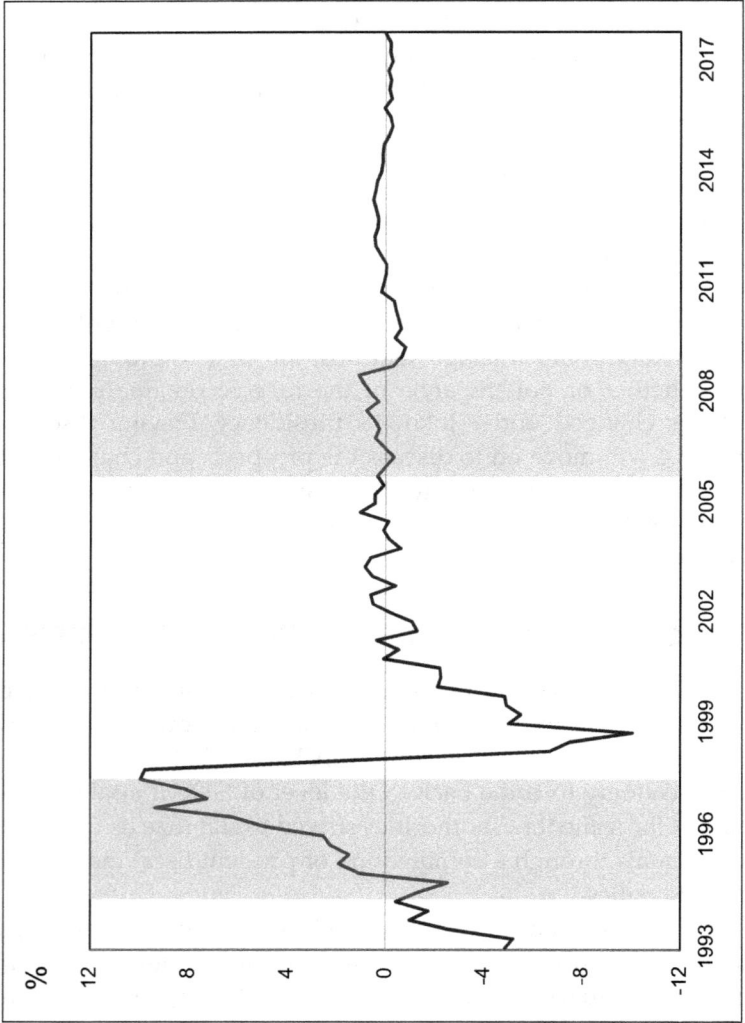

Note: The HP filter is applied to extract the potential trend of output.
Source: Authors' estimates.

The behaviour of investment played an important role in driving the trend of economic performance prior to the AFC. The share of investment in GDP was relatively high, hovering around 30 to 40 per cent of the total GDP (Figure 3.2). This share dropped sharply during the Asian Crisis and has never fully recovered since then. The lower share of investment, however, has in turn reversed the saving–investment gap into positive territory that made room for lower interest rates after the Crisis.

The massive surge in investment prior to the AFC was accompanied by high rates of imports that led to current account deficits despite the country's export-led growth strategy. Figure 3.2 shows how the current account balance turned negative prior to the Asian Crisis and turned positive afterward, mirroring the trend observed in the share of investment. The deficit particularly widened in the period leading up to the Crisis, signifying the country's position as a net international borrower during the episode. Rapid growth in exports and the fall in imports post the Crisis have reversed current account balance.

The way exchange rate was being managed played a huge role in explaining the way investment and current account behaved during this episode. Prior to the Crisis, the rupiah was overvalued with relatively very limited movements. In 1997–98, the currency went through a substantial correction as Indonesia was forced to abandon its heavily managed exchange rate regime and moved to a more flexible regime after reserves to defend the currency depleted abruptly. The overvalued rupiah made imports cheaper in the pre-AFC years. Expectations of continuous appreciation of the exchange rate also lowered the cost of borrowing overseas, further fuelling the boom in investment that relied on external debt and imported capital goods.

The sharp rupiah depreciation seen during the Crisis acted as the needed correction for the misaligned exchange rates. Consequently, imports and loan from abroad immediately became much more expensive. The rupiah correction initially overshot their new but much-weaker equilibrium values, with the value in terms of the U.S. dollar about four times weaker than in 1996. Following these large corrections, investments also plunged but exports increased relative to imports as the country gained exchange rate competitiveness amid the then strong global demand.

Since then, Indonesia has moved to officially adopt a flexible exchange rate regime and passed a regulation for Bank Indonesia (BI) to become a policy-independent institution with an objective of maintaining price

FIGURE 3.2
Investment and Current Account Balance, 1993–2017

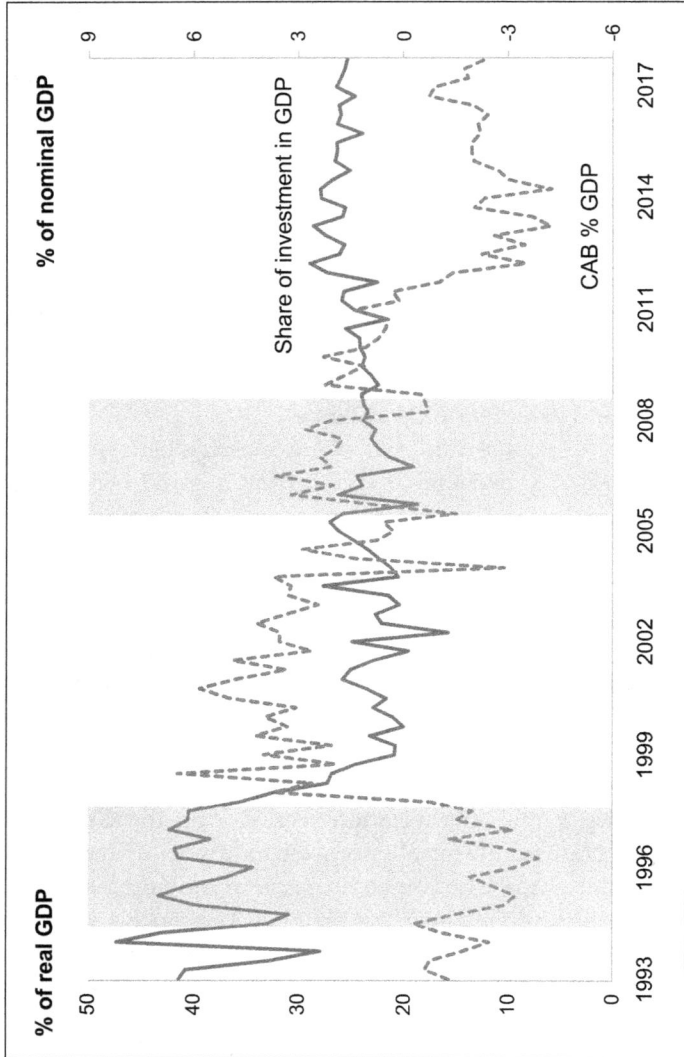

Source: CEIC Data company, Haver Analytics, authors' estimates.

stability. The decline in credit growth lasted for a few years after the Crisis, partly due to the slower pace of growth in GDP and partly due to the big restructuring of the banking system that led to more prudent banking regulations at the same time. The move towards a flexible exchange rate regime and an independent central bank played pivotal roles for building up the country's capacity for more resilience from external shocks.

A more flexible regime ensures that the country is not going to undergo a large misalignment of exchange rate that may expose the economy to severe destabilizing conditions. Park, Ramayandi and Shin (2013) argue that Indonesia was among the economies with domestic interest rate that was too low to maintain the exchange rate value prior to the AFC, and hence was prone to capital outflows. Prior to the Crisis, there was practically no scope for easing interest rates. In fact, higher interest rates were needed to stem capital outflows. This interest rate hike had an adverse effect on the real economy and contributed to the massive dive in economic activity back then. In short, monetary policy was not well posed for an expansion at the onset of the AFC, and hence was impotent to act as a catalyst to the shock that caused the Crisis.

Exchange rate devaluation and the drop in GDP during the AFC have pushed up Indonesia's debt to GDP ratio to about 150 per cent in 1998. Fiscal consolidation then became inevitable after the Crisis when the government was forced to absorb contingent fiscal liabilities as they bailed out bankrupt firms. Nationalization of major domestic banks in Indonesia reduced fiscal space and hence the scope for fiscal stimulus. Mounting external debts due to exchange rate depreciation also reduced the fiscal space. By 2000, debt to GDP ratio still hovered around 100 per cent but declined gradually over time. To ensure fiscal prudence, the government introduced a fiscal rule that limits budget deficit to be capped at a maximum of 3 per cent of GDP.

As share of investment plunged to about 20 per cent after the AFC, source for economic growth since then have mainly shifted to domestic consumption. The latter contributes around 50 to 60 per cent to the country's growth. Although the large population base helped in ensuring substantial consumption contribution to the aggregate economic activity, GDP growth has been contained at between 3 to 5 per cent in between 2000 and 2004. Meanwhile, the progress in economic reforms and restructuring has also put the sovereign debt position into a more comfortable place as debt to GDP ratio is on a declining trend (Figure 3.3), giving way for a fiscal space

FIGURE 3.3
Gross International Reserves and External Debt

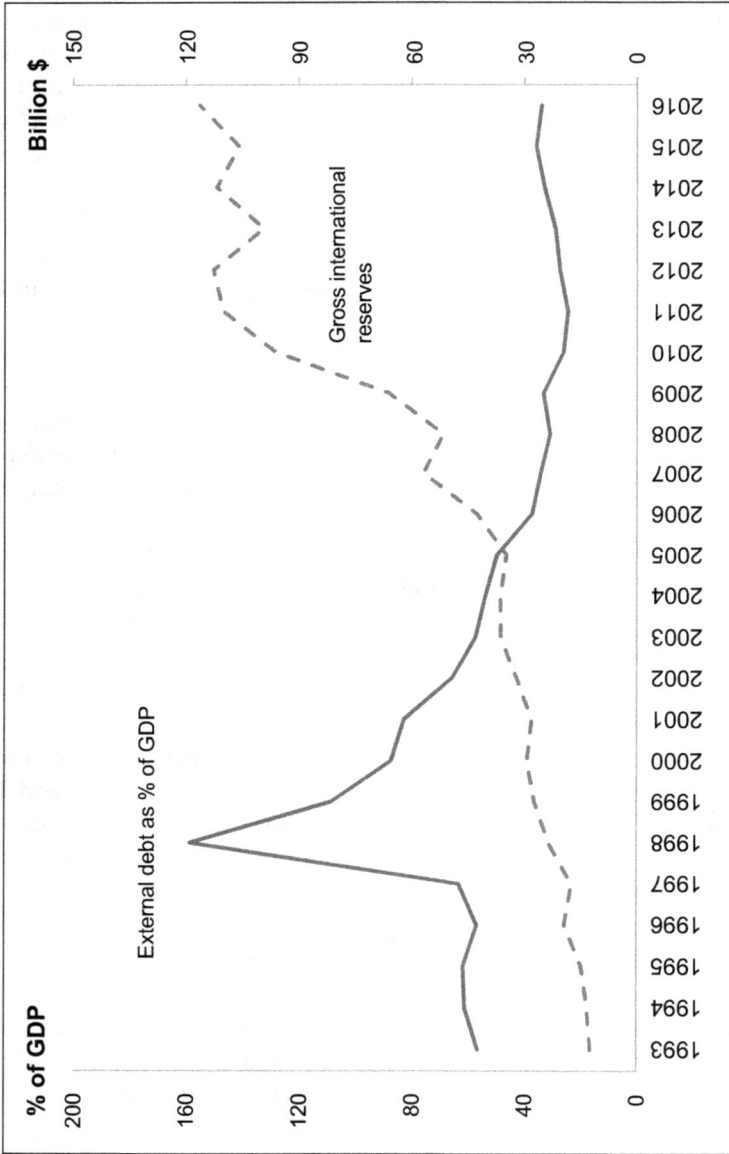

Source: CEIC Data company, Haver Analytics, World Bank WDI, authors' estimates.

to build up. Inflation and exchange rate have calmed down with inflation down to below 7 per cent in 2003–04 and the rupiah stabilized at a new high equilibrium value.

3.3 MACROECONOMIC MANAGEMENT IN THE LAST TWO ADMINISTRATIONS

3.3.1 Susilo Bambang Yudhoyono (SBY) Period (2004–14)

Macroeconomic management during the SBY administration can be broken down into three major episodes, which were divided by two major external shocks that tested the government capacity to navigate macroeconomic stability. The first episode was when SBY just took over the administration until his government was faced with the GFC in 2008 that marked the beginning of the second episode. This was then followed by a brief episode towards the end of his administration, which was marked by the U.S. Federal Reserve tapering announcement in mid-2013.

The beginning of the first term for the SBY government marked by the return of GDP per capita back to be at par with its level prior to the AFC. The economic structure was quite different, however. Relative to the pre-AFC period, the share of investment in GDP remained much lower, consumption share was slightly elevated and remained as the largest pillar for the growth of the economy, and current account was contributing positively to the overall growth of economic activity, thanks to the buoyant global trade conditions.

Inflation remained generally lower than the pre-AFC average, but with some hiccups in 2006 as the administered energy-related components of inflation were adjusted upward in March and October 2005 due to large increases in the global oil prices. Absent such global oil price increases, the trend of aggregate inflation would remain at its low side.[2] This incident highlighted the fact that the policy to subsidize fuel prices for domestic consumption is potentially destabilizing to the economy, particularly when fiscal spending is constrained by a rule that limits budget deficits for the sake of fiscal prudency.

On the policy front, the SBY government continued to maintain the prudent monetary and fiscal policy stance of its predecessors. Monetary policy remained responsive to contain unwanted build up in prices and, although fluctuating, exchange rate remained relatively stable at around

Rp8,000–Rp10,000 per U.S. dollar that is deemed to be somewhat consistent with its market value. Public debts declined to a relatively low share of GDP, particularly in 2005 after the government executed the plan from its previous administration to pay up the long-standing liabilities to the International Monetary Fund (IMF). The debt to GDP ratio dipped below 30 per cent, leaving the government with ample fiscal space to decisively implement large fiscal stimulus programmes when needed.

All these set the economy up for weathering the impact of the GFC in 2008. Compared to the AFC, the economic conditions were in a completely different shape. A number of structural domestic problems that lay at the heart of the AFC were no longer present during the breakout of the GFC (Park, Ramayandi and Shin 2013). Domestic fundamentals were much sounder during the GFC, which was also a largely external crisis for the economy. Structural reforms and more flexible exchange rate regimes in the post-Asian Crisis period strengthened domestic fundamentals, enabling the economy to effectively pursue countercyclical monetary and fiscal policy to cushion the impact of the GFC and laid the foundation for recovery.

The scale of output gap built-up since the 2004–05 recovery was minor relative to the pre-AFC one (see Figure 3.1), implying much lower inflationary pressures from the demand side. Current account was in surplus and the saving-investment gap was nowhere near the pre-AFC episode. Still haunted by the exchange rate collapse during the AFC, Indonesia has been building up international reserves despite more flexible exchange rate regimes. Partly helped by current account balance surpluses, gross international reserve holdings accelerated since 2005 (Figure 3.3), and thanks to this accumulated stockpile of international reserves and the more flexible exchange regime which reduced the scope for misalignment, the magnitude of currency depreciation between 2006 and 2008 was muted relative to that of the AFC.

Ample international reserves provided the country with more ammunition to defend its currency during the Global Crisis, and adequate fiscal space helped to provide fiscal stimulus to support aggregate demand and growth at a time when private demand and external demand were imploding. In short, Indonesia was in completely different conditions before the GFC. Domestic structural issues occurring before the AFC were absent prior to the GFC. Domestic fundamentals were sounder, supported by the structural reforms and more flexible exchange rate regimes in the post-AFC period. Consequently, the country was able to effectively pursue countercyclical monetary and fiscal policies that cushioned the impact of the Global Crisis. In addition, being less open to trade relative to the neighbours — which experienced negative growth in 2008–09 like Malaysia, Singapore, Thailand — also helped to moderate some of the direct impact from the Crisis.

The economy escaped the worst of the GFC relatively unscathed, growing at a positive 4.6 per cent during the peak of the GFC impact in 2009. However, this achievement did not go without costs. Despite the strong economic fundamentals, the government deployed a number of policy interventions to minimize the GFC impact on the economy. Some of the accumulated fiscal space was used up as the budget deficit — which was comfortably stabilized at below 1 per cent of GDP after relaxing the administered fuel subsidy burden in 2005 — spiked to about 1.5 per cent as a result of the fiscal stimulus. Interest rates were brought down to loosen liquidity, and foreign reserves were depleted by about 10 per cent to stabilize the currency movements. GDP growth was immediately corrected to 6.4 per cent in 2010 and remained a little over 6 per cent in 2011 and 2012.

After managing to weather the GFC well, the SBY economic team was again tested by an external financial shock arising from the U.S. Fed announcement on possible tapering of its ultra-loose monetary policy stance known as the quantitative easing policy. This episode, labelled as the taper tantrum, exerted considerable pressures on financial stability of the emerging market economies. Indonesia was among the five countries most badly affected by the shock. Along with India, Brazil, South Africa and Turkey, Indonesia was grouped as the "fragile five" economies that were hit hardest during the taper tantrum episode as their exchange rate depreciated most heavily and, through a network of regional contagion, both bond and equity[3] prices plunged dramatically.

In response to the taper tantrum shock, Indonesia intervened heavily in the exchange rate market to stabilize the currency and tightened the monetary, fiscal and credit policies to curb domestic demand. Interest rate was raised, domestic credit conditions were tightened and the government was also forced to increase the administered domestic fuel prices by restraining the subsidy to maintain budget deficit at less than 3 per cent of GDP. Basri (2017) argues that these tightening actions were needed to raise the country's credibility in the eyes of investors. Regardless, domestic financial market did stabilize after a few months, but was followed by lower growth momentum in the succeeding years. GDP growth dropped to 5.6 per cent in 2013 before fell further to hover around 5.0 per cent in the years after.

All in all, even after more than a decade away from the peak of the AFC, it seems that policymakers were still very much haunted by its trauma. The half-hearted intention to remove the inefficient domestic fuel subsidy from different administration, including SBY's,[4] was primarily driven by the fear of the possible political implications of such subsidy removal. As a result, the subsidy has always been a burden on the government budget, which is very much dependent on the cycle in the international oil prices. The "Century bailout" in 2008, where the government decided to bail out a relatively small bank, Century, in order to prevent systemic risks to materialize in the banking sector, was very much nuanced by the fear of the banking sector collapse during the AFC. Lastly, the heavy exchange rate interventions during the GFC and the taper tantrum signify the fear of floating tendency that the government had during these events.

Aside from the fuel subsidy, both the exchange rate interventions and the "Century bailout" were followed by more stable economic conditions. However, there were critics that argued possible inefficiency in these outcomes. Nevertheless, such arguments will always be left out as debateable since all alternative possibilities would never be factually proven and can only be supported by counterfactual simulations that rest on some supporting assumptions.

The post-taper tantrum stabilization effect was unfortunately coupled with weaker growth momentum going forward. A slowdown in global growth and trade environment is often cited as the main culprit. This is only true partially as both the global growth and trade environment have, in fact, been weaker in the post-GFC period, when Indonesia was growing at 6-plus per cent a year up to 2012. The heavy-handed tightening stance during the taper tantrum seems to have also contributed to putting a break to the growth momentum. Alongside the weaker growth, deficits in current account and government budget had also grown post the taper tantrum episode.

How long would the slow growth momentum persist in Indonesia? Would the economy be able to turn the corner? These questions become relevant for planning the future of the Indonesian economy. According to an estimate, Indonesia's potential growth averaged at almost 5 per cent in 2000–07 and increased further to 5.8 per cent in 2008–2014 (ADB 2016). These levels are, unfortunately, close to the actual growth rates of the economy during the periods. Although it has helped to stabilize inflation in the economy, this also means that growth in output is not potentially seen to occur much faster in the coming years. Such lower economic growth path may persist over a medium term, with identified critical constraints like inadequate and poor quality of infrastructure, weaknesses in governance and institutions, and unequal access to and poor quality of education.

3.3.2 Jokowi's Era (2014–Present)

The Jokowi government recognizes that a 5 per cent growth rate is not sufficient for Indonesia to create enough jobs to match the growth of its labour force and to eradicate poverty in the country (Hamilton-Hart and Schulze 2016; Suryahadi and Al Izzati, Chapter 12). At the start of his presidency, he made a pledge to bring growth up to 7 per cent within his first term. To do so, Jokowi has been pushing his development policy that combines infrastructure development, fiscal stimulus, together with a number of economic packages (sixteen in total), aiming to simplify business licensing procedures. Yet, five years into his first term, the economy is still struggling to get past 5 per cent growth rate.

One may argue that uncertainties in the global economy and increased trade protectionism are the main factors that have caused Indonesia's weaker growth performance. While the global situation is not as conducive as before, structurally, the Indonesian economy itself is also undergoing critical changes. As mentioned in the previous section, post-AFC, exports are no longer the country's main engine of growth. Manufacturing exports have been losing their competitiveness, partly due to the Dutch disease situation, in which the booming of one sector has reduced the incentive in manufacturing to export, as the domestic demand is readily available (Kuncoro, Chapter 7). For many years, Indonesia's exports depend very much on commodity exports. Thus, when commodity prices fell, Indonesia's key commodity exports also declined. Indeed, the fall in commodity prices explains the continuous decline in exports since 2011. The trend however changed in 2017, as commodity prices started to rebound, Indonesia's exports also increased. Detailed data on exports and imports show that export growth is supported by non–oil and gas products, including coal and crude palm oil (Pardede and Zahro 2017).

Examining Indonesia's balance of payment during the Jokowi's first term, one can see some interesting trends. Current account deficit declined from US$27.5 billion in 2014 to US$17.5 billion in 2017 (Table 3.1). However, the deficit increased again in the first half of 2018 due to poor exports performance and large increase in imports. Large depreciation of the rupiah did not seem to be of help. At the same time, trade in services is always negative as the country lacks competitiveness in this sector (Anas and Wikapuspita, Chapter 8). The biggest contributor to current account deficit is primary income outflows, which has increased from US$29.7 billion in 2014 to US$32.8 billion in 2017. And in the first half of 2018, this primary income outflows reached US$16 billion. This shows that the amount of payments made by overseas investors, whose assets are held in Indonesia, exceed the returns held by domestic investors in foreign countries.

The financial account remains positive but volatile during the Jokowi era. After a big drop in 2015, foreign direct investment (FDI) inflows increased by around 20 per cent in 2016 and 2017. The level of FDI is relatively higher than during the SBY era. This is a positive sign as FDI represents relatively stable, long-term capital. This may also indicate that recent efforts to liberalize FDI regulations, through several economic packages, may have started to come to fruition. That said, a decline in FDI inflows was observed in the first half of 2018, suggesting possible "wait and see" strategy applied by investors as they are pausing for the country's soon coming election year. Likewise, portfolio inflows also grew steadily, following an improved investment outlook in the country between 2015 and 2017. However, these types of capital inflows are known to be volatile as can be seen by significant capital outflows in Q1 2018. Under current global uncertainties, there is a higher likelihood that investors will move their portfolio investment from the emerging markets (including Indonesia) to financial markets in developed countries.

While exports seem less promising for stimulating growth, the government has been focusing on infrastructure spending. A sharp increase in infrastructure spending as percentage of total public spending has been made possible thanks to major reductions in fuel subsidies (Figure 3.4). The latter declined sharply in 2015 and continued its declining trends until 2017. The fall in world oil price has given the authority a

TABLE 3.1
Indonesia's Balance of Payment, 2014–18 (US$ million)

	2014	2015	2016	2017	2018-Q1	2018-Q2
Current account: Goods	6,982.6	14,048.6	15,318.0	18,892.1	2,324.0	288.9
Goods: Exports	175,292.8	149,124.5	144,469.8	168,886.8	44,374.4	43,769.7
Goods: Imports	–168,310.2	–135,075.9	–129,151.8	–149,994.7	–42,050.3	–43,480.7
Current Account: Services	–10,009.7	–8,696.7	–7,083.7	–7,863.7	–1,554.1	–1,789.6
Services: Export	23,530.9	22,220.9	23,323.5	24,668.2	6,864.0	6,488.6
Services: Import	–33,540.6	–30,917.6	–30,407.2	–32,531.9	–8,418.0	–8,278.2
Primary Income	–29,702.6	–28,379.1	–29,647.0	–32,837.9	–7,900.4	–8,154.9
Investment: Direct	–19,271.0	–18,504.3	–17,592.9	–20,189.1	–4,792.1	–4,158.5
Investment: Portfolio	–7,105.9	–6,460.2	–8,318.2	–8,906.9	–2,341.3	–2,951.3
Current Account Balance	–27,509.9	–17,518.7	–16,952.3	–17,527.7	–5,716.8	–8,028.4
Capital Account	26.6	16.6	40.7	46.2	57.9	3.0
Financial Account	44,916.1	16,843.2	29,305.6	29,834.4	2,390.1	4,014.8
Direct Investment	14,733.2	10,704.5	16,135.9	20,151.4	2,930.7	2,487.4
Portfolio Investment	26,066.6	16,182.7	18,995.6	20,662.1	–1,151.3	53.1
Overall Balance	15,248.6	–1098.0	12088.9	11,586.0	–3,854.7	–4,308.7

Source: BI.

FIGURE 3.4
Government Expenditures by Key Sectors, 2005–18 (% of total budget)

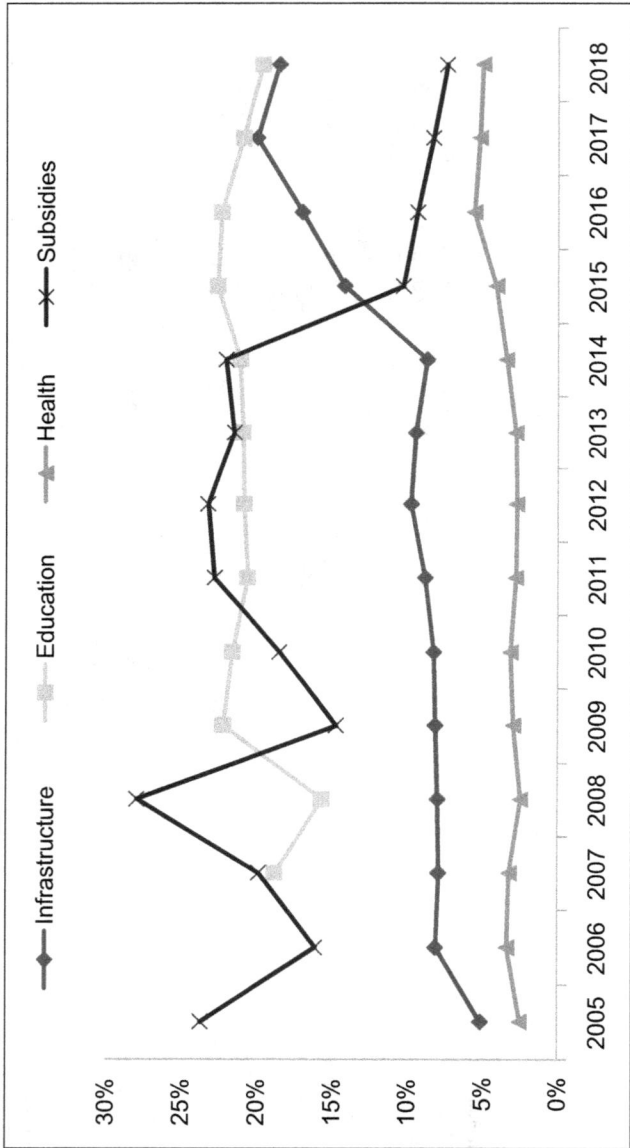

Note: 2018 figure is a projection.
Source: BPK via CEIC.

window of opportunity to substantially reduce energy subsidy. The commitment on this, however, is yet to be tested as the price of oil has started to rebound.

Since 2015, the government has undertaken ambitious infrastructure projects to realize its infrastructure development plans. Financing needs to support these projects have been borne mostly by the government and state-owned enterprises (Salim and Negara, Chapter 9). Relevant state-owned enterprises have been borrowing extensively in order to finance many of the infrastructure development projects. At the same time, the government has not sufficiently encouraged adequate private sector participation in the projects. As a result, the state budget remains the dominant source of financing. Consequently, the infrastructure push contributed to increasing fiscal deficit (Figure 3.5), which has been soaring because of lower than expected tax revenue and the continuing commitment to maintain spending for national priority programmes such as infrastructure, education and health. In 2017, Indonesia's fiscal deficit reached Rp345.8 trillion, or 2.55 per cent of GDP.

The deficit financing generates two conflicting effects on the economy (Stupak 2018). First, the additional public investments are likely to stimulate output either directly (through increase in aggregate demand) and indirectly (through the multiplier effect). Second, the deficit-financed investments may result in crowding out of private investment. This is a result of increased interest rates (induced by increased government borrowing for infrastructure investments). Higher interest rates reduce private investment and interest-sensitive consumer spending (Stupak 2018). Therefore, as the deficit financing increases, the crowding out effect also increases. Figure 3.6 shows a declining trend of domestic credit growth after the second half of 2012 (the end of commodity boom period), which coincides with the period of increased in the government's fiscal deficit. This figure corroborates the crowding out hypothesis.

Fiscal constraint has become a growing problem since the second term of the SBY era, which coincides with the end of the commodity boom. During Jokowi's era, Indonesia experiences much lower than expected tax revenue collection compared to that of the SBY period. In 2016, tax revenue realization reached only around 83 per cent of the tax revenue target (Figure 3.7). Indonesia's weak tax revenues are caused by several factors, including lower commodity prices, lower overall global demand, weak domestic growth, and poor tax compliance. In July 2016, Jokowi

FIGURE 3.5
Government Revenue, Expenditures and Fiscal Deficit, 2004–18

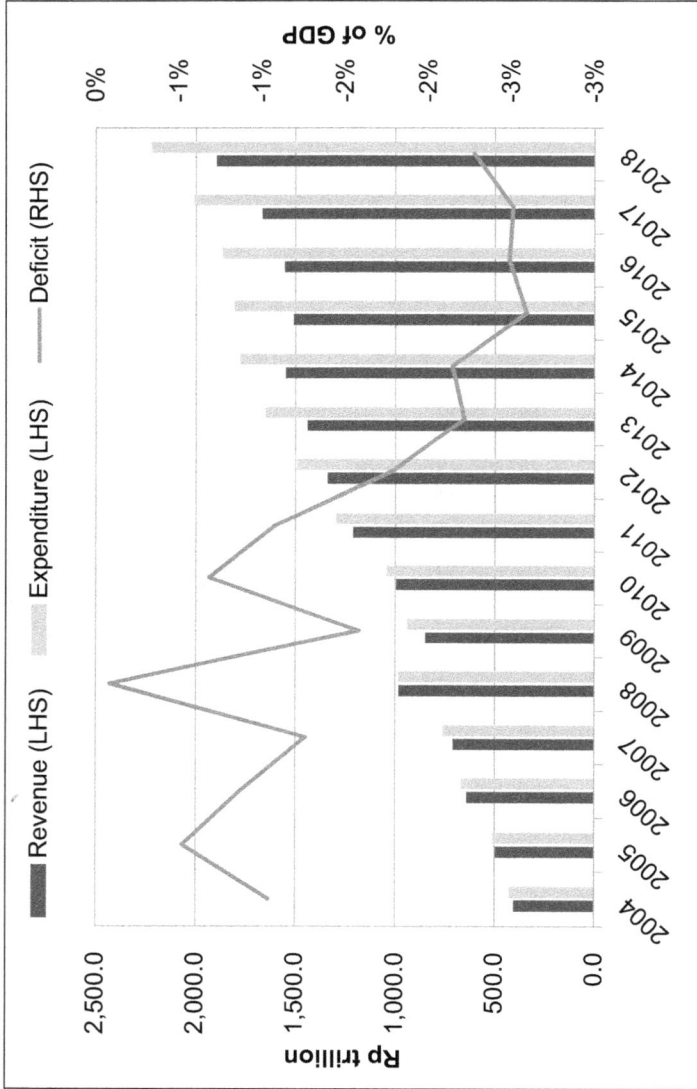

Note: 2018 figures are projection.
Source: BPK via CEIC.

FIGURE 3.6
Domestic Credit Growth in Select ASEAN Countries (% year on year)

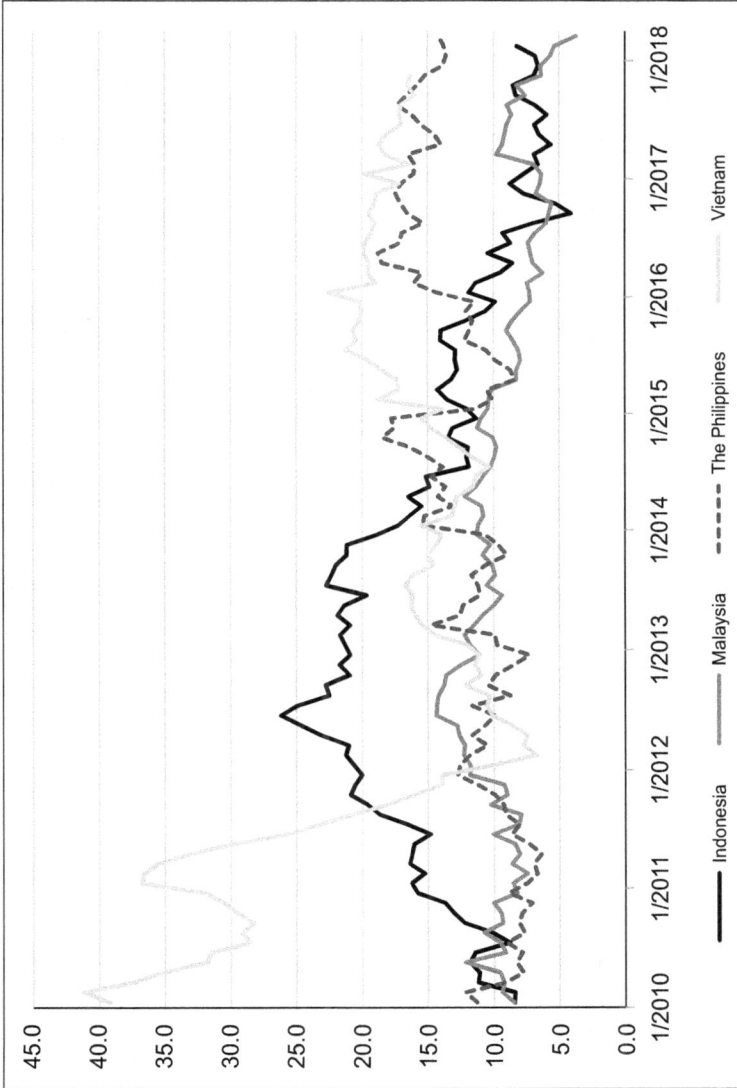

Source: CEIC.

FIGURE 3.7
Tax Revenue Target vs. Realization (Rp trillion)

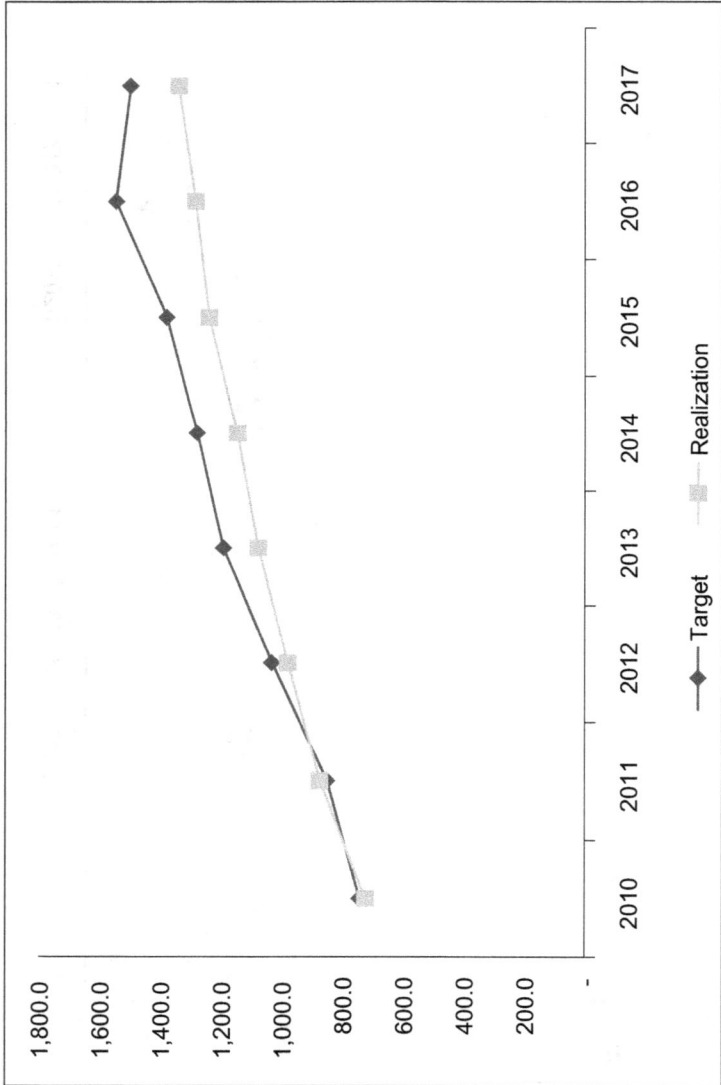

Source: CEIC.

appointed Sri Mulyani Indrawati, replacing Bambang Brodjonegoro, as Finance Minister. Minister Sri has been assigned a challenging task to increase tax revenue collection, to improve Indonesia's low tax to GDP ratio, and to continue pushing on reform in the overall fiscal system. One of the key fiscal initiatives is the implementation of tax amnesty programme,[5] which aims to boost Indonesia's tax revenues through overseas funds repatriations held by rich Indonesians.

Nonetheless, despite the aggressive campaign by the government, the tax amnesty programme (conducted from July 2016 until March 2017) was not able to significantly increase the tax revenue collection in the subsequent year. In 2017, the tax revenue collected increased only by 4.3 per cent from the previous year, or 89.4 per cent of the target.

Indonesia's tax to GDP ratio has been quite low by international standards. In 2016, the figure reached around 10 per cent, much lower compared with Malaysia (14 per cent), the Philippines (14 per cent) and Thailand (16 per cent). The weak tax effort has been caused by a combination of poor policy design and weak enforcement. As argued by Hamilton-Hart and Schulze (2016), the country's tax regulations are very complex and there are too much room for discretionary decisions by tax assessors, resulting in uncertainty over tax assessments. Even worse, the tax administration has been notoriously weak and marred by corruption. This results in much lower collection than its potential revenues. There have been efforts to improve the situation, including an online taxation system, but progress seems to be very slow. It will take some time to build the needed trust between taxpayers and tax authorities as the system improves its predictability, transparency and governance.

Overall, fiscal policy under the Jokowi administration continues to adhere to prudent fiscal rule, i.e., maintain fiscal deficit below 3 per cent limit as mandated by Indonesia's fiscal law. Public debt is also controlled strictly below the 60 per cent limit, which currently stands at 29 per cent of GDP. To keep adhering to these legislations on prudent fiscal rule, the government has been increasingly sought for an "off-budget" financing to fill up its huge financing needs to realize the infrastructure development plans. A number of state-owned enterprises have continuously increased their liabilities in order to fulfil their mandated assignments, for example, infrastructure projects, and keeping low prices for fuel (in the case of Pertamina) and electricity (in the case of Perusahaan Listrik Negara or PLN). According to Standard & Poor Global Ratings, the debt to earnings before interest depreciation and amortization (EBITDA) ratios of Indonesian SOEs have been worsening in recent years.[6] SOEs that were involved in the government's infrastructure projects like electricity power plants and other construction work, particularly, had seen their debt to EBITDA ratios deteriorating, as they needed a large amount of capital to implement many big infrastructure projects.

Another indicator of increasing deficit financing can be seen in Indonesia's outstanding external debt as a share of GDP, which has been growing since 2014. During Jokowi's era, the government's debt has increased from US$209.7 billion at the end of 2014 to US$290.7 billion in 2017, or an increase by 28 per cent (see Figure 3.8). The rising debt level has been caused by an increase in the amount of debt and the weakening rupiah at the same time. Overall, the debt level is still much lower than that in peer countries. However, around 40 per cent of domestically issued debt (Surat Berharga Negara or SBN) is owned by foreigners. This recently becomes a point of vulnerability when the Fed decided to increase the U.S. interest rate.

With regard to monetary policy, as Hamilton-Hart (Chapter 5) argued, three broad objectives are driving the government policy: accelerating domestic economic growth; maintaining financial stability; and promoting social inclusion (controlling inflation). Such a broad mandate risks a loss of focus on financial sector stability. There have been some instances in which political intervention was made. For instance, Bank Indonesia (BI) and the Financial Services Authority (Otoritas Jasa Keuangan, OJK) have been instructed to ensure interest rates fall to a single digit in order to boost domestic credit growth. Moreover, Jokowi has been putting some pressure on banks to lend to particular sectors and categories of borrowers, such as small and medium enterprises. This is then supported by government financial subsidy schemes, such as "people's business credit" (KUR, or Kredit Usaha Rakyat) (Hamilton-Hart and Schulze 2016; Hamilton-Hart, Chapter 5). Such state intervention, if conducted too often, may put BI independence at risk. Along with state intervention, the central bank has cut its policy interest rate eight times since 2016. However, it has then taken a U-turn in the second quarter of 2018 as the rupiah has been under pressure. This is because investors have taken funds out of emerging markets in response to rising interest rates in the U.S. Consequently, BI has had to raise its key interest rate three times since May 2018 to slow down the outflow of funds. As things stand, further rate hikes will definitely

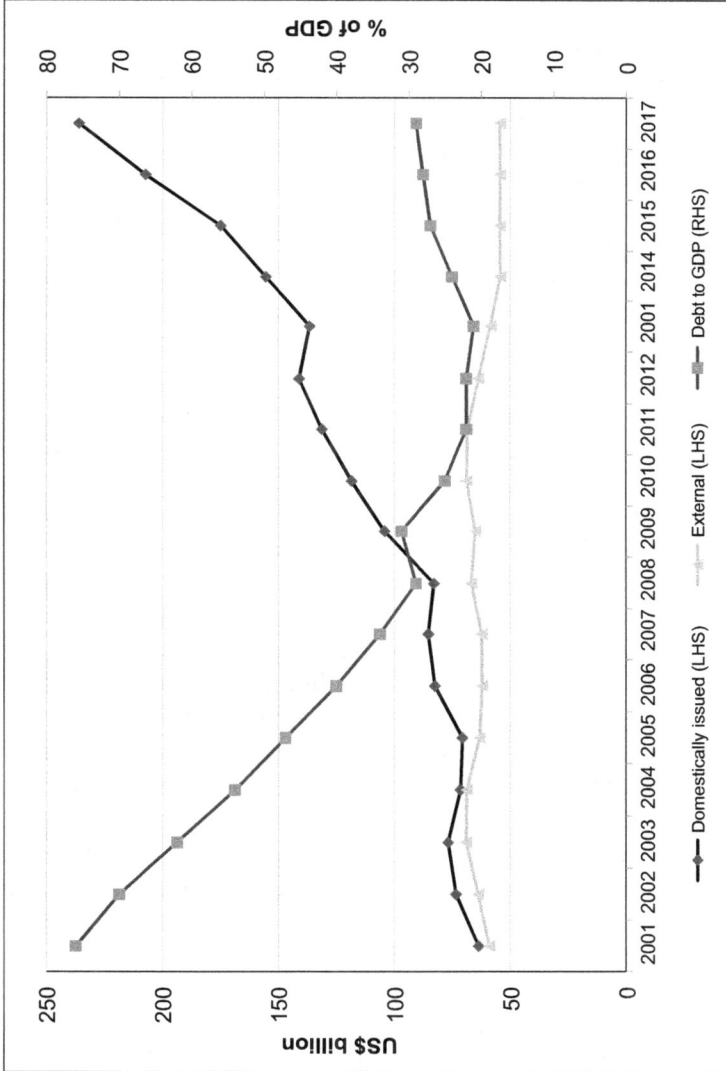

FIGURE 3.8
Indonesian Government Debt, 2001–17

Source: CEIC.

harm the economy, as banks will increase their lending rates to adjust for BI policy rate increases.

The impact of the prior loosening of monetary policy, in the form of lower interest rate has somehow shown mixed results. On one hand, investment growth has picked up since the fourth quarter of 2016 (Pardede and Zahro 2017). On the other hand, while both inflation and interest rates are low, household consumption remains surprisingly lacklustre. Household spending grew at a rate below 5 per cent for several consecutive quarters (Pardede and Zahro 2017). For Indonesia, a strong household spending, which accounts for nearly 60 per cent of its GDP, is necessary for sustaining its long-term growth.

The partial removal of electricity and fuels subsidies has been blamed as the primary cause of weakening consumption. While it is needed to create fiscal space for more productive spending, it nevertheless has adversely affected household purchasing power and is responsible for weakening household consumption. Many Indonesian consumer groups have high marginal propensity to consume, hence their marginal propensity to save is low (Pardede and Zahro 2017). They spend most of their income on food and essential basic commodities. Moreover, this group of consumer faces liquidity constraints and they have poor or no access to credit markets. Many members of this group work in rural areas or in the informal sector in urban areas. During the SBY era, this income group received an unconditional cash transfer. Under the Jokowi administration, such cash transfers have been replaced with conditional cash transfer, such as cash for work programme (Suryahadi and Al Izzati, Chapter 12). Such a change in transfer mechanism, together with energy subsidies reduction, has led to sudden income shock to this household group, and in turn reduced their consumption.

As oil prices start to rebound, the government is forced to make a critical decision whether to reduce energy subsidies further. Considering the political implication of such a policy, the government later decided to halt its subsidy reduction plan. This policy choice means the government must review and cut back a number of spending plans, including those related to infrastructure projects. Indeed, the government has decided to rescale its infrastructure plan, e.g., reducing the number of strategic projects in the pipeline.

Under the SBY administration, monetary authorities often intervened in the exchange rate market to stabilize the currency. This can be seen clearly during the taper tantrum. In the first quarter of 2018, monetary authority does a similar policy to defend the rupiah. The currency has been falling as much as 7 per cent against the U.S. dollar since early 2018. This pressure stems from the Federal Reserve monetary policy that increased the Fed rate. To keep the rupiah below 15,000 per U.S. dollar, BI has intervened regularly in the currency market. As a result, the reserve has declined by 9 per cent in the second quarter 2018, from its peak of US$132 billion in January 2018. See Figure 3.9. It remains to be seen how far BI will intervene to support rupiah against the increased pressure in currency market.

Finally, during the Jokowi era, the government and the parliament have finally passed the bill on financial crisis management, which was passed as Law No. 9/2016 on Financial System Crisis Prevention and Mitigation. In principle, the law is aimed at reducing systemic financial risk by limiting the requirements for the use of public funds to support a distressed bank (Hamilton-Hart and Schulze 2016). The law provides a clear division of labour between the two monetary authorities, BI and OJK, in terms of "macro-prudential" supervision vis-à-vis "micro-prudential" supervision. Moreover, BI and the OJK alongside the Deposit Insurance Corporation (Lembaga Penjamin Simpanan, LPS), have a statutory role in managing financial crises. Nevertheless, it remains to be seen whether or not Indonesia's financial system is resilient enough in responding to external shocks as big as the AFC or GFC.

3.4 MOVING FORWARD

The Jokowi government inherited a better foundation for pushing the medium- and long-term growth rates going forward. However, unlike its predecessor, the government is yet to be tested by significant economic shocks. Some immediate challenges loom ahead if the administration survived its second term. On the external front, several different events will pose challenges to the economy. China's economic slow-down and the trend of trade protectionism and anti-globalization will pose further challenges on the economy's widening current account deficits. Moreover, the normalization of monetary policy in the United States and other advanced economies may entail capital outflow implications to Indonesia, worsening its current account deficit as the country is currently positioned as a net borrower. The increasing trend in international oil prices will

FIGURE 3.9
Rupiah Exchange Rate and International Reserve, 2006–18

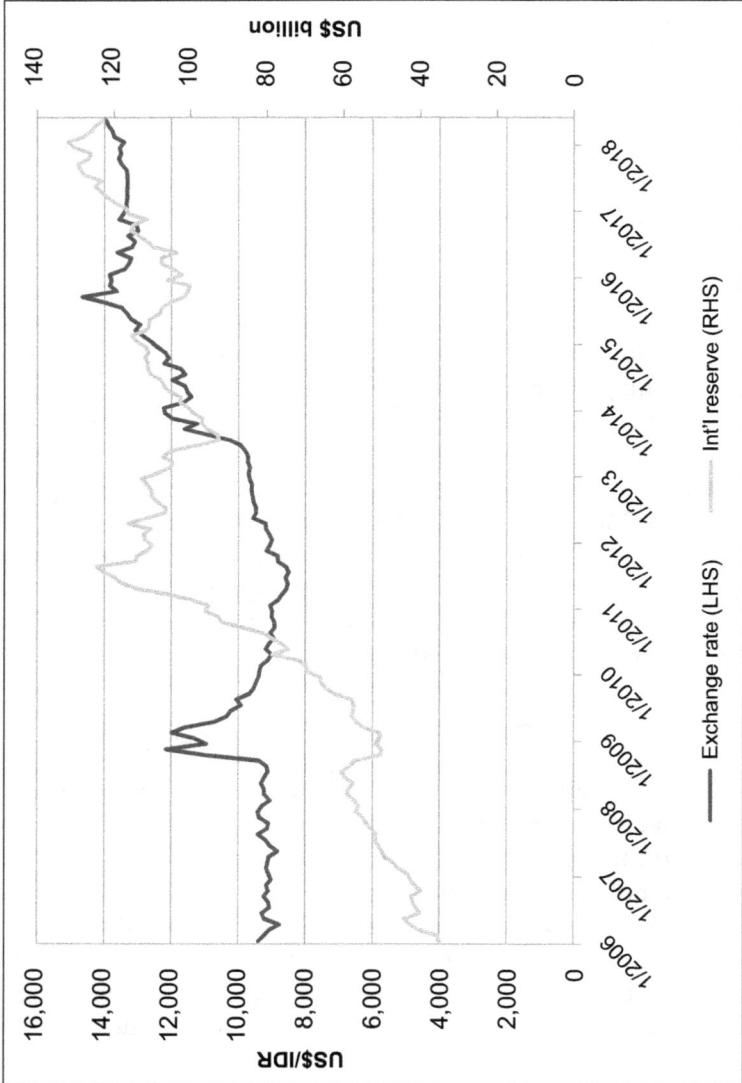

Source: BI.

challenge the government's commitment to reduce fuel subsidy. On the internal front, issues like the fiscal gap, saving investment gap, high-cost economy, weak export performance, and shifts in budget allocation remain.

Having said this, the government may soon be tested on several sets of issues. The first test is related to how the administration deals with an increase in current account deficit. Poor export performance combined with increased import has increased trade deficit. At the same time, available reserves do not seem to provide investors with enough confidence on the strength of the financial system to respond to changes in the Federal Reserve's policy, rising U.S. bond yields and the strengthening U.S. dollar. Given this challenge, in the short-term the government should monitor the implementation of public spending, in particular those related to infrastructure projects and energy subsidies. Those two require a large volume of imported capital goods and raw materials. Gradually increasing the domestic price of fuel may help in reducing the oil import, which is one of the main contributors to trade deficit.

The policy plan to cut imports, including enforcing the local content requirement (TKDN) policy and expanding the use of a 20 per cent blended biodiesel (B20) mix is not an ultimate solution and must be implemented carefully. Local content requirement is prohibited under the WTO regulations. However, many countries have implemented this policy for their respective national-strategic or security reasons. The policy, if overly implemented (or too restrictive), may adversely affect industrial performance and thus its competitiveness (Negara 2018). This is because 90 per cent of Indonesia's total imports consists of capital goods and raw materials. Facilitating a more buoyant environment for export should be prioritized.

In the medium term, the government must continue to address issues that constrain expansion of the manufacturing sector and to boost exports. Thus far, the government has increased infrastructure funding and unveiled policy reforms to stimulate private investment, and is planning to continue doing so as long as necessary. Further reforms to boost productivity, attract long-term investment, and stimulate new sources of growth are definitely required for the economic programmes planned by the current administration.

The second test is about measures to avoid a major fiscal crisis. In recent years, state revenue has been stagnant and tends to decline as a proportion of national output. On the contrary, state spending keeps increasing due to the needs to build infrastructure, to support social expenditures and to maintain energy subsidies. The latter, in particular, will likely to be a key issue for the Jokowi administration, given that world oil prices have been increasing recently. Ideally, to narrow the deficit, Indonesia should raise its domestic fuel and energy prices following increases in the world oil prices. This policy will also reduce the balance sheet pressures in Pertamina and PLN, thus reducing the contingent liabilities risks. However, the administration has been reluctant to further reduce the subsidies on fuel and electricity, considering it as a political risk since 2019 will be an election year. As a result, fiscal deficit is projected to increase. This in turn reduces state capacity to undertake the needed public spending to boost the economy amidst a weakening aggregate demand. Given this fiscal constraint, it is imperative for the government to rescale, prioritize and improve the effectiveness of its spending, especially on health, education, social programmes and infrastructure projects. The latter should be implemented without increasing contingent liabilities on the state-owned enterprises as it may strain the budget further. In the medium to longer term, the tax reform should be continued in order to improve the low tax to GDP ratio. All these initiatives have to be complemented with greater transparency and governance.

Finally, amidst both fiscal and current accounts deficit, the third test would be how to propel the growth prospect going forward. Given the budget deficit limit, an over-expansionary fiscal policy is going to be difficult, if not impossible, to be implemented. At the same time, easing monetary policy has its inherent risk, given the possibility of the U.S. Fed Reserve fund rate hike. The only option for the government is to improve its spending quality and ensure it has the biggest multiplier effect on the economy. To support the reforms progress, improvements in the disbursement of public spending on the social sectors and public infrastructure, both in terms of quantity and quality, is seen as a necessary ingredient to promote the inclusiveness of economic growth.

Notes

All views expressed in this chapter are of the authors and do not reflect the views of the Asian Development Bank (ADB).

1. The rupiah was practically fixed to the U.S. dollar with a fixed depreciation rate normally announced once a year.

2. Ramayandi and Rosario (2010) show that adjusting for the direct impact of the changes in administered fuel prices result in lower inflation that is more consistent with the price movements due to demand pressures faced by the economy.
3. See, for example, discussion in Estrada, Park and Ramayandi (2016).
4. See Yusuf, Patunru and Resosudarmo (2017) for the discussion on history of domestic fuel subsidy in Indonesia.
5. Nota Keuangan and RAPBN 2017.
6. *Jakarta Post*, "SOEs debt ratios worsen: S&P", 22 March 2018 <http://www.thejakartapost.com/news/2018/03/22/soes-debt-ratios-worsen-sp.html> (accessed 22 May 2018).

References

Asian Development Bank. "Asian Development Outlook 2016: Asia's Potential Growth". 2016.

Basri, M.C. "A Tale of Two Crises: Indonesia's Political Economy". In *Two Crises, Different Outcomes: East Asia and Global Finance*, edited by T.J. Pempel and Keiichi Tsunekawa, pp. 41–63. Ithaca: Cornell University Press, 2015.

———. "India and Indonesia: Lessons Learned from the 2013 Taper Tantrum". *Bulletin of Indonesian Economic Studies* 53, no. 2 (May 2017): 137–60.

Estrada, G.B., D. Park and A. Ramayandi. "Taper Tantrum and Emerging Equity Market Slumps". *Emerging Markets Finance and Trade* 52, no. 5 (May 2016): 1060–71.

Hamilton-Hart, N. and G.G. Schulze. "Taxing Times in Indonesia: The Challenge of Restoring Competitiveness and the Search for Fiscal Space". *Bulletin of Indonesian Economic Studies* 52, no. 3 (2016): 265–95.

IMF. *International Monetary Fund Country Report No. 17/48*. Washington, D.C.: International Monetary Fund, 2016.

Negara, S.D. "Indonesia's 2017 Budget Seeks Cautious Economic Expansion". *ISEAS Perspective*, no. 51/2016, ISEAS – Yusof Ishak Institute, Singapore, 15 September 2016.

——— "Assessing the Impact of Local Content Requirements on Indonesia's Manufacturing". In *The Indonesian Economy: Trade and Industrial Policies*, edited by Lili Yan Ing, G.H. Hanson and Sri Mulyani, pp. 213–37. Abingdon and New York: Routledge, 2018.

Park, D., A. Ramayandi and K. Shin. "Why Did Asian Countries Fare Better during the Global Financial Crisis Than during the Asian Financial Crisis". In *Responding to Financial Crisis: Lessons from Asia Then, the United States and Europe Now*, edited by A.S. Posen and C. Rhee, pp. 103–39. Manila and Washington, D.C.: ADB and PIIE Press, 2013.

Pardede, R. and S. Zahro. "Saving not Spending: Indonesia's Domestic Demand Problem". *Bulletin of Indonesian Economic Studies* 53, no. 3 (2017): 233–59.

Qibthiyyah, Riatu and A. Utomo. "Family Matters: Demographic Change and Social Spending in Indonesia". *Bulletin of Indonesian Economic Studies* 52, no. 2 (2016): 133–59.

Ramayandi, A. and A. Rosario. "Monetary Policy Discipline and Macroeconomic Performance: The Case of Indonesia". ADB Economics Working Paper Series 238, Asian Development Bank, 2010.

Stupak, J.M. "Economic Impact of Infrastructure Investment'". *Analyst in Macroeconomic Policy*, 24 January 2018.

Warburton, E. "Jokowi and the New Developmentalism". *Bulletin of Indonesian Economic Studies* 52, no. 3 (2016): 297–320.

Yusuf, A.A., A.A. Patunru and B.P. Resosudarmo. "Reducing Petroleum Subsidy in Indonesia: An Interregional General Equilibrium Analysis". In *Regional Growth and Sustainable Development in Asia*, edited by A.A. Batabyal and P. Nijkamp, pp. 91–112. Cham, Switzerland: Springer, 2017.

4

CONTINUITY OR CHANGE?
Indonesia's Intergovernmental
Fiscal Transfer System under Jokowi

Gerrit J. Gonschorek and Günther G. Schulze

4.1 INTRODUCTION

In 2001, Indonesia embarked on a far-reaching decentralization reform that devolved core responsibilities such as health, primary and secondary education and infrastructure to the districts. While the centre retained authority over foreign affairs, defence, law enforcement, justice, fiscal and monetary policy, and religion, control of all other functions was transferred to the regions — at least in principle (Sjahrir 2016). This implied a huge shift of expenditure from the centre to the regions (districts and provinces), which now spend around a third of the consolidated state budget. Yet, fiscal decentralization, which was accompanied by political

This article was first published in *Journal of Southeast Asian Economies* 35, no. 2 (August 2018).

and administrative decentralization, has remained largely one-sided. While local governments have authority over their spending, they rely heavily on transfers from the centre to finance their expenditure (Schulze and Sjahrir 2014). This particularly concerns districts, which received only 10–16 per cent of their revenue from own sources (tax and non-tax) between 2011 and 2016. Transfers to local governments accounted for around 30 per cent of central expenditure in recent years (Figure 4.1), making the design of the intergovernmental transfer system crucial for the success of the decentralization reform.

From a normative perspective, intergovernmental fiscal transfer systems should fulfil three basic functions. First, they should internalize externalities created by regional spillovers, such as public goods that benefit people from multiple local jurisdictions (Oates 1999), cross-border pollution or the erosion of tax bases in the presence of interjurisdictional competition (Wilson 1999). Second, they should incentivize local governments to mobilize resources and spend their resources efficiently. And third, they should have an equalizing function through which differences in economic development across regions are counterbalanced (Shah 2006; Boadway and Shah 2007). In the case of a one-sided fiscal decentralization, transfers of course have a major financing function (Boadway and Shah 2007). In short, intergovernmental fiscal transfers are an instrument that allow benefitting from the advantages of fiscal decentralization while minimizing its costs in terms of fiscal inequity or negative external effects (Boadway 2007). Yet, in practice, the allocation of transfers is often determined by political considerations like rewarding core voters or targeting swing voters (Gonschorek, Schulze and Sjahrir 2018; Weingast 2009, 2014). Moreover, transfer systems are often designed as a result of lobbying for regional interests. We, thus, cannot expect the system of intergovernmental transfers to fully follow normative criteria; the criteria may also be, in part, contradictory as efficiency considerations may run counter to equity considerations.

Indonesia has three main tiers of government — the centre, provinces and districts. Compared to district governments, provinces have limited responsibilities. They are responsible for supervision and cross-district cooperation, whereas districts are in charge of delivery of public services in education, health and infrastructure. Below districts are village governments, which have recently gained importance, after being entitled to receive their own transfers.

FIGURE 4.1

Share of Intergovernmental Transfers in Central Government Expenditure, 2001–18

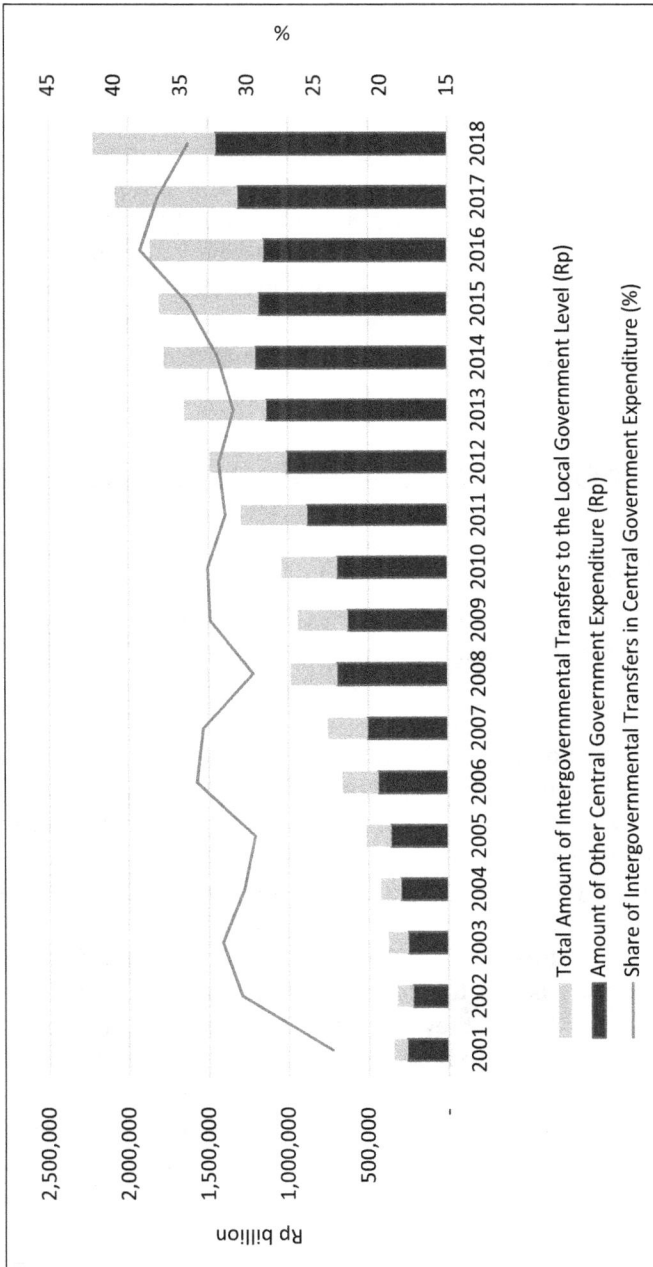

Note: Expenditure in current prices. 2017 based on realization until 28 September 2017; 2018 based on planned budget (APBD).
Source: Authors' illustration based on data by the Ministry of Finance.

The structure of this chapter is as follows. In the second section, we provide a systematic overview of the entire intergovernmental fiscal transfer system in Indonesia. While the country's transfer schemes have been analysed in the past,[1] the analyses are either outdated or only focus on individual components. We, on the other hand, describe the relative magnitude, allocation mechanism and economic rationale (if any) of the different transfer schemes and point out issues that these schemes may have. In the subsequent section, we describe reforms initiated under President Joko "Jokowi" Widodo (elected in 2014) and evaluate whether his administration has a different policy stance towards fiscal decentralization in general and the design of the transfer system in particular. The fourth section concludes.

4.2 INDONESIA'S INTERGOVERNMENTAL FISCAL TRANSFER SYSTEM

4.2.1 Overview

Indonesia's three major transfer mechanisms to support the local governments' budget are: the general allocation grant DAU (*Dana Alokasi Umum*); the specific allocation grant DAK (*Dana Alokasi Khusus*); and the natural resources and tax revenue-sharing system DBH (*Dana Bagi Hasil*).[2] In addition, there are smaller transfers, such as: co-administration and assistance task funds (TP, *Tugas Pembantuan*); deconcentration funds (DK, *Dana Dekonsentrasi*); an incentive fund (DID, *Dana Insentif Daerah*); special autonomy funds (*Dana Otonomi Khusus*); assistance in grants (*Hibah*); and a village fund (*Dana Desa*). Figure 4.2 offers an overview of these funds in 2016.

The relative importance of transfers is very different for districts and provinces. Districts are the core providers for public services. In fact, between 2011 and 2016, they received more than 80 per cent of all DAU, DBH and DAK transferred to subnational jurisdictions. Provinces receive less, but their share recently increased to 17 per cent (see Figure 4.3).

Districts are heavily dependent on transfers. The general allocation grant DAU is, by far, the most important transfer (Figure 4.4). The natural resource sharing scheme, which is very unequally distributed across districts (Agustina, Fengler and Schulze 2012), and the special allocation fund DAK are the second and third most important programmes,

FIGURE 4.2
Intergovernmental Transfers in 2016 (in Rp trillion)

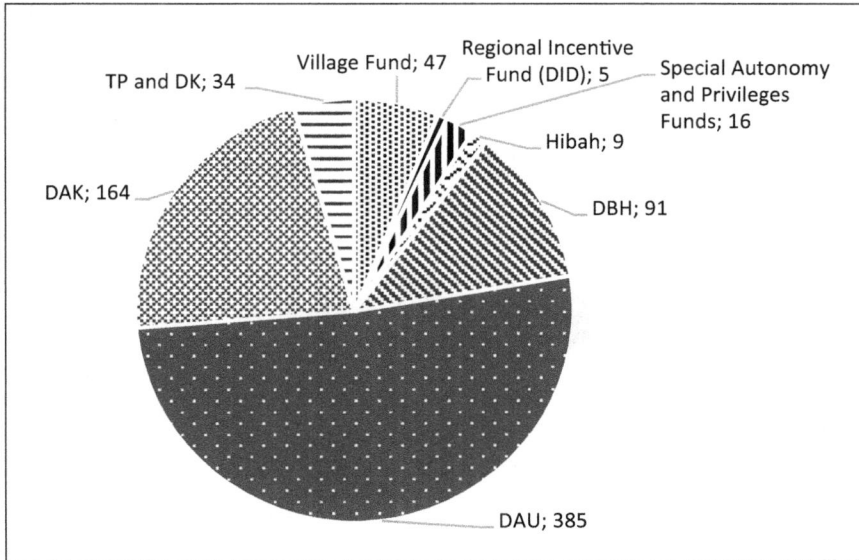

Source: Authors' illustration based on data by the Ministry of Finance.

respectively. Districts raised only around 10–16 per cent of their revenues from own sources (2011–16). This points to a potential structural problem, because a number of studies have shown that governments that raise revenue directly from the people they govern tend to spend the money more responsibly (Rodden 2002; Foremny 2014; Asatryan, Feld and Geys 2015).

In order to increase the revenue raising capacity of the districts, the responsibility for property tax (land and buildings) was gradually devolved to the districts between 2010 and 2014 (Law 28/2009). Since then, districts can set property taxes (including exemptions) up to a maximum of 0.3 per cent of the property value. In 2011, a tax on the transfer of land and buildings was devolved to local governments as well — set at 5 per cent of the gross transfer value (Law 28/2009). However, it should be noted that the largest potential revenue sources — plantations, mining and forestry — are not devolved to the districts. It is debatable whether local governments have

FIGURE 4.3
Share of DAU, DBH and DAK between Provinces and Districts, 2011–16

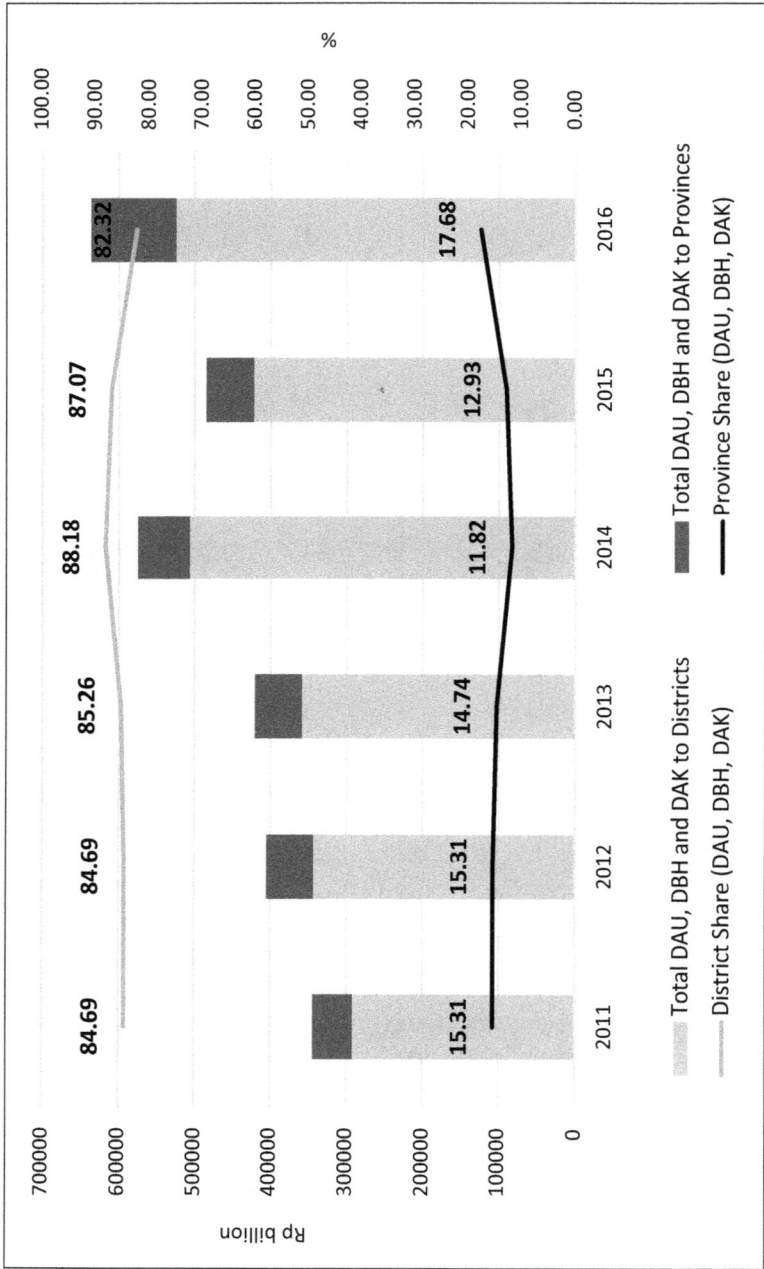

Source: Authors' illustration based on data by the Ministry of Finance.

FIGURE 4.4
Revenue Sources of Districts, 2011–16 (Percentage)

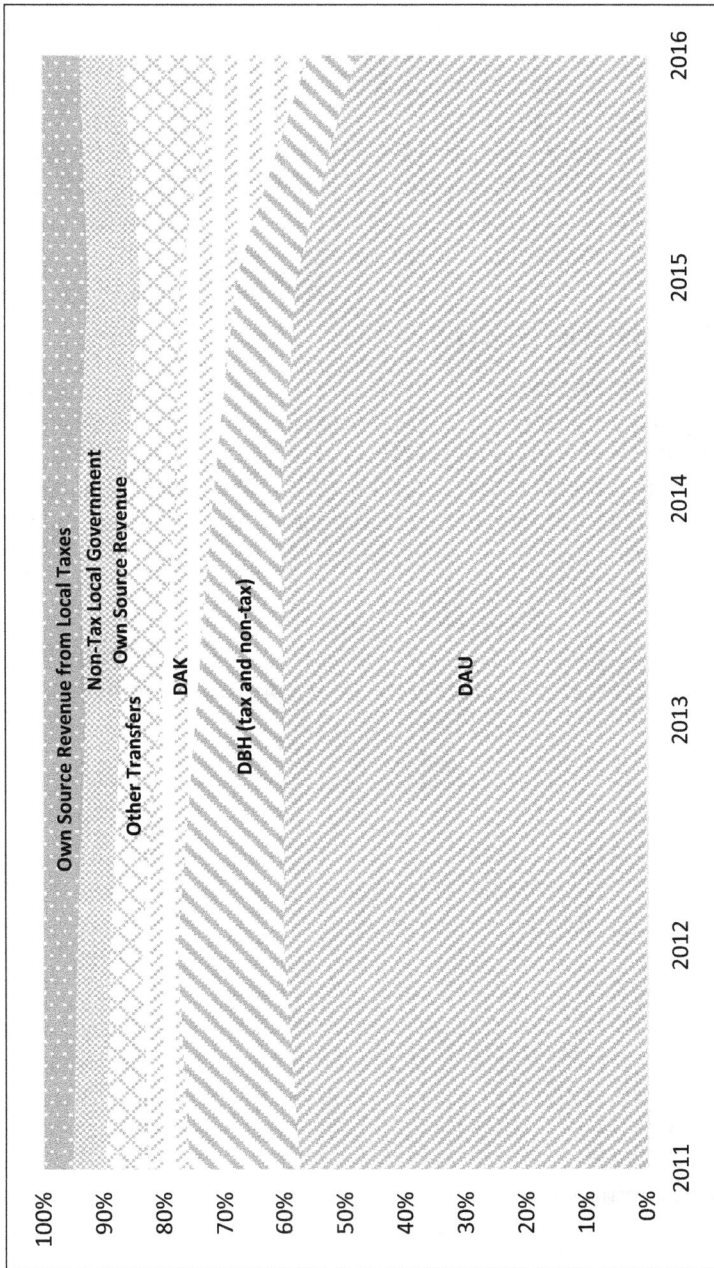

Source: Authors' illustration based on data by the Ministry of Finance.

the capacity and administrative infrastructure for adequate tax collection and whether local tax policy may be distorted by upcoming local direct elections and a potential loss in votes due to unpopular local tax increases (Haldenwang et al. 2015).

The structure of province revenue is substantially different (Figure 4.5). The lion's share comes from own source revenue, even though its relative importance has decreased in recent years due to the increase in DAK revenue (both in nominal and real terms).[3]

4.2.2 General Allocation Fund

The general allocation grant, DAU is a non-earmarked, formula-based general purpose grant. The DAU formula takes into account the fiscal capacity and the fiscal needs of a district, aimed at reducing interregional disparities in economic development. Law 33/2004 stipulates that the amount of DAU funding for each district i is calculated as the sum of a "basic allocation" (BA_i) and a "fiscal gap" (FG_i).

$$DAU_i = BA_i + FG_i \qquad (1)$$

The basic allocation is proportional to the local government's wage bill (WB)

$$BA_i = \gamma \, WB_i \qquad (2)$$

with $\gamma = 0.507$ in the year 2015. In 2015, 49 per cent of the DAU allocations for the districts went to the basic allocation, 51 per cent were determined by the fiscal gap. That basic allocation pool was distributed to the districts pro rata of the personnel expenditures, which resulted in 50.7 per cent of districts' personnel expenditures being covered by the DAU transfers.[4] For provinces the basic allocation accounted for 40 per cent of DAU allocations to provinces in 2015, 60 per cent were determined by the fiscal gap.

The fiscal gap (FG_i) is the difference between the fiscal capacity (FC_i) and the fiscal need (FN_i); the fiscal capacity is the sum of the local governments' *actual* own source revenue and the shared revenue through the DBH funding scheme.

$$FG_i = FN_i - FC_i \qquad (3)$$

FIGURE 4.5
Revenue Sources of Provinces, 2011–16 (Percentage)

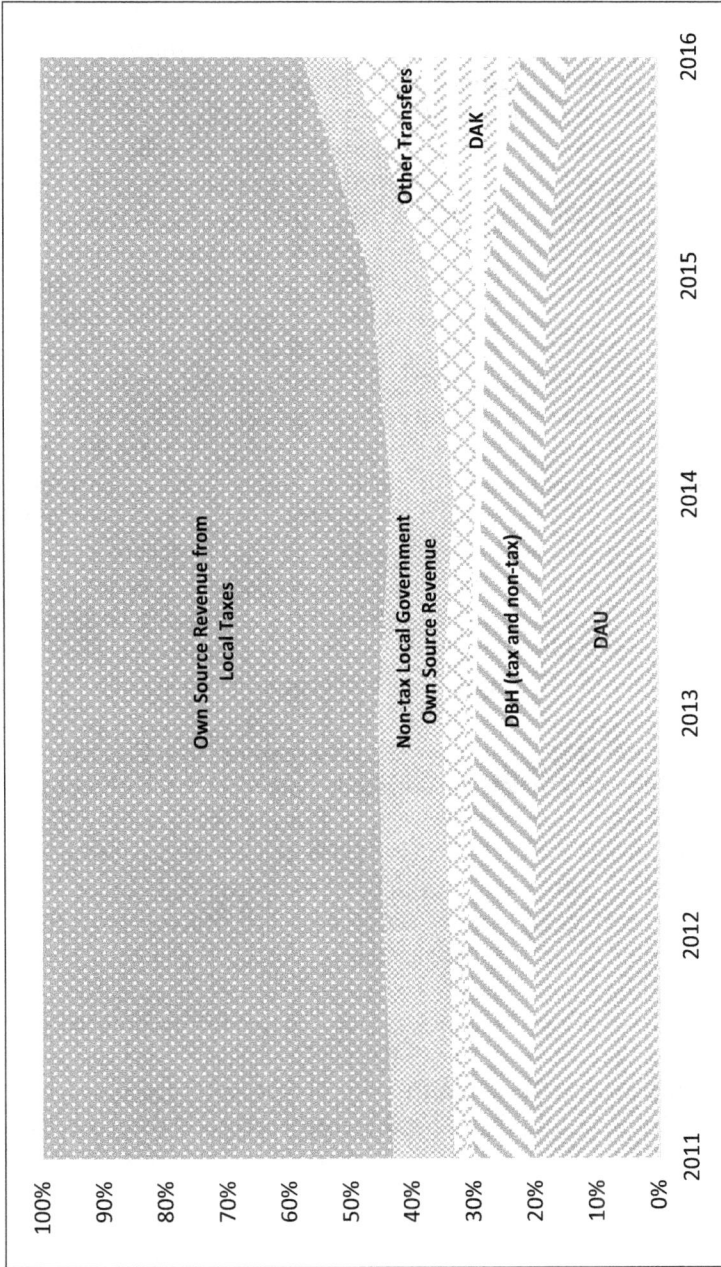

Source: Authors' illustration based on data by the Ministry of Finance.

Fiscal need is determined by a weighted index of population size, the surface area, the inverse of the Human Development Index, a cost price index, and the gross regional domestic product (GRDP) in the previous year (t–1). The formula weights are picked to achieve a given numerical value of the so-called Williamson index (weighted coefficient of variation). The weighted average of all five indices is then multiplied with the average spending across all local governments of this type of government (province or district) to determine the fiscal need of a local government.

The formula underlying the DAU allocation provides the wrong incentives for local governments to improve the efficiency of local administration and increase local tax revenue. This is because of a number of reasons. First, the basic allocation constitutes a classical externality problem. If personnel expenditures are increased, all benefits accrue to the district, but only $(1 - \gamma)$ of the costs are borne by the district, leading to inefficient overstaffing. To mitigate this, local personnel policies are managed by the central government. This, however, significantly limits the autonomy of local governments and thus runs counter to the intended effects of decentralization (Shah, Qibthiyyah and Dita 2012). Rather than imposing an external personnel management by the centre, the source of the problem should be abolished; i.e., the DAU formula should not include a basic allocation that is linked to the input of labour.

Second, using the *actual* own source revenue as a determinant of the fiscal capacity of a local government instead of an estimated *potential* revenue provides strong disincentives to improve local tax collection and compliance (McLeod and Fadliya 2010). Any increase in tax collection would be partly offset by a reduction in transfers.[5] Third, it is not clear why DBH transfers are part of fiscal capacity but DAK transfers are not. Both transfers effectively increase the resources of a region, even if DAK transfers are earmarked. Fourth, McLeod and Fadliya (2010) argue that the DAU formula provides incentives for regional fragmentation.

Last, it is debatable whether the DAU formula captures the needs of districts adequately. The formula is highly complex and non-transparent, and it is unclear whether components such as "area" or the newly introduced "maritime zone" and "GRDP" approximate fiscal needs well. Similarly, there is debate about whether rural and urban districts can be measured along the same metrics used in the formula (Shah, Qibthiyyah and Dita 2012; Farhan 2012). GRDP overstates the fiscal capacity of resource-rich districts. Shah (2012) suggests that transfers should be output based, i.e., on the population to be serviced. School operating grants, for instance, should be tied to the number of school-aged children. Districts should be grouped according to size and rural/urban status, and output based grants should be complemented by infrastructure grants. Khemani (2007) argues that, for India, transfers could be allocated by an independent finance commission, which would lessen politically motivated allocation procedures. While some of these suggestions may be debatable, they clearly show that the formula needs to be revised.

4.2.3 Natural Resources Revenue-Sharing System

The DBH is Indonesia's tax and natural resource revenue-sharing system. Its amount is based on revenue generated by natural resources (forestry, oil, gas, general mining and geothermal energy), personal income tax, and property tax at the subnational-government level (Agustina, Fengler and Schulze 2012). By constitution, the revenue from natural resources should benefit the whole country; however, DBH gives natural resource-rich regions a larger share of resource rents (Harjowiryono 2011). Its objectives are to reduce vertical imbalances (i.e., imbalances between expenditure responsibilities; say, the cost of extraction of natural resources), and to generate total revenue for the central government.[6] Eighty per cent of the revenue from natural resources from forestry, mining, fishery and geothermal energy must be allocated to the region of origin, and 20 per cent remains with the central government. From oil revenue, 15.5 per cent goes back to the region of origin; from gas revenue, the share is 30.5 per cent, the rest remains at the central government level. Twenty-six per cent of the rest is distributed to all (producing and non-producing) regions using DAU transfers (Law 33/2004). As for the revenue allocated to the producing regions, 20 per cent is kept by the provincial government, 40 per cent goes to the producing districts in the province, and the remaining 40 per cent is shared by the non-producing districts. In contrast to DAU, DBH allocations are based on actual net oil and gas revenue (Agustina, Fengler and Schulze 2012).

Critics argue that Indonesia's revenue-sharing system (DBH) and the general formula-based block grant (DAU) partly offset each other. According to the DAU formula, resource-rich districts receive less DAU

transfers as their fiscal gap is decreased by DBH transfers — the larger
DBH transfers are almost fully offset by lower DAU transfers (McLeod
and Fadliya 2010), although significant portions of these resource incomes
may accrue to foreigners or non-residents. This is particularly the case
for Aceh and Indonesia's most remote areas — Papua and West Papua.
By law, these regions receive greater shares from the taxes on resource
revenue; however, the additional gains also increase their fiscal capacity
in the DAU formula, decreasing their DAU entitlements (Shah, Qibthiyyah
and Dita 2012).

4.2.4 Special Allocation Fund

The specific allocation fund DAK is an earmarked fund for physical
capital investments and operational and maintenance needs in line with
national development priorities. It has increased substantially in the last
four years, from around Rp31 trillion in 2014 to Rp163 trillion in 2016,
and is currently budgeted at Rp185 trillion for 2018. DAK allocation is
determined by: general criteria (e.g., fiscal capacity of a local government);
technical criteria (e.g., guidelines by the responsible line ministry); and
special criteria (e.g., specific geographical characteristics of a region). Since
2016, DAK has been divided into physical DAK for capital spending in a
large range of sectors from health to agriculture, and non-physical DAK
to finance operational costs in the local health and education sectors
(see section 4.3).

It is often argued that the criteria to allocate DAK capital grants lack
allocative efficiency, transparency, and accuracy in their definition and
planning (Shah 2012). Shah (2012) states that the DAK allocation lacks a
long-term mapping of the entire country to identify regional deficiencies in
relation to minimum infrastructure standards. This increases the possibility
of ad hoc projects determined by pork-barrel politics. Specifically, it may
favour projects that give the central government greater visibility, and may
create subnational infrastructure that cannot be maintained. Moreover,
the ability of more prosperous districts (richer urban or resource-rich
rural districts) to finance themselves on the capital market should also
be considered and supported by providing technical assistance instead
of DAK grants (Shah 2012). Farhan (2012) notes that the technical criteria
for DAK grant allocation change too frequently and are too complex for
local governments to keep track.

In order to improve the effectiveness of DAK capital grants, Shah (2012) proposes supplementing them with a simple output based grant (based on equal per capita services) to sustain national minimum standards for public services. To implement such minimum service standards in sectors of national priority, DAK grants should (only) be based on identified deficiencies at the local level compared to the service standards spelled out in Indonesia's national five-year development plan (Shah 2012). While such an allocation criterion would be clearer and provide less discretionary scope, it may create disincentives for improvement because the DAK would dry up once deficiencies are eliminated and minimum service standards met.

The World Bank (2017) argues that DAK allocations should be tied to actual project outcomes rather than being pure disbursements in different sectors, as this would ensure better spending quality. DAK physical allocations should focus on specific national programmes rather than just on certain sectors in order to improve result orientation. Moreover, the spending of DAK physical and non-physical allocations should be aligned more closely, since most national priorities for development rely on both capital and non-capital inputs to be successful (World Bank 2017).

4.2.5 Discretionary Transfers

Dana Dekonsentrasi (DK, Deconcentration Funds) and *Tugas Pembantuan* (TP) are discretionary central government transfers that are not part of the local governments' budget. Since 2001, the departments of the central government, which are not responsible for the five "core" responsibilities — foreign affairs, defence, justice, fiscal/monetary policy and religion — have to delegate the implementation of projects financed by these transfers to subnational governments, which act as representatives of the central government.[7] According to Government Regulation 7/2008, DK and TP transfers are allocated on very vaguely defined allocation criteria, stating that allocations should take into account: the financial capacity of the local government; the funding balance in the region; the requirement of regional development; and the criteria of externality, accountability, efficiency, as well as a harmonious national and regional development. Transfers for the implementation of central government tasks of a physical nature are financed by the grant mechanism *Tugas Pembantuan*,[8] whereas tasks of a non-physical nature (e.g., capacity-building or public awareness campaigns) are financed by *Dana Dekon*.[9] Both grants are co-administered — in case of DK, with the provincial governor, and/or with the district head in case of TP. The amount of the two grants combined accounted for around Rp51 trillion in 2009 and was larger than DAK each year between 2001 and 2009. However, it declined to Rp33 trillion in 2016. One reason for this is that TP has been gradually converted into DAK physical since 2015. Moreover, recently, DK has been reduced as it is planned to be discontinued by 2019. This is likely to simplify the intergovernmental fiscal transfer system and make it more transparent as TP and DK were never determined by any objective criteria, giving the central government discretionary scope to pursue political re-election motives (Gonschorek, Schulze and Sjahrir 2018).

4.2.6 Additional Transfer Schemes

In addition to these major transfer schemes, there are smaller transfers to the local governments. These include: grants (*Hibah*) to support local infrastructure development; the Special Autonomy Funds (for Papua and Aceh Province); and a special privilege fund for the Province of Yogyakarta.[10] It should be noted that the special autonomy transfer schemes have been implemented for political reasons and do not have an economic rationale.

A special incentive grant (*Dana Insentif Daerah*, DID) benefits districts with a favourable performance in public service delivery. In order to be eligible for DID, a set of minimum criteria must be fulfilled, such as the use of e-governance in the local government (e.g., in public procurement).[11] Additionally, local governments are ranked by their performance in a range of different sectors related to fiscal management, governance, public service delivery performance, or economic welfare, and are able to win a reward payment in each of these sectors. In order to provide adequate incentives, the performance indicators must be under the control of the local government and give a timely reflection of their performance. Yet, some of the current indicators are beyond direct local government control and measure improvements in sectors where changes take longer than one grant cycle (World Bank 2017). Moreover, DID funds are very small.

A new general purpose fund to villages was introduced in 2014 (PP 43/2014), allocating funds directly to the lowest level of local government, details of which are discussed in subsection 4.3.5. Table 4.1 provides an overview of all existing intergovernmental fiscal transfer schemes.

4.3 REFORMS UNDER THE JOKOWI ADMINISTRATION

In this section, we point out the major changes that have occurred in the intergovernmental fiscal transfer system under Jokowi. We critically evaluate the recent reforms pertaining to: changes in the structure and amount of the transfers; newly introduced requirements on spending purposes; changes in incentive based funds; and the introduction of village funds.

4.3.1 General Fiscal Reforms

The recent abolition of fuel subsidies and a tax amnesty programme have opened up opportunities to scale up transfer programmes and invest in physical and social infrastructure. The Jokowi administration seized the opportunity of falling oil prices to substantially reduce fuel subsidies in January 2015,[12] which had accounted for more than one-fifth of central government spending (World Bank 2017). This reform reduced the share of subsidies from 2.5 per cent of GDP in 2014 to 0.5 per cent of GDP in 2015 (World Bank 2017). Yet, the state-owned enterprise Pertamina did not raise fuel prices accordingly, resulting in losses for the government to cover.[13]

In July 2016, the government introduced a tax amnesty programme to increase tax revenue by Rp165 trillion in redemption payments (Law 11/2016). By the end of the programme in March 2017, Rp111 trillion of tax redemption payments had been collected, much more than many critics had anticipated (Hamilton-Hart and Schulze 2016). In fact, the official target of Rp4,000 trillion in newly declared assets was exceeded by around Rp800 trillion. While it is questionable whether the tax amnesty programme has sustainably broadened Indonesia's tax base by getting wealthy tax payers newly into the system, it has generated extra tax revenue in the short run.[14]

To what extent this larger spending potential benefits the Indonesian people depends, in part, on the effectiveness of the intergovernmental transfer system. In the past, a lacking quality of spending was a more

TABLE 4.1
Intergovernmental Transfers

Transfer	Size (2016) Rp trillion	Aim	Type of Transfer and Main Allocation Criteria	Main Critique
DAU (Dana Alokasi Umum)	385	Reduce horizontal imbalances between regions	Formula-based general purpose equalization grant. Salary expenditure plus part of fiscal gap (fiscal needs — own source revenue and DBH). Fiscal needs: weighted index of population, area, inverse of HDI, construction price index and GRDP	Disincentive for raising tax revenue and reducing personnel.
DAK (Dana Alokasi Khusus)	163.8	Support local governments with limited capacity in the realization of national development priorities	Specific earmarked allocation grant general criteria (e.g. financial capacity of a subnational government), technical criteria (e.g., guidelines established by the responsible line ministry) and special criteria (e.g., specific characteristics of a region).	Lack of transparency in allocation criteria.
DBH (Dana Bagi Hasil)	90.5	Reduce vertical imbalances due to the difference tax revenue raising authorities between different government levels	Tax and natural resource revenue sharing system (Actual) revenues generated by natural resources, personal income tax, and property tax at the subnational-government level.	Very unequally distributed, partly offset by DAU.
TP (Tugas Pembantuan) DK (Dana Dekonsentrasi)	33.5	Support local governments in the fulfilment of decentralized task of physical nature (TP) and non-physical nature (DK)	Central-discretionary government grant financial capacity of the state, the funding balance in the region, the requirement of regional development, criteria of externality, accountability, efficiency, as well as a harmonious national and regional development.	Actual allocation has no relation to districts' level of neediness. Large discretionary scope. Entry point for pork barrel

Special autonomy funds (*Dana otonomi khusus*)	15.9	Finance the implementation of special autonomy in certain regions	Given to Aceh, Papua and much less to special region Yogyakarta	The economic rationale (not the political one) is unclear.
Village funds (*Dana Desa*)	46.9	Foster the effectiveness of national rural development programmes	General purpose grant to village governments, based on equal amounts for village governments and a needs formula (see Table 2).	Village heads need more technical assistance and oversight to avoid the misuse of funds. Allocations should be more determined by local development needs.
Hibah	9.2	Provide assistance for infrastructure development	Capital grants provided by the central government.	Lack of transparency in allocation criteria.
DID (*Dana Insentif Daerah*)	5	Reward local government performance	Performance based grant tied to local government performance in fiscal management, governance, public service delivery performance or economic welfare.	Too small in size, performance categories should be under local government control, provide more information in which specific sectors improvements are necessary, lack of more relative performance measures.

severe problem than the amount of available funding (Lewis 2014*b*; Sjahrir, Kis-Katos and Schulze 2014). Between 2001 and 2009, district governments spent around 30 per cent, on average, for their own administration, excluding sector administration (Sjahrir, Kis-Katos and Schulze 2014) — twice the amount for infrastructure and a clear sign of inefficient spending patterns. In recent years, the share of salaries in district expenditures has decreased from 49 per cent in 2014 to around 40 per cent in 2016, which seems still out of proportion, as it continues to be almost twice as large as the amount spent for capital expenditures or services in 2016.[15] For provinces, the share of salary expenditure decreased from 21 per cent in 2014 to 18 per cent in 2016 (or Rp46 trillion), which is still almost as large as the amount spent on capital (Rp44 trillion) or on goods and services (Rp52 trillion). This suboptimal spending structure may have contributed to the fact that access to public services has not improved significantly in recent years despite increasing amounts of per capita spending (World Bank 2017).

4.3.2 Changes in Size and Structure of Transfers

Since 2014, all three major transfer schemes have substantially increased in absolute size, with the DAK showing the highest absolute increase. The total amount of the three transfers combined grew (in real per capita terms) from Rp1.3 million in 2010 to around Rp2.7 million in Jokowi's first year (2015), and to around Rp4 million in 2017 (in 2010 prices). The development of inter-jurisdictional transfers in constant wholesale prices of 2010 is shown in Figure 4.6. This significant increase in funds for the local governments can be seen as a commitment of the Jokowi administration to decentralization.

In particular, DAK increased substantially in the last four years from around Rp31 trillion in 2014 to Rp163 trillion in 2016; for 2018, it is budgeted at Rp185 trillion. The earmarked DAK grants for national development priorities are divided into physical and non-physical DAK (Law 14/2015 Article 12). DAK physical is used for the development of local health, education, sanitation, roads, and transportation infrastructure. Capital investments, formerly funded through central discretionary TP grants, are currently incorporated in this type of allocation. DAK non-physical finances non-capital investments, mainly in the health and education sectors. DAK physical funds capital investments and infrastructure spending, and

FIGURE 4.6
DAU, DBH and DAK, 2001–18 (in constant prices)

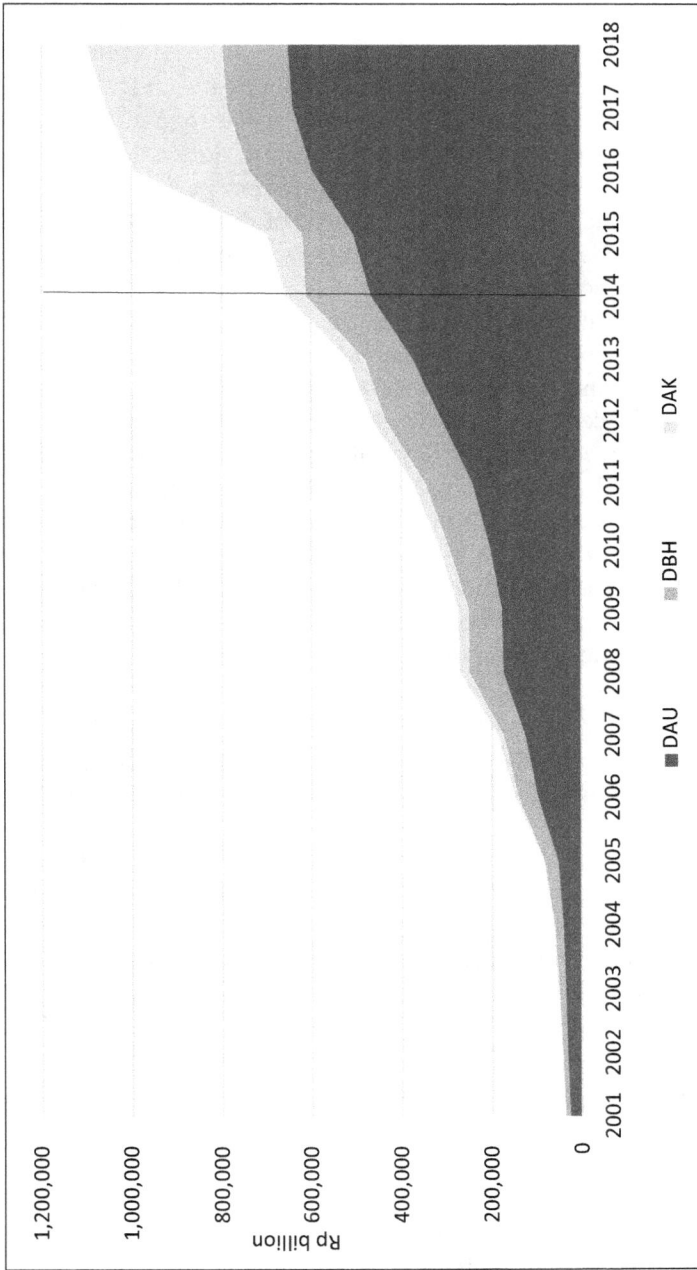

Notes: In constant prices (base year 2010), 2017 based on realization until 28 September 2017; 2018 based on planned budget (APBD).
Source: Authors' illustration, data from the Ministry of Finance.

accounted for an average of Rp68 trillion per annum during the period 2016–18. DAK non-physical stood, on average, at Rp120 trillion per annum during this span. In 2016, the matching requirements for DAK funding was abolished. Previously, local governments needed to match DAK transfers with first 10 per cent, later with 0–2 per cent, depending on their fiscal capacity (Law 27/2014 Article 10(8)). Now, a new performance component has been introduced — the disbursement of the third tranche of DAK is conditional on the compliance with financial reporting standards and fund absorption by local governments, which provides the right incentives to improve financial management and the disbursement of DAK funds.

There have been smaller changes in the DAU allocation. First, the DAU has a dynamic budget ceiling since 2018.[16] The national DAU budget is based on the central government's projected net revenue (taxation and non-taxation revenue, reduced by state revenue shared with the regions),[17] which implies that DAU transfers are effectively tied to the *projected* oil price, while the national budget is determined by the *actual* oil price. If the former exceeds the latter, the central government experiences a budget strain. Since 2018, the ceiling for the DAU budget is flexible and can be readjusted depending on actual central government net revenue. This allows the Indonesian government to react to shocks to their fiscal budget more easily and quickly, but at the same time increases uncertainty on part of the local governments. If such changes to the net domestic revenue occur, regions with limited fiscal capacity, however, still get a specific treatment to maintain their regional allocation ceilings (Law 18/2016 Article 11(11)).

Second, since 2018, the maritime area of a district or province is fully accounted for as part of a region's area size in the fiscal need allocation (Government Regulation 112/PMK.07/2017 Article 47). The argument is that jurisdictions with a very large sea area (such as islands) face higher transport costs to deliver services. This reform increases the calculated fiscal need of regions with access to the sea in the DAU formula, and thus reallocates funds from landlocked to maritime districts. The rationale for this change is not entirely clear as (fully) landlocked districts are typically disadvantaged because they lack access to trading ports and maritime resources.

Third, the provinces now obtain a larger share of DAU than before. Until 2018, districts received 90 per cent of the DAU budget and provinces 10 per cent. In 2018, the share for provinces was increased to 14.1 per cent (Law 15/2017 Article 11(12)) as the responsibilities of provinces have increased in recent years (e.g., in forestry management and high school education) (Law 23/2014).

4.3.3 Requirements on Spending Purpose

In order to improve the quality of spending, a new requirement on the use of funds has been introduced. By a constitutional amendment, the central government and the regional governments already have to spend 20 per cent of their budget on education.[18] Since 2018, 25 per cent of the DAU and DBH funds are earmarked for regional infrastructure expenditures (Law 18/2016 Article 11(15)). This will amount to around Rp122 trillion in the budget year 2018 and mark a major shift in spending patterns.

While DAU had been non-earmarked and local governments could freely choose their expenditure patterns, the new regulation reduces the regional governments' freedom to choose their budget structure. This marks a major change in the attitude on fiscal decentralization. Decentralization theory suggests that local governments should have discretion over their budgets to react to region-specific needs and preferences, and that decentralized decision-making could constitute a laboratory for discovering the optimal policy choices. Yet, this requires that accountability at the local level is functioning, which may not be the case for all regions. While it is undisputed that Indonesia needs to improve its infrastructure (*inter alia* IMF 2016; Salim and Negara, Chapter 9), it is unclear to what extent the new spending requirements will contribute to that end. This will depend on the degree to which this regulation will be implemented in practice, especially whether local governments will have the capacity to identify and implement infrastructure investment projects with high returns effectively, and whether they will be able to disburse these funds quickly enough.[19]

4.3.4 Performance-based Funds (DID)

DID funds have more than quintupled from Rp1.6 trillion in 2015 to Rp8.5 trillion in 2018, but still remain small compared to other non-performance based transfer schemes. Even at its current level, the DID funding represents only 1.26 per cent of the planned funds of the major non-performance based schemes (DAU, DAK and DBH) in 2018 (Rp676 trillion). It has been reported that for more than half of the local governments' incentive funding accounted for less than 1 per cent of their total revenue (World Bank 2017). This is hardly enough to substantially incentivize local governments to improve their performance.

Indicators to evaluate the performance of local governments in "fiscal management" measure the: local taxing power (locally collected tax revenue/redistributed tax revenue); quality of budget planning (realized budget/planned budget); fiscal space (non-earmarked transfers and income/total income); and quality of spending (real capital expenditure/ total expenditure). The "public service delivery" criterion is measured by the number of households with access to clean water, sanitation facilities, and by the condition of roads. The criterion of "governance" consists of more generally formulated measures on local government planning (e.g., quality of local development planning report), innovation (e.g., use of new governance approaches) and the local investment climate in different sectors.[20] "Economic welfare" is determined using the poverty rate and the Human Development Index. In 2017, local governments received a minimum DID allocation after fulfilling three criteria: the use of e-procurement; timely submission of local government reports; and adequate quality of the reports. Since 2018, these criteria are the minimum eligibility criteria for the consideration of DID fund allocations.

While incentive funds make a lot of sense and many indicators are actionable, not all of them are under the local governments' control or responsive to policy changes in the short run. Ideally, performance criteria should incentivize high and low performers alike. For this, the right balance between relative and absolute performance measures needs to be found. If absolute criteria (such as school enrolment rates or access rates to infrastructure) are used exclusively, existing development differences between districts may be deepened as high performers receive more funds and low performers are not rewarded for their improvements. If only relative criteria (like an increase in school enrolment or other access rates) are considered, high performers with smaller room for improvement are not rewarded, even though they perform well.

4.3.5 Village Funds

At the end of his term, President Yudhoyono signed Law 6/2014 on village funds (*Dana Desa*), which replaced the National Community Empowerment

Programme (*Program Nasional Pemberdayaan Masyarakat*, PNPM *Generasi*). The law was endorsed by President Widodo and implemented in 2015 under his rule. It marks the extension of decentralization to the lowest public administration level. The idea is to foster the effectiveness of national rural development programmes by a stronger support for village development (PP 43/2014, Article 98(4)), the hope being that allocation of is less influenced by special interest politics (Antlöv, Wetterberg and Dharmawan 2016).

Under the village law, 10 per cent of Indonesia's central government budget needs to be allocated directly to villages.[21] The funds are distributed first to the districts by the Ministry of Finance and then to the villages within the district. In 2014, it was planned that 100 per cent of *Dana Desa* would be allocated, in equal amounts, to each village (Lewis 2015). Between 2015 and 2017, 90 per cent of the village funds were distributed equally among villages, the remaining 10 per cent were allocated based on a formula that considered the weighted sum of a district's: relative population size; poverty rate; area size; and construction price index. A similar concept was applied for the allocations to the village level within a district (see Table 4.2). In addition to the 10 per cent of *Dana Desa* funds coming directly from the central government budget, villages (by law) should also receive 10 per cent of the district's own source revenue, as well as 10 per cent from all transfers to the district level (excluding Special Autonomy Funds) (PP 43/2014, Article 96(2), Article 97(2)). The use of village funds is monitored by the Ministry of Villages, Development of Disadvantaged Regions and Transmigration (*Kemendesa*, PDTT).

The assessment of Indonesia's recently introduced village funds — between 2014 and 2017 — shows rather mixed results. According to the Ministry of Villages, Development of Disadvantaged Regions and Transmigration, village funds have been used to build, for example, 121,709 kilometres of village roads; 6,504 health centres (*Polindes*); 41,730 irrigation, and more than 82,000 sanitation units.[22] According to the Ministry of Finance, however, poverty has not declined as expected, and the utilization of village funds has not yet been fully felt by the local village communities (Suryahadi and Al Izzati, Chapter 12). District heads are still late in establishing regulations pertaining to village funds, and there are delays in channelling funds from the district to the village level, as well as in reporting on the realization and absorption of funds.

TABLE 4.2
Village Fund (*Dana Desa*) Allocation Reforms, 2015–18

Allocation Criteria:	2015	2016	2017	2018
Allocation Criteria from central to district level	Equally distributed 90%; formula-based 10%	Equally distributed 90%; formula-based 10%	Equally distributed 90%; formula-based 10%	Equally distributed 77%; formula-based 20%; affirmation allocations to underdeveloped villages based on number of poor population 3%
Formula Components and Weights (for central to district allocation)	Poverty rate (35%) construction price (30%) share of district population (25%) area (10%) in Indonesia.	Poverty rate (35%) construction price (30%) share of district population (25%) area (10%) in Indonesia.	Poverty rate (35%) construction price (30%) share of district population (25%) area (10%) in Indonesia.	Number of poor villages (50%) construction price (25%) village area (15%) share of a district's number of villages (10%) in Indonesia.
Allocation Criteria from district to village level	Equally distributed 90%; formula-based 10%	Equally distributed 90%; formula-based 10%	Equally distributed 90%; formula-based 10%	Equally distributed 77%; formula-based allocations 20% affirmation allocations to underdeveloped villages based on number of poor population 3%

Formula Components and Weights (for district to village allocation)	Poverty rate (35%) geographical accessibility index (30%) share of village population (25%) area (10%) in district.	Poverty rate (35%) geographical accessibility index (30%) share of village population (25%) area (10%) in district.	Poverty rate (35%) geographical accessibility index (30%) share of village population (25%) area (10%) in district.	Number of poor population (50%) geographical accessibility index (25%) area (15%) share of population (10%) in district. (PMK 199/2017 Pasal 11)
Laws, Government Regulations (PP) and Ministerial Decrees (PMK)	PP47/2015 as an amendment of PP43/2014. PP22/2015 as an amendment of PP60/2014. Law 3/2015 as an amendment of Law 27/2014.	Law 14/2015, PMK 93 07/2015 (rule apply starting in May 2015), PP No 47/2015 49 PMK 07/2016 (rules apply starting in march 2016)	Law 18/2016, PP 8/2016 as an amendment of PP 60/2014, 50/PMK 07/2017 (rules apply starting in April 2017) PMK 225/2017 (rules apply starting in December 2017)	Law 15/2017, 228 PMK 07/2017, 122/PMK 07/2017, 199/PMK 07/2017, PMK 226/2017

Note: Table 4.2 refers to the allocation of central government village fund budget.

Village heads need technical assistance and oversight to avoid the misuse of the village funds, which are transferred to a single village account under the direct control of the village head (Antlöv, Wetterberg and Dharmawan 2016) (PP 43/2014, Article 98(4)). Berenschot and Sambodoh (2017) argue that village heads, given that they have the discretion to use these funds, could allocate them based on political calculus — since potential gains from being a village head have increased and village head elections are likely to become more competitive. If the village representative councils (BPD) do not operate as an effective counterforce, the village law will end up restoring the power and influence that village heads used to have in the past regarding the distribution of benefits and the selection to social assistance programmes (Berenschot and Sambodoh 2017). Previously, villages were hardly monitored by district governments, mostly due to limited capacity at district level (Antlöv, Wetterberg and Dharmawan 2016). Moreover, the village law does not provide any basis to regulate proper financial management at the local level (Novrizal and Podger 2014). Hence, there is a need to balance the increased powers of village heads with improved management and accountability mechanisms. Antlöv, Wetterberg and Dharmawan (2016) argue that the village law reinforced the legislative powers of the BPDs to monitor village heads and that it introduced village assemblies to allow for communal participation in the planning process. However, the misuse of funds by village heads remains an issue and is a reason for concern.[23]

Village funds are accompanied with the requirement to limit village operational expenditure to 30 per cent (e.g., village head salaries). 70 per cent must be used for development, village community development, and the empowerment of village communities. Since 2018, 20 per cent of the 70 per cent is earmarked for village community empowerment, with the aim to increase accountability and to control the village head. The Ministry of Villages, Development of Disadvantaged Regions and Transmigration has formed the Village Task Force (*Satgas DD*), responsible for overseeing the implementation of the use of village funds. Whether these changes are enough to counter the misappropriation of funds by several village heads and ensure appropriate spending quality is an open question, particularly because the regulations still do not stipulate penalties for the misuse of funds.

Village fund allocations should be determined by local development needs. The criteria for village fund allocations were reformed in 2017.[24]

Now, 77 per cent of the funds are divided equally among villages, 3 per cent is allocated to highly disadvantaged villages with a large number of poor people, and the formula component has increased to 20 per cent (see Table 4.2). This is a favourable step to increase the need orientation of village funds, but the bulk portion continues to be devoted to villages without accounting for their sizes or development needs. This is clearly inefficient.

4.4 CONCLUSION

The intergovernmental fiscal transfer system in Indonesia is an incoherent system of different schemes that are governed by diverse rationales — and not by a grand plan. This may, in part, be a consequence of the different functions that such a system should fulfil, which are partially contradictory as we have argued in the introduction. Simultaneously, it may also be the consequence of divergent political interests that had to be satisfied when designing the system.

Regarding the changes implemented by the current administration and the degree of continuity in — or change of — the system, we make the following observations based on our analysis.

First, many apparent problems of the intergovernmental fiscal system remain unresolved. The basic allocation is still part of the DAU formula, even though allocative efficiency requires that it be discontinued and replaced by a scheme that does not link transfers to (labour) inputs. Likewise, *actual* own-source revenue needs to be replaced by a reasonable estimate of *potential* own source revenue in order to remove disincentives for revenue mobilization, and DAK needs to be included in a fiscal capacity calculation. Determination of "fiscal need" in the DAU formula should be reformed as well, as it is opaque and, to some extent, arbitrary. Despite the devolution of the property tax, own source revenue remains low, which may be, in part, due to missing incentives to collect taxes (as they decrease DAU transfers), and also due to lacking tax bases.

As fundamental problems continue to be unresolved and the system as such remains largely in place in its previous structure, we see continuity rather than change dominating the picture. Yet, there are distinct — somewhat more gradual — changes that we note.

Second, we observe a more interventionist approach to fiscal decentralization, as minimum spending requirements for infrastructure have been introduced in DAU and DBH transfers. This addresses an important deficit in the previous economic policy and is laudable as such, but reduces the local governments' freedom to choose an optimal policy mix. Given that the deficiency in infrastructure is so huge, the local governments' incentives to invest in pro-growth policies might not have been strong enough in the recent past.

Third, we observe a significant increase in overall funds transferred to the regions, which demonstrates a commitment to fiscal devolution of authority to the subnational level.

Fourth, we witness limited attempts to provide incentives for better performance of local governments, mostly in the area of financial management. DAK now includes requirements to that effect, and the small incentive funds that DID has increased significantly in relative terms, but are still much too low to make a significant difference.

Fifth, allocation of funds should be improved through the integration of the discretionary schemes, TP and DK into DAK, even though allocation criteria for DAK are far from being transparent and clear.

Sixth, the implementation of village funds extends Indonesia's fiscal decentralization even further; it may be the biggest change in the intergovernmental transfer system under President Widodo so far. Instead of solving more urgent problems, such as increasing the local own source revenue or the overall quality of spending, it devolves more funds and fiscal responsibilities to another level of local government. While its introduction again shows the current administration's commitment to fiscal decentralization, its design is found wanting. It partly repeats the same mistakes as with the current (and former) DAU design: spending requirements are unclear; there is no effective sanction for the misuse of funds; and the incentive to use the funds for pork-barrel politics is large. The allocated amount is very substantial and may overstrain the planning and absorption capacities of villages. The allocation is largely on a "lump sum per village" basis and is thus essentially unfair — as it disregards population size and needs characteristics. Village funds should be downsized and allocated on a formula determined by relevant needs and characteristics of the village.

In sum, the Jokowi administration has moved in the right direction overall, but has shied away from the more far-reaching (but necessary) reforms of the intergovernmental fiscal transfer system. In the implementation of village funds, which is a major change, the design has been found to be suboptimal.

Notes

We are grateful to the participants of the conference on "The Indonesian Economy Under Jokowi: A New Developmental Model?", held at ISEAS – Yusof Ishak Institute, Singapore on 21–22 March 2018, especially to the organizers Hal Hill and Siwage Dharma Negara for their helpful comments. We also thank Ahmad Zaki Fahmi, Asep Suryahadi and Gema Satria as well as many more friends and colleagues in Indonesia for their valuable comments and suggestions. Gerrit Gonschorek is grateful to SMERU Institute in Jakarta for hosting him during the field work for this article in February and March 2018.

1. *Inter alia* Brodjonegoro and Martinez-Vazquez (2005), Harjowiryono (2011), Shah, Qibthiyyah and Dita (2012), Shah (2012), Agustina, Fengler and Schulze (2012), Lewis (2014*a*, *b*, 2015), Gonschorek, Schulze and Sjahrir (2018).
2. Law No. 25/1999 on fiscal balance between the central government and the regions, Law No. 33/2004 on fiscal decentralization, and its revision under government regulation No. 55 of 2005.
3. The total own source revenue of local governments in real terms (in whole sale prices of 2010) increased from around Rp117 trillion in 2010 to Rp355 trillion in 2016.
4. The basic allocation for a district is the personnel expenditures for the respective district divided by personnel expenditures of all districts times total basic allocation pool.
5. Recent evidence on these disincentives for tax collection is mixed (Lewis and Smoke 2017); yet, the reform of the property tax only marginally increased the own source revenue of districts, which remain heavily dependent on transfers (Figure 4.4).
6. Of course, in political reality, the transfers may not only compensate costs of exploration and environmental degradation but also reward the regions for being home of these natural resources.
7. Government Regulation No. 52/2001, Government Regulation No. 7/2008 and Government Regulation No. 106/2000.
8. Government Regulation 7/2008 Article 49 paragraph 2.
9. Government Regulation 7/2008 Article 20 paragraph 3.
10. Law No. 35/2008, Law No. 11/2006, and Law No. 21/2001.
11. E-procurement has been shown to be instrumental for increasing the quality of contractors and for reducing delays in infrastructure projects in Indonesia (Lewis-Faupel et al. 2016).

12. Budgetary transfers to gasoline shifted to a fixed Rp1,000 per litre subsidy for diesel.

13. We owe this point to M. Chatib Basri's lecture "How to Do Reform in a 'Second Best World': The Case of Indonesia", The Australian National University, Canberra, 22 September 2016; see also Hamilton-Hart and Schulze (2016).

14. Indonesia's tax to GDP ratio stands at a very low level of 10.3 per cent (in 2017).

15. Total district salary expenditure in 2016 was Rp303 trillion, capital expenditure Rp177 trillion and expenditure for goods and services Rp157 trillion. (Authors' calculation based on the Ministry of Finance data.)

16. Law 18/2016 Article 11(10). Before 2018, based on Law 14/2015 Article 11(8), no change was allowed to be made to the amount of DAU budget in response to changing central government revenue.

17. The DAU budget was set at 27.7 per cent of projected central government net revenue, but fixed for the year (Law 14/2015 Article 11(6)). It is now set at least at 28.7 per cent of the central net domestic revenue but can react flexibly to changes to the net domestic revenue of the revised state budget (Law 18/2016 Article 11(10)).

18. Initially, Law 20/2003 Article 49 excluded salaries from the 20 per cent spending rule (see also Arze del Granado et al. 2007). However, the implementation in 2004 began under the assumption that it would include salaries, which was reconfirmed by a Constitutional Court Decision in 2009. Source: Presentation at the Australian-Indonesian High Level Fiscal Policy Dialog by Hieu T.M. Nguyen (Australian National University), 26 March 2018, Ministry of Finance, Jakarta.

19. There have been smaller changes in the tasks on which DID funds can be spent. Moreover, since 2017 revenue from DBH forestry previously distributed to producing districts are now also earmarked for reforestation and rehabilitation activities at the province level (Law 18/2016 Article 11(5)).

20. Changes in this performance measure category are apparently considered for 2019 again, such as introducing indicators for local deregulation and foreign direct investment (FDI). It is questionable if these frequently changing evaluation criteria provide effective incentives for local governments.

21. PP 60/2014, PP 22/2015.

22. Presentation by Edward Lumban Gaol, from the Ministry of Villages, Development of Disadvantaged Regions and Transmigration at the Australian-Indonesian High Level Policy Dialog, 26 March 2018, Ministry of Finance, Jakarta, Indonesia.

23. According to Indonesia Corruption Watch (13 February 2018), corruption at the village level was on the rise between 2015 and 2017; in 2015, there were 17 registered cases, 41 cases in 2016, and 96 cases in 2017. The 154 cases of

corruption at the village level in this period created losses of Rp47.56 billion. Out of the 154 cases, 127 cases were pertaining to village funds; the village head was involved in 112 cases, family members of the village head in 3 cases and 32 cases were perpetrated by village officials. At <https://antikorupsi. org/en/news/village-funds-are-prone-misuse> (accessed 6 March 2018).

24. Law 15/2017, 228 PMK 07/2017, 122/PMK 07/2017, 199/PMK 07/2017, PMK 226/2017.

References

Agustina, C.R.D., W. Fengler and G.G. Schulze. "The Regional Effects of Indonesia's Oil and Gas Policy: Options for Reform". *Bulletin of Indonesian Economic Studies* 48, no. 3 (2012): 369–97 <https://doi.org/10.1080/00074918.2012.728 644>.

Antlöv, H., A. Wetterberg and L. Dharmawan. "Village Governance, Community Life, and the 2014 Village Law in Indonesia". *Bulletin of Indonesian Economic Studies* 52, no. 2 (2016): 161–83 <https://doi.org/10.1080/00074918.2015.112 9047>.

Arze del Granado, F.J., W. Fengler, A. Ragatz and E. Yavuz. "Investing In Indonesia's Education: Allocation, Equity, and Efficiency of Public Expenditures". Poverty Reduction and Economic Management Unit, East Asia and Pacific Region, Jakarta. Washington, D.C.: World Bank, 2007.

Asatryan, Z., L.P. Feld and B. Geys. "Partial Fiscal Decentralization and Sub-national Government Fiscal Discipline: Empirical Evidence from OECD Countries". *Public Choice* 163, no. 3-4 (2015): 307–20 <https://doi.org/10.1007/s11127-015-0250-2>.

Berenschot, W. and P. Sambodoh. "The Village Head as Patron". *Inside Indonesia*, edn 128, April–Jun 2017 <www.insideindonesia.org/the-village-head-as-patron> (accessed 15 March 2018).

Boadway, R. "Grants in a Federal Economy: A Conceptual Perspective". In *Intergovernmental Fiscal Transfers. Principles and Practices*, edited by R. Boadway and A. Shah, pp. 55–73. Washington, D.C.: International Bank for Reconstruction and Development/World Bank, 2007.

Boadway, R.W. and A. Shah, eds. *Fiscal Equalization: Challenges in the Design of Intergovernmental Transfers*. Springer Science & Business Media, 2007.

Brodjonegoro, B. and J. Martinez-Vazquez. "An Analysis of Indonesia's Transfer System: Recent Performance and Future Prospects". In *Reforming Intergovernmental Fiscal Relations and the Rebuilding of Indonesia: The "Big Bang" Program and Its Economic Consequences*, edited by J. Martinez-Vazquez, I.S. Mulyani and J. Alm, pp. 159–98. Cheltenham: Edward Elgar Publishing, 2005.

Farhan, Y. "Policy Recommendations on Revision of Regional Fiscal Balance Funding (Dana Perimbangan): Recommendations Relevant to Revision of Law No. 33/2004 Concerning Fiscal Balance Between the Center and the Regions". Budget Brief 03. Indonesian Forum for Budget Transparency, Jakarta, 2012.

Foremny, D. "Sub-national Deficits in European Countries: The Impact of Fiscal Rules and Tax Autonomy". *European Journal of Political Economy* 34 (2014): 86–110 <https://doi.org/10.1016/j.ejpoleco.2014.01.003>.

Gonschorek, G.J., G.G. Schulze and B.S. Sjahrir. "To the Ones in Need or the Ones You Need? The Political Economy of Central Discretionary Grants, Empirical Evidence from Indonesia". *European Journal of Political Economy* (2018) <https://doi.org/10.1016/j.ejpoleco.2018.04.003>.

Haldenwang, C., A. Elfert, T. Engelmann, S. Germain, G. Sahler and A.S. Ferreira. *The Devolution of the Land and Building Tax in Indonesia*. Bonn: German Development Institute (DIE), 2015.

Hamilton-Hart, N. and G.G. Schulze. "Taxing Times in Indonesia: The Challenge of Restoring Competitiveness and the Search for Fiscal Space". *Bulletin of Indonesian Economic Studies* 52, no. 3 (2016): 265–95 <https://doi.org/10.1080/00074918.2016.1249263>.

Harjowiryono, M. "Development of Indonesia's Intergovernmental Financing System". In *Fiscal Decentralization in Indonesia a Decade after Big Bang*, edited by Ministry of Finance, Republic of Indonesia, pp. 119–40. Jakarta: University of Indonesia Press, 2011.

IMF. "Indonesia: Selected Issues". International Monetary Fund Country Report No. 17/48. International Monetary Fund, Washington, D.C., 2016.

Khemani, S. "Does Delegation of Fiscal Policy to an Independent Agency Make a Difference? Evidence from Intergovernmental Transfers in India". *Journal of Development Economics* 82, no. 2 (2007): 464–84 <https://doi.org/10.1016/j.jdeveco.2006.04.001>.

Lewis, B.D. "Indonesian Intergovernmental Performance Grants: An Empirical Assessment of Impact". *Bulletin of Indonesian Economic Studies* 50, no. 3 (2014*a*): 415–33 <https://doi.org/10.1080/00074918.2014.980378>.

———. "Twelve Years of Fiscal Decentralization: A Balance Sheet". In *Regional Dynamics in Decentralized Indonesia*, edited by H. Hill, pp. 135–55. Singapore: Institute of Southeast Asian Studies, 2014*b*.

———. "Decentralising to Villages in Indonesia: Money (and Other) Mistakes". *Public Administration and Development* 35, no. 5 (2015): 347–59 <https://doi.org/10.1002/pad.1741>.

——— and P. Smoke. "Intergovernmental Fiscal Transfers and Local Incentives and Responses: The Case of Indonesia". *Fiscal Studies* 38, no. 1 (2017): 111–39.

Lewis-Faupel, S., Y. Neggers, B.A. Olken and R. Pande. "Can Electronic Procurement Improve Infrastructure Provision? Evidence from Public Works in India and Indonesia". *American Economic Journal: Economic Policy* 8, no. 3 (2016): 258–83 <https://doi.org/10.1257/pol.20140258>.

McLeod, R.H. and Fadliya. "Fiscal Transfers to Regional Governments in Indonesia". Working Paper No. 2010/14. The Australian National University, Canberra, Australia, 2010.

Novrizal, M. and O. Podger. "Corruption Prevention in Village Finance Governance". Paper presented at the International Conference on "Eradicating Corruption: An Inter-Disciplinary Perspective", sponsored by Universitas Andalas, Utrecht University, KPK, UNODC and TII, in Padang, Indonesia, June 2014.

Oates, W.E. "An Essay on Fiscal Federalism". *Journal of Economic Literature* 37 (1999): 1120–49.

Rodden, J. "The Dilemma of Fiscal Federalism: Grants and Fiscal Performance Around the World". *American Journal of Political Science* 46, no. 3 (2002): 670–87.

Schulze, G.G. and B.S. Sjahrir. "Decentralization, Governance and Public Service Delivery". In *Regional Dynamics in Decentralized Indonesia*, edited by H. Hill, pp. 186–207. Singapore: Institute of Southeast Asian Studies, 2014.

Shah, A. "A Practitioner's Guide to Intergovernmental Fiscal Transfers". World Bank Policy Research Working Paper 4039. World Bank, 2006.

———. "Autonomy with Equity and Accountability: Toward a More Transparent, Objective, Predictable and Simpler (TOPS) System of Central Financing of Provincial-Local Expenditures in Indonesia". World Bank Policy Research Working Paper 6004. World Bank, 2012.

———, R. Qibthiyyah and A. Dita. "General Purpose Central-Provincial-Local Transfers (DAU) in Indonesia: From Gap Filling to Ensuring Fair Access to Essential Public Services for All". World Bank Policy Research Working Paper 6075. World Bank, 2012.

Sjahrir, B.S. "The Impact of Decentralization and Democratization on Public Service Delivery: An Empirical Analysis". PhD dissertation, Freiburg im Breisgau, Germany, 2016.

———, K. Kis-Katos and G.G. Schulze. "Administrative Overspending in Indonesian Districts: The Role of Local Politics". *World Development* 59 (2014): 166–83 <https://doi.org/10.1016/j.worlddev.2014.01.008>.

Weingast, B.R. "Second Generation Fiscal Federalism: The Implications of Fiscal Incentives". *Journal of Urban Economics* 65, no. 3 (2009): 279–93 <https://doi.org/10.1016/j.jue.2008.12.005>.

———. "Second Generation Fiscal Federalism: Political Aspects of Decentralization and Economic Development". *World Development* 53 (2014): 14–25 <https://doi.org/10.1016/j.worlddev.2013.01.003>.

Wilson, J.D. "Theories of Tax Competition". *National Tax Journal* 52, no. 2 (1999): 269–304.

World Bank. "Decentralization that Delivers". *Indonesian Economic Quarterly*. Jakarta: World Bank, 2017.

5

HOW WELL IS INDONESIA'S FINANCIAL SYSTEM WORKING?

Natasha Hamilton-Hart

5.1 INTRODUCTION

The costs of financial system failure in the form of a systemic banking crisis can be extraordinarily high, as illustrated by Indonesia's devastating financial crisis that began in 1997. It took many years for bank lending growth to resume and, by some measures, Indonesia's level of financial development has yet to return to pre-crisis levels. In comparison with this history, Indonesia's financial system has been working very well over the past decade. Government financial policy has the declared aim of promoting a financial system that facilitates economic growth, supports financial inclusion and safeguards financial stability. These goals require a balancing act that, so far, appears to have achieved a degree of success. Measures of growth and performance described in this chapter focus on the significant financial development over the past two decades and

This article was first published in *Journal of Southeast Asian Economies* 35, no. 2 (August 2018).

suggest a financial system that is more resilient than at any stage in the past. Notwithstanding potential costs and risks arising from increasingly interventionist financial policies and an inadequate financial safety net, the banking sector (to date) remains relatively robust in prudential terms. There is evidence of inefficiency arising from structural segmentation of the banking system, which has persisted despite foreign presence in the banking system. The financial sector as a whole has diversified as nonbank capital markets and the nonbank financial service sector have developed, albeit modestly.

The next section of this chapter presents basic data on the structure and performance of Indonesia's financial system. It goes on to discuss the policy framework governing the financial sector, with an emphasis on agencies and policies relating to banks, which remain the dominant players in the financial system. The third section identifies some of the policy conflicts and constraints affecting financial sector performance, with attention to the segmentation of the banking sector, the role of foreign ownership and the potential for financial sector diversification away from current levels of reliance on commercial banks. The final section concludes.

5.2 FINANCIAL SYSTEM STRUCTURE AND PERFORMANCE

Indonesia's financial system remains bank-dominated, with banks accounting for around 76 per cent of the assets of all financial institutions, as shown in Figure 5.1. Insurance companies, pension and mutual funds and all other financial intermediaries together thus account for less than a quarter of all assets held by financial institutions. The dominance of commercial banks is, however, declining slowly — in 2005, for example, they represented 81 per cent of the assets of all financial institutions (IMF and World Bank 2017).

State-owned commercial banks account for around 38 per cent of all banking assets and another 8 to 9 per cent is held by regional development banks, bringing the total public sector share to nearly half (around 46 to 47 per cent) of all banking assets (IMF and World Bank 2017). The share of all bank lending accounted for by state-owned banks is thus noticeably higher than it was just before Indonesia's major financial crisis of the late. 1990s (at 35 per cent in July 1997) and higher than the 43 per cent it stood at by the end of 2005 (Hamilton-Hart 2008). The private banks that account

FIGURE 5.1
Total Financial Assets by Type of Institution, 2015

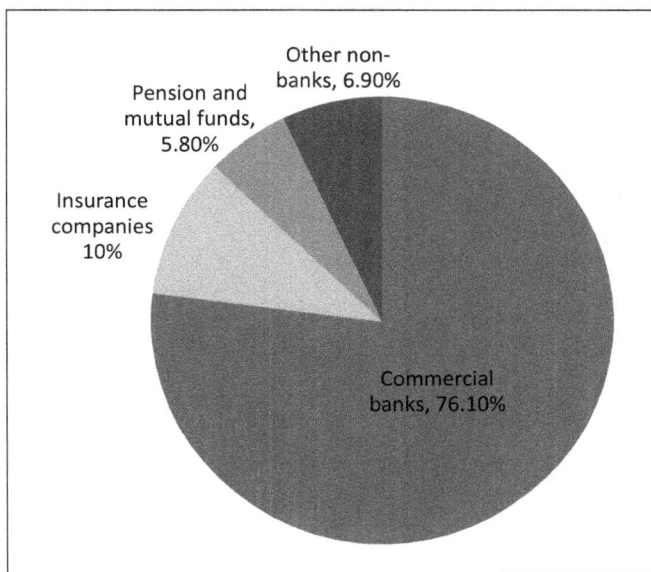

Pension and mutual funds, 5.80%

Other non-banks, 6.90%

Insurance companies 10%

Commercial banks, 76.10%

Source: IMF and World Bank (2017), p. 32.

for the remaining banking sector assets include a substantial presence by foreign-controlled or joint venture banks, either subsidiaries or foreign bank branches. As discussed below, such foreign-controlled banks represent over half of private sector banking assets, 27.6 per cent of all bank assets.

Commercial bank lending continues to increase, as depicted in Figure 5.2, albeit at a slower rate than the annual increases of over 20 per cent for much of the decade until 2014. Despite this credit growth, total lending to the private sector in Indonesia has yet to return to the levels it reached before the crisis of 1997–98, and remains at a modest level when compared to regional peers. As shown in Table 5.1, Indonesia's collapse in bank lending after the 1998 crisis was particularly deep and its recovery has been gradual, although it should be noted that the credit to GDP ratio has not returned to pre-crisis peaks for any of the crisis-hit countries. At 39 per cent of GDP in 2016, bank lending to the private sector in Indonesia is close to the average for all "lower middle income" countries (40 per cent in 2010, rising to 44 per cent in 2016), according to the World Bank data.

FIGURE 5.2
Growth of Commercial Bank Credit, 2012 to November 2017 (% year on year)

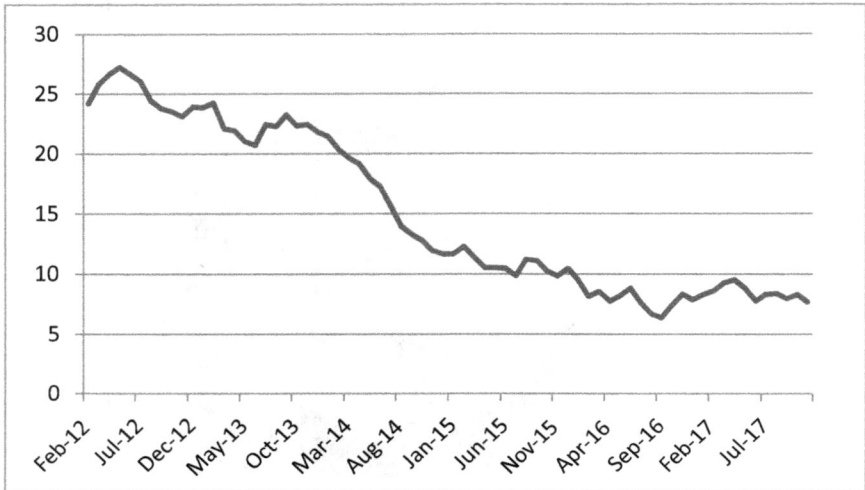

Source: Indonesia Financial Statistics, Table 1.1.

TABLE 5.1
Domestic Credit to Private Sector (Percentage of GDP)

	1997	2000	2005	2010	2015	2016
Indonesia	57.1	18.7	24.8	27.3	39.1	39.4
China	96.7	111.1	111.8	126.3	152.6	156.7
Malaysia	158.4	135.0	106.5	107.1	125.1	123.9
The Philippines	56.5	36.8	29.1	29.6	41.8	44.7
Thailand	166.5	105.1	93.8	115.7	149.8	147.3
Vietnam	19.8	35.3	60.5	114.7	111.9	123.8

Source: World Bank, World Development Indicators, at <https://data.worldbank.org/indicator/FS.AST.PRVT.GD.ZS>.

Since February 2017, the total number of commercial banks in Indonesia has stood at 115, down from 120 at the end of 2013. Commercial banks have, since 2012, been divided into four categories known as BUKU (*Bank Umum Berdasarkan Kegiatan Usaha*) based on size (total tier one capital), corresponding with some variation in permitted activities. The

2012 regulation (14/26/PBI/2012) was issued by the central bank, Bank Indonesia.[1] Table 5.2 shows the structure of the banking sector based on these categories. It shows that as of November 2017, the five large (BUKU 4) banks account for nearly half of all assets, with the next largest 26 banks (BUKU 3) with 34 per cent. Thus, most of the apparently large number of commercial banks are very small, accounting together for only 17 per cent of banking assets.

The new trend in the structure of the banking sector is towards consolidation in the larger banks. The number of BUKU 4 banks increased from four to five in November 2017, while banking assets represented by the BUKU 1 and BUKU 2 banks have declined in absolute as well as relative terms over the last five years. The direction of change in market share according to bank type is shown in Figure 5.3.

After the turmoil of the financial crisis two decades ago, Indonesia's banking sector is now stable and appears resilient on most indicators (IMF and World Bank 2017). Capital adequacy ratios are high across all bank categories, well exceeding regulatory minimums, and have been

TABLE 5.2
Number and Type of Commercial Banks, November 2017

	Tier 1 Capital (Rp)	Tier 1 Capital (US$)	Number of Banks	Total Assets (Rp billion)	Total Assets (% all banking assets)
BUKU 1	100 billion to 1 trillion	7.7 million to 77 million	18	69,241	1
BUKU 2	1 trillion to 5 trillion	77 million to 385 million	53	859,094	12
BUKU 3	5 trillion to 30 trillion	385 million to 2.3 billion	26	2,447,486	34
BUKU 4	Over 30 trillion	Over 2.3 billion	5	3,568,545	49
Syariah	100 billion to 30 trillion	7.7 million to 2.3 billion	13	278,003	4
Total			115	7,222,351	100

Notes: Tier 1 capital consists of paid-up shareholder capital, reserves and other qualifying capital assets.
US$ figures based on exchange rate of US$1 = Rp13,000
Source: Indonesia Banking Statistics, November 2017.

FIGURE 5.3
Commercial Bank Assets by Type of Bank (in Rp billion)

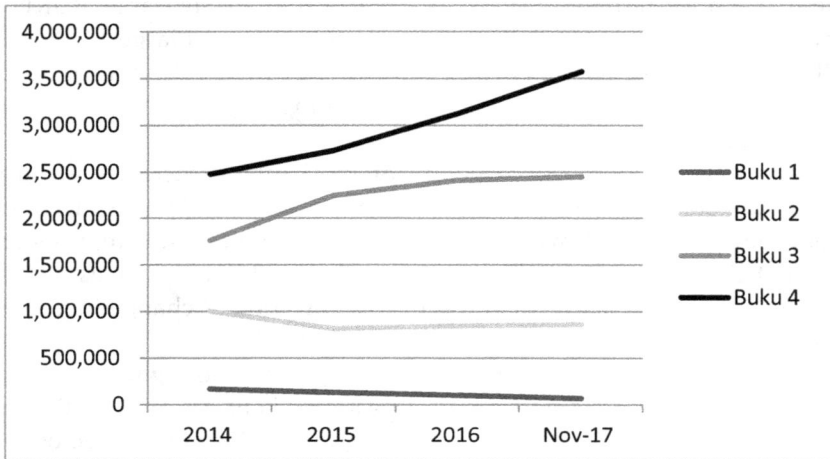

Source: Indonesia Financial Statistics, Table 1.33.

TABLE 5.3
Bank Performance Indicators by Category of Bank, November 2017

Category of Bank	Capital Adequacy Ratio	Return on Assets	Net Interest Margin	Loan to Deposit Ratio	Non-Performing Loans
Average	23.37	2.48	5.31	88.97	2.89
BUKU 1	21.11	1.61	5.45	76.25	2.98
BUKU 2	24.84	1.55	5.12	83.91	3.37
BUKU 3	24.94	1.86	4.38	96.83	2.84
BUKU 4	22.08	3.15	6.00	86.07	2.61

Source: Financial Services Authority, Indonesian Banking Statistics, Tables 1.25–1.28; Tables 3.9–3.13.

steadily increasing in recent years. Banking sector capital adequacy is now substantially higher than among averages in peer countries (IMF 2018). Averages across the different bank categories are mentioned in Table 5.3. Liquidity is good for most banks and the banking sector as a whole is very profitable.

Bank efficiency and productivity are hard to measure. This is mainly because widely used accounting ratios need interpretation, given differences in capitalization, the mix of banking services provided, and other contextual conditions (Vittas 1991). One partial indicator of bank performance is the net interest margin — the difference between average lending and deposit rates. Indonesia continues to have high net interest margins, despite a modest decline over 2017. Efficiency, as measured by overhead costs to total assets, has improved modestly since 2009, when costs were 3.78 per cent of assets, to 3.15 per cent in 2015.[2] On this indicator, Indonesian banks are less efficient than those in the Philippines — a country with similar geographic characteristics and a comparable level of development — where operating costs stood at 3 per cent of total assets in 2009 and 2.33 per cent in 2015.[3] This difference, however, may simply reflect the different rates of bank asset growth in the two countries in recent years, as the Philippine banking sector has expanded very rapidly while credit growth in Indonesia has moderated. In terms of profitability (as measured by return on assets, ROA), the Indonesian banking sector as a whole remains the most profitable among a benchmark set of emerging markets (IMF 2018). High profits and high interest margins combined with relatively high operating costs suggest a somewhat inefficient banking sector. As discussed below, the reasons for this inefficiency are complex and there is no easy prescription for greater efficiency that does not compromise financial stability.

At present, financial stability in the country looks secure. In addition to high capital buffers, credit quality — as measured by the ratio of non-performing loans (NPL) to total credit — is at manageable levels for most banks, despite having risen in the last two years. This rise in the average NPL ratio from 1.7 in 2013 to 2.9 in 2017, depicted in Figure 5.4, occurred despite the Financial Services Authority's decision in 2015 to relax criteria for restructuring loans and to maintain this permissive stance through 2017. Banks have been permitted to restructure loans earlier, the maximum size of loans that can be restructured was increased and two out of three criteria for restructuring could be waived (*Jakarta Post*, 22 July 2016; EIU 2016). Restructured "special mention" loans have also increased in addition to the reported growth in NPLs, which are concentrated in the processing industry and in wholesale and retail trade (Bank Mandiri Institute 2016a).[4] The NPL level remains well below what the central bank regards as the threshold for a "safe" level of 5 per cent (Bank Indonesia 2017), but reaching this threshold would indicate significant problems. Credit quality problems are known to be severe in some small banks, but these are far from being systemically important. The bigger risk arises

FIGURE 5.4
Non-performing Loans, All Banks (% of total credit)

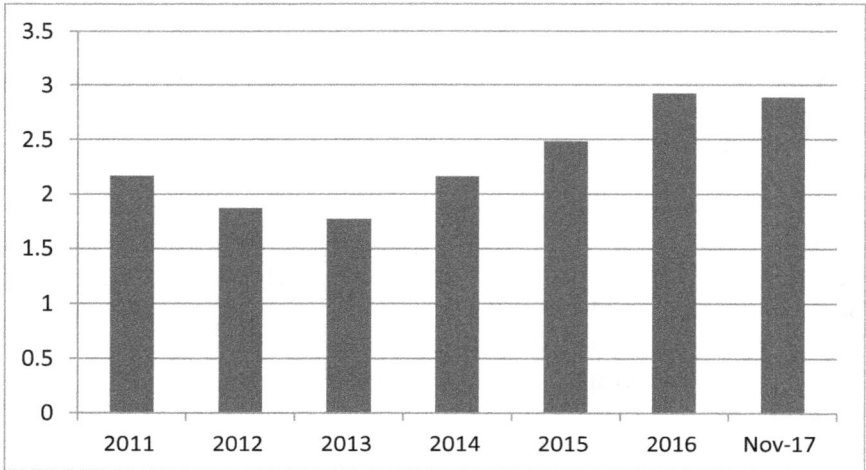

Source: Indonesian Financial Statistics, Table 3.9 (old series Table 4.9a).

from the unknown potential of hidden credit problems in the larger banks, which generally only come to light during a crisis. Given Indonesia's past experience, there is a risk of political interference in the large state-owned banking sector, resulting in state-owned banks lending on political or personal criteria. However, while rumours are widespread, a panel data analysis has found that democratization has reduced the politicization of the banking sector, with positive effects on the performance of state owned banks (Poczter 2017).

5.2.1 Policy and Supervisory Structure

Financial sector policy and supervision has changed over the last decade. The long-mooted proposal to remove the central bank's principal role in bank supervision (proposed in the wake of the late 1990s financial crisis) finally led to the creation of a specialized Financial Services Authority (Otoritas Jasa Keuangan, OJK) in 2011, with the prime responsibility of banking regulation and supervision, as well as the regulation of other financial sector firms and markets. The OJK assumed full responsibility of all its current functions only in 2014, when the central bank, Bank Indonesia, relinquished its "micro-prudential" supervision functions. There remain doubts about its internal structure (under which, each commissioner is responsible for a separate area of financial supervision, thereby creating "silos" in the organization) and lack of staff expertise after approximately a third of the staff seconded from Bank Indonesia returned to the central bank (IMF and World Bank 2017).

The OJK only came into existence after significant struggle. Bank Indonesia had long opposed the transfer of supervisory functions to a separate agency. The bill to establish the OJK was presented to Indonesia's House of Representatives (Dewan Perwakilan Rakyat, DPR) only in 2010, after corruption involving a Bank Indonesia deputy governor was uncovered in the aftermath of the Bank Century bailout in 2008.[5] The bill was then deadlocked in parliament over the issue of representation on the OJK's board of commissioners, and was only passed into a law at the end of 2011. In the end, Bank Indonesia and the Ministry of Finance retained the right to appoint two commissioners, with the remaining six appointed by the DPR. A deputy governor of Bank Indonesia was appointed Chair of the OJK board of commissioners. A nine-member board appointed to serve from 2017 until 2022 consists of five people with central bank backgrounds (some with career exposure in other organizations), two from the Ministry of Finance, and others with a mixture of private and state-owned financial sector experience.[6]

The central bank retains its role with respect to "macro-prudential" regulation of the banking sector. This role gives Bank Indonesia powers to monitor and set regulations on areas of bank activity with systemic implications. For example, it limits the foreign borrowing of both banks and non-financial companies. A 2014 regulation that empowers it to limit exposure to foreign debt may have helped bring about a fall-off in private external debt in the second half of 2016, although this drop is consistent with reduced corporate leverage overall (Bank Indonesia 2017). Bank Indonesia has also taken other organizational steps (like creating a new department for macro-prudential regulation) and issued regulations governing other systemic risks such as loan to value ratios for bank lending. However, it does not have authority over macro-prudential regulation of other (non-bank) systemically important institutions. This is an important limitation in the context of a financial system dominated by horizontally-organized financial conglomerates (as of end-2015, the World Bank identified forty-four conglomerates accounting for 66 per cent of financial sector assets), which include insurance companies (IMF and World Bank 2017).

Bank Indonesia itself had its statutory independence strengthened under a new central bank law passed in 1999. The appointment of Bank Indonesia governors and deputies is subject to parliamentary approval, and the bank is sometimes described as subject to political interference (see Omori 2014). However, it has demonstrated the ability to defy parliamentary pressure. Perhaps most spectacularly, one governor served out his term despite the efforts of the government to remove him in 2000–01 as a result of a corruption conviction (Hamilton-Hart 2008). More routinely, the central bank appears to defend its sphere of authority, although it works in cooperation with other government agencies and seems to internalize many of the financial policy goals of the government.

Bank Indonesia and the OJK both have a statutory role in managing financial crises, alongside the much smaller Deposit Insurance Corporation (Lembaga Penjamin Simpanan, LPS). The LPS was established, after much delay, in 2005 as an element in Indonesia's long-term response to its financial crisis of the late 1990s. It was strongly criticized for opening the door to virtually unlimited public bailout of banks in the event of a crisis (McLeod 2006). Spurred in part by the political furore over the bailout of Bank Century in 2008, a series of laws and regulations amending the roles of LPS, Bank Indonesia and the OJK were subsequently passed, leading to a new law on Financial System Crisis Prevention and Mitigation (PPKSK) in March 2016, after strong parliamentary contention (Qibthiyyah and Utomo 2016). The 2016 law aims to reduce the problem of moral hazard by strictly limiting conditions for public funds to be used to support a distressed bank. The first line role is assigned to the deposit insurance institution that is meant to support solvent but temporarily illiquid banks using its own funds (Nuryazidi 2016). The apparently strong prohibition on state-funded bailouts saw earlier draft chapters (that provided for the use of public funds and guarantees) removed as a result of DPR objections (Asian Banker 2016). The law also establishes a committee structure for crisis decision-making and prevention, with the committee comprising the finance minister, the governor of Bank Indonesia, the chair of the OJK, and (in a non-voting capacity) the chair of the LPS. It defines systemically important banks which can apply to the central bank for short-term lending in the event of a liquidity crisis, subject to adequate collateral and solvency. If the bank is not judged solvent, there is a provision for the committee to take action, including for the LPS to take over an insolvent bank and establishing — what a central bank official termed — a "bridge bank for purchasing assets and liabilities of the systemically important bank" prior to its winding up (Nuryazidi 2016). There is still some scope for limited use of public funds, although in the opinion of the World Bank and IMF joint assessment, provision for such funding is overly restricted by the new law (IMF and World Bank 2017).

The law has little chance of working as planned during a crisis, making this an area of potential vulnerability. This is due to two reasons. First, the LPS has no ability to contain a crisis in the way stipulated by the law, given its lack of funds. The organization, in fact, declared itself significantly underfunded, making an open statement that it had only Rp80 trillion in bailout funds, a tiny fraction of deposits of Rp740 trillion held by small and medium banks, let alone the Rp4 quadrillion held by the twenty large banks judged systemically important (*Jakarta Post*, 24 July 2017). The Rp2 billion (about US$150,000) depositor protection ceiling is "excessively high relative to average retail deposits and per capita GDP" (IMF and World Bank 2017). Second, it is hard to imagine that public funding would not be forthcoming in the event of a crisis that threatened the financial system. The chairman of the banking association and a senior economist from a large domestic bank were reported as believing that no president could allow a financial crisis to paralyse the economy (Asian Banker 2016). In this situation, by mandating unfeasibly strict limits on access to public funds, the law may simply serve to delay a decisive public response and leave decision-makers again taking ad hoc decisions in a crisis situation.

The goals informing financial sector policy in recent years are summarized in the OJK's *Financial Sector Master Plan 2015–2019* (OJK 2016). This document, as well as other public statements by OJK officials, the central bank and senior political leaders, shows that financial sector policy juggles three broad objectives: economic growth, financial stability and social inclusion. As put in the Chairman's foreword to the Master Plan (OJK 2016), it has three priority planks:

Optimizing the supporting role of the financial services sector in accelerating domestic economic growth (contributive), safeguarding financial system stability as a foundation of sustainable development (stable) as well as attaining public financial well-being and nurturing equitable development (inclusive).

Such a broad mandate risks a loss of focus on financial sector stability. From a technocratic viewpoint, the goal of financial stability should be enshrined in law as the "unequivocal" primary focus of the OJK (IMF and World Bank 2017). In the current political climate, however, it is unlikely that such a narrow interpretation of its mandate would be sustainable. Indeed, while providing independent regulatory agencies and central banks with a single overriding mandate has for long been advocated as a means to improve their performance, it is not clear that it is either necessary or sufficient. Relatively effective central banks such as Australia's and the Federal Reserve of the United States have a dual mandate for price stability and macroeconomic growth. In contexts such as Indonesia's, regulator independence and a mandate to focus on narrowly defined goals has not been sustainable when the agency has acted strongly against entrenched interests (Davidson 2017).

The OJK and Bank Indonesia appear to have chosen to tread a path between the political objectives of the government and their own judgement. The risk, of course, arises from the potential conflicts among the three priority areas of the Master Plan. The policies designed to encourage the financial sector's contribution to economic growth, for example, may conflict with the prudential policies that safeguard stability. Similarly, financial inclusion may undermine efficiency and stability objectives. Nonetheless, the financial agencies show no sign of retreating into roles that would limit their activity to either macroeconomic stability or micro-prudential regulation. Instead, overall, financial sector policy shows an increasing willingness to manage the market by attempting — through regulation and informal pressure — to influence banking sector decision-making on a wide range of issues.

One area where financial policy has taken an increasingly activist line is the push for banks to increase their lending. The sector has come a long way in this regard from its post-crisis tendency to hold most assets in the form of government bonds. As a result of the late 1990s crisis, the banking system's loan to deposit ratio sank as low as 26 per cent in 1999, and even in 2005, it stood only at 53 per cent (Hamilton-Hart 2008). This was, for years, an issue of concern for government officials and politicians. However, the banking system has, in recent years, had a much more "normal" loan to deposit ratio of around 90 per cent (and as discussed below, some banks are liquidity constrained). Despite this, as the rate of growth in bank lending has declined, officials have taken steps to encourage more lending. In 2016 and 2017, Bank Indonesia moved to ease liquidity requirements and required reserve ratios, explicitly linking these steps to its goal to encourage more lending, as expressed by the governor of Bank Indonesia (for example, *Jakarta Post*, 5 December 2017). Similarly, the OJK has made calls on the banks to increase lending. For instance, the OJK head was reported as saying the agency was considering allowing zero per cent down payments on some bank loans, to support similar moves by the central bank to ease loan to value and collateral requirements for property and vehicle loans, in order to encourage lending (*Jakarta Post*, 15 August 2016).[7]

A second area of activism is in the renewed push to influence both bank deposit and lending rates. President Joko Widodo announced in February 2016 that he wanted interest rates to "fall, fall, and keep falling" (quoted in Angga 2016). Both the OJK and the central bank have stated that they wished to see lending rates fall to a single digit number. The OJK has introduced deposit rate regulations that stipulate the maximum rates that banks can offer depositors in relation to the central bank's official rate (Hamilton-Hart and Schulze 2016). Other political leaders, too, have frequently called for lower bank lending rates. Vice-President Jusuf Kalla, for example, again called for lower lending rates in 2017 (*Jakarta Post*, 18 January 2017).

Third, under President Joko Widodo, there has been rising pressure on banks to lend to particular sectors and categories of borrowers, supplemented by an increase in government financial subsidy schemes. Bank Indonesia regulations of 2012 and 2015 required banks to have a minimum 10 per cent of their loan portfolio dedicated to lending to small enterprises by the end of 2016. This target was not met, although the central bank reported that fifty-six banks had complied with the mandate (Bank Indonesia 2017).

Early in 2018, the President called on banks to lend more to a greater variety of small and medium enterprises. He was reported as saying, "I want more people to have access to banks" (quoted in *Jakarta Post*, 19 January 2018). His remark comes after a substantial increase in a large scale government financial inclusion programme, the "people's business credit" (KUR, *Kredit Usaha Rakyat*) subsidized lending programme. The KUR programme was introduced in 2007, with support from the World Bank, which issued a largely positive assessment of the programme to subsidize credit to small and micro enterprises and — more recently —

migrant workers through government-funded credit guarantees (World Bank 2014). During the first phase (until 2014), the KUR programme functioned as a credit guarantee scheme involving an initial six banks, later expanding to include the twenty-seven regional development banks, working with state-owned guarantee companies. In this phase, it counted 12.3 million people as borrowers and had Rp175.2 trillion in cumulative credit disbursements, with Rp50.7 trillion outstanding as of November 2014 (Adam and Lestari 2017).

Under the Widodo government, the programme expanded and began to function as a direct credit subsidy scheme. The KUR programme now provides for heavily discounted interest rates, which vary according to borrower type. In 2016, the interest rate subsidy ranged from 4.5 per cent to 12 per cent. Annual disbursement of credit under the programme rose from Rp22.7 trillion (approximately US$1.75 billion) in 2015, to Rp58.7 trillion (US$4.5 billion) up to end July 2016. The cost of the interest subsidy for 2015–16 was US$310 million, according to figures provided by the Coordinating Ministry for Economic Affairs, which has overall oversight of the programme (Hamilton-Hart and Schulze 2016). Later changes in 2016 saw lending rates decrease again from 12 to 9 per cent, and a further increase in the target for total lending under the programme from Rp30 trillion to Rp100 trillion. The actual amount disbursed in 2016 came close to this target, with Rp94.4 trillion in loans issued that year. The number of institutions distributing KUR loans also increased to thirty-seven financial institutions and the range of borrowers expanded to include individuals as well as small enterprises, with special support for KUR lending to export-oriented businesses (Bank Indonesia 2017). The reported NPL rate for KUR loans in 2016 was only 0.4 per cent (Bank Indonesia 2017), which is improbably low given higher rates observed for the earlier, less generous KUR scheme, which saw some banks with NPL ratios on KUR lending as high as between 9.5 and 17.2 per cent (Adam and Lestari 2017). The expanded KUR programme does not represent a better approach to promoting small-scale lending than has been led — successfully and profitably — by Bank Rakyat Indonesia (Patten, Rosengard and Johnston 2001; Seibel, Rachmadi and Kusumayakti 2010; Revindo and Gan 2017). The expansion of the KUR programme is best understood as a consequence of the political objectives and constraints of the Widodo government. President Widodo's policy platform and political constituency require it to be visibly seen to support the interests of "the people" and actively delivering both large- and small-scale developmental projects (Warburton 2016). KUR and other interventions are politically useful as highly visible new initiatives that the government can claim credit for.

5.3 CONFLICTS AND CONSTRAINTS

Any assessment of the financial sector twenty years after Indonesia's devastating financial crisis of 1997–98 should highlight the enormous progress that has been made on many fronts. Bank capitalization, levels of non-performing loans and risk management systems (whether set internally or in response to central bank prudential limits) have all strengthened enormously. In fact, comprehensive surveys by the IMF acknowledge that Indonesia's financial system is prudentially sound (IMF 2018). Indonesia weathered the Global Financial Crisis of 2008 with minimal disruption, in part due to good luck, but also due to underlying resilience in its financial sector risk profile, as well as good decision-making by officials (Basri 2015). While there is always the potential for credit risks to be hidden, a number of stress testing scenarios suggest that Indonesia's banking sector is relatively resilient to a variety of external shocks (IMF and World Bank 2017). Levels of corporate leverage are much lower than before Indonesia's financial crisis of 1997–98 and better monitoring of foreign currency exposure by non-banking corporations — a major source of vulnerability in the 1990s, when such exposure was not systematically monitored — has reduced vulnerability to exchange rate shocks. The scope for unreported related party lending, another major component of vulnerability in the 1990s, has also been partially reduced as some of Indonesia's largest banks have changed ownership as a result of bank restructuring and sales after the crisis, and foreign owners took large stakes in several banks (Carney and Hamilton-Hart 2015). However, more recently, there have been instances of conglomerate groups acquiring banks and many of Indonesia's larger banks are part of broader conglomerate groupings (IMF and World Bank 2017).

There do remain some outstanding sources of potential vulnerability in Indonesia's exposure to short term capital flows, which have been large and, at times, volatile in recent years. However, these swings have been managed through a combination of exchange rate flexibility and targeted interventions to manage capital flows. Further, the banking system is relatively insulated from fluctuations in short-term foreign capital flows, which are largely directed to equity and bond markets. Foreigners account for a high proportion of the value of listed firms (64 per cent as of mid-2016, up from 54 per cent in 2012), although domestic investors make up more than half of all trading (Oxford Business Group 2016). A major part of foreign portfolio inflows continues to be placed in government securities, with foreign investors holding about 37 per cent of government bonds (Bank Indonesia 2017).

Overall, most indicators suggest that Indonesia's banking system is on a much sounder footing in prudential terms than it has ever been. The more common critique of the financial sector as a whole and banking in particular is that it is sluggish and inefficient, and fails to provide adequate access to both savers and borrowers. As put by two long-time observers of Indonesia's financial system, re-regulation after the 1998 crisis produced a "prudentially sound but inefficient, narrow, and homogenized banking oligopoly", in which competition and innovation are at low levels (Rosengard and Prasetyantoko 2011). Other sources point to Indonesia's overall level of financial development — as measured by the ratio of private sector borrowing to GDP — to argue that Indonesia's financial system is under-developed, to the detriment of growth and poverty reduction (Ismail 2015). While these criticisms have some validity, they overstate the problem and underweigh the risk and costs of financial instability.

First, to what extent is there really a lack of competition in the banking sector? On the surface, the persistence of very high levels of banking profits and high net interests margins (on both counts Indonesian banks are at the high end when compared to regional peers) is puzzling, given the large number of banks in Indonesia. Banking profitability is frequently cited as an attractive factor for investors wishing to enter the market or acquire shares in Indonesian banks (DBS 2015; EY 2017; Koh 2015). In a competitive open market, one might expect the pressures of competition to erode these profits. There is, in fact, significant competition in parts of the banking sector (DBS 2017). However, due to segmentation among banks, the largest banks face less competition than suggested by the number of banks in the market.

One indicator is the persistence of a relatively high level of con-centration. As discussed above, the majority of Indonesian banks are very small BUKU 1 or BUKU 2 banks that collectively account for a small and declining share of all banking assets. At the other end, the share of total banking system assets accounted for by the largest five commercial banks remains high at around 55 per cent, as shown in Figure 5.5. This represents a relatively high level of banking concentration, although much lower than in previous decades in Indonesia, and also much lower than in some developed markets such as Australia and New Zealand, where the four largest banks account for around 85 per cent of banking sector assets.

The five largest banks that make up the BUKU 4 category are, as shown in Table 5.3, clearly the most profitable of all banks. Their net interest margins are significantly wider than those of banks in the other categories, and their return on assets is higher. Three of these banks are state-owned (Bank Rakyat Indonesia, Bank Mandiri and BNI) and one (BCA) has been the largest private commercial bank in Indonesia for decades, despite being badly hit by the 1997 crisis and passing into new ownership. Only the newest entry into the BUKU 4 category (in 2017), Malaysian-controlled CIMB-Niaga, represents something of what could be called an "insurgent presence in this elite tier". Some factors appear to prevent the mid-size BUKU 3 banks — among which there is vigorous competition — from competing with the BUKU 4 banks. One indicator is that BUKU 3 banks

FIGURE 5.5
Banking Concentration (Percentage), 1996–2015

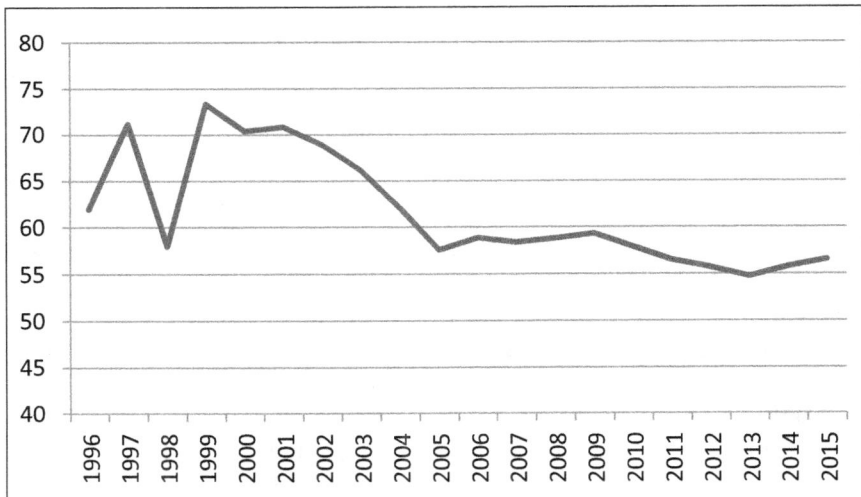

Source: Federal Reserve Bank of St Louis Economic Data, "5-Bank Asset Concentration for Indonesia", <https://fred.stlouisfed.org/series/DDOI06IDA156NWDB>.

are relatively liquidity-constrained. Their average loan to deposit ratio is high at 97 per cent, much higher than for other categories of bank (in fact, in recent years this ratio has been even higher for BUKU 3 banks, and for some individual banks the loan to deposit ratio (LDR) is much higher still). Although banks can turn to other sources of funding such as issuing commercial paper or borrowing on the interbank market, deposits are a stable, low cost source of funding. The high LDR for mid-size banks suggests that they are constrained in accessing deposits. Anecdotal reports suggest that the mostly state-owned BUKU 4 banks benefit from having access to state-sector deposits. One systematic analysis of 89 Indonesian banks has found that "politically connected" banks — which included state-owned banks — benefitted through obtaining a lower cost of funding (Sutopo et al. 2017).

Further, although mandated deposit rate maximums set by the OJK marginally favour the BUKU 3 banks (which can offer rates up to 100 basis points above the central bank rate, compared to 75 basis points for the BUKU 4 banks), this does not appear to be sufficient to outweigh their other disadvantages, including a smaller branch infrastructure and lack of access to large state-sector deposits (Hamilton-Hart and Schulze 2016). Banks also face competition for deposits from government bonds. Since cuts to the central bank's official rate in 2016, bank deposit rate maximums are lower than the yield on government bonds. This price-based factor, as well as the regulatory requirement by the OJK for nonbank financial institutions to hold minimum levels of government bonds, was cited by the central bank as leading to a shift out of deposits by pension funds and insurance companies (Bank Indonesia 2017). Towards the end of 2017, government bond yields were declining, with ten-year yields at 6.8 per cent at the end of September 2017 (Pardede and Zahro 2017); however this is still a much higher return than offered by the deposit rates advertised by large banks such as BCA.[8] Finally, the 2016 law on managing financial crises may have the effect of favouring the large, "systemically important" banks that are perceived to have preferential status in terms of access to funds to cover depositors with deposits above the LPS coverage limit of Rp2 billion (Lingga 2016).

Consolidation in the banking sector may enhance the ability of mid-size banks to compete with the largest five banks, but any impact is likely to be modest. Consolidation is the openly stated aim of the OJK and the goal dates back to the "Indonesian Banking Architecture" launched by the central bank in 2004, which envisaged a banking sector comprising around sixty banks.[9] Although far from reaching this target, consolidation has been occurring, and can be seen in the declining number of total banks operating in Indonesia. In principle, it is meant to result in more capable, financially resilient and competitive banks. In practice, well-known problems of integration following mergers mean that post-merger, combined banks may be bigger in terms of asset base but not necessarily more efficient. For instance, it took HSBC eight years to officially merge its local office with the small bank it acquired in 2009, only merging the two banks in May 2017 (*Jakarta Post*, 9 May 2017), suggesting limited perceived synergies from integration. In the case of mergers involving very small banks with precarious levels of capitalization, consolidation may enhance the prudential soundness of the banking system (when the acquiring bank is sufficiently larger and more robust), but have no real impact on the competitive capacities of the acquiring bank. Consolidation can also involve the largest banks acquiring smaller ones. BCA, for example, is reportedly looking to acquire two medium-sized banks in 2018 (*Jakarta Post*, 29 January 2018).

Consolidation may also be combined with foreign entry or increased foreign presence in the banking sector. Indeed, one of the pathways for foreign banks to acquire a banking licence in Indonesia is to acquire two domestic banks, as the OJK has indicated that it is willing to use its discretion to approve foreign ownership above the usual limit of 40 per cent if they are willing to acquire and merge two domestic banks. This prompted one commentator to quip that "a 2-for-1 sale is something you find in a retail shop, not in a banking sector" — while also affirming that synergies between the two acquired banks were likely to be elusive, and such deals might in fact mean "double the trouble" (Koh 2015).

Since 2012, new rules limit foreign ownership by setting shareholding thresholds for foreign owners of national banks, limiting a single entity from owning more than one bank, and by effectively making it a requirement that the only way for new foreign entrants to enter the market is through acquisition (EY 2017). Are these restrictions a major factor limiting competition in the banking market? Restrictions on foreign entry are probably not a significant reason for the somewhat sluggish performance in parts of the banking sector. In the first place, the banking market is far from closed to foreigners. Foreigners hold major stakes in many of Indonesia's listed "national" banks (Carney and Hamilton-Hart 2015). As of late 2016, foreign-controlled banks accounted for 27.6 per cent of all banking assets (IMF and World Bank 2017). And as described above, the door is relatively open — subject to approval from the OJK — for foreign entities that wish to acquire a local bank. Approvals for such acquisitions have been forthcoming in recent years. As of March 2017, one compilation listed twenty-five merger and acquisition transactions since 2002, twenty of them involving foreign entities acquiring a substantial stake in an Indonesian bank (EY 2017). Since then, Japanese banking giant MUFG announced a deal to buy a 73.8 per cent stake in Bank Danamon from Singapore's Temasek (*Financial Times*, 27 December 2017).

The bigger issue is not foreign access to the Indonesian banking market, but the effects of such access. A recent journalistic overview of Asian banking markets has found that new foreign entrants have found it difficult to challenge incumbents, leading to the conclusion that in highly varied markets subject to nationalistic interventions, "banks are better off being local" (*Financial Times*, 8 June 2016). This is in line with econometric evidence from a large scale panel study, which suggested that foreign banks in emerging markets and low-income countries face informational bottlenecks (Ghosh 2017). Significantly, this study found that higher levels of foreign presence in emerging market and low-income markets *reduced* economic growth. Although counter-intuitive for models that suppose banking sector openness increases competition and efficiency, another large-scale study has found the effects of foreign bank entry depend largely on host country characteristics. Foreign entry was found to have a negative effect on overall levels of intermediation (private credit) in countries with high costs in enforcing credit contracts, limited credit information and limited market share held by foreign banks as group; with negative effects amplified if foreign banks come from distant home countries (Claessens and Van Horen 2014). When applied to Indonesia, these findings have mixed implications. On the negative side, there is limited credit market information and the legal infrastructure for creditor protection continues to have large gaps, suggesting limited benefits from increased foreign presence. On the other hand, most foreign acquisitions have come from banks or entities that are well-established in the Asian region, indicating that they may be more attuned to local business practice. One analysis of the Indonesian banking market has found that foreign-owned banks behaved more competitively and were more efficient than their local counterparts; but the effect was significant only for newly established foreign banks (Mulyaningsih et al. 2015). This implies that once foreign banks are established in the Indonesian market, they may find a profitable niche for themselves, but their presence is unlikely to be transformational.

5.3.1 Is Indonesia Capital-Constrained?

Many commentators and officials routinely observe that Indonesia's level of financial development, as measured by the ratio of private credit to GDP, is undesirably low. A review by the Asian Development Bank (ADB), for example, describes Indonesia's financial sector as "underdeveloped" and claims that financial sector development is "critical for reducing poverty through better access to financial products and services" (Ismail 2015). Difficulties in obtaining bank credit — particularly for small and micro enterprises, agricultural smallholders and low income families — are frequently cited (e.g., Pramudya, Hospes and Termeer 2017). Such difficulties provide the rationale for the KUR programme and other interventions to increase access to finance, as well as the growth of the regional development banks in the post-democratization era. As described above, both political leaders and finance officials frequently call for commercial banks to lend more to all types of borrower. On the savings side, there is a perception that many Indonesians in rural areas lack access to financial services, with lack of access given as a reason for low rates of financial saving among the rural poor (Shrestha and Coxhead 2018, p. 19).

The role of financial development in promoting economic growth is not a straightforward case of more is better (Seven and Yatkiner 2016; Samargandi, Fidrmuc and Ghosh 2015). At very low levels of financial development, a lack of access to savings and borrowing opportunities hinders economic growth. However, not only do the benefits of increasing financial development level off, aggregate financial development ratios should not be conflated with access to banking services. Although only 36 per cent of Indonesia's population aged 15 or over has a bank account (lower than the 42 per cent average for the World Bank's lower middle income group),[10] bank network penetration is reasonably high (Seibel 2005; JICA 2013). The largest commercial banks have branch networks serving most towns and there were also 1,619 rural banks operating at the end of 2017. In remote rural areas, there are people who do not have adequate access to banking services, and from a poverty alleviation perspective, it makes sense to subsidize basic banking services in such areas. It does not follow that national aggregate measures of financial development have much to do, one way or the other, with access to financial services in such areas. The reluctance of commercial banks to lend more to small and micro enterprises due to the high default risks and overheads of such loans has been described as evidence of market failure, hence a rationale for the KUR programme (Adam and Lestari 2017). However, if default rates are high, it makes more sense to see a reluctance to lend at normal commercial rates as evidence of banking markets accurately pricing credit risk. Similarly, interventions to redress the recent slow-down in credit growth, particularly in commercial lending, are misplaced given that the underlying reason is a lack of demand for credit (Pardede and Zahro 2017).

It is the case that Indonesia's financial system remains bank-dominated, and this is often taken as an indicator of financial underdevelopment (Ismail 2015). Indonesia has invested enormously in capital market development over the last decade. To take just one example, the ADB issued two loans to support policy and institutional development to this end in 2007 and 2009, each for US$300 million. Its assessment of the outcomes of the policy programme was that, despite the long list of "policy actions" required for loan disbursement being mainly adopted, the targeted "impacts" (such as equity market capitalization, share of non-bank financial assets and corporate bonds outstanding) were quite limited (ADB 2017). In fact, although non-bank financing is modest, it is far from insignificant. IPOs and new rights issues on the stock exchange increased from Rp53.6 trillion in 2015, to Rp79.2 trillion in 2016 (the total for 2011 was Rp62.8 trillion). Private sector bond issues are also increasing, albeit unevenly, from Rp51.3 trillion 2011 to Rp112 trillion in 2016. However, these bond issues were dominated by financial sector issuers as an alternative to deposits (Bank Indonesia 2017). Other financial sector service firms that provide savings-linked products have proliferated. For example, there were 265 pension fund companies as of 2014, a relatively high number because large companies tend to manage their own employees' pension funds (Djaja, Mardanugraha and Sihombing 2015). Total assets of pension and insurance funds, however, together make up only 12.5 per cent of all financial assets (IMF and World Bank 2017). As noted above, the government bond market is well developed and attracts retail investors as well as financial institutions. Serving the other end of the market, new financial technology firms have moved into micro-lending and peer-to-peer lending services, as well as providing an alternative to banks for payment services. Although this remains a very small sector, it looks set to expand significantly as long as mooted regulations by the OJK does not stifle it.

Overall, it appears that although capital and equity markets remain much smaller than in many other countries, they have developed in a meaningful sense, providing alternatives to the banking system for corporate financing requirements and, in a more limited way, alternatives to bank deposits for retail investors. It is doubtful that "capital market development" should be a priority area for financial policy or that it merits the kind of public spending seen in recent years. Capital market development has been presented as important for financial inclusion.[11] However, even though higher rates of return are available to those who are able to diversify their investments outside of bank deposits, it is not clear that there are positive externalities from bond and stock market development that are significant enough to justify costly public investment that primarily benefits the middle class and wealthy, who have the means to invest in bond and equity markets. Theoretically and empirically, the benefits from disintermediated as opposed to bank-based finance are ambiguous (Levine 2002). In contexts where even financial intermediaries face significant information asymmetries in making credit decisions (and enforcing creditor rights), it seems fanciful that small investors are likely to make better investment decisions when they invest directly in equities and bonds.

5.4 CONCLUSION

How well Indonesia's financial system is judged to be working depends on which performance measures are taken as most important and on how one assesses counter-factual scenarios arising from different policy settings. Critiques of Indonesian policy settings for having failed to encourage greater innovation and efficiency in the banking system, or more diversification through the development of nonbank financial markets, are based on the assumption that these outcomes can realistically be achieved without increasing the risk of financial instability. This chapter has shown that there is certainly room for improvement in a number of areas. However, given Indonesia's political, economic and institutional conditions, improvements in efficiency and diversification can probably only come in small, incremental steps if they are to be sustainable. The kind of dramatic policy measures that might usher in more radical innovation and financial sector growth carry very high risks in any context. The Global Financial Crisis of 2008 showed that financial policymakers in countries such as the United States and the United Kingdom — with high levels of financial market infrastructure, regulatory capacity and legal certainty — can fail spectacularly with enormous costs for ordinary people. In this light, some inefficiency can reasonably be considered an acceptable price for stability.

Notes

1. Available on Bank Indonesia's website, "Perbankan", <http://www.bi.go.id/id/peraturan/perbankan/Pages/pbi_142612.aspx>.
2. Data from Federal Reserve of St Louis, "Bank's [sic] overhead costs to total assets for Indonesia" <https://fred.stlouisfed.org/series/DDEI04IDA156NWDB>.
3. Data from Federal Reserve of St Louis, "Bank's [sic] Overhead Costs to Total Assets for Philippines" <https://fred.stlouisfed.org/series/DDEI04PHA156 NWDB>.
4. This reflects the volume of lending to these sectors. As a proportion of credit to each sector, the NPL ratio is highest for lending to mining and construction.
5. On the Bank Century bailout and formation of the OJK, see Omori (2014). Basri (2015) provides a defence of the decision to bail out the bank given the potential for systemic loss of confidence in the context of the global financial crisis at the time.
6. Profiles on the OJK website, "Commissioner Board 2017–2022" at <http://www.ojk.go.id/en/tentang-ojk/Pages/Dewan-Komisioner.aspx>.
7. Joko Widodo has also made similar calls. See "Jokowi Calls on Lenders to Help Accelerate Economic Growth", *Jakarta Globe*, 19 January 2018 <http://jakartaglobe.id/business/jokowi-calls-on-lenders-to-help-accelerate-economic-growth/>.
8. Interest rates on various savings instruments advertised on the BCA website with effect from December 2017 and February 2018, <https://www.bca.co.id/id/individu/sarana/Kurs-dan-Suku-Bunga/Suku-Bunga-Simpanan>.
9. Bank Indonesia, "Indonesian Banking Architecture – Structure", <http://www.bi.go.id/en/perbankan/arsitektur/struktur/Contents/Default.aspx>.
10. World Bank data for 2014, "Financial inclusion data, Indonesia", <http://datatopics.worldbank.org/financialinclusion/country/indonesia>.
11. An OJK official was reported as describing efforts to increase the role of

domestic investors on the stock exchange as a matter of "financial inclusion" (Oxford Business Group 2016).

References

Adam, Latif and Esta Lestari. "Indonesia's guaranteed microfinance programme (KUR): Lessons from the first stage of implementation". *Journal of Southeast Asian Economies* 34, no. 2 (2017): 322–44.

ADB (Asian Development Bank). "Performance Evaluation Report: Capital Market Development Program Cluster (Subprograms 1 and 2) (Indonesia) (Loans 2379 and 2577)". IN.460-17, 19 December 2017) <https://www.adb.org/sites/default/files/evaluation-document/239536/files/in460-17.pdf>.

Asian Banker. "Financial crisis bill will severely limit Indonesian government action". 12 March 2016 <http://www.theasianbanker.com/press-releases/financial-crisis-bill-will-severely-limit-indonesian-government-action>.

Bank Indonesia. *2016 Economic Report on Indonesia*. Jakarta: Bank Indonesia, 2017.

Basri, Muhammad Chatib. "A tale of two crises: Indonesia's political economy". In *Two Crises, Different Outcomes: East Asia and Global Finance*, edited by T.J. Pempel and Keiichi Tsunekawa, pp. 41–63. Ithaca: Cornell University Press, 2015.

Carney, Richard and Natasha Hamilton-Hart. "What do changes in corporate ownership in Indonesia tell us?". *Bulletin of Indonesian Economic Studies* 51, no. 1 (2015): 123–45.

Claessens, Stijn and Neeltje Van Horen. "Foreign banks: trends and impact". *Journal of Money, Credit and Banking* 46, no. 1 (2014): 295–326.

Davidson, Jamie. "Survival of the weakest? The politics of independent regulatory agencies in Indonesia". In *Asia after the Developmental State: Disembedding Autonomy*, edited by Toby Carroll and Darryl Jarvis, pp. 237–360. Cambridge: Cambridge University Press, 2017.

Djaja, Komara, Eugenia Mardanugraha and Manue Sihombing. "An assessment of the Indonesian financial services sector". International Labour Office, Geneva, 4 August 2015.

EY. "The Indonesian Banking Industry: Unfolding the Opportunity". March 2017 <http://www.ey.com/Publication/vwLUAssets/EY-the-indonesian-banking-industry-unfolding-the-opportunity/$FILE/EY-the-indonesian-banking-industry-unfolding-the-opportunity.pdf>.

Ghosh, Amit. "How does banking sector globalization affect economic growth?". *International Review of Economics and Finance* 48 (2017): 83–97.

Hamilton-Hart, Natasha. "Banking systems a decade after the crisis". In *Crisis as Catalyst: Asia's Dynamic Political Economies*, edited by Andrew MacIntyre,

T.J. Pempel and John Ravenhill, pp. 45–69. Ithaca: Cornell University Press, 2008.

IMF (International Monetary Fund). "Indonesia: Selected Issues". IMF Country Report No. 10/285, August 2010.

———. "Indonesia: 2015 Article IV Consultation". IMF Country Report No. 16/81, March 2016.

———. "Indonesia: 2017 Article IV Consultation". IMF Country Report No. 18/32, February 2018.

IMF and World Bank. *"Republic of Indonesia Financial Sector Assessment"*. World Bank, Washington, D.C., 2017 <https://www.openknowledge.worldbank.org/handle/10986/28391>.

Islam, Ezazul. "Inclusive Finance in the Asia-Pacific Region: Trends and Approaches". MPDD Working Paper WP/15/07, 2015 <www.unescap.org/our-work/macroeconomic-policy-development/financing-development>.

Ismail, Mohd Sani. "Summary of Indonesia's Finance Sector Assessment". ADB Papers on Indonesia, No. 12 (2015) <https://www.adb.org/sites/default/files/publication/178045/ino-paper-12-2015.pdf>.

JICA (Japan International Cooperation Agency). "Basic Study on Financial Inclusion in Indonesia: Final Report". JICA and Japan Economic Research Institute, August 2013.

Koh, Joyce. "Double or nothing is way into lucrative Indonesian banking". Bloomberg News, 24 November 2015 <http://www.bloomberg.com/news/articles/2015-11-23/2-for-1-way-into-indonesia-banking-may-end-up-double-the-trouble>.

Levine, Ross. "Bank-Based or Market-Based Financial Systems: Which Is Better?". *Journal of Financial Intermediation* 11, no. 4 (2002): 398–428.

Lingga, Vincent (2016) "View point: New financial safety law will accelerate bank consolidation". *Jakarta Post*, 20 March. At <http://www.thejakartapost.com/news/2016/03/20/view-point-new-financial-safety-law-will-accelerate-bank-consolidation.html>.

McLeod, Ross. "Indonesia's new deposit guarantee law". *Bulletin of Indonesian Economic Studies* 42, no. 1 (2006): 59–78.

Mulyaningsih, Tri, Anne Daly and Riyana Miranti. "Foreign participation and banking competition: Evidence from the Indonesian banking industry". *Journal of Financial Stability* 19 (2015): 70–82.

Nuryazidi, Mohammad. "Preventing, handling financial system crises". *Jakarta Post*, 17 May 2016.

Omori, Sawa. "The Politics of Financial Reform in Indonesia". *Asian Survey* 54, no. 5 (2014): 987–1008.

Oxford Business Group. "Efforts to Bring New Investors and Listings onto the Indonesian Capital Markets Bode Well for Future". 2016 <https://

oxfordbusinessgroup.com/overview/across-board-efforts-bring-new-investors-and-listings-market-bode-well-future-growth>.

Pardede, Raden and Shirin Zahro. "Saving not spending: Indonesia's domestic demand problem". *Bulletin of Indonesian Economic Studies* 53, no. 3 (2017): 233–59.

Patten, Richard, Jay Rosengard and Don Johnston. "Microfinance Success Amidst Macroeconomic Failure: The Experience of Bank Rakyat Indonesia During the East Asian Crisis". *World Development* 29, no. 6 (2001): 1057–69.

Poczter, Sharon. "Democratization and the depoliticization of the banking sector: Are all banks affected equally?". *Journal of Economic Policy Reform* 20, no. 1 (2017): 26–45.

Pramudya, Eusebius Pantja, Otto Hospes and C.J.A.M. Termeer. "Governing the Palm-Oil Sector through Finance: The Changing Roles of the Indonesian State". *Bulletin of Indonesian Economic Studies* 53, no. 1 (2017): 57–82.

Qibthiyyah, Riatu and Ariane Utomo. "Family Matters: Demographic Change and Social Spending in Indonesia". *Bulletin of Indonesian Economic Studies* 52, no. 2 (2016): 133–59.

Revindo, Mohamad D. and Christopher Gan. "Rural Microfinance Banking and Outreach: A Case of Bank Rakyat Indonesia". In *Microfinance in Asia*, edited by Christopher Gan and Gilbert V. Nartea, pp. 337–56. Singapore: World Scientific, 2017 <https://doi.org/10.1142/9789813147959_0011>.

Rosengard, Jay K. and A. Prasetyantoko. "If the Banks Are Doing So Well, Why Can't I Get a Loan? Regulatory Constraints to Financial Inclusion in Indonesia". *Asian Economic Policy Review* 6, no. 2 (2011): 273–96.

Samargandi, Nahla, Jan Fidrmuc and Sugata Ghosh. "Is the Relationship Between Financial Development and Economic Growth Monotonic? Evidence from a Sample of Middle-Income Countries". *World Development* 68 (2015): 66–81.

Seibel, H., A. Rachmadi and D. Kusumayakti. "Reform, growth and resilience of savings-led commercial microfinance institutions: The case of the microbanking units of Bank Rakyat Indonesia". *Savings and Development* 34, no. 3 (2010): 277–303 <http://www.jstor.org/stable/41803647>.

Seven, Unal and Hakan Yatkiner. "Financial Intermediation and Economic Growth: Does Income Matter?". *Economic Systems* 40, no. 1 (2016): 39–58.

Shrestha, Rashesh and Ian Coxhead. "Can Indonesia Secure a Development Dividend from Its Resource Export Boom?". *Bulletin of Indonesian Economic Studies* 54, no. 1 (2018): 1–24.

Sutopo, Bambang, Irwan Trinugroho and Sylviana Maya Damayanti. "Politically connected bank: Some Indonesian evidence". *International Journal of Business and Society* 18, no. 1 (2017): 83–94.

Vittas, Dimitri. "Measuring Bank Efficiency: Use and Missue of Bank Operating Ratios". WPS 806, World Bank Country Economics Department, 1991 <http://

documents.worldbank.org/curated/en/568891468739781885/pdf/multi-page.
    pdf>.
Warburton, Eve. "Jokowi and the New Developmentalism". *Bulletin of Indonesian
    Economic Studies* 52, no. 3 (2016): 297–320.
World Bank. "Implementation and Completion Report". Report No.
    ICR00003179, 25 June 2014 <http://documents.worldbank.org/curated/
    en/814821468268218664/text/ICR31790P130150IC0disclosed07020140.txt>.

6

RISING ECONOMIC NATIONALISM IN INDONESIA

Arianto A. Patunru

"It would be wrong to see nationalism as either an unmitigated evil or a universal virtue. It can be both, a boon and a curse."
Amartya Sen (2008)

"Protectionism breeds monopoly, crony capitalism and sloth. It does not achieve a happy and serene egalitarian society."
Paul A. Samuelson (2005)

6.1 BACKGROUND

The world is gradually recovering from the 2008–09 Global Financial Crisis. In 2017, for example, economic growth climbed back to 3 per cent. During this transition phase, however, the role of trade has been much smaller — thanks to the maturation of global value chains, the shift to

This article was first published in *Journal of Southeast Asian Economies* 35, no. 3 (December 2018).

robotization and the services economy, fluctuation in commodity prices, as well as rising protectionism around the world.

At the same time, more than 3 billion people still have to struggle to live with US$2.50 or less per day. The richest 10 per cent of the global population owns more than 85 per cent of the global wealth. Even in countries where poverty has gone down, inequality is on the rise — prompting social tensions. These factors are often seen as the main cause of the re-emergence of anti-globalization sentiments and seem to have encouraged world leaders to adopt populist, inward-looking policies. Examples of consequent surprises coming from the voting booths include Duterte, Brexit, and Trump among others. Moreover, often by riding on the back of this disdain for globalization, those in power display increasingly authoritarian inclinations — such as Erdogan in Turkey, Putin in Russia, and Xi in China, to name a few.

Indonesia is no exception. In this country, dissatisfaction with globalization has manifested itself in rising protectionism, rejection of foreign interference, and expressions of distrust of democracy — sometimes with a New Order flavour. The disappointment, nevertheless, is not totally unfounded. As in the case elsewhere, globalization — and nationalism — can bring both good and bad results, "boon and curse", as Amartya Sen put it. Trade creates winners and losers, and in the absence of (1) well-functioning compensation mechanisms and (2) free movement of labour across sectors, the gains may remain concentrated in the hands of a few. And corruption only worsens this situation.

Nationalism in the economic sphere takes the form of protectionism — protecting domestic industries from foreign competition. It usually reveals itself in policies aimed at self-sufficiency in a number of commodities, including those of which Indonesia is a natural net importer. Like several other countries, Indonesia's approach to trade has, in general, been mercantilist, i.e., promoting exports while limiting imports. As most of the protection measures in Indonesia are imposed only on the import side, this chapter focuses mainly on import protection.

The chapter is structured as follows. The next section summarizes the current state of trade and openness in Indonesia. The third section discusses the major tariff and non-tariff measures of protection used by the country's policymakers. The fourth section is a historical take on trade policy in Indonesia — a brief chronology of approaches from the ultra-nationalist era of President Sukarno to the reform era of President Yudhoyono. The subsequent section zooms in on President Joko "Jokowi" Widodo's era, and the final section offers further points for discussion.

6.2 INDONESIA'S TRADE AND OPENNESS

The role of trade in the Indonesian economy had been increasing in the lead up to the Asian Financial Crisis (AFC), with the share of merchandise trade in the national income fluctuating around 40 per cent since the late 1970s before reaching more than 80 per cent just before the crisis (Figure 6.1). The spike in openness between 1997 and 1998 also reflects the collapsing rupiah around the time (the denominator effect, as the measure is percentage of national income). After the Crisis, the figure has been continuously declining and now stands at around 35 per cent.

Figure 6.2 compares Indonesia's openness to that of China, India and Vietnam. Indonesia, in the past, was much more open to trade than any of these countries. By the early 1990s, however, Vietnam had taken the lead.[1] Indonesia, on the other hand, has become less open since the early 2000s, overtaken by China.[2]

Despite the differences in openness, the terms of trade between these countries have actually converged in recent years (Figure 6.3). During the 1960s, Indonesia was far behind India and China, but then its terms of trade improved dramatically from mid-1975 until mid-1985. This might reflect the effect of the two oil booms in 1973–74 and 1979–80. Since then, the trend of Indonesia's terms of trade has been similar to the other countries.

During the AFC, the Indonesian currency depreciated dramatically and continued to stay weak for almost three years (Figure 6.4). As the economy began to recover, along with increasing export revenues, the rupiah too started to strengthen in 2001, and by 2003 it was catching up with regional currencies (Pangestu, Rahardja and Ing 2015). In more recent times, the trend of Indonesia's real exchange rate has been closer to that of India than that of China. It also appears that the rupiah is a bit weaker in Jokowi's era as compared to the figures observed during President Yudhoyono's second term.

Several scholars argue that a weak rupiah is a result of the country's current account deficit. This view often results in a mercantilist approach towards trade — increasing exports and limiting imports. Figure 6.5, however, shows that the relationship between the currency and current

FIGURE 6.1
Openness

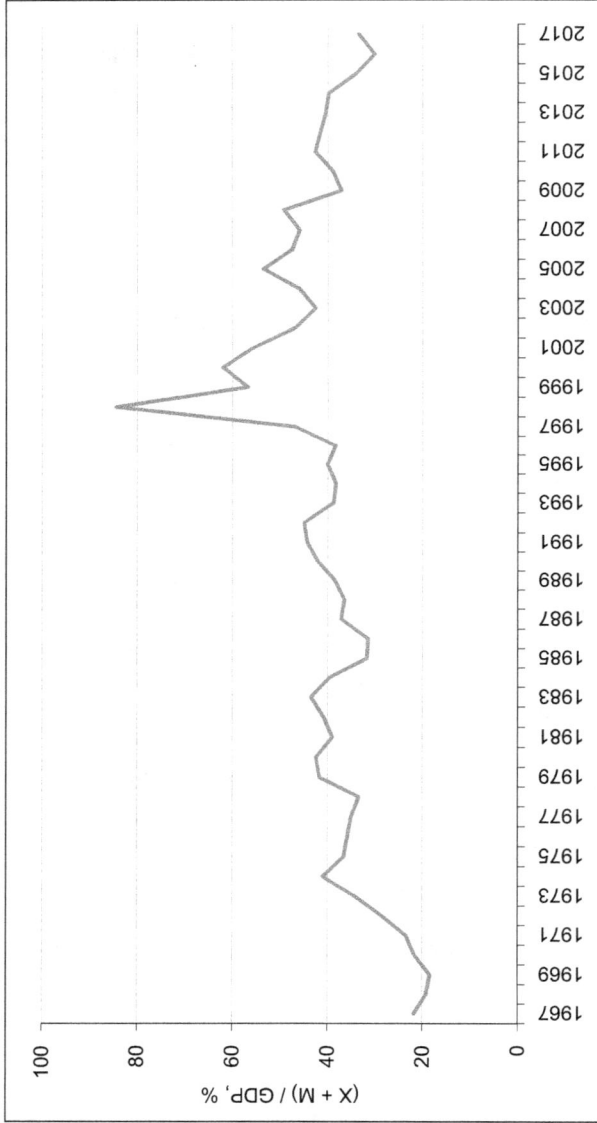

Note: Proxy for openness here is the share of merchandise trade in GDP.
Source: World Development Indicators and BPS (via CEIC Data).

FIGURE 6.2
Real Openness, Compared

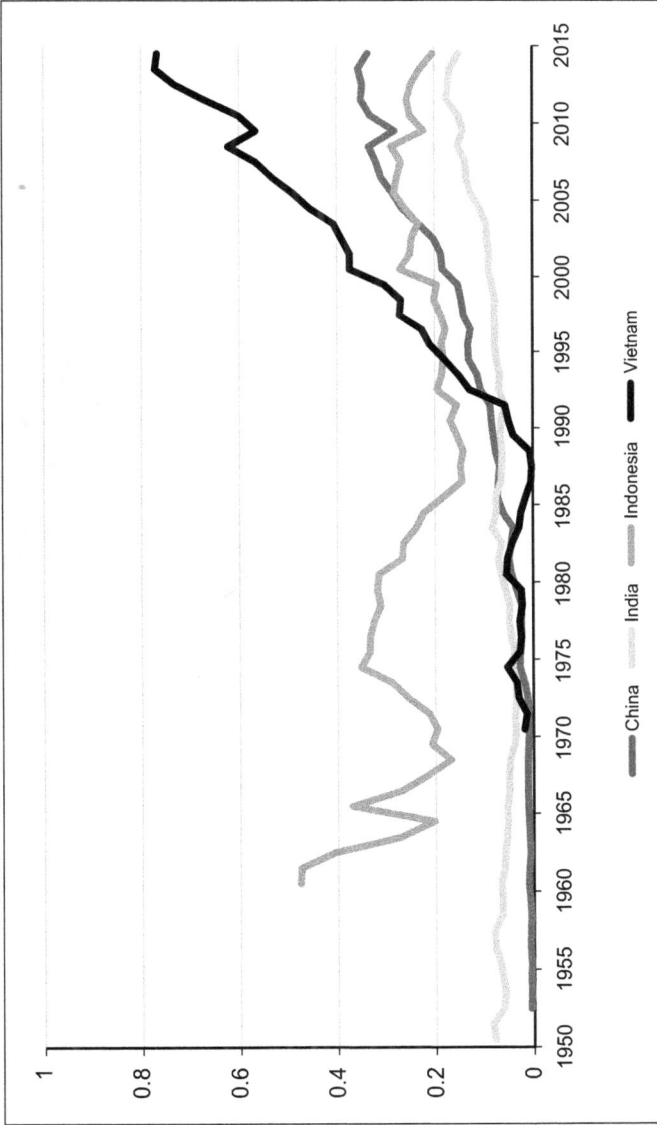

Notes: Real openness is total shares of merchandise exports and imports in the GDP at current PPPs.
Source: Penn World Table 9.0 (see Feenstra, Inklaar and Timmer 2015).

FIGURE 6.3
Real Terms of Trade

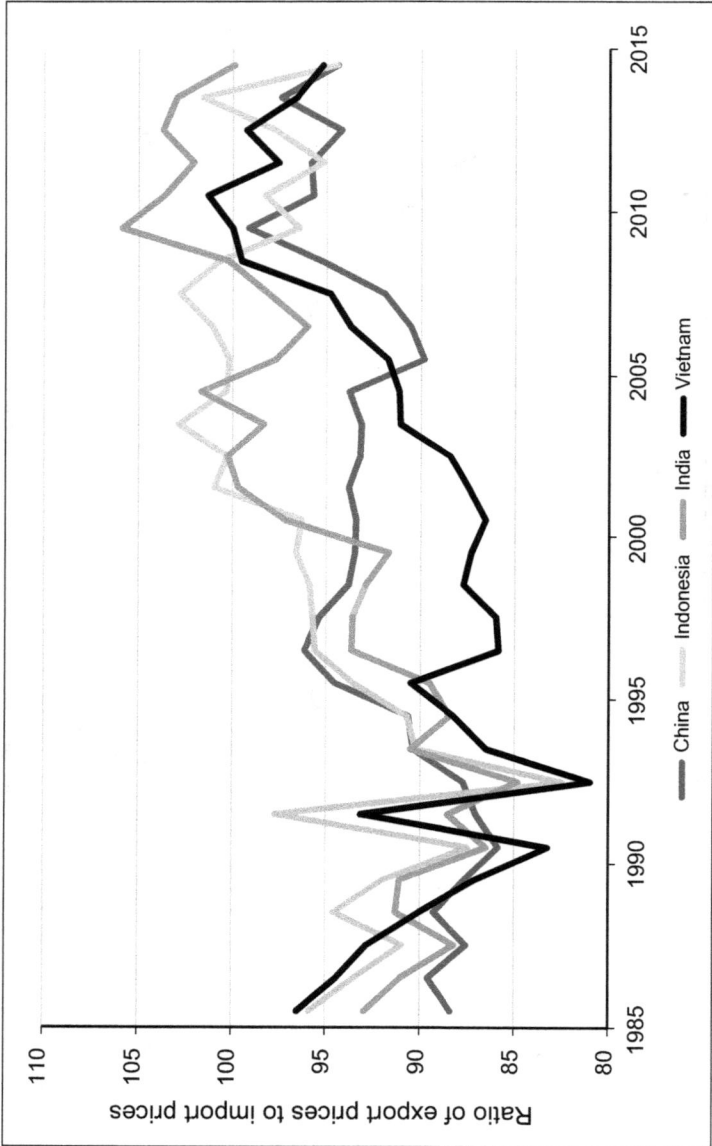

Source: Penn World Table 9.0 (see Feenstra, Inklaar and Timmer 2015).

FIGURE 6.4
Real Effective Exchange Rates (2010 = 100)

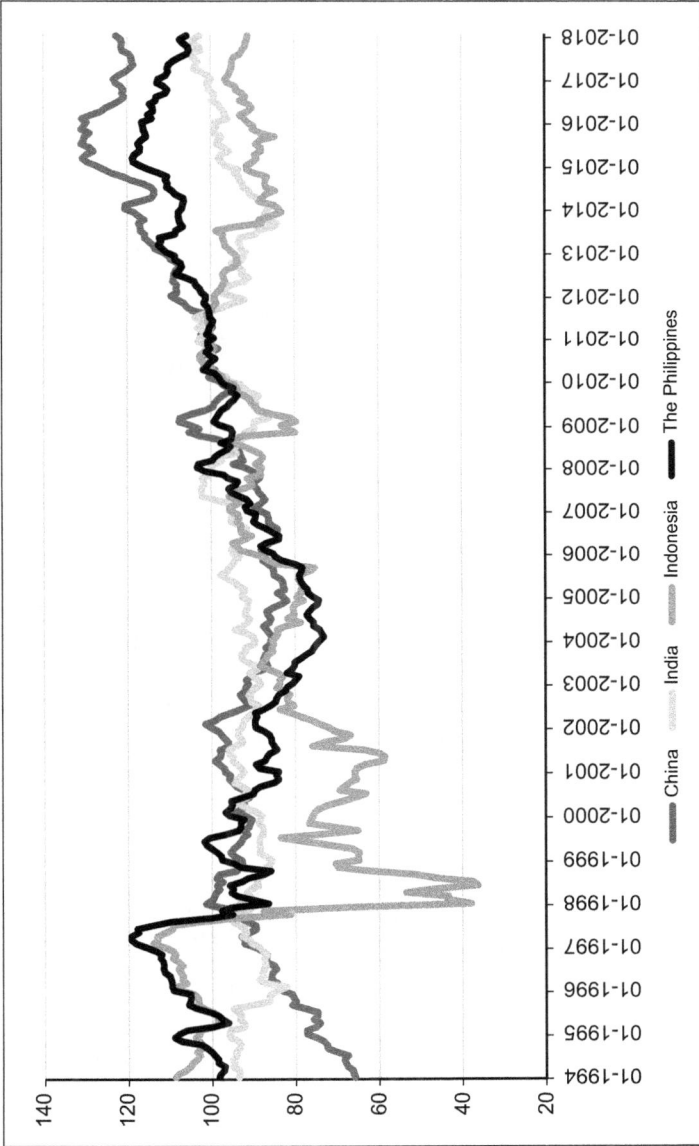

Note: The indices are such that the movement to higher (lower) figures indicates appreciation (depreciation) of the respective country's currency.
Source: BIS.

FIGURE 6.5
Current Account Deficits and Rupiah Depreciation

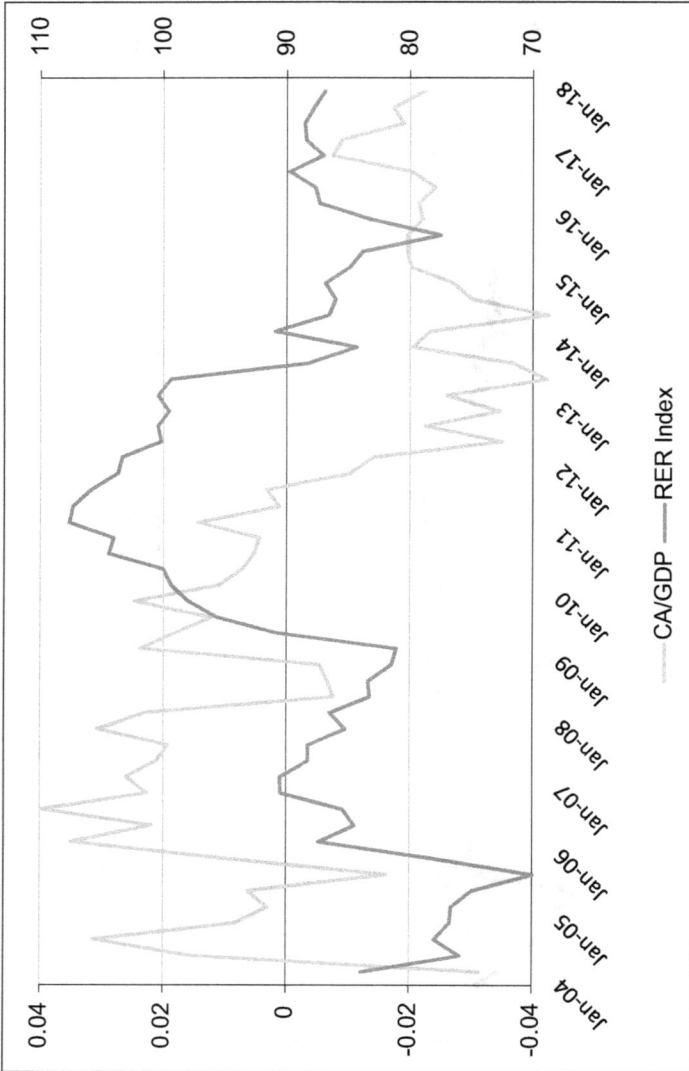

Sources: Current account series are from Bank Indonesia (via CEIC Data), GDP series are from BPS (via CEIC Data), RER Index uses Indonesia's CPI and US CPI series from the IMF, both at 2010=100 (via CEIC Data). The RER index is such that the movement to a higher (lower) level indicates appreciation (depreciation) of the rupiah against the U.S. dollar.

account deficit might be more complicated. Although in some periods depreciation seems to follow the changes in the current account deficit, the pattern breaks down elsewhere.

The mercantilist approach also runs counter to the structure of Indonesia's imports. As shown in Figure 6.6, the vast majority of Indonesian imports, around 75 per cent, is made up of raw materials, followed by 15 per cent capital goods. Consumer goods constitute only 10 per cent. This suggests that Indonesia does need imports in order to be able to produce. Figure 6.7 emphasizes that it is exactly the raw materials for industry that Indonesia imports the most.

6.3 MEASURES OF PROTECTION

In general, Indonesia has been "precariously open" since the late 1960s (Hill and Pane 2018). Two influential studies on effective protection in Indonesia (Fane and Condon 1996; Marks and Rahardja 2012) show how the country has been relatively open, despite a handful of episodes of high protectionism.

As depicted in Figure 6.8, protection in Indonesia in terms of tariff has decreased over time, consistent with the trend elsewhere. The decline was relatively sharp between the 1980s and 2000s, before it fell to very low rates of 3–4 per cent (weighted mean). Under the Jokowi administration, tariffs have increased slightly.

Similar to the case in other countries, whenever tariffs have gone down in Indonesia, non-tariff barriers have rapidly increased. Figure 6.9 compares the number of trade interventions imposed by Indonesia, China, Vietnam and India. The information has been sourced from the Global Trade Alert (GTA) database that tracked the trade interventions among countries since 2009. The database classifies trade measures as colour-coded green, amber, and red to indicate the level of their "harmfulness", with red being the most harmful and green liberalizing. According to the GTA, in most countries, the number of harmful measures exceeds that of liberalizing measures. This might indicate that following the Global Financial Crisis, countries became more protectionist — but the fact that GTA does not have data before 2009 makes it hard to confirm the argument.

Figure 6.9 shows that the number of harmful measures in Indonesia fluctuated more than that in China, Vietnam and India — with the highest being in 2015, or a year into Jokowi's presidency. Recently, in 2017, the

FIGURE 6.6
Proportion of Imports by Categories (%)

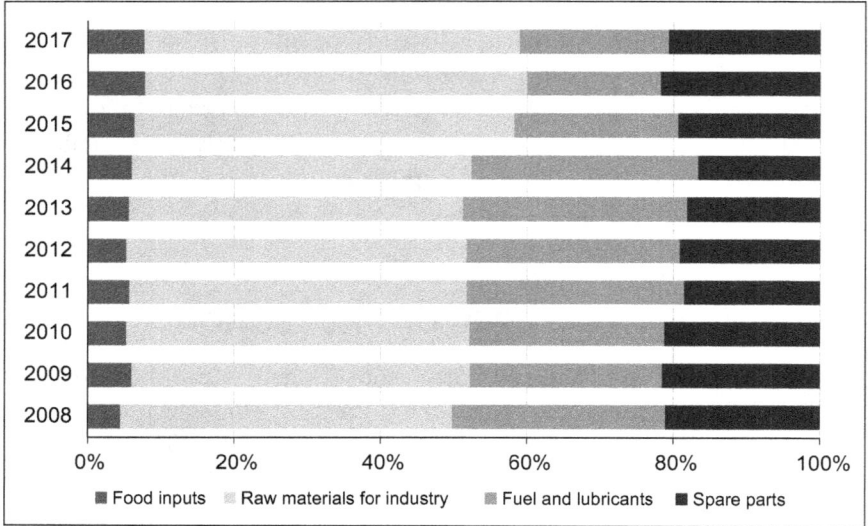

Source: BPS (via CEIC Data).

FIGURE 6.7
Imported Raw Materials by Groups (%)

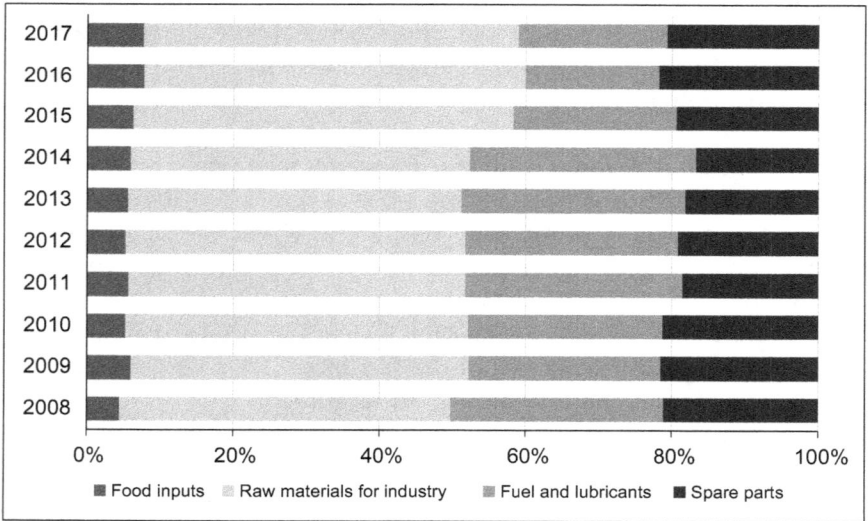

Source: BPS (via CEIC Data).

FIGURE 6.8
Applied Tariff Rates, All Products (%)

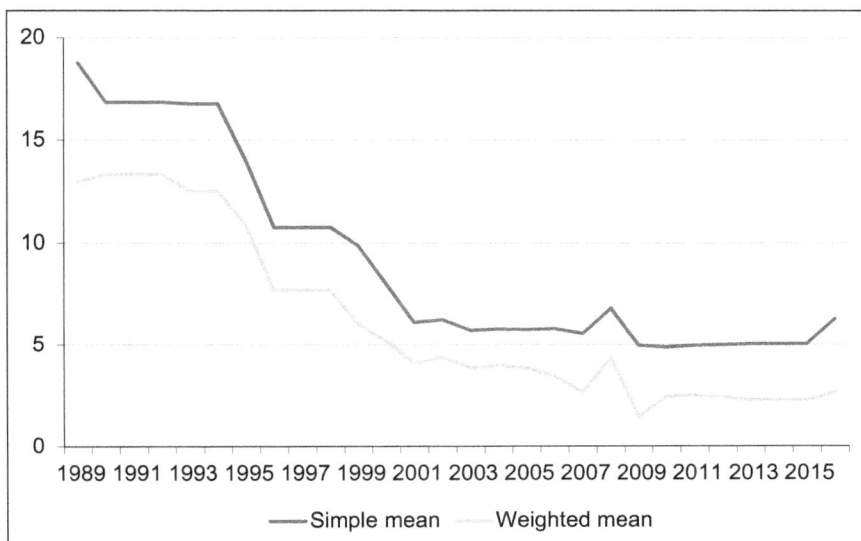

Source: WTO

number is higher in Indonesia than that in China and Vietnam. India, like the United States (not shown) on the other hand, has traditionally shown more protectionist tendencies than other countries.[3] Interestingly, the number of liberalizing measures is also high in Indonesia relative to that in China and Vietnam. Again, it is not very clear in the aggregate whether Indonesia is more protectionist than these other countries.[4]

Table 6.1 provides a breakdown of the "harmful" trade interventions implemented in the four countries since 2009. The number of such measures in Indonesia is 173, comparable to that in China, but higher than that in Vietnam. In fact, Indonesia's protectionism in this regard is higher than many other ASEAN countries.[5] This is particularly true for measures like anti-dumping, FDI restrictions, local sourcing, tax relief and incentives, and import tariff.

Table 6.2 shows the sectors and goods that are affected most often by the trade measures (both in liberalizing and harmful ways) in Indonesia. Food and meat are among the most protected sectors in Indonesia, whereas machinery is the least protected. This is consistent with the fact

FIGURE 6.9
Trade Interventions

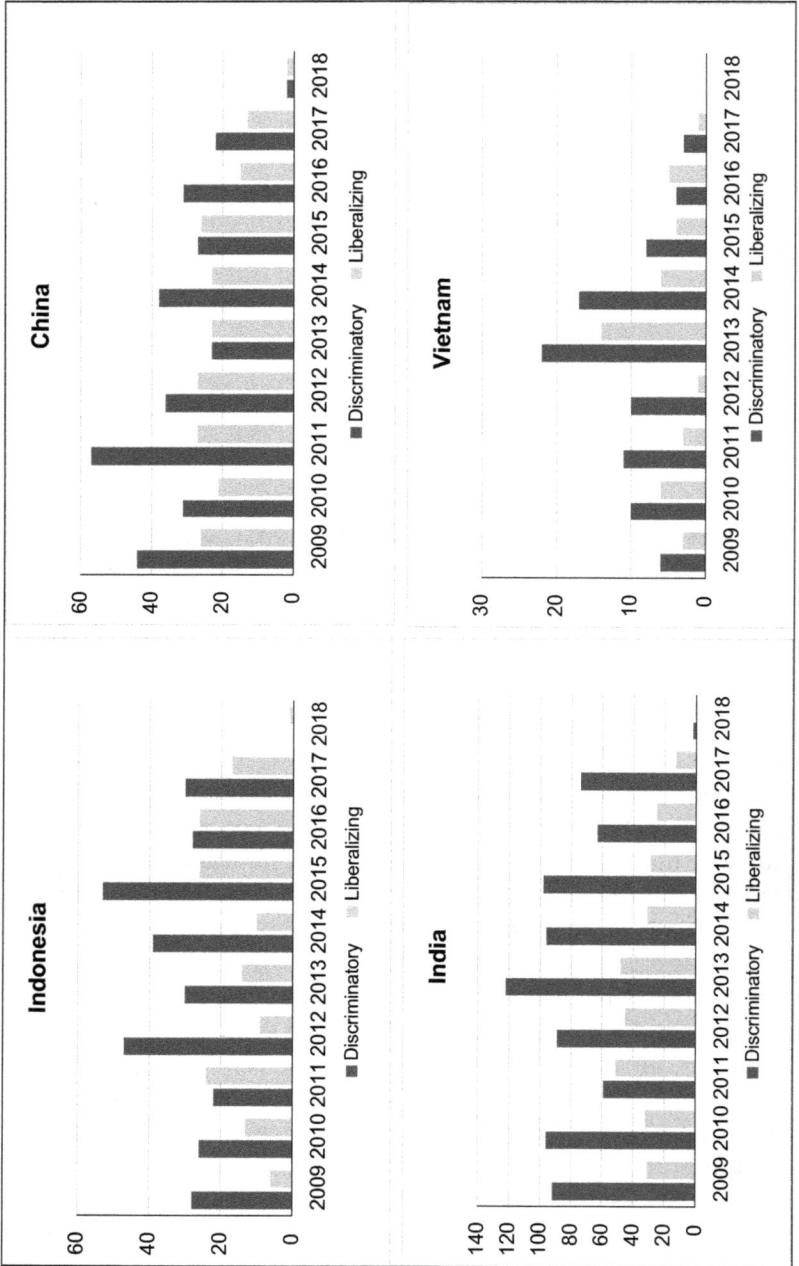

Source: Global Trade Alert <www.globaltradealert.org>.

TABLE 6.1
Trade Measures: Harmful

	Indonesia	Vietnam	China	India
Anti-dumping	15	2	42	155
Anti-subsidy	0	0	7	2
Bailout (capital injection or equity)	1	1	2	3
Competitive devaluation	0	2	0	0
Consumption subsidy	0	0	0	1
Control on personal transactions	2	0	0	0
Controls on commercial transactions	2	0	0	0
Controls on credit operations	1	1	0	0
Export ban	1	0	2	2
Export licensing requirement	4	0	0	2
Export quota	3	0	2	0
Export subsidy	0	0	0	3
Export tax	8	6	3	7
Export-related non-tariff measure, nes	3	0	0	1
FDI: Entry and ownership rule	13	2	8	10
FDI: Financial incentive	0	0	1	0
FDI: Treatment and operations, nes	7	0	5	1
Financial assistance in foreign market	0	0	4	0
Financial grant	1	0	5	2
Import ban	8	2	4	5
Import licensing requirement	7	0	8	4
Import monitoring	0	0	0	0
Import quota	3	1	0	4
Import related non-tariff measure, nes	0	1	0	0
Import tariff	10	25	12	46
Import tariff quota	0	0	2	1
Import-related non-tariff measure, nes	12	0	4	11
In-kind grant	0	0	0	0
Instrument unclear	1	0	2	1
Interest payment subsidy	1	1	1	0
Internal taxation of imports	4	0	7	1
Labour market access	7	2	1	1
Loan guarantee	0	0	0	1
Local labour	0	0	0	0
Local operations	4	1	11	1
Local sourcing	10	0	1	4
Localisation incentive	1	0	0	0
Other export incentive	0	0	1	1

continued on next page

TABLE 6.1 — *cont'd*

	Indonesia	Vietnam	China	India
Post-migration treatment	1	1	0	0
Price stabilization	0	0	1	0
Production subsidy	6	0	1	5
Public procurement access	2	0	0	2
Public procurement localisation	6	1	2	13
Public procurement preference margin	1	0	1	1
Public procurement, nes	0	0	0	0
Safeguard	5	5	1	4
Sanitary and phytosanitary measure	2	0	0	0
State aid, nes	1	0	0	3
State loan	2	1	4	3
Tax or social insurance relief	10	3	10	3
Tax-based export incentive	4	0	28	23
Technical barrier to trade	1	0	1	0
Trade finance	2	1	4	126
Trade payment measure	1	1	0	0
	173	60	188	453

Source: Global Trade Alert <www.globaltradealert.org> (accessed 10 March 2018).

TABLE 6.2
Sectors Affected Most Often

Sector	Interventions
Liberalizing	
Other general-purpose machinery and parts thereof	26
Plastics in primary forms	24
Chemical products n.e.c.	22
Products of iron or steel	21
Domestic appliances and parts thereof	19
Harmful	
Products of iron or steel	20
Meat and meat products	20
Food products n.e.c.	20
Chemical products n.e.c.	19
Computing machinery and parts and accessories thereof	18

Source: Global Trade Alert.

that Indonesia has been pushing for food self-sufficiency, and that it has little resources for producing parts and machinery needed for industries.

6.4 PROTECTIONISM IN INDONESIA BEFORE THE JOKOWI PRESIDENCY

Under President Sukarno, Indonesia was a newly independent economy, struggling to define itself away from colonial influence. In his nation-building efforts, Sukarno relied more on politics than economics. He nationalized hundreds of Dutch companies such as De Javasche Bank into Bank Indonesia, Koninklijke Paketvaart Maatschappij into Pelayaran Nasional Indonesia (Pelni), and Koninklijk Luchvaart Maatschappij into Garuda Indonesia Airways. More than 250 plantation companies were nationalized into PT Perkebunan Nusantara (PTPN), almost 200 companies in the mining and basic industries into Badan Penguasaan Industri dan Tambang (BAPPIT) and 40 trading companies were consolidated into PT Negara. The command economy era ended in 1966 with a very bleak picture. The inflation rate surpassed 500 per cent, half of the government expenditure went into covering the budget deficit, and per capita income was less than that in 1938.

The incoming New Order regime of President Soeharto was accompanied by a series of measures aimed at rehabilitating the economy. The government introduced market-friendly reforms, recommended by able technocrats under the leadership of Widjojo Nitisastro. These included opening up the capital market, welcoming foreign investment, and relaxing trade policies. But the prosperity period did not last long. The commodity boom in the early 1970s and the two oil booms in 1973–74 and 1979–80 brought windfall gains to Indonesia, encouraging the government to move forward with the idea of protectionism — in the form of import substitution, local content requirements, import licensing, and an export ban. Fuel was subsidized from 1976 onwards and attaining food self-sufficiency, especially for rice, became a priority. Then the oil price plunged in the 1980s. The strained budget, coupled with the global recession, forced the government to make a sweeping adjustment. From the mid-1980s to the mid-1990s, Indonesia witnessed strict deregulation, export promotion, and devaluation. However, business groups who had grown strong in the previous, protectionist era still had their way, and were now joined by emerging new cronies. Import monopolies and other facilities offered to these groups, especially those closest to President Soeharto, persisted. Then the AFC struck in 1997, throwing the Indonesian economy into a tailspin, far worse than its neighbours — including the epicentre Thailand. The economy shrank, inflation soared, and unemployment crept up. Once again, the government was forced to adopt more liberal policies. Import restrictions were removed, tariffs were cut, and Indonesia's involvement in international trade agreements increased. Most of these reforms to recover the economy were taken under the short terms of President Jusuf Habibie (1998–99), President Abdurrahman Wahid (1999–2001), and the early period of President Megawati Soekarnoputri (2001–04).

But the interest in free trade was, once again, short-lived. Protectionism started to creep back again in the early 2000s, beginning with restrictive measures for food crops, and followed by trade regulations and licensing requirements on textiles, steel, sugar and cloves. This continued until the second term of President Susilo Bambang Yudhoyono. Subsequently, the government passed new laws on mineral and coal mining (Law 4/2009), horticulture (Law 13/2010), food (Law 18/2012), farmers' protection and empowerment (Law 19/2013), industry (Law 3/2014), trade (Law 7/2014), and standardization (Law 20/2014), all with a serious impact on the openness to trade and investment.[6] Furthermore, import licensing was reinstated, the distribution of imported goods tightened, and the export of raw minerals banned. The Cabinet shake-up of 2011 turned out to side-line the trade reformists and, instead, opened the door for protectionist operatives. Very soon the Ministry of Agriculture and the Ministry of Industry added new products to the list of those requiring permits. It should be noted that the Yudhoyono presidency coincided with the 2008–09 Global Financial Crisis. The fact that "bad times" now came with "bad policies" seemed to have broken what had been known as the "Sadli's Law" — bad times make for good policies and good times make for bad policies, at least on the trade front (see Patunru and Rahardja 2015).[7]

6.5 JOKOWI'S STYLE OF PROTECTIONISM

In contrast to President Yudhoyono who frequented international events and forums, Jokowi seems to be less excited about trade and foreign affairs. Early in his presidency, for example, he surprised observers by skipping the APEC Leaders Forum in Manila in 2015. In the same year, he shortened his visit to the United States and returned home less than half-way through his trip.

The trend towards greater nationalism is on the rise under the current administration. However, Jokowi's stance appears to be a mix between pragmatism and ambivalence. Addressing the Indian Ocean Rim Association Leaders' Summit in March 2017, Jokowi embraced both nationalism and internationalism. Quoting President Sukarno, he reiterated "internationalism cannot live without nationalism" and vice versa — rhetoric that sounds good but the exact meaning of which is unclear.

In other events, Jokowi is always eager to extend his invitation to foreign investors to visit Indonesia, such as the APEC CEO Summit (November 2014 in Beijing), the ASEAN Summit (April 2017 in Manila) and the G-20 Summit (July 2017 in Hamburg). But he is also critical of the existing international order. At the Asian-African Summit (April 2015 in Jakarta), for instance, he mentioned that the current system dominated by the World Bank, the IMF and the ADB is obsolete, and that building a new international economic order is imperative. During another visit to the United States, he said he wanted to join the Trans-Pacific Partnership. He also supports the China-led Asian Infrastructure Investment Bank (AIIB), but openly criticizes China in the South China Sea dispute — despite Indonesia not being a formal party to the dispute. In response to a statement from Beijing in June 2017 that implicitly put Natuna in the territories subject to "overlapping claims", the president demonstratively held a cabinet meeting on board a warship near the Natuna Islands.

In relation to economic policies, Jokowi's stance leans more towards protectionism. Recalling the presidential campaign days, Jokowi's promises included a lower dose of nationalism relative to his rival General Prabowo. However, he started his presidency with a heavy use of protectionist measures, mostly via the Ministry of Trade, the Ministry of Agriculture, and the Ministry of Industry. Although tariffs levied under the Jokowi administration are lower than before, protectionism continues in the form of non-tariff barriers. Data from the Ministry of Trade shows that the use of non-tariff barriers, mostly import restrictions, have increased from 9 per cent of tariff lines in 2011 to 35 per cent in 2016. Critics have pointed out that non-tariff barriers such as quotas, import licences, or export bans are prone to corruption.[8] Moreover, in democratic polities like Indonesia, they may lead to the "protection for sale" phenomenon, whereby protection is given to the highest bidders — or cronies.

Perhaps in response to criticisms, Jokowi reshuffled his Cabinet. Within three years into his presidency, he already had three trade ministers: Rachmat Gobel, Thomas Lembong, and Enggartiasto Lukita. The closest analogy is that of a pendulum oscillating from protectionist to market-friendly back to protectionist again — but it might as well be a reflection of the absence of a clear vision. He also replaced the Minister of Industry Saleh Husin with Airlangga Hartarto, but kept the Minister of Agriculture Amran Sulaiman in the Cabinet despite the two reshuffles. This is an interesting development, considering that the Ministry of Agriculture is arguably the most populist ministry in Jokowi's Cabinet.

How can the rising economic populism and protectionism under Jokowi be explained? In the beginning of Jokowi's presidency, the rupiah appreciated, making exports more expensive. Around the same time, Indonesia's competitiveness dropped as the commodity boom ended. Both these factors increased the demand for protection. Then there is the bandwagon effect. Many countries use an active industrial policy — perhaps in response to the weak global demand. The blame partly goes to the failure of the Doha Round of the WTO, which damaged confidence in the international architecture. Some countries resort to "beggar-thy-neighbour" exchange rate policies while others continue erecting non-tariff barriers. To sum up, despite protectionist measures often leading to negative consequences, they seem to be taking the stage again almost everywhere, including in Jokowi's Indonesia.

The first 100 days of Jokowi were marked by a series of protectionist measures by his ministers, as surveyed by Damuri and Day (2015). For example, Fisheries Minister Susi Pudjiastuti introduced a ban on catching young crustaceans and prohibited the transfer of fish from smaller to larger vessels at sea, to curb illegal fishing. Transportation Minister Ignasius Jonan set minimum prices for airline tickets and discounted airfares, while Trade Minister Rachmat Gobel banned the sale of light alcoholic beverages in convenience stores throughout Indonesia.

In 2015, Jokowi replaced Rachmat Gobel with Thomas Lembong. The latter is known to be a pro-trade reformer. In an interview after his inauguration, Lembong made a remark that protectionist policies always backfire.[9] But just like Gobel, he only had the post for a year. Jokowi's third (and current) trade minister is Enggartiasto Lukita, appointed in 2016, who seems to be less protectionist than Gobel, but not as open as Lembong. Lukita, with Agriculture Minister Sulaiman, has recently been dealing with the controversies around rice and other food commodities.[10]

Protectionism is not just noticeable in policies from the Trade or Agriculture Ministries alone. In January 2017, the government issued a controversial decision to relax an export ban on unprocessed minerals. The ban itself was put into effect in 2014 as a follow up to the 2009 Law on Mineral and Coal Mining. It required mining companies to establish processing capacity in Indonesia — a policy that falls into a broader agenda of domestic value addition. As a result of this earlier policy, several companies invested, albeit reluctantly, on building smelters in Indonesia. By the end of 2016, over US$18 billion in downstream investment had been channelled into thirty-two smelting facilities (Warburton 2018). Jokowi's decision to relax the ban in January 2017 therefore came as a shock and jeopardized three years of investment and development. Warburton (2018) argues that this decision was not related to budgetary pressures, but rather it was a move to protect PT Aneka Tambang, a state-owned mining company, whose profit had suffered during the export ban period.

As it turns out, this mining saga has another controversial aspect that involves an escalated tension between the Indonesian government and Freeport Indonesia, a subsidiary of the American mining giant Freeport-McMoRan Inc., which has long been operating in Indonesia (Dong and Manning 2017). Initially, when the export ban was imposed in 2014, Freeport and another big mining company, Newmont, were given an extension of rights to export ore until 2017. In return, they were required to pay additional taxes and start to build their processing capacity by 2017. Neither of them met the latter condition. While relaxing the import ban, the Indonesian government introduced stricter rules that prevented Freeport from exporting copper concentrate until it adopted a new permit. The company was also required to make a 51 per cent divestment after ten years. This Indonesia–Freeport tension increased business uncertainty in the country.

Prior to the Freeport episode, investment uncertainty was also reflected in a plan to develop Indonesia's first high-speed railway. China and Japan were competing to win the multi-billion dollar contract in 2015. At the last minute, however, Jokowi announced the cancellation of the plan, citing (rightly) that a high-speed railway between Jakarta and Bandung was not economically feasible owing to the short distance. Instead, the government now wanted a slower train and asked both countries to resubmit their proposals.[11] Even before this cancellation, the project had been mired with controversies around the bidding process (Ray and Ing 2016). It finally kicked off in January 2016 with a target of completion by 2019. But the Minister of SOE, Rini Soemarno has expressed her doubts on meeting the target, given the slow progress in land acquisition (see Salim and Negara, Chapter 9).

In addition to the series of protectionist policies stated above, the Jokowi administration is also dealing with two commodities that have long been the subject of discourse on protectionism in the country — rice and fuel. It is safe to say that both goods have been political and politicized. In the case of rice, the government policy (import ban) has continuously resulted in very high domestic prices compared to international prices, whereas in the case fuel, the policy (fuel subsidy) has led to the domestic price being too low when compared to the international market price. The distortion in the rice market primarily hurts the poor, while that in the fuel market is not only regressive, but also inefficient and environmentally unfriendly.

6.5.1 Rice

Indonesia is one of the largest rice importers in the world. But imports have been banned since 2004, and only allowed occasionally under the government's (and in some cases, the Parliament's) approval. This has led to relative increase in domestic prices compared to the international price (Figure 6.10). While the price distortion benefits the largest farmers and traders, including absentee landowners, it harms the poorest consumers, including landless farm workers or peasants (Patunru 2018). More than 80 per cent of the Indonesian population, including most of the poor, are net consumers of rice. For them, lower rice prices are preferable. As Figure 6.10 shows, by the end of 2012, Indonesia's rice price was 65 per cent above the international price, pushing millions of people into poverty.[12]

Nevertheless, Indonesia's food self-sufficiency ambition remains strong and, in fact, is proliferating again under the Jokowi administration — most notably championed by the Ministry of Agriculture. The strength of this ambition often makes the government pass reform opportunities. For example, during the world food price crisis in 2007–08, domestic prices

FIGURE 6.10
Domestic vs. World Rice Prices, 1995–2017 (Rp/kg)

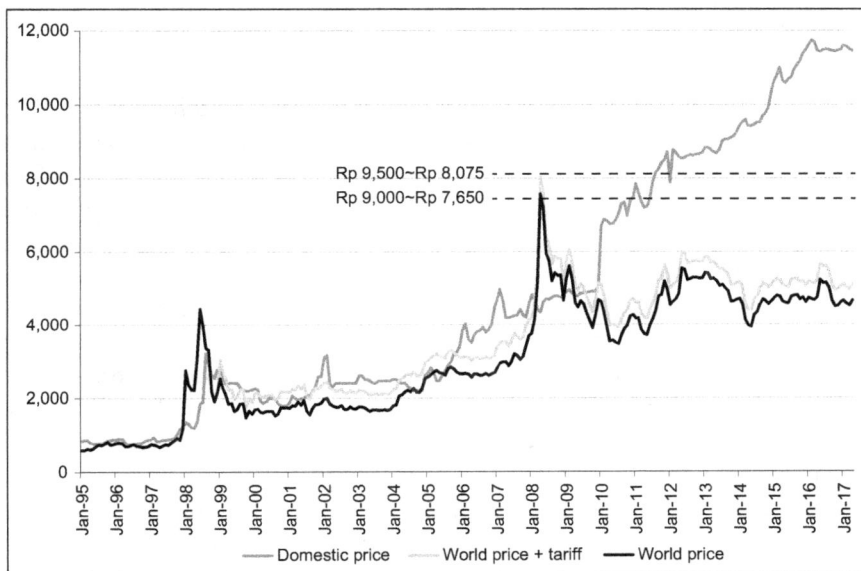

Sources: The domestic prices are of the wholesale prices of IR 64 rice variety, as quoted in Cipinang, the biggest wholesale market in Jakarta, collected from McCulloch (private communication) for series from January 1995 until May 2009 and from BPS afterward. Prices from June 2009 until December 2009 were estimated using the prices of Medium rice variety, adjusted with the average margin between the retail and wholesale prices since November 2006 until May 2009. The world price series is represented by the wholesale prices of Thai 25 per cent brokens rice variety, collected from Bank of Thailand database (via CEIC Data), converted to Indonesian rupiah, added with $20/ton shipping and handling cost and $5/ton import profit. The "world price + tariff" series is the same as the world price but with the addition of 20 per cent tariff in 1999, and specific tariffs of Rp430/kg from January 2000 until December 2006, Rp550/kg from January 2007 until November 2007, and Rp450/kg from December 2007 onward. The two dashed lines (Rp9,500/kg and Rp9,000/kg) correspond to the existing and proposed retail price ceilings, respectively, set by the government (Rp8,075/kg and Rp7,650/kg are my estimated corresponding wholesale prices to match with the vertical axes).

in Indonesia remained relatively stable, which would have been a good time to introduce a reform like a price band policy automatically linked to the world price. But no such reform took place and, just when the world price had calmed down, the domestic price jumped dramatically again.

There are a number of factors that explain why rice protectionism persists in Indonesia. First, it is simply the result of a bandwagon effect.

Many countries are embracing protectionism again, especially when the WTO is not working efficiently. Rice protectionism, in other words, is part of the general protectionism and populism that are trending again.

Second, it is due to the power of lobbying, whereby trade restrictions tend to favour those who are better organized, who, in turn, usually stand to lose from increased trade (Krugman, Obstfeld and Melitz 2015; Olson 1965). In the case of Indonesia's rice market, the call for protection is often voiced by organizations like the Indonesian Farmers Association (HKTI) and the Indonesian Farmers Union Federation (FSPI). Interestingly, the key members of these associations are rich farmers and traders and not the poorest peasants (Patunru and Basri 2011).

The third explanation relates to the view that in Indonesia, self-sufficiency as part of the food sovereignty narrative is necessary rhetoric to strengthen the role and function of the state (Neilson 2018). This is consistent with the view that populism pays politically (Rodrik 2017). These views, however, implicitly assume naïveté or even ignorance on the part of the public. Yet, it is also probably true that people believe that self-sufficiency in rice (and other commodities) is important, despite the argument being built on false premises that: self-sufficiency is the way to ensure food security (food security can actually be obtained without self-sufficiency (Heufers and Patunru 2018)); Indonesia is rice-abundant and should therefore be a natural exporter not importer (only in 7 out of 145 years since 1870, did Indonesia export more than it imported rice[13]); and it is important to be self-sufficient as the world market is thin (the world rice market today is much larger and more stable than in the 1970s (Dawe 2008)). As noted, this level of ignorance may be linked with the proliferation of these false beliefs. But judgement may also involve romanticism. This quote from two top Indonesian agricultural economists supporting rice protection in the country illustrates this: "Since long time ago painters have been drawing yellowing paddy trees or harvesting in the paddy fields with a background of mountains, clear water irrigations or green dykes..." (Amang and Sawit 2001).

But why is the rice self-sufficiency ambition again rising in Jokowi's administration? Ever since the campaign days, Jokowi had promised to achieve self-sufficiency in rice. After taking office in late 2014, he reiterated this promise, claiming that rice imports would stop within two years.[14] It should also be noted that Jokowi belongs to the Indonesian Democratic Party of Struggle (PDI-P), whose chairperson, Megawati Soekarnoputri, is the daughter of the late President Sukarno — an ultra-nationalist. With respect to issues related to food, Neilson (2018) argues that it was President Sukarno who first set the foundational terms of the national-scale self-sufficiency in food, by questioning "why bother talking about political freedom if we don't have freedom to manage our rice?" and by insisting "food is a matter of life and death". Interestingly, Jokowi, too, has often quoted these remarks.

In reality, however, it is hard for Indonesia to be self-sufficient in rice. As a matter of fact, one year after his promise, Jokowi decided that the country needed to import 200,000 to 300,000 tons of rice.[15] Later in October 2017 the Agriculture Minister, Amran Sulaiman proudly announced self-sufficiency in rice (as well as in chilli, corn and onions). But in January 2018, the government imported 500,000 tons of rice, creating a furore in the media.[16] As noted, Jokowi has reshuffled his Cabinet three times — and has already had three different ministers for trade. But Amran Sulaiman has always retained his position, despite limited achievements. This might be, as Power (2016) observed after the second reshuffle, due to his loyalty to the president and his ability to mobilize cash and support — Sulaiman was a key financier during Jokowi's campaign days.

6.5.2 Fuel

Fuel subsidies have been a key feature of the Indonesian economy for decades. It was meant to be a way of channelling the rent from oil revenues to the people, as Indonesia was once an oil-abundant country. But it has been very hard to undo this policy even though the country is no longer rich in oil resources (in fact, Indonesia had to quit OPEC in 2008 after it became a net importer of oil). In the 1970s, oil and gas constituted half of Indonesia's exports, now they account for less than 10 per cent, whereas on the import side the share of oil and gas is around 14 per cent. Indonesia's proven oil reserves now stand at only a fourth of their volume in the 1970s. The oil production capacity is only 800,000 barrels per day (as assumed in the 2018 State Budget), about half the capacity in the 1970s, while consumption is more than 1.5 million barrels per day.

There are at least three problems with the fuel subsidy regime. First, it is regressive in nature. Almost half of the subsidy is actually enjoyed by those in higher income groups and less than 2 per cent reaches the bottom decile (Patunru and Basri 2011; Agustina et al. 2008). A study conducted by the University of Indonesia showed that among the top 30 per cent of the income distribution, 80 per cent own vehicles and thus use fuel, whereas only a third of the households in the bottom 30 per cent do (LPEM-FEUI 2006).

Second, it is unproductive, as it takes resources away from more important sectors such as basic education and health. In 2013, the spending on energy subsidies, around two-thirds of which was on fuel, constituted a quarter of the central government expenditure. This was around one and half times of that spent on education, and around fifteen times of that spent on health (Allford and Soejachmoen 2013). This is in stark contrast with Thailand, for example, which spends about 14 per cent and 30 per cent of government expenditure on health and education, respectively. It is therefore not surprising that malnourishment and illiteracy rates are lower in Thailand than in Indonesia.

The third problem is related to environmental concerns. The subsidy on fuel consumption results in a price higher than the market, thus suppressing the incentive to develop renewable and clean energy sources. The Indonesian government has, on many occasions, stated its intention to transition into low carbon economy (Patunru and Rakhmah 2017). In the National Energy Policy (Government Regulation 79/2014), the government targeted to have at least 23 per cent renewable energy in total energy consumption by 2025. Such ambition is also noted in Indonesia's Intended Nationally Determined Contributions (INDCs) submission to the Paris Agreement in 2015. Nevertheless, the country is heavily dependent on fossil fuels, particularly oil. In 2010, the share of fossil fuels in the total energy consumption was 95 per cent. Therefore, without a significant reform to the existing fuel subsidy regime, it is unlikely for the country to realize these intentions.

Despite these challenges, the fuel subsidy was an important component of the state budget for a long time. Jokowi's decision to remove it in January 2015 was therefore widely applauded (Damuri and Day 2015). It was seen as a bold move, long overdue and useful for creating a fiscal space for more productive needs such as social assistance and infrastructure development.

The Jokowi government increased the price of subsidized fuel from Rp6,500 to Rp8,500 per litre on 18 November 2014 (Figure 6.11). Then, on 1 January 2015, the subsidies for premium gasoline were removed, with the price now lowered to Rp7,600 per litre. To reflect the changes in the

FIGURE 6.11
Fuel and Crude Oil Prices (Rp/litre)

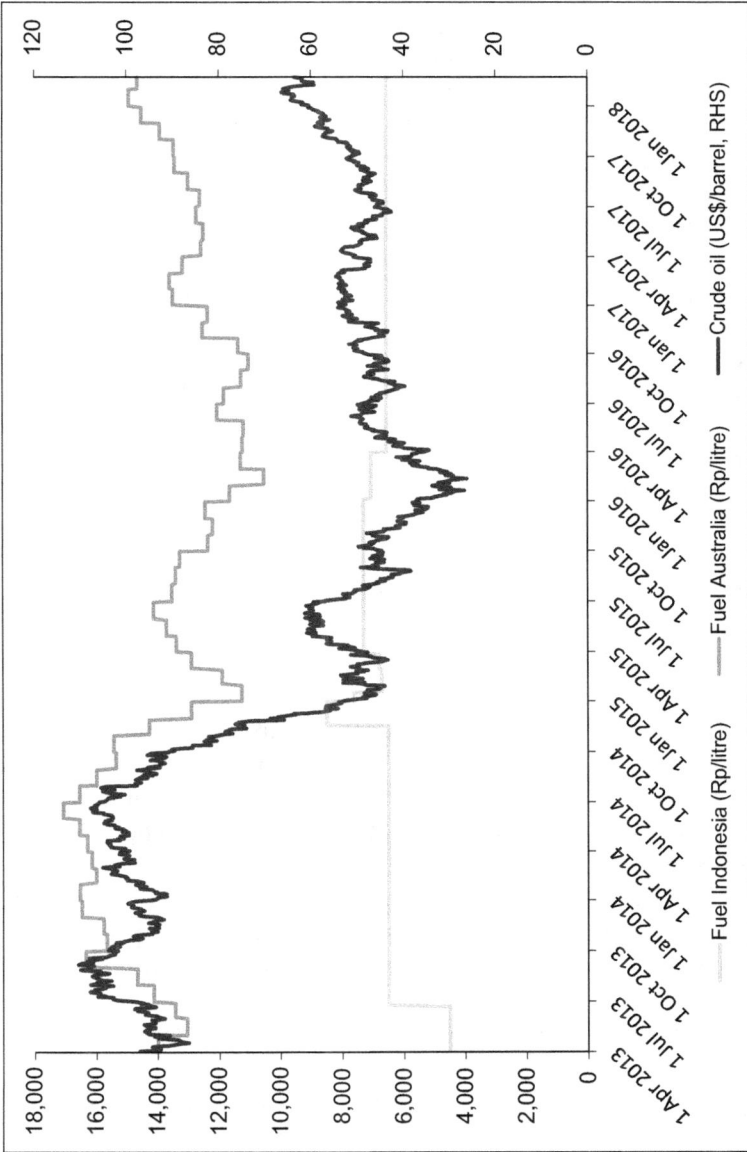

Sources: Indonesia's fuel prices are of gasoline premium as published by Pertamina. Australia's fuel prices are of standard unleaded petrol (ULP) 91 in monthly average from metro areas in Western Australia as reported by Department of Mines, Industry Regulation and Safety (taken from CEIC Data). Crude oil prices are of the West Texas Intermediate (taken from FRED).

world oil price, the domestic price was adjusted again three times before it ended up at Rp7,300 per litre on 28 March 2015. It stayed there for almost a year. In 2016, the government adjusted the price to Rp7,050 per litre on 5 January, and Rp6,550 per litre on 1 April. Since then, there has been no further adjustment.

The choice of timing for the premium fuel subsidy removal was appropriate as it coincided with the global oil price sliding down from around US$60 per barrel to US$50 per barrel, and so public resistance was low. But the prior price increase from Rp6,500 to Rp8,500 per litre took place when the world oil price fell from around US$100 per barrel in mid-2014 to around US$75 per barrel in November 2014.[17] This move was seen as a sign that Jokowi was determined to stay committed to the reform, as it would save him around US$10 billion in the incoming 2015 State Budget. When the subsidy was removed in January 2015,[18] the government was able to reallocate almost US$20 billion from fuel subsidy spending to other, more important posts.[19]

Despite the acclaim received on the decision to scrap the fuel subsidy, it now appears that Jokowi might have lost the golden opportunity to reform the fuel pricing once and for all. The world oil price is now back on the rising trend at more than US$60 per barrel, far above the assumed price of US$45 and US$48 per barrel in the 2017 and 2018 state budgets, respectively.[20] With the fuel price left unadjusted since April 2016, this has again created a heavy burden on the budget. But instead of raising the price, the government asked Pertamina, the state-owned oil and mining company, to cover for the price differences. When the subsidy was scrapped in January 2015, the government explained that the fuel price would be adjusted periodically in response to changes in oil prices and the exchange rate.

But, as noted, this was not the case. In fact, the government seems hesitant to increase the price again, even as the oil price is increasing since June 2016. In hindsight, the government should have tied the fuel price automatically to the oil price in January 2015 (without the need to adjust it periodically). Just like the case of rice in 2007–08, this too was a missed opportunity.

Figure 6.11 also shows a fuel price series that automatically follows the changes in oil price. Due to data availability, it uses the average retail fuel prices around metro areas in Western Australia. It is clear that this series moves very closely with the oil price. But the gap between the Australian and Indonesian fuel prices has been widening, implying an increasing opportunity cost of keeping the fuel price low in Indonesia. As of now, the government has Pertamina to shoulder the burden, but there is a limit. A collapse could bring the old subsidy regime back again, negating Jokowi's legacy of eliminating it in January 2015.

6.6 DISCUSSION

Jokowi's approach to trade is, in general, populist-protectionist. Consequently, it is not very different from his predecessors. Many recent laws and regulations that are very protectionist in nature were actually introduced under the Yudhoyono's administration. Rice- and fuel-protectionism go even further back to the Sukarno and Soeharto eras. But Jokowi seems to have amplified the intensity of such protectionist measures. As the 2019 election approaches, populism is expected to intensify even further.

Globalization can have both positive and negative results, but Indonesia has to continue its reform in order to make the most out of its engagement with the rest of the world. In this regard, improving compensation mechanisms and increasing labour market flexibility are key to reducing the risks and costs of globalization (Patunru, Pangestu and Basri 2018). At the same time, it is important to increase Indonesia's engagement with the international economic architecture as it would help to reduce trade barriers, provide policy discipline to withstand rent-seeking activities, and frame policy reforms (Anas and Narjoko 2018). Despite the multilateral WTO agreement not functioning effectively, Indonesia should not get carried away by the proliferation of costly bilateral agreements. Instead, it should keep resisting the push for protectionist policies while upholding non-discriminatory principles in regional agreements.

Notes

1. Size effect might have a role too; smaller countries usually rely more on trade as compared to bigger countries.
2. In the same period, Malaysia and Singapore were more open than Vietnam.
3. Note that the vertical axes of the panels for Vietnam and India were not aligned.

4. Note, however, that GTA information is mostly based on complaints from trade partners. Therefore, the number of harmful measures might be overstated while liberalizing measures understated.

5. The total number of harmful measures in the same period is twenty-seven in Malaysia, thirty-three in Thailand, twenty in Singapore, and ten in the Philippines.

6. Some of the implementing regulations based on these laws are listed in Patunru and Rahardja (2015). This does not imply that there were no good policies under President Yudhoyono. In fact, some laws issued within his period were considered very useful such as Law 21/2011 on Financial Service Authority, Law 21/2012 on Land Acquisition, Law 5/2014 on Civil Administration, and Law 6/2014 on Villages. Most of these laws, however, deal with domestic issues.

7. An interesting periodization of Indonesia's trade policy over time is studied by Pangestu, Rahardja and Ing (2015) who divide the period into five sub-periods, namely 1965–71: from chaos to rehabilitation; 1971–85: import substitution; 1985–89: devaluation, bold deregulation, export diversification; 1989–2004: recovery and soul-searching; and 2004–15: more reform, more Dutch disease, and the Global Financial Crisis. (Note, however, that the 1989–2004 period has a lot of sub-trends, including the Asian Financial Crisis).

8. In 2016, the Indonesia's Corruption Eradication Commission (KPK) had recommended that the Ministry of Trade should no longer use quantitative restrictions. Presumably, this recommendation was prompted by two high-profile corruption cases that sent a former chairman of the Justice and Prosperity Party and a Constitutional Court Chief Justice to jail for taking bribes related to beef import quotas. This KPK recommendation was then included by the government as part of Presidential Regulation 10/2016.

9. See <https://www.bloomberg.com/news/videos/2015-08-14/indonesia-s-lembong-signals-less-protectionist-policies>.

10. See, for example, <http://www.thejakartapost.com/news/2018/09/21/rice-import-debate-is-old-paradigm-agriculture-minister-says.html>.

11. See <https://www.reuters.com/article/indonesia-railway/scrapping-indonesias-bullet-train-leaves-top-investors-confused-idUSL4N11A14X 20150904>.

12. In July 2017, the domestic prices were already very high, prompting the Trade Minister to lower the ceiling price (see the dashed lines in Figure 6.10). The news immediately met resistance from farmers' associations and the proposed regulation was annulled. In practice, retail ceiling prices are rarely obeyed. But even if it is effective, the figure shows that the resulting domestic prices would still be far above the international price.

13. I thank Pierre van der Eng for data for this point.

14. See <http://www.thejakartapost.com/news/2014/11/06/jokowi-stop-rice-imports-within-two-years.html>.
15. See <http://www.thejakartapost.com/news/2015/10/22/jokowi-finally-agrees-import-rice-thailand-vietnam.html>.
16. See <http://jakartaglobe.id/business/lullaby-gets-govt-import-rice-at-most-unfortunate-time/>.
17. See <https://theconversation.com/indonesias-fuel-subsidy-cut-a-bitter-pill-that-had-to-be-swallowed-34357>.
18. A fixed subsidy of Rp1,000 per litre was still given to diesel and kerosene; but since it is not a fixed price, it was expected that the government would no longer pay the additional bill when the oil price rises. Some subsidy was also still applied to a type of fuel gasoline, namely RON 88, but with an expectation to decrease its supply gradually until it is phased out completely and all consumers have switched to non-subsidized, RON 92 fuel. The remaining subsidy accounted for 1 per cent of the national budget, dropped from 13.5 per cent in the previous year.
19. There was a noticeable increase in infrastructure spending in the state budget from 8.4 per cent in 2014 to 12.6 per cent in 2015, and 15 per cent in 2016.
20. There are slight differences in the crude oil prices as quoted by West Texas Intermediates, Brent Price, Platts, and Indonesia Crude Price (ICP), but in general, these differences are very small.

References

Agustina, Cut Dian R.D., J. Arze del Granado, T. Bulman, Wolfgang Fengler and Mohamad Ikhsan. "Black Hole or Black Gold: The Impact of Oil and Gas Prices on Indonesia's Public Finances". Policy Research Working Paper 4718, September 2008. Washington, D.C.: World Bank, 2008.

Allford, Jason and Moekti P. Soejachmoen. "Survey of Recent Developments". *Bulletin of Indonesian Economic Studies* 49, no. 3 (2013): 267–88.

Amang, Beddu and M. Hasan Sawit. *Kebijakan Beras dan Pangan Nasional: Pelajaran dari Orde Baru dan Orde Reformasi* [National Rice and Food Policy: Lessons from the New Order and the "Reformasi" Order]. Bogor: IPB Press, 2001.

Anas, Titik and Dionisius Narjoko. "International Cooperation and the Management of Globalisation: the Indonesian Experience". In *Indonesian in the New World: Globalisation, Nationalism and Sovereignty*, edited by Arianto A. Patunru, Mari E. Pangestu and M. Chatib Basri, pp. 294–315. Singapore: ISEAS – Yusof Ishak Institute, 2018.

Damuri, Yose R. and Creina Day. "Survey of Recent Developments". *Bulletin of Indonesian Economic Studies* 51, no. 1 (2015): 3–27.

Dawe, David. "Can Indonesia Trust the World Rice Market?". *Bulletin of Indonesian Economic Studies* 44 no. 1 (2008): 115–32.

Dong, Sarah X. and Chris Manning. "Labor Market Development at a Time of Heightened Uncertainty". *Bulletin of Indonesian Economic Studies* 53, no. 1 (2017): 1–25.

Fane, George and Timothy Condon. "Trade Reform in Indonesia, 1987–1995". *Bulletin of Indonesian Economic Studies* 32, no. 3 (1996): 33–54.

Feenstra, Robert C., Robert Inklaar and Marcel P. Timmer. "The Next Generation of the Penn World Table". *American Economic Review* 105, no. 10 (2015): 3150–82 <www.ggdc.net/pwt>.

Heufers, Rainer and Arianto A. Patunru. "Food Security in Indonesia". Paper presented at the Indonesia Study Group, Australian National University, 7 March 2018.

Hill, Hal and Deasy Pane. "Indonesia and the Global Economy: Missed Opportunities?". In *Indonesian in the New World: Globalisation, Nationalism and Sovereignty*, edited by Arianto A. Patunru, Mari E. Pangestu and M. Chatib Basri, pp. 267–93. Singapore: ISEAS – Yusof Ishak Institute, 2018.

Krugman, Paul R., Maurice Obstfeld and Marc J. Melitz. *International Economics: Theory and Policy*. 10th ed. Essex: Pearson Education Limited, 2015.

Marks, Stephen V. and Sjamsu Rahardja. "Effective Rates of Protection Revisited for Indonesia'. *Bulletin of Indonesian Economic Studies* 48, no. 1 (2012): 57–84.

Neilson, Jeffrey. "Feeding the Bangsa: Food Sovereignty and the State in Indonesia". In *Indonesia in the New World: Globalisation, Nationalism and Sovereignty*, edited by Arianto A. Patunru, Mari E. Pangestu and M. Chatib Basri, pp. 73–89. Singapore: ISEAS – Yusof Ishak Institute, 2018.

Pangestu, Mari, Sjamsu Rahardja and Lili Yan Ing. "Fifty Years of Trade Policy in Indonesia: New World Trade, Old Treatments". *Bulletin of Indonesian Economic Studies* 51 no. 2 (2015): 239–61.

Patunru, Arianto A. "Is Greater Openness to Trade Good? What are the Effects on Poverty and Inequality?". In *Trade, Poverty and Income Distribution: The Indonesian Experience*, edited by Richard Barichello, Richard Schwindt and Arianto A. Patunru. Vancouver: University of British Columbia Press, 2018.

———— and M. Chatib Basri. "The Political Economy of Rice and Fuel Pricing in Indonesia". In *Poverty and Global Recession in Southeast Asia*, edited by Aris Ananta and Richard Barichello, pp. 203–28. Singapore: Institute of Southeast Asian Studies, 2011.

———— and Sjamsu Rahardja. *Trade Protectionism: Bad Times and Bad Policy*. Sydney: Lowy Institute for International Policy, 2015.

————, Mari E. Pangestu and M. Chatib Basri. "Challenges for Indonesia in the New World". In *Indonesia in the New World: Globalisation, Nationalism and Sovereignty*, edited by Arianto A. Patunru, Mari E. Pangestu and

M. Chatib Basri, pp. 1–13. Singapore: ISEAS – Yusof Ishak Institute, 2018.

Powers, Tom. "Cashing in". *New Mandala* blog, 8 August 2016.

Rodrik, Dani. "Populism and the Economics of Globalization". NBER Working Paper 23559. Cambridge: National Bureau of Economic Research, 2017.

Ray, David and Lili Yan Ing. "Addressing Indonesia's Infrastructure Deficits". *Bulletin of Indonesian Economic Studies* 52, no. 1 (2016): 1–25.

Salim, Wilmar and Siwage Dharma Negara. "Infrastructure Development under the Jokowi Administration: Progress, Challenges and Policies". *Journal of Southeast Asian Economies* 35, no. 3 (2018): 386–401.

Samuelson, Paul A. " 'Response from Paul Samuelson' to 'The Limits of Free Trade', a comment by Avinash Dixit and Gene Grossman on Samuelson's 'Where Ricardo and Mill Rebut and Confirm Agreements of Mainstream Economist Supporting Globalization'. *Journal of Economic Perspectives* 18, no. 3 (Summer 2004): 135–46, *Journal of Economic Perspectives* 19, no. 3 (Summer 2005): 241–44.

Sen, Amartya. "Is Nationalism a Boon or a Curse?". *Economic and Political Weekly*, 16 February 2008.

Warburton, Eve. "Nationalism, Developmentalism and Politics in Indonesia's Mining Sector". In *Indonesia in the New World: Globalisation, Nationalism and Sovereignty*, edited by Arianto A. Patunru, Mari E. Pangestu and M. Chatib Basri, pp. 90–108. Singapore: ISEAS – Yusof Ishak Institute, 2018.

7

TRENDS IN THE MANUFACTURING SECTOR UNDER THE JOKOWI PRESIDENCY
Legacies of Past Administrations

Ari Kuncoro

7.1 INTRODUCTION

Following the introduction of economic reforms in trade and investment in the mid-1980s, manufacturing gradually replaced agriculture as the mainstay of the Indonesian economy. In terms of exports, the sector even edged out oil's monopoly as the top foreign exchange earner. In other words, manufacturing emerged as the driver of development, pushing the country's GDP to grow at an average of about 8 per cent per annum. This trend abruptly ended in 1998 with the onset of the Asian Financial Crisis (AFC). The post-crisis recovery was led by the commodity boom, mainly

This article was first published in *Journal of Southeast Asian Economies* 35, no. 3 (December 2018).

fuelled by the economic expansion in China. The growth of manufacturing, however, remained sluggish and continues to be so — well into the first term of President Joko "Jokowi" Widodo's administration (2014–19).

Despite a number of initiatives taken by the government, reviving the manufacturing sector has proven to be a difficult task. The role of manufacturing as the primary growth-driver has not been replicated in the post-AFC era. Even though, for a while, moderate economic growth of 5.5 per cent per annum could be maintained with the help of the commodity boom which boosted aggregate demand (especially consumption), the end of the boom in 2012 brought the growth rate down to a steady state level of 5 per cent per annum. The current government's recent strategy to improve growth and employment figures is articulated in President Jokowi's campaign platform, known as *Nawacita* (nine priority programmes). One of its main focus areas is the manufacturing sector.

The purpose of this chapter is to assess the performance of the Indonesian manufacturing sector under the Jokowi government. To boost the sector, several policies have been launched by the Ministry of Industry. External factors like infrastructure, government regulations, the structure of effective rate of protection (ERP), and openness are discussed in this chapter, along with the dynamics of structural change and overall growth in the manufacturing sector. The analysis is based on the data from the Annual Manufacturing Surveys of the Central Bureau of Statistic (BPS).

7.2 POLICY OVERVIEW

7.2.1 Pre-2000 Manufacturing Policies

The rise of Indonesian manufacturing can be traced to the introduction of the Investment Law in 1967 and subsequent Law No. 6 concerning Domestic Investment in 1968. One important question that arises is whether Indonesia has (ever) seriously pursued industrial policies. The answer, however, remains unclear. According to Hill (1996), although many planning documents suggest the intention to pursue sector-specific policies, pragmatism eventually prevailed when it faced new realities as Indonesia reverted to pursue broad-based policies.

The most clear broad-based economic reform measures were introduced between 1967 and the mid-1980s, when protectionism and government intervention were pervasive. The priorities of the manufacturing sector were set by the Ministry of Industry, based on strategic importance of individual industries. These included base metals, petrochemicals, and the automotive (local parts) industries. The objective was to use the petrodollar to develop upstream industries in which state-owned enterprises (SOEs) played a major role.

However, when the results proved to be disappointing, the government was forced to introduce policy changes. While the original strategy always hovered between nationalism and pragmatism, the fall in oil prices in 1982 provided sufficient impetus for policymakers to change their approach and move towards a more open, outward-looking economy.

The watershed moment came in 1986 when the government launched a set of unprecedented, across-the-board reforms, starting with the liberalization of the banking sector in 1983, followed by trade and other regulatory reforms. In all, they encompassed four broad categories related to: exchange rate management; monetary and financial policies; fiscal policy; and trade policy and other regulatory reforms.[1]

The second set of economic reforms was introduced between 1991 and 1995. These were mainly related to investment and trade policies, including: abolishing limitations on foreign ownership; reducing trade barriers in the form of tariff cuts; and opening up previously closed sectors to foreign investment. Under the new investment rule, foreign investors were allowed to either form a joint venture with 95 per cent majority equity ownership without any further divestment obligation, or have full ownership (100 per cent stake) of a business entity in Indonesia with the provision that within ten years some unspecified divestment to locals would take place. Another aspect of the deregulation process was the opening up of nine sectors previously closed to foreign investment, including: sea ports; production, transmission and distribution of electricity; telecommunications; shipping; civil aviation; drinking water; railways; nuclear power generation; and mass media.[2]

The completion of the reform sequence with a significant reduction in tariffs took place in 1995. Among the reforms was the introduction of a simpler industrial permit to replace the permanent business permit. Another development was in the area of customs procedures, with the waiving of pre-shipment inspection of imported goods transported by air as well as custom inspection of export goods that moved between bonded zones and entry ports. Duty-free treatment was also extended to capital goods and other imported inputs used in production, provided that at least 30 per cent was used for restructuring or capacity expansion.

Table 7.1 outlines two key performance indicators — growth and GDP share — of Indonesian manufacturing over three decades, starting from 1983 until 2000–03. During this span, the Indonesian economy evolved from an agriculture dependent country into a manufacturing-dominated economy. One major implication of this transition is that the country's growth dynamic depends on the vitality of manufacturing. In fact, the subdued growth in manufacturing post-2000 provides some explanation about the modest growth of GDP since then.

The striking feature of manufacturing growth over the 1983–2003 period is its inverted U-shaped pattern. The peak was reached in 1994–96, after which the slowdown began. During this time, the non-tradable sectors (such as utilities, construction, communication and finance) witnessed rapid expansion. However, the encouraging growth performance abruptly ended in 1998 when the Asian Financial Crisis struck (Figure 7.1).

In the post-AFC period, manufacturing, given its large share in the economy, has been dragging down the country's GDP growth (Tables 7.1 and 7.2).[3] This can be attributed to several factors including: deterioration

TABLE 7.1
GDP Growth, 1983–2003

Sector	1983–93		1994–96		2000–03	
	Growth Rate (%)	GDP Share (%)	Growth Rate (%)	GDP Share (%)	Growth Rate (%)	GDP Share (%)
Agriculture	3.6	20.6	2.7	17.1	3.2	15.2
Mining	2.2	16.9	6.2	8.7	1.4	9.8
Manufacturing	11.9	13.4	13.0	21.7	5.9	24.5
Utilities	12.6	0.6	14.0	1.2	7.4	0.8
Construction	7.7	5.7	13.7	7.6	5.5	6.0
Trade	7.5	15.4	7.9	16.6	4.9	16.4
Transportation	7.0	4.8	6.8	5.7	7.2	3.6
Communication	10.7	0.6	18.9	1.1	14.5	1.7
Finance	8.8	6.7	9.3	8.7	6.2	8.4
Services	5.2	11.1	3.1	8.9	3.4	9.6
GDP	6.1	100.0	7.9	100.0	4.5	100.0

Notes: The manufacturing sector excludes oil and gas.
Source: CEIC Asia Database.

FIGURE 7.1
Growth Dynamic Prior to 2000: Manufacturing and GDP
(% per annum y.o.y)

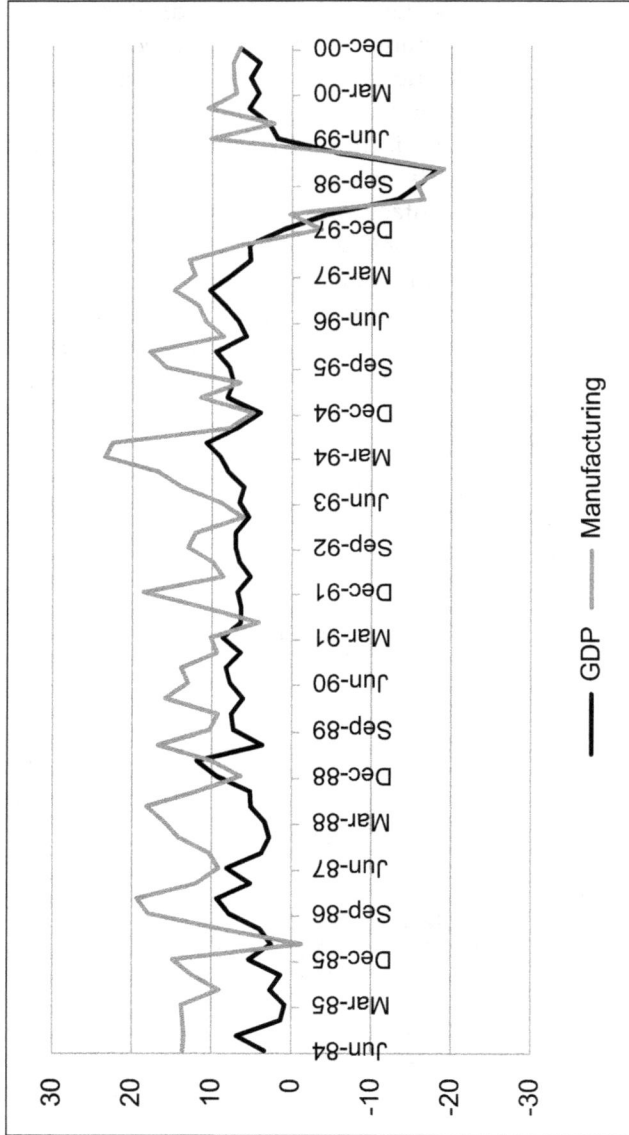

Source: CEIC.

TABLE 7.2
GDP Growth, 2004–17

Sector	2004–09		2010–14		2015–17	
	Growth Rate (%)	GDP Share (%)	Growth Rate (%)	GDP Share (%)	Growth Rate (%)	GDP Share (%)
Agriculture	3.6	14.1	4.2	13.7	3.8	13.7
Mining	1.3	8.9	2.6	10.1	–0.5	10.1
Manufacturing	4.3	24.9	6.4	18.9	4.7	18.9
Utilities	8.7	0.7	6.7	1.1	2.7	1.1
Construction	7.7	6.1	7.2	9.3	6.0	9.3
Trade	6.2	17.0	6.3	16.7	3.9	16.7
Transportation	5.5	3.7	7.4	3.6	7.5	3.6
Communication	26.2	3.4	10.7	4.0	9.4	4.0
Finance	6.9	9.3	7.5	3.6	8.1	3.6
Services	6.0	9.3	6.3	13.6	5.0	13.6
GDP	5.5	100.0	5.7		5.0	

Notes: Manufacturing sector excluding oil and gas.
Source: CEIC Asia Database.

of business climate; labour market rigidity; and competition from low-cost producers such as China. The exchange rate increase due to the commodity boom between 2005 and 2012 may have also played a role.

7.2.2 Post-2000 Manufacturing Performance

The pre-2000 period was marked by comprehensive and across-the-board deregulation that led to rapid expansion of the manufacturing sector. The scale and the pace of deregulation has, however, not been replicated in the post-2000 period.

During the Abdurrahman Wahid (Gus Dur) presidency, manufacturing enjoyed a short burst of recovery from 2000 to 2002. The impeachment of Gus Dur brought Megawati to power in 2001, and manufacturing, once again, experienced a rather big resurgence from 2003 to mid-2004. This was, unfortunately, followed by a downward trend (Figure 7.2). Whether this was the result of inadequate planning on the part of the administration, or just a normal recovery trend remains unclear. It is interesting to note that this period also coincided with the complex decentralization and local democratization processes in Indonesia. It is widely known that entry into political offices is an expensive affair in the country. For instance, to

FIGURE 7.2
Growth Dynamic after 2000: Manufacturing and GDP
(% per annum y.o.y)

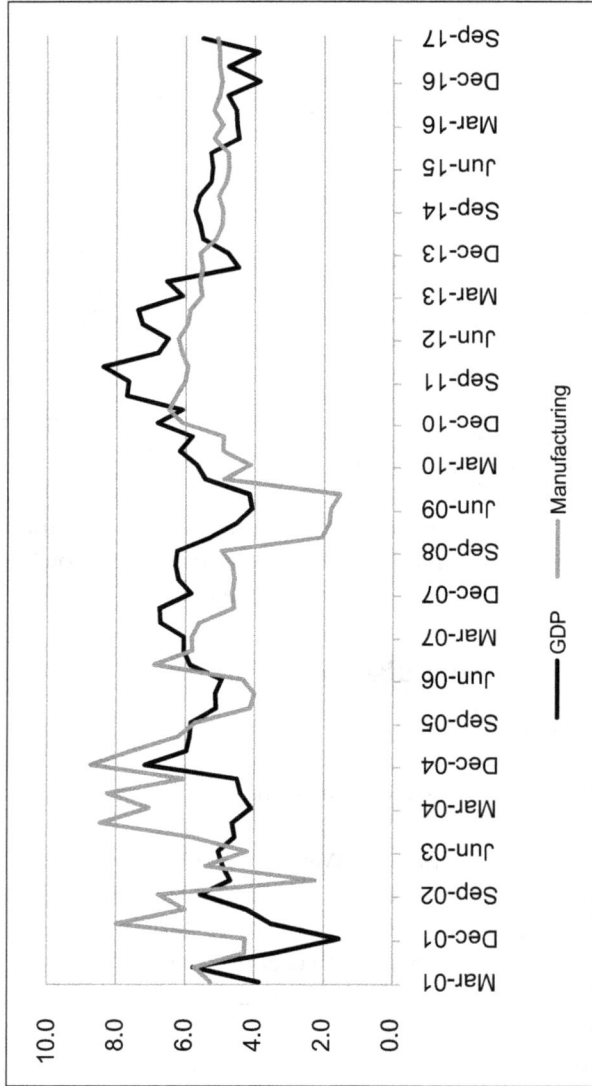

Source: CEIC.

stand for election for the post of district head (or *bupati*), a candidate must first be endorsed by a political party (or a coalition of parties). To recover costs or accumulate funding for the next election, incumbent officers can either sell public projects to the highest bidder during their tenure period or rework regulations to extract rent/bribes from the public and/or the business sector.

Under the Susilo Bambang Yudhoyono (SBY) presidency, the urgency for further deregulation had lessened because the commodity boom had provided some boost to the economy in late 2005. However, the boom was short-lived, and by mid-2006, the slow growth phase had resumed. The Global Financial Crisis (GFC) of 2008 only made things worse. The manufacturing growth rate fell to slightly below 2 per cent at the lowest point. The recovery only began in the first quarter of 2010 when Indonesia's annual growth rate reached about 5 per cent, again spurred by a commodity boom. The momentum was lost in mid-2012 as the boom approached its end. Since then, Indonesian manufacturing has been growing at a "steady state" rate of around 5 per cent per annum.

In 2007, the SBY administration outlined a strategy to revive the sector. Indonesia's Law no. 27 on the long-term development plan for the 2005–25 period (Rencana Pembangunan Jangka Panjang (RPJP) Nasional 2005–2025) reaffirms manufacturing as an engine of growth to improve the country's competitiveness. The main objectives stated in the law include: improving efficiency; modernizing; and increasing the value-added of the manufacturing sector. Small and medium enterprises (SMEs) are specifically mentioned as part of the manufacturing "value chain". At least at the planning document level, this is a major departure from the traditional approach of categorizing economic activities into "sectors"; now sectors are being seen as interrelated business activities. The plan aims to develop value chains through: product processing; diversification; structural deepening; and vertical integration by strengthening inter-industry relations with supporting and complementary industries. It also recognizes the importance of factors external to manufacturing, such as institutional and infrastructure issues. All these developments seem to signify the re-emergence of an industrial policy with a specific focus on cultivating an overall conducive environment, and not just empowering specific industries.

Despite the initiatives taken by the government, the performance of manufacturing has continued to be static. After a brief recovery phase following the GFC in 2008, the sector's growth trajectory was practically flat — suggesting a steady state scenario (Figure 7.2). Contrary to what was stated in the 2007 Industrial Blueprint, manufacturing was neither a driver of the economic growth nor a significant employment creator in the country. This trend continued well into the last quarter of 2014 when Jokowi took office.

7.3 MANUFACTURING UNDER THE JOKOWI ADMINISTRATION: THE *NAWACITA*

The overall vision of *Nawacita* is "sovereignty, self-reliance, and strength through mutual cooperation". It, in a way, shows the path that the country must follow to improve the welfare of its people. For example, the *Nawacita* heavily focuses on strengthening national security to sustain Indonesia's economic independence. Its other objectives include: making the country more equitable, democratic and law-abiding; improving the quality of life for all Indonesian people; making the nation more economically competitive; and preserving Indonesian culture and identity.

The Jokowi administration acknowledges that the country's problems arise from the supply-side factors of the economy. Recent developments related to depreciation of the Indonesian currency and growth slowdown demonstrate the country's vulnerability to external shocks. Prudent macroeconomic management, a flexible exchange rate, external credit worthiness and assistance from development partners have helped to mitigate the impact. Until 2012, the commodity boom had masked the country's supply-side weaknesses. In the longer run, however, the country needs to improve its productivity.

Manufacturing plays a central role in Jokowi's multidimensional development strategy. This includes: (1) security in food, energy, power, maritime and marine development; (2) a human development dimension based on education, health, housing, and national character development; and (3) a regional equity dimension encompassing actions to foster greater equity in opportunity and incomes between villages, border areas, and the country's eastern and western regions.

The Jokowi administration's blueprint on manufacturing development is based on the Law no. 27 (2007), under which manufacturing is still considered vital for the country's growth and development. In particular, the development of inter-sectoral relationships between agriculture, manufacturing and services is given high priority. While the plan is very detailed, the problem lies in finding the right instruments and targeting mechanisms.

In terms of the openness of manufacturing, too, a downward trend has been observed; although, a slight improvement was noted in the third year of the Jokowi presidency (Figure 7.4). Whether or not this was the result of the government's response policy "packages" is hard to tell. In fact, improvement in the international commodity market may have also been a contributing factor. So far, the government has introduced a total of fourteen response packages, indirectly signalling its serious intent to improve the supply-side factors of the economy (Figure 7.3). The packages, in general, constitute a mix of supply side reforms and short-term stimulus

FIGURE 7.3
Government Packages

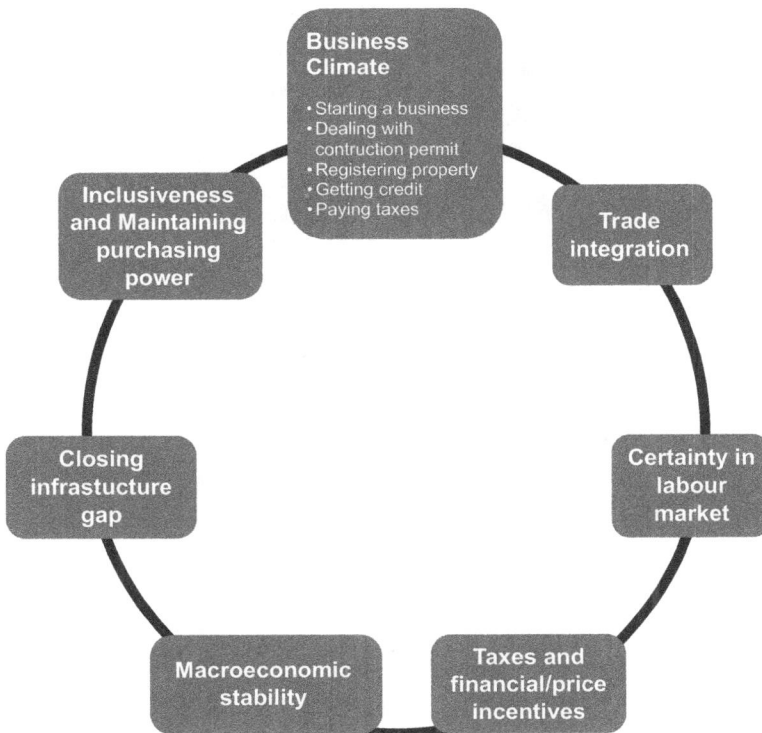

FIGURE 7.4
Export and Import Dynamic (% per annum y.o.y)

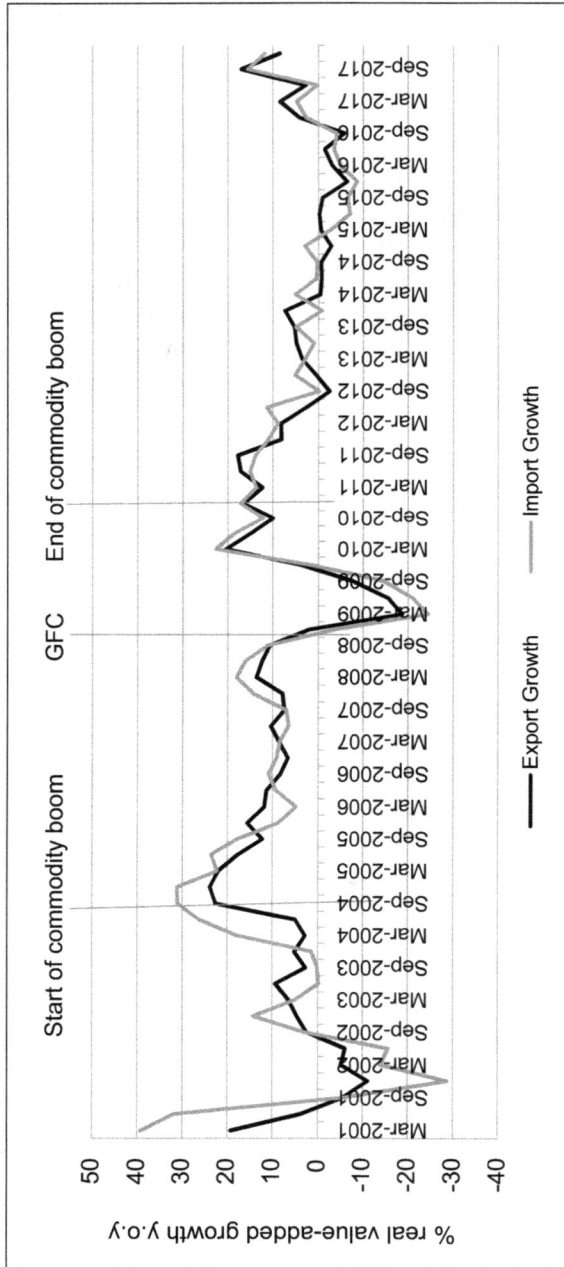

Source: CEIC.

measures. However, unlike the large-scale reforms of the mid-1980s, the policy packages are more like a wish list without a coherent grand strategy (Hill 2016). Consequently, implementation and enforcement remain the biggest challenges.

Recent data suggest that while the commodity boom improved the sector's overall export growth (Figure 7.4), it may also have reduced the incentive to export certain goods like chemicals, cements and machinery, given the services boom in the domestic market (Figure 7.5). This is similar to the Dutch disease phenomenon observed in the 1970s and 1980s.

With regard to sectoral composition, one interesting feature of the manufacturing sector is the dominance of food processing. Since 2012, food and beverage have accounted for the largest share in manufacturing. In 2017, the figure stood at 31.5 per cent, and the share is likely to increase even further in the future (Table 7.3 and Figure 7.6). Textiles and garments also appear to be witnessing accelerated growth (Table 7.3 and Figure 7.7). Transportation equipment (accounting for 9.6 per cent of the manufacturing share) and chemicals (8.1 per cent) occupy the second and third places respectively, but both exhibit declining growth (Table 7.3 and Figure 7.9).

TABLE 7.3
Distribution of Value-Added (% of total manufacturing value-added)

	2012	2013	2014	2015	2016	2017
Food & beverages	26.3	26.4	27.2	27.8	28.9	31.5
Tobacco	4.1	4.3	4.3	4.5	4.3	3.8
Textiles and garments	6.5	6.5	6.2	5.6	5.5	5.6
Wood and wood products	1.2	1.3	1.3	1.3	1.3	1.2
Leather, shoes	3.3	3.2	3.3	3.1	3.0	3.0
Paper and printing	3.9	3.7	3.6	3.6	3.6	3.3
Chemicals and pharmacy	8.7	8.2	8.4	8.3	8.9	8.1
Rubber and plastics	3.9	4.0	3.7	3.9	3.5	3.5
Non-metallic	3.5	3.5	3.6	3.5	3.5	3.4
Basic metals	3.7	3.8	4.0	4.0	3.8	3.9
Electronics	9.6	9.6	9.9	10.2	10.0	9.6
Machinery	1.3	1.4	1.4	1.5	1.4	1.5
Transport equipment	9.1	9.7	9.9	9.5	9.5	9.6
Furniture	1.2	1.2	1.2	1.2	1.2	1.2
Others	0.8	0.9	0.9	0.8	0.8	0.7

Source: CEIC.

FIGURE 7.5
Manufacturing Export Growth (% per annum)

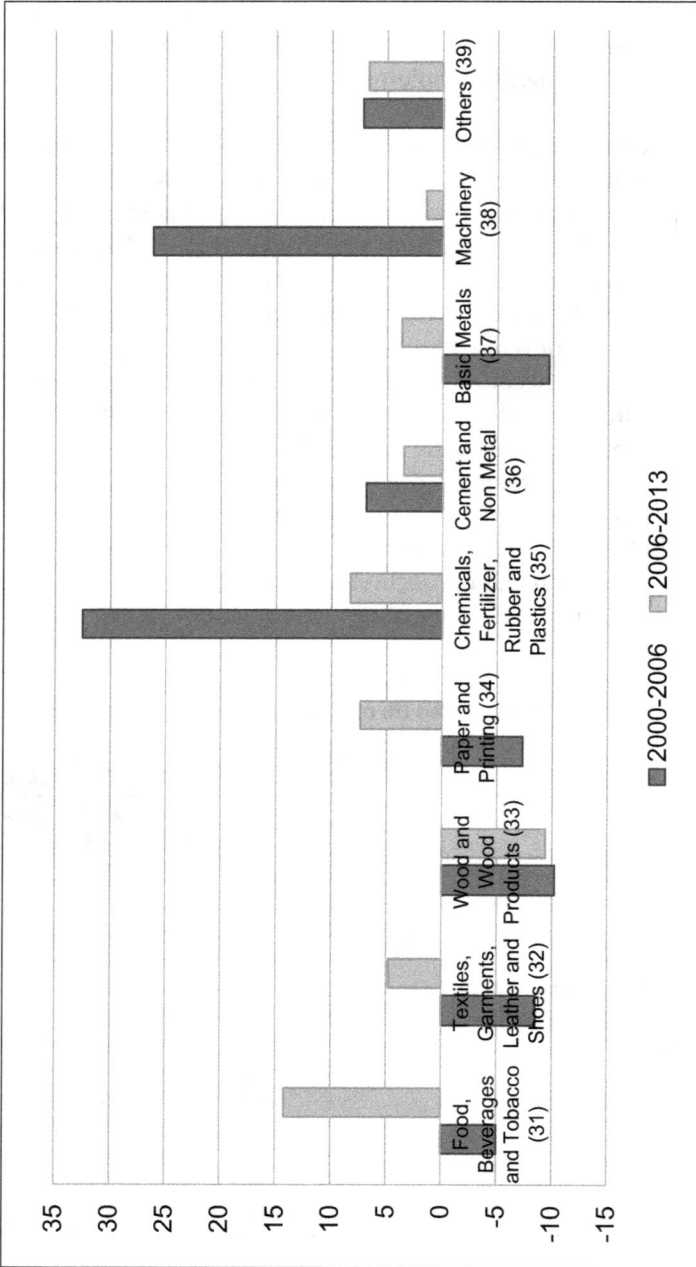

Source: Author's calculation based on data from annual manufacturing surveys (various years).

FIGURE 7.6
Food and Beverage Sector Growth (% y.o.y)

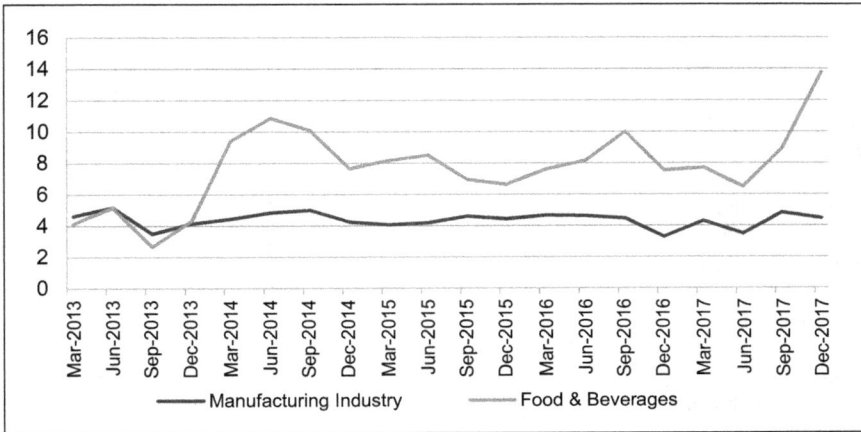

Source: CEIC.

FIGURE 7.7
Textiles and Garments Sector Value-Added Growth (% y.o.y)

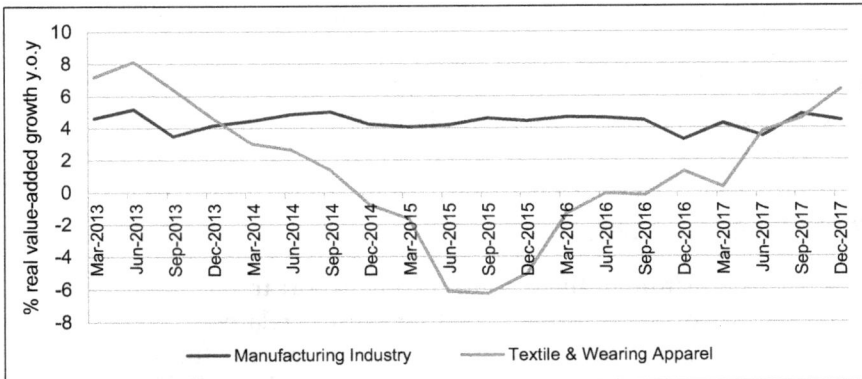

Source: CEIC.

TABLE 7.4
Value-Added Growth (%)

	2013	2014	2015	2016	2017
Food & beverages	4.3	7.6	6.6	7.5	13.8
Tobacco	10.1	3.6	11.1	−1.3	−7.6
Textiles and garments	4.6	−0.8	−5.1	1.3	6.4
Wood and wood products	6.9	4.3	5.8	6.2	−2.7
Leather, shoes	2.1	6.4	−1.8	−1.5	4.9
Paper and printing	−2.0	2.8	2.4	4.0	−4.5
Chemicals and pharmacy	−1.9	6.2	3.9	11.1	−5.5
Rubber and plastics	7.4	−3.9	8.5	−6.1	3.1
Non-metallic	3.4	7.5	3.7	3.4	1.6
Basic metals	9.2	7.8	3.9	−0.3	7.0
Electronics	4.4	7.5	7.4	1.6	0.3
Machinery	6.4	6.8	14.4	−4.5	9.5
Transport equipment	11.1	6.5	−0.2	3.3	5.4
Furniture	4.3	3.6	3.3	1.2	3.8
Others	11.4	3.0	1.2	−3.4	−2.2

Source: CEIC.

It is interesting to note that apart from food and beverage, almost all other groups are practically in a "steady state" situation.

In terms of growth, transportation equipment has been on a downward trend, reflecting the weakening demand since the end of the commodity boom in 2012. However, a slight improvement was seen in late 2017 (Table 7.3 and Figure 7.8). Computers, electronics and optics have performed even worse (Figure 7.9).[4]

7.3.1 Trends in Export

One striking feature of the manufacturing export trend is that it mimics the structure of value added. Starting with a relatively modest share in 1991 (12.1 per cent), food processing still retains the largest share (34.7 per cent in 2015) of total manufacturing exports. This is indicative of Indonesia's stagnant (if not declining) involvement in international production networks (Ando and Kimura 2013). The large share of food also sheds light on the country's "easy approach" to export markets. The second largest share is that of machinery, although it has never exceeded

FIGURE 7.8
Transportation Equipment Sector Value-Added Growth (% y.o.y)

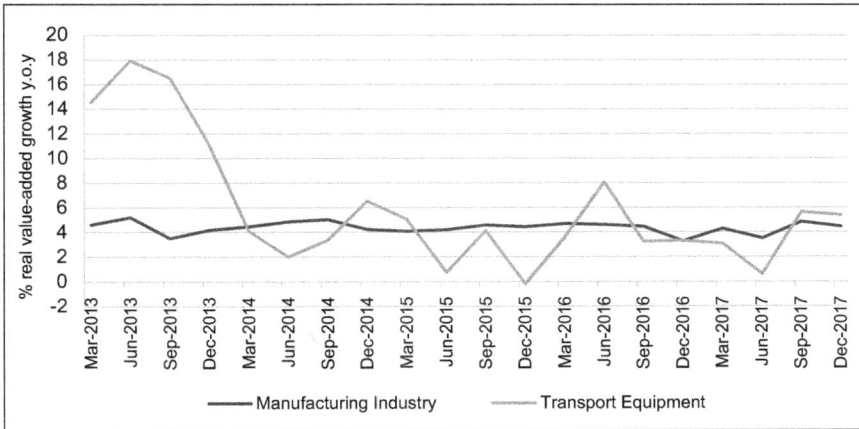

Source: CEIC.

FIGURE 7.9
Computer, Electronic and Optics Sector Real Value-Added Growth (% y.o.y)

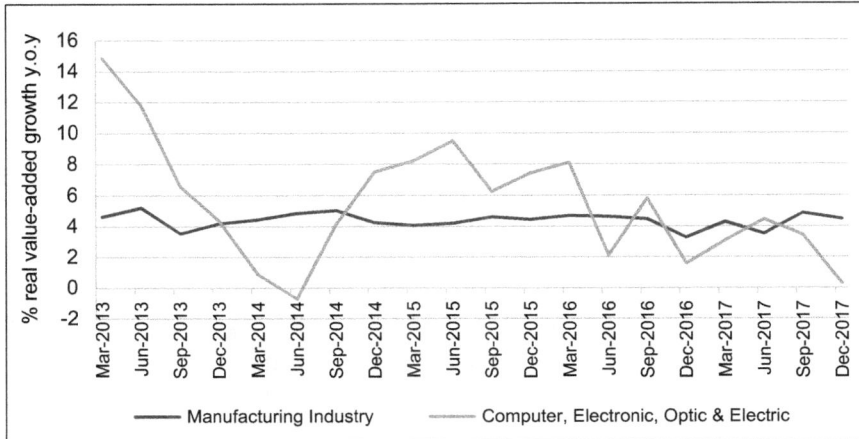

Source: CEIC.

20 per cent (Table 7.5). This reflects the growing importance of Indonesia, especially Java, as the export hub for Japanese automakers specializing in low to medium end vehicles (Aswicahyono, Hill and Narjoko 2010). Chemicals have been relegated to third place.

7.3.2 Product Evolution[5]

Table 7.6 highlights the performance of export goods at the five-digit ISIC level.[6] To be included in this list, an industry must have at least a 5 per cent share in the respective two-digit ISIC industry category. The table shows the top four foreign exchange earners (food, machinery, chemicals, and textiles) specifically for the 1996–2015 period to highlight the impact of the Asian Financial Crisis. Finally, the Herfindahl index (the sum of squared share of exports within the respective two-digit ISIC industrial category) indicates the concentration of a particular industry at the five-digit level within its two-digit ISIC category. The larger the number, the more concentrated are the exports.

The Herfindahl index is increasing for food, which means that food exports are increasingly based on fewer products. In fact, the exports are dominated by cooking palm oil followed by *kretek* cigarettes. Textiles are dominated by garments, which are more connected to international value chains. The share of garment exports in the industry (ISIC 32) was 24 per cent in 2015, compared to only 12.4 per cent in 1996. It should also be taken into account that the Herfindahl index is decreasing for textiles

TABLE 7.5
Distribution of Manufacturing Exports
(percentage of total manufacturing export)

	Food	Textiles	Wood	Paper	Chemicals	Non Metallic	Basic Metals	Machinery
1991	12.1	21.3	36.9	3.6	13.9	1.6	2.8	6.4
1996	11.7	29.2	19.3	2.4	14.1	1.5	2.5	18.0
2006	21.1	17.0	19.1	6.0	19.8	2.6	2.6	19.8
2010	16.2	13.9	15.0	5.7	35.7	0.6	5.6	15.6
2013	32.9	13.6	13.2	5.2	20.1	3.4	2.4	17.6
2014	35.6	11.9	12.7	4.1	18.1	4.7	3.9	18.2
2015	34.7	14.0	13.0	4.6	16.4	3.4	3.7	19.3

Source: Calculated from Industrial Surveys, various years.

TABLE 7.6
Manufacturing Export Performers

Food, Beverages and Tobacco (ISIC 31)					
1996			*2015*		
Industry	*Code*	*(%)*	*Industry*	*Code*	*(%)*
Frozen seafood	31144	22.3	Crude palm oil	31151	32.6
Cooking (palm) oil	31154	11.3	Cigarette *kretek*	31420	14.9
Crude palm oil	31151	11.1	Coconut cooking oil	31151	6.4
Coffee peeling	31163	5.7	Animal food	31281	6.3
Chocolate peeling	31164	5.5	Granulated sugar	31181	3.8
Rice Mill	31262	5.4	Palm cooking oil	31154	2.7
Herfindahl Index = 0.091			Herfindahl Index = 0.142		

Textiles, Garments, Leather and Footwear (ISIC 32)					
1996			*2015*		
Industry	*Code*	*(%)*	*Industry*	*Code*	*(%)*
Weaving	32114	28.4	Garments	32210	24.0
Fibber Preparation	32111	27.3	Knitting	32130	11.7
Garments	32210	12.4	Printing	32116	8.4
Sporting Shoes	32412	11.8	Finishing	32113	7.4
Knitting	32130	9.9	Sporting shoes	32412	7.1
Herfindahl Index = 0.195			Herfindahl Index = 0.101		

Chemicals, Fertilizer, Rubber and Plastic Products					
1996			*2015*		
Industry	*Code*	*(%)*	*Industry*	*Code*	*(%)*
Crumb Rubber	35523	38.2	Crumb Rubber	35523	15.2
Chlorine and Alkaline	35511	15.5	Non-organic gas	35112	13.1
Other non-organic	35119	7.5	Chlorine and Alkaline	35131	11.9
Fertilizer	35112	6.7	Packaging plastic	35606	10.6
Consumer houseware	35695	6.6	Plastic sheet	35511	4.7
Herfindahl index = 0.000142			Herfindahl index = 0.078		

Machinery, Electronic, Transportation and Scientific Equipment					
Industry	*Code*	*(%)*	*Industry*	*Code*	*(%)*
Radio and television	38321	51.8	Automotive component	38433	18.1
Recording media	38324	13.0	Motor vehicle	38431	15.9
Motorcycle	38441	6.7	Vacuum tube	38321	5.4
			Semi-conductor	38321	4.0
			Dry-cell battery	38392	4.0
Herfindahl index = 0.293			Herfindahl index = 0.072		

Source: Calculated from the Annual Manufacturing Surveys, Central Bureau of Statistics.

and garments, which suggests that exports in this sector are now more diversified.

In the case of chemicals, crumb rubber has occupied the top spot throughout the study period. Its share, however, fell from 38.2 per cent in 1996 to 15.2 per cent in 2015. A shifting pattern is also apparent in other parts of the industry. Packaging plastic material and plastic sheets are now part of the top five exported products in the chemicals category. Meanwhile, other non-organic chemicals and consumer houseware had fallen out of the top five in 2015. The Herfindahl index for chemicals has been increasing, which suggests that the industry's exports (ISIC 35) are now more concentrated.

For machinery, the industry is now dominated by the automotive component and motor vehicle industries. Their export shares in 2015 were 18.1 and 15.9 per cent respectively. The Herfindahl index is decreasing, implying that exports are now more diversified than in 1996.

7.3.3 Business Environment

7.3.3.1 Competitiveness Index. Indonesia has moved up the competitiveness ladder (from the forty-first position in 2016 to thirty-sixth in 2017). The new overall ranking is driven mainly by the improvement of constituent rankings like market size (ninth) and robust macroeconomic environment (twenty-sixth). But in terms of others dimensions, Indonesia remains relatively behind. With regard to innovation, the country ranks thirty-first. It fares even worse in technological readiness (eightieth).[7] Similarly, although Indonesia is the world's third largest user of social media platforms like Facebook and Twitter, the use of the Internet to contact customers by the business sector remains limited (World Economic Forum 2017).

7.3.3.2 Ease of Doing Business. Indonesia has improved its standing in the Ease of Doing Business ranking, moving from the 109th position in 2015 to the 72nd place in 2017. Tasks like starting a business, dealing with construction permits, registering property, getting credit, paying taxes, enforcing contracts, and resolving insolvency have all improved in the third year of the Jokowi presidency (Figure 7.10). Cross-border trading, however, continues to be problematic — a symptom of poor logistics. Figure 7.11 shows that the overall logistic performance index (LPI) value in 2016 was not significantly higher compared to the figure recorded in 2007.

FIGURE 7.10
Ease of Doing Business Index

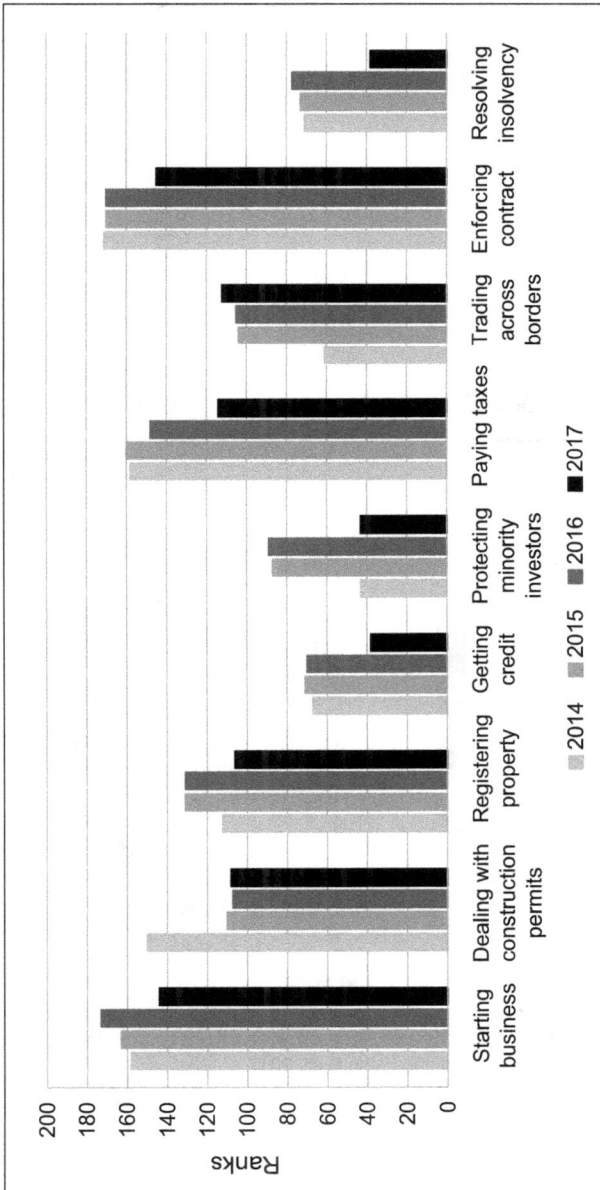

Source: Ease of Doing Business, World Bank 2017.

FIGURE 7.11
Logistic Performance Index

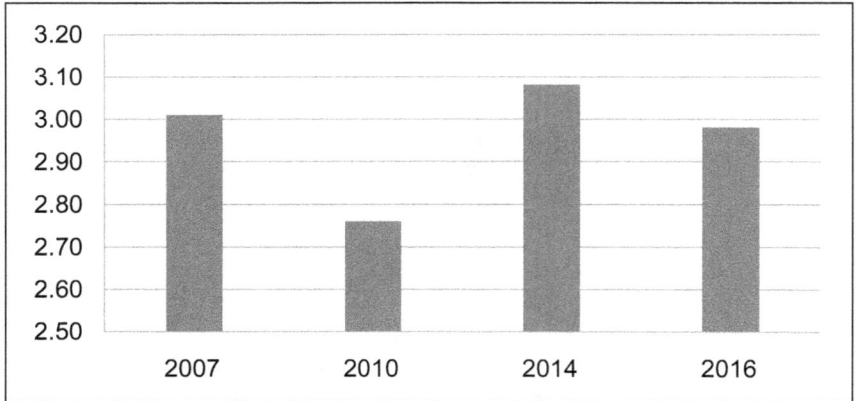

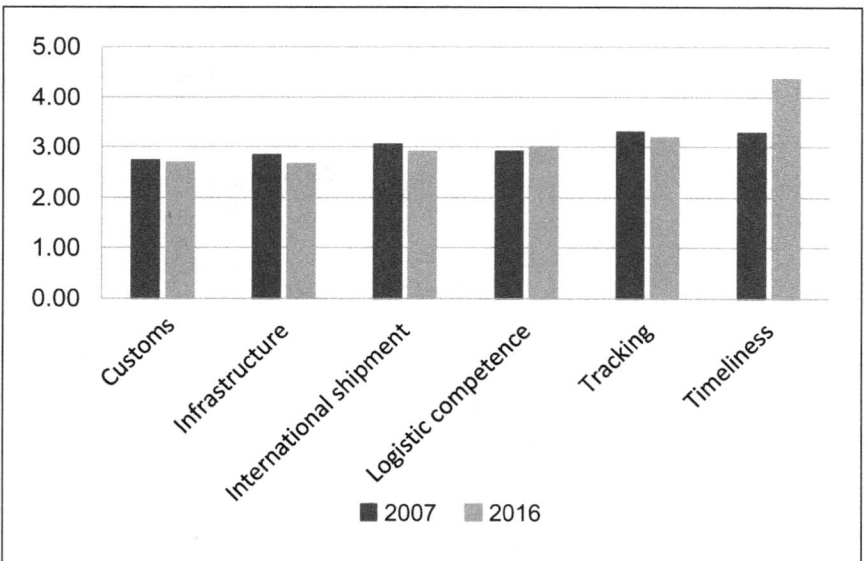

Source: Logistic Performance Index, World Bank 2017.

7.3.3.3 Tariffs. As far as tariffs are concerned, Amiti and Konings (2005) and Widodo (2008) have found that Indonesia's effective rate of protection (ERP) was low, at least until 2005. A recent study by Marks (2017), however, paints a completely different picture. Using a much more elaborate procedure, the study shows that both the nominal rate of protection (NRP) and ERP have actually been increasing. It appears that the worsening of current account balance deficit has tempted the government to resort to non-tariff measures. This started in the SBY era, and appears to have continued in the Jokowi presidency as well. In fact, Indonesia has more non-tariff measures in place compared to India and China (Table 7.7).

Marks (2017) also calculates the impact of non-trade regulations in Indonesia on NRP and ERP (Table 7.8).[8] Indonesia had fewer non-tariff measures (NTMs) in 2008 as compared to 2015 (Figure 7.12). The introduction of NTMs increased dramatically in 2012 under the SBY administration. Things have not changed much under Jokowi either. The only difference is that under SBY, NTMs were directed more towards limiting imports (to reduce the current account deficit), while under Jokowi, the measures have been implemented to curb the export of some essential commodities to stabilize domestic consumer prices. Marks' (2017) calculations regarding the impact of the increase in the number of NTMs on NRP and ERP are shown in Table 7.8.

One major NTM instrument that is often used to promote the development of Indonesia's manufacturing sector is local content requirement (LCR). The strategy was stated in Law No. 27, 2007 (under the SBY administration) in a rather disguised message. LCR is thought to prevent firms from acquiring essential imported inputs, thereby facilitating the development of the domestic sector. This measure, however, has not been implemented efficiently in the country. Firms can still import inputs from abroad by bribing some lower level officials. Also, manufacturing exporters tend to import proportionally higher inputs relative to non-exporters (Figure 7.13). At the same time, they also pay higher bribes, especially after 2006, reflecting the need to get around various NTMs, including the local contents scheme that has been put in place to stem imports (Figure 7.14). But the bribe amount appears to be relatively small (less than 1 per cent of the total costs), and can either be absorbed into profits or passed on to consumers (Figure 7.15).

TABLE 7.7
Non-tariff Measures

	Indonesia	China	Malaysia	Thailand	India
Bailout/state aid measure	6	6	1	1	19
Competitive devaluation	0	0	0	0	0
Consumption subsidy	0	1	0	0	0
Export subsidy	3	11	2	1	25
Export taxes or restriction	18	10	1	2	24
Import ban	6	3	1	0	6
Import subsidy	0	0	1	1	2
Intellectual property protection	0	2	0	0	0
Investment measure	13	17	4	3	12
Local content requirement	15	9	4	0	107
Migration measure	2	1	2	1	2
Other non-tariff barriers	25	9	3	1	12
Other service sector measure	4	3	0	0	1
Public procurement	9	7	0	0	13
Quota (including tariff rate quota)	5	7	0	0	2
Sanitary and phytosanitary measure	4	0	0	0	0
State trading enterprise	0	0	0	0	0
State controlled company	2	1	0	0	1
Sub national government measures	0	2	0	0	1
Tariff measures	12	15	3	1	37
Technical barrier to trade	3	1	0	0	0
Trade defence measure	17	45	7	14	135
Trade finance	1	1	2	0	95
Total	115	131	18	22	356

Source: GTA, accessed 2016.

Initially, the overall export orientation of manufacturing was quite low. At its peak, exports reached 14 per cent of the total manufacturing output prior to the AFC, but it has been lower subsequently. The general motivation behind increasing the NRP and ERP on manufacturing was to reduce the incentive to export and focus more on the domestic market. Figure 7.15 suggests that the export orientation declined significantly after 2006. This could have been caused, partly, by the Dutch disease phenomenon associated with the commodity boom. The second dip began in 2014, most likely because of the increase in NTMs since 2012. The blame, in this

TABLE 7.8
Nominal and Effective Rate of Protection

	(NRP)			(ERP)		
	2008	2015	%	2008	2015	%
Food and beverages	3	10.6	253.3	2.7	13.9	414.8
Textiles, garments and leathers	0.7	3.7	428.6	1.3	3.4	161.5
Wood products	−0.1	0.6	700.0	1.5	1.2	−20.0
Paper products	0.7	1.4	100.0	1.5	1.7	−13.3
Chemicals	1.7	3.2	188.2	18	24.2	−34.4
Oil refining and LNG	0.2	0.4	100.0	0.4	0.7	−75.0
Non-metal products	2	4.7	135.0	6.2	11.2	−80.6
Metals and metal products	3.3	6.7	103.0	6.2	11.2	−80.6
Machinery and transport equipment	4.7	7.7	163.8	7.3	10.6	−45.2
Other manufacturing	2.1	4.3	104.8	4.8	8.5	−77.1
Manufacturing	2.7	6.6	144.4	5.1	12.3	141.2
All sectors in the economy	1.1	3.7	236.4	3.8	8.5	123.7

Source: Adapted from Marks (2017).

FIGURE 7.12
Incremental Non-tariff Measures 2002–15

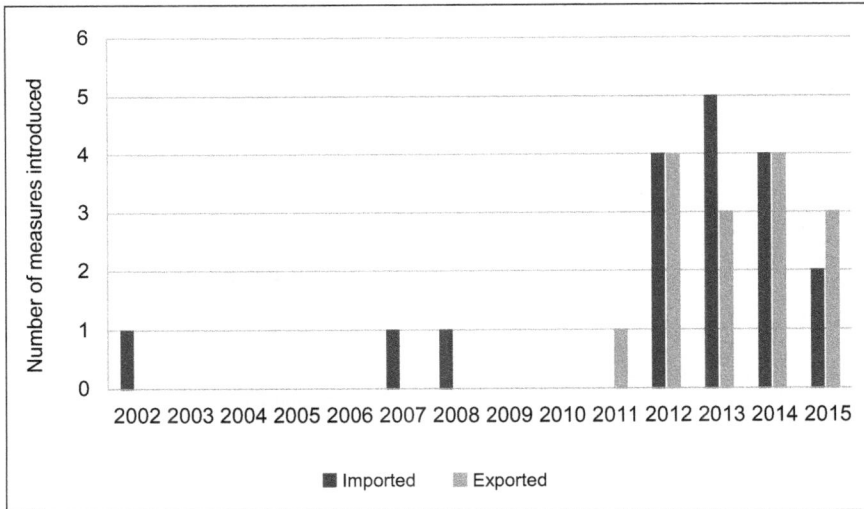

Sources: Marks (2007).

FIGURE 7.13
Imported Inputs as a Percentage of Total Inputs

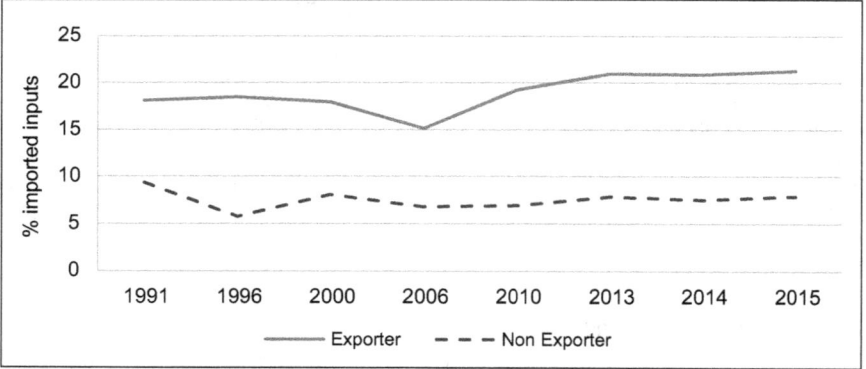

Sources: Calculated from the Annual Manufacturing Surveys, Central Bureau of Statistics.

FIGURE 7.14
Bribe as a Percentage of Total Costs

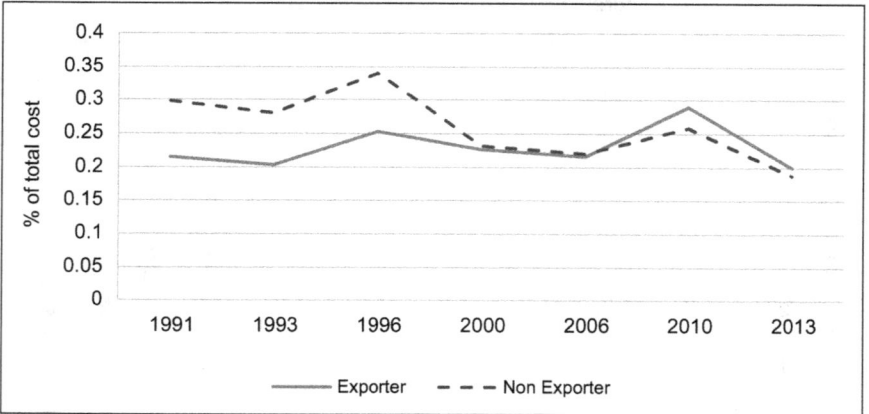

Sources: Calculated from the Annual Manufacturing Surveys, Central Bureau of Statistics.

FIGURE 7.15
Firm Level Percentage of Exported Output

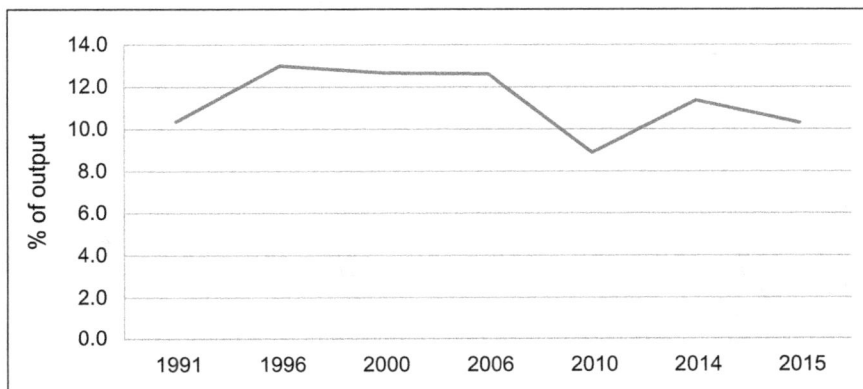

Sources: Calculated from the Annual Manufacturing Surveys, Central Bureau of Statistics.

case, therefore falls on both the SBY administration as well as the Jokowi government. The 2014 decline was not as deep as before, which suggests that firms had paid bribes to circumvent complicated NTMs. Available data, however, are not sufficient to confirm whether this was solely the result of Jokowi's policy. Regardless, it is fair to say that a protectionist stance is on the rise again in Indonesia.

7.3.4 Human Resource

Manufacturing successfully underwent the first phase of export-oriented industrialization following the deregulation measures in the mid-1980s. However, today, the sector primarily specializes in the production of raw materials and a few low value-added goods. In other words, very little has been gained by entering global value chains. In order to move up the ladder to manufacture higher value products, Indonesia must improve the quality of its human resources. It is not surprising to note that Indonesia scored very low in the global talent index — slightly below Vietnam and significantly below Thailand, the Philippines and Malaysia, let alone Singapore (Figure 7.16). This means that excessive reliance on primary and secondary school graduates has to go down, and attaining higher level of education and vocational training needs to be encouraged.

FIGURE 7.16
Global Competitiveness Talent Index

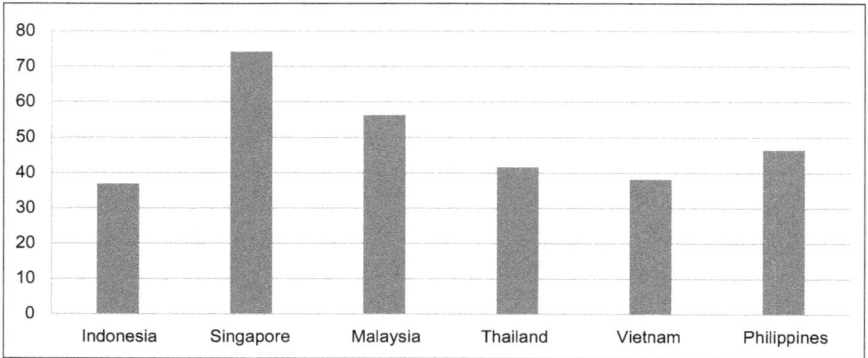

Source: INSEAD (2017).

Many problems have plagued the Indonesian education system. For example, the learning process still relies heavily on recitation and replication of textbook content, while neglecting critical and creative thinking, communication and language skills and logic. Mathematics, one of the fundamentals of logical thinking, is still taught as a memorized subject. One aspect that needs special attention is the quality of teachers. It has often been seen that conceptual mistakes made at the primary level are often repeated at higher levels from one generation of students to another. A national programme for upgrading technical competencies and skills of incumbent teachers/instructors is the need of the hour.

The focus on human resource development is essential because knowledge accumulation through higher educational attainment allows developing countries to jump up the learning curve without having to undergo the lengthy and expensive process of discovery. Indonesia can access ideas and technologies developed elsewhere and put them into practice after some modifications.

7.4 CONCLUSION

In Indonesia, manufacturing has transformed from being the driver of economic growth into a sector that is fully dependent on the growth of domestic demand. The commodity boom in the 2005–12 period created a Dutch disease situation in which a boom in one sector reduced the export incentive in manufacturing, given that domestic demand is readily available.

Currently, manufacturing exports are based on very few products, palm oil being the chief export. There is also evidence that Indonesian manufacturing has not been as successful as its nearest neighbours in exploiting the international value chain. Being more inward-looking, manufacturing now depends on other sectors for generating growth. While some industries — like textiles and automotive — still look promising, to keep the momentum going for manufacturing exports, the country needs additional reforms including: better logistics; fewer non-tariff barriers; and improved human resource quality.

In the initial year following the end of the commodity boom, Indonesia's current account balance deteriorated rapidly. Under the SBY government, the increasing use of the non-tariff measures may have had a nationalistic undertone, but in reality, such barriers were put in place to reduce imports for balance of payment reasons. The Jokowi administration's economic development plan, on the other hand, is contained in the *Nawacita*. The new objective is to find novel sources of growth to complement the dwindling drive of manufacturing and commodity sectors, and provide price and employment stability for the Indonesian people. Under the current government, while Indonesia's investment ratings have improved, the protectionist stance has also started to make a comeback. The overall impact of the reintroduction of non-tariff measures on manufacturing can be seen in the continuously low export orientation of the sector, even after the Dutch disease effect of the commodity boom has started to dissipate.

Notes

1. The reform programmes were designed to: (1) sustain the momentum of long-term economic development by reducing the country's heavy reliance on the oil sector in the government budget and exports; and (2) have a more balanced economic structure moving away from the dominance of the oil sector.
2. One sector that remained closed to foreign investment, despite much expression of interest, was domestic distribution and retail.
3. Using the Granger causality test, manufacturing is found to be the driver of GDP growth before the AFC, but the direction of causality is reversed post-crisis.

4. It is also suggested that the growth of demand for some manufacturing has fallen due to change of the consumption habits of the Indonesian middle class. Consumption is found to be shifting towards leisure and experience, in other words, moving towards dining, travelling and sport. On the other hand, the real income has not increased very much (Kuncoro 2017; Pardede and Zahro 2018).
5. The method used in this section draws heavily from Kuncoro (2018).
6. Information is being updated to account for the latest five-digit manufacturing data which are only available until 2015.
7. As postulated by Braga and Willmore (1991).
8. According to their calculations, effective rate of protection (ERP) fell in 2005 and 2008, but subsequently ERP began to rise again.

References

Amiti, M. and J. Konings. "Trade Liberalization, Intermediate Inputs and Productivity: Evidence from Indonesia". *American Economic Review* 97, no. 5 (2007): 1161–68.

Ando, M. and F. Kimura. "Production Linkage of Asia and Europe via Central and Eastern Europe". *Journal of Economic Integration* 28, no. 2 (2013): 204–40.

Aswicahyono, H., H. Hill and D. Narjoko. "Industrialization after a Deep Economic Crisis: Indonesia". *Journal of Development Studies* 46, no. 6 (2010): 1084–108.

Braga, H. and L. Willmore. "Technological Imports and Technological Effort: An Analysis of Their Determinants in Brazilian Firms". *Journal of Industrial Economics* 39, no. 4 (1991): 421–31.

Hill, Hal. "Indonesia's Industrial Policy and Performance: Orthodoxy Vindicated". *Economic Development and Cultural Change* 1 (1996): 147–74.

INSEAD. *2017 Global Talent Competitiveness Index*, 2017 <www.insead.edu/news>.

Kuncoro, Ari. "Anomali Data Makro dan Mikro". *Kompas.id*, 9 August 2017 <https://kompas.id/baca/opini/2017/08/09/anomali-data-makro-dan-mikro/>.

————. "Development of Exports in Indonesian Manufacturing". In *The Indonesian Economy: Trade and Industrial Policies*, edited by Lili Yang Ing, Gordon H. Hanson and Sri Mulyani Indrawati. London: Routledge, 2018.

Marks, S.V. "Non-Tariff Trade Regulations in Indonesia: Nominal and Effective Rates of Protection". *Bulletin of Indonesian Economic Studies* 53, no. 3 (2017): 333–57.

Pardede, R. and S. Zahro. "Saving not Spending: Indonesia's Domestic Demand Problem". *Bulletin of Indonesian Economic Studies* 53, no. 3 (2017): 233–59.

World Bank. *Doing Business 2017*, World Bank Group Flagship Report, 2017 <www.doingbusiness.org>.

Widodo, T. "Structure of Protection in Indonesian Manufacturing". *ASEAN Economic Bulletin* 25, no. 2 (August 2008): 161–78.

8

INDONESIA'S SERVICES SECTOR
Performance, Policies and Challenges

Titik Anas and Thaliya Wikapuspita

8.1 INTRODUCTION

In any developing country, the services sector plays a crucial role in promoting economic growth. Unfortunately, the competitiveness and productivity levels of Indonesia's services sector are significantly lower than those of the country's peers in the region. The Groningen Growth and Development Centre (GGDC) database, for example, shows that Indonesia's labour productivity figures are very low when compared to other Asian countries. It is therefore not surprising that the country, for some time now, has been a net importer of services. The policies designed to improve the performance of the sector have been relatively restrictive in terms of foreign investment and workers, as reflected by the Foreign Direct Investment (FDI) Policy Index, the Services Trade Restrictiveness Index (STRI), and Indonesia's services liberalization commitment under its Free Trade Agreements.

This chapter evaluates the performance of Indonesia's services sector under the Joko "Jokowi" Widodo presidency and shows that some policies have, in fact, proved to be quite useful. For example, the government established the Creative Economy Agency (Badan Ekonomi Kreatif) with a mandate to facilitate the development of creative economy (which mainly includes the services sector). The policy towards foreign investment has also been relaxed, with the introduction of new "negative list" in 2016 which permits high foreign share in certain industries. In March 2018, the government enacted Regulation no. 20 on foreign workers to simplify recruitment procedures.

However, these policy changes are still quite restrictive when compared to the international best practice, and do not significantly improve the overall performance of the services sector. This chapter shows that such restrictive policies have led to a shortage of capital and professionals, resulting in the poor performance of the services sector in the country.

The chapter is structured as follows. The second section discusses Indonesia's recent services sector performance. The subsequent section focuses on the relationship between newly implemented sectoral policies and the resultant performance. The fourth section highlights the remaining challenges for the sector, while the final section concludes and offers some policy recommendations.

8.2 THE SERVICES SECTOR IN INDONESIA

The contribution of the services sector to Indonesia's economy is quite significant, roughly accounting for 41 per cent of GDP over the past twenty-five years. Figure 8.1 shows that the services sector is the largest sector in the country (41 per cent share of GDP), followed by manufacturing (25 per cent), agriculture (15 per cent), and other industries (19 per cent). However, when compared to other countries, the contribution of Indonesia's services sector is relatively low. Figure 8.1c shows that the world average of services contribution to GDP was 62.6 per cent and the ASEAN average was 46 per cent for the same period. Among the ASEAN-5 nations, Indonesia's services sector is the smallest (Figure 8.1d).

The sector, however, has grown relatively fast in the past few years. Figure 8.1b shows that the sector's growth between the mid-1980s and 1990s was always lower than that of the manufacturing sector. But, since 2003, the trend has reversed. Nevertheless, following the stagnation of the Indonesian economy over the past five years, the services sector has also slowed down, growing at an average of 6.1 per cent.

FIGURE 8.1
Services Sector, Share, Growth, 1992–2016

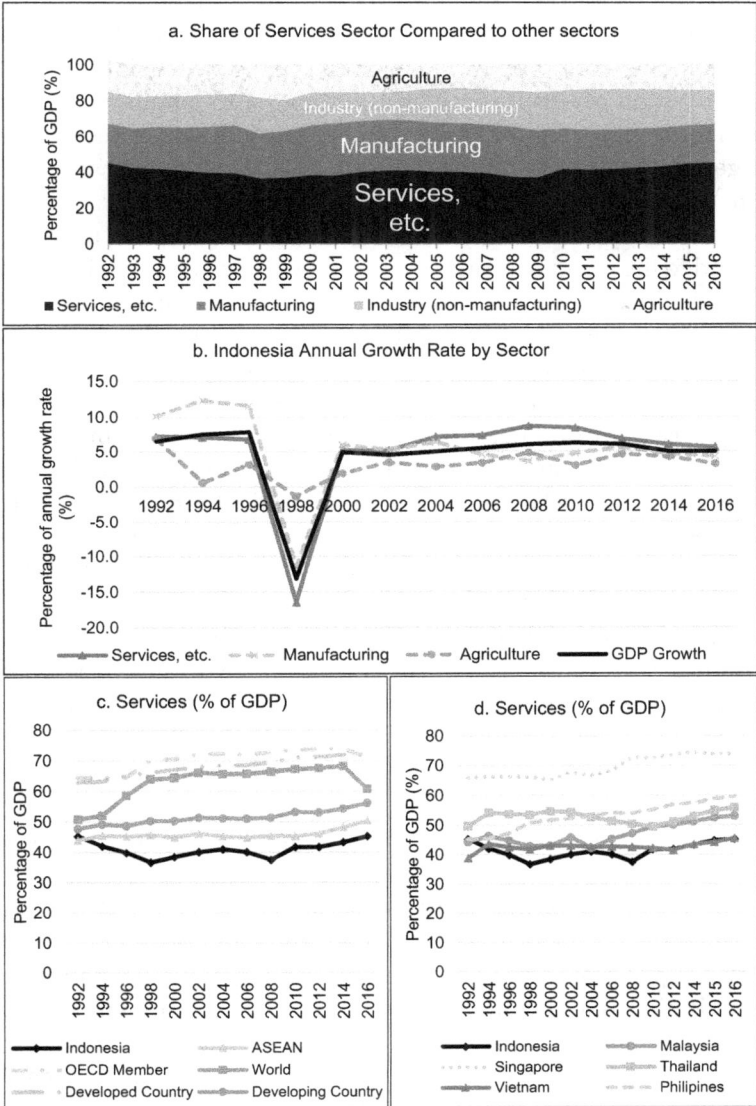

a. Share of Services Sector Compared to other sectors

Agriculture
Industry (non-manufacturing)
Manufacturing
Services, etc.

■ Services, etc.   ■ Manufacturing   ▨ Industry (non-manufacturing)   Agriculture

b. Indonesia Annual Growth Rate by Sector

Services, etc.   Manufacturing   Agriculture   GDP Growth

c. Services (% of GDP)

Indonesia   ASEAN
OECD Member   World
Developed Country   Developing Country

d. Services (% of GDP)

Indonesia   Malaysia
Singapore   Thailand
Vietnam   Philipines

Notes: Last update for share of services to GDP: 1 February 2017 (data 1990–2009) & 22 December 2017 (data 2010–2016)
Source: World Bank (2018*b*).

For Indonesia, the services sector is also important in terms of labour absorption. In the past twenty-five years, 40 per cent of total employment is in the services sector, only slightly lower than the agriculture sector at 42 per cent (Figure 8.2a). The contribution of services sector towards employment is similar to the world trend. However, compared to developed countries, the contribution of services sector in Indonesia to employment is much lower (Figure 8.2b). Similarly, the share of services sector in employment in Singapore, Malaysia and the Philippines is also higher than Indonesia (Figure 8.2c).

Additionally, the services sector has shown lower productivity compared to the manufacturing sector, although it remains higher than that of the agriculture sector. In contrast to manufacturing and agriculture, the productivity of the services sector has consistently increased (Figure 8.3). Global comparison of several services sectors, including construction, trade, hotel and restaurant; transportation, warehouse and communication; financial services, insurance, real estate and business; government services; and personal and social services for a few countries[1] shows that Indonesia's services sector has relatively low labour productivity compared to the other Asian countries. However, there is an exception. In the construction sector, Indonesia's labour productivity is higher than China, India, the Philippines, and Thailand. Similarly, for personal, social and community services, Indonesia's labour productivity is higher than the Philippines and India. However, for financial, insurance, real estate and business services, Indonesia ranks the second lowest. For transport, warehouse and communication, Indonesia ranks eighth. On the other hand, its labour productivity in the trade, hotel and restaurant is the lowest among the ten countries.

A more detailed figure of Indonesia's employment in services sector suggests that the sector is dominated by traditional services such as trade, hotel and restaurant and construction. In 2013, 42 per cent of employment in the services sector was within trade, hotel and restaurants services, 12 per cent in the construction, and 9 per cent in transport and communication (Findlay and Pangestu 2016). The employment in these sectors is dominated by low-skilled workers, majority primary school graduates or less. Figure 8.4 compares the employment in 2005 and 2017 and confirms the same. However, it also shows that there is a significant decline in the number of primary school graduates and increase in the number of senior high school graduates working in these two sectors.

FIGURE 8.2
Services Share in Employment, 1992–2016

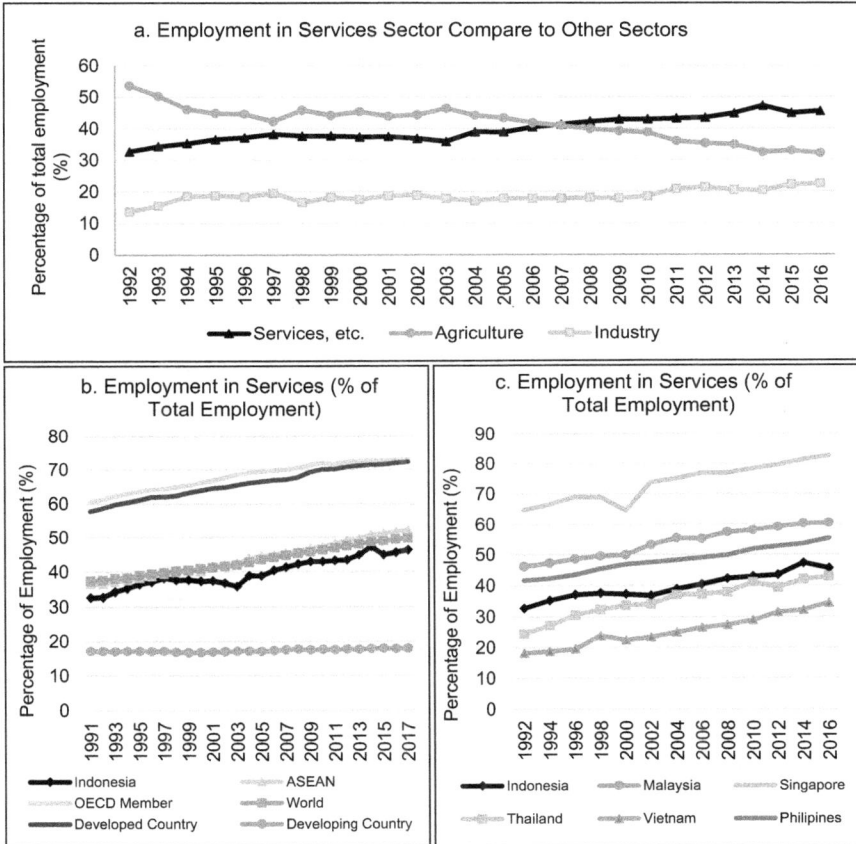

a. Employment in Services Sector Compare to Other Sectors

b. Employment in Services (% of Total Employment)

c. Employment in Services (% of Total Employment)

Source: World Bank (2018*a*).

Figure 8.4 also shows that workers with tertiary education (diploma and university graduates) are largely employed in financial services, real estate, rental and business services which require high skills.

Indonesia is a net importer of services, with an average deficit of US$9 billion per annum in the past twenty-five years. Indonesia's import of services is relatively large compared to the average import by developing countries of 21 per cent (Figure 8.5a). Among ASEAN-6 countries,

FIGURE 8.3
Labour Productivity, 2010–17

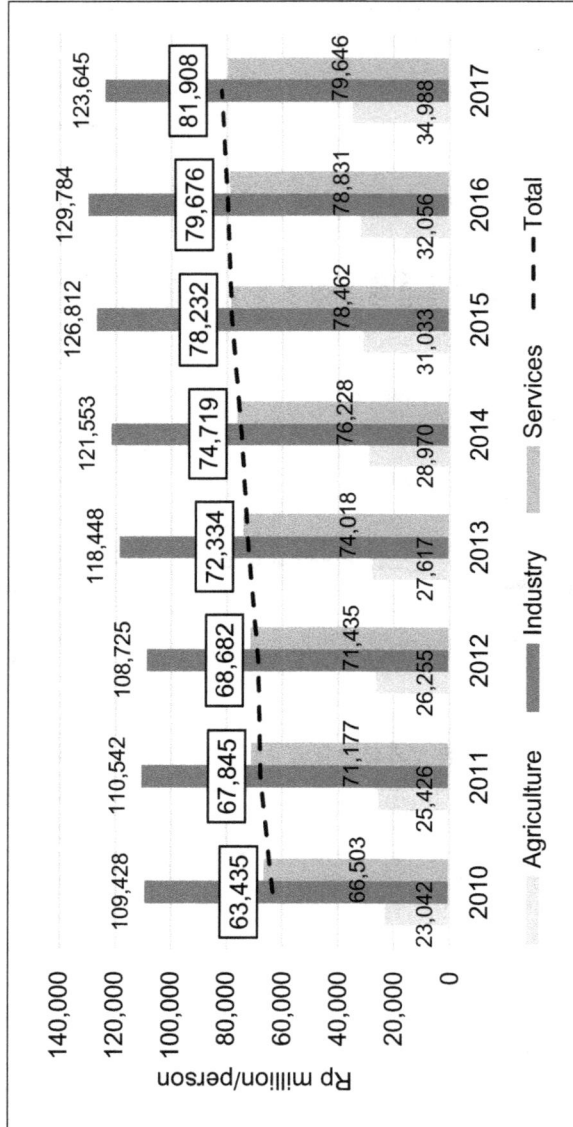

Source: Author's calculation using data from Statistics Indonesia (BPS).

FIGURE 8.4
Employment in Services Sector by Education Level, 2005 and 2017

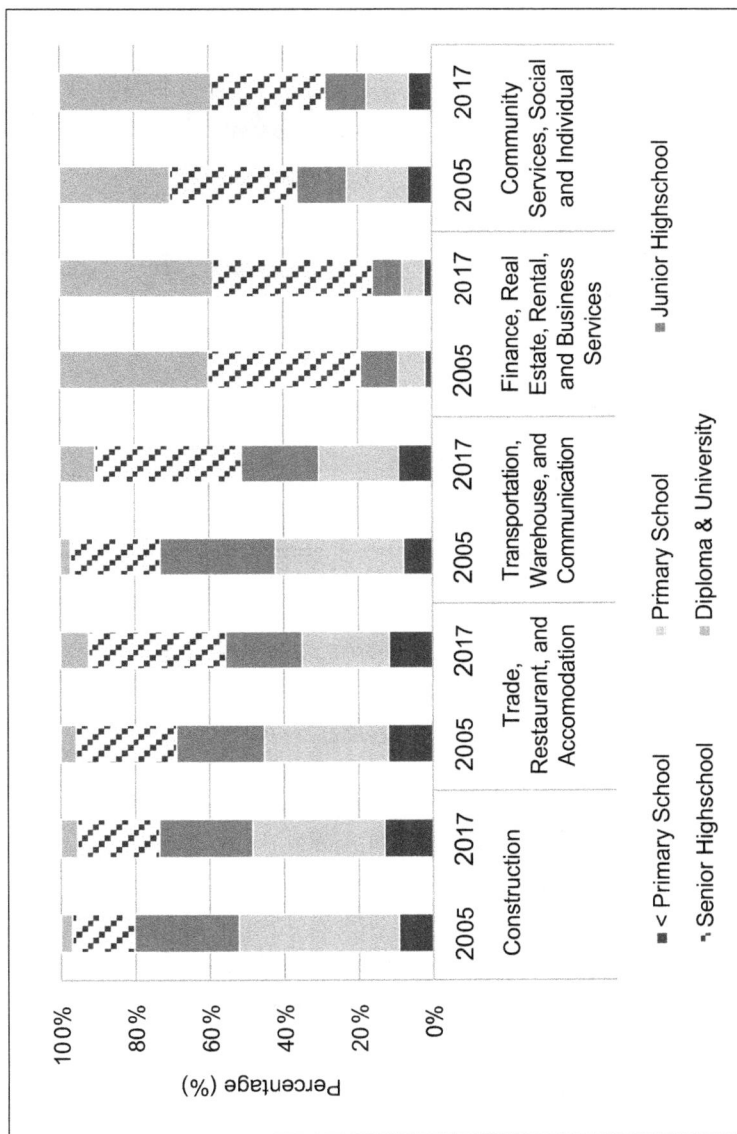

FIGURE 8.5
Services Trade, 1990–2016

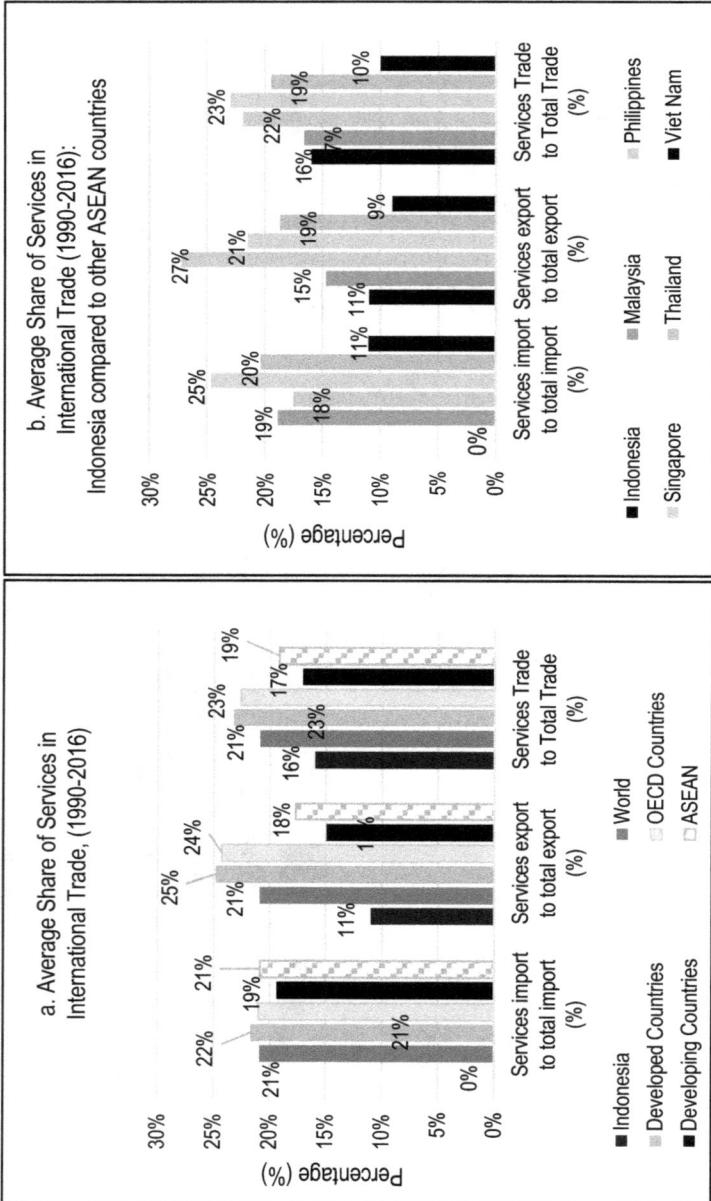

Source: UNCTADstat (2018).

Indonesia is the second largest importer of services after Singapore (Figure 8.5b). On the other hand, export of services is small, about 11 per cent of total exports, slightly higher than Vietnam. The largest trade deficit is in the transport services followed by other services, trade-related Intellectual Property Rights (IPRs), insurance, financial services and manufacturing services. Trade surplus is in remittances, travel and recreational services.

With the rise of global production network and second unbundling,[2] the availability of multi-countries input-output data revealed that the services sector plays more important role in economic activities. Miroudot and Cadestin (2017) showed that the share of services input in the manufacturing sector is considerably high, accounted about 53 per cent (in-house and outsourced) of total input in the manufacturing sector. The authors also suggest that using valued-added method, services exports account for about two-thirds of total export, much higher than what is indicated by the conventional balance of payment figure. The paper also showed that the increasing importance of services in the global value chain (GVC).

Thangavelu, Wenxiao and Oum (2017), using the OECD Trade in Value Added (TIVA) dataset, analyse the increasing importance of the services sector in Asia and Pacific countries. The authors show that the contribution of foreign services added value is higher in several countries. However, for the case of Indonesia, the Philippines and Thailand, the trend seems to be opposite: the contribution of services sector in manufacturing exports in 2011 was lower than 1995 and the share of domestic value added of services sector is also higher.

For the case of Indonesia, Figure 8.6 shows the trade in value-added from 1995 to 2011. It can be seen that in contrast to the global trend, the contribution of services sector in the Indonesian manufacturing exports declined from 27 per cent in 1995 to 25 per cent in 2011.

Also, foreign direct investment (FDI) in the services sector is generally lower than in manufacturing. During the period of 2010–17, total FDI inflows to services sector were US$53 billion, about 26 per cent of total FDI inflows in Indonesia. However, there is an increasing trend in the past four years. In 2017 alone, there was an inflow of US$8.7 billion into the services sector, more than twice the value of 2013 (see Figure 8.7). The largest inflows went to transport, communication and warehouse services, about 41 per cent, followed by inflows to office building, industrial estate and housing services, about 21 per cent.

FIGURE 8.6
Value-Added Exports, 1995–2011

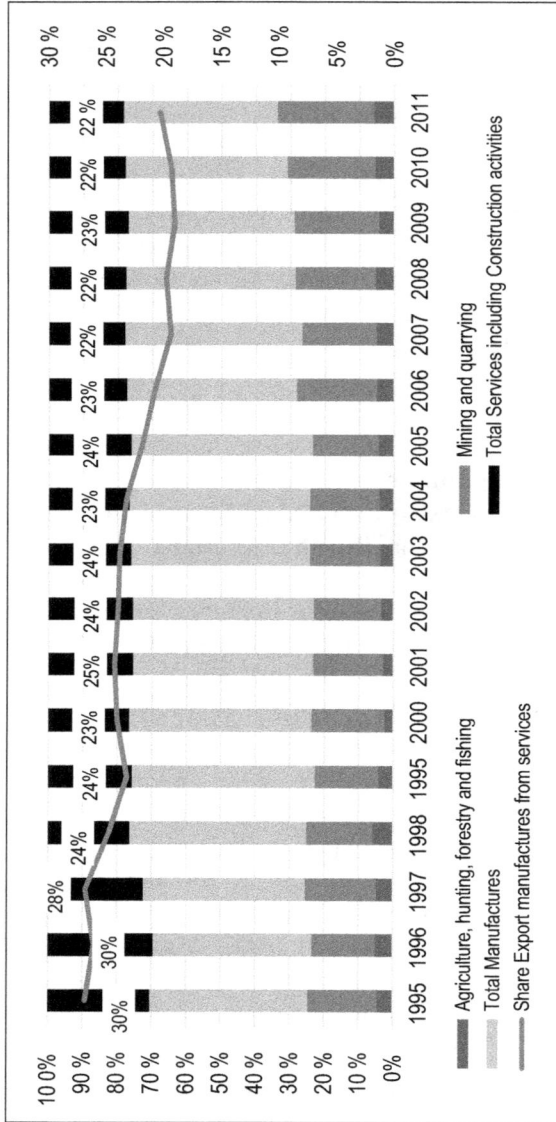

Source: OECD (2016).

FIGURE 8.7
Foreign Direct Investment Inflow, 2010–17 (US$ million)

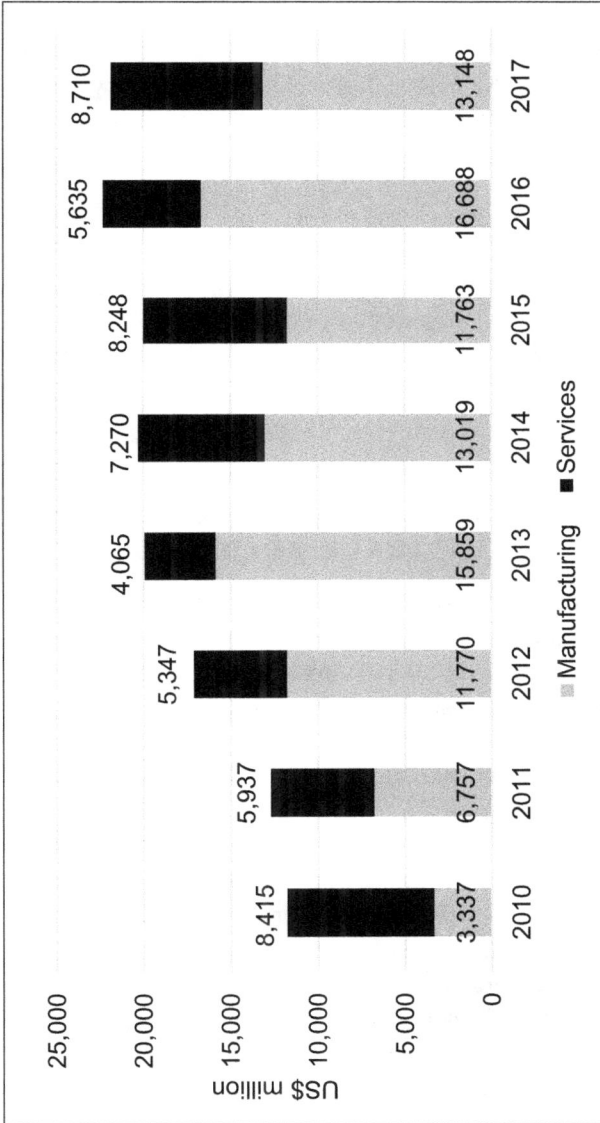

Notes: This data does not include investment in Oil and Gas, Finance, and Insurance Sector.
Source: The Investment Coordinating Board of the Republic of Indonesia (BKPM) (2018).

In terms of employment of foreign workers, the number is relatively small, between 70,000 and 90,000 during the period 2007–16 (Figure 8.8a). Foreign workers mainly came from China, Japan, Korea, India, some of OECD countries, and Malaysia. Most of foreign workers work in trade and services sector (Figure 8.8b). In terms of job types, foreign workers work mainly as high-skilled professional, manager, directors, and advisors/consultants as required by the labour law and regulation (Figure 8.8c).

Although there is a significant increase in the number of foreign workers in 2018, nearly 126,000 (Manning and Pratomo, Chapter 11), this is still relatively small compared to the total employment. If we compare with neighbouring countries (Singapore, Malaysia and Thailand), the number of foreign workers in Indonesia is much smaller. Singapore employed 3,673,100 foreign workers in 2016 while Malaysia and Thailand employed 1,866,400 and 1,476,841, respectively.[3]

8.3 BIASED AGAINST SERVICES: TRADE POLICIES

This section focuses on trade policy in the services sector. Given the nature of services, trade policies govern not only trade flow of services as it is in the goods market (coined as cross-border supply of services) but also flow of consumer, investment and workers.

In theory, services trade can take place through four modes of supply. First, cross-border supply (Mode 1) is when services supplier and consumers do not cross borders to provide and consume the services. Examples of the services delivered as Mode 1 is an online course. Second, consumption abroad (Mode 2) occurs when consumers cross borders to consume services. Examples of services delivered under Mode 2 are inbound or outbound tourists consuming services in the host country. Third, commercial presence (Mode 3) is when foreign companies cross borders to provide the services. This refers to foreign companies investing in a particular service sector in a domestic market. Fourth, movement of natural person (services supply Mode 4) refers to workers crossing borders to provide services. An example of this mode would be engineers or doctors crossing borders to offer their services.

FIGURE 8.8
Foreign Workers in Indonesia, 2007–16

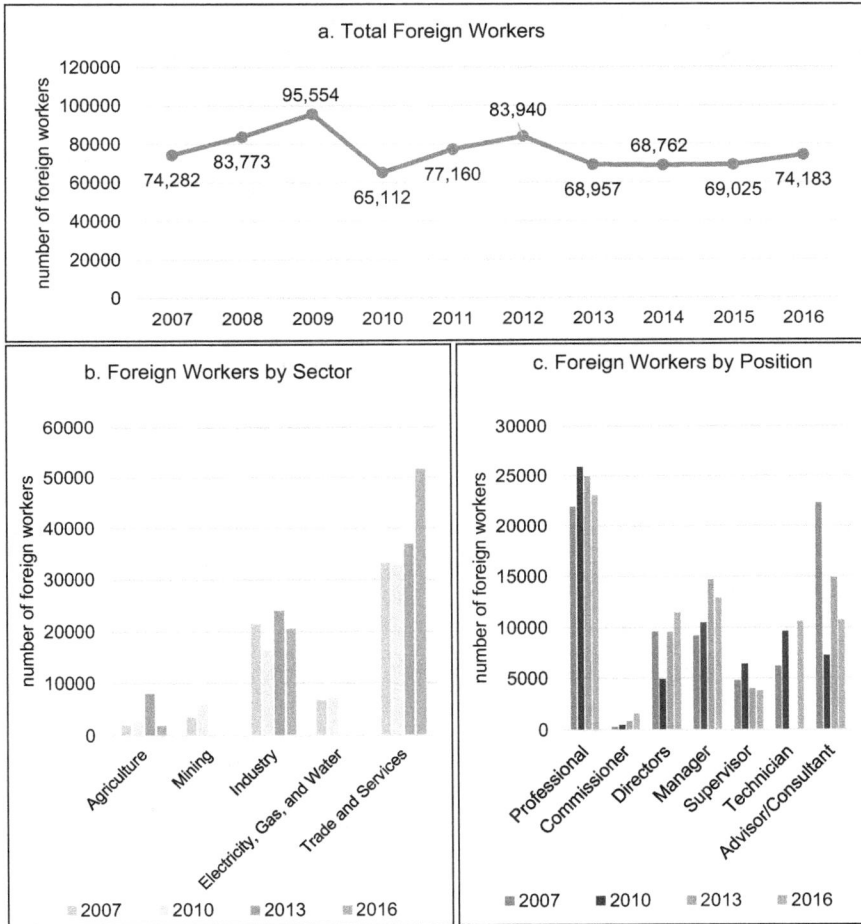

a. Total Foreign Workers

b. Foreign Workers by Sector

c. Foreign Workers by Position

Source: Ministry of Manpower on "Statistik Mobilitas Penduduk dan Tenaga Kerja 2010–2017", Statistics Indonesia.

In Indonesia, services trade in the form of cross-border supply and consumption abroad is relatively open. However, restrictions on commercial presence (foreign investment) and/or movement of natural persons (foreign workers) exist. Recently, a number of sectors have become more open.

8.3.1 Commercial Presence

Indonesia's economic policies became biased against services, i.e., more restrictive than other sectors (agriculture, mining and manufacturing) during the past twenty-five years. Foreign investment policies in particular were more open in the non-services sectors, including agriculture and mining (Duggan, Rahardja and Varela, 2013).

While it is true that, in general, the policies towards services sector are more restrictive than other sectors, it is important to note that there was a trend towards a more open investment policy for the services sector. Figure 8.9 shows that policy changes between 2014 and 2017 reflected this trend. Focusing on the Joko Widodo era, the OECD FDI Policy Index revealed that a few services sectors were becoming more open in 2017, such as the financial sector, communication, media, hotel and restaurant, transport, retail, wholesale and distribution. However, no changes seem to take place in real estate investment, business services and construction. Currently, a large number of services sector, such as real estate and rental services, remain closed to foreign investment, although some services sectors are already open with certain cap on foreign equity. The improvement in FDI Policy Index is the result of the new Negative List of Investment (*Daftar Negatif Investasi*, DNI) published in May 2016.

8.3.2 FDI Policy Changes on Services Sector in 2016

In May 2016, the Joko Widodo government published the new DNI in an attempt to boost investment. The 2016 DNI relaxed foreign equity limits in a number of sectors. Particularly for services sectors, a more open policy can be seen in a few subsectors of business services, communication, distribution and transport. The changes had been much driven by Indonesia's commitment in ASEAN as reflected by a number of sectors are subject to larger foreign equity limit only for ASEAN.

Business Services

Some of the sectors under business services classification (which are more open) include: (1) survey services/community pools and market research, which allow ASEAN investors with maximum foreign investment of 70 per cent; (2) MICE (Organizing Meetings, Incentive Trips, Conferences

FIGURE 8.9
Services Trade Restrictiveness Index Indonesia, 2014 and 2017

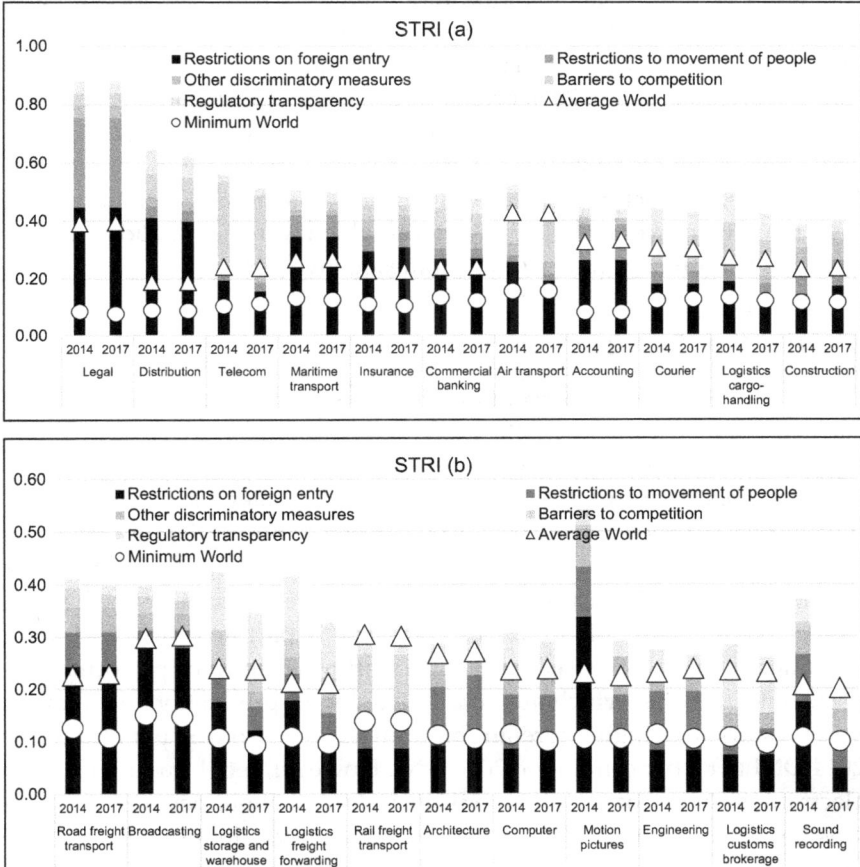

STRI (a)

- Restrictions on foreign entry
- Other discriminatory measures
- Regulatory transparency
- Minimum World
- Restrictions to movement of people
- Barriers to competition
- Average World

2014 2017 categories: Legal, Distribution, Telecom, Maritime transport, Insurance, Commercial banking, Air transport, Accounting, Courier, Logistics cargo-handling, Construction

STRI (b)

- Restrictions on foreign entry
- Other discriminatory measures
- Regulatory transparency
- Minimum World
- Restrictions to movement of people
- Barriers to competition
- Average World

2014 2017 categories: Road freight transport, Broadcasting, Logistics storage and warehouse, Logistics freight forwarding, Rail freight transport, Architecture, Computer, Motion pictures, Engineering, Logistics customs brokerage, Sound recording

Notes: Services Trade Restrictiveness Index : 0 (less restrictive) ; 1 (more restrictive)
Source: OECD, 2018.

and Exhibitions) services, which allow higher foreign investment cap, from 51 per cent in 2014 DNI to maximum 67 per cent for all investors and maximum 70 per cent for ASEAN investors; and (3) training services which are open for foreign investment share of 67 per cent.

However, some of the sectors under classification of business services are also more restrictive towards foreign investment. Construction consulting services using high technology and/or high risk and/or work value more than Rp10 billion which used to be open to 100 per cent foreign ownership are now subject to a maximum foreign equity of 67 per cent for all foreign investments and 70 per cent for ASEAN investors. Similarly, certain construction consulting services, which were not included in the 2014 negative list, are now subject to 49 per cent maximum foreign investment. Meanwhile, inspection and examination of electricity installation on low/medium power installation services which were not included in 2014 negative list are now reserved for domestic investors.

Distribution Services

Distribution services that are more open to foreign investment include retail trade through post and Internet, which were reserved for domestic investors in the 2014 DNI, are now made open for foreign investors in the form of partnership. Department stores with floor size of sales 400 m² to 2,000 m², which were reserved for local investors, are now open for foreign investors with maximum foreign share of 67 per cent. However, special permit is required from the Ministry of Trade with requirements that they have to be located in a mall rather than a stand-alone department store. Addition of outlets is allowed based on export performance (pay performance). Distributor services which are not affiliated with production are allowed for investors with higher foreign share, an increase from 33 per cent in the 2014 DNI to 67 per cent in the 2016 DNI. However, retail trading through electronic systems for various goods (including alcoholic beverages) which was not listed in the 2014 DNI, is now reserved for domestic investors.

Communication Services

Many subsectors under communication services are now open for investors with higher foreign ownership. Foreign investment cap for fixed, mobile and integrated telecommunications network services has been increased slightly from 65 per cent to 67 per cent. A significant increase of foreign equity limit takes place in services such as content telecommunication services (ring tone, premium messaging), call centre and other value-added telephony services, Internet service provider, data communication system services and Internet telephony service for public use. Based on the 2014 DNI, investment in these sectors are subject to majority domestic shareholders (i.e., maximum foreign share is 49 per cent). However, the 2016 DNI allowed maximum foreign of 67 per cent.

Recreational and Cultural Services

A large number of subsectors in the services sector classified as recreational and cultural are also made more open to foreign investment. The maximum foreign equity limit increased from 51 per cent to 67 per cent for all investors and 70 per cent for ASEAN investors in sectors such as museum management services (CPC 96321), management of historical and archaeological relics (in the form of temples, palaces, inscriptions and ancient buildings), pool house (CPC964), bowling centre (CPC964), impresario services (CPC 96191), karaoke, natural tourism object in outer conservation zone and golf course.

Transportation Services

Foreign equity limit is also relaxed for a number of transport services. Under the cabotage rules in marine transportation, foreign equity limit in overseas marine transport modes for passenger and cargo services has been increased from 60 per cent in 2014 to 70 per cent in 2016 for ASEAN investors. Foreign equity limit is also increased in maritime cargo handling services (CPC 7412) from 60 per cent to 67 per cent for all investors and 70 per cent for ASEAN countries when investing in four ports in eastern Indonesia, i.e., Bitung, Ambon, Kupang and Sorong.

In transport supporting services, however, there is a setback. Investment in port facility (dock, building, delays of container terminal vessels, liquid bulk terminals, dry bulk terminal and Ro-Ro terminal) now requires special permit from the Ministry of Transportation related to minimum capital requirements. Similarly, salvage and/or underwater work services also require special permits.

In air transport, foreign investment limit has been increased from 49 per cent to 67 per cent in the supporting business at terminal, air transport support services and services related to airport and transportation management services, aircraft cargo expedition services, and general sales agent (GSA) services for foreign air transport company.

The provision and operation of ferry ports and ports in rivers and lakes sectors are now open for 49 per cent foreign investment. Similarly, operation of motor vehicle periodic testing and construction of land transport passenger terminal (limited to public facilities and public goods terminal only) are also open for 49 per cent foreign investment.

Construction Services

Based on the 2016 DNI, a number of construction subsectors are getting more restrictive. High voltage power utilization installation was open for foreign investment in the 2014 DNI. However, based on the 2016 DNI, foreign investment share in this sector has been capped at a maximum of 49 per cent. Construction and installation of electricity on installation of low/medium voltage power utilization which was open in the 2014 DNI is now reserved for domestic investors. Construction services using high technology and/or high risk and/or work value more than Rp50 billion is only for investors with maximum foreign share of 67 per cent for general investors and 70 per cent for ASEAN investors. Construction services using simple and medium technologies and/or small and medium risk and/or work value up to Rp50 billion is now reserved for small and medium enterprises (SMEs).

Hotels and Restaurants

Based on the 2016 DNI, all subsectors in hotels and restaurants sector are made more open. Restaurants, bars, cafés and homestays are included in the 2014 DNI. However, these sectors are not included in the 2016 DNI, which means that the sectors are open for 100 per cent foreign investment. Hotels (including no-star, one-star, and two-star hotels) have become more open in 2016. The foreign investment limit has been increased from 51 per cent in 2014 to 67 per cent in 2016. For catering services, foreign investment limit has been increased from 51 per cent to 67 per cent and 70 per cent for ASEAN countries. For motels, foreign investment allowed in 2014 was 49 per cent and 51 per cent if they have partnership with micro, small, and medium enterprises (MSMEs). In the 2016 DNI, the foreign investment limit has been increased to 67 per cent and 70 per cent for ASEAN countries.

8.3.3 Movement of Natural Persons

Indonesia's policy regarding foreign workers is stipulated in the labour law (Law number 13/2003). The basic principles adopted by the law are as follows. First, employers except for individual employer are allowed to employ foreign workers.[4] Second, foreign workers are allowed for certain position and for certain time period (Article 42.4). The positions and time period are further regulated by Ministerial decree (Art. 42.5). Third, foreign workers are not allowed for position related to human resource and other positions stated in the implementing regulations of the law (Art. 46). Fourth, companies employing foreign workers are required to employ an Indonesian worker as assistant to the employed foreign workers and arrange relevant trainings for the local workers (Art. 45).

Although the law provides leeway for the government to set its policies with regard to occupations that can be open for foreign workers, the Minister of Manpower regulations opted for restrictive policies. This is indicated by the long list of jobs closed to foreign workers.[5] As a result, the number of foreign workers in Indonesia is relatively small compared to Singapore, Malaysia or Thailand.

When a company decides to employ foreign workers, the labour law requires it to submit its recruitment plan (Rencana Penempatan Tenaga Kerja Asing, RPTKA) by outlining the purpose and duration of employment, and the positions to be held by the foreign workers. The detail of the process of applying for the permit and the submission of RPTKA is outlined in Presidential Regulation No. 72/2014. Furthermore, the law also requires companies to pay compensation to the government for every foreign worker employed (Labour Ministry Regulation No. 12/2013).

Although in principle there is no change in the foreign workers policy, in March 2018 the government issued a Presidential regulation regarding utilization of foreign expatriates (PR 20/2018) to revoke Presidential Regulation No. 72 of 2014 dated 11 July 2014. PR 20/2018 is basically relaxing the procedures to employ foreign workers and explicitly stating social, religious, educational and cultural institutions are allowed to employ foreign workers.

Prior to the enactment of PR 20/2018, companies intending to employ foreign workers are required to submit an RPTKA and apply for a licence to use foreign workers (Ijin Menggunakan Tenaga Asing, IMTA).

With the new regulation, there is no requirement to apply for IMTA. With an approved RPTKA, the company is allowed to employ foreign workers. In addition, the relevant minister has to approve the RPTKA within two days after the requirement is fulfilled. For urgent position, companies can even submit the RPTKA two days after the arrival of the foreign worker.

The Joko Widodo government was heavily criticized after the enactment of PR 20/2018. The opposition parties and public in general claimed that the government does not protect local workers and is being too open to foreign workers.[6]

8.3.4 Services Trade Restrictiveness Index (STRI)

A more comprehensive quantified trade policy restrictions on services sector, which are comparable across countries is available for 2014–17 period when the OECD Services Trade Restrictiveness Index (STRI) became available. The STRI translates qualitative policies related to government services trade, including investment and labour movement policies. STRI collects policy information with regard to the four modes of supply of services and transforms the information into quantitative measures and converts it into an index which allows cross-country and sectoral comparisons.

The STRI is calculated based on a number of aspects: (i) restrictions on foreign entry; (ii) restrictions on the movement of people; (iii) other discriminatory measures; (iv) barriers to competition; and (v) regulatory transparency (Grosso et al. 2014). The STRI is available for twenty-two sectors and forty-four countries including Indonesia, which represents over 80 per cent of global services trade. Although it is more comprehensive than the FDI Policy Index, which is available since 1997, the STRI is available only from 2014 to 2017.

Using the STRI, it can be shown that the policy gap in Indonesia from the best practice (i.e., fully open to foreign competition) is quite large. In 2014, the level of restrictions for a large number of Indonesia's services sectors was much higher than the world average, except for engineering, rail freight, architecture and custom brokerage services. The year 2017 witnessed more open policies for a number of sectors, including distribution, telecommunication, maritime transport, commercial banking, air transport, accounting, courier, logistic cargo-handling, road freight transport, broadcasting, logistics storage and warehouse, logistics freight forwarding, computer, motion picture, engineering, logistics customs brokerage, and sound recording. A significant change took place in the motion picture services followed by sound recording and logistics services due to improvement in investment-related policies.

The improvement in the 2017 STRI score for Indonesia as reported by OECD (2018) is due to the removal or relaxation of restrictions on foreign investment following the enactment of the Government Regulation No. 44/2016 regarding the DNI. However, comparing Indonesia with world minimum (the best practice), the level of restrictions in services based on the 2017 STRI remains high for twenty-two sectors surveyed in STRI.

8.4 SERVICES, RESTRICTIONS AND COMPETITIVENESS

There are several studies available on services. Eschenbach and Hoekman (2006) examine the impact of services policy reforms to growth using data from twenty-four transition economies during 1990–2004. Using financial and infrastructure services policy reform as indicators for services reforms, the authors found a statistically significant positive association between per capita GDP growth and services policy reforms. Mattoo, Rathindran and Subramanian (2006) compared the impact of services trade liberalization to goods trade liberalization on output growth using telecommunication and financial services as case studies. The authors showed that countries with fully open services sector, telecommunication and financial services in this case, grew up to 1.5 percentage points faster than other countries.

Another stream of studies shows the impact of services reforms on the performance of the sector. Using data from eighty-six developing countries during the period 1985–99, Fink, Mattoo and Rathindran (2003) showed that privatization and competition improved performance in the services sectors. Anas and Damuri (2005) showed how more open foreign investment and competition triggered the emergence of low-cost carriers in Southeast Asia, including Indonesia. Anas and Findlay (2017), using Indonesia's air transport as a case study, showed that reforms in the sector made it more competitive, reflected by lower price, higher traffic and routes.

Other studies examined the contribution of services to manufacturing competitiveness. Arnold et al. (2016) used panel data from 4,000 Indian firms for the period 1993–2005 to analyse the impact of India's services policy reform on its manufacturing sector. The authors found that reform in banking, telecommunication, insurance and transport services significantly contributed to the productivity of manufacturing firms in India.

Using OECD measures of domestic regulation and detailed French data on firm-level bilateral export of professional services, Crozet, Milet and Mirza (2015) showed that the possibility of French firms to export was small in highly regulated market. The estimation result showed that an increase in domestic regulation (in this case non-manufacturing regulation index (NMR) will result in a decline of firms' export values.

A number of studies employ STRI to show the impact of services policy restrictions on its own performance. He and Findlay (2014) evaluate the impact of policies on services sector performance. The authors use the services shares in the gross value of goods exports from TIVA database for performance indicators and the OECD STRI as policy indicators. The authors showed that more restrictive policies are associated with lower services share in exports.

Hoekman and Shepherd (2015) employed the World Bank Enterprise Surveys database and STRI to examine the impact of services productivity to manufacturing firm's productivity. The authors showed that on average, improvement of services productivity by 10 per cent will increase manufacture productivity by 0.3 per cent and manufacture export by 0.2 per cent.

The policy restrictiveness quantified in the STRI database were also used by Nordås and Rouzet (2017) to show that the trade cost resulting from the restrictions are high, even higher than the remaining tariff for trade in goods. The ad valorem equivalent of the restrictions is in the range of 142 per cent to 1,800 per cent for courier services, 115 per cent to 1,191 per cent for commercial banking, 31 per cent to 149 per cent for telecommunication services and 32 per cent to 154 per cent for construction services. The authors also showed that reducing policy restrictiveness on services sector positively affect the manufacturing exports. Furthermore, the authors showed that the trade cost associated with the restrictions was higher to the smaller and less productive companies.

An earlier study by Nguyen-Hong (2000) showed the impact of policy restrictions in engineering services on price and cost margin of firms. The author used restrictiveness index of engineering services in twenty Asia and Pacific countries with eighty-four engineering service companies to show that foreign barriers to establishment and ongoing operations were significant and positive determinants of the price-cost margins of engineering service firms.

8.4.1 FDI Restrictions and FDI Inflows into Services Sector

Past studies using multi-country data show that the FDI policy restrictions affect FDI inflows negatively. Using data of seventy-three developed countries for the period of 1980–2006 and developing countries including Indonesia for the period 2004–05, Golub (2009) showed that foreign investment restrictions in the services sector were negatively correlated with FDI flow into the sectors.

Ghosh, Syntetos and Wang (2012) analyse the determinants of inward investment using inward FDI stocks in the twenty-three OECD countries during the period of 1981–2004. The authors found that the impact of FDI restrictions on FDI stocks was negative and statistically significant. The authors also found that GDP, R&D intensity and tele-communication investment per capita were important determinants of inward FDI.

Another study by Duggan, Rahardja and Varela (2013) evaluates the impact of FDI restriction on the services sector on the performance of manufacturing sector in Indonesia. Their study used the OECD FDI Restrictiveness Index of services sector as proxy of policy restrictions, the manufacturing firm level data and Input-Output table to link the services to the manufacturing sector. The authors found that relaxing FDI in the service sector was associated with improvements in perceived performance of the service sector. The authors also found that the relaxation the FDI policy in services sector accounted for 8 per cent of the observed increase in manufacturers' total factor productivity (TFP) over the period of their analysis.

Following previous cross-countries studies, we use a bivariate econometric model to measure the correlation between FDI inflows and FDI restrictiveness index.

$$\text{Log } (FDI)_{it} = c + \beta_1 \log (FDIr)_{it} + u_{it} + a_i + \varepsilon_t$$

The FDI restrictiveness index (FDIr) is from the OECD and the FDI is proxied by the realization value of FDI from the Investment Coordinating Board (BKPM). The data consists of seventeen subsectors in nine services sectors from 1997 to 2017 period, which are construction, distribution (wholesale and retail), transport (surface, maritime, and air), hotels and restaurants, media (radio and TV broadcasting and other media), communications (fixed telecoms and mobile telecoms), financial services (banking and other finance), business services (legal, accounting and audit, and architectural and engineering), and real estate investment. However, there are some limitations in this econometric exercise since the data for the Indonesian services sector is quite small.

The Durbin-Wu-Hausman test was conducted to determine which panel model to use between the random effects model and the fixed effect model. The null hypothesis of this test is a random effect model. So, if the probability value in the test result is more than 0.05, then the model we have to use is a random effect. The test result is corresponding with the hypothesis above (the probability value is 0.62). Therefore, we used the random effect model in this analysis.

Table 8.1 shows that the FDI restrictiveness index is negatively associated with FDI inflows. The coefficient of FDI restrictiveness index is –1.13, which means if the FDI restrictiveness index is increased by 1 per cent, the FDI inflows will decline by 1.13 per cent. This result is consistent

TABLE 8.1
Estimation Result

	Dependent Variable: log of FDI
log of FDI Restrictiveness Index	–1.13
	(0.34)**
Constant	15.62
	(0.74)**
R-squared	0.05
Number of Observation	211

Notes: * $p < 0.05$; ** $p < 0.01$
The estimation using random-effect model.
Source: Author's calculation.

with cross-country analysis from earlier studies from Ghosh, Syntetos and Wang (2012) and Golub (2009).

8.5 REMAINING CHALLENGES

The 2016 FDI Policy Index and the 2017 STRI shows that Indonesia's policies towards twenty-two services sector remain highly restrictive relative to the best practice. The high STRI index is mainly due to restrictions on foreign investment and flows of skilled workers. The restrictions on foreign investment limit the availability of investments, technology and innovation in the services sector in Indonesia. Similarly, the restrictions on foreign workers limit domestic supply capacity. These restrictions are not only negatively affecting services sector but also other sectors. To improve the service sector performance, policies towards foreign investment and workers need to be relaxed.

8.5.1 Higher Education[7]

Another aspect that needs to be addressed in an attempt to increase Indonesia's supply-side capacity of the services sector is the higher education sector. Evidence shows that Indonesia is facing shortage of skilled workers. As reported in Di Gropello, Kruse and Tandon (2011) and Findlay et al. (2018), the restrictions on foreign workers were in place due to general nationalistic sentiments (Manning and Aswicahyono 2012).

Suryadarma et al. (2018) showed that despite significant increase in public spending, Indonesia's educational outcome in the primary and secondary students remains low. Similar concerns were also evident for tertiary education. Allen (2016) shows that 40 per cent of people with tertiary education remained unemployed in Indonesia. Findlay et al. (2018) showed that 27 per cent of university graduates in Indonesia receive lower income than the median income of high-school graduates. The relatively low salaries of some university graduates show that they are working in low-paid occupations that require lower skills. The authors further elaborate that 10 per cent of tertiary education graduates work in unskilled occupations while 40 per cent are employed in semi-skilled roles.

In contrast, analysis of the private sector reveals difficulties in finding skilled workers in Indonesia. The World Bank 2008 survey shows two-thirds of employers reported to have difficulties in finding employees for professional and management roles. Moreover, Allen (2016) shows that 51.5 per cent of workers are under-qualified in Indonesia.

The low quality of graduates is the outcome of the relatively poor quality of tertiary education in international comparison or even when compared to Malaysia, Singapore and Thailand. None of Indonesia's universities reached the top 800 of the Times Higher Education ranking while universities in Malaysia, Singapore and Thailand are on this list. Singapore's universities are even in the top 60. Indonesia's scholars and academics also rank low in terms of cited publication. Similarly, Indonesia's performance in innovation and creativity is also low relative to the three countries.

Findlay et al. (2018) shows that trade openness is the common characteristic behind the success of tertiary education institutions in Malaysia, Singapore and Thailand. Trade openness means that foreign investment and foreign workers in the sector are also welcome. While Indonesia is relatively restrictive on foreign investment in the education sector as well as in the employment of foreign lecturers, Malaysia, Singapore and Thailand are relatively open. This can be seen in STRI index developed in Findlay et al. (2018).

8.6 CONCLUSION AND POLICY RECOMMENDATIONS

In Indonesia, the contribution of the services sector to GDP is much less than the world average. Productivity is also low. The domestic supply-side capacity is weak.

The sector has been subject to restrictive trade policies. This had contributed to the poor performance of the sector. Although the past twenty years have witnessed policies becoming more open, the improvement is rather limited to accelerate the growth of the sector.

During Joko Widodo's period, the trend of a more open services sector has continued. Two main reforms have been made with regard to services sector liberalization during this period. First, the 2016 DNI has opened up some sectors to foreign investment. Second, the 2018 Presidential

Regulation regarding foreign workers aims to simplify the procedures to employ foreign workers.

The reforms during Joko Widodo's period, however, were also too limited to accelerate the growth of the services sector. A large number of subsectors under the sector remains subject to foreign investment restrictions, and jobs open for foreign workers remain limited. Having a 49 per cent cap for shipping while having cabotage[8] continues to restrain the growth of the logistic sector. Similarly, limiting foreign skilled workers in modern business will only limit the growth of the sector.

We recommend further foreign investment liberalization in the services sector, a review of the list of occupations open to foreign workers and a reform in tertiary education in the country. These policies will gradually improve domestic capacity of service sector, which in turn will improve the performance of services sector in particular and the economy in general.

Notes

1. The Groningen Growth and Development Centre (GGDC) database provides labour productivity for a few services sector of 11 countries di Africa, 11 countries in Asia, 2 countries in Middle East and North Africa, 9 countries in Latin America, the United States and a few countries in Europe <http://www.rug.nl/research/ggdc/data/10-sektor-database>.
2. The second unbundling is defined as the unbundling of factories and offices to allow not only goods but also tasks are traded. The principal cause of the second unbundling is a drastic fall in trade costs for goods, people, and especially for ideas.
3. Malaysia, Ministry of Finance Malaysia (2018); Singapore, Ministry of Manpower, 2018; Sritubtim, M.P., 2017.
4. The labour law defines employers as individuals, entrepreneurs, legal establishment or other institutions which employ workers and pay workers salaries or other benefit.
5. Workers are stipulated in several Labour Minister decrees (Permenakertrans 357/2013, 359/2013, 14/2015, 15/2015 and 707/2015).
6. <https://nasional.kompas.com/read/2018/04/11/07444811/gerindra-dan-pks-kritik-kebijakan-jokowi-soal-perpres-tenaga-kerja-asing>.
7. This section drawn from Findlay et al. (2018).
8. Cabotage is restriction on movement of goods or passengers between two places in the same country by a transport operator from another country.

References

Allen, Emma R. "Analysis of Trends and Challenges in the Indonesian Labor Market". *Asian Development Bank (ADB) Paper on Indonesia*, no. 16, 2016, pp. 1–38.

Anas, Titik and Yose Rizal Damuri. "Strategic Directions for ASEAN Airlines in a Globalizing World The Emergence of Low Cost Carriers in South East Asia". REPSF Project No. 04/008, 2005.

———— and Christopher Findlay. "Indonesia: Structural Reform in Air Transport Service". APEC Policy Support Unit, May 2017.

Arnold, Jens Matthias, Beata Javorcik, Molly Lipscomb and Aaditya Mattoo. "Services Reform and Manufacturing Performance: Evidence from India". *The Economic Journal* 126, Issue 590 (2016): 1–39.

Crozet, Matthieu, Emmanuel Milet and Daniel Mirza. "The Impact of Domestic Regulations on International Trade in Services: Evidence from Firm-Level Data". *Journal of Comparative Economics* 44, no. 3 (2016): 585–607 <http://dx.doi.org/10.1016/j.jce.2015.11.004>.

Di Gropello, Emanuela, Aurelien Kruse and Prateek Tandon. *Skills for the Labor Market in Indonesia: Trends in Demand, Gaps, and Supply*. World Bank, 2011.

Duggan, Victor, Sjamsu Rahardja and Gonzalo Varela. "Service Sector Reform and Manufacturing Productivity: Evidence from Indonesia". Policy Research Working Paper. no. WPS 6349. Washington, D.C.: World Bank, 2013.

Eschenbach, Felix, and Bernard Hoekman. "Services Policy Reform and Economic Growth in Transition Economies". *Review of World Economics* 142, no. 4 (2006):746–64.

Findlay, Christopher and Mari Pangestu. "The Services Sector as a Driver of Change: Indonesia's Experience in the ASEAN Context". *Bulletin of Indonesian Economic Studies* 52, no. 1 (2016): 27–53.

Fink, Carsten, Aaditya Mattoo, and Randeep Rathindran. 2003. "A N Assessment of Telecommunications Reform in Developing Countries." *Policy Research Working Per* 15(October): 443–66.

Ghosh, Madanmohan, Peter Syntetos and Wang Weimin. "Impact of FDI Restrictions on Inward FDI in OECD Countries". *Global Economy Journal* 12, no. 3 (2012) <http://doi.org/10.1515/1524-5861.1822>.

Golub, Stephen S. "Openness to Foreign Direct Investment in Services: An International Comparative Analysis". *World Economy* 32, no. 8 (2009): 1245–68 <http://doi.org/10.1111/j.1467-9701.2009.01201.x>.

Grosso, Massimo Geloso et al. *Services Trade Restrictiveness Index (STRI): Construction, Architecture and Engineering Services*. OECD Publishing, 2014.

He, Xiaobo and Christopher Findlay. "Policy Restrictions and Services Performance: Evidence from 32 Countries". *Journal of International Commerce, Economics and Policy* 5, no. 1 (2014): 1440003.

Hoekman, Bernard and Ben Shepherd. "Services Productivity, Trade Policy and Manufacturing Exports". *World Economy* 40, no. 3 (2015): 499–516.

Investment Coordinating Board of the Republic of Indonesia (BKPM). "Perkembangan Investasi". 2018 <https://nswi.bkpm.go.id/data_statistik> (accessed 17 March 2018).

Manning, Chris and Haryo Aswicahyono. "Trade and Employment in Services: The Case of Indonesia". International Labour Organization, Employment Working Paper No. 132, 2012.

——— and Devanto Pratomo. "Labour Market Developments in the Jokowi Years". *Journal of Southeast Asian Economies* 35, no. 2 (2018): 165–84.

Mattoo, Aaditya, Randeep Rathindran and Arvind Subramanian. "Measuring Services Trade Liberalization and Its Impact on Economic Growth: An Illustration Measuring Services Trade Liberalization and Its Impact on Economic Growth : An Illustration." *Journal of Economic Integration* 21(1): 2006. 64–98.

Mattoo, Aaditya, Randeep Rathindran and Arvind Subramanian. "Measuring Services Trade Liberalization and Its Impact on Economic Growth: An Illustration". *Journal of Economic Integration* 21, no. 1 (2006): 64–98.

Miroudot, Sébastien and Charles Cadestin. *Services in Global Value Chains*. OECD Publishing, 2017.

Nguyen-Hong, Duc. "Restriction on Trade in Professional Services". *Staff research paper*. 2000 <http://www.pc.gov.au/research/completed/professional-restrictions/rotips.pdf>.

Nordås, Hildegunn K. and Dorothée Rouzet. "The Impact of Services Trade Restrictiveness on Trade Flows". *World Economy* 40, no. 6 (2017): 1155–83.

OECD. "Services Trade Restrictiveness Index". 2016*a*.

———. "Trade in Value Added (TiVA): December 2016". 2016*b*.

———. "OECD FDI Regulatory Restrictiveness Index". 2018 <http://stats.oecd.org/Index.aspx?datasetcode=FDIINDEX#> (accessed 8 February 2018).

Sritubtim, M.P., 2017. [Author please supply full bibliographic information.]

Statistics Indonesia (BPS). "Penduduk 15 Tahun Ke Atas Yang Bekerja Menurut Lapangan Pekerjaan Utama 1986–2017". *National Labour Force Survey (SAKERNAS)*. 2017 <https://www.bps.go.id/statictable/2009/04/16/970/penduduk-15-tahun-ke-atas-yang-bekerja-menurut-lapangan-pekerjaan-utama-1986---2017.html> (accessed 12 March 2018).

Suryadarma, Daniel, Sandra Kurniawati, Luhur Bima and Asri Yusrina. "Education in Indonesia: A White Elephant?". *Journal of Southeast Asian Economies* 35, no. 2 (2018): 185–99.

Thangavelu, Shandre Mugan, Wang Wenxiao and Sothea Oum. "Servicification in Global Value Chains: The Case of Asian Countries". ERIA Discussion Paper Series 2017.

UNCTAD. "UNCTADstat". 2018.

World Bank. "Employment in Services (% of Total Employment) (Modeled ILO Estimate) | Data". 2018*a*.

————. "World Development Indicators". 2018*b* <http://databank.worldbank.org/data/reports.aspx?source=world-development-indicators> (accessed 15 January 2018).

9

INFRASTRUCTURE DEVELOPMENT UNDER THE JOKOWI ADMINISTRATION
Progress, Challenges and Policies

Wilmar Salim and Siwage Dharma Negara

In many ways, the policy and management bottlenecks in the infrastructure sector are a microcosm of the problems of the overall management of government in Indonesia.

Peter McCawley (2016)

9.1 INTRODUCTION

Infrastructure investment has been identified as one of the key catalysts for unlocking a country's overall economic potential, promoting growth, creating jobs and reducing poverty. Efficient infrastructure is also needed to

This article was first published in *Journal of Southeast Asian Economies* 35, no. 3 (December 2018).

lower distribution costs, make prices of goods and services more affordable, and improve living standards (ADB 2017). Good infrastructure brings better social and economic mobility, leading to better living conditions. For Indonesia, a country with a large population and an archipelagic territory, developing efficient infrastructure is important for ensuring sustainable and inclusive growth.

Infrastructure investments have been traditionally financed by public funds (OECD 2014). After the 1997–98 Asian Financial Crisis, Indonesia's infrastructure spending fell from around 9 per cent of GDP in the mid-1990s to around 2 per cent in 2001 (OECD 2015). By 2014, infrastructure spending had increased to 3.6 per cent of GDP. This level, however, was relatively low compared to Asia's other high growth economies, which spent around 6 per cent of GDP on this rubric (OECD 2015). The political decision to maintain fuel subsidies in the wake of rising world oil prices had shrunk Indonesia's limited fiscal space, thus preventing the country from adequately funding infrastructure investment. As a result, Indonesia's infrastructure crumbled, leaving much of the population with insufficient access to basic facilities, including electricity, water and sanitation. Lack of quality transport and logistics infrastructure has, in turn, constrained local businesses from competing globally.

Under President Joko "Jokowi" Widodo, Indonesia aims to boost its infrastructure development. Specifically, Jokowi's *Nawacita* (nine priority programmes) prioritizes accelerating infrastructure development to connect the peripheries with growth centres and, promoting connectivity between islands in the archipelago (KSP 2016). Moreover, President Jokowi has created the Committee for the Acceleration of Priority Infrastructure Delivery (KPPIP), a special task force that has a mandate to coordinate policies among various stakeholders and to unblock stalled national strategic projects and priority projects. Arguably, Jokowi's development strategy has narrowly focused on building infrastructure and attracting infrastructure investment to address inequality, reduce poverty and promote growth (Warburton 2016).

This chapter discusses the progress and challenges facing infrastructure development in Indonesia from the era of Susilo Bambang Yudhoyono until the current administration.[1] The study focuses on this period because there is, in fact, a continuity in the leaders' vision and political commitment to infrastructure investment for accelerating growth. At the same time, there is a continuity of policy and management bottlenecks that make the progress of infrastructure development not as smooth as expected. As McCawley (2015) argues, many of these problems are not new and the central issues are related to a lack of clear strategy, consistent implementation, and strong law enforcement.

This chapter is organized as follows. The next section discusses the state of infrastructure under President Susilo Bambang Yudhoyono. The third section compares and contrasts Jokowi's infrastructure agenda with that of his predecessor. The fourth section focuses on the structural problems facing the infrastructure sector, including issues related to land acquisition, planning, and financing. This chapter also discusses some concerns regarding national priority projects and the state-led approach to promote infrastructure development, and also whether Indonesia should borrow more for its infrastructure investment. The final section provides concluding remarks and some policy recommendations.

9.2 STATE OF INFRASTRUCTURE UNDER THE YUDHOYONO ADMINISTRATION (2004–14)

When Susilo Bambang Yudhoyono became the sixth Indonesian president, the state of the country's infrastructure ranked among the lowest in the region. According to the World Bank (2014), the lack of infrastructure investment had deterred investors, hence preventing Indonesia's economic growth from reaching its potential. In fact, the World Bank estimated that Indonesia's dilapidated infrastructure contributed to a 1 per cent loss of economic growth each year since 2004 (World Bank 2014).

The Yudhoyono administration had big ambitions to improve the state of infrastructure to boost growth. During Yudhoyono's first term, Indonesia hosted several infrastructure summits to attract investors, both foreign and domestic. In January 2005, the first infrastructure summit was held in Jakarta, and was attended by more than 500 investors from all around the world. The government offered a total of ninety-one public–private partnership (PPP) projects worth US$22 billion to the private sector. The reaction to these offerings, however, was disappointing (World Bank 2007). This was because there were many policy obstacles to prepare bankable projects, and many projects were not well prepared. A second Infrastructure Summit was held in December 2006, where ten PPP projects valued at US$14.7 billion were identified to be the focus of efforts to improve the quality of project preparation. But like the first summit, although investors generally showed cautious optimism, most opted for a wait-and-see approach (McCawley 2015).

McCawley (2015) explains the key issues why the summit failed to attract private investors, including: shortage of well-prepared and well-documented projects available for investors to examine; lack of clear regulations that set guidelines for activities within the infrastructure sector; and economic nationalism hindering market access to the sector. Moreover, Article 33 of the Indonesian Constitution stipulates that economic sectors which are important to the state and crucial for public welfare are controlled by the state and must be developed to give the maximum benefit to the people. This article is always used by special interest groups to oppose privatization, liberalization or any reforms that might reduce the state's control in any particular sector (McCawley 2015).

After the failure of the first Infrastructure Summit, the government took some important remedial steps. In 2005, new regulations were put in place requiring competitive bidding of PPPs and appropriate risk management of guarantees for PPPs (World Bank 2007). In 2006, the government prepared a wide-ranging "Infrastructure Policy Package" aimed at: encouraging competition; eliminating discriminatory practices that obstruct the private sector's participation in infrastructure provision; and redefining the government's role (including separating policy-making, regulatory and operational responsibilities) (World Bank 2007). In 2007, the PPP initiatives to boost infrastructure investment were complemented with major increase in budgeted public spending. This was made possible by the government's improved fiscal situation driven by revenue from the commodity boom.

In addition to introducing the new law and regulations, the Yudhoyono administration also set up new institutions to support project preparation. One of the key institutions is the state-owned infrastructure financing company, PT Sarana Multi Infrastruktur (PT SMI), established in early 2009 with 100 per cent shares owned by the government through the Minister of Finance (SMI 2017). The company is assigned to provide financing, advisory services and project preparation plans for various infrastructure projects in conjunction with private and/or multilateral financial institutions within the PPP scheme. The longer term goal is to transform this state-owned company into an Indonesian Development Financing Institution. Through PT SMI, the government can provide Viability Gap Funding support to make returns on investment for the private sector investment become adequately attractive. PT SMI holds 34 per cent of the share of PT Indonesia Infrastructure Finance (PT IIF). The latter is a private non-bank financial institution established under the Ministry of Finance regulation to focus on investing in commercially feasible infrastructure projects. Other shareholders of PT IIF include the Asian Development Bank (ADB), the International Financial Corporation (IFC), the German Development Bank (DEG), and Sumitomo Mitsui Banking Corporation (SMBC).

To provide a stronger legal foundation for private sector participation in infrastructure investment, the Yudhoyono administration passed the Presidential Regulation No. 13/2010 (amended to Presidential Regulation No. 56/2011) on Public–Private Partnerships (PPP). Then, in 2011, President Yudhoyono launched The Masterplan for the Acceleration and Expansion of Indonesia's Economic Development Plan (MP3EI 2011–2025). It emphasizes the need for heavy investments in infrastructure and improvement in the investment climate to boost average annual growth to 8–9 per cent between 2015 and 2025. This document was endorsed by the government as a legal document through the Presidential Regulation No. 32/2011 to provide directions on key infrastructure targets, including the estimated financial needs for key infrastructure projects. The document also indicates the government's intention to encourage more private sector participation in infrastructure development. The MP3EI projected that more than 70 per cent of the US$468 billion infrastructure investment needs would be contributed by the private sector through public–private partnerships. Considerable time and effort were dedicated to develop and disseminate the MP3EI, but it lacked a coherent strategy for planning and delivery. The MP3EI, however, has been largely forgotten and is rarely referred to by officials under the current government (Ray and Ing 2016).

To achieve the MP3EI goals, the government needs to prepare detailed implementation plans and a supporting legal framework for the execution of various projects. One of the key frameworks is related to land acquisition, which has traditionally been the main stumbling block for infrastructure projects. At the end of 2011, the Yudhoyono government and the parliament approved the new Land Acquisition Law (UU No. 2/2012). This law was an important legal breakthrough aimed at solving common land acquisition problems with regard to infrastructure development. It deals with the revocation of land rights to serve public interest, puts time limits on each procedural phase, and ensures safeguards for land-right holders. With the

Presidential Regulation No. 71/2012, Yudhoyono instructed his ministers to expedite the implementation of the law.

Several key infrastructure projects were initiated during the Yudhoyono presidency. For instance, in the power sector, the government initiated two fast-track programmes to develop a number of power plants all over the archipelago. To meet national electricity demand until 2021, Indonesia requires 57 GW of new generating capacity (PLN 2013). The first 10,000 MW fast-track programme (FTP-1) was started in 2006. The Government mandated the state-owned electricity firm, PT Perusahaan Listrik Negara (PLN), to build coal-fired power plants (Pembangkit Listrik Tenaga Uap or PLTU) at forty-two locations in Indonesia. These include ten power plants with an aggregate capacity of 6,900 MW in Java-Bali and thirty-two power plants with an aggregate capacity of 2,252 MW outside Java-Bali. The second fast-track programme (FTP-2) was started in 2012, aimed at accelerating the development of 10,000 MW of new power capacity. Unlike FTP-1, the FTP-2 mainly uses renewable energy, including geothermal- and hydro-energy. The two fast-track programmes could not be completed on schedule because of several issues, including: poor planning; land acquisition problems; poor selection of contractors; and a lengthy process of issuing business permits, among others.[2]

The Yudhoyono administration also initiated investment in roads, which fell sharply after the crisis in 1997. One of the key road projects started by the administration was the development of the 116-km-long Cikampek–Palimanan, the longest toll road in Indonesia. The Cikampek–Palimanan toll road is expected to reduce traffic distance on Pantura (North Java) highway by about 40 km and save travel time by almost two hours.[3] The project cost was estimated to reach Rp13.8 trillion (US$1.4 billion) and owned by a joint venture company PT Lintas Marga Sedaya (LMS), with 55 per cent of the shares owned by Malaysia Plus Expressways Berhad, and 45 per cent by PT Bhaskara Utama. The construction of the toll road began in early 2013 and was completed in mid-2015. This project is one example of several projects that crossed over two presidencies.

Overall, between 2011 and 2014, the Yudhoyono government spent around US$73 billion for financing 383 infrastructure projects.[4] By the end of his presidency, the push towards improving infrastructure in the country had achieved some progress. According to the Global Competitiveness Index 2014–2015, infrastructure and connectivity in Indonesia have shown improvement. The country managed to move up twenty places since

2011, as a result of improvement in eighteen of the twenty-one indicators. However, the overall quality of infrastructure in Indonesia — such as ports, roads, airports and electricity supply — lags much behind its neighbouring countries (WEF 2014).

Yudhoyono seemed to lose his focus on infrastructure development in the second term of his presidency. He was hesitant to remove the costly fuel subsidies and free the needed fiscal space to increase spending on infrastructure. At the same time, he was also reluctant to fill the financing gap by borrowing loans, as he was concerned about the risk of increasing external debt. Indeed, one of his legacies is that he set a standard for prudent fiscal management. His administration managed to lower the country's external debt to GDP ratio from 54.9 per cent in 2004 to slightly below 33 per cent in 2014 (Bank Indonesia 2017).[5] His critics, however, felt that he was too occupied with "self" international image correction while neglecting domestic issues. Moreover, some of his political party members were involved in major corruption scandals, further dragging his domestic political image down.

Despite several summits and an ambitious masterplan (MP3EI), infrastructure remained a major area of under performance during the Yudhoyono decade (McCawley 2015; Ray and Yan Ing 2016). Decentralization and the autonomy of local governments and legislative councils have frequently been blamed for complicating the implementation of various infrastructure programmes. Many projects brought in by the central government were stalled as the local institutions either chose to wait-and-see (without offering improved services or facilities), or pursued complicated follow-up measures regarding taxes and land concessions. In addition, Yudhoyono was also perceived as being an extremely cautious leader who seemed reluctant to make any firm decision, including removing fuel subsidies amidst increased burden on the state budget. Also, the meddling parliament deterred private investors. Inter-jurisdictional cooperation, too, was problematic, resulting in an ambiguous role of local governments and complex project execution.

9.3 JOKOWI'S INFRASTRUCTURE AGENDA (2014–19)

While Ray and Yan Ing (2016) argue that the MP3EI has been largely forgotten, a number of projects listed in the document have been put under Jokowi's infrastructure agenda. Therefore, it can be argued that Jokowi's infrastructure policy has been a continuation of his predecessor's with some modification. In the national five year plan (RPJMN 2015–2019), the Jokowi administration has pledged to build: 5,000 km of railways; 2,600 km of roads; 1,000 km of toll roads; forty-nine dams; twenty-four seaports; and power plants with a combined capacity of 35,000 megawatts (Bappenas 2014). Therefore, the big infrastructure plan set by the SBY government remains quite relevant. What can differentiate the Jokowi administration from his predecessor is the execution of the plan.

According to RPJMN 2015–2019, there are four key sectors in which the Jokowi administration will invest a significant amount of resources (Bappenas 2014). The first is the maritime sector. Jokowi has stated that Indonesia has been neglecting its maritime potential for decades. Since the Soeharto era, the country's development has primarily focused on economic activities on land. Seeing the maritime potential, Jokowi intends to transform the country into a global maritime axis (*poros maritim*).[6] One of the key pillars of his plan is to support the maritime economy by improving the country's port infrastructure, shipping industry, and maritime tourism sector. On maritime connectivity, Jokowi has promoted a *tol laut* (sea toll) programme to move cargo from land to sea for more efficient goods movement. Creating a thriving roll-on/roll-off (ro-ro) shipping industry that connects western and eastern parts of Indonesian archipelago is one of the cornerstones of this programme. The sea toll scheme is aimed at improving inter-island connectivity to reduce price disparities and the development gap between the two regions.

In contrast to his predecessor, Jokowi preferred to promote the sea toll programme instead of the US$20 billion Sunda Strait Bridge.[7] The latter was designed to connect Java and Sumatra with a land transport road. However, Jokowi saw that the sea toll concept was more attuned with his maritime development plan. It was also expected to generate tangible benefits to the country through a more balanced development approach. In addition, Jokowi has an ambition to cut down dwelling times for cargo vessels from 5.5 days to 4.7 days.[8] Studies show that the lack of regular inter-island freighter services and inefficient port handling are among the main causes of the high logistics costs in Indonesia (World Bank 2014; Sandee 2016). This is why the government has been emphasizing efforts to improve the performance of ports and shipping infrastructure.

Second, the president has also stated that Indonesia will attain food self-sufficiency (*ketahanan pangan*) within three to five years.[9] In view of this agenda, the government has been pushing the development of infrastructure to support the agriculture sector. A number of dam projects are listed as the national strategic projects under the Presidential Regulation No. 3/2016. The government has also increased spending to develop rural areas through Village funds (see Gonschorek and Schulze, Chapter 4), and to create 9 million hectares of agriculture land.[10]

Nevertheless, to achieve food self-sufficiency, Indonesia needs not only improved irrigation but also better and more efficient distribution networks. For example, there are many agricultural commodities that still rely on a multiplicity of transportation methods to be shipped out of the production centres due to poor road networks. As Sandee (2016) argues, an archipelago like Indonesia has to address its geographical challenges (in terms of intra-island connectivity, inter-island connectivity and international connectivity) and deal with the policy challenges.

Third, in view of the need to improve distribution networks and lower logistics costs in the economy, Jokowi has been pushing investment for roads and railways in order to improve inter-regional land connectivity. The Logistics Performance Index of the ASEAN member states in 2016 shows that, in terms of international logistics performance indicators, Indonesia is lagging behind Singapore, Malaysia and Thailand, and is only slightly better than Vietnam. However, in terms of infrastructure quality, Indonesia also ranks lower than Brunei and Vietnam; and on international shipments, Indonesia even ranks lower than Vietnam, Cambodia, and the Philippines. To improve logistics infrastructure, the government has allocated almost 50 per cent of the total transportation expenditure for the railway networks development. In addition, to make the geographic concentration of investment more balanced, 57 per cent of the expenditure will go outside the capital region (Bappenas 2014).

Fourth, Jokowi is also keen to increase energy supply in the country. As the demand for electricity continues to exceed supply, it is estimated that the high-growth regions of Java and Bali will soon face a power crisis (PLN 2016). The state-owned electricity company, PT PLN, has warned that the two islands' electricity reserve margin — the measurement of excess electricity reserves that a system has during peak demand — could fall to 18 per cent, far lower than the ideal level of 30 per cent, within the next five years. Given this risk of an energy deficit, the government has set an ambitious target for the development of 35 GW power stations. There are many doubts regarding this target, including among the cabinet members.[11] One of the key concerns is related to PLN's capacity to finance such a large project. However, Jokowi has tried to defend his policy by stating that the country will experience frequent blackouts if investment in the power generation sector is not increased.

Under the Jokowi administration, state spending on infrastructure has increased significantly, especially after the government managed to reduce the fiscal burden from fuel subsidies. In 2016, spending on infrastructure was estimated to have reached Rp317 trillion (15 per cent of total state budget). For 2017, the amount was estimated to have increased to Rp401 trillion (19 per cent of total state budget or 2.8 per cent of GDP). On the contrary, the share of government subsidy for energy (out of total state spending) has been declining, from 15 per cent in 2014 to 4 per cent in 2017 (Figure 9.1). This is the key difference between the Jokowi administration and the previous government. In total, by 2017, the Jokowi administration had spent almost Rp1,478.9 trillion from thirty-seven projects and one programme for infrastructure (Utomo 2018).

9.4 STRUCTURAL CHALLENGES IN INFRASTRUCTURE DEVELOPMENT

Three major challenges to infrastructure development in Indonesia have been identified: land clearance; planning and project preparation; and financing (Utomo 2017). As mentioned before, land acquisition problems traditionally have been the main stumbling block for infrastructure projects in the country. Although the Yudhoyono administration issued several regulations to tackle the issue (starting with Presidential Regulation No. 36/2005 on Land Provision for Development for the Public Interest, which then evolved into Law No. 2/2012 on Land Acquisition with its implementing regulations), land clearance remains the biggest contributor (around 30 per cent) to the problems in infrastructure development (Utomo 2017). Two interrelated issues with land clearance are: lack of compensation fund and the lengthy negotiation process.

Davidson (2016) explains the core of the problem as a mismatch between national and local interests. On one hand, the central government is interested in getting the land cleared as soon as possible so that construction could start for national level projects. On the other hand, if such projects are located in areas where the land belongs to local residents (thus requiring the local government's intervention to negotiate), a significant amount of

FIGURE 9.1
Budget Allocation for Key Sectors (percentage of Total State Budget)

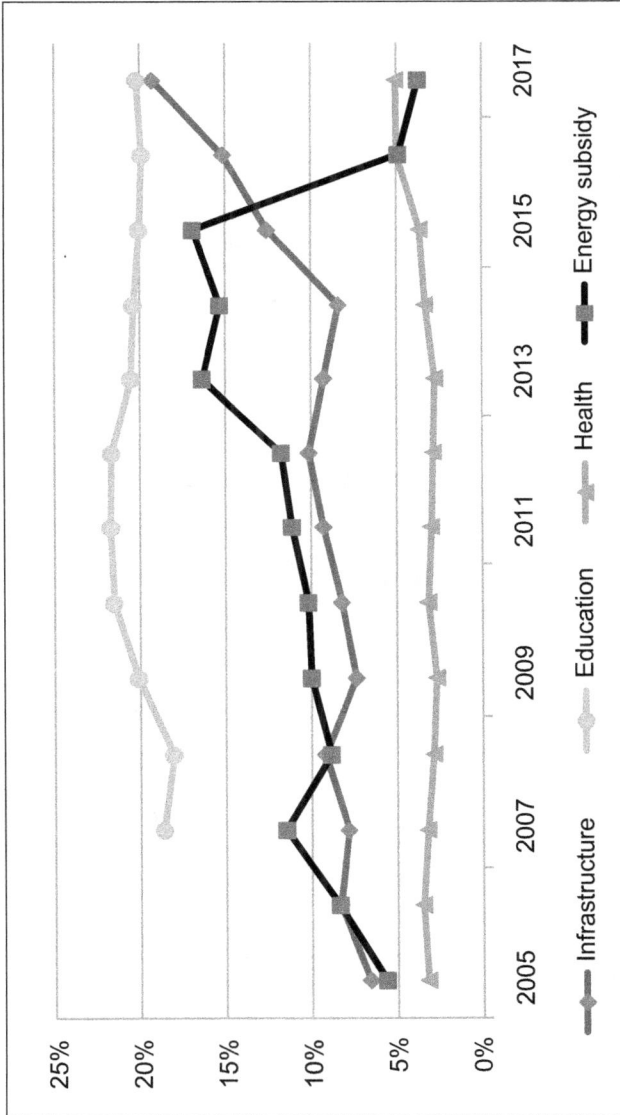

Source: Ministry of Finance, via CEIC.

time goes into dealing with angry residents who have to be relocated with small compensation fees. This may end up in a vicious cycle. Delaying land acquisition means an increase in land value, which means that more money is needed for compensation — which is not available. There are many infrastructure projects that have been stalled for decades due to delays in land clearance.

Two obstacles to efficient land clearance have stemmed from the broader political environment (Davidson 2016): suspicion among residents; and financial uncertainties. Due to poor practices in the past, people are more suspicious of the "public interest rhetoric" of infrastructure development by the government, which is shadowed by private interests. The suspicion also stems from the lack of trust towards the notoriously corrupt National Land Agency (BPN). Thus, some landowners are not willing to sell their properties even though they are for the public interest. Meanwhile, financial uncertainties of the project have caused hesitation on the part of project holders to appropriate money for land acquisition. The Trans-Java tollway land acquisition process is an example. Uncertainties regarding the ownership of licences made the investor reluctant to pay for land acquisition, which led to uncertainties among landowners and project contractors. Between 2006 and 2014, there were multiple changes in project ownership on several sections of the toll road, before it was finally owned by the state-owned construction company, PT Waskita Karya.

The second challenge in infrastructure is related to planning and project preparation (Utomo 2017). Embedded in this challenge are coordination issues among stakeholders and the quality of the project document. In most cases, infrastructure development involves many stakeholders, which includes central and local governments, village governments and residents, investor and contractors, and so on. Therefore, it is difficult to find a consensus among the competing interests of the stakeholders during project planning.

Besides coordination, the quality of project document and design are also important consideration in project preparation. Many investors are not convinced by the project design quality, as it is not made according to international standards (Utomo 2017). Thus, it hinders full participation by the private sector in infrastructure development. The involvement of the private sector is crucial, especially when the government expects a major contribution from them on infrastructure financing needs worth Rp4,000 trillion.

The third challenge is financing. As discussed above, during the Yudhoyono administration, the private investment needed to finance infrastructure development had not materialized even after several summits. According to the RPJMN 2015–2019, around 50 per cent of infrastructure financing is expected to come from the state budget, 30 per cent from the private sector, and 20 per cent from state-owned enterprises. Actually, there are four sources of infrastructure financing that could be administered by the government: the state budget; the state-owned enterprise; the private sector; and partnerships between the government and private entities. The government has tried to venture more into the last scheme, however, during the Yudhoyono presidency, only a few projects were implemented under the PPP scheme.

OECD (2015) mentions several issues with regard to public–private partnerships in infrastructure projects in Indonesia. First, the overlap between economy-wide regulations and sector-specific laws detailing modalities for private investment creates ambiguity for investors and procurement entities embarking on PPPs. Second, restrictions on foreign participation remain high and most of these sectors are regulated by non-independent agencies. Third, since there are no clear PPP regulations, there is little interest from the private sector to take part in infrastructure projects.

Despite an increase in public spending, Indonesia's infrastructure gap is, by far, the largest in ASEAN (Figure 9.2).[12] According to Bappenas' calculation, Indonesia needs Rp4,796 trillion (US$356 billion) to meet its targets for infrastructure development between 2015 and 2019.[13] The central and regional government budgets can only cover around 41.3 per cent (or equal to Rp1,482 trillion) of the total investment needs. Funding from state-owned enterprises (SOEs) is expected to contribute around 22.2 per cent (Rp799 trillion). Therefore, the rest, or around 36.5 per cent, of the investment gap is expected to be filled by the private sector. Unfortunately, private sector investment has not been strong enough to fill this void. As a result, the overall allocation to infrastructure spending remains low, about 18.5 per cent of the total state budget and 2.8 per cent of the GDP.

Even though most of the infrastructure investment comes from the government budget, the country's tax collection remains weak. Indonesia has the lowest tax to GDP ratio in the region, with only 10.3 per cent of tax/GDP ratio.[14] The tax amnesty programme (from July 2016 until March

FIGURE 9.2
Infrastructure Spending as a Share of GDP in Select ASEAN Countries (percentage of GDP)

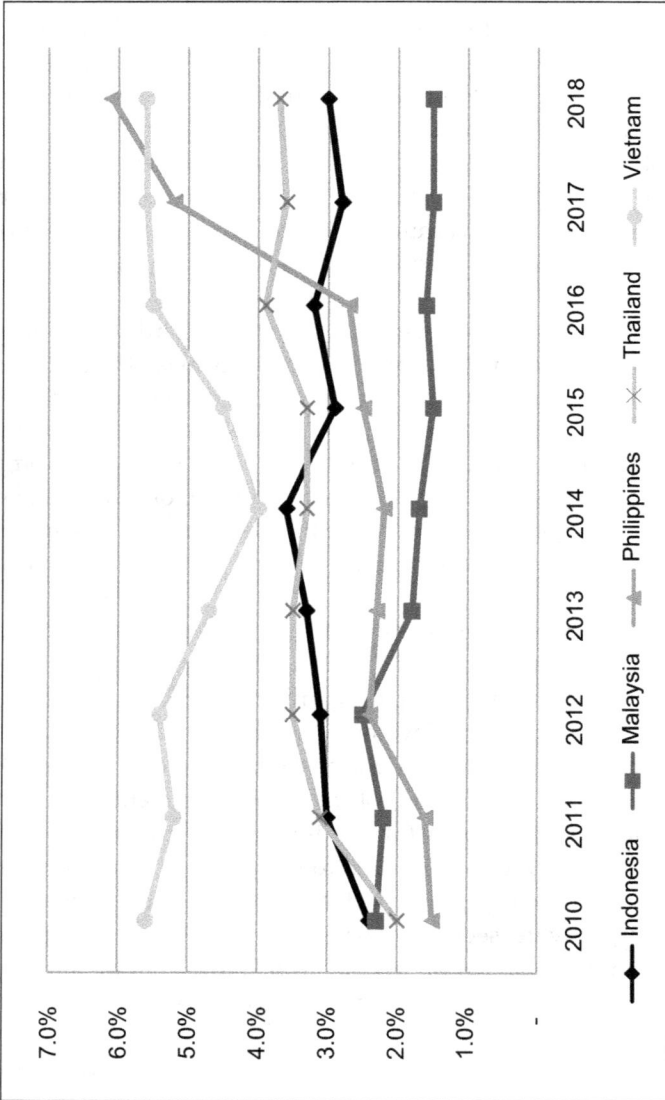

Notes: 2017 and 2018 figures are forecasted figures. Indonesia figures are budgeted (not realized) data. They include 25 per cent of total regional government allocation for infrastructure.
Source: CEIC, HSBC.

2017), dubbed to be the most successful in the world, was a one-off effort to boost tax collection. However, more sustained efforts are needed.

9.5 POLICY RESPONSES BY THE JOKOWI ADMINISTRATION

In order to overcome the abovementioned challenges, the Jokowi administration has taken a number of measures. First of all, a set of regulations was introduced to tackle the challenges of land clearance and financing — both at presidential as well as the ministerial levels. Some of these regulations include: Presidential Regulation No. 30/2015 on Land Acquisition; Presidential Regulation No. 38/2015 on Partnership between Government and Business Entity; Presidential Regulation No. 82/2015 on Direct Lending; Minister of Agraria and Spatial Planning Regulation No. 6/2015 on Land Acquisition; and Minister of Finance Regulation No. 190/2015 on Availability Payment. These were accompanied by a set of economic policy packages issued in the last quarter of 2015. A total of eight economic policy packages were launched, collectively aimed at: reorganizing regulations that hinder economic growth; restructuring the bureaucracy; and offering incentives to create conducive investment climate and strengthen Indonesia's economy (KPPIP 2018).

Second, several infrastructure projects have been designated as "nationally strategic". Based on Presidential Regulation No. 3/2016, many infrastructure projects have been listed as strategic nationally — either by the central government, local government and/or business entity — to accelerate their implementation. The regulation stipulates the type of permits and non-permits that can be accelerated by either a minister or head of national agency, or governor, or mayor of district or municipality. It also stipulates among other things: the compliance with spatial plan; land provision; government guarantee; and procurement procedure. In all, there are 225 projects under twenty-three categories plus twenty projects under power infrastructure in a separate list. Dams (sixty projects), toll roads (forty-seven), and special economic/ industrial zones (twenty-four) occupy more than half of these projects. A Committee for the Acceleration of Priority Infrastructure Delivery (KPPIP) that was established earlier (by Presidential Regulation No. 75/2014) supports the implementation of this regulation. Its mandate is to assist, facilitate, coordinate, and give recommendations for the revision of or new regulations in order to expedite infrastructure development.

Third, the current administration has established and strengthened several institutions to support infrastructure development throughout the country. The establishment of the public service agency on state asset management (BLU-LMAN) is an example; it is the only government agency dealing with financing land acquisition for national strategic projects. Before this agency existed, land acquisition for infrastructure projects was executed by an ad-hoc team formed by each ministry, for example, the Public Works Ministry. That, however, was far from effective. With BLU-LMAN, land acquisition is more coordinated and time-efficient (Utomo 2017). In addition, the government has also centralized permit procedures under a one-stop permit service, and investment coordination under the Investment Coordination Agency (BKPM). The administration has also provided more capital to Limited Liability Company PT Sarana Multi Infrastruktur (PT SMI) by shifting capital from the Government Investment Centre. PT SMI has now become the centre for infrastructure financing with the capacity to fund infrastructure projects managed by state-owned enterprises (SOEs), regional government-owned enterprises (ROEs), and regional governments (KPPIP 2018).

Fourth, in order to deal with the challenge of planning and project preparation, KPPIP has been mandated to draft the project preparation document according to the international standard, including the pre-feasibility study document, outline business cases, as well as financing scheme appropriation (Utomo 2017). The project preparation document now contains information about: the project; investment value needed; the rate of return of investment; financial benefit, including facilities offered by the government; and investment risk projection. In addition, a Project Development Facility (PDF) is also provided by the Ministry of Finance to help the Government Contracting Agency (GCA) to prepare for a pre-feasibility study and bidding documents, and assist in the PPP project transactions until it reaches financial closure (DJPPR 2017).

Lastly, to deal with the challenge of financing, the government now offers several fiscal instruments to encourage more public private partnerships. A legal base for the PPP scheme has been put in place under Presidential Regulation No. 38/2015 on Partnership between Government and Business Entity. In order to attract private investment, several innovative fiscal policies have been developed by the government, like availability payment, viability gap fund, and government guarantees for direct lending. Availability payment is made to the business entity for the availability of infrastructure that satisfies the quality and criteria set in the PPP contracts. It is expected to increase project feasibility to stimulate investor interest. The Viability Gap Fund (VGF) is a form of contribution of some of the construction cost, given in cash to a PPP project that is economically viable but not financially feasible. It can be offered when there is no other alternative to make the PPP project financially feasible (DJPPR 2017). Meanwhile, a government guarantee is given if the GCA is obliged to pay compensation to the project company in case of infrastructure risks, as long as those risks are based on risk allocations agreed in the PPP agreement.

Through Presidential Regulation No. 82/2015 (on Central Government Warranty for Infrastructure Finance Using Direct Lending from International Financial Institutions to a State Owned Enterprise), the scope of projects eligible for such a warranty has broadened. This warranty can be provided to an SOE that is entirely owned by the government. The government is also preparing alternative fiscal instruments, such as: government bonds to attract investment from the public at large; non-budgetary infrastructure financing to attract long-term funds (insurance fund, pension fund, tax amnesty fund) and private equity investment; and a Limited Concession Scheme (LCS) based on private funds which are given concession to manage assets owned either by the government or an SOE (Utomo 2017).

With the help of the different types of facilities mentioned above, several toll roads (such as Balikpapan–Samarinda, Manado–Bitung, Panimbang–Serang, and Yogyakarta–Bawen) and Drinking Water Provision System (SPAM) Umbulan in East Java are being developed under the PPP scheme. Similarly, the availability payment scheme has been used in Palapa Ring infrastructure development to expand broadband coverage (Utomo 2017).

9.6 SOME REMAINING CONCERNS

There are several issues that the Jokowi administration continues to face. First is the large number of national strategic projects (225), which is almost too big to handle. As discussed, Presidential Regulation No. 3/2016 has a list of 225 national strategic projects under twenty-three categories, and an additional twenty projects under the power infrastructure category. Although the regulation is accompanied by several economic policy packages and several fiscal instruments, the outcome has not materialized in all infrastructure categories. The ambitious 35 GW electricity power plant programme that was launched in 2015 has seen less than 4 per cent progress. Around 49 per cent continues to remain under construction, 36 per cent has been contracted, and the remaining is still at the procurement and planning stage.[15] The progress is slow because electricity sales are only half of the estimate (of 8 per cent in 2017), forcing the state electricity firm (PLN) to postpone the commercial operation of the programme. This suggests that there was a problem with the demand projection that was used to design the project.

Another slow-progress project is the controversial Jakarta–Bandung high-speed rail. The Minister of State-Owned Enterprises, Rini Soemarno, said in February 2018 that the project will fail to meet its completion target of 2019. Apparently, only 54 per cent of the land needed for the project has been acquired.[16] This shows that land acquisition in Indonesia continues to be a challenge, despite new regulations and institutions. Due to this, the disbursement of project loan from China Development Bank has been repeatedly delayed. Jokowi, who had high expectations regarding the success of the project, has, in fact, called for the project to be re-evaluated.[17] Although it does not involve any state budget, the project is listed as one of the national strategic projects under Presidential Regulation No. 3/2016. The government, through the Minister of State-Owned Enterprises, had also established a consortium of four Indonesian SOEs, i.e. PT Kereta Api Indonesia (KAI), PT Wijaya Karya (WIKA), PT Perkebunan Nusantara VIII, and PT Jasa Marga, that held 60 per cent of the project shares. All of these SOEs have huge financing needs, as they have also been tasked with supporting other infrastructure projects simultaneously.

What the Jokowi administration is doing to accelerate infrastructure development resembles the state-led approach or the statist-nationalist orientation (Warburton 2016). To implement massive infrastructure projects all over the country, the government has injected large portions of budgetary funds to SOEs. There is now a concern, however, about the possible crowding-out of more efficient private providers (Ray and Ing

2016) — the SOE domination can potentially hinder their market access. The overburden of projects on individual SOEs has also led to many construction accidents in the past couple of years.[18]

One of the reasons to boost infrastructure spending is to create a multiplier effect such that many local private providers can also benefit. The investment needs are very large for SOEs to handle everything all by themselves (Gustely 2015; Suzuki 2017). In such a case, the private sector is the natural partner for SOEs that need capital financing, better planning and delivery of infrastructure at a particular scale (Ray and Ing 2016). It can also be argued that the state-led approach, if designed correctly, can lead to downstream spillover for the private sector. The remaining challenge then for the government is how to create institutional and market conditions that are attractive for private capital (OECD 2014). Here, enforcing Law No. 5/1999 to prohibit monopoly and uncompetitive business practices through increasing transparency and accountability is a must. The implementation of e-procurement for government projects is a good example of how the regulation can help.

In order to find alternatives for financing, Jokowi has openly welcomed foreign and multilateral support for infrastructure investment. One potential source for financing is China. In fact, over the last few years, China has become an important source of infrastructure development financing for a number of developing countries in the region. While his predecessor was reluctant, Jokowi made Indonesia join the China-led Asia Infrastructure Investment Bank (AIIB) and become one of its key shareholders. He also attended the Belt and Road Initiative Forum in Beijing in May 2017, and followed up the visit with proposals for cooperation under the BRI framework.[19]

To date, Indonesia has received loans worth US$2.4 billion from AIIB. Overall, Chinese loans to Indonesia have increased gradually, from around US$800 million in 2007 to US$15.7 billion in 2017. It is interesting to note that most of the loans from China go to the private sector (92 per cent), and only a small portion (8 per cent) is diverted to the government.[20] Even though loans from China to Indonesia have been increasing, the size is still relatively small compared to those from Japan. In terms of its share to total external debt, Chinese loans have increased from around 0.6 per cent in 2008 to 4.5 per cent of Indonesia's total foreign loans in 2017. In contrast, Japan's share of total external debt in Indonesia has been declining, from 23.5 per cent in 2008 to 8.3 per cent in 2017. Given this trend, one can foresee the share of Chinese loans rapidly growing, especially if some BRI proposed projects are approved.

This leads to the third concern: Indonesia's increasing public debt. As the country has received a favourable investment grade from several key rating agencies,[21] it has been enjoying the advantage of getting low-interest loans from global investors. While practical, this alternative may have political costs as the Jokowi administration has been criticized as accumulating debt much faster than its predecessor.[22] Indonesia's external debt has been increasing significantly from around Rp2,500 trillion in 2014 to Rp4,000 trillion in 2017 — leading the debt to GDP ratio to above 30 per cent. However, compared to other neighbouring countries, Indonesia's external debt to GDP ratio is not worrisome (Figure 9.3). The ratio is far below the limit set in the law (60 per cent). Nevertheless, it is better to be cautious about how the debt is spent, whether to support infrastructure projects that will contribute to GDP growth or not. Losing the focus on debt management may cost Jokowi's political standing in the 2019 re-election, as the opposition would focus more on the debt figure than the actual ratio.

9.7 CONCLUDING REMARKS

Efficient infrastructure is important to promote economic and social development. Under both the Yudhoyono government as well as the Jokowi administration, Indonesia has taken big steps to revitalize the sector. The ultimate objective is to boost economic growth and improve the competitiveness of the Indonesian economy. Based on this study, it can be argued that Jokowi's infrastructure policy is a continuation of that of his predecessor. While the MP3EI is no longer being used, some of the key infrastructure projects under the masterplan have been retained as Jokowi's national strategic projects. Table 9.1 summarizes the key differences between the two administrations with regard to infrastructure development.

What differentiates Jokowi's policy from that of Yudhoyono is that the former has taken a more pragmatic approach to push infrastructure development in the country. One of his boldest policies has been to shift budget allocations away from fuel subsidies, and towards infrastructure spending. In fact, under the current administration, Indonesia has experienced significant growth in terms of infrastructure spending, from

FIGURE 9.3
External Debt to GDP Ratio in Select ASEAN Countries

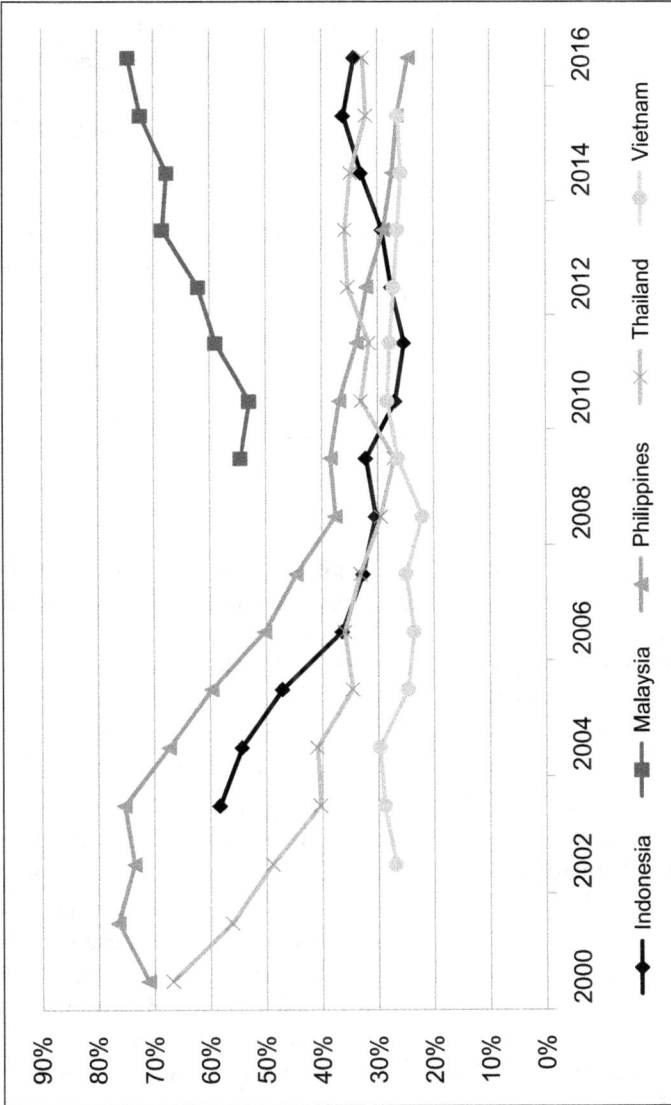

Indonesia — Malaysia — Philippines — Thailand — Vietnam

Source: CEIC.

TABLE 9.1

Key Policies and Strategies on Infrastructure Development

Aspect	S.B. Yudhoyono	Joko Widodo
Legal framework	On land acquisition and PPP	On land acquisition, PPP and financing
Key document	MP3EI	National Strategic Projects (PSN)
Agency created	PT. SMI	BLU-LMAN and KPPIP
Key sectors	Energy, transportation, fuel subsidy	Maritime, agriculture, transportation, energy
Percentage of state budget for infrastructure	6–10 per cent	12–19 per cent
Alternative funding mechanism	PPP scheme	Various schemes: availability payment; viability gap funding; guarantee for direct landing; etc

Source: Authors' summary.

less than 10 per cent in 2013 to 19 per cent of the total national budget in 2017. In addition, Jokowi has also openly welcomed foreign and multilateral support.

However, Jokowi's infrastructure development has not progressed as smoothly as he had expected. Some projects have seen positive developments (Java toll road, Jakarta MRT, airport train, Jatigede dam, *inter alia*) while others have witnessed poor progress (Jakarta–Bandung High-Speed Rail, 35 GW electricity project, mineral smelters, *inter alia*). Realistically, launching 245 nationally strategic infrastructure projects was unrealistically ambitious to begin with — given the country's limited financing and technological capacity. In order to appease his political supporters, Jokowi needs to find ways to expedite these projects.

This can be done by re-evaluating all projects listed as nationally strategic in nature, and being more selective in prioritizing them. It is important for Jokowi to revisit the *Nawacita* and the RPJMN 2015–2019. The third point in the *Nawacita* focuses on building Indonesia from the periphery by reinforcing the regions. This priority agenda has been translated into maritime development being the first key sector in RPJMN 2015–2019. However, in the list of national strategic projects, seaport development is of secondary importance. Furthermore, the word periphery is supposed to refer to the islands off-Java, Madura and Bali, which are less populated. Those should be the focus of development and not on Java where most of the projects are concentrated.

Re-evaluation of projects must also include reassessing the assumptions used and projections made in the project proposals. In the time lapsed between the proposal stage and now, a variable like infrastructure demand could have changed due to the changing global economy. The case of much lower electricity sales compared to projections is an example of overestimation of demand.

Lastly, the national strategic projects must be in line with greater national development plans which have a longer time-frame (like the National Spatial Plan; and sectoral master plans such as the Master of Plan of Transportation) in order to achieve integrated regional development, and to really build Indonesia from the periphery as intended in the *Nawacita*.

Notes

1. See McCawley (2015) for a comprehensive survey of infrastructure policy in Indonesia since 1965 until 2015.
2. <https://www.merdeka.com/uang/pln-pelajari-kegagalan-sby-bangun-proyek-pembangkit-ftp-1-dan-2.html> (accessed 2 March 2018).
3. <http://setkab.go.id/diresmikan-presiden-jokowi-tarif-tol-cikampek-palimanan-rp-96-000/> (accessed 2 March 2018).
4. See article in *Jakarta Globe*, "SBY Cements Infrastructure Credentials, Advises Jokowi to Build on Momentum" <http://jakartaglobe.beritasatu.com/economy/sby-cements-infrastructure-credentials-advises-jokowi-build-momentum/> (accessed 2 March 2018).
5. See "Statistik Utang Luar Negeri Indonesia" <http://www.bi.go.id/en/iru/economic-data/external-debt/Documents/SULNI-Jan-2018.pdf> (accessed 2 March 2018).
6. Rendi A. Witular, "Jokowi launches maritime doctrine to the world", *Jakarta Post*, 13 November 2014 <http://www.thejakartapost.com/news/2014/11/13/jokowi-launches-maritime-doctrine-world.html> (accessed 26 December 2017).
7. See *Kompas*, "Ini Pertimbangan Utama Jokowi Tak Lanjutkan Rencana Jembatan Selat Sunda" [The main reason Jokowi does not continue Sunda-Strait bridge], 1 November 2014 <http://bisniskeuangan.kompas.

com/read/2014/11/01/065100626/Ini.Pertimbangan.Utama.Jokowi.Tak.
Lanjutkan.Rencana.Jembatan.Selat.Sunda?utm_source=bisniskeuangan&utm_
medium=bp-kompas&utm_campaign=related&> (accessed 26 December
2017).

8. Sabrina Asril, "Jokowi Kecewa 'Dwelling Time' di Tanjung Priok Masih
   5,5 Hari", *Kompas*, 17 June 2015 <http://bisniskeuangan.kompas.com/
   read/2015/06/17/122153726/Jokowi.Kecewa.Dwelling.Time.di.Tanjung.Priok.
   Masih.5.5.Hari> (accessed 26 December 2017).

9. *Kompas*, "Jokowi: Pemerintah Fokus Benahi Pangan dan Infra-struktur",
   15 September 2015 <http://ekonomi.kompas.com/read/2015/09/15/
   093402726/Jokowi.Pemerintah.Fokus.Benahi.Pangan.dan.Infrastruktur>
   (accessed 26 December 2017).

10. Fabian Januarius Kuwado, "Jokowi Resmikan Bendungan Pertama dari 49 yang
    Direncanakan di Indonesia", *Kompas*, 9 January 2018 <http://nasional.kompas.
    com/read/2018/01/09/16592601/jokowi-resmikan-bendungan-pertama-dari-
    49-yang-direncanakan-di-indonesia> (accessed 10 January 2018).

11. <https://finance.detik.com/energi/3660193/ramalan-rizal-ramli-soal-proyek-
    35000-mw-yang-bisa-bikin-pln-bangkrut> (accessed 2 March 2018).

12. HSBC, "ASEAN Report".

13. *Kompas*, "Bappenas kekurangan proyek", 9 September 2017 <https://kompas.
    id/baca/ekonomi/2017/09/09/bappenas-kekurangan-proyek/> (accessed
    27 December 2017).

14. Yoga Sukmana, "Rasio Pajak Masih Rendah, Sri Mulyani Heran", *Kompas*,
    12 July 2017 <http://ekonomi.kompas.com/read/2017/07/12/191629826/
    rasio-pajak-masih-rendah-sri-mulyani-heran> (accessed 27 December
    2017).

15. <http://www.thejakartapost.com/news/2018/03/04/jokowis-35000-mw-
    program-only-reaches-3-8-percent-progress.html> (accessed 21 March
    2018).

16. <http://www.thejakartapost.com/news/2018/02/19/jakarta-bandung-
    railway-project-wont-meet-target-minister.html> (accessed 21 March 2018).

17. *Jakarta Post*, "High-speed rail land acquisition to be settled in March", 9 February
    2018 <http://www.thejakartapost.com/news/2018/02/09/high-speed-rail-
    land-acquisition-to-be-settled-in-march.html> (accessed 21 March 2018).

18. Winda A. Charmila, "Government halts all elevated projects", *Jakarta Post*,
    20 February 2018 <http://www.thejakartapost.com/news/2018/02/20/
    government-halts-all-elevated-projects.html> (accessed 21 March 2018).

19. *Jakarta Post*, "Indonesia, China sign $23.3b in contracts", 14 April 2018
    <http://www.thejakartapost.com/news/2018/04/14/indonesia-china-
    sign-23-3b-in-contracts.html> (accessed 30 April 2018).

20. Calculated from "Statistik Utang Luar Negeri Indonesia" <http://www.bi.go.

id/en/iru/economic-data/external-debt/Documents/SULNI-Jan-2018.pdf>
(accessed 2 March 2018).

21. Yudith Ho, "Indonesia wins Fitch Rating upgrade months after S&P move", *Jakarta Post*, 21 December 2017 <http://www.thejakartapost.com/news/2017/12/21/indonesia-wins-fitch-rating-upgrade-months-after-sp-move.html> (accessed 27 December 2017).

22. "Mabuk Utang", *Majalah Sindo Weekly* No. 20/VI/2017.

References

ADB. *Meeting Asia's Infrastructure Needs*. Manila: Asian Development Bank, 2017 <https://www.adb.org/sites/default/files/publication/227496/special-report-infrastructure.pdf>.

Bappenas (National Development Planning Agency). *Rencana Pembangunan Jangka Menengah Nasional (RPJMN) 2015–2019* [National Medium-Term Development Plan (RPJMN) 2015–2019]. Jakarta: Bappenas, 2014.

Brilianto, Herfan. "Addressing the Infrastructure Deficit in Indonesia and Beyond". East Asia Forum, 17 February 2014 <http://www.eastasiaforum.org/2014/02/17/addressing-the-infrastructure-deficit-in-indonesia-and-beyond/>.

Davidson, Jamie S. *Indonesia's Changing Political Economy: Governing the Roads*. Cambridge: Cambridge University Press, 2015.

———. "Eminent Domain and Infrastructure under the Yudhoyono and Widodo Administrations". In *Land and Development in Indonesia: Searching for the People's Sovereignty*, edited by John McCarthy and Kathryn Robinson. Singapore: ISEAS – Yusof Ishak Institute, 2016.

DJPPR. "Indonesia PPP Day 2017". 2017 <http://www.djppr.kemenkeu.go.id/ppp>.

Gonschorek, Gerritt J. and Günther G. Schulze. "Continuity or Change? Indonesia's Intergovernmental Fiscal Transfer System under Jokowi". *Journal of Southeast Asian Economies* 35, no. 2 (August 2018): 143–64.

Gustely, Edward. "How Do Foreign Investors Perceive Opportunities in Indonesian Infrastructure?". *Prakarsa: Journal of the Indonesia Infrastructure Initiative* 22 (October 2015): 6.

Hamilton-Hart, Natasha and Günther G. Schulze. "Taxing Times in Indonesia: The Challenge of Restoring Competitiveness and the Search for Fiscal Space". *Bulletin of Indonesian Economic Studies* 52, no. 3 (2016): 265–95.

Heath, Jared. "Infrastructure in Indonesia: Building the Framework for Effective PPPs". 19 November 2013 <http://www.corrs.com.au/thinking/insights/infrastructure-in-indonesia-building-the-framework-for-effective-ppps/>.

KPPIP. "Perkembangan Pembangunan Infrastruktur di Indonesia". 2018 <https://kppip.go.id/tentang-kppip/perkembangan-pembangunan-infrastruktur-di-indonesia/>.

KSP. "2 Tahun Kerja Nyata Jokowi – JK". 2016 <https://web.kominfo.go.id/sites/default/files/KSP%202%20Tahun%20Jokowi%20JK.pdf>.

Lee, John. "Indonesia's Road Infrastructure: Accelerating the Private Sector Contribution". *Prakarsa: Journal of the Indonesia Infrastructure Initiative* 22 (October 2015): 22–27.

McCawley, Peter. "Infrastructure Policy in Indonesia, 1965–2015: A Survey". *Bulletin of Indonesian Economic Studies* 51, no. 2 (2015): 263–85 <doi: 10.1080/00074918.2015.1061916>.

Morris, Nicholas and Irene Tsjin. "How to Solve Indonesia's Infrastructure Crisis". East Asia Forum, 10 June 2015 <http://www.eastasiaforum.org/2015/06/10/how-to-solve-indonesias-infrastructure-crisis/>.

Negara, Siwage Dharma. "Indonesia's Infrastructure Development under the Jokowi Administration". In *Southeast Asian Affairs 2016*, edited by Malcolm Cook and Daljit Singh. Singapore: ISEAS – Yusof Ishak Institute, 2016.

OECD. "Private Financing and Government Support to Promote Long-Term Investment in Infrastructure". 2014.

———. "Investment: Upgrading Indonesia Infrastructure". *Indonesia Policy Brief*, March 2015.

PLN. "Power Supply Business Plan (RUPTL) PT PLN (Persero) 2012–2021". 2013 <http://energy-indonesia.com/02electrcitylaw/0130213RUPTL.pdf> (accessed 2 March 2018).

———. "Power Supply Business Plan (RUPTL) PT PLN (Persero) 2016–2025". 2016. <http://www.djk.esdm.go.id/pdf/RUPTL/RUPTL%20PLN%202016-2025.pdf> (accessed 2 March 2018).

Ray, David, and Lili Yan Ing. "Addressing Indonesia's Infrastructure Deficit". *Bulletin of Indonesian Economic Studies* 52, no. 1 (2016): 1–25.

Sandee, Henry. "Improving Connectivity in Indonesia: The Challenges of Better Infrastructure, Better Regulations, and Better Coordination". *Asian Economic Policy Review* 11 (2016): 222–38.

SMI. "PT Sarana Multi Infrastruktur (Persero): Company Profile". 2017 <https://www.ptsmi.co.id/wp-content/uploads/2017/09/Company-Profile-PT-SMI-July-2017-EN.pdf> (accessed 2 March 2018).

Suzuki, Wataru. "Indonesia lives dangerously with $355bn infrastructure drive". *Nikkei Asian Review*, 21 November 2017 <https://asia.nikkei.com/Features/Asia-Insight/Indonesia-lives-dangerously-with-355bn-infrastructure-drive> (accessed 3 March 2018).

Utomo, Wahyu. "Tantangan Pembangunan Infrastruktur di Indonesia".

6 November 2017 <https://kppip.go.id/opini/tantangan-pembangunan-infrastruktur-indonesia/>.

———. *Progres dan Prospek Pembangunan Infrastruktur*. 2018.

Warburton, Eve. "Jokowi and the New Developmentalism". *Bulletin of Indonesian Economic Studies* 52, no. 3 (2016): 297–320.

World Economic Forum (WEF). "The Global Competitiveness Report 2014–2015". 2014 <http://www3.weforum.org/docs/WEF_GlobalCompetitiveness Report_2014-15.pdf>.

World Bank. "Indonesia Infrastructure Development Policy Loan". Program Information Document (PID)- Appraisal Stage, Report No. AB3407, 2007.

———. "Indonesia: Avoiding the Trap". *Development Policy Review 2014*.

———. "Indonesia Economic Quarterly: Closing the Gap". October 2017.

10

EDUCATION IN INDONESIA
A White Elephant?

Sandra Kurniawati, Daniel Suryadarma,
Luhur Bima and Asri Yusrina

10.1 INTRODUCTION

In January 2018, President Joko Widodo stated that his government would
start to focus on improving the country's human resources (*Kompas Daily*,
3 January 2018).[1] He added that improved human resources is a necessary
condition to be able to take full advantage of Indonesia's demographic
dividends and be globally competitive.

The president's assessment is correct. Hanushek and Woessmann (2008)
find that cognitive skills have large and causal relationships with earnings,
distribution of income, and economic growth. In addition, Hanushek et al.
(2017) find that returns to these skills are larger in faster growing economies.
Since strong economic growth is usually a sign of a dynamic and rapidly
changing economy, the authors state that their finding is consistent with

This article was first published in *Journal of Southeast Asian Economies* 35, no. 2 (August 2018).

the hypothesis that highly skilled individuals are better at adapting to, and taking advantage of change.

The policy implication of the findings in the previous paragraph is straightforward: countries must ensure that their labour markets are highly skilled. From a policymaker's perspective, it means that increasing the educational attainment of the population is a necessity. And, overall, countries have largely succeeded in doing so (Pritchett 2001). The World Bank's Edstats show that the average educational attainment of adults globally has increased from 6.4 years in 1990 to 8.3 years merely two decades later.[2]

The problem, however, is that learning levels remain low for many countries. Pritchett (2013) states that in India, over a quarter of fifth graders could not read a simple sentence while only slightly more than half could perform subtraction. Mullis et al. (2012) find that only 43 per cent of Indonesian eighth grade students have some understanding of whole numbers, decimals, operations, and basic graphs. In contrast, 99 per cent of Singaporean eighth grade students have this knowledge. Therefore, the amount of learning produced by Indonesian and Singaporean education systems in the eight years of schooling are vastly different. In addition, there has been very little improvement among the weak performers. For example, Suryahadi and Sambodho (2013) show that Indonesia's performance in eighth grade TIMSS mathematics has declined between 2003 and 2011. Hanushek and Woessmann (2008) conclude that merely increasing education attainment, without focusing on the amount of learning actually accrued by students, has no correlation with economic growth.

This chapter examines numeracy and literacy levels among fifteen-year-olds in Indonesia and put them in a global perspective. Simple simulations are conducted to examine what it would mean for Indonesia to be globally competitive, as President Widodo desires (as expressed in his recent statement). This chapter describes several major education policies that President Widodo and his predecessor, President Yudhoyono have enacted. It also discusses the effects of these policies in terms of improving the skills of Indonesians, and whether they have the potential to make the country globally competitive. This chapter focuses on primary and secondary education, and leaves early childhood, vocational, and tertiary education issues for other studies.

It is important to note that education is a slow-moving sector, where the returns to investing in academic training systems and the impact of policies can only be apparent after the beneficiaries complete their education and join the labour market. In addition, as we discuss below, many education policies enacted by President Yudhoyono are still in place, albeit some under different names. Therefore, comparing the success of President Widodo with President Yudhoyono in this sector is, in some sense, too early and virtually impossible.

The next section provides a brief overview of the Indonesian primary and secondary education system, including the amount of public funds allocated to the sector. The third section discusses the level of numeracy and literacy in the country and undertakes some simulations. The subsequent section describes the current education policies in Indonesia and their impacts. The final section concludes.

10.2 PRIMARY AND SECONDARY EDUCATION SYSTEM IN INDONESIA: A BRIEF OVERVIEW

Being the fourth most populous country in the world, Indonesia's education system is large. The country's primary and secondary education sector (covering grades one to twelve) has more than 266,000 schools, where 45 million students are taught by 2.7 million teachers. Around 85 per cent of the students are enrolled in regular schools, which could be in the form of public, private non-religious, and private religious schools. The rest are in *madrasah*s — Islamic schools that are largely privately operated.[3]

The primary education level is overwhelmingly public; 87 per cent of students go to public schools. The proportion between public and private is more balanced at the secondary level. Overall, 75 per cent of junior secondary and 58 per cent of senior secondary students are enrolled in public schools. Newhouse and Beegle (2006) find that at the junior secondary level, public schools benefit from positive selection, i.e., public school enrolment is positively correlated with household wealth and primary school test score. Therefore, it seems that public schools are the preferred choice relative to private schools or *madrasah*s. At the senior secondary level, Newhouse and Suryadarma (2011) find the same pattern: students with higher junior secondary test scores and better educated parents appear to choose public schools.

Since 2001, the delivery of early childhood, primary and secondary education has been devolved to local governments. Provincial governments are in charge of senior secondary level (grades ten to twelve), consisting of general and vocational schools. The district governments are in charge of early childhood education, and also primary and junior secondary level (grades one to nine).

According to data from the Ministry of Education and Culture, the net enrolment rate in Indonesia is practically universal at the primary level at 93 per cent, around 81 per cent at the junior secondary level, and 60 per cent at the senior secondary level (Ministry of Education and Culture 2016). Education transitions between levels have also continued to increase over time, and there is little gender difference (Suharti 2013). In addition, Suharti (2013) notes that the gap in educational attainment between children from poor and rich households is non-existent at the primary level and, in fact, continues to narrow at the secondary levels. Therefore, while increasing access to senior secondary education remains a priority, the government is increasingly turning to improving the quality of primary and junior secondary levels.

Figure 10.1 shows the amount of public spending on education from 2001 to 2014, classified by source — central, provincial, and district government. It is important to note, however, that the vast majority of provincial and district government spending on education comes from central government transfers. As a proportion of total public spending, the government spent between 10 per cent and 15 per cent of its budget on education from 2001 to 2008. In 2005, parliament amended the constitution, requiring the government to spend 20 per cent of its budget on education. This was achieved for the first time in 2009, and the rate has remained around 20 per cent since.

Where has the money gone? Figure 10.1 shows that in 2014, 60 per cent of education spending was carried out by the district and provincial governments. In addition, the central government also provides direct transfers to primary and secondary schools in the form of a school operational assistance grant (known as BOS). In 2014, the BOS transfer reached Rp24 trillion (equivalent to US$2 billion).[4] Therefore, just looking at 2014, around 70 per cent of education spending was on primary and secondary education levels.

Al-Samarrai and Cerdan-Infantes (2013) find that teachers have benefited the most from the increase in education spending. For example, about half of the US$7 billion increase between 2006 and 2009 (in 2009 constant prices) was spent on hiring more teachers — which has resulted

FIGURE 10.1
Education Spending in Indonesia, 2001–14

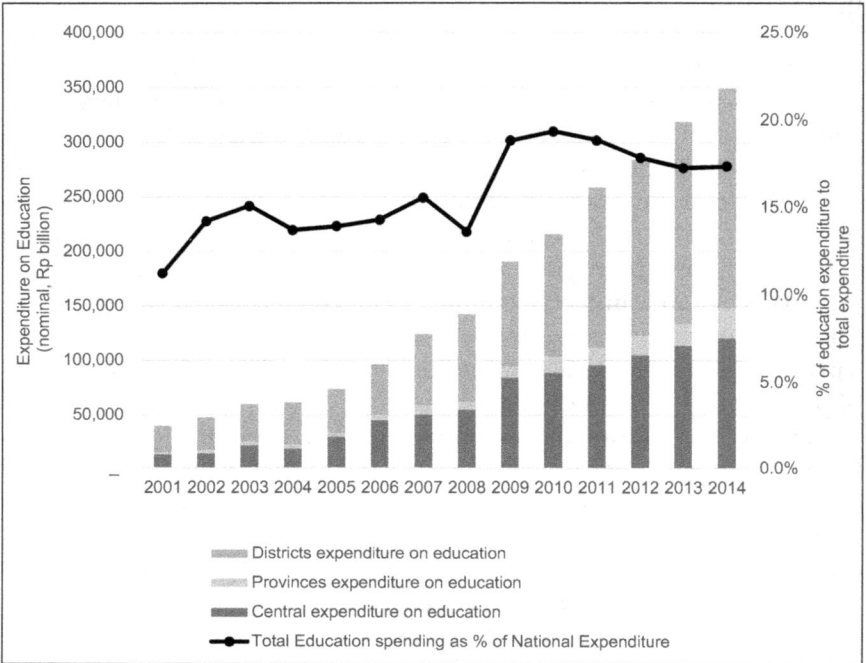

Source: Yusrina, Bima and Pradhan (2017).

in Indonesia having one of the lowest student to teacher ratios in the world — and increasing teacher salaries (discussed in section 10.4). At the district level, 80 per cent of the salaries went to teachers. From the BOS allocations, about 16 per cent are allocated to teachers (Artha 2017).

In summary, the Indonesian government invests a significant amount of its resources into the education sector. In proportional terms, spending on education has increased from around 10 per cent of national expenditure in 2001 to 20 per cent in 2009, and remained at that rate since. Most of the spending goes to primary and secondary education, especially for hiring more teachers and increasing their salaries. In the next section, we explain whether the increased spending has resulted in higher learning.

10.3 NUMERACY AND LITERACY IN INDONESIA

For the purpose of our analysis, we use data from the Programme for International Student Assessment (PISA), a triennial international survey that tests the skills and knowledge of fifteen-year-olds. Administered by the OECD (Organization for Economic Cooperation and Development), PISA started in 2000, and until 2015, had been undertaken six times. PISA participants include not only OECD nations, but also non-OECD countries. In total, eighty-eight countries and economies (for example, China and Shanghai participate separately) have participated at least once.

The tests are conducted in the national language of the countries. The skills and knowledge tested by PISA are on: numeracy; science; reading; collaborative problem solving; and financial literacy. However, only the numeracy, science, and reading tests have been undertaken since the first PISA. The focus of the Assessment is on the application of knowledge and skills for tasks relevant in adult life, as opposed to memorization.[5] As this chapter is interested in examining how the education system provides skills relevant for adult life (including in the labour market), PISA is appropriate.

Indonesia has participated in PISA since 2000. Therefore these assessment rounds can be used to examine the trend in skills of fifteen-year-old Indonesians and compare them with other participating countries. This chapter uses the 2003, 2006, 2009, 2012, and 2015 PISA tests — specifically the mathematics and reading tests.

Figure 10.2 shows the mathematics skills of Indonesian students over time, relative to two metrics: the 25th percentile score and the 75th percentile score. The former represents a low level of skills, while the latter represents the level of skills that could be considered to be globally competitive.

Three facts can be observed about the mathematics skills of fifteen-year-olds. First, Indonesia is below the 25th percentile globally. This is true up to the latest PISA round in 2015. Second, the country has been catching up. In particular, the gap between Indonesia's performance and the 25th percentile has continued to decline, from more than 113 points in 2003 to around 20 points in 2015. Similarly, the gap between Indonesia and the 75th percentile has also narrowed, from 163 points to 114 points over the observed period. This suggests that Indonesia is close to catching up with the 25th percentile, but is still far from being globally competitive. Third, the reduction in the gap between Indonesia and the 25th percentile is, to some extent, caused by the decline in the performance of the 25th percentile.

FIGURE 10.2
PISA Mathematics, 2003–15

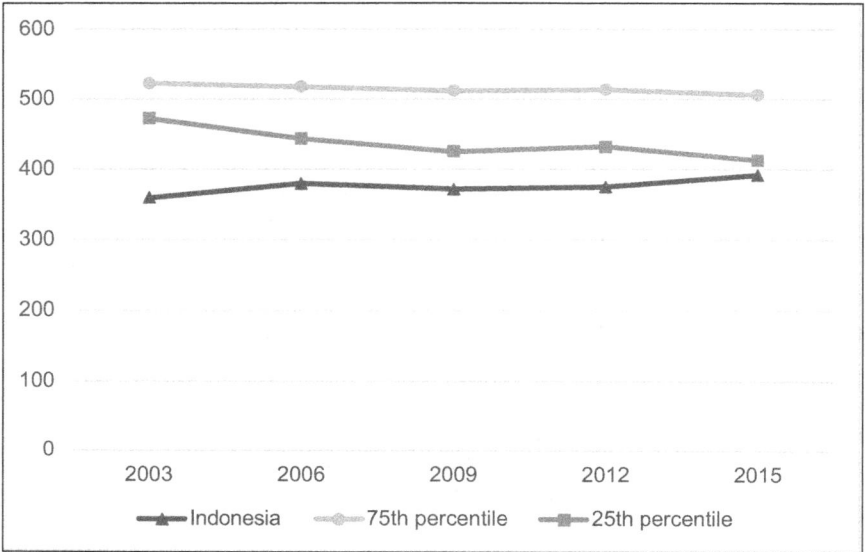

Source: PISA.

In 2003, the gap between the 25th and 75th percentile was quite small, at 50 points. In 2015, the gap almost doubled to 93 points. It is important to note that the main cause appears to be deterioration in the performance of the 25th percentile, rather than the improvement in the 75th percentile. Thus, inequality in mathematics skills is rising globally, triggered by a decline in the worst performers rather than an enhancement in the top performers. While beyond the scope of this chapter, one cause of this could be the ever increasing access to education, where children — mostly from poor families — who previously could not attend schools before are now in school. However, this also demonstrates that education systems across many parts of the world have not been able to deliver quality education for all. When it comes to Indonesia, it appears that the way the country is narrowing the gap — with the 75th percentile moving further away from the 25th percentile — is a positive outcome.

Figure 10.3 shows the trend in PISA reading tests. Overall, the three observations from Figure 10.2 remain. Indonesia started off quite far behind

FIGURE 10.3
PISA Reading, 2003–15

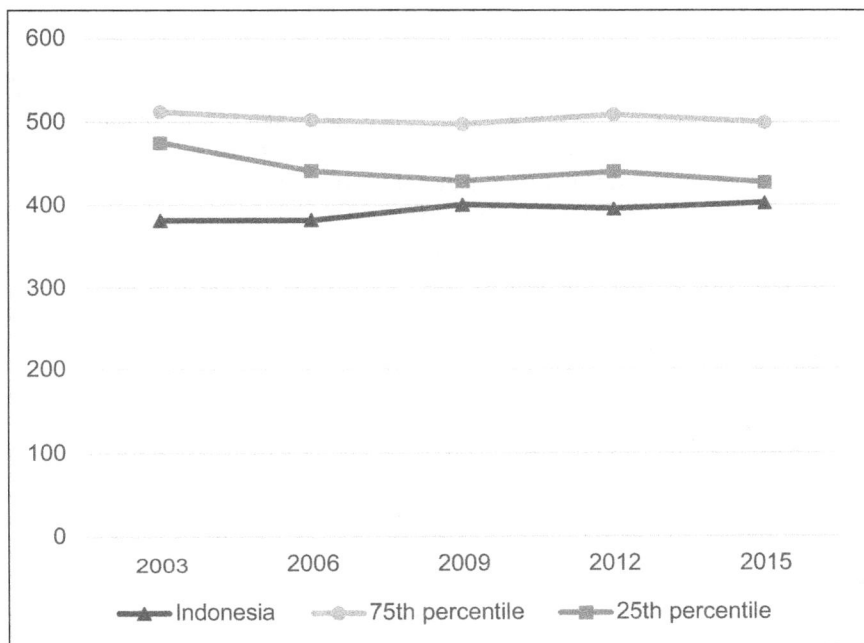

Source: PISA.

in 2003, and has since closed the gap with both the 25th percentile and the 75th percentile. However, the decline in reading gap has been slower than in mathematics. Proportionally, the gap between Indonesia and the 75th percentile narrowed by 30 per cent between 2003 and 2015. The decline in reading over the same period was 26 per cent.

Overall, the gap between Indonesia and the 75th percentile (globally competitive level) has declined in both mathematics and reading. This trend leads to two further questions. First, how long would it take for Indonesia to catch up to the 75th percentile and become globally competitive, as President Widodo wishes? Second, if Indonesia wants to catch up faster (say in 2024, at the end of President Widodo's second term (should he win a second term); or in 2030, in order to take advantage of the demographic dividends), what level of mathematics and reading skills should Indonesian children demonstrate, compared to the ones we observe in Figures 10.2 and 10.3?

To address these questions, a simple extrapolation is conducted using the PISA data, extending the study by Beatty and Pritchett (2012). Table 10.1 shows the results. If it is assumed that the long-term decline in gap between Indonesia and the 75th percentile from 2003 to 2015 persists, then Indonesia would need twenty-eight years to catch up to the 75th percentile in mathematics performance, and thirty-five years for reading performance (column 5). Since the Assessment is derived from fifteen-year-olds, then assuming that some of them would start working after completing senior secondary school and others after four-year university, Indonesia will be globally competitive around 2060. Therefore, while the mathematics and reading skills of Indonesian students have improved between cohorts, the improvement is too small for the nation to be globally competitive anytime soon. By 2060, the demographic dividend would have been long gone.

The second question is based on the extent of improvement needed in the overall education system, especially before individuals reach the age of fifteen, for Indonesia to be in the 75th percentile faster? From Table 10.1, it is found that the average annual reductions in gap between Indonesia and the 75th percentile in mathematics and reading are 4 and 3 points respectively. Table 10.2 shows different improvements in mathematics and reading skills annually to catch up to the 75th percentile. Suppose Indonesia aims to have a skilled labour force by 2030 (at the height of the demographic dividends), then the country must reach the 75th percentile around 2023–27, i.e., close to a decade from 2015. Column 3 in Table 10.2

TABLE 10.1
Number of Years Needed for Indonesia to Reach the 75th Percentile in PISA

	Gap in 2003 (points)	Gap in 2015 (points)	Decline in Gap, 2003–15 (points)	Average annual decline in gap (points)	Years needed for gap to reach zero (years)
	(1)	(2)	(3)	(4)	(5)
Math	163	114	49	4	28
Reading	131	97	33	3	35

Source: PISA, author estimation.

TABLE 10.2
Improvement Needed to Reach 75th Percentile, Various Targets

	Gap in 2015 (points)	Annual Decline in Gap Needed for Indonesia to be in the 75th Percentile (points)				Increase in Education Sector Performance Needed (%)			
		5 yrs	10 yrs	15 yrs	20 yrs	5 yrs	10 yrs	15 yrs	20 yrs
	(1)	(2)	(3)	(4)	(5)	(6)	(7)	(8)	(9)
Math	114	23	11	8	6	455.0	177.5	85.0	38.7
Reading	97	19	10	6	5	595.6	247.8	131.9	73.9

Source: PISA, author estimation.

shows that for this to happen, the gap must be reduced by 11 and 10 points annually for mathematics and reading, respectively, starting from 2015. Correspondingly, Column 10 shows that the education system must raise its performance by 178 per cent for mathematics and 248 per cent for reading.

Such an improvement is very challenging for an education system to attain. While education has received a significant boost in investments over the past decade, progress has been far from substantial. Since investments in the sector have already reached 20 per cent of government expenditure, as shown in Figure 10.1, further increase may be very difficult. Therefore, the only way to improve skills is by enhancing the productivity of the education system with the same level of investment.

Before moving to the next section, it should be pointed out that children from low socioeconomic status households perform much worse than their high socioeconomic status counterparts. In the specific case of numeracy, however, the gap has not narrowed (Al-Samarrai and Cerdan-Infantes 2013). Therefore, while the enrolment gap between children from poor and rich households has narrowed, the condition is less encouraging in terms of numeracy. This may indicate that children from poor households are enrolling in inferior schools.

The following section discusses some of the education policies that the Yudhoyono and Widodo governments have enacted. It focuses on both presidencies because the effect of education policies on learning outcomes tends to materialize in the long run, if at all. For the policies we evaluate, impact estimates are also provided. For those that are relatively new and not included in this study, it offers a discussion on their potential impact on improving the productivity of the country's education system.

10.4 EDUCATION POLICIES AND THE IMPACT ON LEARNING OUTCOMES

This section describes six main education policies implemented in Indonesia since 2004, at the start of the Yudhoyono presidency. For this analysis, the scholarship schemes for children from poor families, *Bantuan Siswa Miskin* (during Yudhoyono's presidency) and *Kartu Indonesia Pintar* (during Widodo's presidency) are excluded because they are considered social protection programmes aimed at getting children into school and ensuring that they do not drop out. As such, the programmes are not relevant to the topic of this chapter, i.e., quality of education in the country. For the same reason, the government's conditional cash transfer programmes (*Program Keluarga Harapan* and PNPM *Generasi*), under which, school participation is a requirement are also excluded. Finally, the district-level education policies are side-stepped because many of them focus on providing higher allowance for teachers and have virtually no effects on learning (Bima and Yusrina 2018).

The first two policies that are discussed are the ones that take up a significant amount of Indonesia's education budget: (1) the "teacher certification"; and (2) the "school operational assistance". Afterwards, the "teacher competence test", the new "in-service teacher development" programme, the new "pre-service teacher training" programme, and the "computer-based testing" scheme are discussed.

10.4.1 A Brief Review of the Correlates of Student Learning Outcomes

Many of the policies we discuss below have either not been rigorously evaluated, or are relatively new. With the exception of the teacher certification programme, so far, there is no estimation of the impact of these policies on learning outcomes. For this reason, we believe it would be informative to provide a brief review of the correlates of education quality in Indonesia, usually proxied by student test scores in various subjects. The evidence would allow us to determine whether the education policies could be expected to have any considerable impact.

Examining the correlation between teacher characteristics and student performance, Suryadarma et al. (2006) use survey data from 100 primary schools across Indonesia, and find that teacher absenteeism rates have a statistically significant and negative correlation with mathematics performance. In addition, factors like teachers with other occupations, teachers with permanent (civil servant) status, and female teachers are all negatively correlated with mathematics performance of students. In a survey of 360 primary and junior secondary schools in twenty districts that match students with their teachers, World Bank (2016) finds that teachers with formal qualification (such as a bachelor's degree) are only moderately better. Also, the study finds that paying teachers more does not make them teach better. Finally, the research shows that teacher content knowledge is very important in determining student performance. This is especially important because many teachers in Indonesia have been found to possess very low content knowledge. However, Popova, Evans and Arancibia (2016), in their systematic review of twenty-six in-service teacher training programmes around the world with rigorous impact evaluations, find that there is little detail on teacher training interventions. While they find that programmes that provide complementary materials, focus on a specific subject, and include follow-up visits tend to show higher gains, overall, there is little evidence on the types of training programmes that may generate large gains.

In the context of teachers and principals, an often-ignored topic relates to incentives. Kurniasih, Utari and Akhmadi (2018) find that the Indonesian constitution views education as a way to build character. Bjork (2006) finds that, in Indonesia, schooling has been viewed as a means to instil patriotism. A particularly striking example from Bjork (2006) is the observation that no teachers were absent during the Monday flag-raising ceremony, but some left the school immediately after the ceremony was over. Panjaitan (2017) finds rampant cheating in national school examinations in Indonesia, and that teachers and principals are complicit in these practices. These anecdotes show that the incentives for teachers and principals are not aligned with the objective of educating students. Therefore, policies that do not consider the incentive structures would have little chance of succeeding in the country.

On school level characteristics, Suryadarma et al. (2006) find that that quality of school facilities predict better performance. Well-functioning toilets are especially important for girls' performance. The authors also conclude that the student-to-teacher ratio has a concave relationship with performance, and the optimal ratio appears to be at twenty-five students per teacher. World Bank (2018) finds that relevant and accurate student assessments, both formative and summative, would significantly improve learning outcomes.

One particularly relevant aspect for Indonesia, given the large public investment in education, is the correlation between the amount of funds allocated to education and student performance. Suryadarma (2012) finds no correlation between district-level spending and student performance. Likewise, at the school level, Suryadarma et al. (2006) find zero correlation between amount of school fees and student performance in mathematics or dictation tests. One reason could be corruption, but another reason is that the funds are not spent on things that matter for education quality. The latter could happen when teachers and principals are not incentivized to care about learning, which seems to be the case in Indonesia.

10.4.2 Major Education Policies in Indonesia since 2004

10.4.2.1 Teacher Certification. The main purpose of this policy is to ensure that teachers have sufficient skills. World Bank (2016) states that the motivation for the programme comes from Indonesia's low performance in the 2000 PISA. Policymakers felt that teacher quality has been inadequate and must be upgraded. To gain buy in, the policy promises a significant increase in remuneration for certified teachers. With the certification allowance being equivalent to base pay, certified teachers essentially receive a doubling of income. While there are various estimations with regard to the cost of this policy — ranging from US$5.6 billion (Fahmi, Maulana and Yusuf 2011) to virtually all of the public education budget (Al-Samarrai and Cerdan-Infantes 2013) — it is clear that this policy is very expensive.

In order to be certified, the initial policy design required teachers to obtain a bachelor's degree, pass a written competency test, be observed in the classroom, and submit a portfolio of past training and experience. The original idea was that teachers without these qualifications would have a clear financial incentive to upgrade their skills (World Bank 2016). In practice, however, the initial design was significantly watered down due to pressure from the teachers' union. Only the portfolio assessment, experience, and bachelor's degree requirement were retained (Chang et al.

2013). Suryahadi and Sambodho (2013) note that there also exist other channels to receive certification, such as passing the in-service teacher development programme (see further below in this section) or completing a master's or doctoral degree.

The certification programme started in 2006 and has certified around 20,000 teachers annually. The initial aim was to have all teachers certified by 2015. While detailed data on the proportion of teachers certified is not available, it appears that this target has been missed.

Teacher certification is one of the very few government education policies in Indonesia whose impact has been rigorously evaluated. Given the watering down of the certification requirements, lack of conditionality on receiving the allowance, and the finding that formal qualification by itself has very small effects on learning outcomes, there is little hope that the certification programme has any effect on learning outcomes. De Ree et al. (2017), indeed, find that the scheme improves teacher satisfaction and reduces the incidence of teachers holding outside jobs. However, there is no improvement in student learning outcomes across the whole distribution of test scores. Fahmi et al. (2011) arrive at the same conclusion, despite using a different research methodology. Similarly, Kusumawardhani (2017) shows that the certification policy does not improve teacher content knowledge or attendance.

10.4.2.2 School Operational Assistance. The programme, known by its Indonesian acronym, BOS, is a direct per-student grant from the central government to schools. The government began implementing the scheme in 2005 as part of compulsory education (World Bank 2015). The grant is provided to both public and private schools at primary and secondary levels, and can be used on an approved list of expenditure — ranging from administration to teacher allowance.

As of 2014, BOS covered 43 million primary and junior secondary school students annually, costing around US$2 billion (or equivalent to 7 per cent of the total education budget). Artha (2017) finds that the bulk of BOS is spent on buying school supplies, paying for student extracurricular activities, and teacher salaries (including providing additional teacher allowances, as well as hiring more teachers). These three areas made up 48 per cent of BOS spending in 2015.

The BOS grant can affect education participation and learning through three channels: increased funding and reduced household burden; direct support to poor students; and strengthened school-based management. World Bank (2015) finds little effect of BOS on reducing household education spending. Instead, as discussed in the previous paragraph, a large proportion of the grant is used to hire more teachers. However, the report finds that junior secondary enrolment among poor households appear to benefit from BOS, although there is no impact on transition rate to senior secondary. Finally, there is no impact of the scheme on school-based management. In summary, out of the three potential channels, only the one on direct support to poor students appears to have worked. Therefore, there is little surprise that there is no statistically significant impact of BOS allocation on national examination scores at the primary or junior secondary level (Artha 2017).

10.4.2.3 Teacher Competence Test. As part of the teacher certification programme, the government introduced a teacher competence test (known by its Indonesian acronym UKG). After much pushback from teacher unions, the first competence test was administered in 2012, covering pedagogical knowledge and content knowledge. In total, just above a million teachers participated in the first test. The result, with an average of 47 (out of 100), was discouraging. The government had set the passing threshold at 65.

Although controversial and subject of criticism from many parties (from those who do not believe teachers should be tested, to those who think the test does not actually measure skills that matter for teachers), for the first time, the government has a mapping of teachers' knowledge level. As a diagnostic tool, the competence test is invaluable.

10.4.2.4 In-service Teacher Professional Development. With the UKG results in hand, the government has the ability to map teachers' weaknesses, down to the individual level. To improve the quality of teachers, the government implements an in-service teacher professional development programme called *Guru Pembelajar* (teacher learner), which has now been renamed as *Pengembangan Keprofesian Berkelanjutan* (PKB) (continuing professional development). This programme began in 2014, and still continues.

To participate in this scheme, teachers should be a member of a teacher community, such as the Primary Teachers' Working Group (KKG), or the Secondary School Subjects Teachers' Working Group (MGMP). The Center for Teacher and Education Personnel Development and Empowerment

(P4TK) is the technical unit at the Ministry of Education and Culture that is responsible for managing and supervising the PKB programme and the UKG post-test.

The current set up of the programme is as follows:

(i)   Teachers undertake face-to-face training in the modules of UKG that they failed;

(ii) Each module is around sixty hours, consisting of thirty hours of training, ten hours of on-the-job mentoring, and twenty hours of review/feedback/sharing workshop; and

(iii) Upon completion of the sixty hours, a teacher needs to sit in another UKG related to the specific modules that he/she failed. Anecdotal stories say that the pass rate in this UKG post-test is 100 per cent.

We are not aware of any rigorous evaluation of the programme, either on the quality of implementation or regarding its impact on teacher knowledge, teaching practice, or student learning outcomes.

10.4.2.5 One-year Professional Training for Pre-service Teachers. This brand new programme, called *Pendidikan Profesi Guru* (PPG, Teacher Professional Education) started in September 2017, and aims to increase the quality of teacher candidates in the country. It is a one-year programme modelled after other professional programmes for aspiring doctors, lawyers, and psychologists. After finishing a four-year degree, Indonesians who want to pursue a career in teaching can enrol in the PPG scheme. To widen the pool of high-quality teachers, PPG is open to both graduates from teacher-colleges, as well as non-teacher colleges. It is arguably the government's main vehicle to improve teacher quality and is therefore subsidized.

According to the Ministry of Research Technology and Higher Education (which is responsible for higher education, including teacher colleges), this additional year towards teaching, in theory, would improve the quality of teacher candidates. The first channel is through the selection process. The PPG applicants need a minimum GPA of 3.0/4.0 to pass the first screening. After that, these applicants go through a series of online standardized tests to assess their professional, pedagogic, social, and personal competencies. They also undergo a psychological test to determine their talent and interest in teaching. The chosen PPG students study in selected LPTK across the country. During the programme, they sit through various teaching workshops and practice classroom teaching (microteaching). This is the second channel by which PPG hopes to improve teacher quality.

Despite the rigorous selection process and few changes in curriculum, the programme is still too new to be evaluated thoroughly. However, the reliance on a selective admission system is encouraging. If strictly enforced, it could (potentially) enhance teaching quality and eventually lead to better learning outcomes.

10.4.2.6 Computer-based Testing. A noteworthy feature of the Indonesian education system is the high-stakes national examination at the end of junior secondary and senior secondary levels. Students must pass these examinations in order to graduate. Additionally, district governments regularly use national examination pass rates to measure education quality. The result is extensive cheating. Panjaitan (2017) documents the extent of this practice and finds that teachers and principals, under pressure from district officials and parents, are active participants in the scheme. The government has attempted to address this issue, too. In 2016, the Ministry of Education and Culture removed performance in the national examination as a condition for graduation. Instead, school-based examinations now determine whether a student graduates. While this policy effectively turns the national examination to a diagnostic (formative assessment) tool rather than a summative evaluation tool, cheating in the national examination remains rampant.

The problem with cheating is that the results do not reflect the true amount of learning that students attain. Therefore, it cannot be used as a diagnostic tool or employed to measure the impact of particular policies or practices.

In 2013, the Ministry of Education and Culture piloted computer-based testing (CBT) in two schools. Practically, CBT means that each student receives a unique test, as the items are randomly drawn from a centralized item bank.

There are several ways that cheating becomes more difficult with CBT:

(i) Each student receives a unique exam, so students cannot copy answers from other nearby students;

(ii) Teachers cannot supply students with answers to the test because there are virtually infinite tests; and

(iii) The test is retrieved online and has a time limit, making it impossible to prepare answers before the test is taken.

In 2015, the Ministry piloted CBT in 556 junior and senior secondary schools across the country. The pilot revealed a significant reduction in test scores in the participant schools. The decline in test scores was larger in schools that initially had a lower integrity index, suggesting that this was, at least partially, the result of reduced cheating, rather than student difficulty with navigating the new test format. In 2016, 4,382 junior and senior secondary schools participated in CBT, while in 2017, the number has increased to 30,577 (Ministry of Education and Culture 2017). The Ministry plans to roll out CBT in 70 per cent of junior secondary schools and 100 per cent of senior secondary schools by 2018.

While the CBT is not implemented with an explicit aim to improve teaching or learning outcomes, the severely diminished prospect of cheating, together with its still-high-stakes nature, has the potential to incentivize teachers to actually teach better. With the easy ways of cheating eliminated, teaching properly is the only way their students can perform well in the examination. Therefore, while there is yet to be an evaluation of the impact of CBT on teaching and student learning outcomes, the potential is certainly there.

Table 10.3 presents a summary of the policies we discuss in this section. Out of the six policies, four address the issue of low teaching skills. This implies that the government realizes that teaching skills/knowledge is the most important hurdle that needs to be overcome. However, the main lesson from the two most expensive policies, teacher certification and BOS, is that providing resources unconditionally would not lead to any significant gains; these programmes must be tied directly to student learning outcomes. Similarly, just providing training would also not lead to any learning improvement, let alone gains that are large enough for Indonesia to quickly catch up to the other countries.

10.5 CONCLUSION

President Widodo views human resources as a necessary condition for Indonesia to be globally competitive. Indeed, evidence from across the globe shows that highly skilled individuals not only earn more, but also cope better, even thrive, in a rapidly changing environment.

TABLE 10.3
Summary of Central Government Education Policies in Indonesia

Policy	Year started	Constraint the Policy Aims to Alleviate	Provide Incentives Directly Tied to Learning (Yes/No)	Impact on Learning
Teacher certification	2005	Low teaching skills	No	Statistically not different from zero
School operational assistance	2005	School-level resources; support for children from poor families; weak school-based management	No	Statistically not different from zero
Teacher competence test	2012	Lack of information on teacher knowledge	No	N/A because this is a diagnostic tool, although World Bank (2016) finds positive correlation between teacher knowledge and student performance.
Program Keprofesian Berkelanjutan (in-service teacher professional development programme)	2014	Low teacher knowledge	No	Unknown
Program Pendidikan Guru (one year pre-service teacher training)	2017	Low teaching skills	No	Unknown
Computer-based Testing	2015	Inaccurate assessment of student learning	Yes, unintended	Unknown

Source: Authors' assessment

This chapter finds that Indonesia is on a positive long-term trajectory with regard to producing skilled individuals. However, the trajectory is not sufficiently steep to achieve significant improvements in the medium term. Making simple out-of-sample projections using Indonesia's performance in PISA mathematics and reading from 2003 to 2015, it is found that the country will only reach the global 75th percentile (in the two areas) in 2060. Given that Indonesia has essentially doubled its public investment in education in recent years, it is observed that the returns have been very small.

Increasing the slope of mathematics and reading skills requires either a significantly larger investment, or better returns on the current investment. Indonesia does not have much room for the former option. This chapter's findings suggest that the education system must increase its productivity by 180 per cent in mathematics and 250 per cent in reading in order to produce a globally competitive workforce by 2030, as opposed to 2060.

Based on a review of the central government's major education policies, it is found that they are quite costly. The two most expensive policies, teacher certification and school operational assistance, have a combined cost that uses up almost all of the public education allocation. These two policies, however, have no discernible effects on improving student learning outcomes. The main reason, as de Ree et al. (2017) and World Bank (2015) suspect, is because of the lack of accountability. The programmes are, essentially, unconditional transfers to teachers and schools.

Given that it would be virtually impossible to roll back these programmes without suffering significant political costs, it is recommended that the government add accountability measures to all education policies that use learning as the ultimate performance indicator. In fact, the teacher certification and school operational assistance programmes should be urgently reformed to bring about some positive change. Fundamentally, the government needs to start imposing certain conditions before teachers and schools continue receiving these transfers. One such condition must be observable progress in student learning outcomes that is commensurate with the cost of these policies. Without such accountability measures, Indonesia has little chance of becoming globally competitive anytime soon.

Notes

1. See <https://nasional.kompas.com/read/2018/01/03/16514421/2018-jokowi-ingin-pemerintah-fokus-tingkatkan-sdm>.

2. <http://databank.worldbank.org/data/reports.aspx?source=Education%20
    Statistics>.
3. <http://referensi.data.kemdikbud.go.id>.
4. See <http://www.djpk.depkeu.go.id/attach/pmk-nomor-201pmk-072013/
    PMK_BOS_2014_optimize.pdf>.
5. See <http://www.oecd.org/education/school/2960581.pdf>.

References

Al-Samarrai, Samer and Pedro Cerdan-Infantes. "Where did all the Money Go? Financing Basic Education in Indonesia". In *Education in Indonesia*, edited by D. Suryadarma and G.W. Jones. Singapore: Institute of Southeast Asian Studies, 2013.

Artha, Rima. "The Impact of School Operational Assistance Allocation on Student Performance at the District Level". Unpublished manuscript. University of Indonesia, Depok, 2017.

Beatty, Amanda and Lant Pritchett. *From Schooling Goals to Learning Goals: How Fast can Student Learning Improve?* CGD Policy Paper 012. Washington, D.C.: Center for Global Development, 2012.

Bima, Luhur and Asri Yusrina. "More Prosperous Teachers have No Impact on the Quality of Education". 2018 <https://theconversation.com/more-prosperous-teachers-have-no-impact-on-the-quality-of-education-90690> (accessed March 2018).

Chang, Mae Chu, Sheldon Shaeffer, Samer Al-Samarrai, Andrew B. Ragatz, Joppe de Ree and Ritchie Stevenson. *Teacher Reform in Indonesia: The Role of Politics and Evidence in Policy Making*. Washington, D.C.: World Bank, 2013.

de Ree, Joppe, Karthik Muralidharan, Menno Pradhan and Halsey Rogers. "Double for Nothing? Experimental Evidence on an Unconditional Teacher Salary Increase in Indonesia". *Quarterly Journal of Economics* (2017) <https://doi.org/10.1093/qje/qjx040>.

Fahmi, Mohamad, Achmad Maulana and Arief Anshory Yusuf. "Teacher Certification in Indonesia: A Confusion of Means and Ends". Working Paper in Economics and Development Studies No. 201107. Padjadjaran University, Bandung, 2011.

Hanushek, Eric and Ludger Woessmann. "The Role of Cognitive Skills in Economic Development". *Journal of Economic Literature* 46, no. 3 (2008): 607–68.

———, Guido Schwerdt, Simon Wiederhold and Ludger Woessmann. "Coping with Change: International Differences in the Returns to Skills". *Economics Letters* 153 (2017): 15–19.

Kurniasih, Heni, Valentina Y.D. Utari and Akhmadi. *Character Education and Its*

Implications for Learning in Indonesia's Education System. RISE Insight. Oxford: RISE Directorate, 2018.

Kusumawardhani, Prita Nurmalia. "Does Teacher Certification Program Lead to Better Quality Teachers? Evidence from Indonesia". *Education Economics* 25, no. 6 (2017): 590–618.

Ministry of Education and Culture. *APK/APM tahun 2015/2016*. Jakarta: Ministry of Education and Culture, 2016.

Mullis, Ina V.S., Michael O. Martin, Pierre Foy and Alka Arora. *TIMSS 2011 International Results in Mathematics*. Chestnut Hill, MA: Lynch School of Education, Boston College, 2012.

Newhouse, David and Kathleen Beegle. "The Effect of School Type on Academic Achievement: Evidence from Indonesia". *Journal of Human Resources* 41, no. 3 (2006): 529–57.

———— and Daniel Suryadarma. "The Value of Vocational Education: High School Type and Labor Market Outcomes in Indonesia". *World Bank Economic Review* 25, no. 2 (2011): 296–322.

Panjaitan, Debby Elfrida. "Student Cheating in National Examinations: A Case of Indonesia". Master's dissertation. Osaka Jogakuin University, Osaka, 2017.

Popova, Anna, David Evans and Violeta Arancibia. *Training Teachers on the Job: What Works and How to Measure It*. Policy Research Working Paper 7834. Washington, D.C.: World Bank, 2016.

Pritchett, Lant. "Where has all the Education Gone?". *World Bank Economic Review* 15, no. 3 (2001): 367–91.

————. *The Rebirth of Education: Schooling ain't Learning*. Washington, D.C.: Center for Global Development, 2013.

Suharti. "Trends in Education in Indonesia". In *Education in Indonesia*, edited by D. Suryadarma and G.W. Jones. Singapore: Institute of Southeast Asian Studies, 2013.

Suryadarma, Daniel. "How Corruption Diminishes the Effectiveness of Public Spending on Education in Indonesia". *Bulletin of Indonesian Economic Studies* 48, no. 1 (2012): 85–100.

————, Asep Suryahadi, Sudarno Sumarto and F. Halsey Rogers. "Improving Student Performance in Public Primary Schools in Developing Countries: Evidence from Indonesia". *Education Economics* 14, no. 4 (2006): 401–29.

Suryahadi, Asep and Prio Sambodho. "An Assessment of Policies to Improve Teacher Quality and Reduce Teacher Absenteeism". In *Education in Indonesia*, edited by D. Suryadarma and G.W. Jones. Singapore: Institute of Southeast Asian Studies, 2013.

World Bank. *Growing Smarter: Learning and Equitable Development in East Asia and Pacific*. Washington, D.C.: World Bank, 2018.

————. *Indonesia: Teacher Certification and Beyond*. Report No. 94019-ID. Washington, D.C.: World Bank, 2016.

————. *Improving Education through the Indonesian School Operational Assistance Program (BOS)*. Policy Brief. Jakarta: World Bank, 2015.

Yusrina, Asri, Luhur Bima and Menno Pradhan. *Learning Profile of Basic Education in Indonesia*. Jakarta: SMERU Research Institute, 2017.

11

LABOUR MARKET DEVELOPMENTS IN THE JOKOWI YEARS

Chris Manning and Devanto Pratomo

11.1 INTRODUCTION

In 2014, President Joko "Jokowi" Widodo took office with strong nationalist party credentials. He is also the first president with significant and successful business experience. It is an unusual combination of a nationalist inclination combined with a pragmatic approach that focuses on action and results more than programmes and planning. Both these characteristics suggest an approach that is different from that of his predecessor Susilo Bambang Yudhoyono (SBY) in regard to social issues and the labour market.

Like Yudhoyono, Jokowi has strongly supported agriculture and food self-sufficiency, as well as self-reliance in the public documents that set

This article was first published in *Journal of Southeast Asian Economies* 35, no. 2 (August 2018).

out his five-year term plans and policy directions.[1] The country's overall economic policy framework has not undergone a dramatic change in focus under Jokowi — continuities are especially evident in regard to macroeconomic policies. But microeconomic reform has emerged as a priority. Simplification of administrative processes and concrete reform packages across a wide range of areas of the economy have quickly become a hallmark of his presidency. Jokowi has been more wedded to the nuts and bolts of microeconomic reform than Yudhoyono. This bodes well for employment and skills.

When it comes to labour market issues, Jokowi's approach has emphasized combining fair wages with greater business certainty to make sure sufficient *better jobs* are created. In the policy domain, he has been assisted by the Minister of Manpower, Hanif Dhakiri, who has also been pragmatic and committed to labour reforms in contrast to several predecessors in this position. In areas like international migration, Jokowi reaffirmed the government's strong commitment to improve labour standards. On the ground, there was a major shake-up as his cabinet sought to promote more investment (and hence more jobs) and improved living standards for working families. Emphasis has been on programmes that raise the productivity and skills of workers, which fits well with the president's private sector background. With some modifications, most programmes oriented directly towards poverty alleviation — a hallmark of the Yudhoyono era — have continued. But like in other areas of public policy, the sheer volume of policy initiatives has not always been backed up with institutional arrangements that ensure effective implementation.

This study looks at labour issues and policies during the Jokowi presidency in the context of developments since the Asian Financial Crisis (AFC) and regime change in 1998, paying special attention to comparisons with Yudhoyono's second term (2009–14). The outline is as follows. The next section sets the scene with a brief look at Indonesia's standing in regard to labour market performance from a comparative Asian experience. The third section looks at the employment and productivity record under Jokowi, the fourth at wage policies and trends, and the fifth at Jokowi's approach to skill issues. In the subsequent section, we examine the policies towards migrant workers, where social concerns have begun to outweigh economic goals. The final section concludes.

11.2 THE LABOUR MARKET UNDER JOKOWI: SOME COMPARATIVE PERSPECTIVES

Indonesia was already well established as a middle-income country when the Jokowi administration took over in October 2014. At that point, the labour market faced a dual set of challenges related to the economy of both the past and the future. Incomes, wages and productivity were (and continue to be) very low, and a major challenge has been to try and move a significant share of the workforce — well over one-third — out of low-productivity and vulnerable jobs in agriculture and the informal sector (Manning and Purnagunawan 2016). Success in this endeavour mostly depends on the rate and pattern of economic growth, that is, generating enough jobs through growth and employment-friendly investments.

The other, no less pressing, challenge is to equip an increasingly well-educated segment of the workforce with skills to raise productivity and support a technological transition, as Indonesia competes with other middle-income countries in moving up the income scale (McKinsey 2012). Part of this challenge is to take advantage of the digital revolution, which has heralded a significant change in economic structure and begun to propel the economy in new directions (Pangestu and Dewi 2017). Achieving this involves not only encouraging higher-technology investments, but also arming people with skills that are relevant to the new digital technology. Some initiatives are already being taken in the short to medium term to try to bridge the skills gap. In the longer term, however, it is widely acknowledged that there needs to be a transformation of basic and applied education — at all levels — if productivity is to be raised significantly.[2]

We set this discussion on employment, productivity, wages and skills in Indonesia in the context of progress and problems experienced by other comparable Asian economies that have grown quickly over the past few decades.[3] Overall, since the AFC hit hard in 1998, achievements in the country have been intermediate from an international perspective, in terms of both supply and demand indicators of the labour market. While it is distinctive on some scores, on most indicators Indonesia's rankings have been broadly in line with what might be expected from a large country well on its way to transitioning to upper middle-income status.

- *On the labour supply side,* five characteristics in particular help determine the size and quality of Indonesia's workforce: first, moderately fast growth in the working-age population in the Asian context — in Indonesia, close to 2 per cent growth in 2015, falling to around 1.5 per cent per annum by 2025; second, a high but declining dependency ratio offering the prospect of around fifteen years of "demographic bonus" until around 2030; third, urbanization that has been quite rapid in the Southeast Asian context, although not so when compared with Vietnam, Lao PDR, or China in recent years;[4] fourth, quite high female participation rates in the workforce (close to 50 per cent in 2017) for a predominantly Muslim population, but at the same time "stickiness" in female activity rates over the past few years (Cameron and Suarez 2015; Manning and Pratomo 2018); and finally, still quite low but nonetheless big improvements in average (expected) years of schooling — estimated at just under 13 years in 2015, up from 10.6 in 2000[5] — accompanied by the disturbing problem of low quality schooling at all levels.

- *In terms of employment and productivity,* Indonesia still has some distance to go before being classified as a mature middle-income country. It still has just under one-third of its workforce in agriculture (2017) which is moderately high by regional standards. The share of employment in manufacturing (14 per cent in 2017) is close to the low figure currently recorded in the Philippines, but far below the share in Malaysia and Thailand at similar stages of development. Also, output per worker — estimated at just under US$24,000 per worker per year in 2017 — is intermediate in the Asian context, well above that in India and Vietnam, but low compared to China (just over US$27,000) in 2017.[6]

- Finally, Indonesia does not rank high in terms of *labour utilization.* The total and youth unemployment rates (the latter just under 20 per cent in 2017) have always been high by Southeast Asian standards, with the exception of the Philippines. This is also true for the proportion of working age youth who are neither in employment nor in school (around 25 per cent in 2015–16) — another indicator of under-utilization of the workforce.

11.3 JOKOWI'S RECORD ON JOBS AND PRODUCTIVITY

The record of the Jokowi government, so far, has been quite impressive in terms of jobs outside agriculture, compared to most Indonesian administrations in the post-crisis period. This can be observed not only in services, but also manufacturing. It should, however, be noted that the country has not performed so well in regard to labour productivity. This brings to the fore issues both on the supply side — policies to mobilize and augment skills — as well as industrial performance and policies. In this section, we discuss some of the factors behind this contrasting experience.

11.3.1 Employment

Figure 11.1 provides data on employment in the country's major sectors under Jokowi (2014–17) along with the second Yudhoyono administration (2009–14), and patterns in the early post-Soeharto period (2001–09).[7] Consistent with growth of the digital economy globally, Indonesia is well on its way to becoming a service-based economy. In this context, three features of the Jokowi period are noteworthy. First, agricultural employment has started to fall quite steeply in absolute numbers, following a slower decline during the Global Financial Crisis of 2008–09. Employment dynamics also have parallels with what had occurred almost three decades earlier when many workers left the primary sector in search of non-agricultural jobs in the decade before the AFC. Between 2014 and 2017, agricultural employment has fallen by nearly 3 per cent (or around 1 million people per annum). Seemingly, this was a combination of job losses at the end of the commodity boom, and more workers being drawn out of low paid agriculture into better jobs — mainly in a range of services industries (Figure 11.2).

Second, manufacturing employment has continued to revive under Jokowi, a process that began in the second Yudhoyono period (2009–14). Output in industry and manufacturing recovered after the AFC in the early 2000s, but jobs in these sectors did not rebound. As is widely known, Indonesia experienced "jobless growth" in manufacturing for the first decade after the crisis until the first Yudhoyono years (World Bank 2010). However, this did not continue when the resource boom came to an end around 2011. In part, this might be attributed to the Jokowi government's strong support for labour-intensive industries (such as garments and footwear) — especially in the president's home province of Central Java — in areas like Kendal in the north, as well as in upland regions such as Boyolali and Salatiga. The main problem is that the recovery of exports

FIGURE 11.1
Employment Growth in Major Sectors, Indonesia Since the Crisis (Percentage)

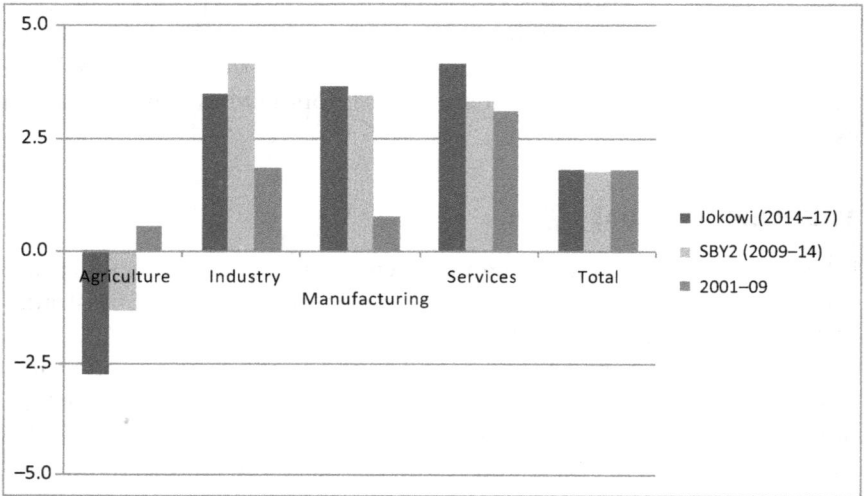

Note: *Industry* consists of mining, manufacturing, utilities and waste disposal and construction. Services consists of trade, restaurants and hotels, transport and communications, business and finance and personal, community and social services (including government and security).
Source: BPS, National Labour Force Survey (SAKERNAS), August round, various years.

FIGURE 11.2
Employment Growth in Service Industries, Indonesia Since the Crisis
(Percentage p.a.)

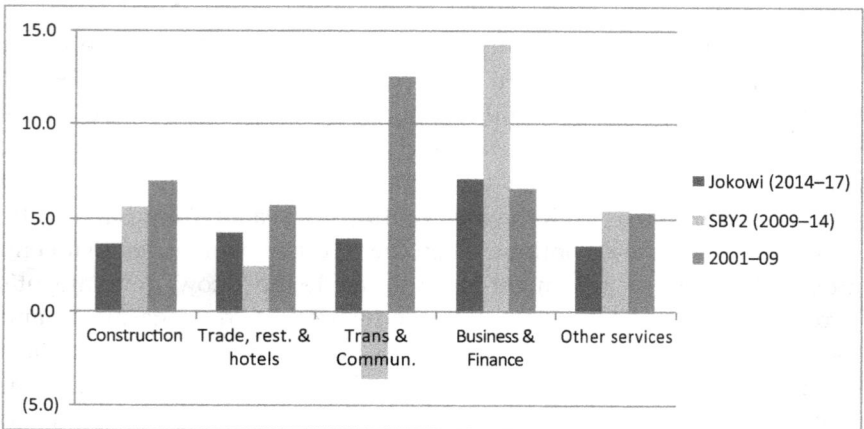

Source: BPS, National Labour Force Survey (SAKERNAS), August round, various years.

in these industries has been slow compared to the New Order period, mainly due to domestic obstacles (especially infrastructure), competition from China and Vietnam, and the slowdown in world trade.

The third feature refers to the accelerated increase in the share of formal sector workers.[8] Figure 11.3 shows that the upturn in the number of formal sector workers was quite steep from 2015 onwards. In addition, the share of informal, non-agricultural jobs fell from 40 per cent to just over 30 per cent between 2010 and 2017. This started during the second Yudhoyono term and formal sector growth was, to a considerable extent, counterbalanced by a fall in agricultural employment. Many of these new formal sector jobs were in the broad group of activities classified as trade, restaurants and hotels, and include the rapidly growing tourist industry (see Figure 11.2). It seems quite likely that many of the new formal sector workers outside agriculture are now employed on fixed term contracts, partly related to the stringent hiring and firing regulations for permanent jobs.

This growing share of formal sector jobs suggests that the high costs of hiring and firing permanent hires implicit in the country's very high rates of severance pay may *not* have had a sustained effect on employment

FIGURE 11.3
Employment Agriculture, Formal and Informal Sectors, Indonesia, 2010–17

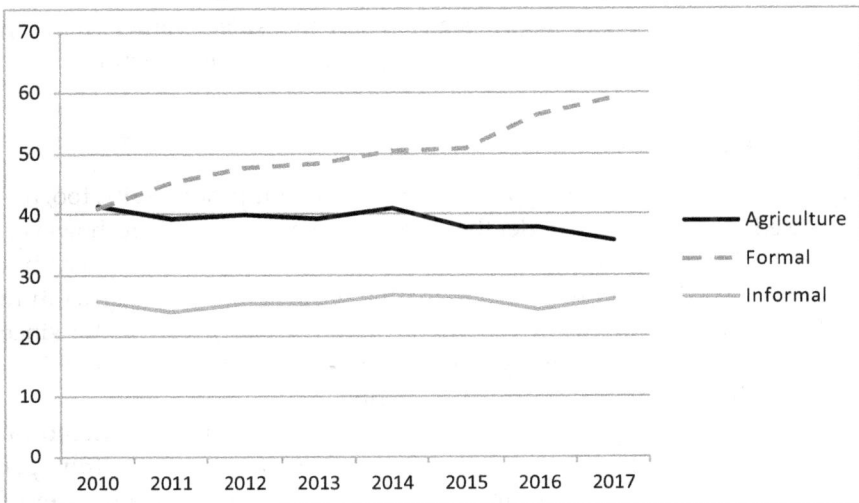

Source: BPS, National Labour Force Survey (SAKERNAS), August round, various years.

growth.[9] Indonesia seems to have created a similar percentage of jobs relative to the working age population as other countries in the region in the last years of Yudhoyono and under Jokowi. Data from the national labour force survey suggest that unemployment and underemployment fell quite steeply among both males and females, right from the Yudhoyono years. This continued under Jokowi too, declining from 6 per cent to 5.5 per cent for both sexes between 2014 and 2017, according to Dong and Manning (2017).[10]

Two explanations suggest themselves. First, compliant firms had adjusted to the 2003 regulations by around 2010. They appear to have employed more casual workers and limited contract workers after a period of alarm within businesses and disputes over high rates of severance pay in the labour law in the early 2000s. Second, there is considerable anecdotal evidence that the large majority of small and medium firms — accounting for around 60–70 per cent of all employment in manufacturing — did not comply with minimum wage and severance pay regulations (World Bank 2010). In practice, they were not expected to, either by the regulators or by the unions; the latter mainly focused on bigger establishments.

In the area of services, there has been rapid growth in jobs in businesses and financial services, which has opened up opportunities for more educated individuals, especially women in the workforce. A growth rate in jobs of around 7 per cent during the Jokowi period is a continuation of the trends experienced in this subsector from the crisis onwards (see Figure 11.2). This is a positive sign not only for skilled workers entering the labour market, but also for Indonesian businesses in general.

11.3.2 Labour Productivity

Apart from a reasonable employment record, labour productivity, too, has increased at a decent pace under the current administration. There, however, is a twist. Labour productivity in total (across all sectors combined) has increased mostly because of a combination of rising output in agriculture and a significant number of individuals moving out of that sector since 2014 (Figure 11.4). Particularly noteworthy has been the slow growth in productivity in industry and manufacturing.

What factors might have been at play here? Clearly, rising agricultural productivity is a positive development in a sector where output per worker was less than half of that in other sectors, and only a quarter of

FIGURE 11.4
Productivity Growth in Major Sectors, Indonesia After the Asian Financial Crisis
(Percentage p.a.)

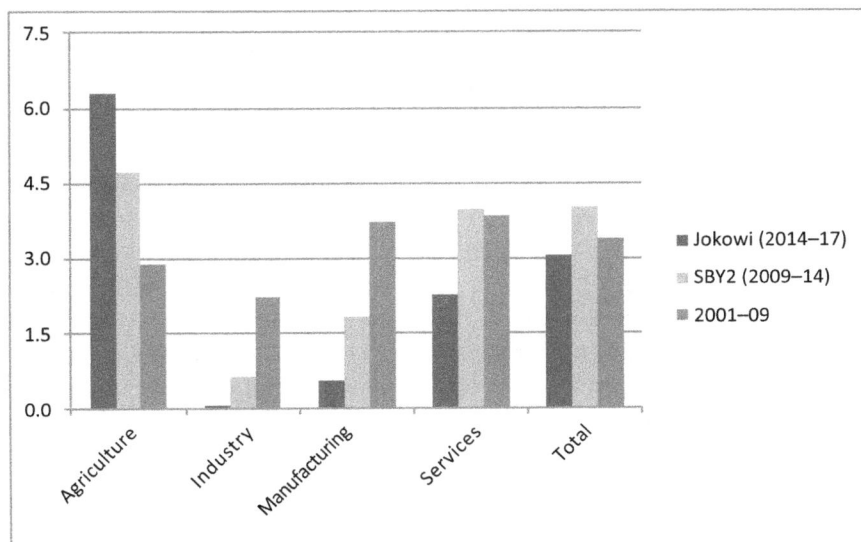

Source: BPS, National Accounts and National Labour Force Survey (SAKERNAS), August round, various years.

that in industry and in manufacturing, even in 2017. But the slow rate of increase in output per worker in manufacturing and services has been a cause of concern for the government. With respect to services, these trends are surprising, given the comparatively high rates of job growth in the more modern segment of sector. There is no good explanation for this development in what is a very heterogeneous sector. However, these developments help explain the attention that the government has been paying to skills development and training.

11.4 WAGE POLICY AND OUTCOMES: SOME PROGRESS IN A CONTROVERSIAL AREA

The minimum wage was a focus of labour demands after the country's regime change in 1998 and the consolidation of political and social reforms during the early 2000s.[11] Likewise, wage policy has been an area of significant reform under Jokowi. Specifically, the administration has been focusing on creating a more predictable environment for businesses, as well as developing a safety net for workers.[12]

The contrast with the previous government (2009–14) has been marked. The Jokowi administration has sought to step back from the more populist approach under Yudhoyono, which had discarded what it considered had been a "cheap wages" approach in labour policy in the past. Jokowi, in contrast, gave the responsibility of reformulating the minimum wage policy to his "business-oriented" vice-president, whose main advisor on economic policy is Sofian Wanandi, former head of Apindo, the Indonesian Employers Association. Apindo had overseen the negotiation of minimum wages with the central and local governments across the country since the AFC. It had argued strongly for wage restraint as businesses coped with slower economic growth after the end of the resources boom period. Under Jokowi, representations have been less vocal from the more active section of the union movement that had pushed for much higher wages under Yudhoyono.[13]

Previously, minimum wages were negotiated on a "tripartite" basis — between businesses, unions and government members of wage councils — at the district and/or provincial level. The system allowed for annual minimum wage increases based on two main criteria: (1) local economic conditions; and (2) changes in the prices of a basket of commodities and services that made up the Decent Living Needs Index (*Kebutuhan Hidup Layak* or KHL) at the district and/or provincial level. In practice, there were large differences across regions in the percentage increase in minimum wages recommended by the local wage councils, and the estimated changes in the cost of living on which they were mainly based.

After an extended negotiation period in the first half of 2015, the government issued a new countrywide regulation for setting minimum wage levels (Government Regulation No. 78/2015) to come into effect from 1 January 2016. This regulation cut through a number of complicated and uncertain processes by mandating uniform minimum wage increases across all regions. The new formula was based on the rate of growth of the national economy and the national increase in cost of living over the previous twelve months.[14] In one go, Indonesia managed to switch from a highly decentralized (and uncertain) system to a much more centralized (and predictable) one. While minimum wages still differed significantly across regions (based on the historical experience of fifteen years of decentralized bargaining), the rate of increase was now much more uniform across the country.

In January 2016, the recommended increase was ratified in most regions using the new formula. The recommended increases were 11.5 per cent in 2016, 8.3 per cent in 2017 and 8.7 per cent in 2018.[15] By international standards, this was a fairly good outcome for labour, given that unions could still negotiate for raises above these levels. While some governors increased the minimum wage (at the district level) in their province by more than the recommended increase in 2016, only four have done so in 2018. Also, a few governors have publicly indicated their displeasure with the new regulation, but the majority of them have complied with the central government policy. It is safe to say that, in this case, the Jokowi administration has proved to be an adept negotiator.[16]

Evidence from the last two years shows that the gap between high wage and low wage provinces has narrowed under Jokowi, compared to Yudhoyono's second term (Table 11.1). This is especially noticeable between the high wage and more urban areas in Banten, West Java and East Java province on one hand, and the more rural locations on the other. Thus, one of Jokowi's achievements in labour policy has been to help create a less fragmented structure of minimum wages geographically.

As noted by Dong and Manning (2017), one response to the rapidly rising minimum wages around the major industrial areas was a movement of capital in labour-intensive industries to lower wage locations. For example, many factories producing garments moved to smaller urban and semi-urban regions like Sukabumi and Cirebon in West Java; Semarang, Kendal, and Boyolali in Central Java; and Mojokerto in East Java — where wages were half (or even less than half) of those in Greater Jakarta, Surabaya, and neighbouring districts.

Consistent with employment trends, real average wages (adjusted for inflation) paid in different sectors have improved under Jokowi, compared to the Yudhoyono period. This has been possible because of the nominal wage increases, and the conservative monetary policy stance of the Central Bank Governor Agus Martowardojo.[17] Nonetheless, these increases have not been uniform across socio-economic groups. This is shown by the much more rapid rise in monthly earnings among regular workers compared to both casual workers and purely self-employed individuals. The contrasts are apparent for both agricultural and non-agricultural workers (Figures 11.5a and 11.5b).[18]

TABLE 11.1
Minimum Wages in High and Low Wage Districts Across Java, 2006–18

Province	Group	District	Wage in 2018 (Rp million)	Annual Percentage Increase		
				Early SBY 2006–10	Late SBY 2010–14	Jokowi 2014–18
Jakarta			3.6	11	18	18
Banten	High Wage	Kota Cilegon	3.6	18	18	10
		Kota Tangerang	3.6	19	19	10
	Low Wage	Kab. Pandeglang	2.4	16	10	13
		Kab. Lebak	2.3	16	11	11
	Average		*3.2*	*18*	*17*	*10*
West Java	High Wage	Kab. Karawang	3.9	10	20	12
		Kota Bekasi	3.9	19	19	12
	Low Wage	Kab. Ciamis	1.6	10	11	11
		Kota Banjar	1.6	11	10	11
	Average		*2.3*	*19*	*16*	*11*
Central Java	High Wage	Kota Semarang	2.3	12	10	12
		Kab. Demak	2.1	12	11	12
	Low Wage	Kab. Wonogiri	1.5	11	19	11
		Kab. Banjarnegara	1.5	18	18	12
	Average		*1.7*	*10*	*19*	*11*
Yogyakarta	High Wage	Kota Yogyakarta	1.7	12	11	19
		Kab. Sleman	1.6	12	10	18
	Low Wage	Kab. Kulon Progo	1.5	12	19	18
		Kab. Gunungkidul	1.5	12	17	19
	Average		*1.6*	*12*	*10*	*19*
East Java	High Wage	Kota Surabaya	3.6	11	19	12
		Kab. Gresik	3.6	11	19	12
	Low Wage	Kab. Pacitan	1.5	11	12	10
		Kab. Ponorogo	1.5	12	11	10
	Average		*2.0*	*11*	*13*	*11*
All Java			2.1	10	13	11

Source: Ministry of Manpower, Administrative Data, various years.

FIGURE 11.5a
Agricultural Real Wages by Work Status Group, Indonesia 2009–17
(Rp '000/mth)

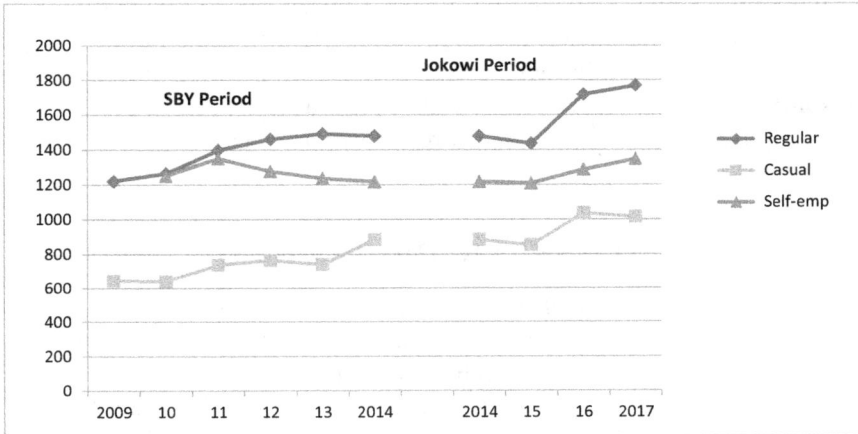

Source: BPS, National Labour Force Survey (SAKERNAS), August round, various years.

FIGURE 11.5b
Non-Agriculture, Real Wages by Work Status Group, Indonesia 2009–17
(Rp '000/mth)

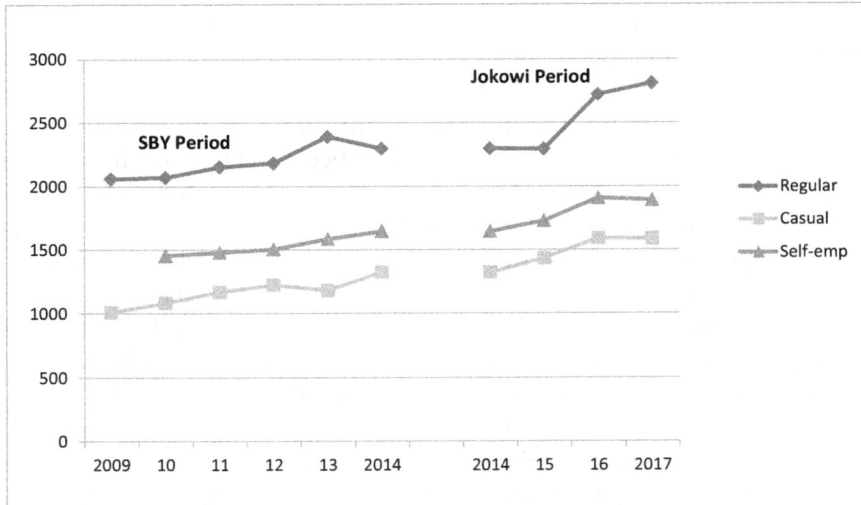

Source: BPS, National Labour Force Survey (SAKERNAS), August round, various years.

These wage trends also lend indirect support to some of the findings of Suryahadi and Al Izzati (Chapter 12). Their analysis shows that those in the bottom quintiles in regard to income distribution have not fared as well under Jokowi as they did under Yudhoyono. Relative to regular employees, casual and self-employed workers who are on lower wages and in more vulnerable jobs appear to have suffered a similar fate. In absolute terms, however, wages of all work status groups (except purely self-employed workers in agriculture or farmers) rose more quickly from 2014 onwards.

11.5 SKILLS AND TRAINING

A shortage of workers with the right skills for the jobs on offer has been reflected in a number of endemic labour market problems in Indonesia, including low levels of productivity and high youth unemployment rates (Ginting, Manning and Taniguchi 2018). Consequently, "supply side" efforts to raise productivity — through investments in education and training — have been a goal of successive governments stretching back to the Soeharto era. As a former businessman, Jokowi has given greater emphasis to increased productivity through skills acquisition than any of his predecessors in the post-Soeharto period. In fact, the National Medium Term Development Plan (RPJMN) 2015–19, which sets out priorities for the Jokowi government, has a strong focus of enhancing labour productivity and not just creating more jobs.

But until very recently, the focus had continued to be on expanding the number of enrolments and the quantity of jobs rather than their quality. Also, insofar as investment in skills became a priority, the quality of vocational schools has been of serious concern related to outdated curriculum, shortages of qualified teachers and a failure to link efforts on the supply side with the needs of business. Finally, private enterprise has tended to underinvest in training workers. As Figure 11.6 shows, this has been a problem especially in small-scale industry and has persisted through to recent years since the first international enterprise surveys were conducted by the World Bank in 2007–09 (Kadir and Bachrul 2016). Indonesia recorded a low incidence of firm participation in training across all size categories (small, medium and large firms) compared to other ASEAN countries that participated in the survey. One might hazard a guess that a combination of dysfunctional labour regulations that discourage

FIGURE 11.6
Percentage of Firms Offering Training to Their Workers, Indonesia and
Some ASEAN Countries, 2007–09 and 2015–16

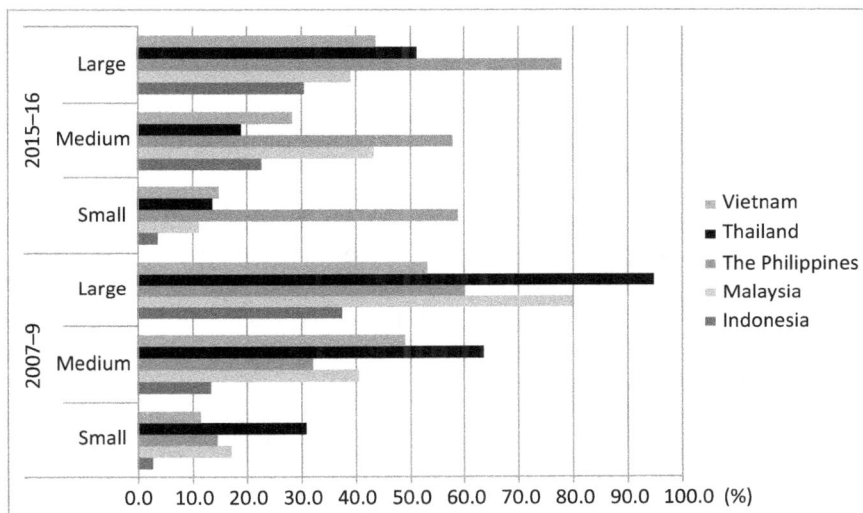

Source: World Bank, *Enterprise Surveys*, 2007–09 and 2015–16.

permanent hires and the short perspective of the much of the business community has contributed to this state of affairs.

For skills generation, Jokowi has sought to: engage businesses more actively in vocational school and apprenticeship programmes; focus on strategic industries; and prepare migrant workers for more skilled jobs abroad. Quality assurance is being promoted through competency-based testing by the National Body for Professional Certification (*Badan Nasional Sertifikasi Profesi* or BNSP) — developed during the Yudhoyono period — as part of the Indonesian Qualifications Framework. This includes setting standards for skilled occupations in collaboration with industry partners.[19] The system now acknowledges different pathways for vocational students into work or through further study after graduation, and at the same time provides a more uniform level of skills for firms to choose from.

In typical Jokowi style, increasing productivity through skills promotion has been promoted through crash programmes, especially in two areas: a short-term solution through expanding apprenticeships with major companies in a range of industries; and a longer term strategy through continued focus on vocational high schools; the latter includes improvements to the government vocational training centres, especially by establishing closer links between business and vocational schools. More recently, there have also been renewed talks of establishing a training fund mainly for workers displaced from their jobs because of technological change.

11.5.1 Apprenticeships and Training Fund

To complement the longer term training efforts in vocational high schools, a new apprenticeship programme — developed jointly by the government, APINDO (Indonesian Employers' Association), and Kadin (Chamber of Commerce and Industry) — engaged around 350 firms in a pilot programme which began in 2017 (Dong and Manning 2017). This initiative has been taken partly because the president, ministers and senior government officials have become increasingly concerned about the future of jobs in Indonesia and the need to prepare for a deepening of the "Fourth Industrial Revolution" or Industry 4.0, mainly in light of international reports of spreading digital technology and automation.[20]

The concern and the remedial initiatives have two important implications for skills and training. First, existing employees and new job seekers have to be better prepared with digital and cyber skills for new kinds of jobs increasingly on offer. Second, support and retraining opportunities for employees displaced from work because of the new technology is needed so that the transition to new jobs can be as seamless as possible. With respect to the latter in particular, the government has resurrected the idea of a training fund that has long been discussed but not implemented, partly because of bureaucratic wrangling (Dong and Manning 2017). In late 2017, the Minister of Manpower announced the possibility of a new "Workers Fund" as both a financial cushion for retrenched workers and a vehicle for acquisition of new skills for displaced workers.[21]

BJPS *Ketenagakerjaan* (or the Workers Social Security Fund) has been mentioned as one source for funding for this initiative, together with possible contributions from businesses (sections of which have reservations about supporting the scheme). Formal discussions of this idea is a first step to moving towards a partial unemployment benefits scheme. The scheme might not only provide training initiatives; support for displaced workers could also lead to relaxing some of the more extreme elements of the severance pay system that many have seen as an obstacle to more private sector investment in training.[22]

11.5.2 Expanding Vocational Education

For more than a decade, the government has sought to expand vocational education at the senior high school level (*Sekolah Menengah Kejuruan* or SMK) as one solution to the shortage of skilled blue-collar workers and middle-level manpower (Taniguchi, Francisco and Naval 2018). The number of SMK more than doubled in a decade from the mid-2000s (to just over 10,000), accounting for close to half of all senior high school level enrolments. However, such a rapid increase could only be achieved at the expense of quality. It is reported that only a small number of SMKs engaged with business in setting curriculum, standards and productive interaction between classroom study and practical work. Other issues include the quality of teachers, the curriculum design, and limited opportunities for practical work (Kadir and Bachrul 2016).

The president, too, has argued that it is time to ensure that vocational schools "equip students with the practical skills needed to meet industry demands" partly with the support of foreign donors (*Jakarta Post*, 29 November 2016). Greater private sector engagement in training has been encouraged in the maritime, electronics, shipping, agriculture and manufacturing sectors following Jokowi's visit to Germany in 2016. The Ministry of Education now requires all SMKs to work with an industry partner and students to engage in three- to six-month student internship programmes in host companies. The German international aid agency GIZ (*Deutsche Gesellschaft für Internationale Zusammenarbeit*), renowned globally for its assistance to vocational schools, has been engaged by the government to help build the capacity of SMKs in selected industries.

New efforts are also underway to revive the 160 Vocational Training Centres (BLKs or *Balai Latihan Kerja*) across Indonesia that are managed by the Ministry of Manpower and some regional governments. These institutions offer short training courses (of around 140 hours) for basic skills in various subject areas including: auto-mechanics; IT; machine shop; secretarial skills; bookkeeping; sewing and dress-making; and building and construction. Most of the BLKs face a raft of problems, like recruiting and keeping qualified teachers with industrial experience, as well as acquiring and maintaining equipment (Taniguchi, Francisco and Naval 2018). Efforts are underway to turn the situation around. Specifically, the Minister of Manpower has set a special team (composed of major business figures, government and academic advisers) to manage skills development in this sector and (re)training of up to 1,000 instructors, with funding support from the Ministry of Finance.

Jokowi's pragmatism and business orientation have not only helped to make the government, businesses and workers more aware of Indonesia's pressing problem of a skills deficit, but also to get a range of training programmes off the ground. However, a much longer time horizon than the electoral cycle is needed to generate continued improvements in the quality of education and training, absorption of new graduates into productive jobs and significant improvement in output per worker. Sustained implementation by the end of this presidency (and well into the next one) will be crucial for the country's transformation to a higher level, skill-intensive economy.

11.6 INTERNATIONAL MIGRATION: CONTINUED REASSESSMENT

Asserting tighter management over the emigration of Indonesian workers abroad as well as regulating the inflow of foreign workers into Indonesia are two other important dimensions of the labour policy. In both areas, the Jokowi government has adopted new approaches, in addition to building on initiatives of previous administrations.

11.6.1 Tighter Controls and More Protection for TKI

Although the government continued to support international migration as one source of reducing unemployment at home, the number of registered overseas workers (*Tenaga Kerja Indonesia* or TKI) showed a significant drop in 2015. This is mainly related to the administration's moratorium policy — banning the outflow of migrant workers for work in nineteen Middle East countries from 2015, due to reports of exploitation of female domestic workers in the region.[23] Although this was not the first time the Indonesian government had declared a temporary halt on sending workers overseas (see Manning and Sukamdi forthcoming), the 2015 moratorium reduced the number of TKI processed and registered by government agencies even further. In fact, the number dropped from well over half a million at the peak in 2011, to stabilize at around 200,000–300,000 migrants per annum in 2015–17 (BPS 2017; see Figures 11.7 and 11.8).

While the moratorium has been welcomed, there is also a downside. Bans on migration to these countries have been criticized as it forces some people to stay at home without work — leading to a loss of annual remittances of up to US$3 billion for low-income households and villages in Indonesia (Patunru and Uddarojat 2015). The post-moratorium survey by Migrant Care has shown that the policy tends to push some workers to migrate illegally through unregistered agents or individually, providing them with no legal protection and making them potentially vulnerable to the exploitative practices of human traffickers.[24]

Associated with this policy of restricting TKI flows, the Indonesian government also began to pay closer attention to the rights of TKI during the first three years of the Jokowi government. The Minister of Manpower,

FIGURE 11.7
Labour Migrant Flows from Indonesia by Gender 2009–17

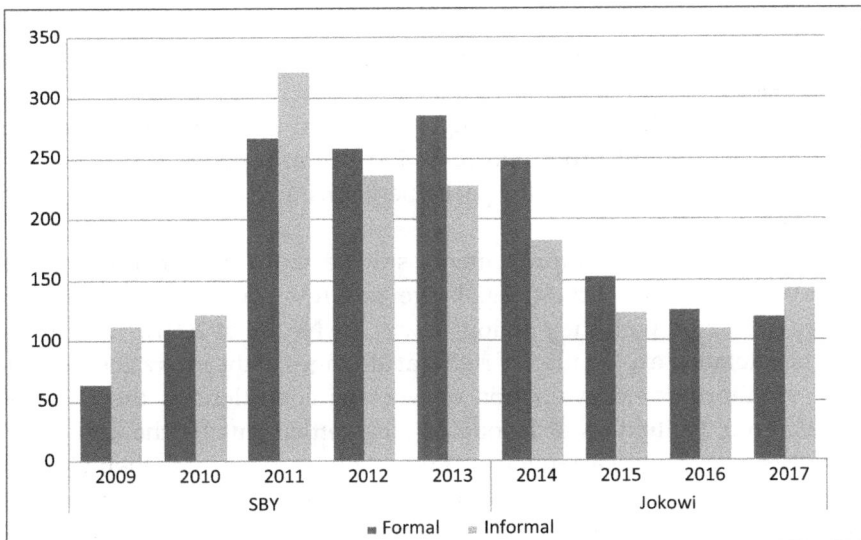

FIGURE 11.8
Labour Migrant Flows from Indonesia by Sector, 2009–17 (in million)

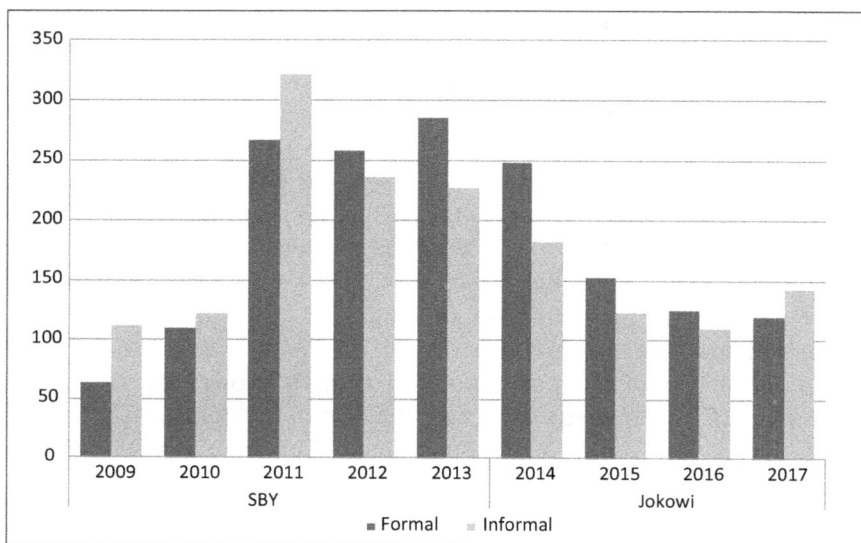

Source: BNP2TKI (various years).

Hanif Dhakiri, the son of a former migrant worker, is well known for his outspoken criticism of the ill-treatment of Indonesian migrant workers abroad.[25] In fact, his strong backing contributed to the ratification of the new law on migrant protection (Law No. 18) in October 2017, after the draft law had languished in the parliament during President Yudhoyono's second term (2009–14).

While the key to improvements still lie with implementation, the new bill reflects important legislative progress on migrant protection issues compared with the previous law (Law No. 39 in 2004).[26] Examples include: detailed explanation of rights at all stages of the migration process (like monitoring and evaluation of working conditions at the point of destination); facilitation of labour dispute settlements by the appointed overseas officials; and arrangements for migrants to return to their place of origin. The bill also covers a greater role of local governments, including providing assistance and services at the time of departure and return of migrant workers, and one-stop services at the provincial level. With regard to training and placement, the bill also makes provisions for the vocational training and placement of more skilled migrant workers.

It should also be noted that the government has also encouraged the roles of villages, the lowest level of the government, through *Desa Peduli Buruh Migran* (*Desbumi*) or the Village Care for Migrant Workers Villages Programme, by providing more monitoring, greater certainty during recruitment, and assisting in the placement and protection of Indonesian migrant workers.[27] Another initiative has been the ratification of the "ASEAN Consensus on the Protection and Promotion of the Rights of Migrant Workers" signed in November 2017, after eight years of negotiation. Although legally non-binding, it is a first step towards better protection of migrant workers in ASEAN.[28] Overall, these (and other) government initiatives have been a response to the long-standing criticism from NGOs about government inaction in these areas, despite ongoing challenges in implementation (Susilo, Hidayah and Mulyadi 2013).

In an effort to avoid more potential human rights violations and exploitation, the Jokowi government has continued to promote more formal sector employment abroad. The number of formal sector jobs (such as production work in manufacturing, drivers and seafarers) has outpaced the flow of domestic workers in the informal sector since 2012 (See Figure 11.9, and Manning and Pratomo 2018).[29]

11.6.2 Indonesia's Diaspora

Besides management of TKI, the Jokowi government has also started to pay more attention to the Indonesian diaspora and appreciate them as a social and economic asset to the country — a process that had already begun during Yudhoyono's second term.[30] The Indonesian diaspora has been estimated at around 8 million people (Muhidin and Utomo 2015). Malaysia is the top destination country, hosting about 35 per cent of Indonesian-born migrants. Besides supporting an annual congress held in Jakarta, President Jokowi also signed the Presidential Decree No. 76, in August 2017, legalizing the Indonesian Diaspora Card (Kartu Masyarakat Indonesia di Luar Negeri, KMILN), thereby formalizing the national identity of the Indonesian community living overseas. One specific target here is to attract more foreign investment.

FIGURE 11.9
Number of Foreign Workers Registered in Indonesia by Country of Origin, 2013–16

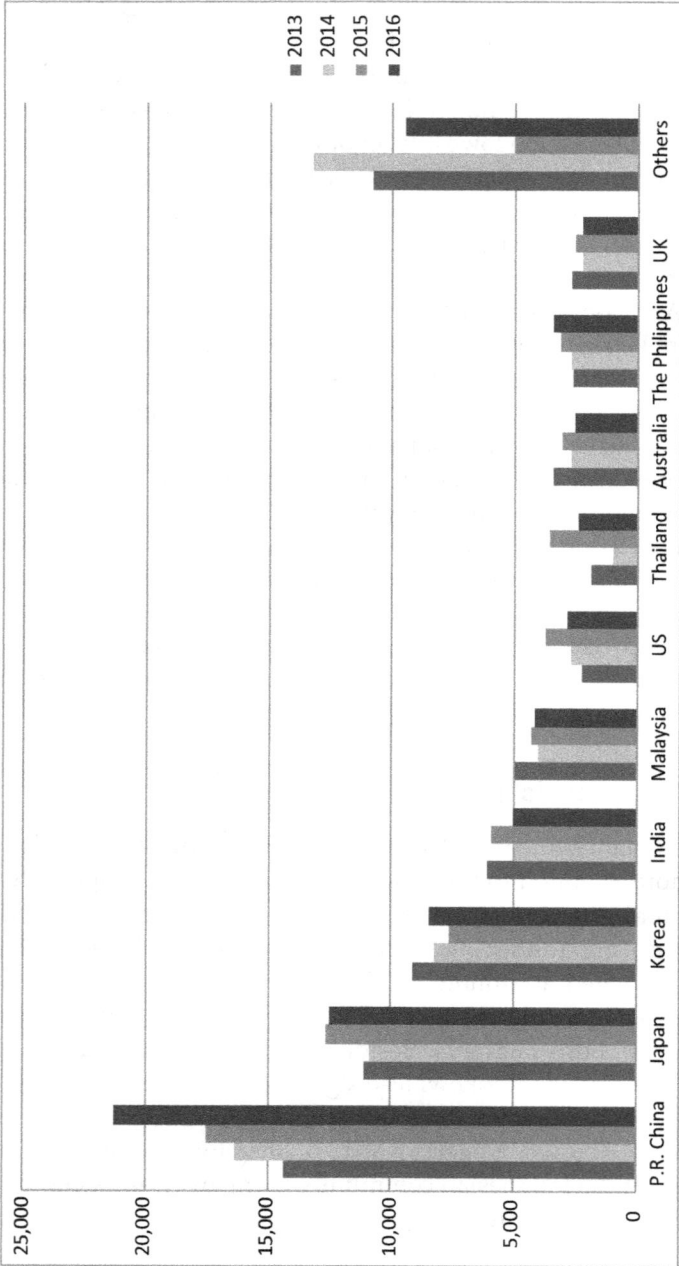

Source: Ministry of Manpower, Administrative Data, various years.

11.6.3 Foreign Workers in Indonesia

In contrast to the Indonesian workers overseas, the number of foreign workers in Indonesia (*Tenaga Kerja Asing*, or TKA) is miniscule — at about 70,000 in 2016–17, rising to 126,000 in 2018 (as a fraction of total employment, less than 1 per cent). Jokowi has trodden carefully in policies towards TKA, aware of a (potential) strong opposition to their presence, particularly by those seeking to mobilize nationalist opposition to the government. In 2016, the government was confronted by the wild rumours about the number of illegal Chinese workers in the country — a figure of 10 million went viral on social media (Dong and Manning 2017). In reality, the number of registered Chinese workers in Indonesia was only about 20,000 in 2016, according to the Ministry of Manpower (see Figure 11.9).[31] Even if illegal (unregistered) migrants working mainly on energy and mineral projects are included, it is most unlikely that the total number could exceed 50,000.

As a fraction of total employment, the share is also very small compared to the estimated number of foreign workers in the neighbouring countries — Singapore, Malaysia, and Thailand — where they are reported to account for 36, 15 and 4 per cent of the workforce respectively.[32] More than half of foreign workers in Indonesia originated from Northeast Asian countries, including China, Japan, and Korea. The others come from India, some from OECD countries and some from neighbouring countries, such as Malaysia. Most of them are employed in high-skilled jobs, as professionals, consultants, or managers in the industry and services sectors (Manning and Pratomo 2017).

While being wary of taking a strong stand in this area, the president, together with the proactive head of the Investment Coordinating Board (BKPM), Thomas Lembong, has linked the recruitment of foreign experts to attempt to boost foreign investment and economic growth. President Jokowi has dropped some of the more restrictive policies in regard to foreign workers, which were introduced partly in response to popular concerns about TKA inflows after the implementation of the ASEAN Economic Community (AEC) at the end of 2015.[33] More recently, the president also issued the Presidential Regulation No. 20/2018 in February 2018 on foreign workers (effective from July 2018) as an administrative reform to simplify work permit procedures and facilitate investment, particularly in occupations that cannot be filled by local workers. The regulation has received widespread criticism from opposition figures. It is a sensitive political issue and 2019 is an election year.[34]

11.7 CONCLUSION

From an economic perspective, President Jokowi can be judged to have had a number of successes in regard to labour markets and employment. Employment has held up and wages have improved, despite slower growth than in the decade before he came to power. Wage and migration policies and legislation have achieved their twin goals of more predictable wage increases in the major industrial areas, as well as reducing the exposure of Indonesia workers to abuse abroad, respectively. The government has started a range of new initiatives in the area of skills and training. Although it lags behind its neighbours, it has continued to encourage the deployment of foreign talents in Indonesia, despite strong criticism from several corners. Productivity levels are still very low, especially in agriculture and services. But these have been improving as people move out of agriculture and more educated job seekers move into higher skilled occupation in services — many of them created in the digital economy.

The biggest challenge still appears to be improving the skills of blue-collar workers so as to raise their productivity, wages and living standards. Various of strategies are being tried. This includes mobilizing local resources — especially through the support of big business, and reaching out to donor agencies and experienced training institutions and their governments abroad. It is too early to evaluate the success of these efforts. Nonetheless, the government's initiatives have taken a broader approach and been more innovative than those tested by previous administrations.

Finally, there is also a dilemma for the Jokowi administration about how to embrace and mobilize the trade union movement more effectively to support skills development. This is especially important because the government's economic goals do not always fit easily with union objectives of raising wages much faster than would result through market forces. The preliminary announcement of plans to provide support and training for displaced workers may win some support from trade unions. Commentators have repeatedly argued for greater efforts to engage unions and business in more intensive collective bargaining at the plant and industry level, rather than rely on regulations from Jakarta. This could help skills development through eliciting business commitments to invest more in training — as a precursor to higher productivity and better wage solutions. Finally, tackling the politically difficult task of revising severance pay laws — which in their present form tend to run counter to efforts to raise productivity and wages — still needs to be on the agenda of a pro-labour development strategy.

Notes

1. See the National Medium Term Development Plan (RPJMN) and the *Nawacita*, the nine guiding principles for government programmes 2015–19.
2. See the articles "Introduction: The Indonesian Economy in Transition — Policy Challenges in the Jokowi Era and Beyond" and "Education in Indonesia: A White Elephant?" in this issue.
3. These comparisons are based on data from the World Bank Development Indicators and ADB dataset on *Leading Indicators of Social and Economic Development*.
4. Data are for 2010–2015/16. Taken from Asian Development Bank, *Key Indicators for Asia and the Pacific 2017* (Manila), p. 118.
5. See UNDP, *Human Development Report*, 2016.
6. All figures in PPP dollars, 2011 prices, from World Bank Open Data <https://data.worldbank.org/indicator/SL.GDP.PCAP.EM.KD?view=chart>.
7. The data on which these statements are based is taken from the annual August round of the National Labour Force Survey, and thus covers most of the first to the last year of the second Yudhoyono administration (beginning October 2009 through to October 2014) and the first three years of the Jokowi administration from October 2014.
8. This formal sector group covers wage workers employed either on a permanent or contract basis, employers and self-employed professionals, managers or clerical staff, as defined by the national statistics agency, BPS.
9. See, especially Manning and Roesad (2007) in regard to the high rates of severance or payments to dismissed workers. The main burden was a doubling of quite high basic payments for dismissal or downsizing due to "economic cause".
10. In 2016, for the first time in thirty years female unemployment rates fell below those of males (5.5 per cent compared with 5.7 per cent respectively). Underemployment was recorded at just under seven per cent in 2016, down almost one percentage point from when Jokowi came to power in 2014.
11. These issues are covered in an unpublished White Paper on employment and wages prepared by Bappenas in 2002–03.
12. See also Dong and Manning (2017) for a discussion of some of these issues. This section updates and expands on material covered in that paper.

13. Said Iqbal, the dynamic leader of the Metal Workers Union and the associated confederation KSPSI, had lost some credibility as a union leader after he became actively engaged in politics on the losing side in the 2014 election campaign.
14. Mainly for pragmatic reasons — credible data could only be produced on regional prices and GDP after long delays — the reform did not encompass regional variations in either prices or economic performance.
15. Thus the most recent recommended increase in 2018 of 8.7 per cent was based on the national statistics agency, BPS, estimate of the national inflation rate of 4 per cent and a national growth rate of 4.72 per cent in the preceding twelve months.
16. The government offered a carrot to the unions in the form of low-cost housing especially for factory workers.
17. CPI increases had slipped back from five to 6 per cent per annum during the final Yudhoyono term to 3 to 4 per cent in 2016–17.
18. Wage increases occurred across all major industries in 2016, and were especially marked among mainly regular workers in rapidly growing business and finance, although they had levelled off somewhat by 2017.
19. For further information on BNSP, see <https://bnsp.go.id>.
20. In April 2018 the President launched a roadmap for "Making Indonesia 4.0" led by the Ministry of Industry and including digital technology to be promoted in five priority sectors. See *Investments-Indonesia*, 6 April 2018 <https://www.indonesia-investments.com/business/business-columns/widodo-launches-roadmap-for-industry-4.0-making-indonesia-4.0/item8711?>.
21. See *Jakarta Post*, 11 November 2017 <http://www.thejakartapost.com/news/2017/11/17/govt-considers-establishing-workers-fund.html>.
22. These issues are canvassed in detail in World Bank (2010).
23. See <http://www.migrantcare.net/2017/06/hasil-survey-mobilitas-prt-migran-pasca-moratorium-di-bandara-soekarno-hatta/>.
24. See <http://www.thejakartapost.com/academia/2017/11/16/the-problem-with-aseans-new-migrant-workers-pact.html>.
25. The Minister made national headlines by climbing a fence to inspect conditions in an overcrowded holding centre in Jakarta for TKI aspirants from West Java. See <https://nasional.kompas.com/read/2014/11/05/11184321/Gerbang.Tak.Dibuka.Menaker.Teriak.dan.Lompat.Pagar.Saat.Sidak.Penampungan.TKI>.
26. See <http://www.migrantcare.net/2017/12/undang-undang-no-18-tahun-2017-tentang-pelindungan-pekerja-migran-indonesia>.
27. See <http://www.thejakartapost.com/news/2016/08/31/govt-pledges-to-better-protect-migrant-workers.html>.
28. See <http://www.thejakartapost.com/academia/2017/11/16/the-problem-with-aseans-new-migrant-workers-pact.html>.

29. The exception was 2017 when the demand for domestic work in Hong Kong, China increased as a by-product of the impact of moratorium to the Middle East countries.

30. Following the simplest definition, the Indonesian diaspora refers to Indonesians by birth and ancestry who live (permanently) outside of Indonesia.

31. Thomas Lembong, Chairman of Indonesian government agency Investment Coordinating Board (BKPM), also spoke in favour of FDI from China, which he argued had brought in capital worth more than US$1.6 billion and also created about 1 million jobs for local Indonesians. See <http://indonesiaexpat. biz/featured/real-score-number-foreigners-working-indonesia/>.

32. Ibid.

33. These restrictions included the requirement that foreigners must have Indonesian language proficiency if they wished to work in the country and the obligation that all companies in Indonesia place ten local workers under the supervision of each foreign employee to ensure sufficient transfer of knowledge. See <https://www.indonesia-investments.com/news/news-columns/indonesia-amends-local-staff-per-foreign-worker-expat-regulation/item6098?>.

34. Former President Yudhoyono was one voice to speak strongly against foreign workers at around this time, asking for more clarification about numbers from Jokowi, the current President, even though Jokowi and the minister had repeatedly provided information to the public on this matter. The *Jakarta Post* was one newspaper that mounted a spirited defence of the new legislation. See <http://www.thejakartapost.com/academia/2018/04/26/editorial-we-welcome-foreign-workers.html>.

References

Allen, E.R. "Analysis of Trends and Challenges in the Indonesian Labor Market". ADB Papers on Indonesia No. 16, Asian Development Bank, Manila, 2016.

Badan Pusat Statistik (BPS, Statistics Indonesia). *Statistik Mobilitas Penduduk dan Tenaga Kerja*. Jakarta, 2017.

Bappenas. "Rencana Pembangunan Jangka Menengah Nasional (RPJMN)". Jakarta, 2015.

Cameron, L., D. Suarez and B. Rowell. "Gender Inequality in Indonesia". Australia-Indonesia Partnership in Economic Governance, Jakarta, October 2015.

Caraway, T. and M. Ford. "United in Disappointment". *Inside Indonesia*, no. 123 (January–March 2016) <http://www.insideindonesia.org/united-in-disappointment>.

Di Gropello, E. "Role of Education and Training Sector in Addressing Skill Mismatch in Indonesia". In *Education in Indonesia*, edited by D. Suryadarma and G. Jones, pp. 236–66. Singapore: Institute of Southeast Asian Studies, 2013.

Dong, S and C. Manning. "Labour Market Developments at a Time of Heightened Uncertainty". *Bulletin of Indonesian Economic Studies* 53, no. 1 (2017): 1–25.

Ginting, E., C. Manning and K. Taniguchi, eds. *Indonesia: Enhancing Productivity through Quality Jobs*. Manila: Asian Development Bank, 2018.

Kadir, S. and B. Bachrul. "Technical and Vocational Education and Training in Indonesia: Challenges and Opportunities for the Future". Lee Kuan Yew School of Public Policy, Microsoft Case Study on Series on Technical and Vocational Education and Training, Singapore, 2016.

Manning, C. and K. Roesad. "The Manpower Law of 2003 and Its Implementing Regulations: Genesis, Key Articles and Potential Impact". *Bulletin of Indonesian Economic Studies* 43, no. 1 (2007): 39–86.

———— and R.M. Purnagunawan. "Has Indonesia Passed the Lewis Turning Point and Does it Matter". In *Managing Globalization in the Asian Century*, edited by H. Hill and J. Menon, pp. 457–85. Singapore: ISEAS – Yusof Ishak Institute, 2016.

———— and D. Pratomo. "Labour Supply and Attachment to the Workforce". In *Indonesia: Enhancing Productivity through Quality Jobs*, edited by E. Ginting, C. Manning and K. Taniguchi, pp. 29–67. Manila: Asian Development Bank, 2018.

———— and Sukamdi. *International Labour Migration: A Very Mixed Blessing*. Singapore: ISEAS – Yusof Ishak Institute, forthcoming.

McKinsey Global Institute. "The World at Work: Jobs, Pay, and Skills for 3.5 Billion People". McKinsey Global Institute, June 2012.

McBeth, J. "Indonesia's Troubled Quest for Food Self-sufficiency". *Strategist* (ASPI), 19 December 2016.

Muhidin, S. and A. Utomo. "Global Indonesian Diaspora: How Many Are There and Where Are They?". *Journal of ASEAN Studies* 3, no. 2 (2015): 93–101.

Pangestu, M., and G. Dewi. "Indonesia and the Digital Economy: Creative Destruction, Opportunities and Challenges". In *Digital Indonesia: Connectivity and Divergence*, edited by E. Jurriëns and R. Tapsell, pp. 227–56. Singapore: ISEAS – Yusof Ishak Institute, 2017.

Patunru, A. and R. Uddarojat. "Reducing the Financial Burden of Indonesian Migrant Workers". CIPS Policy Recommendations No. 1, Center for Indonesian Policy Studies, June 2015 <www. cips-indonesia.org>.

Suryahadi, A. and R. Al Izzati. "Cards for the Poor and Funds for Villages: Jokowi's Initiatives to Reduce Poverty". SMERU Working Paper 2018.

Susilo, W., A. Hidayah, and Mulyadi. *Selusur Kebijakan (Minus) Perlindungan Buruh Migran Indonesia*. Jakarta: Migrant Care, 2013.

Taniguchi, T., R. Francisco and D. Naval. "Education, Skills, and Labor Productivity".

In *Indonesia: Enhancing Productivity through Quality Jobs*, edited by E. Ginting, C. Manning and K. Taniguchi, pp. 170–204. Manila: Asian Development Bank, 2018.

Wicaksono, T.Y. and C. Manning. "Globalisation and Labour: The Indonesian Experience". In *Indonesia in the New World: Globalisation, Nationalism and Sovereignty*, edited by A.A. Patunru, M. Pangestu and M.C. Basri, pp. 201–24. Singapore: ISEAS – Yusof Ishak Institute, 2018.

World Bank. *Indonesia Jobs Report*. Washington, D.C.: World Bank, 2010.

———. *Indonesia: Enterprise Survey 2015*. Washington, D.C.: World Bank, 2015 http://microdata.worldbank.org/index.php/catalog/2665/study-description.

12

CARDS FOR THE POOR AND FUNDS FOR VILLAGES
Jokowi's Initiatives to Reduce Poverty and Inequality

Asep Suryahadi and Ridho Al Izzati

12.1 INTRODUCTION

Joko "Jokowi" Widodo was sworn in as the new president of Indonesia in October 2014, replacing Susilo Bambang Yudhoyono (SBY) who had governed Indonesia for ten years from 2004 to 2014. At the time of the transition, the picture of the Indonesian economy was not too positive. Economic growth had steadily declined since its peak in 2011 and poverty reduction had stagnated since 2012. Meanwhile, inequality, as measured by the Gini Ratio, had steadily increased and reached its highest point ever of 0.41 in 2011 and remained at this level thereafter. An underlying

This article was first published in *Journal of Southeast Asian Economies* 35, no. 2 (August 2018).

fundamental beneath these trends was the continuously declining commodity prices since 2011. During the previous decade, Indonesia had been riding a commodity boom — a steady increase in the prices of primary commodities.

Figure 12.1 depicts the trends of economic growth, poverty rate, and Gini Ratio during the 2002–17 period. It shows that Indonesia's economic growth rate has steadily increased from 4.5 per cent in 2002 to 6.35 per cent in 2007, but the Global Financial Crisis (GFC) brought it down to 4.58 per cent in 2009. The recovery was relatively quick, reaching 6.49 per cent in 2011. However, it has steadily declined since then, bottoming out at 4.88 per cent in 2015. It has progressively increased in the following two years, reaching 5.17 per cent in 2017.

During this period of positive economic growth, the poverty rate has generally declined, falling from 18.2 per cent in 2002 to 10.64 per cent in 2017. The exception was in 2006 when the poverty rate increased to 17.75 per cent from 15.97 per cent in the previous year due to increases in fuel and rice prices. Meanwhile, the Gini Ratio has steadily increased from 0.32 in 2004 to 0.41 in 2011, remaining at this level until 2015. It then slightly decreased to 0.393 by 2017.

The stagnating poverty reduction and high inequality level posed a double challenge in social welfare for Jokowi when he took over the presidency at the end of 2014. He immediately launched a couple of initiatives in this area, which he had flagged during his presidential campaign. First, he introduced the KIP (*Kartu Indonesia Pintar*, Smart Indonesia Card) and KIS (*Kartu Indonesia Sehat*, Indonesia Health Card), two major social assistance programmes in the areas of education and health, respectively. Second, he started the disbursement of village funds, which is mandated by the Law No. 6/2014 on Villages, replacing the PNPM (*Program Nasional Pemberdayaan Masyarakat*, National Community Empowerment Programme). Other initiatives were introduced later, including the expansion of the PKH (*Program Keluarga Harapan*, Family of Hope Programme), the Indonesian version of a conditional cash transfer programme.

This study aims to evaluate the impact of these initiatives on efforts to increase social welfare, particularly reducing poverty and inequality. The approach employed is based on the seminal paper by Dollar and Kraay (2002), which assesses the correlation of average income growth (defined as economic growth) with income growth of the poor. In this study, we

FIGURE 12.1
Trends in Economic Growth, Poverty Rate, and Inequality Level
in Indonesia, 2002–17

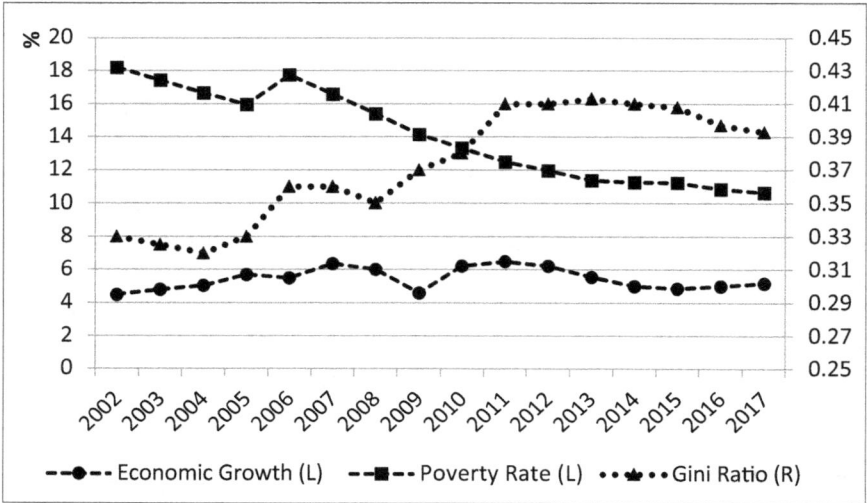

Source: Statistics Indonesia (various years).

correlate real economic growth with the real consumption growth of each quintile of per capita household consumption for three periods: 2004–09; 2009–14; and 2014–17. The first two periods refer to the first and second Yudhoyono governments, while the last period refers to the first three years of the Jokowi presidency. The objective is to examine whether economic growth has become more or less pro-poor during the Jokowi period compared to the previous periods.

12.2 LITERATURE REVIEW

Dollar and Kraay (2002) hypothesize that income of the poor rises proportionally with average income. They define average income as real per capita GDP, while the income of the poor as per capita income of the poorest 20 per cent of the population. The study uses the Generalized Method of Moment (GMM) system of estimation that, by design, combines both the levels and changes of the data. The main finding of the analysis is that the authors cannot reject the null hypothesis that average income of the poorest fifth rises with average income equiproportionately. Apart from average income as the main predictor, the paper also uses several other specifications of estimation, including: regional dummies; time trend; interactions of income with decade dummies; interactions of regional dummies with income; and interaction of incomes with negative growth dummy.

Using those specifications, they find that the coefficient of average incomes ranges from 0.9 to 1.3 and most often is 1. It means that each 1 per cent increase of average income will increase the average income of the poorest fifth also by 1 per cent. They conclude that growth of average incomes does benefit the poor and, hence, growth is good for the poor. Dollar, Kleineberg and Kraay (2015) extended their work using data from 151 countries for the period between 1967 and 2011. Their results still lead to the same conclusion that growth is good for the poor.

In the Indonesian context, Balisacan, Pernia and Asra (2003) show the correlation between growth and poverty. They estimate the log of average per capita consumption (instead of GDP per capita) to the log of consumption of the poor. The elasticity is about 0.7 for the period 1993 to 1999. Meanwhile, Miranti (2010) examines the elasticity of growth to poverty for three periods of development. The first period is called liberalization (1984–90), the second period is referred to as slower liberalization (1990–96), and the third period is recovery from the Asian Financial Crisis (AFC) (1999–2002). The results from the study show that growth was pro-poor during those periods. Meanwhile, Miranti, Duncan and Cassells (2014) re-estimate that model for the decentralization period (2002–10). The findings suggest that in the decentralization era, elasticity of average consumption to poverty is greater, but rising inequality has reduced the impact of economic growth on poverty reduction.

Timmer (2004) compares Indonesia's pro-poor growth process to other countries in the region (from mid-1960s until 1990s) and concludes that Indonesia's growth has always benefited the poor. Although during the 1967–2002 period Indonesia experienced both weak and strong pro-poor growth, the country recorded one of the best poverty reductions in Asia during the entire span. The results from Timmer (2004) indicate that persistent pro-poor growth requires simultaneous and balanced interaction between the growth and distribution process.

Another way to measure the rate of pro-poor growth is by using a Growth Incidence Curve (GIC), as proposed by Ravallion and Chen

(2003). The curve depicts the annualized growth rate of per capita income or expenditure for each percentile of the distribution between two points in time. Therefore, a GIC is useful not only for demonstrating how the gains from economic growth are distributed in the population, but also for monitoring income growth of the poor.

For example, Ravallion and Chen (2003) show that during the 1990–99 period, China experienced a rise in inequality because growth of per capita household income of the richest segment of the population was higher than that of the poorest. On the other hand, a study conducted by the World Bank (2018) shows that during the last decade, in most Latin American countries, income growth of households at the bottom of the income distribution was significantly higher than those at the top, resulting in a decline in inequality. Similarly, Bridonneau (2016) shows that different countries in Asia and Africa exhibit different GIC patterns, while the pattern of each country can change over time.

Kraay (2006) identifies three potential sources of pro-poor growth: first, a higher growth of average incomes; second, higher sensitivity of poverty to growth in average incomes; and third, a poverty-reducing pattern of growth in relative incomes. Using a decomposition method, the study finds the first source as the dominant factor. Hence, he suggests that countries should focus on the policies and institutions that drive average income growth.

12.3 JOKOWI'S INITIATIVES ON SOCIAL POLICY

Jokowi's direct initiatives on improving social welfare consist of two broad categories. First, expanding the coverage of social assistance programmes and making them more effective. Second, rolling out and continuously enlarging the village fund, a grant for villages mandated by Law No. 6/2014 on Villages. The remainder of this section discusses each initiative in turn.

12.3.1 Social Assistance through Cards

During the 2014 presidential campaign, Jokowi often flagged two cards — KIP and KIS — as his main tools to assist the poor on accessing education and health services. The introduction of these cards followed the successful implementation of similar cards at regional levels when Jokowi became the Mayor of Surakarta in Central Java and later Governor of Jakarta.

Since social protection programmes in the areas of education and health were already in operation since the late 1990s as part of the JPS (*Jaring Pengaman Sosial*, Social Safety Net) programme (which was launched as an effort to alleviate the social impact of the AFC that hit Indonesia during 1997–98), the implementation of these initiatives is integrated with the existing programme.

KIP was integrated with the BSM (*Bantuan Siswa Miskin*, Assistance for Poor Students) programme, a scholarship programme for students from poor families. In 2014, the programme provided scholarships of Rp450,000 per year for a primary school student, Rp750,000 per year for a junior high school student, and Rp1,000,000 per year for a senior high school student — covering a total of 11.2 million students. The Jokowi government has increased the coverage of the KIP programme to 19.7 million students by 2016.

Meanwhile, KIS was integrated with the PBI (*Penerima Bantuan Iuran*, Premium Assistance Recipients) programme of the JKN (*Jaminan Kesehatan Nasional*, National Health Insurance) programme. This scheme is part of the SJSN (*Sistem Jaminan Sosial Nasional*, National Social Security System), which is mandated by Law No. 40/2004 on SJSN. The law requires that the JKN premium of the poor is paid for by the government through the PBI programme. In July 2013, the premium assistance was Rp19,225 per PBI recipient and the total number of recipients reached 86.4 million people. In 2017, the premium assistance was increased to Rp23,000 per recipient and the total number of participants of the KIS programme was expanded to 92.4 million.

Actually, the second term of Yudhoyono government introduced a card for social assistance recipients, called the KPS (*Kartu Perlindungan Sosial*, Social Protection Card) in 2013. The holder of this card is entitled to receive the benefit of the Rastra (*Beras untuk Keluarga Sejahtera*, Rice for Prosperous Families) scheme, a heavily subsidized rice price programme. In addition, a KPS holder is also entitled to receive the benefit of BLSM (*Bantuan Langsung Sementara Masyarakat*, Community Temporary Direct Assistance) programme, an unconditional cash transfer initiative which is usually invoked if there is a shock to the community, such as an increase in fuel prices.

The Jokowi government changed the KPS card into another card called KKS (*Kartu Keluarga Sejahtera*, Prosperous Family Card), which continues to give its holders entitlement to receive the benefit of the Rastra programme.

In 2014, 15.5 million households were Rastra recipients, and the figure has slightly increased to 15.8 million households in 2017.

Meanwhile for the BLSM recipients, the Jokowi government introduced a new card called KSKS (*Kartu Simpanan Keluarga Sejahtera*, Prosperous Family Saving Card). The last BLSM during the Yudhoyono government was in 2013, providing a benefit of Rp600,000 in two phases, with the number of recipients being 15.5 million households. The Jokowi government, on the other hand, implemented the BLSM programme in late 2014 and early 2015 for six months with the number of recipients growing to 15.8 million households, each receiving Rp1,000,000 in three phases.

One social assistance programme that did not experience much change in term of its design is the PKH (*Program Keluarga Harapan*, Family of Hope Programme), a conditional cash transfer programme. The Jokowi government has continuously increased the coverage of this programme, indicating the priority put by the government on PKH as the main mechanism to address poverty and inequality problems in the country. In 2014, PKH covered 2.8 million households, which was then increased to 3.5 million in 2015, 5.9 million in 2016, and 6 million in 2017. Furthermore, its coverage is planned to be increased to 10 million households in 2018. The benefit received by each recipient household varies in accordance with the household structure. Specifically, it ranged from Rp800,000 to Rp3,700,000 per year per household in 2016. In 2017, the PKH switched to a single benefit of Rp1,890,000 per household.

Table 12.1 shows the coverage, while Table 12.2 shows the budget of the major social assistance programmes during 2014–18. Table 1 indicates that, from 2014 to 2018, there has been an increase in the number of beneficiaries covered by the various programmes. The number of KIP beneficiaries almost doubled, from around 11 to 21 million students between 2014 and 2015. The number of KIS beneficiaries also increased from around 88 to 92 million individuals between 2015 and 2016. However, the programme that has continuously expanded — rather significantly — is PKH, starting from just 2.8 million beneficiary households in 2014 to 10 million in 2018.

In line with the increase in the number of beneficiaries, Table 12.2 shows that the budget of major social assistance programmes has also significantly increased during the 2014–18 period. Again, PKH has experienced the largest increase, as its budget has more than tripled — from around Rp5.5 trillion in 2014 to Rp17.3 trillion in 2018.

TABLE 12.1
Number of Beneficiaries of the Major Social Assistance Programmes, 2014–18 (million)

Programme	2014	2015	2016	2017	2018
KIP/BSM[b]	11.1	20.95	19.68	19.71	19.7
KIS/PBI[b]	86.4	88.2	92.4	92.4	92.4
Rastra[a]	15.5	15.5	15.5	15.8	15.6
KSKS/BLSM[a]	15.5	15.8	—	—	—
PKH[a]	2.8	3.5	5.9	6	10

Notes: a. Household, b. Individual/student
Source: World Bank (2017), Bappenas (2017).

TABLE 12.2
Budget of the Major Social Assistance Programmes, 2014–18 (Rp trillion)

Programme	2014	2015	2016	2017	2018
KIP/BSM	6.6	6.4	10.6	11.7	10.5
KIS/PBI	19.9	19.9	24.8	25.5	25.5
Rastra	18.2	21.8	22.1	19.8	21
KSKS/BLSM	6.2	9.4	—	—	—
PKH	5.5	6.5	7.8	11.3	17.3

Source: World Bank (2017), Bappenas (2017).

The targeting of social assistance programmes in Indonesia has evolved a long way since the social safety net (JPS) programmes of the late 1990s. Currently, the application of a uniform targeting mechanism, through a national registry of around 26 million poor and vulnerable households (the Unified Database, or UDB), has improved the targeting of social assistance benefits towards the needy (World Bank 2017).

McCarthy and Sumarto (Chapter 13) are sceptical with the top-down approaches in targeting of the social assistance programmes. They suggest that community-based targeting, developed using existing community practices, will produce better and more acceptable results. Actually, in recent years, innovations by including community consultation (*musyawarah desa* or Musdes) and self-targeting (*Mekanisme Pendaftaran Mandiri* or MPM) have been piloted and adopted.

12.3.2 Village Development through Grants

In addition to social assistance to households, the government also provides block grants to villages, the *Dana Desa* (village fund), as mandated by Law No. 6/2014 on Villages. These grants to villages replaced the grants to communities under the PNPM (*Program Nasional Pemberdayaan Masyarakat*, National Community Empowerment Programme), which was implemented from 2007 to 2014. Although the law was signed by President Yudhoyono near the end of his second term, it was only implemented in 2015 when Jokowi had been inaugurated as his successor.

During the 2014 presidential campaign, Jokowi made a promise to provide a grant of Rp1 billion to each village every year. Table 12.3 recapitulates the distribution of the village fund from 2015 to 2018. In 2015, the government started to disburse the village fund at an average amount of Rp280 million for each village. The amount was continuously increased in subsequent years, reaching Rp800 million per village in 2018. As a consequence, the total village fund distributed has tripled in just four years, from around Rp20 trillion in 2015 to Rp60 trillion in 2018.

The use of the village fund in each village is determined through a planning meeting called Musrenbangdes (*Musyawarah Perencanaan Pembangunan Desa*, Village Development Plan Consultation), with the results formally formulated in a village budget called APBDes (*Anggaran Pendapatan dan Belanja Desa*, Village Income and Expenditure Budget). Most villages allocate the largest portion, more than 70 per cent, of the fund for infrastructure development, in particular roads. Only a small share is allocated for community empowerment (Syukri et al. 2018).

TABLE 12.3
The Distribution of Village Fund, 2015–18

Year	Average Fund per Village (Rp million)	Number of Villages	Total Village Fund (Rp trillion)
2015	280	74,754	20.8
2016	628	74,754	46.9
2017	776	74,954	58.2
2018	800	74,954	60.0

Source: Ministry of Finance (various years).

12.4 MODEL AND DATA

To assess the impact of Jokowi's social welfare initiatives on poverty and inequality, we examine whether economic growth has become more or less pro-poor during Jokowi's period, compared to previous presidencies. A framework that can be used for this purpose is the model estimated by Dollar and Kraay (2002), in which they correlate economic growth with income growth of the poorest quintile. While Dollar and Kraay (2002) estimate the model in a multi-country setting, we adopt the model for Indonesia using district level data. We make use of consumption instead of income and carry out some extensions where we estimate not only the elasticity of the poorest quintile (Q1), but also the middle (Q2, Q3, and Q4) and the richest (Q5) quintiles of per capita household consumption.

The expectation is that Jokowi's social welfare initiatives will boost the consumption growth of the poor. However, the framework used here cannot evaluate the impact of social welfare policies on consumption growth in isolation. The results of the analysis will show the net effect of all social and economic policies and shocks that take place in the economy on household consumption growth.

12.4.1 Model of Economic Growth and Consumption Growth of the Poor

Following Dollar and Kraay (2002), the model is formulated as:

$$y^q_{dt} = \alpha_0 + \alpha_1 Y_{dt} + \alpha_2 X_{dt} + \mu_d + \varepsilon_{dt} \tag{1}$$

where q, d, and t refer to quintile, district, and years respectively. y^q_{dt} is the logarithm of mean per capita consumption of quintile q in district d at time t, Y_{dt} is the logarithm of GDP per capita in district d at time t, and X_{dt} is a vector of control variables (which, in this case, consists of island and year dummies). Meanwhile, μ_d and ε_{dt} are the cross-section district heterogeneity and time series error terms, respectively. The coefficient of interest is α_1 that shows the elasticity of the impact of average income towards per capita consumption of household in each quintile.

Since this is an analysis of a single country, we use the same source of data for the left and right hand side variables (Statistics Indonesia, BPS). As a result, there is no problem of inconsistent definition and/or measurement of variables, which often plague multi-country studies. To ensure robustness, we estimate the model using several regression techniques.

First, we estimate the model using Ordinary Least Squares (OLS) technique. However, this estimation suffers from reverse causality problem and unobserved variables, resulting in downward bias of the estimates. Second, to control for unobserved heterogeneity, we run a panel fixed-effect estimation, bearing in mind that the reverse causality problem still remains. Third, to solve the reverse causality and unobserved heterogeneity problems, we use first difference estimation technique. To do this, the model in equation (1) is modified into:

$$y^q_{dt} - y^q_{dt-1} = \alpha_1(Y_{dt} - Y_{dt-1}) + \alpha_2(X_{dt} - X_{dt-1}) + (\varepsilon_{dt} - \varepsilon_{dt-1}) \qquad (2)$$

However, a new problem appears in the form of autocorrelation. Hence, fourth, in line with Dollar and Kraay (2002), we combine equations (1) and (2) into a system equation and use GMM-system estimation technique to estimate the model. At this point, we use the Hansen test for over-identification and Arrelano-Bond's second order test for serial correlation. Unfortunately, the results show that we now have an over identification problem and the serial correlation issue continues.

Therefore, fifth, to overcome the over identification and serial correlation problems, we include year and island dummy variables in the GMM-system estimation. Since we estimate the model using data from relatively short periods of time following the presidential periods, this fits with the GMM-system technique that supports estimation of panel data with many individuals but few time periods (i.e., large N and small T panel data).

12.4.2 Data

The unit of observation of the data used in the analysis is district (*kabupaten* and *kota*). The data consists of district per capita GDP, district average of real per capita household consumption by quintile (constant 2000 price), and several district level control variables. The district per capita GDP is calculated from the data of district level Gross Regional Domestic Product (GRDP) at constant 2000 price. Meanwhile, the per capita household consumption is calculated from the data collected through the National Socio-Economic Survey (Susenas), a household survey covering basic demographic and detailed household consumption variables. Since Susenas is not a household panel data, the quintiles can consist of different households over time.

We use the district Consumer Price Index (CPI) to deflate the nominal household consumption to obtain the real consumption data using constant 2000 price. Since the district per capita GDP is calculated in annual terms, we transform the monthly household per capita consumption into annual value as well. The source of all this data is Statistics Indonesia (BPS).

Between 2004 and 2017, many districts in Indonesia split. To avoid any discrepancy, we re-aggregate the divided districts into their original districts. Our final data includes a balance panel of 377 districts, covering the period of 2004–17. In accordance with the objective of this study, we estimate the model using data from three periods synchronized with presidential periods: 2004–09 (SBY1), 2009–14 (SBY2), and 2014–17 (JKW).

12.5 EMPIRICAL ESTIMATION AND DISCUSSION

12.5.1 Growth Incidence Curve

To visually depict what happened to household consumption during the three periods of analysis, Appendix Figure 12.A1 shows the growth incidence curve (GIC) in each period. As explained in the literature review section, GIC is measured as the annual growth of each percentile of per capita household consumption.

Several observations can be made from the curves. First, the growth of per capita household consumption for all segments of the population is positive in all periods, implying that, in general, the welfare of Indonesian people has continuously increased. Second, however, the mean of the growth of per capita household consumption has declined from one period to another, suggesting that the pace of welfare improvement has declined over time. Third, during the first two periods, the GIC curves are positively sloped, meaning that the growth of consumption is higher the richer the population. This is the underlying cause of increasing inequality observed during the period. Fourth, during the Jokowi period, the curve is inverse U-shaped, implying that the welfare improvement for the middle class is higher than for the poorest and richest population groups. This explains why inequality has slightly declined during the last two years.

12.5.2 Is Growth Good for the Poor in Indonesia?

The results of our estimations using various estimation techniques are shown in Appendix Tables 12.A1 to 12.A5. Table 12.A1 shows the estimation results using OLS, Table 12.A2 using fixed effect, Table 12.A3 using first differences, Table 12.A4 using GMM-system with the log GDP per capita instrumented using second lag of the independent variables, and Table 12.A5 using GMM-system with control for year and region dummies. Different from Table 12.A4, the estimation results in Table 12.A5 pass the Hansen test for over-identification and Arellano-Bond test for serial correlation. Hence, we use the results in Table 12.A5 as the main findings of our analysis.

We present the coefficients of log per capita GDP in Table 12.A5 in the form of a graph in Figure 12.2. Since the estimations have controlled for region and year dummies, the results obtained have taken into account both regional characteristics that do not vary over time, as well as specific time shocks that affect all regions nationally. This means that, in addition to district specific controls, the results have also controlled for global level variables, such as changes in commodity prices, and national level variables, such as the change in tax collection effort by the national government.

The figure shows that during the SBY1 and SBY2 periods, the elasticities of per capita consumption growth of the poorest 20 per cent to per capita GDP growth are close to 1, replicating the results obtained by Dollar and Kraay (2002). During the SBY1 period, the elasticities of the middle quintiles are slightly less than 1. During the SBY2 period, the elasticities of Q2 and Q3 quintiles are significantly lower at around 0.5, while that of Q4 quintile is 1. However, in both periods, the elasticities of the richest 20 per cent are significantly higher, at 1.2. This means that while growth was good for the poor, growth benefited the richest section of the population even more.

During the Jokowi period, unfortunately, elasticity of the poorest 20 per cent is significantly less than 1, at 0.7. Furthermore, the higher the quintile of per capita household consumption the higher the elasticity. The richest 20 per cent, meanwhile, maintain their elasticity at around 1.2. This means that, for every 1 per cent per capita GDP growth, per capita consumption of the poorest 20 per cent grows by 0.7 per cent, while that of the richest 20 per cent grows by 1.2 per cent. Hence, compared to the previous periods, growth is not as good for the poor, while it is better for the middle class and even more for the richest.

FIGURE 12.2
Elasticities of Per Capita Consumption Growth to Per Capita GDP Growth

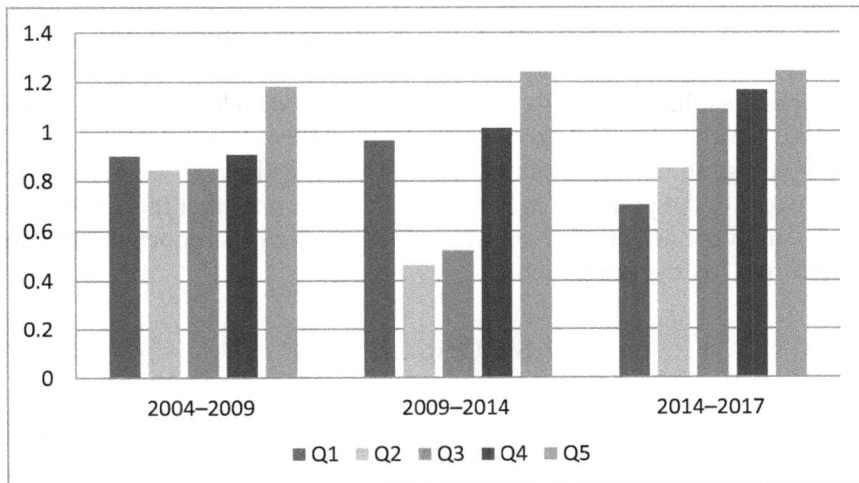

Source: Authors' calculations.

Manning and Pratomo (Chapter 11) find that real wages have increased significantly in recent years. Wage data from the national labour force survey (Sakernas), which they used in their analysis, refers to formal sector wages. Since formal sector workers are most likely to be located in the middle quintiles in the household per capita expenditure distribution, their finding is consistent with Figure 12.2 (which shows significant increases in the elasticities of the middle quintiles during Jokowi's presidency).

12.5.3 Heterogeneity Analysis

To see whether the decline in the elasticity of per capita consumption growth of the poorest 20 per cent to per capita GDP growth during Jokowi period occurs uniformly across Indonesia, we perform two heterogeneity analyses. First, we split the sample into municipality districts (*kota*) and regency districts (*kabupaten*) and re-estimate the model separately. The results are presented in Tables 12.B1 and 12.B2 respectively. They show that the elasticity for the poorest 20 per cent in municipality districts is significantly lower at less than 0.7, while in regency districts it is still relatively close to 1, at 0.9.

Second, we divide the sample into districts in Java and those outside Java, and again re-estimate the model separately. The results are presented in Tables 12.C1 and 12.C2 respectively. They show that the elasticity for the poorest 20 per cent in the districts in Java is significantly lower at around 0.7, while in the districts outside Java the elasticity is still around one.

These results are actually consistent with the development priority of Jokowi, which is summarized in the motto *"Membangun dari pinggiran"* (developing from the periphery). However, considering that more than 60 per cent of the poor live in Java, these results imply that it is important to devote more attention to assist the livelihood of the poor who live in Java as well as the urban poor.

12.6 CONCLUSION

When Jokowi took over the Indonesian presidency at the end of 2014, the economic and social conditions of the country were not favourable; economic growth had been declining, poverty reduction had stagnated and inequality was high. He has since launched several social policy initiatives to improve the welfare of the nation's poor and vulnerable. These include expanding the coverage of several social assistance programmes as well as making them more effective. In addition, he started and has continuously increased the village fund, a grant for villages mandated by the 2014 Village Law.

This chapter analyses the impact of these initiatives on poverty and inequality trends in the country. Adopting the framework developed by Dollar and Kraay (2002), we correlate economic growth with real per capita household consumption growth by quintile at the district level for three periods: 2004–09, 2009–14 and 2014–17. The last period refers to Jokowi's presidency, while the first two periods refer to the first and second term of President Yudhoyono. In this study, we try to assess whether economic growth has become more or less pro-poor under Jokowi.

The results of the analysis indicate that economic growth has become less pro-poor during the first three years of the Jokowi government. Compared to the ten years of the SBY administration, where the elasticity of per capita consumption growth to per capita GDP growth of the poorest 20 per cent population was stable at around 1, the elasticity has decreased to around 0.7 during the Jokowi period. This means that, for every 1 per cent economic growth, real consumption of the poor grows less at 0.7 per cent.

The clear winner of the Jokowi period is the middle class. Growth elasticities of consumption of the middle quintiles (Q2–Q4) have increased significantly, especially compared to the second term of the SBY period. Meanwhile, the richest 20 per cent maintains their high elasticity, at around 1.2. This high level of elasticity has been consistently enjoyed by the richest population since the first SBY period.

These results clearly indicate that, during the first three years of the Jokowi period, the poor were less connected to economic growth compared to the middle class and the rich. This implies that the president's strategy to assist the poor through the expansion of social assistance programmes and village fund is not sufficient. While this approach has helped the poor to maintain a positive real consumption growth, it does not really propel them to rise above subsistence level. Hence, a complementary strategy to connect the poor to economic growth — through job creation and income generation — is needed. Furthermore, the results of the heterogeneity analyses indicate it is important to place more attention on assisting the livelihood of the poor who live in Java and the urban poor.

APPENDIX

FIGURE 12.A1

Growth Incidence Curve (GIC) of Household per Capita Consumption

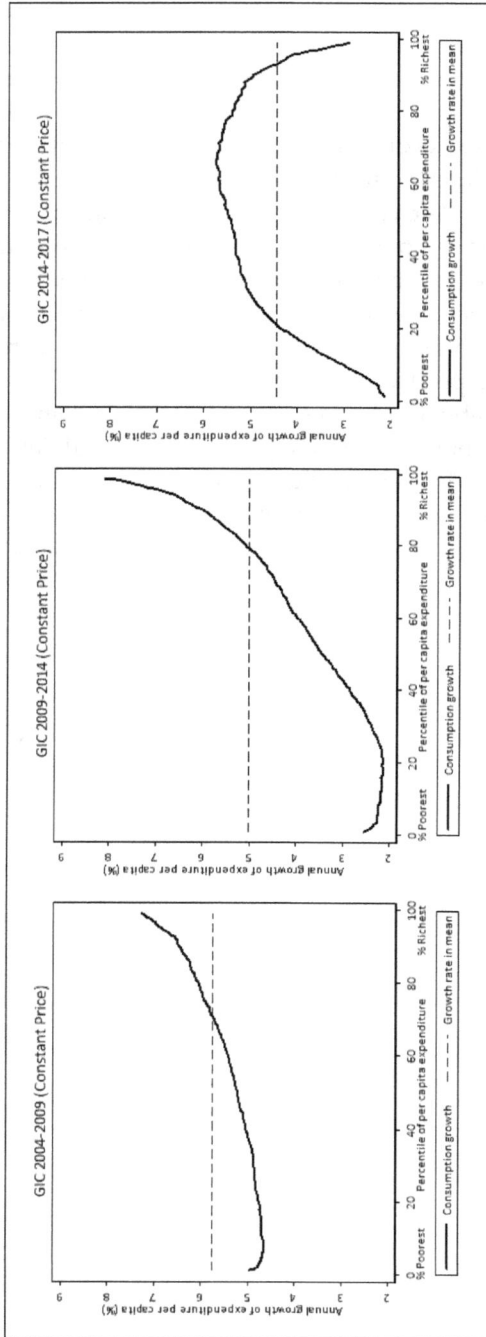

Source: SUSENAS, authors' estimation.

TABLE 12.A1
Estimation Result from OLS

	Dependent: Log of per capita consumption				
	Period 1 (2004–09)				
	Q1	Q2	Q3	Q4	Q5
Log of per capita GRDP	0.252***	0.276***	0.288***	0.301***	0.308***
	(0.034)	(0.031)	(0.029)	(0.028)	(0.029)
Constant	9.840***	9.807***	9.841***	9.884***	10.326***
	(0.535)	(0.488)	(0.459)	(0.440)	(0.450)
Number of observations	2,262	2,262	2,262	2,262	2,262
Adjusted R2	0.345	0.376	0.389	0.391	0.322

	Dependent: Log of per capita consumption				
	Period 2 (2009–14)				
	Q1	Q2	Q3	Q4	Q5
Log of per capita GRDP	0.245***	0.274***	0.295***	0.314***	0.331***
	(0.028)	(0.027)	(0.028)	(0.030)	(0.032)
Constant	10.117***	9.988***	9.911***	9.905***	10.279***
	(0.441)	(0.429)	(0.448)	(0.476)	(0.505)
Number of observations	2,262	2,262	2,262	2,262	2,262
Adjusted R2	0.369	0.400	0.403	0.398	0.352

	Dependent: Log of per capita consumption				
	Period 3 (2014–17)				
	Q1	Q2	Q3	Q4	Q5
Log of per capita GRDP	0.250***	0.282***	0.305***	0.313***	0.314***
	(0.026)	(0.027)	(0.031)	(0.035)	(0.042)
Constant	10.120***	9.960***	9.889***	10.088***	10.742***
	(0.411)	(0.432)	(0.491)	(0.566)	(0.673)
Number of observations	1,508	1,508	1,508	1,508	1,508
Adjusted R2	0.358	0.385	0.399	0.393	0.366

Notes: Standard error in parenthesis, * $p<0.1$; ** $p<0.05$; *** $p<0.01$

TABLE 12.A2
Estimation Result from Fixed Effect

	Dependent: Log of per capita consumption				
	Period 1 (2004–09)				
	Q1	Q2	Q3	Q4	Q5
Log of per capita GRDP	0.633***	0.721***	0.702***	0.662***	0.584***
	(0.077)	(0.082)	(0.073)	(0.069)	(0.063)
Constant	3.898***	2.881**	3.403***	4.271***	6.039***
	(1.199)	(1.284)	(1.129)	(1.074)	(0.984)
Number of observations	2,262	2,262	2,262	2,262	2,262
Adjusted R2	0.304	0.336	0.322	0.287	0.132

	Dependent: Log of per capita consumption				
	Period 2 (2009–14)				
	Q1	Q2	Q3	Q4	Q5
Log of per capita GRDP	0.270***	0.294***	0.444***	0.685***	1.103***
	(0.089)	(0.088)	(0.102)	(0.127)	(0.174)
Constant	9.720***	9.677***	7.560***	4.070*	−1.879
	(1.397)	(1.385)	(1.602)	(2.002)	(2.740)
Number of observations	2,262	2,262	2,262	2,262	2,262
Adjusted R2	0.066	0.079	0.136	0.212	0.254

	Dependent: Log of per capita consumption				
	Period 3 (2014–17)				
	Q1	Q2	Q3	Q4	Q5
Log of per capita GRDP	0.677***	0.971***	1.160***	1.217***	0.848***
	(0.067)	(0.100)	(0.113)	(0.123)	(0.113)
Constant	3.320***	−1.002	−3.714**	−4.308**	2.235
	(1.063)	(1.592)	(1.795)	(1.951)	(1.793)
Number of observations	1,508	1,508	1,508	1,508	1,508
Adjusted R2	0.229	0.352	0.387	0.380	0.182

Notes: Standard error in parenthesis, * $p<0.1$; ** $p<0.05$; *** $p<0.01$

TABLE 12.A3
Estimation Result from First-difference

	Dependent: Log of per capita consumption				
	Period 1 (2004–09)				
	Q1	Q2	Q3	Q4	Q5
Log of per capita GRDP	0.317***	0.248***	0.182***	0.120**	−0.065
	(0.035)	(0.049)	(0.047)	(0.049)	(0.093)
Number of observations	1,885	1,885	1,885	1,885	1,885
Adjusted R2	0.068	0.040	0.022	0.008	0.000

	Dependent: Log of per capita consumption				
	Period 2 (2009–14)				
	Q1	Q2	Q3	Q4	Q5
Log of per capita GRDP	0.292***	0.012	0.052	0.210**	0.396***
	(0.056)	(0.051)	(0.051)	(0.077)	(0.090)
Number of observations	2,262	2,262	2,262	2,262	2,262
Adjusted R2	0.033	−0.000	0.001	0.012	0.021

	Dependent: Log of per capita consumption				
	Period 3 (2014–17)				
	Q1	Q2	Q3	Q4	Q5
Log of per capita GRDP	0.525***	0.758***	0.996***	1.134***	0.981***
	(0.062)	(0.089)	(0.116)	(0.142)	(0.124)
Number of observations	1,508	1,508	1,508	1,508	1,508
Adjusted R2	0.083	0.148	0.190	0.200	0.105

Notes: Standard error in parenthesis, * $p<0.1$; ** $p<0.05$; *** $p<0.01$

TABLE 12.A4
Estimation Result from GMM-system

	Dependent: Log of per capita consumption				
	Period 1 (2004–09)				
	Q1	Q2	Q3	Q4	Q5
Log of per capita GRDP	1.054***	0.961***	0.901***	0.835***	0.484***
	(0.042)	(0.038)	(0.037)	(0.038)	(0.047)
Constant	−2.636***	−0.846	0.306	1.584***	7.585***
	(0.651)	(0.584)	(0.580)	(0.594)	(0.740)
Number of observations	2,262	2,262	2,262	2,262	2,262
Number of instrument	3	3	3	3	3
Overidentification restrictions (Hansen test)	0.176	0.290	0.297	0.388	0.180
First-order serial correlation (Arellano-Bond test)	0.000	0.000	0.000	0.000	0.000
Second-order serial correlation (Arellano-Bond test)	0.869	0.000	0.000	0.000	0.000

	Dependent: Log of per capita consumption				
	Period 2 (2009–14)				
	Q1	Q2	Q3	Q4	Q5
Log of per capita GRDP	0.917***	0.304***	0.549***	1.016***	1.476***
	(0.053)	(0.042)	(0.043)	(0.052)	(0.068)
Constant	−0.468	9.520***	5.910***	−1.149	−7.755***
	(0.832)	(0.661)	(0.676)	(0.822)	(1.068)
Number of observations	2,262	2,262	2,262	2,262	2,262
Number of instrument	3	3	3	3	3
Overidentification restrictions (Hansen test)	0.687	0.108	0.584	0.802	0.506
First-order serial correlation (Arellano-Bond test)	0.000	0.000	0.000	0.000	0.000
Second-order serial correlation (Arellano-Bond test)	0.035	0.070	0.000	0.000	0.000

	Dependent: Log of per capita consumption				
	Period 3 (2014–17)				
	Q1	Q2	Q3	Q4	Q5
Log of per capita GRDP	0.889***	1.249***	1.584***	1.832***	1.358***
	(0.047)	(0.053)	(0.067)	(0.088)	(0.133)
Constant	−0.055	−5.412***	−10.446***	−14.059***	−5.858***
	(0.738)	(0.846)	(1.064)	(1.402)	(2.105)
Number of observations	1,508	1,508	1,508	1,508	1,508
Number of instrument	3	3	3	3	3
Overidentification restrictions (Hansen test)	0.200	0.015	0.001	0.000	0.000
First-order serial correlation (Arellano-Bond test)	0.000	0.000	0.000	0.000	0.000
Second-order serial correlation (Arellano-Bond test)	0.092	0.526	0.490	0.992	0.305

Notes: Standard error in parenthesis, * $p<0.1$; ** $p<0.05$; *** $p<0.01$
All estimations are estimated using system GMM with two-step estimation, GRDP is instrumented using 2nd or 3rd lags of GRDP, and robust standard error.

TABLE 12.A5
Estimation Result from GMM-system with Year and Island Dummies

	Dependent: Log of per capita consumption				
	Period 1 (2004–09)				
	Q1	Q2	Q3	Q4	Q5
Log of per capita GRDP	0.908***	0.844***	0.851***	0.907***	1.182***
	(0.089)	(0.070)	(0.067)	(0.072)	(0.102)
Year dummies	Yes	Yes	Yes	Yes	Yes
Island dummies	Yes	Yes	Yes	Yes	Yes
Constant	−0.400	1.090	1.290	0.706	−3.017*
	(1.391)	(1.073)	(1.028)	(1.096)	(1.543)
Number of observations	2,262	2,262	2,262	2,262	2,262
Number of instrument	14	14	14	14	14
Overidentification restrictions (Hansen test)	0.131	0.799	0.642	0.683	0.874
First-order serial correlation (Arellano-Bond test)	0.000	0.000	0.000	0.000	0.000
Second-order serial correlation (Arellano-Bond test)	0.445	0.974	0.717	0.523	0.002

	Dependent: Log of per capita consumption				
	Period 2 (2009–14)				
	Q1	Q2	Q3	Q4	Q5
Log of per capita GRDP	0.964***	0.463***	0.521***	1.013***	1.240***
	(0.096)	(0.045)	(0.047)	(0.047)	(0.065)
Year dummies	Yes	Yes	Yes	Yes	Yes
Island dummies	Yes	Yes	Yes	Yes	Yes
Constant	−1.057	7.176***	6.658***	−0.839	−3.686***
	(1.483)	(0.671)	(0.748)	(0.720)	(1.009)
Number of observations	2,262	2,262	2,262	2,262	2,262
Number of instrument	14	14	14	13	16
Overidentification restrictions (Hansen test)	0.136	0.000	0.000	0.920	0.554
First-order serial correlation (Arellano-Bond test)	0.000	0.000	0.000	0.000	0.000
Second-order serial correlation (Arellano-Bond test)	0.171	0.008	0.013	0.470	0.530

| | Dependent: Log of per capita consumption | | | | |
| | Period 3 (2014–17) | | | | |
	Q1	Q2	Q3	Q4	Q5
Log of per capita GRDP	0.704***	0.850***	1.090***	1.166***	1.243***
	(0.056)	(0.063)	(0.099)	(0.133)	(0.126)
Year dummies	Yes	Yes	Yes	Yes	Yes
Island dummies	Yes	Yes	Yes	Yes	Yes
Constant	2.968***	1.093	−2.310	−3.185	−3.711*
	(0.880)	(0.971)	(1.516)	(2.050)	(1.948)
Number of observations	1,508	1,508	1,508	1,508	1,508
Number of instrument	13	13	13	13	13
Overidentification restrictions (Hansen test)	0.143	0.773	0.000	0.000	0.000
First-order serial correlation (Arellano-Bond test)	0.000	0.000	0.000	0.000	0.000
Second-order serial correlation (Arellano-Bond test)	0.399	0.270	0.335	0.602	0.751

Notes: Standard error in parenthesis, * $p<0.1$; ** $p<0.05$; *** $p<0.01$
All estimations are estimated using system GMM with two-step estimation, GRDP is instrumented using 2nd or 3rd lags of GRDP, and robust standard error.

TABLE 12.B1
Estimation Result GMM-system for Municipality

	Dependent: Log of per capita consumption				
	Period 1 (2004–09)				
	Q1	Q2	Q3	Q4	Q5
Log of per capita	1.066***	0.859***	0.872***	0.902***	1.293***
GRDP	(0.292)	(0.166)	(0.163)	(0.179)	(0.281)
Year dummies	Yes	Yes	Yes	Yes	Yes
Islands dummies	Yes	Yes	Yes	Yes	Yes
Constant	−2.432	1.191	1.256	1.038	−4.588
	(4.623)	(2.607)	(2.551)	(2.811)	(4.427)
Number of observations	534	534	534	534	534
Number of instrument	14	14	14	14	14
Overidentification restrictions (Hansen test)	0.736	0.613	0.610	0.840	0.851
First-order serial correlation (Arellano-Bond test)	0.026	0.000	0.000	0.000	0.000
Second-order serial correlation (Arellano-Bond test)	0.415	0.303	0.611	0.333	0.051

	Dependent: Log of per capita consumption				
	Period 2 (2009–14)				
	Q1	Q2	Q3	Q4	Q5
Log of per capita	0.895***	0.277***	0.237*	1.087***	1.250***
GRDP	(0.161)	(0.101)	(0.121)	(0.116)	(0.152)
Year dummies	Yes	Yes	Yes	Yes	Yes
Islands dummies	Yes	Yes	Yes	Yes	Yes
Constant	0.233	10.472***	11.446***	−1.817	−3.784
	(2.570)	(1.603)	(1.933)	(1.845)	(2.420)
Number of observations	534	534	534	534	534
Number of instrument	14	14	14	13	16
Overidentification restrictions (Hansen test)	0.470	0.000	0.000	0.877	0.959
First-order serial correlation (Arellano-Bond test)	0.005	0.000	0.000	0.000	0.000
Second-order serial correlation (Arellano-Bond test)	0.957	0.283	0.924	0.184	0.116

	Dependent: Log of per capita consumption				
	Period 3 (2014–17)				
	Q1	Q2	Q3	Q4	Q5
Log of per capita	0.675***	1.084***	1.705***	1.759***	1.624***
GRDP	(0.125)	(0.187)	(0.387)	(0.568)	(0.368)
Year dummies	Yes	Yes	Yes	Yes	Yes
Islands dummies	Yes	Yes	Yes	Yes	Yes
Constant	3.680*	−2.365	−11.826*	−12.381	−9.916*
	(2.054)	(3.044)	(6.193)	(9.050)	(5.868)
Number of observations	356	356	356	356	356
Number of instrument	13	13	13	13	13
Overidentification restrictions (Hansen test)	0.559	0.871	0.015	0.000	0.131
First-order serial correlation (Arellano-Bond test)	0.000	0.000	0.003	0.002	0.000
Second-order serial correlation (Arellano-Bond test)	0.756	0.575	0.067	0.562	0.209

Notes: Standard error in parenthesis, * $p<0.1$; ** $p<0.05$; *** $p<0.01$
All estimations are estimated using system GMM with two-step estimation, GRDP is instrumented using 2nd or 3rd lags of GRDP, and robust standard error.

TABLE 12.B2
Estimation Result GMM-system for Regency

	Dependent: Log of per capita consumption				
	Period 1 (2004–09)				
	Q1	Q2	Q3	Q4	Q5
Log of per capita GRDP	1.157***	0.916***	0.869***	0.913***	1.323***
	(0.168)	(0.112)	(0.097)	(0.106)	(0.198)
Year dummies	Yes	Yes	Yes	Yes	Yes
Islands dummies	Yes	Yes	Yes	Yes	Yes
Constant	−4.165*	−0.093	0.911	0.529	−5.184*
	(2.527)	(1.664)	(1.451)	(1.576)	(2.923)
Number of observations	1,728	1,728	1,728	1,728	1,728
Number of instrument	14	14	14	14	14
Overidentification restrictions (Hansen test)	0.410	0.725	0.888	0.874	0.187
First-order serial correlation (Arellano-Bond test)	0.000	0.000	0.000	0.000	0.000
Second-order serial correlation (Arellano-Bond test)	0.235	0.699	0.613	0.760	0.031

	Dependent: Log of per capita consumption				
	Period 2 (2009–14)				
	Q1	Q2	Q3	Q4	Q5
Log of per capita GRDP	1.321***	0.276***	0.416***	1.018***	1.339***
	(0.133)	(0.067)	(0.064)	(0.055)	(0.073)
Year dummies	Yes	Yes	Yes	Yes	Yes
Islands dummies	Yes	Yes	Yes	Yes	Yes
Constant	−6.553***	9.707***	7.926***	−1.011	−5.237***
	(2.006)	(1.034)	(1.052)	(0.838)	(1.121)
Number of observations	1,728	1,728	1,728	1,728	1,728
Number of instrument	14	14	14	13	16
Overidentification restrictions (Hansen test)	0.520	0.000	0.000	0.266	0.392
First-order serial correlation (Arellano-Bond test)	0.003	0.000	0.000	0.000	0.000
Second-order serial correlation (Arellano-Bond test)	0.177	0.015	0.005	0.090	0.740

	Dependent: Log of per capita consumption				
	Period 3 (2014–17)				
	Q1	Q2	Q3	Q4	Q5
Log of per capita GRDP	0.909***	0.828***	1.159***	1.317***	1.485***
	(0.056)	(0.075)	(0.101)	(0.167)	(0.182)
Year dummies	Yes	Yes	Yes	Yes	Yes
Islands dummies	Yes	Yes	Yes	Yes	Yes
Constant	−0.224	1.314	−3.381**	−5.414**	−7.325***
	(0.873)	(1.128)	(1.509)	(2.484)	(2.722)
Number of observations	1,152	1,152	1,152	1,152	1,152
Number of instrument	11	14	14	14	14
Overidentification restrictions (Hansen test)	0.382	0.291	0.145	0.000	0.000
First-order serial correlation (Arellano-Bond test)	0.000	0.000	0.000	0.000	0.000
Second-order serial correlation (Arellano-Bond test)	0.497	0.297	0.699	0.481	0.385

Notes: Standard error in parenthesis, * $p<0.1$; ** $p<0.05$; *** $p<0.01$
All estimations are estimated using system GMM with two-step estimation, GRDP is instrumented using 2nd or 3rd lags of GRDP, and robust standard error.

TABLE 12.C1
Estimation Result GMM-system for Java

	Dependent: Log of per capita consumption				
	Period 1 (2004–09)				
	Q1	Q2	Q3	Q4	Q5
Log of per capita GRDP	0.837***	0.768***	0.780***	0.939***	1.226***
	(0.111)	(0.092)	(0.098)	(0.128)	(0.075)
Year dummies	Yes	Yes	Yes	Yes	Yes
Provincial dummies	Yes	Yes	Yes	Yes	Yes
Constant	1.094	2.472*	2.497	0.207	−3.813***
	(1.746)	(1.437)	(1.539)	(2.014)	(1.174)
Number of observations	744	744	744	744	744
Number of instrument	16	16	16	15	15
Overidentification restrictions (Hansen test)	0.185	0.274	0.258	0.318	0.314
First-order serial correlation (Arellano-Bond test)	0.000	0.000	0.000	0.000	0.000
Second-order serial correlation (Arellano-Bond test)	0.260	0.576	0.987	0.314	0.012

	Dependent: Log of per capita consumption				
	Period 2 (2009–14)				
	Q1	Q2	Q3	Q4	Q5
Log of per capita GRDP	0.798***	0.438***	0.770***	0.920***	1.379***
	(0.076)	(0.061)	(0.062)	(0.075)	(0.106)
Year dummies	Yes	Yes	Yes	Yes	Yes
Provincial dummies	Yes	Yes	Yes	Yes	Yes
Constant	1.643	7.718***	2.702***	0.621	−5.963***
	(1.201)	(0.961)	(0.967)	(1.182)	(1.678)
Number of observations	744	744	744	744	744
Number of instrument	15	15	15	16	16
Overidentification restrictions (Hansen test)	0.635	0.000	0.024	0.331	0.909
First-order serial correlation (Arellano-Bond test)	0.000	0.000	0.000	0.000	0.000
Second-order serial correlation (Arellano-Bond test)	0.812	0.101	0.245	0.275	0.257

	Dependent: Log of per capita consumption				
	Period 3 (2014–17)				
	Q1	Q2	Q3	Q4	Q5
Log of per capita GRDP	0.727***	0.955***	1.239***	1.352***	1.531***
	(0.088)	(0.116)	(0.186)	(0.227)	–(0.216)
Year dummies	Yes	Yes	Yes	Yes	Yes
Provincial dummies	Yes	Yes	Yes	Yes	Yes
Constant	2.700*	–0.590	–4.892*	–6.350*	–8.513**
	(1.404)	(1.830)	(2.942)	(3.591)	(3.426)
Number of observations	496	496	496	496	496
Number of instrument	14	14	14	14	14
Overidentification restrictions (Hansen test)	0.922	0.576	0.000	0.000	0.000
First-order serial correlation (Arellano-Bond test)	0.001	0.001	0.000	0.000	0.000
Second-order serial correlation (Arellano-Bond test)	0.902	0.212	0.504	0.233	0.786

Notes: Standard error in parenthesis, * $p<0.1$; ** $p<0.05$; *** $p<0.01$
All estimations are estimated using system GMM with two-step estimation, GRDP is instrumented using 2nd or 3rd lags of GRDP, and robust standard error.

TABLE 12.C2
Estimation Result GMM-system for Outside Java

	Dependent: Log of per capita consumption				
	Period 1 (2004–09)				
	Q1	Q2	Q3	Q4	Q5
Log of per capita	1.250***	1.004***	0.977***	1.022***	1.305***
GRDP	(0.181)	(0.118)	(0.111)	(0.118)	(0.170)
Year dummies	Yes	Yes	Yes	Yes	Yes
Islands dummies	Yes	Yes	Yes	Yes	Yes
Constant	−5.747**	−1.549	−0.899	−1.348	−5.263**
	(2.859)	(1.851)	(1.746)	(1.851)	(2.671)
Number of observations	1,518	1,518	1,518	1,518	1,518
Number of instrument	12	12	12	12	12
Overidentification restrictions (Hansen test)	0.398	0.728	0.720	0.679	0.568
First-order serial correlation (Arellano-Bond test)	0.000	0.000	0.000	0.000	0.000
Second-order serial correlation (Arellano-Bond test)	0.631	0.684	0.721	0.827	0.021

	Dependent: Log of per capita consumption				
	Period 2 (2009–14)				
	Q1	Q2	Q3	Q4	Q5
Log of per capita	1.163***	0.437***	0.549***	0.966***	1.248***
GRDP	(0.125)	(0.066)	(0.073)	(0.062)	(0.081)
Year dummies	Yes	Yes	Yes	Yes	Yes
Islands dummies	Yes	Yes	Yes	Yes	Yes
Constant	−4.353**	7.472***	5.930***	−0.390	−4.219***
	(1.968)	(1.040)	(1.142)	(0.979)	(1.272)
Number of observations	1,518	1,518	1,518	1,518	1,518
Number of instrument	12	12	12	11	12
Overidentification restrictions (Hansen test)	0.508	0.000	0.000	0.008	0.059
First-order serial correlation (Arellano-Bond test)	0.007	0.000	0.000	0.000	0.000
Second-order serial correlation (Arellano-Bond test)	0.175	0.056	0.050	0.193	0.986

| | Dependent: Log of per capita consumption | | | | |
| | Period 3 (2014–17) | | | | |
	Q1	Q2	Q3	Q4	Q5
Log of per capita	0.955***	0.873***	1.176***	1.343***	1.408***
GRDP	(0.063)	(0.079)	(0.113)	(0.177)	(0.171)
Year dummies	Yes	Yes	Yes	Yes	Yes
Islands dummies	Yes	Yes	Yes	Yes	Yes
Constant	−1.179	0.535	−3.986**	−6.326**	−6.720**
	(0.991)	(1.246)	(1.790)	(2.786)	(2.704)
Number of observations	1,012	1,012	1,012	1,012	1,012
Number of instrument	10	11	11	11	11
Overidentification restrictions (Hansen test)	0.405	0.106	0.113	0.000	0.000
First-order serial correlation (Arellano-Bond test)	0.000	0.000	0.000	0.000	0.000
Second-order serial correlation (Arellano-Bond test)	0.744	0.751	0.732	0.049	0.796

Notes: Standard error in parenthesis, * $p<0.1$; ** $p<0.05$; *** $p<0.01$
All estimations are estimated using system GMM with two-step estimation, GRDP is instrumented using 2nd or 3rd lags of GRDP, and robust standard error.

TABLE 12.D1
Summary Statistics (All sample)

	Period 1 (2004–09)				
	Observation	Mean	Std. Dev	Min	Max
Log of per capita consumption (Quintile 1)	2262	13.75	0.31	12.78	14.80
Log of per capita consumption (Quintile 2)	2262	14.10	0.32	13.18	15.21
Log of per capita consumption (Quintile 3)	2262	14.33	0.33	13.40	15.49
Log of per capita consumption (Quintile 4)	2262	14.57	0.35	13.66	15.84
Log of per capita consumption (Quintile 5)	2262	15.12	0.39	14.11	16.80
Log of per capita GRDP	2262	15.56	0.72	14.01	19.20

	Period 2 (2009–14)				
	Observation	Mean	Std. Dev	Min	Max
Log of per capita consumption (Quintile 1)	2262	13.98	0.28	13.00	14.81
Log of per capita consumption (Quintile 2)	2262	14.31	0.30	13.38	15.22
Log of per capita consumption (Quintile 3)	2262	14.56	0.32	13.60	15.63
Log of per capita consumption (Quintile 4)	2262	14.86	0.34	13.89	16.10
Log of per capita consumption (Quintile 5)	2262	15.50	0.38	14.49	17.15
Log of per capita GRDP	2262	15.76	0.69	14.04	19.04

| | | Period 3 (2014–17) | | | |
	Observation	Mean	Std. Dev	Min	Max
Log of per capita consumption (Quintile 1)	1508	14.09	0.28	13.24	15.02
Log of per capita consumption (Quintile 2)	1508	14.45	0.30	13.64	15.49
Log of per capita consumption (Quintile 3)	1508	14.74	0.32	13.88	15.82
Log of per capita consumption (Quintile 4)	1508	15.07	0.33	14.14	16.10
Log of per capita consumption (Quintile 5)	1508	15.73	0.35	14.76	17.15
Log of per capita GRDP	1508	15.91	0.67	14.17	18.96

TABLE 12.D2
Summary Statistics (Municipality)

	Period 1 (2004–09)				
	Observation	Mean	Std. Dev	Min	Max
Log of per capita consumption (Quintile 1)	534	14.04	0.28	12.78	14.80
Log of per capita consumption (Quintile 2)	534	14.42	0.28	13.73	15.21
Log of per capita consumption (Quintile 3)	534	14.67	0.28	13.95	15.49
Log of per capita consumption (Quintile 4)	534	14.94	0.29	14.15	15.84
Log of per capita consumption (Quintile 5)	534	15.54	0.36	14.57	16.80
Log of per capita GRDP	534	16.01	0.76	14.66	19.20

	Period 2 (2009–14)				
	Observation	Mean	Std. Dev	Min	Max
Log of per capita consumption (Quintile 1)	534	14.23	0.23	13.55	14.81
Log of per capita consumption (Quintile 2)	534	14.60	0.25	14.02	15.22
Log of per capita consumption (Quintile 3)	534	14.89	0.26	14.22	15.63
Log of per capita consumption (Quintile 4)	534	15.22	0.28	14.45	16.10
Log of per capita consumption (Quintile 5)	534	15.90	0.33	14.99	17.15
Log of per capita GRDP	534	16.22	0.73	14.95	19.04

| | Period 3 (2014–17) | | | |
	Observation	Mean	Std. Dev	Min	Max
Log of per capita consumption (Quintile 1)	356	14.32	0.23	13.79	14.93
Log of per capita consumption (Quintile 2)	356	14.74	0.26	14.14	15.40
Log of per capita consumption (Quintile 3)	356	15.07	0.26	14.35	15.72
Log of per capita consumption (Quintile 4)	356	15.43	0.27	14.65	16.10
Log of per capita consumption (Quintile 5)	356	16.13	0.29	15.25	17.15
Log of per capita GRDP	356	16.37	0.71	15.12	18.96

TABLE 12.D3
Summary Statistics (Regency)

	Period 1 (2004–09)				
	Observation	Mean	Std. Dev	Min	Max
Log of per capita consumption (Quintile 1)	1728	13.67	0.26	12.84	14.66
Log of per capita consumption (Quintile 2)	1728	14.01	0.27	13.18	14.94
Log of per capita consumption (Quintile 3)	1728	14.22	0.27	13.40	15.15
Log of per capita consumption (Quintile 4)	1728	14.45	0.27	13.66	15.36
Log of per capita consumption (Quintile 5)	1728	14.99	0.30	14.11	16.05
Log of per capita GRDP	1728	15.42	0.64	14.01	18.46

	Period 2 (2009–14)				
	Observation	Mean	Std. Dev	Min	Max
Log of per capita consumption (Quintile 1)	1728	13.90	0.24	13.00	14.73
Log of per capita consumption (Quintile 2)	1728	14.22	0.25	13.38	15.15
Log of per capita consumption (Quintile 3)	1728	14.46	0.26	13.60	15.53
Log of per capita consumption (Quintile 4)	1728	14.75	0.27	13.89	15.86
Log of per capita consumption (Quintile 5)	1728	15.38	0.31	14.49	16.39
Log of per capita GRDP	1728	15.62	0.61	14.04	18.32

		Period 3 (2014–17)			
	Observation	Mean	Std. Dev	Min	Max
Log of per capita consumption (Quintile 1)	1152	14.02	0.25	13.24	15.02
Log of per capita consumption (Quintile 2)	1152	14.37	0.26	13.64	15.49
Log of per capita consumption (Quintile 3)	1152	14.64	0.27	13.88	15.82
Log of per capita consumption (Quintile 4)	1152	14.95	0.26	14.14	16.08
Log of per capita consumption (Quintile 5)	1152	15.61	0.26	14.76	16.63
Log of per capita GRDP	1152	15.77	0.58	14.17	18.17

TABLE 12.D4
Summary Statistics (Java)

	Period 1 (2004–09)				
	Observation	Mean	Std. Dev	Min	Max
Log of per capita consumption (Quintile 1)	744	13.79	0.31	13.08	14.80
Log of per capita consumption (Quintile 2)	744	14.13	0.34	13.52	15.21
Log of per capita consumption (Quintile 3)	744	14.34	0.35	13.73	15.49
Log of per capita consumption (Quintile 4)	744	14.58	0.37	13.97	15.84
Log of per capita consumption (Quintile 5)	744	15.16	0.43	14.38	16.80
Log of per capita GRDP	744	15.52	0.75	14.42	18.52

	Period 2 (2009–14)				
	Observation	Mean	Std. Dev	Min	Max
Log of per capita consumption (Quintile 1)	744	13.99	0.27	13.48	14.81
Log of per capita consumption (Quintile 2)	744	14.31	0.30	13.76	15.22
Log of per capita consumption (Quintile 3)	744	14.56	0.33	13.96	15.63
Log of per capita consumption (Quintile 4)	744	14.86	0.37	14.21	16.10
Log of per capita consumption (Quintile 5)	744	15.53	0.43	14.73	17.15
Log of per capita GRDP	744	15.76	0.74	14.68	18.80

| | Period 3 (2014–17) | | | |
	Observation	Mean	Std. Dev	Min	Max
Log of per capita consumption (Quintile 1)	496	14.11	0.25	13.59	15.00
Log of per capita consumption (Quintile 2)	496	14.47	0.30	13.91	15.49
Log of per capita consumption (Quintile 3)	496	14.78	0.34	14.10	15.82
Log of per capita consumption (Quintile 4)	496	15.12	0.35	14.35	16.10
Log of per capita consumption (Quintile 5)	496	15.83	0.38	15.04	17.15
Log of per capita GRDP	496	15.93	0.73	14.87	18.96

TABLE 12.D5
Summary Statistics (Outside Java)

	Period 1 (2004–09)				
	Observation	Mean	Std. Dev	Min	Max
Log of per capita consumption (Quintile 1)	1518	13.74	0.30	12.78	14.65
Log of per capita consumption (Quintile 2)	1518	14.09	0.32	13.18	15.12
Log of per capita consumption (Quintile 3)	1518	14.32	0.32	13.40	15.33
Log of per capita consumption (Quintile 4)	1518	14.56	0.33	13.66	15.62
Log of per capita consumption (Quintile 5)	1518	15.10	0.37	14.11	16.27
Log of per capita GRDP	1518	15.58	0.70	14.01	19.20

	Period 2 (2009–14)				
	Observation	Mean	Std. Dev	Min	Max
Log of per capita consumption (Quintile 1)	1518	13.97	0.28	13.00	14.79
Log of per capita consumption (Quintile 2)	1518	14.31	0.30	13.38	15.18
Log of per capita consumption (Quintile 3)	1518	14.56	0.31	13.60	15.54
Log of per capita consumption (Quintile 4)	1518	14.86	0.33	13.89	15.99
Log of per capita consumption (Quintile 5)	1518	15.49	0.35	14.49	16.75
Log of per capita GRDP	1518	15.76	0.66	14.04	19.04

| | Period 3 (2014–17) | | | | |
	Observation	Mean	Std. Dev	Min	Max
Log of per capita consumption (Quintile 1)	1012	14.08	0.29	13.24	15.02
Log of per capita consumption (Quintile 2)	1012	14.45	0.30	13.64	15.39
Log of per capita consumption (Quintile 3)	1012	14.73	0.31	13.88	15.70
Log of per capita consumption (Quintile 4)	1012	15.04	0.32	14.14	16.05
Log of per capita consumption (Quintile 5)	1012	15.68	0.32	14.76	16.75
Log of per capita GRDP	1012	15.90	0.63	14.17	18.57

References

Balisacan, Arsenio M., Ernesto M. Pernia and Abuzar Asra. "Revisiting Growth and Poverty Reduction in Indonesia: What do Subnational Data Show?". *Bulletin of Indonesian Economic Studies* 39, no. 3 (2003): 329–51.

Bappenas. *Social Assistance Table*. Jakarta: Kementerian Perencanaan Pembangunan Nasional Republik Indonesia, Internal Documentation, 2017.

Bridonneau, Sophie. *What I Have Learnt about the Use of Growth Incidence Curves: Use Them but Stay Critical*. Chronic Poverty Advisory Network, 2016. <http://www.chronicpovertynetwork.org/blog/2016/8/5/what-i-have-learnt-about-the-use-of-growth-incidence-curves-use-them-but-stay-critical> (accessed 10 June 2018).

Dollar, David and Aart Kraay. "Growth is Good for the Poor". *Journal of Economic Growth* 7, no. 3 (2002): 195–225.

———, Tatjana Kleineberg and Aart Kraay. "Growth is Still Good for the Poor". *European Economic Review* 81 (2015): 68–85.

Kraay, Aart. "When is Growth Pro-Poor? Evidence from a Panel of Countries". *Journal of Development Economics* 80, Issue 1 (2006): 198–227.

Manning, Chris and Devanto Pratomo. "Labour Market Developments in the Jokowi Years". *Journal of Southeast Asian Economies* 35, no. 2 (2018): 165–84.

McCarthy, J. and M. Sumarto. "Social Protection Program in Indonesia: Understanding the Politics of Distribution". *Journal of Southeast Asian Economies* 35, no. 2 (2018): 223–36.

Ministry of Finance. *Peraturan Menteri Keuangan tentang Rincian Dana Desa* [Minister of Finance Regulation on Village Fund]. Jakarta: Kementerian Keuangan Republik Indonesia, various years.

Miranti, Riyana. "Poverty in Indonesia 1984–2002: The Impact of Growth and Changes in Inequality". *Bulletin of Indonesian Economic Studies* 46, no. 1 (2010): 79–97.

———, Alan Duncan and Rebecca Cassells. "Revisiting the Impact of Consumption Growth and Inequality on Poverty in Indonesia during Decentralisation". *Bulletin of Indonesian Economic Studies* 50, no. 3 (2014): 461–82.

Ravallion, Martin and Shaohua Chen. "Measuring pro-poor growth". *Economics Letters* 78, no. 1 (2003): 93–99.

Statistics Indonesia. *Statistical Yearbook of Indonesia*. Jakarta: Statistics Indonesia, various years.

Syukri, Muhammad, Palmira Permata Bachtiar, Asep Kurniawan, Gema Satria Mayang Sedyadi, Kartawijaya, Rendy Adriyan Diningrat and Ulfah Alifia. *Studi Implementasi Undang-Undang No. 6 tahun 2014 tentang Desa: Laporan Baseline* [A Study of the Implementation of the Law No. 6/2014 on Village: A Baseline Report]. Laporan Penelitian SMERU. Jakarta: The SMERU Research Institute, 2018.

Timmer, C. Peter. "The Road to Pro-poor Growth: The Indonesian Experience in Regional Perspective". *Bulletin of Indonesian Economic Studies* 40, no. 2 (2004): 177–207.

World Bank. *Indonesia Social Assistance Public Expenditure Review Update: Towards a Comprehensive, Integrated, and Effective Social Assistance System in Indonesia.* Washington, D.C.: World Bank, 2017.

———. *LAC Equity Lab: Economic Growth — Growth Incidence Curve (GIC).* <http://www.worldbank.org/en/topic/poverty/lac-equity-lab1/economic-growth/growth-incidence-curve> (accessed 10 June 2018).

13

DISTRIBUTIONAL POLITICS AND SOCIAL PROTECTION IN INDONESIA
Dilemma of Layering, Nesting and Social Fit in Jokowi's Poverty Policy

John McCarthy and Mulyadi Sumarto

13.1 INTRODUCTION

Since 1990, rates of extreme poverty have fallen by more than half. With rapid income growth, a global middle class has arisen in emergent middle-income countries such as Indonesia. However, the majority of the global poor also reside in these middle-income countries (Sumner 2012), as sustained growth has not worked evenly to alleviate persistent poverty. In this context, social protection policies (SPPs) have emerged as the key response. Social protection encompasses all interventions from public, private, voluntary organizations and informal networks,

This article was first published in *Journal of Southeast Asian Economies* 35, no. 2 (August 2018).

to support communities, households and individuals in their efforts to prevent, manage and overcome a defined set of risks and vulnerabilities (Barrientos and Hulme 2008). In many respects, the turn to social protection represents a laudable move in social policy. With the state embracing the need to provide for its most vulnerable as a moral duty, we can see social protection as an effort to expand progressive social contracts to marginal groups (Hickey 2012).

In the case of Indonesia, rising inequality emerged as a critical political concern after the Gini coefficient increased from 0.33 in 2002 to 0.41 in 2016. After reducing the multibillion U.S. dollar fuel subsidy as soon as he stepped into office, President Joko "Jokowi" Widodo has overseen a rapid expansion of SPPs — publically distributing an Indonesia Health Card (KIS) that provides free healthcare services and the Prosperous Family Saving Card (KKS) in public events. Likewise, the health programme (*Program Jaminan Kesehatan Nasional* or JKN) is being expanded to cover 36 million families, the rice for welfare — *Beras untuk Keluarga Sejahtera* (Rastra) — programme will include 15.7 million families, while the Family Hope Programme (*Program Keluarga Harapan,* PKH) will provide cash transfer benefits to 10 million families. As depicted in Figure 13.1, the national expenditure for social protection programmes has increased more than ten times between 2005 and 2017. However, this does not represent aggregate growth in terms of GDP, as contributions have fallen from 0.9 per cent of GDP to 0.7 per cent of GDP over the same period (World Bank 2017). This is still far below the World Bank target for social spending and as a percentage of GDP is among the lowest worldwide (Samboh 2017).

The turn to social protection programmes poses a range of policy challenges with respect to rates of coverage, financing, targeting, impacts, and governance. While these questions are extensively researched by developmental economists, social protection involves significant distributional challenges of a political and social nature that also merit analysis. Moving beyond the productivist paradigm of the past, the SPPs repose the poverty problem in terms of how to redistribute public resources and access to opportunities in a way that best addresses the vulnerability of the most marginal. In other words, the policies encompass a politics of distribution around how resources should be allocated, who is entitled to receive them, and why (Ferguson 2015)?

Looking at the case of Indonesia, this chapter is concerned with two questions: first, how did distributional politics shaping policy thinking

FIGURE 13.1

Government Expenditure in Social Protection Programme*, 2005–17 (in Rp billion)

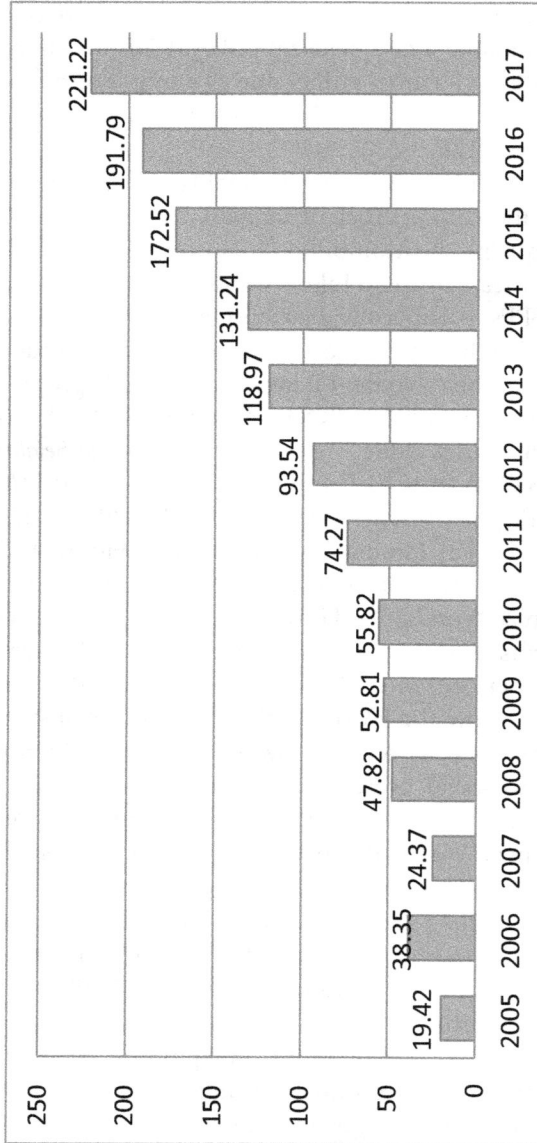

Note: *This covers social protection and other social programmes under the poverty reduction programme managed by TNP2K.
Source: Unpublished data from the Ministry of Finance.

lead to framing key social protection interventions in particular ways, and second, how do distributional practices work out on the ground and with what effect? We focus on two main programmes most relevant to the poor: the rice for the poor — *Beras untuk Keluarga Miskin* (Raskin, now renamed Rastra) scheme and the PKH programme. While PKH and Raskin are both targeted in nature, each involves different politics and practices of distribution which we explore below.

The SPPs here involve multi-level governance and exemplify two quite different approaches. On one hand, social protection can involve introducing new institutional arrangements on top of, or alongside existing ones. Such "layering" is seen when the state SPP overlays the local community institutions and local social protection practices which provide (to varying degrees) informal social protection (such that exist) according to locally embedded notions of entitlement and practices of distribution (Sumarto 2017). It seeks to minimize the role of locally elected and village actors who may be distrusted, perceived as less competent in administrative terms, or seen as likely to distribute public resources through patronage networks. This layering approach requires the formal, rational-bureaucratic institutions to develop sufficient state capacity to deliver benefits effectively (Hickey 2012). This approach, however, may reflect priorities of decision-makers and experts and be less responsive to local values and needs and, if it is not seen to work well, pose particular problems of legitimacy and effectiveness. The challenge is that a gap might emerge between the state notions of who should be entitled to help (the deserving poor) and the village-based principles of entitlement.

On the other hand, policymakers can attempt to "nest" lower level processes in wider state arrangements in ways that allow these local levels to devise their own measures without being challenged by higher levels (Marshall 2008). According to Ostrom (1995; 2005), where lower levels make collective choices for themselves, decisions are more socially legitimate and less contested. By making use of local knowledge, this may increase the likelihood that informal institutional arrangements can be harnessed to exclude untrustworthy individuals, and provide for rules that are better adapted to the local situation. Further, nesting can also lower enforcement or implementation costs, strengthen local perceptions of the legitimacy of rules, and make it easier to fashion rules that can be monitored affordably (Ostrom 1999). Of course, there is a downside from a policy perspective. For instance, community-based targeting of social protection beneficiaries runs the risk of elite capture of programme benefits (Devereux et al. 2017). The hope for local legitimacy of nested arrangements could be at the expense of effective targeting, unless a "robust" system is developed where higher level institutions provide effective enforcement and control to ensure that distribution accords to certain principles.

This chapter considers Indonesia's SPP dilemmas in terms of the tension between the layered and the nested approach. In the case of the Rastra programme, given the shortcomings of the targeted, layered approach, the state allowed village-level decisions to be more or less nested within the larger, more inclusive organizational unit of the state. However, it is now turning back to a more layered approach. In a similar manner, after placing great faith in the layered approach, the PKH programme has begun to make some tentative moves towards integrating some nested principles within, what remains, a layered approach. Unless Indonesia switches to a more universal system of social protection where all households in particular categories receive benefits, the central problem of finding a more polycentric approach to social protection — one that better resolves the tensions between layering and nesting — will need to be resolved soon for the country to develop a distributional system that fits its social and political-economic situation and cultural practices.

13.2 THE POLITICS OF DISTRIBUTION: MANAGING SPPS AFTER 1998

The trajectory of SPP development in Indonesia needs to be understood in the context of earlier policy developments. The literature on the dynamics of policy development (e.g., Mahoney and Thelen 2015; Pierson 2000; Steinmo 2010) discusses this in terms of "path dependence" — the causal relevance of preceding stages in a temporal sequence (Pierson 2000). This suggests that we need to understand how the choices that policymakers face are limited by the decisions made in the past. Thus, to fully understand contemporary developments, we need to briefly review the programme, especially the management of institutions prior to the recent phase of SPPs.

SPPs have developed in a progressive and dynamic fashion over the past few decades. International institutions (like the World Bank) have played a key role in introducing a selective programme for poor households, for the most part, with informal livelihoods. The development of social protection for poor households in Indonesia began with the implementation of the social safety net (SSN) programme. During the 1997 economic crisis, Indonesia witnessed increasing inflation and a precipitous contraction of the economy, spiralling unemployment and poverty, forcing the government to agree to a structural adjustment programme (SAP). As a condition for borrowing from the World Bank and the International Monetary Fund (IMF), Indonesia agreed to implement the SSN programme (Sumarto 2017). Before this, during the Soeharto period, the state only provided social protection to formal workers. While the country owes a lot to the World Bank for introducing SPPs for poor households, this does not mean that the programme is beyond criticism. Similar SAP programmes across several countries in Asia, Africa, and Latin America failed to mitigate the economic risks faced by the poor (Saprin 2004). Indeed, the programme now faces significant problems of design, targeting, administrative capacity, and implementation that pose serious challenges. Given the relatively limited number of people who receive modest benefits, critics argue that the programme has yet to make a significant contribution to poverty alleviation (Kontan 2017).

It is important to stress that the basic concept for the distribution of social protection to poor households derived from the World Bank and IMF structural adjustment programmes in Latin America. In Latin America, conditional cash transfers using social registries have emerged as the prevalent type of social protection and have since been advocated as the "best practice" model for poverty alleviation in the global south (Gubrium, Pellissery and Lodemel 2014). Advocates of the model suggest that it: provides an income transfer in times of need; represents a social investment in human capital amongst those caught in intergenerational cycles of poverty; and is politically palatable because it targets benefits for the "deserving" poor (Dornan and Porter 2013).

Thus, the essential elements of the Indonesian programme reflect the model brought by the World Bank from Latin America. As it is not the fruit of Indonesian government planning, for the people of Indonesia, this programme is "something that fell from the sky". Yet, given the very tough socioeconomic situation, politically the SSN scheme was accepted without any significant objections. At that point, there were no alternative policies for resolving the serious economic difficulties of the moment. With the exception of Malaysia, East Asian countries facing similar problems also borrowed foreign aid and accepted conditionalities. However, from the very beginning, the programme posed serious challenges, especially because the Indonesian government was not well prepared to run it.

State administrative arrangements went through several iterations. First, in 1998 when the World Bank introduced the SSN programme, Bappenas led its implementation (Bappenas 1999). Given its experience of handling social protection issues in the past, Bappenas was considered the best prepared (at least conceptually) to run the programme.

Second, after Indonesia paid the loans to respond to the economic crisis, in 2005, the Yudhoyono administration abolished the SSN programme and transformed it into a poverty alleviation scheme. The goal remained similar — offering social protection to poor households. Under the umbrella of poverty eradication, Yudhoyono developed a number of initiatives, expanding from five in 1998 to more than fifty in 2008, with many programmes spread across all ministries (Sumarto 2017). In these circumstances, Bappenas no longer coordinated the implementation of poverty reduction. While there is no clear explanation for why Yudhoyono's government replaced Bappenas, politically the change was predictable; the president wanted to give his ministers discretionary power over the funding and management of social protection programmes. This social protection budget may also have served as a source of largesse for the political parties to which a particular minister was affiliated.

Third, in 2009, after winning his second election, Yudhoyono realized that managing a very large number of programmes spread across several ministries presented many difficulties. For that reason, in 2010, he established a national team for the acceleration of poverty reduction — *Tim Nasional Percepatan Penanggulangan Kemiskinan* (TNP2K) — as an ad hoc institution to harmonize, coordinate and monitor all poverty reduction schemes under the chairmanship of the vice president (Sumarto 2013). Basically, TNP2K took over the previous role of Bappenas even while implementation of the poverty reduction programme remained under the ministries. While the majority of SSN programme funding came in the form of loans from the World Bank, a large portion of funding for TNP2K came from aid funds provided by the Australian government (Wilmsen, Kaasch and Sumarto 2017).

Fourth, President Jokowi has made increasing the welfare of citizens and addressing social inequality key priorities of his presidency. In this regard, his administration has made several changes. Previously, the Poverty Management Act (*Undang-Undang Penanganan Fakir Miskin* 2011) had provided the Ministry of Social Affairs the authority to manage the data for social protection programmes, but now the Ministry itself took over this role from TNP2K. The President has also issued a regulation on the Office of the Presidential Staff (KSP), placing it in charge of controlling, managing and monitoring his priority programmes, including the social protection schemes. Moreover, Jokowi, like his predecessor, established an ad hoc institution (like TNP2K) to monitor and control the social protection programme that operates directly under him.

Considering this trajectory of change, we can see that the institutional arrangements for managing social protection programmes in Indonesia have been in a state of flux (Table 13.1). At the same time, development planners in key state institutions have steered the programme with rather minimal involvement from civil society actors or political parties. Meanwhile, as we will consider in the next section, the predominant World Bank model for social protection has also become institutionalized. All this suggests that Indonesia is still grappling with questions of "social" and "institutional fit" — how can social protection institutions and practices be brought in line with social expectations and local practices?

13.3 DISTRIBUTIONAL APPROACHES AND THE PROBLEM OF MISS-TARGETED DISTRIBUTION

Social protection invariably involves developing a targeting mechanism. Two systems are generally applicable, namely proxy-means testing (PMT)

TABLE 13.1
Institutional Arrangement of Indonesian Social Protection Programmes, 1998 to Present

Period	Program	Managing Agency	Executing Agency
1. 1998– 2005	SSN programme	Bappenas	Bappenas
2. 2005–10	Poverty alleviation programme	N/a	Ministries
3. 2010–15	Poverty alleviation programme	TNP2K	Ministries
4. 2015 – present	Poverty alleviation programme	• Ministry of Social Affairs • KSP	Ministries

Source: Authors, compiled from various sources.

and community-based targeting (CBT). The former is a distribution approach that relies on statistical calculation, using survey data to predict household welfare (Stoeffler, Mills and Ninno 2016). It scores households against their possession of a set of proxies that are correlated with consumption, and uses this to rank households and then allocate resources to beneficiaries selected according to certain criteria (Kidd, Gelders and Bailey-Athias 2017). In contrast, CBT involves the state getting community groups or intermediary agents to carry out one or more of the following activities: (1) identify recipients for cash or in-kind benefits; (2) monitor the delivery of those benefits; and/or (3) engage in some part of the delivery process (Conning and Kevane 2001). While variations of these two approaches have been used widely in developing countries, considerable debate continues over the relative merits of the rival approaches. Due to limited research comparing the two approaches, the literature is yet to establish that PMT is more effective than CBT or vice versa (Stoeffler, Mills and Ninno 2016).

From the time of SSN, on the advice of the World Bank, state agencies applied a PMT approach. In line with the World Bank's economic focus, this targeting system stresses efficiency rather than equity.[1] Moreover, the development planners in the Indonesian government also prioritize efficiency because, given the condition of state finances, the budget for social protection remains limited. With very high inflation in 1997, Indonesia could not follow a universal approach to social protection at that point. Although economic conditions and state budget for social protection have improved since then (e.g., SPP budget of approximately 1.6 per cent of GDP),[2] Indonesia still cannot afford to pursue the universal welfare programmes found, say, in western Europe which spends up to 27 to 30 per cent of GDP on social protection.

For the targeted distributional model to work, the accuracy of data regarding poor households is seen as critical. Unfortunately, to begin with, the government only had limited household-level data for supporting a PMT approach. Even though the Central Bureau of Statistics (BPS) collected poverty data, this was aggregate data at the national level. The National Family Planning Coordinating Board was the only agency that had data regarding poor households, but that too was aimed at supporting the implementation of family planning schemes rather than social protection ones. Moreover, family planning facilitators at the subdistrict level collected this data without necessarily having the skills required to ensure accuracy. Nonetheless, in the absence of other data, the Indonesian government turned to the National Family Planning Coordination Board (*Badan Kependudukan dan Keluarga Berencana Nasional*, BKKBN) poverty data, causing significant targeting errors in the early iterations of the programme (Sumarto 2013).

After the policy moved from the SSN programme to poverty alleviation schemes, between 2005 and 2015, the Indonesian government conducted three rounds of PMT-oriented surveys, in 2005, 2008 and 2011 (Table 13.2). Government planners knew that, given that the unconditional cash transfer programme (*Bantuan Langsung Tunai*, BLT) would distribute cash in significant amounts to poor households, miss-targeting BLT funds could generate conflict (Sumarto 2013). In 2008 and 2011, the government undertook the second and third surveys, PPLS-2008 and PPLS-2011. The 2011 process used the 2010 census data that included all households and was, therefore, considered more complete. The PPLS-2011 selected 40 per cent of households, the lowest economic strata, to create a registry of 15.5 million households, and became the point of reference for distributing social protection benefits.

In attempting to rank the poorest 40 per cent of the population for distributing benefits, large exclusion- and inclusion-errors emerged. In 2015, when the Ministry of Social Affairs took over, it introduced elements of a community-based targeting (*Pemutakhiran Basis Data Terpadu* or PBDT), introducing a nesting in what remains a highly layered approach. Village leaders joined a "Public Consultation Meeting" (FKP) to vet the initial list of "vulnerable households" and then households would be surveyed using the socioeconomic survey tool. Those overseeing the process would also check with poor informants to see if anyone else should be included

TABLE 13.2
PMT-oriented Surveys

Name of survey	Survey name	Surveyor	Lead agency
PSE-2005	PSE	BPS	Bappenas
PPLS 2008	PPLS	BPS	N/A
PPLS-2011	2010 census survey for developing the UDB	BPS	TNP2K

Source: Authors, compiled from various sources.

in the list. Following this procedure, the state statistics agency surveyed those on the edited beneficiary register, and the response data would then be analysed statistically to update the Unified Database (UDB) and create an improved beneficiary list, with the PMT ultimately deciding who obtains the benefits.

Interviews with village leaders, village- and district-level statistics officials in Aceh revealed what people referred to as "field risks", "emotional factors" and "political nuances" that shape the survey process. Village leaders are reluctant to delete supporters or people close to them, wishing to include as many people as possible to avoid conflict. They also worry that cutting back the list too far would decrease the amount of benefits the village would receive from other programmes (McCarthy, Hadi and Maliati 2017). Poverty is, to a certain degree, relative — there are no clear cut-off points or criteria regarding who should be included in the list generated by village-level consultations. At the same time, field officers undertaking the survey faced the hazards that bedevil survey work. For instance, scorecards may be filled inaccurately (SMERU 2011), respondents' ignorance or self-interest may shape how they respond, villagers might hide assets to increase the possibility of being categorized as poor, while the poor might inadvertently suggest they owned assets which they only rent or manage under tenancy arrangements, *inter alia*. Overall, surveyor competency, authority and discernment are critical.

The literature also points to a number of difficulties with the PMT methodology (Kidd, Gelders and Bailey-Athias 2017). First, indicators are determined based on the ease with which they can be observed by enumerators, pointing to a real danger of misleading simplification — given the primary focus on using assets as proxies for consumption. While the use of multiple indicators may reduce such distortions, assumptions made in the selection of proxies and underpinning the analysis of household surveys significantly change who is selected (Kidd, Gelders and Bailey-Athias 2017). Devereux et al. (2017) suggest that PMT may also be affected by a poor correlation between proxies and household consumption; surveys may be inaccurate; and there may be sampling errors in survey design and difficulties in verifying proxies. Also, in cases where households accumulate from past work and then fall into poverty, assets are often a poor indicator of present income. Other studies have shown that accumulating households become "inclusion-errors" while declining households are excluded. Indeed, a range of studies have questioned the wisdom of the

PMT approach (e.g., Brown, Ravallion and van de Walle 2016; Kidd and Wylde 2011; Kidd, Gelders and Bailey-Athias 2017).

13.4 DISTRIBUTION PRACTICES

Let us now turn to the distributional practices shaping how SPPs work out on the ground, starting with the Rastra initiative. This programme emerged from a range of SSN schemes that aimed to address food security issues during the financial crisis and El Niño event of 1997–98, and remains Indonesia's principal SSN. The idea was to distribute subsidized rice to severely affected poor families every month.

As the programme developed, we can see three principles of distribution that are in tension with one another. First, in keeping with the tradition of needs-based welfare payments, the state set out to identify and then distribute subsidized rice to the neediest, using the databases described above. However if village leaders in charge of implementing the programme chose to distribute rice according to the beneficiary list based on the state's assessment of need, it would entail distributing subsidized rice to only a small proportion of the village. Very early on in the programme, village leaders found that the targeting formula left out many people who were felt to be deserving of assistance — according to the socially accepted or locally embedded notions of entitlement, including large numbers of those who are near poor. A second option presented itself: if communities considered equality as the criterion, the rice would be distributed equally among all villagers, without taking differences in levels of need into account. Under a third possibility, as villagers needed to pay for the subsidized rice, contribution could be a criterion: subsidized rice would be distributed to individuals who were able to purchase the rice. The problem was that under these alternatives, the poor might receive fewer benefits. Nevertheless, the latter two criteria would later be widely accepted in the local domain.

In practice, individual areas or villages have developed their own practices of rice distribution that respond to these different criteria. Given that the practice of rice distribution would be accepted if social protection was distributed selectively to poor households and those in need, in some villages, the leadership decided to distribute rice only amongst those seen as being relatively needy. However, in some places, village leaders divided the rice to those who demanded it, while in other villages, the rice was distributed amongst all villagers without formal employment (McCarthy, Hadi and Maliati 2017). Although practices differ, they are generally referred to as *bagidil* and *bagito*. *Bagidil* and *bagito* are Javanese acronyms meaning "fair rice distribution" and "equal rice distribution", respectively (Sumarto 2013). These terms (hereafter referred to as *bagito*) reflect the gap between the targeting logic of the SPP programme and the logic of distribution prevalent in villages.

To varying degrees, rural communities maintain reciprocal and redistributive practices that bind together the social fabric of village life. This is often symbolized by the concept of *gotong-royong*, or mutual cooperation, reciprocity, and collective action (Bowen 1986; Sullivan 1986). It also includes informal forms of social support and mutual assistance during times of illness, death, and food insecurity, as well as interdependencies and reciprocities encompassing mutual assistance with housing, income maintenance, and neighbourhood security (Sumarto 2017). It should also be noted that villages are highly differentiated. Given that village-based social protection practices typically depend on the ability to contribute and to reciprocate, and the very poor are often unable to reciprocate fully, the very poor are often not well protected (Nooteboom 2015). However, in view of this ethic, villagers do find it unacceptable if some obtain an entitlement while neighbours of similar socioeconomic standing are left out. Community leaders fear that if social jealousy is not resolved, it can lead to social disharmony. From the early days of the programme, the government accepted the *bagito* practice, both because of concerns about the emergence of social disharmony, and also because the government acknowledged that their assessments on the eligible households were not accurate (Sumarto 2013).

Here we see the gap between village practices and policy-making. Village practices are based on cultural constructs, political expectations and the common view that it is more important to share widely. Even if the distributional system involves considerable inclusion errors, from a local perspective, sharing widely is better than if many poor families are left out. In sharp contrast, through the regulation governing the Rastra programme, the government explicitly declares that the scheme is only for poor households. However, under the *bagidil* practice, community leaders in some cases divide Rastra both to poor households, as well as a section of non-poor households, thus reducing the amount received by poor households. The practice of *bagito*, therefore, cannot be accepted by state policymakers as a legitimate distribution mechanism. Given this background, from an outside perspective, Raskin is seen as the least successful of the social protection interventions.

Researchers have also found faults in the inaccurate targeting, insufficient data and poor coverage leading to substantial exclusion- and inclusion-errors, as well as the frequency of distribution achieved by Raskin (Perdana and Maxwell 2005). It has been found that the programme makes irregular and unpredictable transfers to poor households. Also, poor families face difficulties in paying for the subsidized rice at the point of delivery, and many sell the rice cheaply to speculators who, in turn, sell it for a higher price. There have also been allegations of fraud and lost rice, as well as complaints about the quality and price of the rice received by beneficiaries (Timmer, Hastuti and Sumarto 2018). Consequently, analysts have called for quick reforms to be introduced.

The present administration is reforming the scheme to: improve its targeting; provide better choice; increase access to nutritious food; eliminate the price paid by the rice recipients; and increase the efficiency of the delivery system. Since 2017, the Ministry of Social Affairs has trialled two systems. Under the first initiative, the *Bantuan Pangan Non Tunai* (BPNT) programme, 1.2 million beneficiaries in major cities have received a card (*Kartu Keluarga Sejahtera*) to purchase staples, including rice, eggs and cooking oil, up to Rp110,000 from e-Warong. It is envisaged that the system will eventually be rolled out on a national scale. In the meantime, in rural areas, only beneficiaries identified by the unitary database as "deserving" would receive 10 kilograms of Rastra rice a month, free of charge. As the rice would only be available to those with the card, this would represent a fall in the number of beneficiaries under the programme.

However, this initiative is already proving to be controversial. In early 2018, newspapers carried stories of village heads rejecting the new programme due to concerns of widespread resentment and social jealousy amongst recipients and non-recipients (*Kompas*, 20 January 2018). Although not formally allowed, in some areas, the village officials have been facilitating ways for Rastra recipients to share the rice with other poor households not on the beneficiary list. However, in other villages the new distributional method is being fully implemented by village leaders, fearing the repercussions of not following instructions.[3]

This represents an attempt to revert to a layered approach that prioritizes the need-based criterion of the state's targeting and implementation methods. In re-embracing a layered approach to improve targeting, the state has let go of the benefits of increased legitimacy associated with the more inclusive, nested system. In doing so, Rastra will face the same complexities affecting the conditional cash transfers.

The PKH is a conditional cash transfer scheme. Indonesia has more or less adopted the Brazilian model, widely seen as "best practice". As the PKH aims to assist the bottom 10 per cent, targeting is critical. In two survey villages, an Acehnese community based poverty analysis was undertaken (McCarthy, Hadi and Maliati 2017). This involved using a wealth-ranking exercise that graded a random sample of households against the community's own definitions of poverty — *fakir* and *miskin* — and then categorized those receiving the PKH benefit against the community's ranking. The survey revealed that only 14 per cent of those whom the wealth-ranking exercise identified as poor according to community standards actually obtained PKH. Among the poor who met the PKH criteria, only 27 per cent obtained the PKH benefits. In contrast, the community's own *zakat* system (which used the community's own *fakir/miskin* categories), provided assistance to 70 per cent of those classified as poor. At the same time, 50 per cent of the PKH recipients in the sample were non-poor by the community's own criteria. As many poor villagers watch neighbours gain access to benefits, they harbour bitter feelings of disappointment and blame village leaders. This creates problems for social cohesion, leaving communities polarized between those receiving benefits and those who feel that some of the beneficiaries are undeserving. Consequently, villagers seek a system that is more responsive to local views, demands and moral claims (McCarthy, Hadi and Maliati 2017).

While the results from this survey may not be statistically representative of the wider population, they do point to the problems with the process and also triangulate with other studies. For instance, one study estimates that the PMT usually has targeting errors of more than 50 per cent and tends to be arbitrary in its selection of beneficiaries (Kidd, Gelders and Bailey-Athias 2017). Drawing on research based on several countries, Kidd and Wylde (2011) noted that exclusion and inclusion vary between 57 and 71 per cent when only 10 cent of the population is covered — the current coverage target for PKH. A critical World Bank study similarly argues that the standard PMT method is particularly deficient in reaching the poorest (Brown, Ravallion and van de Walle 2016).

To sum up, while PKH benefits do make a significant contribution to those who receive them, the system is also giving rise to serious problems, with many poor villagers watching neighbours (undeservingly) gain benefits. Villagers expect a social protection system that is more responsive to local views, demands and moral claims. At the same time, critics in the press have expressed dismay that the targeting system still has so many inclusion- and exclusion-errors despite a number of efforts to remedy the problem.[4]

Policymakers are responding with technical innovations to address these challenges. This includes a new system to validate data and update the database more regularly — the Independent Update Mechanism (MPM). Further, a new "verification and validation" system is being introduced to check the lists through community deliberation and the reapplication of the survey and PMT.[5] However, it remains to be seen whether these "patches" can overcome the methodological problems identified in the PMT approach. As the final decision over who is included will still lie with the PMT, community deliberation may have little effect.

13.5 DISCUSSION AND CONCLUSION: LAYERING, NESTING AND POLYCENTRIC APPROACHES

Let us return to the first question that animated this study: how have politics and policy thinking framed Indonesia's key social protection interventions? The World Bank has successfully spread and institutionalized the development knowledge and practices underlying conditional cash transfer programmes in twenty-six countries (Clemens and Kremer 2016). Using these ideas at the time of crisis, Indonesian decision-makers accepted that social protection schemes based on selecting the most deserving beneficiaries will be the most effective (and politically acceptable) way to proceed.

However, this presents two issues. The social protection model remains, in many ways, an imported "exotic species" that borrows from foreign experience, rather than indigenous development. The discourses justifying Indonesia's social protection programme and the instruments applied in implementing it remain highly derivative of the World Bank's experience elsewhere. This approach involves layering, a mode of change that entails introducing a new institution on top of existing ones (Mahoney and

Thelen 2010) and translates to creating technical instruments, programmes and arrangements for social protection and placing them on existing informal ones (Sumarto 2017). Such arrangements prioritize efficiency over equity.

Over the last decade, with responsibilities spread over a range of state agencies, the authority for managing the social protection programme has repeatedly shifted; in many respects, institutional arrangements are yet to crystalize in a stable form. To date, the programme tends be dynamic, running on a rather ad hoc basis using a trial and error approach. After the World Bank introduced the SSN programme years ago, it continues to be a "grafted" one — it has yet to take root in an integrated fashion with a clear institutional home. In other words, Indonesia's social protection system still faces a question of social and institutional fit (Epstein et al. 2015). This raises another question — how to ensure that the country's welfare regime evolves in a fashion that fit with Indonesia's social and political-economic situation and cultural practices?

There are several factors that affect the layered approach as it now attempts to function. As discussed, the social protection framework presents critical problems. Livelihoods are difficult to model, especially given a target population with unclear and diffuse attributes. Moreover, the statistical approach needs to make assumptions and quantify livelihoods using proxies based on a simplifying logic in order to model consumption, income and saving. In fact, there is considerable debate over the astuteness of this PMT approach. While some researchers focus on the methodology problem, others question its implementation (see Brown, Ravallion and van de Walle 2016; Kidd and Wylde 2011; Kidd, Gelders and Bailey-Athias 2017; Devereaux et al. 2017).

The process of evaluating livelihood and working out who is eligible emerges from a complex social and bureaucratic process that involves dealing with relational complexities (McCarthy, Hadi and Maliati 2017). It is difficult to extract social protection from the context and the processes that shape it. These include both the social dynamics shaping focus group identification of the poor, as well as those shaping survey implementation. If we add the social complexity that elides precise simplification and quantification by statistical modelling, it is clear that there is no simple technical fix. Hence, the layered approach needs to come to terms with the social context. Further, the logic of targeting encounters an inclusive local ethic of obligation — the poor exist within a dense network of debt and obligation involving neighbours, family, and patrons whom they call upon at times of need. These are relations of dependence and exploitation from which the very poor may be excluded (Nooteboom 2015). However, for households enmeshed in networks of reciprocity and mutual dependence, if they are to continue to draw on them, they need to reciprocate, and receiving state entitlements while others miss out for no apparent reason raises moral and social questions. Put simply, it involves hoarding benefits and (unreasonably) discriminating against members of the community who otherwise participate in village life and who are seen as entitled. Hence, unless the targeting system is mapped onto social values, like Aceh's *zakat* practice, Indonesian villages take it upon themselves to "modify" the state benefit schemes (benefiting only a section of the population) by redistributing amongst the layers of the population that make a case for inclusion. Indeed, over the past several years, villages have (repeatedly) redistributed misdirected social benefits to maintain social cohesion.

So what are the possible ways forward? In answering this question, we need to keep in mind two caveats. First, as in other political systems, we can see a path dependency at play (Lichbach and Zuckerman 2009). Once Indonesia embraces the PMT model, the cost of reverting to another model is likely to be very high. While there may be times when other choices could be made, investments in the current institutional arrangements mean that the existing approach is now so embedded that it is difficult to envisage an easy reversal of the initial choice to pursue this model. Thus, institutional jockeying between state agencies for control of the programme coincides with internal debates over how the social protection scheme might best be targeted and implemented and indeed to what extent it provides the best remedy for poverty rather than whether the predominant model with its embedded assumptions is the best fit for Indonesia.

Second, during layering, policymakers might expect a gradual change through amendments or additions to the old institution (Mahoney and Thelen 2010) where the new institution grows at the edge of the old one (Streeck and Thelen 2005). In other words, with layering between formal institutional arrangements, we might expect mutual adjustment. However, this type of adjustment is unlikely to occur in cases of informal–formal layering. To some extent, the informal institutions provide social support for community members to overcome socioeconomic risks, and policymakers cannot amend these institutions (Sumarto 2017). We see this in the case of Rastra and PKH, where the state has yet to make effective adjustments to community institutions and practices. To date, even if deliberative processes are included in the typical procedure, the top-down targeting (based on proxies) has the final word and overrides village preferences. Yet, the targeting logic and the collective ethics and practices of villages need to run simultaneously, or accommodate each other.

When agencies try to impose standardized approaches and organizational structures in localities with very different ideas of equitable distribution and decision-making (alongside pre-existing norms and arrangements for managing resources) different outcomes are bound to emerge. This is because local-level constraints shape how designs work on the ground. Policy strategies that look good on paper are often transformed at the point of delivery, creating wide discrepancies between expected and actual outcomes, which is currently being observed.

Critical institutionalists (Cleaver and Koning 2015) emphasize the multi-scalar complexity of institutions, focusing on the problems that arise when local arrangements located within wider frames of governance affect multi-layered management in large and complex systems in unexpected ways. A wider body of research suggests that, if good policy interventions are to take varied institutional and cultural landscapes into account, donors and state agencies need to work with existing institutions in a way that is sensitive to embedded realities. Also, improving the institutional and/or social fit entails building on (rather than avoiding) the complex social processes that exist for allocating benefits. This involves embracing an inclusive ethic of moral obligation, mutuality and dependence. As poverty is, to a certain degree, relative and that it may be difficult to identify the most needy from the outside, village deliberation processes need clear cut-off points or criteria regarding who should be included in the list of beneficiaries — something not provided by the PMT.

Devereaux et al. (2017) suggest that, in the absence of an optimal targeting mechanism, operative programmes should be based on specific objectives, well-targeted, efficiently designed and effectively implemented strategies that fit the context. Therefore, in the case of Indonesia, the current approaches to social protection might continue to be adjusted rather than abandoned altogether. Although several changes are being made, greater efforts are required to "Indonesia-nize" the programmes by adapting them to local conditions, concepts and practices. To sum up, progress clearly depends upon trialling multiple targeting methods, learning from the logic of existing distributional systems in the country, and assimilating knowledge from perspectives beyond the predominant economistic model.

Notes

1. For instance, the World Bank recommends that a borrowing country provide targeted social protection rather than universal ones on the grounds that the former is more efficient (Okun 2010).
2. Unpublished data from the Ministry of Finance.
3. Field observations in Aceh, North Sumatra and Java.
4. See Media Indonesia (2017); VIVA.co.id (2016); rakyatjambi.co (2017); Berita Metro (2016).
5. Peraturan Menteri Sosial 28/2017 tentang pedoman verifikasi dan validasi data terpadu pengangan fakir miskin dan orang tidak mampu. [Regulation of the Minister of Social Affairs 28/2017 on guidelines for verification and validation of integrated data for managing poor and disadvantaged people.]

References

Bappenas. "Penjelaan Menteri Negara Perencaaan Pembangunan Nasional/ Kepala Bappenas pada rapat intern Komisi VIII Dewan Perwakilan Rakyat Republic Indonesia tentang Program Jaring Pengaman Sosial (JPS)". Bappenas, Jakarta,1999.

Barrientos, A. and D. Hulme, eds. *Social Protection for the Poor and Poorest: Concepts, Policies and Politics*. New York: Palgrave Macmillan, 2008.

Berita Metro. "Bidikan Program Pengentas Kemiskinan Belum Tepat Sasaran". 15 December 2016.

Bowen, J.R. "On the Political Construction of Tradition: Gotong Royong in Indonesia". *Journal of Asian Studies* 45, no. 3 (1986): 545–61.

Brown, C., M. Ravallion and D. van de Walle. "A Poor Means Test? Econometric Targeting in Africa". World Bank Policy Research Working Paper 7915. Washington, D.C., December 2016.

Cleaver, F.D. and J. de Koning. "Furthering Critical Institutionalism". *International Journal of the Commons* 9, no. 1 (2015): 1–18.

Clemens, M. and M. Kremer. "The New Role for the World Bank". *Journal of Economic Perspectives* 30, no. 1 (2016): 53–76.

Conning, J. and M. Kevane. "Community-based Targeting Mechanisms for Social Safety Nets: A Critical Review". *World Development* 30, no. 3 (2001): 375–94.

Devereux, S., E. Masset, R. Sabates-Wheeler, M. Samson, A.M. Rivas and D. te

Lintelo. "The Targeting Effectiveness of Social Transfer". *Journal of Development Effectiveness* 9, no. 2 (2017): 162–211.

Dornan, P. and C. Porter. "The Implications of Conditionality in Social Assistance Programmes". In *Social Policy in a Developing World,* edited by R. Surender and R. Walker, pp. 155–71. Northampton: Edward Elgar Publishing, 2013.

Epstein, G., J. Pittman, S.M. Alexander and S. Berdej. "Institutional Fit and the Sustainability of Social-Ecological Systems". *Current Opinion in Environmental Sustainability* 14 (2015): 34–40.

Ferguson, J. *Give a Man a Fish: Reflections on the New Politics of Distribution.* Durham: Duke University Press, 2015.

Freeland, Nicholas, "Poxy Means Testing: It's Official!". Development Pathways <http://www.developmentpathways.co.uk/resources/poxy-means-testing-official/>.

Gubrium, E.K., S. Pellissery and I. Lodemel. *The Shame of It. Global perspectives on anti-poverty policies.* Bristol: Policy Press, 2014.

Hastuti, S. Mawardi, B. Sulaksono, A.S. Devina, R.P. Artha and Ratna Dewi. *The Effectiveness of the Raskin Program.* Jakarta: SMERU Research Institute, 2008.

Hickey, S. "Turning Governance Thinking Upside-down? Insights from 'the politics of what works'". *Third World Quarterly* 33, no. 7 (2012): 1231–47.

Kidd, S. and E. Wylde. "Targeting the Poorest: An Assessment of the Proxy Means Test Methodology". AusAID, Canberra, 2011.

———, B. Gelders and D. Bailey-Athias. "Exclusion by Design: An Assessment of the Effectiveness of the Proxy Means Test Poverty Targeting Mechanism". International Labour Office, Social Protection Department (SOCPRO), Geneva, 2017.

Kompas. "Karawang Distribusikan 12.000 Ton Rastra Pertama di Jabar". 20 January 2018.

Kontan.co.id. "Analis: Program Keluarga Harapan tidak efektif". 22 August 2017.

Lichbach, M.I. and A.S. Zuckerman. *Comparative Politics: Rationality, Culture, and Structure.* Cambridge: Cambridge University Press, 2009.

Mahoney, J. and K. Thelen. "A Theory of Gradual Institutional Change". In *Explaining Institutional Change. Ambiguity, Agency, and Power,* edited by J. Mahoney and K. Thelen, pp. 1–37. Cambridge: Cambridge University Press, 2010.

——— and K. Thelen. "Comparative-Historical Analysis in Contemporary Political Science". In *Advances in Comparative-Historical Analysis,* edited by J. Mahoney and K. Thelen, pp. 3–36. Cambridge: Cambridge University Press, 2015.

Marshall, G.R. "Nesting, Subsidiarity, and Community-based Environmental Governance beyond the Local Level". *International Journal of the Commons* 2, no. 1 (2008): 75–97.

McCarthy, J., S. Hadi and N. Maliati. "Agrarian Change and Social Protection: Towards a Relational Analysis of the Government of Poverty in Indonesia's Rural Periphery". Paper presented at the Euroseas conference, Oxford, September 2017.

Media Indonesia. "Tepat Sasaran Atasi Kemiskinan". 11 August 2017.

Merrey, D.J. and S. Cook. "Fostering Institutional Creativity at Multiple Levels: Towards Facilitated Institutional Bricolage". *Water Alternatives* 5, no. 1 (2012): 1–19.

Nooteboom, G. *Forgotten People: Poverty, Risk and Social Security in Indonesia. The Case of the Madurese.* Leiden: Brill, 2015.

Okun, A.M. *Equality and Efficiency: The Big Trade Off.* Brookings Institution Press, 2010.

Ostrom, E. *Governing the commons: The Evolution of Institutions for Collective Action.* New York, NY: Cambridge University Press, 1990.

———. *Understanding Institutional Diversity.* Princeton, NJ: Princeton University Press, 2005.

Perdana, A. and J. Maxwell. "Poverty Targeting in Indonesia". In *Poverty Targeting in Asia*, edited by John Weiss, pp. 79–135. Cheltenham: Asian Development Bank Institute and Edward Elgar, 2005.

Pierson, P. "Increasing Return, Path Dependence, and the Study of Politics". *American Political Science Review* 4, no. 2 (2000): 251–67.

Rakyatjambi. "Pelaksanaan Program PKH di Tanjabtim Tidak Tepat Sasaran". 2017 <https://rakyatjambi.co/pelaksanaan-program-pkh-di-tanjabtim-tidak-tepat-sasaran/>.

Samboh, E. "High Noon for Jokowi's Social Welfare Ambitions". *Jakarta Post*, 12 January 2017.

SAPRIN. *Structural Adjustment: The Sapri Report.* London: Zed Books, 2004.

Steinmo, S. *The Evolution of Modern States: Sweden, Japan, and the United States.* Cambridge: Cambridge University Press, 2010.

Stoeffler, Q., B. Mills and C.D. Ninno. "Reaching the Poor: Cash Transfer Program Targeting in Cameroon". *World Development* 83 (2016): 244–63.

Streeck, W. and K. Thelen. "Introduction: Institutional Change in Advanced Political Economies". In *Beyond Continuity: Institutional Change in Advanced Political Economies*, edited by W. Streeck and K. Thelen, pp. 1–39. Oxford: Oxford University Press, 2005.

SMERU. "Rapid Appraisal of the 2011 Data Collection of Social Protection Programs (PPLS 2011)". Research Report , SMERU Institute, Jakarta, 2011.

Sullivan, J. "Kampung and State: The Role of Government in the Development of Urban Community in Yogyakarta". *Indonesia*, no. 41 (1986): 63–88.

Sumarto, M. (M. Mulyadi). "Welfare Regime, Social Conflict, and Clientelism in

Indonesia". Unpublished PhD thesis, Australian National University, Canberra, 2013.

————. "Welfare Regime Change in Developing Countries: Evidence from Indonesia". *Social Policy and Administration* 51, no. 6 (2017): 940–59.

Sumarto, S., A. Suryahadi and S. Bazzi. "Indonesia's Social Protection During and After the Crisis". In *Social Protection for the Poor and Poorest: Concepts, Policies and Politics*, edited by A. Barrientos and D. Hulme, pp. 121–45. New York: Palgrave Macmillan, 2008.

Sumner, A. "Where Do the World's Poor Live? A New Update", IDS Working Paper 393 (2012).

Timmer, P.C., H. Hastuti, S. Sumarto. "Evolution and Implementation of the Rastra Program in Indonesia", MPRA Munich Personal RePEc Archive Paper No. 81018, 2016.

VIVA.co.id. "Perlu Evaluasi Efektifitas Program Pengentasan Kemiskinan". 2017 <https://www.viva.co.id/berita/politik/804012-perlu-evaluasi-efektifitas-program-pengentasan-kemiskinan>.

Wilmsen, B., A. Kaasch and M. Sumarto. "The Development of Indonesian Social Policy in the Context of Overseas Development Aid". UNRISD Working Paper No. 5 (2017).

World Bank. *Towards a Comprehensive, Integrated, and Effective Social Assistance System in Indonesia*. Indonesia Social Assistance Public Expenditure Review Update. Washington, D.C.: World Bank, 2017.

14

HAS INDONESIAN FOOD POLICY FAILED?

Maria Monica Wihardja

14.1 INTRODUCTION

Food policy goes far beyond simple agricultural production, encompassing issues such as food and nutrition security, poverty alleviation, women's participation, structural transformation and value addition. Food policy also has a macroeconomic dimension, as it has implications for inflation, fiscal policy, and affects the trade balance. Failure to manage food policy has the potential to disrupt politico-socio-economic stability.

This chapter discusses whether Indonesian food policy has failed, mainly focusing on rice policy, but also looking at cocoa, sugar and salt policies as an illustration. The same shortcomings and challenges apply to many other food commodities and hence some of the policy recommendations can be generalized, with minor adjustments depending on the food commodity.

While significant long-standing food policy challenges remain, such as striking a balance between consumer and producer welfare, in recent years many changes have been introduced. They are (i) the omnipresent use of enforcement officials (both military and civilian) to "discipline" the market (including "food mafias" or hoarders); (ii) the extensification of agricultural production by opening new rice fields outside Java and increasing the crop plantation index to increase production; (iii) putting a binding cap on retail prices of some food commodities to counter high prices; and (iv) the crowding-out of private investment by state-owned enterprises and the lack of market competition. While there have been significant improvements in some aspects of food policy, such as the development and rehabilitation of irrigation systems and dams (*Kompas* 2018*b*) and the use of Area Sampling Frames methodology to more accurately produce rice production statistics according to international best practices, these seem to be overshadowed by the continuing shortcomings.

This chapter discusses four main topics: (i) food policy goals; (ii) the performance of these goals; (iii) why they may have failed or succeeded; and (iv) policy recommendations.

14.2 FOOD POLICY GOALS

At the highest strategic level, the *Nawacita* — the vision and mission of President Joko Widodo and Vice-President Jusuf Kalla for their 2014–19 term — mandates that "food sovereignty" should be the ultimate goal of food policy in Indonesia. A passage in the *Nawacita* explains how to achieve food sovereignty. First is increasing on-farm production by improving irrigation systems, opening new rice fields and restoring soil fertility. Second is providing financial and capital access to farmers and micro, small and medium enterprises (MSMEs). Third is increasing the value-added of farmers' products through post-harvest technology and capturing longer value chains.

The pursuit of food sovereignty is a continuation of the policies of the previous administration. Unlike the *Nawacita*, Law No. 18/2012 (the "Food Law") goes beyond the food sovereignty target. Article 2 of the Food Law states that food policy should be based on eight principles: sovereignty (*kedaulatan*), independence (*kemandirian*), security (*ketahanan*), safety (*keamanan*), benefits (*manfaat*), equality (*pemerataan*), sustainability (*keberlanjutan*) and justice (*keadilan*). Food independence is more commonly referred to as "food self-sufficiency".

In addition to the *Nawacita* and the 2012 Food Law, high-level food policy is also contained in other documents, including the Government

Work Programme 2017 issued by the National Development Planning Agency (Bappenas). In this programme, food sovereignty has four priority programmes: (i) to increase the production of paddy and other food commodities; (ii) to increase the quality of food consumption patterns and community nutrition; (iii) to increase the efficiency of food distribution and food access systems; and (iv) to improve the management of disturbances to food production.[1]

Following the *Nawacita*, the budget for food sovereignty has been increased from 3.8 per cent of the national budget in 2014 (Rp67.3 trillion) to 5.0 per cent in 2017 (Rp103.1 trillion) (Ministry of Finance 2017). Most government spending on food sovereignty is allocated for input subsidies and irrigation systems (Rusono 2016). The increase in the food sovereignty budget reflects the government's staunch commitment to improving food availability and accessibility. However, the ways in which the *Nawacita*, the Food Law and the Government Work Programme are interpreted and operationalized through ministerial programmes and operations is a matter of considerable importance.

Agricultural value chains from farm to table tend to be very long. There are many stakeholders in food value chains, including farmers, traders, retailers, logistic firms, banks and other financial institutions. It also involves state-owned enterprises and many social organizations such as cooperatives and farmers' associations. Furthermore, the long farm-to-table value chain requires coordination across several ministries and many other government agencies as well as levels of government.

A major source of potential policy failure appears to lie in the narrow way in which the Ministry of Agriculture interprets and translates the *Nawacita* into policy, the misalignment of higher order goals into the ministerial budget allocation, and the incoherence of the agricultural, trade and industrial policies, as discussed in more detail below.

14.3 POOR PERFORMANCE TOWARDS ACHIEVING FOOD POLICY GOALS

Given the ambitious objectives and targets set by the *Nawacita*, the Food Law 2012, and the Government Work Programme 2017, it is important to ascertain the extent to which these objectives and targets have been achieved. This analysis is undertaken by using two indicators to measure policy progress in meeting their ultimate goals: improving producer welfare and consumer welfare. The next subsection argues that overall the ultimate food policy goals are not met, indicated by declining farmers' terms-of-trade and real agricultural wages as well as the omnipresent pest or plant pest attacks (producer welfare); and continued high inflation in many of food commodities (consumer welfare).

14.3.1 Producer Welfare

Based on labour productivity, farmers' terms-of-trade (a welfare measurement for agricultural household enterprises), real agricultural wages (a welfare measurement for agricultural paid workers), and farm profitability, there is little evidence of much improvement of producer welfare over the past three years. In fact, some indications point to a worsening of producer welfare.

In 2013, there were 26.14 million farm households in Indonesia, a decline from 31.23 million farm households in 2003. Among these farm households, the largest number of households was in paddy cultivation subsector, totalling 14.2 million households (Table 14.1).

TABLE 14.1
Number of Farm Households in Indonesia, 2003–13

	2003	2013
Food crops	18,708,052	17,728,185
Paddy	14,206,355	14,147,942
Secondary crops	10,941,919	8,624,243
Horticulture	16,937,617	10,602,147
Plantations	14,128,539	12,770,090
Livestock	18,595,824	12,969,210
Fisheries	2,489,681	1,975,233
Fish cultivation	985,418	1,187,563
Fish catching	1,569,048	864,495
Forestry	6,827,937	6,782,856
Agricultural services	1,846,140	1,075,935

Notes: One household may be working on multiple crops, thus the number of farm households is not the sum of the numbers of households for each of the sector.
Source: Agriculture Census 2013, BPS.

According to Indonesia's National Social Economic Survey (Susenas), about half the population in the bottom 40 per cent and two-thirds of the population in the bottom 5 per cent of the income distribution worked in the agriculture, forestry and fisheries sector in 2017, generally at low levels of productivity and with minimal capital. Although value-added per worker in the agriculture sector had increased between 2015 and 2017 mostly due to workers transitioning out of the sector, value-added per worker is much lower in the agriculture sector relative to other sectors (one-quarter of that of the manufacturing sector and one-half of that of the services sector). The slow pace of employment transition to higher productivity sectors becomes a "productivity drag" on the entire economy. Agricultural development remains a significant contributor to poverty reduction in rural areas (Suryahadi and Hadiwidjaja 2011), where most farmers live and where the poverty rate is almost double that of urban areas: 13.37 per cent vs. 7.26 per cent in September 2017 (Susenas).

Around one-quarter of workers in the agriculture sector work as unpaid family workers, although there has been a slight shift in the share of unpaid family workers out of total employment in the agriculture sector from 29 per cent in 2015 to 26 per cent in 2017. In absolute terms, the number declined from 10.9 million to 9.5 million unpaid family workers (Sakernas). Meanwhile, the shares of own-account and casual workers have increased, although these kinds of jobs are still considered as informal jobs (BPS 2017). Because of excess supply of labour in the agriculture sector, as seen in the share of unpaid family workers, farm profitability may not necessarily increase when these unpaid family workers move out of the sector.

The high labour intensity per hectare (ha) of farm area results in a very high labour cost per ha (although many of the workers are unpaid, as discussed above), which increases the total production cost per ha. Relative to other neighbouring Asian countries, Indonesian farmers have relatively high production costs (IRRI 2016; FAO 2016). The cost of production per kg of paddy is high in Indonesia compared with China, India, the Philippines, Thailand and Vietnam, due to very high labour and rental costs per ha. The Cost Structure of Paddy Cultivation Household Survey 2017 conducted nationwide by Indonesia's Central Bureau of Statistics (Badan Pusat Statistik, or BPS) shows that wetland paddy farmers pay about 26 per cent out of the total cost of production for rent and about 50 per cent for labour. These high production costs are passed on to consumers in the form of higher output prices. The widening divergence between domestic and international rice price over the past decade has only been made possible because of high import protection that obscures high and increasing domestic production costs.

Indonesia's high labour costs in the total production cost per ha reflect a low degree of mechanization. Indonesia's small average farm size is often cited as a constraint to mechanization, but countries with a smaller average farm size, such as China, still have highly mechanized farming. In China, all farmers surveyed use a combine-harvester, while none of the farmers surveyed in Indonesia use them (IRRI 2016). The majority of farmers surveyed in China also use a four-wheel tractor, while in Indonesia the majority of farmers still use a two-wheel tractor. Thanks to higher mechanization and other factors, countries such as Vietnam and China only spend about 7 per cent and 3 per cent, respectively, out of total production costs on labour costs. In terms of land productivity, during the high (low) yielding season, the mean paddy yield in Indonesia is 6.11 ton per ha (5.42 ton per ha), compared to 7.46 ton (6.10 ton) in China and 8.56 ton (6.33 ton) in Vietnam, although these differences cannot be isolated to the different degrees of mechanization alone (IRRI 2016).

Farmers' terms-of-trade (FTT) — the ratio of price received to price paid index, for food crop farmers — and real wage for agricultural paid workers (*buruh tani*) indicate worsening farmer welfare. Compared with January 2015 (at the start of the Widodo administration), FTT in food crops and the real wages for agricultural workers were lower in March/April 2018 (Figures 14.1 and 14.2). From January 2015 to February 2018, the price paid index for buying food by food crop farmers increased by 16.8 per cent,[2] much higher than the increase in the index for price received by food crop farmers of 13 per cent (BPS 2017). This shows that the decline in FTT for food crops is due to prices paid by food-crop farmers increasing more than prices received by food-crop farmers, and most of the increase in prices paid by food-crop farmers comes from the food they paid to consume.

Moreover, the outbreak of Brown Plant Hopper infestation in 2017 was unprecedented, as reflected in the Cost Structure of Paddy Cultivation Household Survey, which shows that 77.16 per cent of survey respondents across Indonesia experienced pest/plant pest attacks in 2017 and one-third experienced pest/plant pest attacks that reduced their productivity by more than 25 per cent. This adversely affected farm profitability.

In the past three years, farmers benefit the least from retail rice price increases. The compound annual growth rate (CAGR) of the farm-gate

FIGURE 14.1

Farmers' Term of Trade and Changes on Food Price, January 2015–March 2018 (%, year on year)

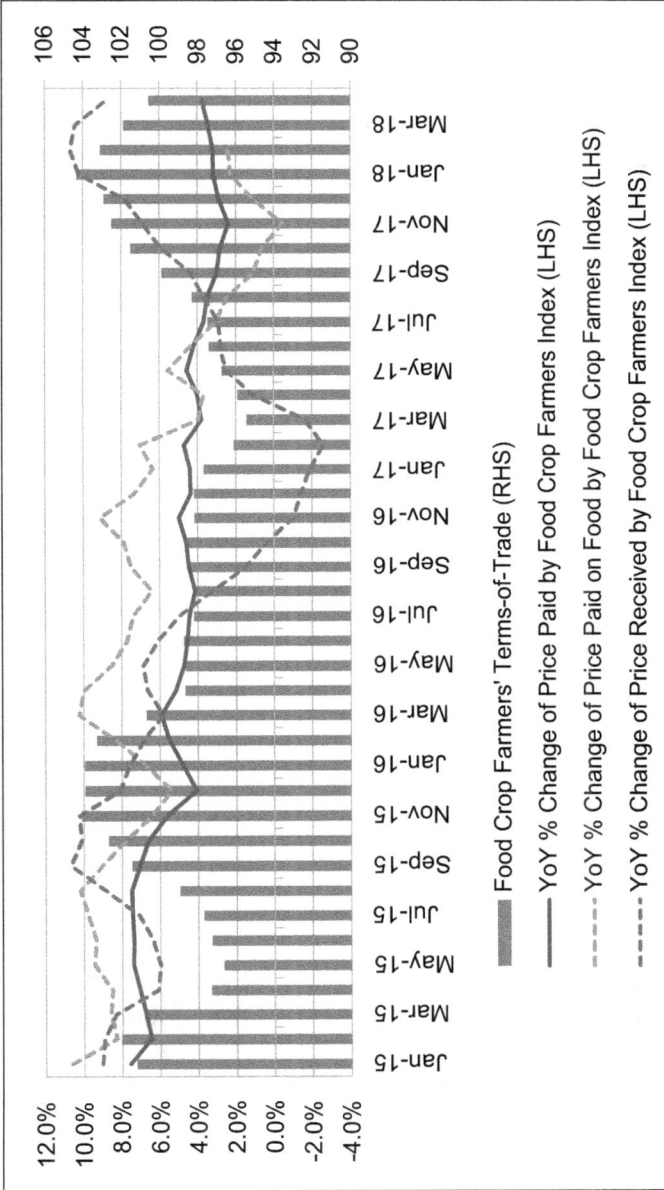

Food Crop Farmers' Terms-of-Trade (RHS)

YoY % Change of Price Paid by Food Crop Farmers Index (LHS)

YoY % Change of Price Paid on Food by Food Crop Farmers Index (LHS)

YoY % Change of Price Received by Food Crop Farmers Index (LHS)

Source: BPS, author's calculation.

FIGURE 14.2
Real Wage of Agricultural Paid Worker Per Day, January 2015–March 2018 (in rupiah)

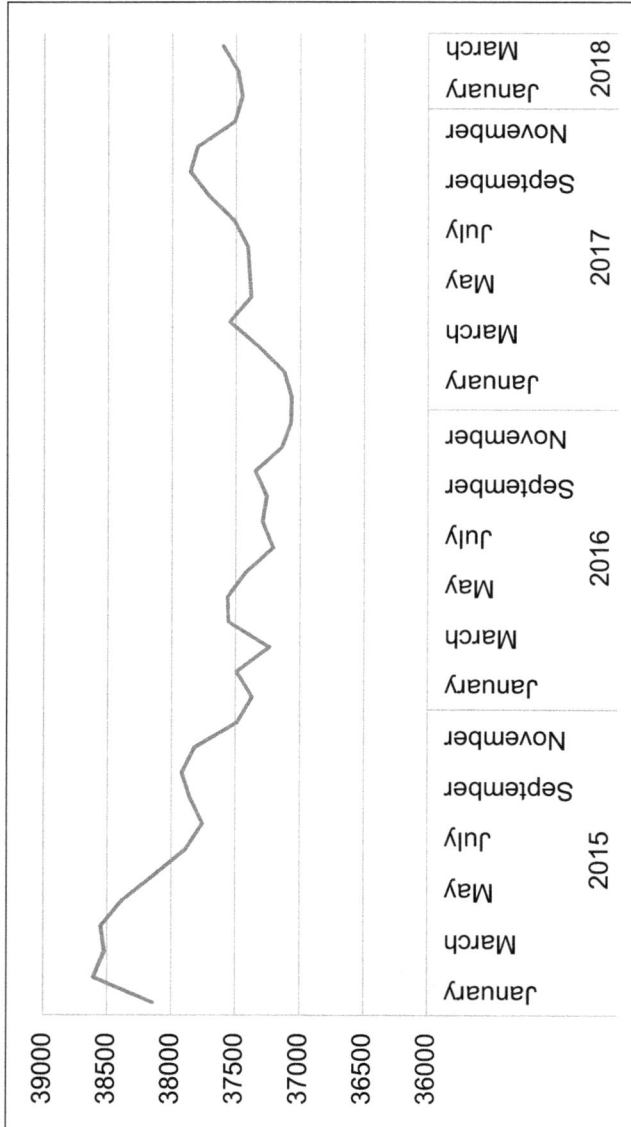

Source: BPS, author's calculation.

price of dried harvested unhusked paddy is 2.8 per cent, compared to 5.8 per cent for dried milled unhusked paddy price at miller, 5.8 per cent for wholesale rice price, and 5.0 per cent for retail rice price. High retail rice price growth is not translated directly into high farm-gate price growth in the short run although the farm-gate price and the retail price move together over time (co-integrated).

Another effect of an increase in the retail rice price operates through the labour market or agricultural paid workers (*buruh tani*), but this effect is generally small and only happens over the longer run (Dawe et al. 2010).

14.3.2 Consumer Welfare

Higher food prices erode the purchasing power of consumers, especially poor consumers whose food basket accounts for almost two-thirds of their total expenditure. In rural areas, rice consumption alone accounted for almost one-quarter of the total consumption of the reference poor-household group (i.e. the poverty line). Food inflation is a major contributor to Indonesia's general inflation. This affects how the government sets its nominal interest rate policy, further affecting growth. The CAGRs of Consumer Price Index (CPI) for food, and processed food/beverages and tobacco, between January 2015 and January 2018 were 4.54 and 5.22 per cent, respectively, compared with the 3.63 per cent CAGR for general CPI (BPS 2017). Food prices are ranked second, after economic issues, as the most important issues perceived by the public, as shown in a political survey conducted by Indo Barometer in March 2017 (*Kompas* 2017).

Historically, Indonesia's domestic rice price had increased faster than those of other Asian countries. From 2004 to 2016, Indonesia had the highest annual average increase in real domestic rice prices (3.9 per cent) compared with Asian countries, including Vietnam, Thailand, China, the Philippines, India, Lao PDR, Pakistan, Cambodia, Nepal, Bangladesh and Sri Lanka (FAO, 2017b) (Figure 14.3). Between 2014 and 2016, Indonesia also has the third highest average retail rice price in all Asian countries analysed, while Vietnam — the largest rice exporter to Indonesia — had the lowest average retail rice price (all converted to rupiah per kg) (FAO 2017b).

Given the potentially significant adverse impact of increases in the rice price for net rice consumers, McCulloch (2008) and Warr (2014) estimate the percentage of net consumers and net producers using the Susenas

FIGURE 14.3
Average Annual Inflation of Domestic Real Prices of Rice, 2004–16

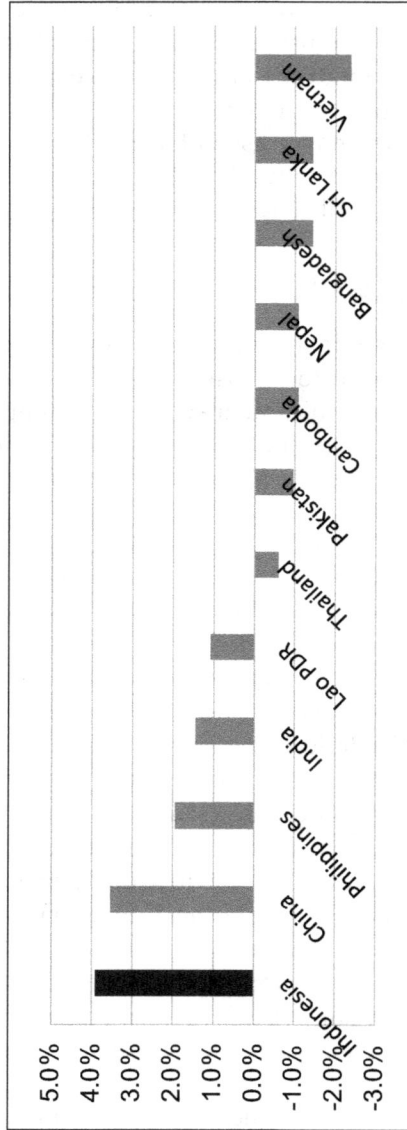

Source: FAO 2017b.

TABLE 14.2
Percentage of Net Consumers and Net Producers

Poverty Status	Net Producers	Net Consumers		Total Households
		Rice Producers	Non-Rice Producers	
Non-Poor	4,571,759	2,647,248	47,731,402	54,950,408
	8.3%	4.8%	86.9%	100%
Poor	875,689	608,756	5,072,780	6,557,225
	13.4%	9.3%	77.4%	100%
National	5,447,448	3,256,004	52,804,182	61,507,632
	8.9%	5.3%	85.8%	100%

Source: Susenas Core and Module 2013, WB staff calculations.

Rice Production Module 2004 and Indonesian Family Life Survey 2007, respectively. An update of the statistics using Susenas 2013 is given in Table 14.2. The finding is consistent with McCulloch (2008) and Warr (2014) that the majority of Indonesians are net consumers of rice. Around 87 per cent of poor households were net consumers of rice in 2013. A higher retail rice price hurts poor net rice consumers more, given their typically higher share of expenditure on rice than rich net rice consumers.

In response to Indonesia's high, rising and volatile food prices, the government set non-legally binding reference farm-gate and retail prices for rice, corn, soybean, consumption sugar, cooking oil, shallots, frozen meat (including buffalo meat), beef, chicken meat and eggs (Minister of Trade Regulation No. 27/2017).

In the case of rice prices, the government even moved to set a binding maximum retail price (*harga eceran tertinggi,* or HET) in 2017. HET distinguishes between medium-quality rice (max. 20 per cent broken), premium-quality rice (max. 15 per cent broken) and "special rice", whose specifications are determined by the Ministry of Agriculture. HET also distinguishes between rice surplus and deficit areas, and areas that are difficult to reach. For medium-quality rice, HET was set at Rp9,450/kg for Java, Lampung and South Sumatera, and Rp10,250/kg for Papua. Any sale of rice over HET — whether in a wet market selling unpacked rice or in a modern retail store selling packaged rice — will incur sanctions or get arrested by a special taskforce working under the police. A Ministry of Trade regulation that is supported by a Ministry of Agriculture regulation was issued to regulate HET and implemented since 1 September 2017.

However, since coming into effect even the wholesale rice price (mostly medium-quality rice) has been much higher than the regulated HET for the medium-quality rice price. From September 2017 to January 2018, wholesale rice price increased from Rp11,552/kg to Rp12,276/kg. This highlights the ineffectiveness of the regulation, while at the same time distorting the rice market, including farmers' incentives to grow paddy and millers' incentives to mill medium-quality rice, and hurting business climate.

14.4 WHY INDONESIA'S FOOD POLICIES MAY HAVE FAILED

The main reason for the failure to achieve the objectives set by the *Nawacita*, the Food Law 2012, and the Government Work Programme 2017 is due to the flawed way in which these objectives are translated into policies that are reflected in ministerial budgets and programmes, many of which are designed without transparent and clear data, analysis or evidence. Many of these policies and programmes need "policing" (enforcement officials) on the ground, creating sporadic enforcement of the regulations and hurting the business climate. Every so often, there is incoherence between agricultural, industrial and trade policies and programmes, exemplified by policies in the rice and cocoa industries. There is also a lack of competition, with state-owned enterprises crowding out the private sector and the government trying to impose trade restrictions on all food crops.

14.4.1 Ministerial Interpretation of High-Order Goals

The Ministry of Agriculture translates higher-order food-policy objectives (the *Nawacita*, the Food Law 2012, and the Government Work Programme 2017) more narrowly to boost production to achieve 100 per cent self-sufficiency for all food crops and target food commodities for export, even those that Indonesia has no comparative advantage in. For example, for food crops (paddy and secondary crops such as corn), the target for 2019 is to be self-sufficient and have a continuous surplus of rice; to be self-sufficient in corn in a sustainable way starting 2017; to accelerate the increase of production and the reduction of imports of soybean; and to support the export of food crops (Ministry of Agriculture, Directorate General for Food Crops, 2016).

Ministerial programmes tend to be flawed partly because they are based on weak evidence arising from the poor data quality for most of the main food commodities. This also leads to ad-hoc and reactive policies by the government.

14.4.1.1 Lack of High Quality Data and Lack of an Early Warning System. Food issues are rife with conflicting data quoted by different ministers. This affects almost all food commodities, from rice and cocoa to salt production data. Not only do ministers report different data, but associations, academicians and farmers do too. In April 2016, President Widodo made a public statement that Indonesia's Central Bureau of Statistics (BPS) would be the exclusive agency for publicizing data. A Presidential Regulation on One-Data is also being drafted, which will oblige all policymakers to use the same data for policymaking. While the production data collection methodology is being improved by different agencies, including BPS and the Ministry of Agriculture, data improvement will take time. The longer Indonesia has to wait for food data, especially food production data, to improve and to be "triangulated", the more damaging this becomes for policymaking. With unreliable data, the food policy is "Widodo's smoke and mirrors" (McBeth 2018). Even with data that are officially available and reliable, such as the National Logistics Agency's (Bulog) operational and managerial data, these data are often not used for early warning purposes. This was evident from the 13 per cent wholesale rice inflation in March 2015 that could have been avoided if procurement, stocks and distribution data had been monitored more closely (Wihardja 2016).

14.4.1.2 Ad-hoc Food Policy. The issuance of some food policies has been unprecedented and proved damaging. For example, in February 2017, Presidential Regulation No 20/2017 was issued. This regulation was issued amidst negative year-on-year inflation of the paddy price at the farmer level between July 2016 and March 2017. The regulation gave the Minister of Agriculture authority over rice policies (including trade and procurement policies) — normally under the authority of the Minister of Trade and the Coordinating Minister for Economic Affairs — for the period of six months. Under the regulation, policies on the government's purchase price (including allowing flexibility in the purchase price), conducting market operations, rice imports, and the management of government rice stocks were all under the authority of the Minister of Agriculture. The regulation, which has been intended to stabilize the rice price, proved less than successful. By July 2017, rice prices had started to increase because Bulog's procurement — despite the use of Bintara Pembina Desa (Babinsa, i.e., the military) to procure rice from farmers — was so far behind target and rice imports were not allowed. The exclusive power given to the Minister of Agriculture over rice policies, including rice import policies, prevented other ministers, including the Coordinating Minister for Economic Affairs, from influencing the many critical decisions that were necessary to make. This is a contradiction to Presidential Instruction No. 17/2017, which requires that for policies with a national scale, and a strategic and major impact on Indonesians, decisions have to be made under the coordination of the coordinating ministers and, if necessary, the President.

14.4.1.3 Reactive but Not Responsive. Food policy is more often a reaction to noise in the media or in political surveys. It is not designed to respond to long-term issues, such as increasing the productivity of both land and labour through R&D, better external services and market competition. A clear example of this is seen in the two rice price spikes at the start of 2015 and 2018, when the government reacted to the surge in retail rice prices above 10 per cent by immediately importing rice. In the case of rice, data clearly suggest that the two rice price spikes were due to poor rice policy management: Bulog's total stock depleted to less than 1 million tons, the government's rice stocks went negative, market operations were late or too little, Jakarta's wholesale rice market's stocks depleted to below 30,000 tons, Bulog's domestic procurement was well below the targeted amount, no rice imports were ordered despite rising prices (and even announcing that no rice imports would be made, confirming to the market that there would be stock shortages), and the distribution of rice for the poor was delayed, serving to increase demand in the rice market. Only after the rice price spiked did the government finally react by accelerating the replenishment of government rice stocks, increasing market operations and placing orders for rice imports. Similarly, in the case of salt, only when the processed food and beverages industry threatened to close its operations because of a shortage of industrial salt in early 2018, did the government react by issuing a Presidential Regulation to modify the salt import policy (Katadata 2018*a*). Evidently early warning indicators or long-term issues were ignored.

14.4.1.4 Sporadic Enforcement of Regulations. The involvement of the military and the police in regulating food production, procurement, stocks and prices hurts the business climate. There are numerous examples of regulations whose implementation needs the involvement of enforcement institutions. Presidential Regulation No. 71/2015 on anti-hoarding was issued to regulate prices, and manage stocks and logistics, as well as export and import policy of the "main and important" commodities. This is an example of regulations in which monitoring of compliance is unfeasible because, for at least some commodities such as rice, not only do stocks change hands very rapidly, but there are also millions of traders to monitor and hence punishment/sanctions can only be undertaken sporadically. Another example of sporadic enforcement is setting a binding maximum retail rice price, as discussed above.

14.4.2 Misalignment between Objectives and Budget Allocations

The Ministry of Agriculture's annual budget, which is biased towards agricultural programmes to increase the production of paddy and corn, and mostly go towards buying equipment and machinery, is far from being aligned to the high-order goals.

With the objective of boosting production to achieve self-sufficiency in all food crops, the Ministry of Agriculture has further detailed some strategies (Ministry of Agriculture, Directorate General for Food Crops 2016): intensification, extensification, securing production, increasing the quality of products and reducing crop losses. These strategies are then translated into operational steps, including the use of new superior seeds, increasing the Crop Plantation Index (Index Pertanaman), opening new paddy fields, strengthening the early monitoring system to detect plant-disturbing organism, socialization of an integrated pest management system, distributing harvest and post-harvest machinery, widening the use of processing technology, and better storage infrastructure.

But, what might look like a very detailed set of goals by the Ministry of Agriculture is barely reflected in the ministry's budget. In 2017, the Ministry of Agriculture's budget reached Rp22.1 trillion, compared with

Rp17.93 trillion in 2013. However, a closer look shows that 61 per cent of the budget was spent on equipment and machinery to be given to communities/local governments (Directorate General of Budget, Ministry of Finance; author's calculation). Meanwhile, another 30 per cent of the total budget was allocated for administrative-related spending, i.e., employees, travel and operational/offices. Less than 5 per cent was allocated for extension services, agricultural training and education, while only 4.2 per cent was allocated for programmes to increase production and value addition of horticulture, and only 2 per cent was allocated for programmes to increase diversification and community food security.

Looking at the programme level, more than 60 per cent of the budget was spent on two programmes: the programme for the provision and development of agricultural infrastructure and facilities (32.08 per cent) and the programme for increasing production, productivity and quality of food crops (30.05 per cent). An even closer look shows that 81 per cent and 83 per cent of sub-budgets allocated to these two programmes, respectively, were used to buy equipment, machinery and other goods (Directorate General of Budget, Ministry of Finance; author's calculation).

Overall, there seems to be a wide gap between the objectives set by the government, including crop diversification, and the budget allocated for programmes that should support the achievement of these objectives.

14.4.3 Incoherence of Agricultural, Industrial and Trade Policies and Programmes

Agricultural value chains from farm to table tend to be very long. Along these long value chains, cross-ministerial synergies are critical. Price risks, as well as food wastage, along value chains can be better managed if policies are synergized.

Examples include the rice and corn sectors. Policies to increase the production of paddy and corn (sometimes through legal means to force farmers to plant all year long) without providing proper post-harvest facilities to help keep paddy and corn dry make farmers worse off. This is because they have to pay for the production costs, while being constrained to sell harvested paddy or corn at sub-optimal farm-gate prices as the paddy and corn they produce may become wet during the rainy season. Also, regulating retail rice prices while not improving efficiency along the value chain, such as production losses during the milling stage, becomes an impossible task, with adverse impacts when millers and traders stop producing/selling altogether. This has a further impact on the incentives of farmers to produce. In addition, many of these fragmented policies were passed without providing a sufficient grace period for stakeholders to adjust to them.

Another case in point is the cocoa sector. In the case of cocoa, since the government imposed an export tax on raw cocoa beans in 2010 to boost domestic cocoa production (down-streaming), the capacity of the cocoa downstream industry increased significantly, from 360,000 tons in 2010 to 560,000 tons in 2011. Capacity continued to increase and in 2017 stood at 800,000 tons (Figure 14.4). However, contradicting the effort to downstream the domestic cocoa production, the domestic production of cocoa beans (the upstream industry) in Indonesia declined significantly, according to the Association of Cocoa Industry of Indonesia (AIKI 2018), from 559,000 tons in 2010 to 260,183 tons in 2017 (Figure 14.4). This triggered a significant increase in the volume of imports of cocoa beans from 24,831 tons in 2010 to 226,613 tons in 2017. Meanwhile, total cocoa exports, including beans and processed cocoa, did not increase significantly between 2016 and 2017. The trade policy of taxing exports of cocoa beans and the industrial policy of increasing the capacity of processing cocoa beans are not aligned with agricultural production policy aimed at increasing the production of cocoa beans.

14.4.4 Lack of Market Competition

There is ample evidence of anti-competitive behaviour and regulations in Indonesia that serve to increase retail food prices and input costs. We take rice, sugar and salt as examples.

Import monopolies in the main food commodities in Indonesia are often in the hands of state-owned enterprises such as Bulog for medium-quality rice (Trade Ministerial Regulation No. 19/2014), PT. Garam for salt for consumption (Trade Ministerial Regulation No. 125/2015), and Bulog and two other state-owned enterprises (PT. Perkebunan Indonesia and PT. Perusahaan Perdagangan Indonesia) for plantation white sugar for consumption (Trade Ministerial Regulation No. 117/2014).

In the case of both sugar and salt, markets for consumption are so much more regulated than markets for the industry. Sugar and salt for consumption can only be imported by state-owned enterprises for the

FIGURE 14.4
Production and Processing Capacity of Raw Cocoa Beans
in Indonesia, 2007–17 (in tons)

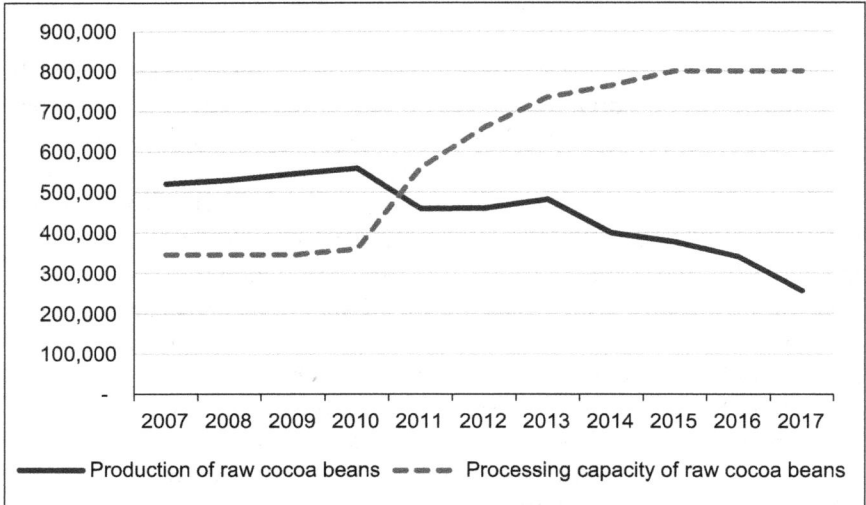

Source: Indonesia's Cacao Industry Association (2018).

purpose of stabilizing domestic prices, while industrial sugar and salt are imported by importer-producers or industries that use industrial sugar and salt as raw materials. However, because sugar and salt for consumption and industrial use are close substitutes, and the prices of industrial sugar and salt tend to be much lower than those of consumption sugar and salt partly due to lower prices for imported industrial sugar and salt, there is always an incentive for importer-producers such as sugar refineries to leak imported sugar and salt destined for industry to the consumer market. While the dichotomy between industrial and consumption sugar and salt may have been created to protect domestic farmers, it also creates price and market distortions.

Imports of industrial sugar (mostly raw sugar, which is then refined by importer-producers of sugar refineries into refined sugar) and refined salt are based on quotas. Even when production is sufficient, the quality of domestic salt and, to a lesser extent, sugar for industry may not meet the standards of the domestic industry. This often puts the government in a politically difficult position and creates infighting between ministries. The Ministry of Fisheries and Marine Affairs always states that domestic production of salt is sufficient and there is no need to import, while the Ministry of Industry states that there is a shortage of quality salt for industry. For this reason, Presidential Regulation No. 9/2018 was issued mandating that import recommendations for industrial salt be issued by the Ministry of Industry instead of the Ministry of Fisheries and Maritime Affairs.

The distribution of sugar is also restricted. For example, refined sugar can only be traded inter-island by the producers themselves, who must first obtain an Approval Letter to Trade Refined Sugar Inter-Island issued by the Directorate General of Domestic Trade at the Ministry of Trade, and have an established cooperation scheme with industrial users. Moreover, because of the leakage issues from the industrial to the consumption sugar market, in 2017, the Government issued Trade Ministerial Regulation No. 40/2017, mandating large, medium, small and micro enterprises that wanted to buy imported raw sugar processed into refined sugar to buy this through an exclusive government-appointed procurer.

In some cases, state-owned enterprises act as a monopoly of provision of production inputs. The most well-known case is in fertilizer. PT. Pupuk Indonesia is the only fertilizer producer that is eligible for government subsidies that amounted to Rp31.15 trillion in 2017 — the largest non-energy subsidy. Fertilizer subsidies given to PT. Pupuk Indonesia reduce the incentive for fertilizer producers to compete in the fertilizer market, as most production is subsidized. When domestic price of gas increased, far higher than the international price of gas, more government funds are spent for relatively less fertilizer supplied. Meanwhile, a large amount of subsidized fertilizer (allegedly up to 50 per cent) leaks to palm oil plantations. Before 2018, the government also subsidized rice, corn and soybean seeds through PT. Sang Hyang Sari, another state-owned enterprise. Many farmers complained that the quality of subsidized seeds was mixed, while some in the private sector complained that subsidized seeds crowded out the market for the private sector.

In some other cases, state-owned enterprises act as a monopsony of agricultural outputs. In the case of white sugar for consumption, in

August 2017 the Coordinating Minister for Economic Affairs issued Letter No. S-202/M.EKON/08/2017 instructing the sugar owned by sugar cane farmers and state-owned enterprises (which comes from sugar cane farmers through crop-sharing schemes of 70 per cent for farmers and 30 per cent for state-owned enterprises that process the farmers' sugar cane), have to sell their sugar to Bulog (Katadata 2018b). The letter also stated that sugar in bulk (*curah*) could only be sold by Bulog. The National Council of People's Sugar Cane Farmers (Dewan Pimpinan Nasional Petani Tebu Rakyat Indonesia) claimed that the government's purchase price was lower than the production costs, and farmers were unable to sell to the market at higher prices (Katadata 2018b).

Given regulatory uncertainties, crowding out of the private sector by state-owned enterprises and the omnipresent use of enforcement officials to regulate the market, it is not surprising that domestic and foreign direct private investment in the agriculture sector (*excluding* estate crops) in the past three years are very subdued, especially in subsectors where markets are very regulated such as rice, horticulture, cattle farming (Table 14.3). Foreign direct investment is the biggest in the poultry industry, sugar cane plantation and cereal crops (not paddy), beans and oil-producing grains in the case of domestic private investment. But, it is weak elsewhere.

In summary, the lack of competition and subdued private investment due to the crowding-out of the private sector by state-owned enterprises, imperfect market structures (monopoly, monopsony, oligopoly and oligopsony) and trade restrictions carry costs that hurt both consumers and producers.

14.5 POLICY RECOMMENDATIONS: VISIONARY FOOD POLICY ROAD MAP

There is no simple solution in finding a perfect balance in food policy that benefits both consumer and producer welfare (including all participants along the value chain) equally. Many countries face such a food policy dilemma and Indonesia is no exception. However, the diagnostics above do point towards some logical policy levers that would help improve food policy in Indonesia. To implement better food policies, however, a number of enabling factors need to be addressed first.

TABLE 14.3
Total Domestic and Foreign Investment in the Agriculture Sector, 2015–17

Subsectors	Total Domestic Investment 2015–17 (Rp million)	Total Foreign Direct Investment 2015–17 (US$ thousand)
Cereal crops (not paddy), beans, oil-producing grains	810,996	8,688.10
Paddy cultivation	10,785	2,510.40
Vegetable, Fruits and Tubers Farming	79,387	14,628.70
Sugar Cane Plantation	1,829,448	17,862.80
Other One-Season Crop Farming	151,956	14,295.00
Tropical Fruit Plantation	22,817	—
Plantation Plant for Beverages	11,426	10,472.70
Cattle and Buffalo Farming	132,116	31,860.20
Sheep and Goat Farming	—	183.50
Pig Farming	97,318	648.50
Poultry Farming	1,358,653	240,755.40
Other Farming	45,605	4,407.00

Source: Investment Coordinating Board, author's calculation.

14.5.1 Policies to Boost Consumer Welfare

Food policy should target the convergence of the domestic food price with the long-term trend in the international food price, in the least costly way to producers (farmers, millers and traders along the value chain). For example, Indonesia's rice price has diverged significantly from the international rice price and it is increasingly difficult to justify such a sustained departure of the average domestic price from the global market on either efficiency or equity grounds. One way of correcting Indonesia's food price policy would be to move towards a tariff system.

In the case of rice, as a step towards a tariff system, the government could open private sector bidding within a quota system, as in the case of the Philippines, or adopt a tariff-rate quota system, similar to that used in China.[4] The upper bound of import tariffs within the tariff-rate quota system could be set such that it complies with international, regional and bilateral agreements, while still protecting farmers from a sudden surge of cheaper imported rice. This high tariff could be lowered as domestic rice prices become more competitive. In this way, the livelihoods of farmers and related players in the rice sector would not be threatened.

The government should also be sensitive to market segmentation and product differentiation. As more consumer demand shifts towards "commercial" food products differentiated by brands and not by commodities, new markets for high-quality products with higher prices should be allowed to meet the demand of this niche market. Potential innovation, value addition through marketing, branding and packaging should be allowed and encouraged. Consumers of these high-quality products are ready to pay higher prices for what they want. This niche market allows farmers and those who participate in producing these niche products to gain more from value addition. Market segmentation requires product differentiation. The government should not be afraid of high prices, even for rice, if more expensive niche products are intended for consumers who are ready to pay for these high-quality types.

14.5.2 Policies to Boost Producer Welfare

Producer here does not mean only farmers, but every participant along the entire value chain. The approach towards producer welfare should not be a sector-wide approach but a value-chain approach. This means that objectives, policies and programmes across related ministries need to be harmonized and synergized, under the Coordinating Ministers. Moreover, there is an intricate intertwined system that determines land and labour productivity, as well as farmers' incomes. Factors that determine this relationship include the cost of production (especially rental costs and agricultural workers' wages), output prices, land size and ownership, government subsidies, intensity of labour use, and the degree of mechanization. This further necessitates cross-ministerial and agency coordination and collaboration. The government's current agrarian reforms need to be evaluated against the welfare benefits of capital-deprived farmers.

Extension services need to be revitalized.[5] Farmers need to be empowered and not forced regarding when or how to plant. During the Widodo administration, the use of the military (the so-called Babinsa) has overshadowed the presence of extension service workers.

There is also significant scope to improve farmers' access to capital.[6] The government could also explore new initiatives such as a government-backed guarantee fund to promising but less capitalized start-ups and young entrepreneurs who want to help farmers to access capital and markets, while improving product quality. The government's subsidized credits for farmers (KUR) that are slow to disburse could be channelled through these innovative start-ups and young entrepreneurs. India is one example where the ecosystem of digital technologies enables start-ups and young entrepreneurs to prosper in the agriculture sector (Firdaus 2018; Global Innovation Index 2016: Innovation Feeding the World).

Lending to the agriculture and food sectors does not just mean providing access to financing, but also access to knowledge and networks. This is why non-specialized banks in general fail to lend to smallholder farmers and entrepreneurs in businesses involving on-farm production. What distinguishes agriculture and food industry-specialized banks and non-specialized banks such as the state-owned banks is that specialized banks have both domestic and global knowledge (about products, production cycles, prices, value chains, climate and environmental risks, etc.) and domestic and global networks. The agriculture sector, albeit potentially a very profitable business, is perceived as risky and hence the risk-adjusted return is often seen as being too low. Local banking officials use large networks in localized areas to gather information about borrowers. Asymmetric information needs to be addressed by developing such large networks.

14.5.3 Enabling Factors

14.5.3.1 Improve Data Quality. The government should improve food production data. It is difficult to design good policy in the absence of high-quality and transparent data. To avoid sectoral interests, BPS should be the exclusive body collecting and releasing official food production and consumption data, as mandated by the President. The forthcoming Presidential Regulation on One Data should be used as an umbrella to triangulate differences in the existing data. International best practice should be adopted, such as the scientific sampling surveys to measure crop production adopted by Japan, the Republic of Korea and Australia. The Philippines' Statistical Authority, independent from the Ministry of Agriculture, could be an example to follow. A "smoke and mirrors" food policy creates a lose-lose situation for producers, consumers and the private sector.

14.5.3.2 Better Budget Allocation with Monitoring of Programmes and Policies.
Ministerial budgets also need to be reviewed to ensure they are spent on
the right programmes and projects. Cost effectiveness (including social
externalities) of fertilizer and irrigation programmes, which consume the
largest share of the food sovereignty budget, need to be carefully reviewed
and audited. In the case of irrigation, the planned single management
system across different levels of the irrigation network should be
accelerated. In the case of fertilizer subsidies, any policy change to phase
out fertilizer subsidies and replace them with cash transfers to farmers
needs to first resolve three issues: (i) who is entitled to subsidized fertilizer
(the current regulation stipulates that fertilizer subsidies are for all farmers,
both rich and poor); (ii) what data should be used to target recipients of
targeted cash transfer; and (iii) are private providers of fertilizer ready to
supply market needs when there is no more subsidized fertilizer by the
government?

14.5.3.3 Increase the Role of Private Sector. Reflecting from the rice sector,
experience from other countries indicates that a more balanced participation
of public and private sectors in domestic and international procurement,
and storage and distribution, helps to increase efficiency (good case studies
in Vietnam and Singapore), prevent politicization of public stockpiling
and prevent the crowding-out of the private sector (lessons learned from
Thailand).

Regulatory barriers impeding private investment and investment
climate in the agriculture sector, such as the 30 per cent foreign equity
ownership limit in the horticulture sector and the omnipresent use of
enforcement officials, should be addressed and changed.

14.5.3.4 Invest in Research and Technology. Compared with Malaysia, China,
India, Thailand and the Philippines, Indonesia has underinvested in
agricultural R&D, contributing to the underperformance of the agricultural
innovation system (World Bank 2016). Brazil has a very successful
agriculture sector and among its key policy instruments is to invest heavily
in science and technology through Embrapa, the state's R&D system, and
colleges of agriculture. This has enabled Brazil to increase production
through increased productivity and not land expansion. During Brazil's
rapid agricultural development, productivity was projected to account
for about 70 per cent of the increase in agricultural output (Contini and
Martha 2010).

Notes

All views expressed in this chapter are of the author and do not represent the views of any affiliation with which she is or has been affiliated. The author would like to dedicate this book chapter to Jan Walliser and thank Ndiame Diop for invaluable comments and guidance.

1. Details of the sub-programmes can be found in the Government Work Programme 2017, which is publicly available.
2. The data for this index only run until February 2018 (BPS).
3. See Friedman and Levinsohn (2002), as a reference to the QUAIDS (Quadratic Almost Ideal Demand System) methodology.
4. A tariff-rate quota system allows for a limited quantity of rice imports at a reduced tariff rate.
5. In the case of rice, according to the Cost Structure of Paddy Cultivation Household Survey in 2017, 70.72 per cent of farm households did not receive any extension services in the past year.
6. In the case of rice, the Cost Structure of Paddy Cultivation Household Survey in 2017 shows that 73.78 per cent of farmers still sell their paddy through intermediaries (*tengkulak/penebas*). Associated with banking access, more than half of all farmers still use the debt bondage system (*ijon*), while more than one-third of farmers say bank procedures are too complicated for them to follow.

References

Asosiasi Industri Kakao Indonesia. "Kebutuhan Bahan Baku Industri Kakao". 2018.

Badan Pusat Statistik. "Results of Cost Structure of Paddy Cultivation Household Survey". 2017.

Begazo and Sara Nyman. "Competition and Poverty". View Point, Public Policy for the Private Sector. World Bank, 2016.

Bisnis Indonesia. "Revitalisasi Pabrik Gula Mendesak". 2017 <http://industri.bisnis.com/read/20171212/257/717665/revitalisasi-pabrik-gula-mendesak>.

Boyce, James K., Peter Rosset and Elizabeth A. Stanton. "Land Reform and Sustainable Development". Political Economy Research Institute, University of Massachusetts, Amherst, 2005.

Briones, Roehlano M. "Rice price controls: Lessons from the Philippines". Paper presented at the CSIS Seminar on "Quest for an Effective Rice Policy: Is the Ceiling Price the Right Policy?", Jakarta, 7 September 2017.

Caballero-Anthony, Mely, Paul Teng, Jonatan Lassa, Tamara Nair and Maxim Shrestha. "Public Stockpiling of Rice in Asia Pacific". NTS Report No. 3, Singapore, 2016.

Contini, E. and G.B. Martha, Jr. "Brazilian agriculture, its productivity and change". Bertebos Conference on "Food security and the futures of farms: 2020 and toward 2050". Royal Swedish Academy of Agriculture and Forestry, Falkenberg, 29–31 August 2010.

Coordinating Ministry of Economic Affairs, Working Unit for Fertilizer Subsidy Formulation. "Profil Petani, Data Sensus Pertanian 2013". 2017.

Dawe, David. "Government and private rice stocks in Asia". Mimeographed. 2015.

———. "Data and calculation of import 1904–2010". Mimeographed. 2016.

Dawe, David. "International experience with rice price stabilization". Paper presented at the CSIS Seminar on "Quest for an Effective Rice Policy: Is the Ceiling Price the Right Policy?", Jakarta, 7 September 2017.

Dawe, David, Steven Block, Ashok Gulati, Huang Jikun and Ito Shoichi. "Domestic rice price, trade and marketing policies". In *Rice in the Global Economy: Strategic Research and Policy Issues for Food Security*, edited by S. Pandey et al., Chapter 3.2. Manila: International Rice Research Institute, 2010.

Detik. "8 Perusahaan Kantongi Izin Impor Gula Mentah". 2018 <https://finance. detik.com/berita-ekonomi-bisnis/d-3411171/8-perusahaan-kantongi-izin-impor-gula-mentah>.

Food and Agriculture Organization (FAO). "Corporate Private Investment in Agriculture in Indonesia". 2011.

———. FAOSTAT. 2014 <http://www.fao.org/faostat/en/#data>.

———. "Regional Perspective on Rice Policy". Paper presented at Technical Consultation Meeting on Indonesia Rice Policy and Practices: A Stakeholder Consultation Including Farmers Perspective and Policy Implication, Coordinating Ministry of Economic Affairs, FAO Workshop, Jakarta, 8 December 2016.

———. FAOStat Statistical Database. 2017*a* <faostat.fao.org>.

———. "Staff Calculation". 2017*b*.

Firdaus, M. "Transformasi Agribisnis menghadapi Tantangan Global". Paper presented at the Investment Coordinating Board, "The Role of Private Investment in Agribusiness Sector to Improve Agricultural Productivity and Farmer Welfare", 28 May 2018.

Friedman, Jed and James Levinsohn. "The Distributional Impacts of Indonesia's Financial Crisis on Household Welfare: A 'Rapid Response' Methodology". *World Bank Economic Review* 16, no. 3 (2002): 397–423.

Harun, Rosnani and Engku Elini Engku Ariff. "The Role of Institutional Support in Malaysia's Paddy and Rice Industri". Economic and Social Science Research Centre, MARDI, Malaysia, 2016.

International Rice Research Institute. *Competitiveness of Philippine Rice in Asia*, edited by Flordeliza Bordey, Piedad F. Moya, Jesusa Beltran, David C. Daw. Nueva Ecija: Philippine Rice Research Institute, 2016.

Jacoby, Hanan. "Food Prices, Wages, and Welfare in Rural India". World Bank Policy Research Working Paper, April 2013.

Katadata. "Garam Industri, Ini Isi PP yang Diteken Jokowi". 16 March 2018a <https://katadata.co.id/berita/2018/03/16/akhiri-kemelut-impor-garam-industri-ini-isi-pp-yang-diteken-jokowi>.

———. "Petani Tebu Laporkan Dugaan Monopoli Gula Bulog ke KPPU". 2018b. <https://katadata.co.id/berita/2017/09/18/petani-tebu-laporkan-dugaan-monopoli-gula-bulog-ke-kppu>.

Koalisi Rakyat untuk Kedaulatan Pangan (KRKP). "Report on Social Audit of Subsidized Fertilizer in East Sumba, East Flores, North Lombok, North Luwu and Maro". KRKP and Oxfam, 2017.

Kompas. "Survei: Ekonomi, Harga Kebutuhan dan Isu SARA Jadi Persoalan Penting". 22 March 2017.

———. "Sebelum Tutup, Ini Sederet Kasus Kartel Yang Ditangani KPPU". 28 February 2018a <https://ekonomi.kompas.com/read/2018/02/28/090145926/sebelum-tutup-ini-sederet-kasus-dugaan-kartel-yang-ditangani-kppu>.

———. "Pencapaian Target Pembangunan Jaringan Irigasi Terus Diupayakan". 21 May 2018b.

Marwanti, Sri, Endang Siti Rahayu, Joko Sutrisno, Darsono and Susi Wuri Ani. "Memperkokoh Industri Perberasan di Jawa Tengah: Sinergitas Penggilingan Padi Besar dengan Penggilingan Padi Kecil di Sragen". Paper presented at Rice Seminar, Surakarta, 16 May 2017.

McBeth, John. "Widodo's smoke and mirrors hide hard truth". *Asia Times.* 23 January 2018 <http://www.atimes.com/article/widodos-smoke-mirrors-hide-hard-truths/

McCulloch, Neil. 2008. "Rice Prices and Poverty in Indonesia". *Bulletin of Indonesian Economic Studies* 44, no. 1 (2018): 45–64 <doi:10.1080/00074910802001579>.

McKinsey Global Institute. "The Archipelago Economy: Unleashing Indonesia's Potential". 2012.

Menon, Nidhiya, Yana Rodgers and Alexis Kennedy. "Land Reform and Welfare in Vietnam: Why Gender of the Land-Rights Holder Matters". World Bank, 2013 <http://www.worldbank.org/content/dam/Worldbank/document/Gender/Vietnam%20Land%20Rights%20and%20Women%20Yana%20et%20al.pdf>.

Ministry of Agriculture, Directorate General for Food Crops. "Kebijakan Tanaman Pangan & Implementasi Upsus Pajale". Paper presented at Technical Consultation Meeting on Indonesia Rice Policy and Practices: A Stakeholder Consultation Including Farmers Perspective and Policy Implication, Coordinating Ministry of Economic Affairs, FAO Workshop, Jakarta, 8 December 2016.

Ministry of Finance. "Output Realization APBNP 2016". March 2017.

Ministry of Trade (Head of Trade Assessment and Development Agency, BP3). "Pengaruh Harga Komoditas Pangan Dunia Terhadap Daya Tarik Investasi Swasta Sektor Agribisnis Pangan". Paper presented at the Investment Coordinating Board, "The Role of Private Investment in Agribusiness Sector to Improve Agricultural Productivity and Farmer Welfare", 28 May 2018.

Natawidjaja, Ronnie S. "Model Sinerjitas Kerjasama Industri PPK dan PPB di Indramayu dan Sekitarnya". Paper presented at House of Rice, 15 December 2017.

Reuters. "Indonesia loses WTO appeal in food fight with New Zealand, U.S.". 10 November 2017 <https://www.reuters.com/article/us-indonesia-usa-wto/indonesia-loses-wto-appeal-in-food-fight-with-new-zealand-u-s-idUSKBN1D92EE?il=0>.

Rusono, Nono. "Sustainability of Food Self-Sufficiency Policy". Paper presented at Technical Consultation Meeting on Indonesia Rice Policy and Practices: A Stakeholder Consultation Including Farmers Perspective and Policy Implication, Coordinating Ministry of Economic Affairs, FAO Workshop, Jakarta, 8 December 2016.

Satriawan, Elan. "Does Supplementary Food Program Help Children during the Crisis? Evidence from Indonesian Panel Data". Selected Paper prepared for presentation at the American Agricultural Economics Association Annual Meeting, Long Beach, California, 23–26 July 2006.

Sombilla, Mercedita A. "Food (Rice) Policy in the Philippines: What Needs to Change". Paper presented at the CSIS Seminar on "Quest for an Effective Rice Policy: Is the Ceiling Price the Right Policy?", Jakarta, 7 September 2017.

Suryahadi, A. and G. Hadiwidjaja. "The Role of Poverty Reduction in Indonesia". Jakarta: SMERU Research Institute, 2011.

Suryahadi, A., J. Marshan and V.T. Indrio. "Structural Transformation and the Release of Labour from Agriculture". In *Indonesia: Enhancing Productivity through Quality Jobs*, edited by Edimon Ginting, Christopher Manning and Kiyoshi Taniguchi, pp. 100–29. Manila: Asian Development Bank, 2018.

Timmer, C. Peter. "Does Bulog Stabilise Rice Prices in Indonesia? Should It Try?". *Bulletin of Indonesian Economic Studies* 32, no. 2 (1996): 45–74 <doi:10.1080/00074919612331336938>.

Warr, Peter. "Food Insecurity and Its Determinants". Paper presented at Conference of Indonesian Society of Agricultural Economists, Bogor, 28 August 2014.

Wickramasinghe, U., S. Syed and H. Siregar, eds. "The Role of Policies in Agricultural Transformation: Lessons from Brazil, Indonesia, and the Republic of Korea". Working Paper No. 106, CAPSA-ESCAP, 2012.

Wihardja, Maria Monica. "Penyebab Tingginya Harga Beras di Indonesia". WB Presentation at CSIS Public Forum, Jakarta, 4 May 2016.

World Bank. "Improving Quality of Spending in Indonesia. 2017 Budget and Beyond". *Public Expenditure Review*, 2016.

————. "Menutup Celah. Mengatasi Ketimpangan di Indonesia". Paper presented at the Coordinating Ministry of Economic Affairs' Seminar on "Indonesia Menuju Ekonomi Berkeadilan", 30 May 2017.

15

ILLEGAL FISHING WAR
An Environmental Policy during
the Jokowi Era?

Budy P. Resosudarmo and Ellisa Kosadi

15.1 INTRODUCTION

Indonesia, comprising over 17,000 islands, is the world's largest archipelago and is blessed with a rich diversity of resource endowments, ecology and population. It extends about 6,000 km along the equator between the Indian and Pacific oceans, linking the continents of Asia and Australia. This fourth most populous nation in the world (about 260 million in 2016) is the largest member state of the Association of Southeast Asian Nations (ASEAN), accounting for nearly 40 per cent of its population and approximately 36 per cent of its gross national product in 2016 (CEIC Database). Considering these diverse characteristics, Indonesia certainly presents a challenging

This article was first published in *Journal of Southeast Asian Economies* 35, no. 3 (December 2018).

natural resource and environmental policy environment (Resosudarmo 2012; Hill 2014).

For a long time, particularly since the mid-1960s, Indonesia has been able to utilize its natural resources — gas, forest, coal and various types of ore, among others — to push for economic and human development in the country. Since the mid-1990s, the debate over whether the rate of natural resource extraction in Indonesia has been too fast and consequently over-exploitative, began to emerge as a top national issue. At the same time, the growth of economic activities, particularly in urban areas, has resulted in several alarming environmental issues, such as a high level of air pollution and a deterioration in river quality (Resosudarmo 2005; ADB 2013).

By the mid-2000s, the evidence of natural resource over-exploitation and environmental challenges in Indonesia attracted global attention. Among these issues were: the rate of Indonesia's deforestation was among the highest in the world (Resosudarmo et al. 2012*b*; Margono et al. 2014); several megacities in the country were experiencing alarmingly bad air quality; river water pollution was reaching levels that could seriously affect the health of the general public (Resosudarmo and Napitupulu 2004; Cochrane 2015); Indonesia being one of the top exporters of coal — despite its coal reserve being smaller than several other countries (Burke and Resosudarmo 2012; PwC 2012) and; over-fishing occurring everywhere in the nation's sea water areas (Resosudarmo, Napitupulu and Campbell 2009; Muawanah, Pomeroy and Marlessy 2012). The concern that shocked many Indonesians and people worldwide, however, was that Indonesia is one of the top three carbon dioxide (CO_2) emitters in the world, just after China and the United States, due to its deforestation activities (PEACE 2007; Jotzo 2012).

By the end of the 2000s, pressure on the Indonesian government to properly and seriously start managing its natural resources gathered strength from both the domestic and international community. The then president of Indonesia, Susilo Bambang Yudhoyono (SBY), did respond to this pressure, particularly making the programme to reduce Indonesia's CO_2 emission his top priority (Resosudarmo and Yusuf 2009; Resosudarmo, Ardiansyah and Napitupulu 2013). Before these efforts could generate any outcome, SBY's presidential term came to an end in 2014. His successor was Joko Widodo, popularly called "Jokowi". Local and international civil society groups had high expectations that Jokowi would make the better management of Indonesia's environment a top priority, and that he would develop strong environmental programmes. It could be argued that Jokowi has developed several important and successful environmental policies. In fact, his efforts to combat illegal fishing led by his Minister of Marine Affairs and Fisheries, Susi Pudjiastuti is his most prominent environmental policy and an example of his strong commitment. Nevertheless, whether Jokowi has actually made any significant contribution to improve the country's environment management remains unclear. Determining this is the first objective of this chapter. The second objective is to examine in detail what his illegal fishing war amounts to, and whether it has been an effective environmental policy.

15.2 ON THE ENVIRONMENT: JOKOWI VERSUS SBY

This section compares Jokowi's general attitude towards environmental issues with SBY's to determine whether the former has made a top priority out of better managing Indonesia's environment.

When elected for the second time in 2009, SBY was fully confident of his political power, winning a re-election in the first round by a significant margin over his competitor (Aspinall, Mietzner and Tomsa 2015). The Indonesian economy had been growing fairly well — by more than 5 per cent (Resosudarmo and Yusuf 2009) — making him confident of being able to smoothly navigate any upcoming challenges. He was also proud to be a part of the 2008 G20 meeting in Washington, D.C. Furthermore, he received reports conducted by international institutions stating that Indonesia would improve on its ranking, from approximately the sixteenth largest economy to become one of the world's top ten economies (McKinsey & Company 2012). It is suspected that his confidence and Indonesia's favourable economic situation triggered his ambition to create a certain Presidential legacy — similar to those of Sukarno who is known as the founding father of Indonesia, and Soeharto who is seen as the father of Indonesian development (Reid 2012; Resosudarmo, Ardiansyah and Napitupulu 2013).

After hosting the 13th Conference of the Parties to the UNFCCC (COP) in 2007, by which time it was widely known that Indonesia was among the top three CO_2 emitters in the world, the country was under strong international and domestic pressure to better manage its environment. SBY decided to take up this challenge by forming a National Council of

Climate Change (NCCC) in 2008. At the 2009 G20 meeting in Pittsburgh, he announced that Indonesia had decided on a national climate change action plan that "will reduce our emissions by 26 per cent by 2020 from BAU (Business As Usual)", and that, with international support, Indonesia "could reduce emissions by as much as 41 per cent". Much of the potential for reduction (more than 80 per cent) relates to forestry, peat-land and agriculture, where Indonesia makes its greatest contribution to global CO_2 emission (Resosudarmo, Ardiansyah and Napitupulu 2013; BAPPENAS 2012). Among developing countries, Indonesia certainly was among the first countries to announce their emission reduction commitment (Seymour, Birdsall and Savedoff 2015); demonstrating its willingness to lead developing countries on the issue of climate change.

The NCCC, at the end of 2009, developed the National Strategy in reducing CO_2 emission by 2020 (Resosudarmo, Alisjahbana and Nuridianto 2012a; BAPPENAS 2012), proving that he was serious about climate change issues being one of his top priorities. He might have seen this as an opportunity to create a legacy as the father of Indonesia's environment, by emerging as the leader among developing countries on the issue of climate change (Anderson and McKenna 2009; Resosudarmo, Ardiansyah and Napitupulu 2013).

In 2010, SBY added "pro-environment" to his development mantra, originally only "pro-growth, pro-job and pro-poor". In September 2013, he established Indonesia's Reducing Emissions from Deforestation and Forest Degradation plus (REDD+) Management Agency, a "super body" directly under his supervision (Presidential Degree No. 62/2013). In May 2011, he set a moratorium on forest conversion until May 2015 (Presidential Instruction No. 10/2011 and No. 6/2013). By the end of 2011, over thirty REDD+ demonstration activities were documented throughout Indonesia (Burke and Resosudarmo 2012; Resosudarmo et al. 2012b; Hein 2013). Despite some scepticism whether the REDD+ plus programmes would work as expected, SBY and the team kept pushing their schemes and ensuring they were among the top national priorities.

In October 2014, Jokowi was elected by a relatively small vote margin. While he had limited experience in national politics and, particularly, in international affairs compared to his competitor, he was known as "Mr Clean", representing the common people and not the political elite. He received overwhelmingly strong support from civil society groups, a significant number of which were environmental and non-government organizations (NGOs). People had high expectations that Jokowi would bring economic growth through clean government and law enforcement. His environmental civil society supporters certainly expected him to put the better management of Indonesia's environment as his top priority.

Jokowi's *Nawacita* — his top nine priority programmes — actually did not address environmental issues much. During the first three years of his presidency, he mostly discussed infrastructure and business development programmes to boost the Indonesian economy. Jokowi's cabinet, in general, is thin on members from his civil society supporters — let alone from any environmental society or NGOs. Furthermore, he decided to merge the Ministry of Environment and the Ministry of Forestry, which in reality is dominated by the Ministry of Forestry. This indicates that Jokowi put forestry issues, mostly forest production, above environmental challenges.

What disappointed many environmental groups, however, was that Jokowi demolished the REDD+ Management Agency and the NCCC. He put climate change issues under the authority of a new Directorate General for Climate Change Control, which does not report directly to him. By doing so, Jokowi downgraded the importance of climate change issues and the implementation of the REDD+ programme; they are no longer a top priority. In a way, he ended Indonesia's leadership in the area of climate change among developing countries.

Jokowi has developed several policies that have (or could have) significant positive or negative environmental consequences during his presidency. His decision to cut the country's fuel subsidy from approximately Rp276 trillion to Rp65 trillion in 2015 could be the most significant climate change policy in Indonesia's history. SBY, for whom the environment was part of the development motto, was never able to implement this policy. However, the main reason why Jokowi cut this subsidy was to obtain more funding for his infrastructure projects, rather than due to any environmental considerations (Aswicahyono and Hill 2014).

In 2015, Jokowi did extend the period of the moratorium on forest conversion, but consistency regarding this policy has been rather fragile and so the sustainability of this decision remains to be seen. For example, in 2016, Jokowi announced that he would like to accelerate the implementation of his biofuel (B15 and B20) programmes (Surbakti 2016). However, at the moment, mostly only crude palm oil is available to produce this biofuel and so could provide a strong incentive for new forest conversion activities. Another issue related to forest conversion is that, early in his presidency, Jokowi promised to conduct a significant land reform programme to distribute more than 9 million hectares of land to marginal/small farmers and establish 1 million hectares of irrigated paddy fields (Sulistyo 2017). If improperly implemented, these policies could lead to further forest conversion.

In an effort to control forest fires and to rehabilitate peat land areas, Jokowi set up a new Peat Restoration Agency in 2016. Nevertheless, it is not yet clear whether enough funding has been allocated to this agency for it to achieve its target. In 2017, Jokowi hardly drew attention to this agency, unlike SBY, who spoke about his ambition to reduce Indonesia's CO_2 emission. Recently, Jokowi promoted his Social Forestry programme with the target of transferring the management of approximately 12 million hectares of forestland to local communities by 2019 (Pramadiba 2017). He discussed this policy more from the angle of welfare distribution to combat poverty rather than to maintain the environment. It remains to be seen whether or not this policy will protect forestland or further increase forest conversion. Based on Jokowi's general attitude towards the environmental issues mentioned in this section, this chapter argues that, up until now, he has not made better management of Indonesia's environment a top priority.

On the specific issue of combatting illegal fishing (illegal fishing war), Jokowi has attracted wide media attention. What exactly this policy is and how successful it might be is still a source of debate. The rest of this article will examine this policy and estimate its impact on Indonesia's policy sector.

15.3 INDONESIA'S ILLEGAL FISHING WAR

Illegal fishing in Indonesian waters covers a relatively broad range of fishing activities, including: fishing without a licence; fishing with a fake licence; fishing with a "wrong" ship or gear; and fishing in the "wrong" waters. Both Indonesians and foreigners have been involved in these illegal fishing activities. It is also suspected to involve military personnel (Fegan 2005). It was estimated that the amount of fish caught and exported through illegal fishing activities has been between US$12.5 billion and US$20 billion annually (CEA 2016; *Detik Finance*, 1 December 2014). However, there is not enough information available to the public to determine how exactly this loss has been estimated. It is also difficult to find a reliable estimate on the number of fleets participating in illegal fishing activities in Indonesia. Among large fleets (above 30 gross tonnes), there were probably more than 7,000 ships involved in the mid-2000s (Buchary, Pitcher and Pramod 2006; Resosudarmo, Napitupulu and Campbell 2009).

Illegal fishing is not solely Indonesia's problem. It exists everywhere around the world (Sumaila, Alder and Keith 2006; Agnew et al. 2009). The more general term for this phenomenon is Illegal, Unreported and Unregulated (IUU) fishing. In a 1999 report to the United Nations (UN) General Assembly, the UN Secretary General stated that IUU fishing has been one of the most significant problems affecting world fisheries (DAWR 2015). Since then, efforts have been made to combat illegal fishing in many countries around the world (*UN News*, 1 September 2009). Indonesia, too, has been fighting illegal fishing for some time. Since the formation of the Ministry of Marine Affairs and Fisheries (MMAF) in 1999, combating illegal fishing has been one of its important programmes (Baird 2004). However, at least until the early 2010s, it was not very successful. Improper and inconsistent implementation of the programmes have often been cited as the reasons (Resosudarmo, Napitupulu and Campbell 2009).

When Jokowi became president, the issue of illegal fishing quickly came to his attention and he wanted to resolve it. The first occasion when he announced his intention and support to combat illegal fishing was probably at a regular training of the National Security Agency (Lemhannas) conducted at the Jakarta Palace in November 2014, i.e., relatively early in his presidency. Here, Jokowi stated his intention to sink illegal fishing boats without trial (BBC Indonesia, 28 November 2014).

His Minister for Marine Affairs and Fisheries, Susi Pudjiastuti, while not discussing much of her grand strategy to manage Indonesia's marine resources, seems to be determined to implement Jokowi's plans to combat illegal fishing activities, particularly by foreign fleets. She has argued that foreigners have stolen large quantities of Indonesia's marine resources because of which the country has lost significant amounts of wealth each year. The fact is that illegal foreign fleets do not pay any fees for landed fish and, if the fish were not stolen, they could be extracted by Indonesians. She also partly argued that combating illegal fishing could improve the stock of fish in Indonesian waters (Pregiawati 2017).

On 5 December 2014, with help from the Navy, Susi blew up and sank three illegal foreign fishing fleets caught surrounding the Riau islands (BBC Indonesia, 5 December 2014). While she received strong criticism for blasting and sinking the fleets without trial, Susi continued the practice in 2015, 2016 and 2017. Her main argument for doing so was that Fishery Law No. 45/2009 stated that, with enough evidence, a fishery officer is allowed to take special action, including sinking illegal fishing fleets (Asril 2014; Pasopati 2015). Over time, Susi also developed several ministerial regulations to support her actions. Some are as follows.

Shortly after becoming a minister, on 3 November 2014, she announced a moratorium on issuing new fishing permits or renewing old ones, mostly affecting fleets above 30 gross tonnes (GT), until 30 October 2015 (Ministerial Regulation No. 56/2014 then No. 10/2015) to allow time for the ministry to carry out an audit of foreign-owned or foreign-built fleets operating in Indonesian waters. At the end of 2014, she announced the Ministerial Regulation (MR) No. 57/2014 to ban transshipments (transferring fish caught from one ship to another in mid-ocean). This ban is stated again in the MR No. 15/2016. She also banned the use of trawlers and purse seine nets (Ministerial Regulation No. 02/2015), and fishing activities in the Gulf of Tolo (east of Sulawesi) and Banda Sea; i.e. Fishery Management Areas No. 714 (Ministerial Regulation No. 04/2015).

Formalized by Presidential Decree No. 115/2015, Susi established the Illegal-fishing Eradication programme, known as Satgas 115, to: combat illegal fishing; develop policy recommendations; carry out fisheries licence reform; monitor and support enforcement operations; and strengthen coordination among enforcement agencies by developing tracking systems (CEA 2016). In mid-2015, she closed down five large fisheries, mostly domestic owned, suspected to be involved in illegal fishing (Suryowati 2015). In 2017, it was announced that vessels operating in Indonesian waters were required to produce a letter of feasibility (Ministerial Regulation No. 01/2017). In the same year, a Standard Operational Procedure for illegal fishing eradication was developed (Ministerial Regulation No. 37/2017).

Due to the intensity of the activities surrounding the combat of illegal fishing, and blasting and sinking illegal fishing fleets without any trial, the media began using the phrase "Indonesian illegal fishing war" (Herman 2014; Reuters, 3 April 2017; Parameswaran 2017).

It is important to note that the case of sinking illegal fishing boats caught on 5 December 2014 might have been the first such instance during the Jokowi presidency, but this was probably not the first time this had happened in Indonesia or somewhere else. The main difference is that, under the current administration, the process of sinking illegal fishing fleets by blasting them is led by a high-profile government officer, the minister of MMAF and supported by the Navy. Also, the number of ships sunk during the Jokowi era has been much larger than ever before.

Table 15.1 shows that the estimated number of fleets sunk by the end of 2017 is more than 300. Susi Pudjiastuti blasted most of these ships. Since October 2017, she started sinking illegal fishing boats that were caught by creating holes in the body of these ships. Table 15.1 also shows the likely origin of the illegal fishing boats that were sunk. Most of them are foreign boats arriving from neighbouring countries.

15.4 SUCCESS CLAIMS, COMPLAINTS AND DOUBTS

Since the implementation of regulations related to the illegal fishing war, Susi and her staff in the MMAF have argued that:

* The number of foreign fleets carrying out illegal fishing in Indonesian waters has declined (Sembiring 2017);
* Fish stocks in several Indonesian waters have recovered (Pregiwati 2017);

TABLE 15.1
Estimated Number of Illegal Fishing Fleet Sunk

Year		2014	2015	2016	2017
Number of fleets sunk		8	107	115	127
Country of origin	Domestic fleets	n.a.	4	5	4
	Malaysia	n.a.	6	27	13
	Thailand	n.a.	21	0	1
	Vietnam	n.a.	39	59	90
	The Philippines	n.a.	34	22	19
	China	n.a.	1	1	0
	Others	n.a.	2	2	0

Source: Figures for 2014 from: KumparanNEWS, 26 July 2017; 2015 from Azzura (2015); 2016 from Firman (2017); 2018 from Putera (2018).

- The Indonesian fishery sector grew by 40 per cent within twelve months of implementing the new policies (Garrett 2015);
- Harvests of local and smaller fishing boats dominating Indonesian waters have increased — for example, by 17 per cent per trip in North Sulawesi (Hutauruk 2016; Industri.Bisnis.Com, 14 May 2016); and
- Philippine and Thai fishery exports have declined, making Indonesia the number one fish exporter in Southeast Asia by 2017 (Sukmana 2017).

Despite these achievements, a number of complaints that the illegal fishing war and several related regulations have negatively affected the domestic fishing industry have also surfaced, particularly on the part of several regional governments. The strongest complaint came from the head of Bitung district in North Sulawesi. He argued that after the implementation of the illegal fishing war, Bitung's fish production dropped by approximately 50 per cent, leading to rapid increase in unemployment in the district (Putra 2016; *Tribun Bitung*, 17 September 2017). This is a serious problem, given that Bitung is one of the most important fishery industry hubs in Indonesia. At least up till 2015, seven out of the fourteen Indonesian tuna canning companies were located there (*Tribun Manado*, 17 September 2017).

Another significant complaint came from the governor of Maluku, who claimed that the illegal fishing war had caused local unemployment to increase and per capita income to decrease in 2015 (*Koran Suara Maluku*, 9 April 2015). He also stated that fishing crew layoffs were still continuing as of late 2017 (*Berita Maluku*, 3 October 2017). For Maluku, the fishery sector is one of the most important contributors to the local economy.

The rest of this chapter will discuss whether or not these claims and complaints are supported by the data that is available to the general public, and more importantly, whether they are the direct results of the implementation of the illegal fishing war.

In existing literature, there are some doubts regarding the causality between the illegal fishing war and the facts stated in the claims and complaints. The source of these doubts is as follows. The scope of illegal fishing in Indonesia is huge — it involves a large number of domestic as well as foreign fleets. Among the latter, Chinese fleets have been fairly significant (Pauly et al. 2014). Although the number of fleets sunk during Jokowi's illegal fishing war is significant, it is most likely smaller compared to the number of fleets participating in illegal fishing activities throughout the country. Furthermore, China is the major foreign player, and the number of Chinese fleets sunk so far is trivial, as is the case with domestic fleets. The illegal fishing war might deter fleets from the neighbouring ASEAN countries, but that is not the case with Chinese fleets. Domestic fleets, seeing some of their competitors gone, might, in fact, expand their operations. Unfortunately, precise data on how many fleets have carried out illegal fishing in Indonesian territory is not available.

15.5 NATIONAL INDICATORS

It is impossible for the public to fully check whether or not Jokowi's illegal fishing war has had any significant impact on the economy in general and on fishing activities in particular, because the limited national and regional indicators that are available are mostly based on reported activities. For example, there is no formal indicator recording the amount of fish caught by illegal fishers every year. What is available is the amount of fish caught by legal fishers. Hence, the inference regarding the impact of the illegal fishing war can only be based on formal fishing activities, i.e., a decrease in the amount of fish caught by illegal fishers is associated with an increase in the amount caught by legal fishers due to more fish being available. Furthermore, an increase in formal fish production will increase the value-added of the fishery sector. Table 15.2 lists the assumptions about the impact of the illegal fish war and regulations on the amount of fish caught and the value-added of the fishery sector at national and regional levels.

It was expected that the moratorium on new or renewed fishing permits until the end of 2015 would also decrease formal fish production in 2015. Another expectation was that the ban on trawls and purse seine nets would decrease formal fish production in Eastern Indonesia. The negative impact of the illegal fishing war was, therefore, higher in Eastern Indonesia. This would most likely offset the possible increase in formal fish production in 2015, due to a fall in the number of illegal fishing operations and the ban on transshipments. Since 2016, the moratorium has ended and formal fish production is expected to have risen in that year.

Let us first look at the long-term data on the total amount of fish sold (landed fish) in all "Fishery Auction Places" throughout Indonesia collected by Statistics Indonesia (BPS). Figure 15.1 shows the volume of

TABLE 15.2
Expected Impact of the Illegal Fishing War and Related Regulations

Illegal Fishing War	Formal Fish Production
Reduction in the amount of illegal fishing[a]	Increase in formal fish production in all provinces
Moratorium on new fishing permits and renewals until 30 October 2015	Decrease in formal fish production in all provinces in 2015
Banning transhipments	Increase in formal fish production in all provinces
Banning the use of trawls and purse seine nets	Decrease in formal fish production in all provinces in 2015
Banning fishing activities in Gulf of Tolo (east of Sulawesi) and Banda Sea	Decrease in formal fish production in Eastern Indonesia in 2015

Note: a. Due to (1) blasting and sinking illegal fishing fleets; (2) closing down several large fisheries suspected to be involved in illegal fishing; and (3) the formation of Satgas 115 (and its policies).

total landed fish from 2004 to 2016 (solid line), and the trend of landed fish from 2004 to 2014 — projected to 2015 and 2016 (dashed line). It can be seen that the total landed fish decreased in 2015 compared to 2014. This drop could be due to the illegal fishing war. However, the drop was only slightly below the projected trend of landed fish (dashed line). In 2016, the amount of landed fish increased compared to 2015, but again it was not far from the project trend. Based on the figures, it can be predicted that the Indonesian illegal fishing war might have had an impact on the total volume of landed fish, but it is not very significant at the national level.

In 2014, when the illegal fishing war began, the fishery sector's value-added stood at Rp288.9 trillion — approximately 2.3 per cent of Indonesia's GDP for that year (CEIC Database). It should be noted that the fishery sector in this instance typically represents the value of the harvest from both marine captured and aquaculture activities, but does not include processed and canned fish products. In the same year, the value of fishery exports, typically including processed fish products, was around US$3.5 billion — approximately 2 per cent of total Indonesian exports for that year (Comtrade Database).

FIGURE 15.1
Total Fish Sold (Landed Fish) at Fishery Auction Places throughout Indonesia, 2004–16
(in thousand tonnes)

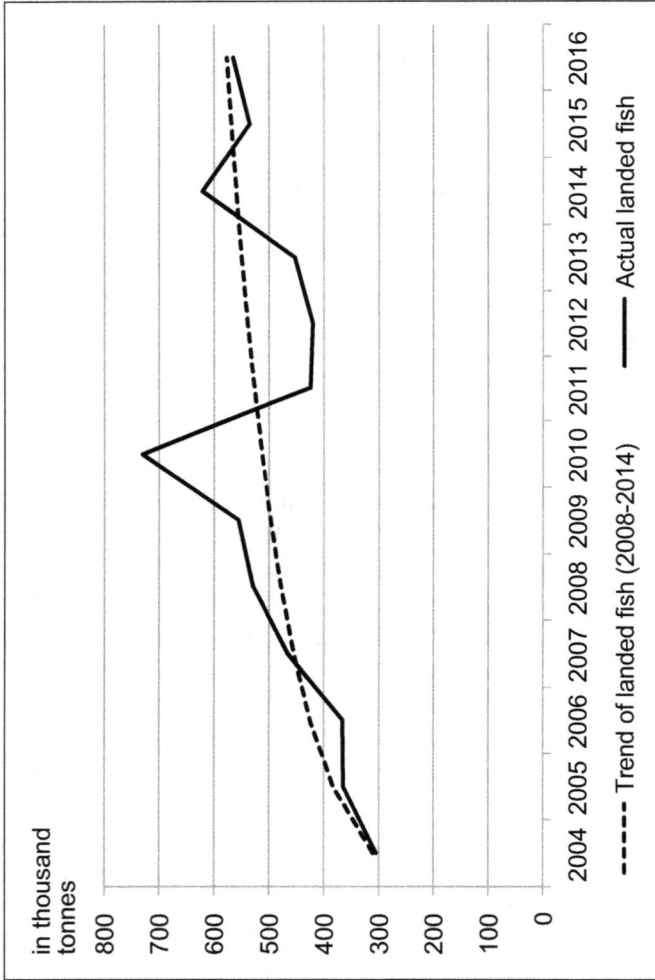

Note: Trend of landed fish is $y = 103.65 \cdot \ln(x) + 311.11$, where x = *year* – 2003.
Source: Statistics Indonesia (BPS).

Figure 15.2 presents the Indonesian fishery sector's real value-added; i.e. the sector's contribution to GDP, and export value indexed at 100 in 2004. The figure also provides trends of the fishery sector's value-added and exports based on data between 2004 and 2014, and projections for 2015 and 2016. For the national fishery sector's value-added, it can be seen that the actual numbers for 2015 and 2016 are not very different from the projected figures. This might suggest that the implementation of Jokowi's illegal fishing war has not had much impact on Indonesia's overall formal fishing industry. By 2016, the fishery sector's value-added in most provinces had reverted to their long-term trends.

The observation that the trend of the fishery sector's value-added (which also indicates the level of activity of the sector as a whole) has been relatively similar to the long-term trend raises the question whether or not the implementation of the illegal fishing war has been successful in recovering fish stocks in Indonesian territory waters. Had there been a long-term large decline in the activities of the fishery sector, we could have expected the fish stocks to recover. This, however, is not supported by the available data.

Regarding the value of fishery exports, it can be seen that the implementation of illegal fishing war reduced the amount of fish exported in 2015. This is most likely due to the temporary moratorium on fishing permits. When the moratorium was removed, the value of exports increased again in 2016 — relatively close to the value of exports in 2014. The phase where there was a decline in exports, but not in the overall fishery sector, indicates that the implementation of the moratorium affected large fishing concerns (those who are able to export their products) more than small fishing concerns (that send most of their produce to domestic markets). In addition, there is not sufficient evidence to prove that sinking illegal fishing boats would reduce illegal fishing operations in Indonesian territory and thereby make more fish available to formal fishing boats.

The fact that national fishery exports declined in 2015 while the sector's value-added did not, indicates that there could be a substitution between the decline of fish exports and an increase in the domestic sale of fish; i.e., domestic fish suppliers might have benefited from the implementation of the illegal fishing war in 2015. However, all indicators appear to have reverted to the normal trend in 2016.

FIGURE 15.2
Indexes of Fishery Value-Added and Export Value, 2004–17

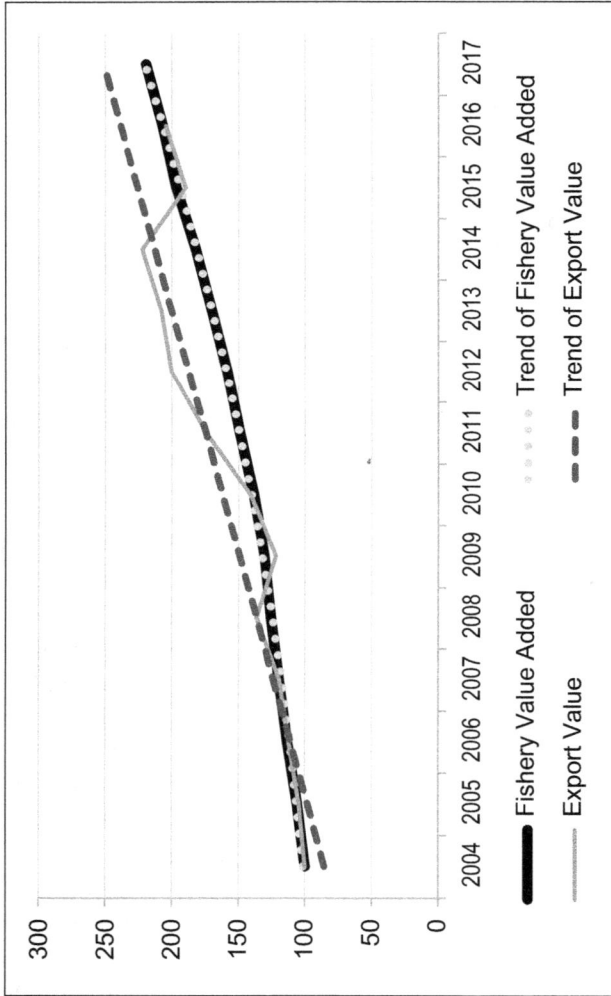

Note: The original data for Fishery sector's value-added is in rupiah at constant 2010 prices and for fishery export is in U.S. dollar. Trend of Fishery Value-Added is $y = 0.3831 \cdot x^2 + 3.3655 \cdot x + 97.845$ and Trend of (fishery) Export Value is $y = 12.75 \cdot x + 72.64$, where $x =$ year $- 2003$.
Source: CEIC Database for fishery sector's value-added; Comtrade Database for fishery export.

15.6 REGIONAL AND LOCAL INDICATORS

At the regional level, too, data on the fishery sector is limited. Table 15.3 shows several indicators related to the sector at the provincial level. From the level of the fishery sector's value-added, it can be seen that in 2014, East Java, South Sulawesi (including West Sulawesi), Riau, Lampung and West Java were the top five most important provinces for the Indonesian fishery sector. Based on the data on the share of the fishery sector's value-added in the provincial Gross Domestic Product (GDP), the top four provinces in which the sector was an extremely important part of the economy were Maluku, Southeast Sulawesi, Gorontalo and North Sulawesi. In general, provinces in Eastern Indonesia were more dependent on fishing compared to those in the western part of the country.

From the "Average Annual Growth: 2004–14" column, it can be seen that East Kalimantan (including North Kalimantan), East Java, South Sulawesi (including West Sulawesi), Banten and Gorontalo are the provinces with the fastest growing fishery sectors in the country for the period 2004–14. The "Growth in 2015" column shows the provincial fishery sector's value-added growth in 2015. It can be observed that the effect of the illegal fishing war varies across provinces. Approximately eighteen provinces experienced a lower growth in 2015 compared to their average annual growth between 2004 and 2014. However, only three provinces experienced negative growth in 2015, namely North Sulawesi, North Maluku and Southeast Sulawesi. As mentioned in the previous section, the implementation of the illegal fishing war has not had much impact on the national fishery sector. In 2016, fishery sector growth in Southeast Sulawesi and North Maluku recovered to the long-term growth trend, but that was not the case in North Sulawesi. It can therefore be concluded that the impact of the illegal fishing war has affected North Sulawesi the most.

Figure 15.3 shows the value of fish production in North Sulawesi and the city of Bitung, from 2010 to 2016 at 2010 constant prices (real value). As the numbers suggest, up to 2013, approximately 30 per cent of the North Sulawesi fish production took place in Bitung.

Figure 15.3 also shows the trends in North Sulawesi and Bitung's fish production from 2010 to 2014 and projections for 2015 and 2016 (the dash and dotted lines, respectively). It can be seen that the real value of fish production in Bitung dropped considerably in 2015 before recovering

TABLE 15.3
Provincial Fishery Value-Added

	Provincial Fishery Value-Added				
	Level in 2014 (Rp trillion; current prices)	Share of Provincial GDP in 2014 (%)	Average Annual Growth[a]: 2004–14 (%)	Growth[a] in 2015 (%)	Growth[a] in 2016 (%)
Aceh	5.8	4.5	1.9	2.8	2.4
North Sumatra	12.0	2.3	5.7	5.7	5.7
West Sumatra	5.7	3.5	5.5	8.8	3.7
Riau	17.1	2.5	6.9	4.3	1.1
Jambi	3.0	2.1	4.6	5.7	4.0
South Sumatra	10.3	3.4	5.7	2.6	1.1
Bangka Belitung	3.7	6.4	5.6	3.0	3.6
Riau Islands	4.0	2.2	4.9	7.0	7.3
Bengkulu	3.2	7.2	2.6	1.1	4.5
Lampung	14.9	6.5	6.0	3.4	3.2
DKI Jakarta	0.7	0.0	2.6	3.1	1.7
West Java	12.5	0.9	4.2	6.8	4.2
Banten	2.3	0.5	8.0	4.5	4.5
Central Java	9.6	1.0	2.8	3.3	5.1
DI Yogyakarta	0.4	0.4	7.1	7.2	1.3
East Java	37.4	2.4	9.1	5.8	5.1
Bali	6.7	4.3	5.7	0.8	5.2
West Kalimantan	2.2	1.6	5.3	2.9	3.0
Central Kalimantan	2.2	2.5	3.7	5.3	0.5
South Kalimantan	4.3	3.3	4.1	4.0	5.3
North+East Kalimantan	10.5	4.0	12.6	8.0	1.3
North Sulawesi	6.6	8.2	6.0	−3.2	2.3
Gorontalo	2.1	8.4	7.9	7.4	7.5
Central Sulawesi	5.7	6.3	6.3	6.3	2.4
West+South Sulawesi	26.0	7.9	8.8	10.8	8.3
Southeast Sulawesi	8.6	11.0	7.5	−1.2	12.7
West Nusa Tenggara	3.4	4.2	4.3	5.0	3.7
East Nusa Tenggara	3.2	4.7	4.7	5.4	5.7
Maluku	4.4	13.8	5.5	0.4	2.4
North Maluku	1.9	7.7	4.2	−2.2	5.1
West Papua	3.1	5.4	4.9	3.7	5.4
Papua	7.0	5.3	4.5	7.6	3.4
Total	240.7	2.3	6.2	4.8	4.1

Note: a = Growth calculated at constant 2010 prices.
Source: CEIC Database.

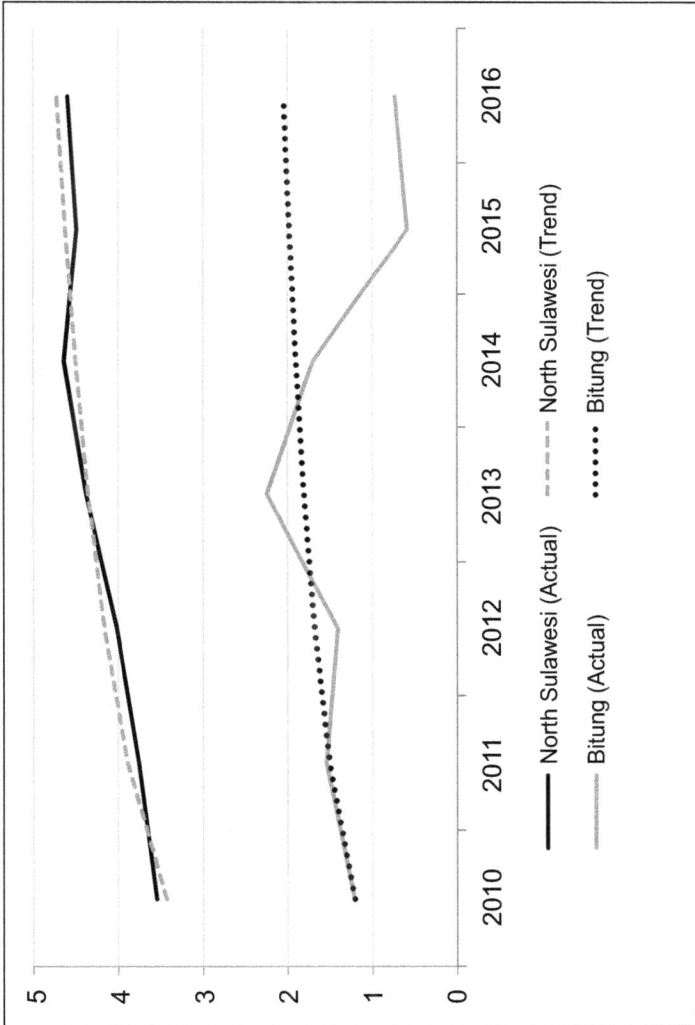

FIGURE 15.3
Values of Fish Production in North Sulawesi and Bitung, 2010–16

Note: Values of fish production are in trillion rupiah at constant 2010 prices. North Sulawesi (Trend) is $x = 0.6674 \cdot \ln(x) + 3.4274$ and Bitung (Trend) is $y = 0.4299 \cdot \ln(x) + 1.2095$, where $x = year - 2009$.
Source: Statistics Indonesia (BPS) Regional North Sulawesi Office and Bitung Office.

slightly in 2016. The fish production of Bitung, however, was still far below (less than half) the usual trend of fish production there. It can be concluded that the implementation of the illegal fishing war has significantly affected the industry in Bitung. Another possible contributing factor could be the declining competitiveness of the city's fishing industry.

The real value of fish production in North Sulawesi in 2015 and 2016 indicates that the value dropped in 2015 and recovered in 2016. This, however, does not really change the overall pattern of fish production in North Sulawesi. Therefore, it is safe to assume that the decline in fish production in Bitung has been substituted by an increase in production in other areas in North Sulawesi.

The data suggests that the impact of the illegal fishing war at the local level varies considerably. In some areas, it has negatively affected the fishing industries in 2015, while it resulted in significant gains in other areas. Nevertheless, in most local areas, fish production was approaching the long-term trend in 2016.

15.7 FINAL REMARKS

This chapter aims to determine whether Jokowi made environment management a top priority. Since combating illegal fishing in Indonesia has been one of his most well-known initiatives, this study also examines what constitutes the illegal fishing war and whether it has been an effective and successful environmental policy.

On comparing Jokowi's attitude towards environmental policy to that of SBY, the latter was willing to announce Indonesia's commitment to reduce CO_2 emissions at a prestigious global leaders' meeting and implement the REDD+ programme. Jokowi, on the other hand, does not seem to have made the better management of the Indonesian environment his top priority and has been relatively quiet about the targets to improve environmental quality.

However, Jokowi has implemented certain schemes that could positively (or negatively) affect the environment. His policy to curb the fuel subsidy, for instance, should benefit the environment. That said, he did it mainly to obtain more funding for his infrastructure projects, rather than for concern for the environment. His land reform and social forestry programmes that aim to reduce poverty in rural areas could significantly affect deforestation. However, it remains to be seen whether these will increase or decrease forest conversion. The environmental policy that has attracted the most media attention is his initiative to combat illegal fishing in Indonesia, led by his Minister of Marine Affairs and Fisheries. While the policy aims to conserve fish stock, it is mainly driven by a reaction to foreign fleets stealing Indonesian fish.

The main strategy behind this illegal fishing war, at least between 2014 and 2017, has been to blast and sink illegal fishing fleets to deter illegal fishing operations in Indonesian waters. There are also several other related regulations, such as a ban on: transshipments; the use of trawls and purse seine nets; and fishing activities in the Gulf of Tolo and Banda Sea — all of which affect formal fishing activities.

It is hard to figure out whether or not the illegal fishing war has reduced illegal fishing activities in Indonesia. This is because there is neither enough record nor comprehensive monitoring of such activities before and after the implementation of the illegal fishing war. By the end of 2017, more than 300 illegal fishing boats had been caught, blasted and sunk. However, if the magnitude of illegal fishing is really as great as has been estimated — between US$12.5 billion and US$20 billion, involving approximately 7,000 fleets comprising boats of above 30 gross tonnes — it is difficult to know the extent to which this policy has been useful. Furthermore, most of the fleets sunk have been from neighbouring countries. Few domestic fleets were sunk, even though it is known that domestic participation in illegal fishing is not insignificant. Only a handful of Chinese fleets have been sunk, despite several reports suggesting many such fleets conducting illegal fishing activities in Indonesia.

The conclusions on the impact of the illegal fishing war on formal fishing activities are as follows. First, at the national level, the impact has been relatively trivial. The real value-added of Indonesia's fishery sector has not deviated much from its long-term trend so far. The value of fishery export declined a bit in 2015, but then caught up again in 2016.

Second, the impact on the provincial formal fishery sectors seems to be varied. In most provinces, the influence was relatively small in the first year of the implementation, except in North Sulawesi, Southeast Sulawesi and North Maluku. In the second year, the provincial sector patterns returned to their long-term patterns — except in the case of North Sulawesi. These facts indicate that the effect of the illegal fishing war has been localized to a few regions, and in most cases, it dissipated by 2016.

Third, the case of North Sulawesi shows that within local economies, the illegal fishing war has negatively affected larger fishing companies but could benefit small fishers. On whether or not the illegal fishing war has been able to conserve fish stocks in the country's waters, the answer is not clear. Overall, the fishery sector has showed a decline in activity for a relatively longer period, so it is difficult to conclude that fish stocks were given enough time to recover.

Based on the findings of this chapter, if Jokowi would like to be known as a pro-environment leader of Indonesia, he certainly has to take much bigger steps towards environment conservation and set corresponding targets. Whether he actually wants this to be his legacy remains to be seen.

References

ADB (Asian Development Bank). "Downstream Impacts of Water Pollution in the Upper Citarum River, West Java, Indonesia: Economic Assessment of Interventions to Improve Water Quality". Water and Sanitation Program Technical Paper No. 85194. Manila: Asian Development Bank, 2013.

Agnew, David J., John Pearce, Ganapathiraju Pramod, Tom Peatman, Reg Watson, John R. Beddington, Tony J. Pitcher. "Estimating the Worldwide Extent of Illegal Fishing". *PLoS ONE* 4, no. 2 (2009): e4570 <doi:10.1371/ journal.pone.0004570>.

Anderson, Anthony and Simon McKenna. "The Road from Bali to Copenhagen and beyond ...". In *Sustainability and Climate Change (S&CC) Indonesia* no. 1/09 (2009). Jakarta: PwC < https://www.pwc.com/id/en/publications/assets/scc_01.pdf> (accessed 1 April 2018) .

Aspinall, Edward, Marcus Mietzner and Dirk Tomsa, eds. *The Yudhoyono Presidency: Indonesia's Decade of Stability and Stagnation*. Singapore: Institute of Southeast Asian Studies, 2015.

Asril, Sabrina. "Susi Pudjiastuti: Soal Tenggelamkan Kapal, TNI dan Polri Harus Dukung". Kompas.com, 24 November 2014 <https://nasional.kompas.com/read/2014/11/24/2235462/Susi.Pudjiastuti.Soal.Tenggelamkan.Kapal.TNI.dan.Polri.Harus.Dukung> (accessed 31 March 2018).

Aswicahyono, Haryo and Hal Hill. "Survey of Recent Developments". *Bulletin of Indonesian Economic Studies* 50, no. 3 (2014): 319–46.

Azzura, Siti N. "Menteri Susi tenggelamkan 107 kapal pencuri ikan sepanjang 2015". Merdeka.com, 28 December 2015 <https://www.merdeka.com/uang/menteri-susi-tenggelamkan-107-kapal-pencuri-ikan-sepanjang-2015.html> (accessed 31 March 2018).

Baird, Rachel. "Illegal, Unreported and Unregulated Fishing: An Analysis of the

Legal, Economic and Historical Factors Relevant to its Development and Persistence". *Melbourne Journal of International Law* 5, no. 2 (2004): 299–334.

BAPPENAS. "Rencana Aksi Nasional Penurunan Emisi Gas Rumah Kaca (RAN-GRK)". Jakarta: Kementerian Perencanaan Pembangunan Nasional/Badan Perencanaan Pembangunan Nasional (BAPPENAS), 2012 <https://www. bappenas.go.id/files/8414/1214/1620/naskah_akademis.pdf> (accessed 1 April 2018).

BBC Indonesia. "Pantaskah kapal pencuri ikan ditenggelamkan?". BBC Indonesia, 28 November 2014 <http://www.bbc.com/indonesia/forum/2014/11/141127_forum_kapal_asing> (accessed 30 March 2018).

———. "Angkatan Laut RI tenggelamkan kapal asing". BBC Indonesia, 5 December 2014. <http://www.bbc.com/indonesia/berita_indonesia/2014/12/141205_indonesia_kapal_asing> (accessed 30 March 2018).

Berita Maluku. "DPRD: Moratorium Perikanan Berdampak Pada Nihilnya Ekspor Maluku". 3 October 2017 <http://dewan.beritamalukuonline.com/2017/10/dprd-moratorium-perikanan-berdampak.html> (access 1 April 2018).

Buchary, Eny, Tony J. Pitcher and Ganapathiraju Pramod. "An Estimation of Compliance of the Fisheries of Indonesia with Article 7 (Fisheries Management) of the UN Code of Conduct for Responsible Fishing". In *Evaluations of Compliance with the FAO (UN) Code of Conduct for Responsible Fisheries*, edited by Tony J. Pitcher, Daniela Kalikoski and Ganapathiraju Pramod. Vancouver: University of British Columbia, 2006.

Burke, Paul and Budy P. Resosudarmo. "Survey of Recent Developments". *Bulletin of Indonesian Economic Studies* 48, no. 3 (2012): 299–324.

CEA (California Environmental Associates). "Indonesia Fisheries: 2015 Review", Prepared for The David and Lucile Packard Foundation, 2016 <https://www. packard.org/wp-content/uploads/2016/09/Indonesia-Fisheries-2015-Review. pdf> (accessed 1 April 2018).

Cochrane, Joe. "As Indonesia Prospers, Air Pollution Takes Toll". *New York Times*, 26 September 2016 <https://www.nytimes.com/2015/09/27/world/asia/as-indonesia-prospers-air-pollution-takes-toll.html> (accessed 1 April 2018).

DAWR (Australian Department of Agriculture and Water Resources). "Overview: Illegal, Unreported and Unregulated (IUU) Fishing". Canberra: DAWR, 2015 <http://www.agriculture.gov.au/fisheries/iuu/overview_illegal_unreported_and_unregulated_iuu_fishing> (accessed 30 March 2018).

Detik Finance. "Menteri Susi: Kerugian Akibat Illegal Fishing Rp 240 Triliun". 1 December 2014 <https://finance.detik.com/berita-ekonomi-bisnis/d-2764211/menteri-susi-kerugian-akibat-illegal-fishing-rp-240-triliun> (accessed 31 March 2018).

Fegan, Brian. "Offshore fishing". In *The Politics and Economics of Indonesia Natural*

Resources, edited by Budy P. Resosudarmo, pp. 168–69. Singapore: Institute of Southeast Asian Studies, 2005.

Firman, Muhammad. "Susi Pudjiastuti tenggelamkan 115 kapal selama 2016". Katadata.co.id, 6 January 2017 <https://katadata.co.id/berita/2017/01/06/susi-pudjiastuti-tenggelamkan-115-kapal-selama-2016> (accessed 1 April 2018).

Garrett, Jemima. "Indonesian minister who revels in destruction of illegal fishing boats creates job surge for small-scale fishers". *ABC News Online*, 14 December 2015 <http://www.abc.net.au/news/2015-12-14/destruction-of-illegal-fishing-boats-in-indonesia-jobs-boom/7027122> (accessed 30 March 2018).

Hein, Jonas. "Reducing Emissions from Deforestation and Forest Degradation (REDD+), Transnational Conservation and Access to Land in Jambi, Indonesia". EFForTS Discussion Paper Series No. 2. Göttingen : University of Göttingen, 2013.

Herman, Steve. "Indonesia Declares War on Illegal Foreign Fishing Vessels". *VOA News*, 23 December 2014 <https://www.voanews.com/a/indonesia-declares-war-on-illegal-foreign-fishing-vessels/2570346.html> (accessed 31 March 2018).

Hill, Hal, ed. *Regional Dynamics in a Decentralized Indonesia*. Singapore: Institute of Southeast Asian Studies, 2014.

Hutauruk, Dharma. "Perikanan Bitung Tanpa Kapal Asing Apa yang Terjadi". *Lautindo.com*, 16 May 2016 <http://lautindo.com/perikanan-bitung-tanpa-kapal-ikan-asing-apa-yang-terjadi/> (accessed 30 March 2018).

Industry.bisnis.com. "Dominasi Kapal Lokal, Produktivitas Perikanan Bitung Meningkat". 14 May 2016 <http://industri.bisnis.com/read/20160514/99/547464/dominasi-kapal-lokal-produktivitas-perikanan-bitung-meningkat> (accessed 30 March 2018).

Jotzo, Frank. "Can Indonesia Lead on Climate Change?". In *Indonesia Rising: The Repositioning of Asia's Third Giant*, edited by Anthony Reid, pp. 93–115. Singapore: Institute of Southeast Asian Studies, 2012.

Koran Suara Maluku. "Moratorium Sektor PERIKANAN Mengakibatkan Ribuan anak Maluku Terancam jadi Pengangguran". 9 April 2015 <http://pipp.djpt.kkp.go.id/detail_berita/1467> (accessed 30 March 2018).

KumparanNEWS. "Menteri Susi tenggelamkan 317 kapal asing pencuri ikan selama menjabat". Kumparan.com, 26 July 2017 <https://kumparan.com/@kumparannews/menteri-susi-tenggelamkan-317-kapal-asing-pencuri-ikan-selama-menjabat> (accessed 31 March 2018).

Margono, Belinda A., Peter V. Potapov, Svetlana Turubanova, Fred Stolle and Matthew C. Hansen. "Primary Forest Cover Loss in Indonesia over 2000–2012". *Nature Climate Change* 4 (2014): 730–35.

McKinsey & Company. "The Archipelago Economy: Unleashing Indonesia's

Potential". Jakarta: McKinsey & Company, 2012 <https://www.mckinsey. com/~/media/mckinsey/global%20themes/asia%20pacific/the%20 archipelago%20economy/mgi_unleashing_indonesia_potential_executive_ summary.ashx> (accessed 30 March 2018).

Muawanah, Umi, Robert W. Pomeroy and Cliff Marlessy. "Revisiting Fish Wars: Conflict and Collaboration over Fisheries in Indonesia". *Coastal Management* 40, no. 3 (2012): 279–88.

Parameswaran, Prashanth. "Indonesia's War on Illegal Fishing Nets New China Vessel". *The Diplomat*, 6 December 2017 <https://thediplomat.com/2017/12/ indonesias-war-on-illegal-fishing-nets-new-china-vessel/> (accessed 30 March 2018).

Pasopati, Giras. "Setahun jadi Menteri, Susi Tenggelamkan Kapal Tanpa Diadili". *CNN Indonesia*, 20 October 2015 <https://www.cnnindonesia.com/ ekonomi/20151020121906-92-86037/setahun-jadi-menteri-susi-tenggelamkan-kapal-tanpa-diadili> (accessed 30 March 2018).

Pauly, Daniel, Dyhia Belhabib, Roland Blomeyer, William W.W.L Cheung, Andres M. Cisneros-Montemayor, Duncan Copeland, Sarah Harper, Vicky W.Y. Lam, Yining Mai, Frederic LeManach, Henrik Osterblom, Ka Man Mok, Liesbeth van der Meer, Antonio Sanz, Soohyun Shon, U Rashid Sumaila, Wilf Swartz, Reg Watson, Yunlei Zhai1 and Dirk Zeller. "China's distant-water fisheries in the 21st century". *Fish and Fishery* 15 (2014): 474–88.

PEACE (Pelangi Energi Abadi Citra Enviro). "Indonesia and Climate Change: Working Paper on Current Status and Policies". Jakarta: PEACE, 2007 <https:// siteresources.worldbank.org/INTINDONESIA/Resources/Environment/ ClimateChange_Full_EN.pdf> (accessed 31 March 2018).

Pramadiba, Istman M. "Targetkan 12 Juta Hektar Hutan Sosial, Ini Tantangan Jokowi". *Tempo.co*, 30 October 2017 <https://nasional.tempo.co/read/1029088/ targetkan-12-juta-hektar-hutan-sosial-ini-tantangan-jokowi> (accessed 30 March 2018).

Pregiwati, Lilly A. "Menteri Susi: Kenaikan MSY Salah Satu Manfaat Perang Melawan Illegal Fishing". *KKP Berita*, 16 June 2017 <http://kkp.go.id/ artikel/1655-menteri-susi-kenaikan-msy-salah-satu-manfaat-perang-melawan-illegal-fishing> (accessed 30 March 2018).

Putera, Andri D. "Tahun 2017, Susi tenggelamkan kapal pencuri ikan dari Negara-negara ini". *Kompas.com*, 11 January 2018 <https://ekonomi.kompas.com/ read/2018/01/11/160116226/tahun-2017-susi-tenggelamkan-kapal-pencuri-ikan-dari-negara-negara-ini > (accessed 30 March 2018).

Putra, Idris R. "Akibat aturan Menteri Susi, ribuan tenaga kerja Bitung terancam PHK". *Merdeka.com*, 19 October 2016 <https://www.merdeka.com/uang/ akibat-aturan-menteri-susi-ribuan-tenaga-kerja-bitung-terancam-phk.html> (accessed 29 March 2018).

PwC (PricewaterhouseCoopers). *Mining in Indonesia: Investment and Taxation Guide.* 4th ed. Jakarta: PricewaterhouseCoopers, 2012.

Reid, A., ed. *Indonesia Rising: The Repositioning of Asia's Third Giant.* Singapore: Institute of Southeast Asian Studies, 2012.

Resosudarmo, Budy P., ed. *The Politics and Economics of Indonesia Natural Resources*, Singapore: Institute of Southeast Asian Studies, 2005.

————. "Implementing a National Environmental Policy: Understanding the 'Success' of the 1989–1999 Integrated Pest Management Programme in Indonesia". *Singapore Journal of Tropical Geography* 33, no. 3 (2012): 365–80.

———— and Lucentezza Napitupulu. "Health and Economic Impact of Air Pollution in Jakarta". *Economic Record* 80, no. Special (2004): S65–S75.

———— and Arief A. Yusuf. "Survey of Recent Development". *Bulletin of Indonesian Economic Studies* 45, no. 3 (2009): 287–316.

————, Lydia Napitupulu and David Campbell. "Illegal Fishing in the Arafura Sea". In *Working with Nature against Poverty: Development, Resources and the Environment in Eastern Indonesia*, edited by Budy P. Resosudarmo and Frank Jotzo, pp. 178–200. Singapore: Institute of Southeast Asian Studies, 2009.

————, Ariana Alisjahbana and Ditya A. Nurdianto. "Energy Security in Indonesia". In *Energy Security in the Era of Climate Change*, edited by Luca Anceschi and Jonathan Symons, pp. 161–79. Hampshire: Palgrave Macmillan, 2012*a*.

————, Ani A. Nawir, Ida A.P. Resosudarmo and Nina L. Subiman. "Forest Land Use Dynamic in Indonesia". In *Livelihood, the Economy and the Environment in Indonesia*, edited by Anne Booth, Chris Manning and Thee K. Wie, pp. 20–50. Jakarta: Yayasan Obor, 2012*b*.

————, Fitrian Ardiansyah and Lucentezza Napitupulu. "The Dynamics of Climate Change Governance in Indonesia". In *Climate Governance in the Developing World*, edited by David Held, Charles Roger and Eva-Maria Nag, pp. 72–90. Cambridge: Polity Press, 2013.

Reuters. "Indonesia blows up illegal fishing boats". 3 April 2017 <https://www.reuters.com/article/us-indonesia-fishing-idUSKBN1750UP> (accessed 30 March 2018).

Sembiring, Lidya J. "Ribuan Kapal Illegal Fishing, Menteri Susi: Sulit Dipercaya, tapi Itulah Fakta dari Data!". *Okezone Finance*, 15 July 2017 <https://economy.okezone.com/read/2017/07/15/320/1737212/ribuan-kapal-illegal-fishing-menteri-susi-sulit-dipercaya-tapi-itulah-fakta-dari-data> (accessed 31 March 2018).

Seymour, Frances, Nancy Birdsall and William Savedoff. "The Indonesia-Norway REDD+ Agreement: A Glass Half-Full". CGD Policy Paper No. 56. Washington, D.C.: Center for Global Development, 2015.

Sulistyo, Eko. "Nawacita Reforma Agraria". *Koran Sindo*, 23 September 2017

<http://ksp.go.id/wp-content/uploads/2017/09/Sindo2.jpeg> (accessed 30 March 2018).

Sukmana, Yoga. "Perkembangan Sektor Perikanan Bikin 'Surprise' ". Kompas.com, 15 July 2017 <https://ekonomi.kompas.com/read/2017/07/15/163608326/perkembangan-sektor-perikanan-bikin-surprise-> (accessed 1 April 2018).

Sumaila, Ussif R., Jackie Alder and Heather Keith. "Global Scope and Economics of Illegal Fishing". *Marine Policy* 30, no. 6 (2006): 696–703.

Surbakti, Tesa O. "Dorong EBT, Pabrik Biodiesel Didirikan". *Media Indonesia*, 6 April 2016 <http://www.mediaindonesia.com/read/detail/38737-dorong-ebt-pabrik-biodiesel-didirikan> (accessed 1 April 2018).

Suryowati, Estu. "Menteri Susi Cabut Izin Lima Perusahaan Perikanan". *Kompas. com*, 22 June 2015 <https://travel.kompas.com/read/2015/06/22/140120826/Menteri.Susi.Cabut.Izin.Lima.Perusahaan.Perikanan> (accessed 31 March 2018).

Tribun Bitung. "Lomban Kembali Curhat Soal Perikanan Bitung Ke Anggota Dewan". 17 September 2017 <http://manado.tribunnews.com/2017/09/17/lomban-kembali-curhat-soal-perikanan-bitung-ke-anggota-dewan> (accessed 1 April 2018).

Tribun Manado. "5.900 Warga Bitung Hengkang, Terdampak Lesunya Sektor Perikanan". 29 July 2017 <http://manado.tribunnews.com/2017/07/29/5900-warga-bitung-hengkang-terdampak-lesunya-sektor-perikanan> (accessed 30 March 2018).

UN News. "More than 90 countries agree to UN-backed treaty to stamp out pirate fishing". 1 September 2009 <https://news.un.org/en/story/2009/09/311022-more-90-countries-agree-un-backed-treaty-stamp-out-pirate-fishing> (accessed 1 April 2018).

INDEX

Note: Page number followed by "n" refer to endnotes